HANDBOOK *of*
APPLIED
SOCIAL
RESEARCH
METHODS

HANDBOOK of APPLIED SOCIAL RESEARCH METHODS

Leonard Bickman
Debra J. Rog
Editors

SAGE Publications
International Educational and Professional Publisher
Thousand Oaks   London   New Delhi

For information:

 SAGE Publications, Inc.
2455 Teller Road
Thousand Oaks, California 91320
E-mail: order@sagepub.com

SAGE Publications Ltd.
6 Bonhill Street
London EC2A 4PU
United Kingdom

SAGE Publications India Pvt. Ltd.
M-32 Market
Greater Kailash I
New Delhi 110 048 India

Printed in the United States of America

Library of Congress Cataloging-in-Publication Data

Main entry under title:

Handbook of applied social research methods / edited by Leonard
    Bickman and Debra J. Rog.
        p.   cm.
    Includes bibliographical references and index.
    ISBN 0-7619-0672-X (cloth: acid-free paper).
    1. Social sciences—Research—Methodology. 2. Social sciences—
Methodology.   I. Bickman, Leonard, 1941–   .   II. Rog, Debra J.
H62.H24534   1997
300'.7'2—dc21   97-4858

This book is printed on acid-free paper.

98 99 00 01 02 10 9 8 7 6 5 4 3 2 1

Acquiring Editor:	C. Deborah Laughton
Editorial Assistant:	Eileen Carr
Production Editor:	Astrid Virding
Production Assistant:	Denise Santoyo
Copy Editor:	Judy Selhorst
Typesetter/Designer:	Rebecca Evans
Indexer:	L. Pilar Wyman
Cover Designer:	Candice Harman

Contents

Introduction

Why a Handbook of Applied Social Research Methods?

Leonard Bickman
Debra J. Rog

A handbook is typically compiled to provide a comprehensive representation of the work in a particular area. It is intended to summarize and synthesize major topics and issues. Designed with a broad perspective, a handbook directs the reader to additional resources for more in-depth treatment of any one topic or issue. Thus a handbook serves as a "handy" reference guide, covering key yet often diverse themes and developments in a given area.

Applied social research methods span several substantive arenas, and the boundaries of application are not well defined. The methods can be applied in educational settings, environmental settings, health settings, business settings, and so forth. In addition, researchers conducting applied social research come from several disciplinary backgrounds and orientations, including sociology, psychology, business, political science, education, geography, and social work, to name a few. Consequently, a range of research philosophies, designs, data collection methods, analysis techniques, and reporting methods can be considered to be "applied social research." Applied research, because it consists of a diverse set of research strategies, is difficult to define precisely and inclusively. It is probably most easily defined by what it is *not,* thus distinguishing it from basic research. Therefore, we begin by highlighting several differences between applied and basic research; we then present some specific principles that apply to most of the approaches to applied social research discussed in this handbook.

■ *What Is Applied Social Research?*

With increasing frequency, public and private institutions are calling upon social scientists and other analysts to help them tackle real-world social problems. The requests they make are extremely varied. They include requests for researchers to study physicians' efforts to improve patients' compliance with medical regimens, to determine whether drug use is decreasing at a local high school, to provide up-to-date information on the operations of new educational programs and policies, to evaluate the impacts of environmental disasters, and even to analyze the likely effects of yet-to-be-tried programs to reduce teenage pregnancy. Researchers are asked to estimate the costs of everything from shopping center proposals to weapons systems, and to speak to the relative effectiveness of alternative programs and policies. Increasingly, applied researchers are being asked to contribute to major public policy debates and decisions.

Applied research uses scientific methodology to develop information to help solve an immediate, yet usually persistent, societal problem. The applied research environment is often complex, chaotic, and highly political, with pressures for quick and conclusive answers yet little or no experimental control. Basic research, in comparison, also is firmly grounded in the scientific method, but has as its goal the creation of new knowledge about how fundamental processes work. Control is often provided through a laboratory environment.

These differences between applied and basic research contexts can sometimes seem artificial to some observers, and highlighting them may create the impression that researchers in the applied community are "willing to settle" for something less than rigorous science. In practice, applied research and basic research have many more commonalities than differences; however, it is critical that applied researchers (and research consumers) understand the differences. Basic research and applied research differ in purposes, context, and methods. For ease of presentation, we discuss the differences as dichotomies; in reality, however, they fall on continua.

☐ *Differences in Purpose*

Knowledge use versus knowledge production. Applied research strives to improve our understanding of a "problem," with the intent of contributing to the solution of that problem. The distinguishing feature of basic research, in contrast, is that it is intended to expand knowledge (i.e., to identify universal principles that contribute to our understanding of how the world operates). Thus it is knowledge, as an end in itself, that motivates basic research. Applied research also may result in new knowledge, but often on a more limited basis defined by the nature of an immediate problem. Although it may be hoped that basic research findings will eventually be helpful in solving particular problems, such problem solving is not the immediate or driving goal of basic research.

Broad versus narrow questions. The applied researcher is often faced with "fuzzy" issues underneath which lie multiple, often broad research questions, and is asked to address them in a "messy" or uncontrolled environment. For example, what is the effect of the provision of mental health services to people living with AIDS? What are the causes of homelessness?

Even when the questions are well defined, the environment is complex, making it difficult for the researcher to eliminate competing explanations (i.e., events other than an intervention could be likely causes for changes in attitudes or behavior). Obviously, aspects of an individual's life other than services received will affect that person's well-being. The number and complexity of measurement tasks and dynamic real-world research settings pose major challenges for applied researchers. They also often require that researchers make conscious choices (trade-offs) about the relative importance of answering various questions and the degree of confidence necessary for each answer.

In contrast, most basic research investigations are narrow in scope. Usually, the basic researcher is investigating a very specific topic and a very tightly focused question. For example, what is the effect of white noise on the short-term recall of nonsense syllables? Or what is the effect of cocaine use on fine motor coordination? The limited focus enables the researcher to concentrate on a single measurement task and to use rigorous design approaches that allow for maximum control of potentially confounding (disturbance) variables. In an experiment on the effects of white noise, the laboratory situation enables the researcher to eliminate all other noise variables from the environment, so that the focus can be exclusively on the effects of the variable of interest, the independent variable.

Practical versus statistical significance. There are differences also between the analytic goals of applied research and those of basic research. Basic researchers generally are most concerned with determining whether or not an effect or causal relationship exists, whether or not it is in the direction predicted, and whether or not it is statistically significant (e.g., the difference observed between the presence and absence of white noise on short-term recall would not be expected by chance).

In applied research, both practical significance and statistical significance are important. Besides determining whether or not a causal relationship exists and is statistically significant, applied researchers are interested in knowing if the effects are of sufficient size to be meaningful. It is critical, therefore, that the applied researcher understand the level of outcome that will be considered "significant" by key audiences and interest groups. For example, what level of reduced drug use is considered a practically significant outcome of a drug program? Thus, besides establishing whether the intervention (independent variable) has produced statistically significant results, applied research has the added responsibility of determining whether the level of outcome attained is important or trivial.

*Handbook
of Applied
Social
Research
Methods*

xii

Theoretical "opportunism" versus theoretical "purity." Applied researchers are more likely than basic researchers to use theory instrumentally. Related to the earlier concept of practical significance, the applied researcher is interested in applying and using a theory only if it identifies variables and concepts that will likely produce important, practical results. Purity of theory is not as much a driving force as is utility. Does the theory help solve the problem? Moreover, if several theories appear useful, then the applied researcher will combine them—hopefully in a creative and useful way.

For the basic researcher, on the other hand, it is the underlying theory that is of prime importance. Thus the researcher will strive to have variables in the study that are flawless representations of the underlying theoretical constructs. In a study examining the relationships between frustration and aggression, for example, the investigator would try to be certain that the study deals with aggression and not another related construct, such as anger, and that frustration is actually manipulated, and not boredom.

☐ *Differences in Context*

Open versus controlled environment. The context of the research is a major factor in accounting for the differences between applied research and basic research. As noted earlier, applied research can be conducted in many diverse contexts, including business settings, hospitals, schools, prisons, and communities. These settings, and their corresponding characteristics, can pose quite different demands on applied researchers. Lengthy negotiations are sometimes necessary for a researcher even to obtain permission to access the data.

Basic research, in contrast, is most typically conducted in universities or similar academic environments, and is relatively isolated from the government or business worlds. The environment is within the researcher's control and is subject to close monitoring.

Client initiated versus researcher initiated. The applied researcher often receives research questions from a client, and sometimes these questions are poorly framed and incompletely understood. Clients of applied social research can include federal and congressional agencies, state governments and legislatures, local governments, oversight agencies, professional or advocacy groups, private research institutions, foundations, business corporations and organizations, and service delivery agencies, among others. The client is often in control, whether through a contractual relationship or by virtue of holding a higher position within the researcher's place of employment. Typically, the applied researcher must constantly be negotiating with the client about project scope, cost, and deadlines. Based on these parameters, the researcher may need to make conscious trade-offs in selecting a research approach that affects what questions will be addressed and how conclusively they will be addressed

University basic research, in contrast, is usually self-initiated, even when funding is obtained from sources outside the university environment, such as through government grants. The idea for the study, the approach to executing it, and even the timeline are generally determined by the researcher. The reality is that the basic researcher, in comparison with the applied researcher, operates in an environment with a great deal more flexibility, less need to let the research agenda be shaped by project costs, and less time pressure to deliver results by a specified deadline. Basic researchers sometimes can even undertake multi-year incremental programs of research intended to build theory systematically, often with supplemental funding and support from their universities.

Research team versus solo scientist. Applied research is most often conducted by research teams. These teams are likely to be multidisciplinary, sometimes as a result of competitive positioning to win grants or contracts. Moreover, the substance of applied research often demands multidisciplinary teams, particularly for studies that address multiple questions involving different areas of inquiry (e.g., economic, political, sociological). These teams must often comprise individuals who are familiar with the substantive issue (e.g., health care) and others who have expertise in specific methodological or statistical areas (e.g., economic forecasting).

Basic research is typically conducted by an individual researcher who behaves autonomously, setting the study scope and approach. If there is a research team, it generally comprises the researcher's students or other persons the researcher chooses from the same or similar disciplines.

☐ *Differences in Methods*

External versus internal validity. A key difference between applied research and basic research is the relative emphasis on internal and external validity. Whereas internal validity (the extent to which a causal relationship can be soundly established) is essential to both types of research, external validity (the extent to which the study results are generalizable) is much more important to applied research. Indeed, the likelihood that applied research findings will be used often depends on the researchers' ability to convince policy makers that the results are applicable to their particular setting or problem. For example, the results from a laboratory study of aggression using a bogus shock generator and involving participants of different races are not likely to be as convincing or as useful to policy makers who are confronting the problem of violent crime in the inner city as are the results of a well-designed survey describing the types and incidence of crime experienced by inner-city residents.

The construct of effect versus the construct of cause. Applied research concentrates on the construct of effect. It is especially critical that the outcome

Handbook
of Applied
Social
Research
Methods

xiv

measures are valid—that they accurately measure the variables of interest. Often it is important for researchers to measure multiple outcomes and to use multiple measures to assess each construct fully. Improvements in mental health, for example, may include measures of daily functioning, psychiatric status, and use of hospitalization. Moreover, measures of real-world outcomes often require more than self-report and simple paper-and-pencil measures (e.g., self-report satisfaction with participation in a program). If attempts are being made to address a social problem, then real-world measures directly related to that problem are desirable. For example, if one is studying the effects of a program designed to reduce intergroup conflict and tension, then observations of the interactions among group members will have more credibility than group members' responses to questions about their attitudes toward other groups. In fact, there is much research evidence in social psychology that demonstrates that attitudes and behavior often do not relate.

Basic research, on the other hand, concentrates on the construct of cause. In laboratory studies, the independent variable (cause) must be clearly explicated and not confounded with any other variables. It is rare in applied research settings that control over an independent variable is so clear-cut. For example, in a study of the effects of a treatment program for drug abusers, it is unlikely that the researcher can isolate the aspects of the program that are responsible for the outcomes that result. This is due to both the complexity of many social programs and the researcher's inability in most circumstances to manipulate different program features to discern differential effects.

Multiple versus single levels of analysis. The applied researcher, in contrast to the basic researcher, usually needs to examine a specific problem at more than one level of analysis, not only studying the individual, but often larger groups, such as organizations or even societies. For example, in one evaluation of a community crime prevention project, the researcher not only examined individual attitudes and perspectives, but also measured the reactions of groups of neighbors and entire neighborhoods to problems of crime. These added levels of analysis may require that the researcher be conversant with concepts and research approaches found in a variety of disciplines, such as psychology, sociology, and political science, and that he or she develop a multidisciplinary research team that can conduct the multilevel inquiry.

Similarly, because applied researchers are often given multiple questions to answer, because they must work in real-world settings, and because they often use multiple measures of effects, they are more likely to use multiple research methods. Although using multiple methods may be necessary to address multiple questions, it may also be a strategy used to triangulate on a difficult problem from several directions, thus lending additional confidence to the study results. Although it is desirable for researchers to use experimental designs whenever possible, often the applied researcher is called in after a program or intervention is in place, and consequently is precluded from building random assignment into the allocation of program resources. Thus applied researchers often use quasi-experimental studies. The obverse, however, is rarer; quasi-experimental designs are generally not found in the studies published in basic research journals.

■ *The Orientation of This Handbook*

This volume is designed to be a resource for professionals and students alike. It is intended to supplement the **Applied Social Research Methods Series** by offering a digest of 18 of the series volumes related to the design of applied research, the collection of both quantitative and qualitative data, and the management and presentation of these data to a range of audiences. The contributors represent a variety of disciplines (sociology, business, psychology, political science, education, economics) and work in diverse settings (academic departments, research institutes, government, the private sector). Through a concise collection of their work, we hope to provide in one place a diversity of perspectives and methodologies that others can use in planning and conducting applied social research.

Similar to our goal as editors of the book series, our attempt in this handbook is to offer a hands-on, how-to approach to research that is sensitive to the constraints and opportunities in the practical and policy environments, yet is rooted in rigorous and sound research principles. Abundant examples and illustrations, often based on the authors' own experience and work, enhance the potential usefulness of the material to students and others who may have limited experience in conducting research in applied arenas.

Despite the diversity of perspectives, methods, and approaches within this volume, several central themes are stressed across the chapters. We describe these themes in turn below.

The iterative nature of applied research. In most applied research endeavors, the research question—the focus of the effort—is rarely static. Rather, to maintain the credibility, responsiveness, and quality of the research project, the researcher must typically make a series of iterations within the research design. The iteration is necessary not because of methodological inadequacies, but because of successive redefinitions of the applied problem as the project is being planned and implemented. New knowledge is gained, unanticipated obstacles are encountered, and contextual shifts take place that change the overall research situation and in turn have affects on the research. The first chapter in this handbook, by Bickman, Rog, and Hedrick, describes an iterative approach to planning applied research that continually revisits the research question as trade-offs in the design are made. In Chapter 3, Maxwell also discusses the iterative, interactive nature of qualitative research design, highlighting the unique relation-

*Handbook
of Applied
Social
Research
Methods*

xvi

ships that occur in qualitative research among the purposes of the research, the conceptual context, the questions, the methods, and validity.

Multiple stakeholders. As noted earlier, applied research involves the efforts and interests of multiple parties. Those interested in how a study gets conducted and its results can include the research sponsor, individuals involved in the intervention or program under study, the potential beneficiaries of the research (e.g., those who could be affected by the results of the research), and potential users of the research results (such as policy makers and business leaders). In some situations, the cooperation of these parties is critical to the successful implementation of the project. Usually, the involvement of these stakeholders ensures that the results of the research will be relevant, useful, and, hopefully, used to address the problem it was intended to study.

Many of the contributors to this volume stress the importance of consulting and involving stakeholders in various aspects of the research process. Bickman, Rog, and Hedrick describe the role of stakeholders throughout the planning of a study, from the specification of research questions to the choice of designs and design trade-offs. In Chapter 9, McKillip describes the critical role that decision makers and other stakeholders play in needs analysis. Similarly, in Chapter 5, on planning ethically responsible research, Sieber emphasizes the importance of researchers' attending to the interests and concerns of all parties in the design stage of a study.

In Chapter 17, Stewart and Shamdasani describe focus groups as one method of obtaining stakeholder input. Finally, several contributors consider the framing of results so that they can reach the attention of decision makers and other potential users (see Henry, Chapter 18; Yates, Chapter 10; Yin, Chapter 8).

Ethical concerns. Research ethics are important in all types of research, basic or applied. When the research involves or affects human beings, the researcher must attend to a set of ethical and legal principles and requirements that can ensure the protection of the interests of all those involved. Ethical issues, as Boruch notes in Chapter 6, commonly arise in experimental studies when individuals are asked to be randomly assigned into either a treatment condition or a control condition. However, ethical concerns are also raised in most studies in the development of strategies for obtaining informed consent, protecting privacy, guaranteeing anonymity, and/or ensuring confidentiality, and in developing research procedures that are sensitive to and respectful of the specific needs of the population involved in the research (see Sieber; Fetterman, Chapter 16). As Sieber notes, although attention to ethics is important to the conduct of all studies, the need for ethical problem solving is particularly heightened when the researcher is dealing with highly political and controversial social problems, in research that involves vulnerable populations (e.g., individuals with AIDS), and in situations where stakeholders have high stakes in the outcomes of the research.

Enhancing validity. Applied research faces challenges that threaten the validity of studies' results. Difficulties in mounting the most rigorous designs, in collecting data from objective sources, and in designing studies that have universal generalizability require innovative strategies to ensure that the research continues to produce valid results. Lipsey, in Chapter 2, describes the link between internal validity and statistical power, and how good research practice can increase the statistical power of a study. In Chapter 7, Reichardt and Mark outline the threats to validity that challenge experiments and quasi-experiments and various design strategies for controlling these threats. Henry, in his discussion of sampling in Chapter 4, focuses on external validity and the construction of samples that can provide valid information about a broader population. Other contributors in Part III (Fowler, Chapter 12; Lavrakas, Chapter 15; Mangione, Chapter 13; van Kammen and Stouthamer-Loeber, Chapter 13) focus on increasing construct validity through the improvement of the design of individual questions and overall data collection tools, the training of data collectors, and the review and analysis of data.

Triangulation of methods and measures. One method of enhancing validity is to develop converging lines of evidence (Yin). As noted earlier, a clear hallmark of applied research is the triangulation of methods and measures to compensate for the fallibility of any single method or measure. The validity of both qualitative and quantitative applied research is bolstered by triangulation in data collection. Yin, Maxwell, and Fetterman stress the importance of triangulation in qualitative research design, ethnography, and case study research. Similarly, Bickman, Rog, and Hedrick support the use of multiple data collection methods in all types of applied research.

Qualitative and *quantitative.* Unlike traditional books on research methods, this volume does not have separate sections for quantitative and qualitative methods. Rather, both types of research are presented together as approaches to consider in research design, data collection, analysis, and reporting. Our emphasis is to find the tools that best fit the research question, context, and resources at hand. Often, multiple tools are needed, cutting across qualitative and quantitative boundaries, to research a topic thoroughly and provide results that can be used.

A variety of tools are described in this handbook. Experimental and quasi-experimental approaches are discussed (Boruch; Reichardt and Mark; Lipsey), alongside qualitative approaches to design (Maxwell), including case studies (Yin) and ethnographies (Fetterman). Data collection tools provided also include surveys (in person, mail, and telephone) and focus groups (Stewart and Shamdasani).

Technological advances. Recent technological advances can help applied researchers to conduct their research more efficiently, with greater precision,

*Handbook
of Applied
Social
Research
Methods*

xviii

and with greater insight than in the past. Clearly, advancements in computers have improved the quality, timeliness, and power of research. Analyses of large databases with multiple levels of data would not be possible without high-speed computers. Statistical syntheses of research studies, called meta-analyses (Cooper and Lindsay, Chapter 11; Lipsey), have become more common in a variety of areas, in part due to the accessibility of computers. Moreover, with personal computers, researchers can manage complex studies, such as longitudinal surveys (van Kammen and Stouthamer-Loeber), with the aid of spreadsheets that provide tracking of interviews attempted, completed, and so on. Even qualitative studies can now benefit from computer technology, with software programs that allow for the identification and analysis of themes in narratives (Stewart and Shamdasani), programs that simply allow the researcher to organize and manage the voluminous amounts of qualitative data typically collected in a study (Maxwell; Yin), and laptops that can be used in the field to provide for efficient data collection (Fetterman). In addition to computers, other new technology provides for innovative ways of collecting data, such as through videoconferencing (Fetterman) and electronic focus groups (Stewart and Shamdasani). Finally, with the increasing sophistication of graphical software, research results can be displayed in more creative ways, to communicate with a variety of audiences (Henry).

However, the researcher has to be careful not to get caught up in using technology that only gives the appearance of advancement. Lavrakas points out that the use of computerized telephone interviews has not been shown to save time or money over traditional paper-and-pencil surveys.

Research management. The nature of the context in which applied researchers work highlights the need for extensive expertise in research planning. Applied researchers must take deadlines seriously, and then design research that can deliver useful information within the constraints of budget, time, and staff available. The key to quality work is to use the most rigorous methods possible, making intelligent and conscious trade-offs in scope and conclusiveness. This does not mean that any information is better than none, but that decisions about what information to pursue must be made very deliberately, with realistic assessments of the feasibility of executing the proposed research within the required time frame. Bickman, Rog, and Hedrick, Boruch, and van Kammen and Stouthamer-Loeber all describe the importance of research management, from the early planning stages through the communication and reporting of results.

■ *Conclusion*

We hope that the contributions to this handbook will help to guide readers in selecting appropriate questions and procedures to use in applied research.

Consistent with a handbook approach, the chapters are not intended to provide the detail necessary for readers to use each method or to design comprehensive research; rather, they are intended to provide the general guidance readers will need to address each topic more fully. This handbook should serve as an intelligent guide, helping readers to select the approaches, specific designs, and data collection procedures they can best use in applied social research.

Part I

Planning Applied Research

The five chapters in this section set the stage for applied research, describing key elements and approaches to designing and planning applied social research. The first chapter, by Bickman, Rog, and Hedrick, presents an overview of the design process. It focuses on the iterative nature of planning research as well as the multimethod approach that we recommend. The authors stress the trade-offs that are involved in the design phase, as the investigator balances the needs for the research to be timely, credible, and of high quality. Bickman and his colleagues stress that as researchers make trade-offs in their research designs, they must continue to revisit the original research questions to ensure either that they can still be answered, given the changes in the design, or that they are revised to reflect what can be answered.

One of the aspects of planning applied research covered in Chapter 1, often overlooked in teaching and in practice, is the need for researchers to make certain that the resources necessary for implementing the research design are in place. These include both human and material resources as well as other elements that can make or break a study, such as site cooperation. Many applied research studies fail because the assumed community resources never materialize.

The next three chapters outline the principles of three major areas of design: experimental designs, qualitative research designs, and descriptive designs. In Chapter 2, Lipsey discusses the importance of design sensitivity in the planning of experiments. Attention to statistical power is key in experiments, in contrast to surveys and other forms of descriptive research. Power, as defined by Lipsey, is the ability to detect an effect of a treatment or intervention if it is really there. In a review of previous studies, Lipsey found that almost half were underpowered and thus lacked the ability to detect reasonable-sized effects. The failure of research to be sensitive to the effects that are present has been recognized by editors and grant reviewers to the extent that a power analysis has increasingly become a required component of a research design. Lipsey carefully explains the components of research that influence statistical power and shows how the statistical power of a planned study can be calculated. In highlighting the components that affect statistical power, Lipsey illustrates numerous ways in which the sensitivity of the research design can be strengthened to increase the design's overall statistical power. Most important, he demonstrates how the researcher does not have to rely only on increasing the sample size to increase the power, but how good research practice (e.g., the use of valid and reliable measurement, maintaining the integrity and completeness of both the treatment and control groups) can increase the effect size and, in turn, increase the statistical power of the study.

In Chapter 3, Maxwell presents a new model of research design, representing the logic and process of qualitative research. Calling it an "interactive" model of research design, Maxwell outlines five key components in the model: purposes, conceptual context, research questions, methods, and validity. Although these components are not unique to qualitative research design, Maxwell contends that what is unique are the relationships among the components. For example, research questions should be related to the study purposes and informed by the conceptual framework. Similarly, the purposes should be informed by the conceptual knowledge, and the relevant theory and knowledge needed to develop the conceptual framework should be driven by the purposes of the research and the questions that are posed. Qualitative design is consequently flexible, due to the simultaneous nature of many of the research activities. Despite this flexibility, Maxwell demonstrates, it is important for the researcher to have an underlying scheme that provides some guidance for a coherent research study.

As Henry points out in Chapter 4, sampling is a critical component of almost every applied research study, but it is most critical to the conduct of descriptive studies involving surveys of particular populations (e.g., surveys of homeless individuals). Focusing primarily on probability sampling, Henry describes a practical sampling design framework to help researchers structure their thinking about making sampling decisions in the context of how those decisions affect total error. Total error, defined as the difference between the true population value and the estimate based on the sample data, involves three types of error: error due to differences in the population definition, error due to the sampling approach used, and error involved in the random selection process. Henry's framework outlines the decisions that affect total error in the presampling, sampling, and postsampling phases of the research. In his chapter, however, he focuses on the implications of the researcher's answers to the questions on sampling choices. In particular, Henry illustrates the challenges in making trade-offs to reduce total error, keeping the study goals and resources in mind.

Planning applied social research is not just application of methods; it also involves attention to ethics and the rights of research participants. In Chapter 5, Sieber discusses three areas of ethics that need to be considered in the design of research: strategies for obtaining informed consent; issues related to, and techniques for ensuring, privacy and confidentiality; and how investigators can recognize research risk and, in turn, maximize the benefits of research. Sieber places special emphasis on these areas in the conduct of research with vulnerable populations (e.g., individuals with AIDS) and with children.

1

Applied Research Design

A Practical Approach

Leonard Bickman
Debra J. Rog
Terry E. Hedrick

■ *Overview of the Planning Process*

The conduct of applied research can be viewed as consisting of two major phases, planning and execution (see Figure 1.1), that encompass four stages. In the planning phase, the researcher is concerned with defining the scope of the research and developing a research plan. During execution, the researcher implements and monitors the plan (design, data collection and analysis, and management procedures), followed by reporting and follow-up activities.

In this chapter we focus on the first phase, the planning of applied research. Figure 1.2 summarizes the research planning approach advocated here, highlighting the iterative nature of the design process. Stage I of the research process begins with the researcher's development of an understanding of the relevant problem/societal issue and involves the researcher's working with clients and other consumers to refine and revise study questions to make sure that they are both useful and researchable. After developing potentially researchable questions, the investigator then moves to Stage II: development of a research design and plan. This stage involves multiple decisions and assessments, including selecting a design and proposed data collection strategies.

Almost simultaneous with design and data collection decisions, the researcher must determine the resources necessary to conduct the study. This is an area where social science academic education is most often deficient, and

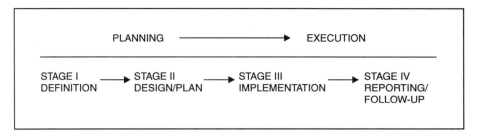

Figure 1.1. The Conduct of Applied Research

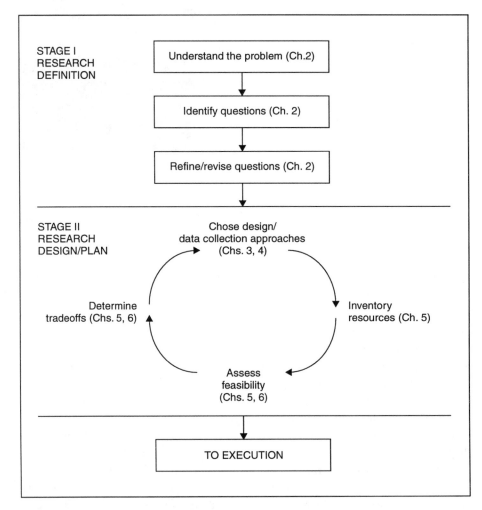

Figure 1.2. Applied Research Planning

perhaps is one reason academically oriented researchers may at times fail to deliver research products on time.

Research design and planning also include the researcher's assessment of the feasibility of carrying out the study design within the requisite time frame and with the available resources, and analysis of the trade-offs to be made in the design and other planning decisions. The researcher should discuss the full plan, and analysis of any necessary trade-offs, with the research consumer, and agreement should be reached on its appropriateness.

As Figure 1.2 illustrates, the planning activities in Stage II often occur simultaneously, until a final research plan is developed. At any point in the Stage II process, the researcher may find it desirable to revisit and revise earlier decisions, perhaps even finding it necessary to return to Stage I and renegotiate the study questions or timeline with the research client or funder. In fact, the researcher may find that the design that has been developed does not, or cannot, answer the original questions. The researcher needs to review and correct this discrepancy together with the client before moving on to Stage III. The culmination of Stage II is a comprehensively planned applied research project, ready for full-scale implementation. With sufficient planning completed at this point, the odds of a successful study are significantly improved.

■ *Stage I: Defining the Focus of the Research*

□ *Understanding the Problem/Issue*

To ensure that the study is ethically and accurately planned, the researcher needs to be educated about the issue at hand. Strategies he or she might use in gathering needed information include the following:

- Hold discussions with the research clients or sponsors (legislative members; foundation, business, organization, or agency personnel; and so on) to obtain the clearest possible picture of their concerns.
- Review relevant literature (research reports, transcripts of legislative hearings, program descriptions, administrative reports, agency statistics, media articles, and policy/position papers by all major interested parties).
- Gather current information from experts on the issue (all sides and perspectives) and major interested parties.
- Conduct information-gathering visits and observations to obtain a real-world sense of the context and to talk with persons actively involved in the issue.

□ *Developing a Conceptual Framework*

Every study, whether it is acknowledged or not, is based on a conceptual framework that specifies the variables of interest and the expected relationships between them. The framework may be relatively straightforward or it may be complex, as in the case of impact studies positing several kinds of effects. Social science theory may serve as the basis for the conceptual framework in some studies. For example, theories of cognitive development may drive investigations of children's learning abilities. Other studies, such as program and policy evaluations, may be based not on formal academic theory but on statements of expectations of how policies or programs are purported to work. Bickman (1987, 1990) and others (e.g., Chen & Rossi, 1992) have written extensively about the need for and usefulness of program theory to guide evaluations.

One mechanism for refining the focus of a study, particularly in program or policy evaluations, is the development of a logic model to display the logic of the program (i.e., how the program goals, resources, activities, and outcomes link together) (Rog, 1994; Rog & Huebner, 1992; Yin, Chapter 8, this volume). The use of the logic model in program research is based on the evaluability assessment work of Wholey and others (e.g., Wholey, 1987), which advocates describing and displaying the underlying theory of a program prior to conducting a study of outcomes. Logic models can be used to structure the development of an intervention, to focus an evaluation of the intervention's effectiveness, and to communicate changes in implementation over the life of program.

☐ *Identifying the Research Questions*

As is noted in the introduction to this handbook, one of the major differences between basic research and applied research is that the basic researcher is often more autonomous than the applied researcher. Basic research, when externally funded, is typically conducted through a relatively unrestrictive grant mechanism; applied research is more frequently funded through contracts and cooperative agreements. There is usually a "client" or sponsor who specifies (or at least guides) the research agenda and requests the research results. Most often, studies have multiple stakeholders: sponsors, interested beneficiaries, and potential users (Bickman & Rog, 1986). This means that the questions to be addressed by an applied study tend to be posed by individuals other than the primary researcher, often by nontechnical persons in nontechnical language. One of the first activities of the applied researcher and his or her clients should be to develop a common understanding of the research agenda—the research questions. Phrasing study objectives as questions is desirable in that it leads to more clearly focused discussion of the type of information needed. It also makes it more likely that key terms (e.g., welfare dependency, drug use) will be operationalized and clearly defined. Later, after additional information has been gathered and reviewed, the parties will need to reconsider whether these questions are the "right" questions and whether it is possible, with a reasonable degree of confidence, to obtain answers for these questions within the available resource and time constraints.

☐ *Clarifying the Study Questions*

In discussing the research agenda with clients, the researcher may identify multiple types of questions. Researchers frequently are asked to produce comprehensive information on both the implementation ("what is" and "what is the difference between what is and what should be") and the effects ("what caused what") of an intervention. These broad research agendas pose significant challenges for planning in terms of allocating data collection resources among the various study objectives.

In clarifying and setting the research agenda, the researcher should guard against biasing the scope of the research. The questions left unaddressed by a study can be as important as or more important than the questions answered. If the research addresses only questions likely to support the position of one political entity in a controversy and fails to develop information relevant to the concerns voiced by other interested parties, it will be seen as biased, even if the results produced are judged to be sound and conclusive. Thus, to the degree possible, the research agenda should be as comprehensive as is necessary to address the concerns of all parties. If resource constraints limit the number of questions that may be addressed, at minimum the researcher should state explicitly what would be necessary for a comprehensive study, and how the research meets or does not meet those requirements.

Ideally, the development of the conceptual framework should occur simultaneously with the identification of the research question. Once the conceptual framework has been agreed upon, the researcher can further refine the study questions—grouping questions and identifying which are primary and secondary questions. Areas that need clarification include the time frame of the data collection, how far the client wants to generalize, and what subgroups the client wants to know about. The level of specificity should be very high at this point, enabling a clear agreement on what information items will be produced. These discussions between researcher and research clients many times take on the flavor of a negotiation—a negotiation of study scope.

□ *Negotiation of Study Scope*

Communication between researcher and research client (the sponsor and all other interested parties) is essential in all stages of the research process. To ensure maximum and accurate utilization of results, the researcher should interact continuously with the research clients—from the initial discussions of the "problem" to recommendations and follow-up.

In the planning phase, we advocate several specific communication strategies. As soon as the study is sponsored, the researcher should meet with the client to develop a common understanding of the research questions, the client's time frame for study results, and anticipated uses for the information. In this meeting the parties can also discuss preliminary ideas regarding a conceptual framework for the study. Even in this initial stage, it is important for the researcher to begin the discussion of what the final reports and products should look like. This is an opportunity for the researcher to explore whether the client expects only to be provided information on study results or whether the client anticipates that the researcher will offer recommendations for action. It is also an opportunity for the researcher to determine whether he or she will be expected to provide interim findings to the client as the study progresses.

For externally funded research, it is also important for the researcher to have an understanding of the amount of funds or resources that will be available to support the research. Cost considerations will determine the scope of the project, and the investigator needs to consider these while identifying and reviewing the research questions. In some studies, the costs are determined prior to any direct personal contact with the research client. In others, researchers may help to shape the scope and the resources needed simultaneously.

As the researcher does a more comprehensive review of the literature relevant to the proposed study and an initial assessment of resources, he or she may determine that the research questions need to be refined, and that there is a need for researcher and client to discuss the research approaches under consideration to answer these questions, as well as the study limitations. This gives the researcher an opportunity to introduce constraints into the discussion regarding available resources, time frames, and any trade-offs contemplated regarding the likely conclusiveness of answers to the questions.

Generally, most research clients want to support sound, well-executed research and are sympathetic to researchers' needs to preserve the integrity of the research. Some clients, however, have clear political, organizational, or personal agendas, and will push researchers to provide results in unrealistically short time frames or to produce results supporting particular positions. Other times, the subject of the study itself may generate controversy, a situation that requires the researcher to take extreme care to preserve the neutrality and credibility of the study. Several of the strategies discussed below attempt to balance client and researcher needs in a responsible fashion; others concentrate on opening research discussions up to other parties (e.g., advisory groups). In the earliest stages of research planning, it is possible to initiate many of these kinds of activities, thereby bolstering the study's credibility, and often its feasibility.

■ *Stage II: Developing a Research Design*

Having developed at least a preliminary study scope during Stage I, the researcher moves to Stage II, developing a research design and plan. During this stage, the applied researcher needs to perform five activities almost simultaneously: selecting a design, choosing data collection approaches, inventorying resources, assessing the feasibility of executing the proposed approach, and determining trade-offs. These activities and decisions greatly influence one another. Thus a researcher may revisit preliminary design selections after conducting a practical assessment of the resources available to do the study, and may change data collection plans after discovering weaknesses in the data sources during planning.

The design serves as the architectural blueprint of a research project, linking data collection and analysis activities to the research questions and ensuring that the complete research agenda will be addressed. The credibility of the research, its usefulness, and its feasibility rest with the design that is implemented. *Credibility* refers to the validity of a study and whether the design is sufficiently rigorous to provide support for definitive conclusions and desired recommendations. *Usefulness* refers to whether the design is appropriately targeted to answer the specific questions of interest. A sound study is of little use if it provides definitive answers to the wrong questions. *Feasibility* refers to whether the research design can be executed given the requisite time and other resource constraints. All three factors are important to the conduct of high-quality applied research.

□ *Features of the Design*

Maximizing Validity

A credible research design is one that maximizes validity—it provides a clear explanation of the phenomenon under study and controls all possible biases or confounds that could cloud or distort the research findings. Four types of validity are typically considered in the design of applied research (Bickman, 1989; Cook & Campbell, 1979):

- *Internal validity:* the extent to which causal conclusions can be drawn
- *External validity:* the extent to which it is possible to generalize from the data and context of the research study to broader populations and settings (especially those specified in the statement of the original problem/issue)
- *Construct validity:* the extent to which the constructs in the conceptual framework are successfully operationalized (e.g., measured) in the research study
- *Statistical conclusion validity:* the extent to which the study has used appropriate design and statistical methods to enable it to detect the effects that are present

All types of validity are important in applied research, but the relative emphases may vary, depending on the type of question under study. With impact questions, for example, more emphasis may be placed on internal and statistical conclusion validity than on external validity. The researcher of an impact study is primarily concerned with finding any evidence that a causal relationship exists and is typically less concerned (at least initially) about the transferability of that effect to other locations. For descriptive questions, external and construct validity may receive greater emphasis. Here the researcher may consider the first priority to be developing a comprehensive and rich picture of a phenomenon. The need to make cause-effect attributions is not relevant. Construct validity, however, is almost always relevant.

Identifying the Key Variables and Concepts

The process of refining and revising the research questions undertaken in Stage I should have yielded a clear understanding of the key research variables and concepts. For example, if the researcher is charged with determining the extent of high school drug use (a descriptive task), key variables might include drug type, frequency and duration of drug use, and drug sales behavior. If the study has an impact focus, the researcher must not only identify key variables, but must specify them as independent or dependent variables. Independent variables are the purported causes of change in dependent variables. Again, using the drug use example, if the researcher is to determine whether a recent drug education program led to decreased drug use, the implementation of the drug education program would be specified as the independent variable and several variables might be posited as potential dependent variables (e.g., frequency of use, type of use).

Attention should be given at this point to reassessing whether the researcher is studying the right variables—that is, whether these are "useful" variables.

Outlining Comparisons

An integral part of design is identifying whether and what comparisons must be made—that is, which variables must be measured and compared with other variables, or with themselves over time. In simple descriptive studies, there are decisions to be made regarding the time frame of an observation and how many observations are appropriate over time. In normative studies, there are further decisions to make concerning what information is appropriate to compare to a "standard," and where that standard will be drawn from or how it will be developed. In correlative studies, the design is again an extension of simple descriptive work, with the difference that two or more descriptive measures are arrayed against each other over time to determine whether they co-vary. Impact studies, by far, demand the most judgment and background work. To make causal attributions (X causes Y), we must be able to compare the condition of Y when X occurred with what the condition of Y would have been without X.

Level of Analysis

Knowing what level of analysis is necessary is also critical to answering the "right" question. For example, if we are doing a study of drug use among high school students in Toledo, are we interested in drug use by individual students, aggregate survey totals at the school level, aggregate totals at the school district, or for the city as a whole?

Correct identification of the proper level of analysis has important implications for both data collection and analysis. The Stage I client discussions should clarify the desired level of analysis. It is likely that the researcher will have to help the client think through the implications of these decisions, providing information about research options and the levels of findings that would result. In addition, this is an area that is likely to be revisited if initial plans to obtain data at one level (e.g., the individual student level) prove to be prohibitively expensive or unavailable. A design fallback position may be to change to an aggregate analysis level (e.g., the school), particularly if administrative data at this level are more readily available and less costly to access.

Population, Geographic, and Time Boundaries

Population, geographic, and time boundaries are related to external validity issues. How these matters are decided will affect the generalizability of the research results—for instance, whether the results will be representative of all high school students, all high school students graduating within the past 3 years, all students in urban areas, and so on. Population generalizability and geographic generalizability are probably the most commonly discussed types of generalizability, and researchers frequently have heated debates concerning whether the persons they have studied and the locations where they conducted their studies will allow them to address larger social problems or programs of interest.

Time boundaries also can be crucial to the generalizability of results, especially if the study involves extant data that may be a few years old. With the fast pace of change, questions can easily arise about whether survey data on teenagers from even just 2 years prior are reflective of current teens' attitudes and behaviors.

When the researcher cannot study all people, all locations, or all time periods relevant to the problem/program under scrutiny, he or she turns to sampling. Sampling allows the researcher to study only a subset of the units of interest and then generalize to all these units with a specifiable degree of error. It offers benefits in terms of reducing the resources necessary to do a study; it also sometimes permits more intensive scrutiny, by allowing a researcher to concentrate on fewer cases. More details on sampling can be found in Henry (1990; see also Chapter 4, this volume).

Level of Precision

Knowing how precise an answer must be is also crucial to design decisions. The level of desired precision may affect the rigor of the design to be chosen. When sampling is used, the level of desired precision also has important ramifications for how the sample is drawn and the size of the sample used. In initial discussions, researcher and client should reach an understanding regarding the precision desired or necessary. It is essential that the researcher have the answers to these kinds of questions during Stage II; if they are not clarified, the research design may later turn out to be inadequate for the client's purposes.

☐ *Choosing a Design*

There are three main categories of applied research designs: descriptive, experimental, and quasi-experimental. In our experience, developing an applied research design rarely allows for implementing a design straight from a textbook; rather, the process more typically involves the development of a hybrid, reflecting combinations of designs and other features, that can respond to multiple study questions, resource limitations, dynamics in the research context, and other constraints of the research situation (e.g., time deadlines). Thus our intent here is to provide the reader with the tools to shape the research approach to the unique aspects of each situation. Those interested in more detailed discussion should consult Reichardt and Mark's work on quasi-experimentation (Chapter 7, this volume) and Boruch's essay on randomized experiments (Chapter 6). In addition, our emphasis here is on quantitative designs; for more on qualitative designs, readers should consult Maxwell (Chapter 3), Yin (Chapter 8), and Fetterman (Chapter 16).

Descriptive Research Designs

Description and purpose. The overall purpose of descriptive research is to provide a "picture" of a phenomenon as it naturally occurs, as opposed to studying the impacts of the phenomenon or intervention. Descriptive research can be designed to answer questions of a univariate, normative, or correlative nature—that is, describing only one variable, comparing the variable to a particular standard, or summarizing the relationship between two or more variables.

Key features. Because the category of descriptive research is broad and encompasses a number of different types of designs, one of the easiest ways to distinguish this class of research from others is to identify what it is not: It is not designed to provide information on cause-effect relationships.

Variations. There are only a few features of descriptive research that vary. These are the representativeness of the study data sources (e.g., the subjects/entities)—that is, the manner in which the sources are selected (e.g., universe, random sample, stratified sample, nonprobability sample); the time frame of measurement—that is, whether the study is a one-shot, cross-sectional study or a longitudinal study; whether the study involves some basis for comparison (e.g., with a standard, another group or population, data from a previous time period); and whether the design is focused on a simple descriptive question, on a normative question, or on a correlative question.

When to use. A descriptive approach is appropriate when the researcher is attempting to answer "what is" or "what was" questions, normative questions, or correlative questions.

Strengths. Exploratory descriptive studies can be low cost, relatively easy to implement, and able to yield results in a fairly short period of time. Some efforts, however, such as those involving surveys, may sometimes require extensive resources and intensive measurement efforts. The costs depend on factors such as the size of the sample, the nature of the data sources, and the complexity of the data collection methods employed.

Limitations. Descriptive research is not intended to answer questions of a causal nature. Major problems can arise when the results from descriptive studies are inappropriately used to make causal inferences—a temptation for consumers of correlational data.

Experimental Research Designs

Description and purpose. The primary purpose in conducting an experimental study is to test the existence of a causal relationship between two or more variables. In an experimental study, one variable, the independent variable, is systematically varied or manipulated so that its effects on another variable, the dependent variable, can be measured.

Key features. The distinguishing characteristic of an experimental study is the random assignment of individuals or entities to the levels or conditions of the study. Random assignment is used to control all biases at the time of assignment and to ensure that only one variable—the independent (experimental) variable—differs between conditions. Through random assignment, all individuals have an equal likelihood of being assigned either to the treatment group or to the control group. If the total number of individuals or entities assigned to treatment and control groups is sufficiently large, then any differences between the groups should be small and due to chance.

Variations. The most basic experimental study is called a *post-only design,* in which individuals are randomly assigned either to a treatment group or to a control group and the measurement of the effects of the treatment is conducted at a given period following the administration of the treatment. There are a number of variations to this simple experimental design that can respond to specific information needs as well as provide control over possible confounds or influences that may exist. Among the features that can be varied are the number and scheduling of posttest measurement or observation periods, whether a preobservation is conducted, and the number of treatment and control groups used.

When to use. An experimental study is the most appropriate approach to study cause-effect relationships. There are certain situations that are especially conducive to randomized experiments (Cook & Campbell, 1979): when random assignment is expected (i.e., certain scarce resources may already be provided on a "lottery" or random basis), when demand outstrips supply for an intervention, and when there are multiple entry groups over a period of time.

Strengths. The overwhelming strength of a randomized experiment is its control over threats to internal validity—that is, its ability to rule out potential alternative explanations for apparent treatment or program effects.

Limitations. Randomized experiments can be difficult to implement with integrity, particularly in settings where the individuals responsible for random assignment procedures lack research training or understanding of the importance of maintaining compliance with the research protocol (Bickman, 1985; Cochran, 1978).

Quasi-experimental Designs

Description and purpose. Quasi-experimental designs have the same primary purpose as experimental studies—to test the existence of a causal relationship between two or more variables. They are the design of necessity when random assignment is impossible.

Key features. Quasi-experiments attempt to approximate true experiments by substituting other design features for the randomization process. There are generally two ways to create a quasi-experimental comparison base—through the addition of nonequivalent comparison groups or through the addition of pre- and posttreatment observations on the treated group; preferably, both methods should be used.

If comparison groups are used, they are generally referred to as *nonequivalent* comparison groups, based on the fact that they cannot be exactly equivalent with the treatment group because they were not formed by random assignment. The researcher, however, strives to develop procedures to make these groups as equivalent as possible, to provide necessary information and control so that competing explanations for their results can be ruled out.

Variations. Quasi-experiments vary along several of the same dimensions that are relevant for experiments. Overall, there are two main types of quasi-experiments: those involving data collection from two or more nonequivalent groups and those involving multiple observations over time. Quasi-experimental designs can vary along the following dimensions: the number and scheduling of postmeasurement or observation periods; the number and scheduling of premeasurement or observation periods; the nature of the observations—whether the preobservation uses the same measurement procedure as the postobservation, or whether both are using measures that are proxies for the real concept; the manner in which the treatment and comparison groups are determined; and whether the treatment group serves as its own comparison group or a separate comparison group or groups are used.

Some of the strongest time series designs supplement a time series for the treatment group with comparison time series for another group (or time period). Another powerful variation occurs when the researcher is able to study the effects of an intervention over time under circumstances where that intervention is both initiated and later withdrawn.

When to use. A quasi-experimental design is not the method of choice, but rather a fallback strategy for situations in which random assignment is not possible. Situations such as these include when the nature of the independent variable precludes the use of random assignment (e.g., exposure or involvement in a natural disaster); retrospective studies (e.g., the program is already well under way or over); studies focused on economic or social conditions, such as unemployment; when randomization is too expensive, not feasible to initiate, or impossible to monitor closely; when there are obstacles to withholding the treatment or when it seems unethical to withhold it; and when the timeline is tight and a quick decision is mandated.

Strengths. The major strength of the quasi-experimental design is that it provides an approximation to the experimental design and supports causal inferences. Although often open to various types of threats to internal validity (see Reichardt & Mark, Chapter 7, this volume), the quasi-experiment does provide a mechanism for chipping away at the uncertainty surrounding the existence of a specific causal relationship. Additional nonequivalent comparison groups also can bolster an experimental design, particularly if it is narrowly focused.

Limitations. The greatest vulnerability of quasi-experimental designs is the possibility that the comparison base created is biased, that it does not give an accurate estimate of what the situation would have been in the absence of the treatment or program.

■ *Selecting Data Collection Approaches*

Concurrent with deciding on a design, the researcher is investigating possible data collection approaches. Studies, particularly those investigating multiple research questions, often encompass several data collection efforts. We begin this section with a discussion of the data collection issues the researcher must consider during the planning stage, including the sources of data available, the form in which the data are available, the amount of data needed, the accuracy and reliability of the data, and whether the data fit the parameters of the design. We then review the major methods of data collection that are used in applied research and discuss the need for an analysis plan.

☐ *Sources of Data*

The researcher should identify the likely sources of data to address the research questions. Data are often described as falling into one of two broad categories: primary and secondary. Among the potential primary data sources that exist for the applied researcher are people (e.g., community leaders, program participants, service providers, the general public), independent descriptive observations of events and activities, physical documents, and test results. Secondary sources can include administrative records, management information systems, economic and social indicators, and various types of documents (e.g., prior research studies, fugitive unpublished research literature) (see Stewart & Kamins, 1993).

☐ *Form of the Data*

The form in which the data are found is a very important factor for any applied research project and may even determine the overall feasibility of the study. Some projects are easy to conduct—the data sources are obvious and the data are already gathered, archived, and computerized. The researcher need only request access and transfer files. Other projects are extremely difficult—identifying appropriate sources for the needed information may be confusing, and it may turn out that the procedures necessary for obtaining the information are expensive and time-consuming. Gathering data may sometimes be so difficult that the study is not feasible—at least not within the available level of resources.

Possible forms of data include self-reports (e.g., attitudes, opinions, memories, characteristics, and circumstances of individuals), computerized or manual (i.e., hard copy) research databases or administrative records, observations (e.g., events, actions, or circumstances that need to be described or recorded), and various kinds of documentary evidence (e.g., letters, invoices, receipts, meeting minutes, memoranda, plans, reports).

Self-Report Data

When dealing with self-reported data, the researcher may ask individual research participants to provide, to the best of their ability, information on the areas of interest. These inquiries may be made through individual interviews, through telephone or mail surveys, or through written corroboration or affirmation.

Extant Databases

When dealing with extant data from archival sources, the researcher is generally using the information for a purpose other than that for which they were originally collected. There are a number of secondary data sources, such as those developed by university consortia, federal sources such as the Bureau of the Census, state and local sources such as Medicaid databases, and commercial sources such as Inform, a database of 550 business journals.

Given the enormous amount of information routinely collected on individuals in U.S. society, administrative databases are a potential bonanza for applied researchers. More and more organizations, for example, are computerizing their administrative data and archiving their full databases at least monthly. Management information systems, in particular, are becoming more common in service settings for programmatic and evaluation purposes as well as for financial disbursement purposes.

Administrative data sets, however, have one drawback in common with databases of past research—they were originally constructed for operational purposes, not to meet the specific objectives of the researcher's task. When the data are to be drawn from administrative databases, the researcher should ask the following questions: Are the records complete? Why were the data originally collected? Did the database serve some hidden political purpose that could induce systematic distortions? What procedures have been used to deal with missing data? Do the computerized records bear a close resemblance to the original records? Are some data items periodically updated or purged from the computer file? How were the data collected and entered, and by whom?

Observational Data

Observational procedures become necessary when events, actions, or circumstances are the major form of the data. If the events, actions, or circumstances are repetitive or numerous, this form of data can be very expensive to collect. Because the subject of the data collection is often complex, the researcher may need to create detailed guidelines to structure the data collection and summary.

Documents

Documentary evidence may also serve as the basis for an applied researcher's data collection; particular kinds of documents may allow the researcher to track what happened, when it happened, and who was involved. Examples of documentary data include meeting minutes, journals, and program reports. Investigative research may rely on documentary evidence, often in combination with testimonies or interviews.

☐   *Amount of Data*

The research planner must anticipate the amount of data that will be needed to conduct the study. Planning for the appropriate amount involves decisions regarding the number and variety of data sources, the time periods of interest, and the number of units (e.g., study participants), as well as the precision desired. As noted earlier, statistical conclusion validity is an important factor in the planning of research. Statistical conclusion validity concerns primarily those factors that might make it appear that there were no statistically significant effects when, in fact, there were effects. The greater the ability of the research to detect effects that are present, the greater the statistical power of the study.

Technically, effect size is defined as the proportion of variance accounted for by the treatment, or as the difference between a treatment and control group measured in standard deviation units. The purpose of using standard deviation units is to produce a measure that is independent of the metric used in the original dependent measure. Thus we can discuss universal effect sizes regardless of whether we are measuring school grades, days absent, or self-esteem scores. This makes possible the comparison of different studies and different measures in the same study. Conversion to standard deviation units is obtained by subtracting the mean of the control group from the mean of the treatment group and then dividing this difference by the pooled or combined standard deviations of the two groups.

There are a number of factors that could account for not finding an effect when there actually is one. As Lipsey (1990; see also Chapter 2, this volume) indicates, there are four factors that govern statistical power: the statistical test, the alpha level, the sample size, and the effect size. Many researchers, when aware of power concerns, mistakenly believe that increasing sample size is the only way to increase statistical power. Increasing the amount of data collected (the sample size) is clearly one route to increasing power; however, given the costs of additional data collection, the researcher should consider an increase in sample size only after he or she has thoroughly explored the alternatives of increasing the sensitivity of the measures, improving the delivery of treatment, selecting other statistical tests, and raising the alpha level. If planning indicates that power still may not be sufficient, then the researcher faces the choice of not conducting the study, changing the study to address more qualitative questions, or proceeding with the study but informing the clients of the risk of "missing" effects below a certain size. (More information on how to improve the statistical power of a design can be found in Lipsey, Chapter 2, this volume.)

☐   *Accuracy and Reliability of Data*

Data are useless if they are not accurate, valid, and reliable. The concept of construct validity (i.e., Are we measuring what we intend to measure?) is relevant whether one is using extant data or collecting primary data. The researcher is concerned that the variables used in the study are strong operationalizations of key variables in the study's conceptual framework.

The researcher must also be concerned with the possibility of large measurement errors. Whenever there is measurement of a phenomenon, there is some level of error. The error may be random or systematic. It is important for the researcher to remember that just about all measures contain some degree of error; the challenge is to minimize the error or understand it sufficiently to adjust the study. If the error is systematic (i.e., not random), the researcher may be able to correct statistically for the bias that is introduced. However, it is often difficult for the researcher to discover that any systematic error exists, let alone its magnitude. Random error can best be controlled through the use of uniform procedures in data collection.

☐ *Design Fit*

Even when accurate and reliable data exist or can be collected, the researcher must ask whether the data fit the necessary parameters of the design. Are they available on all necessary subgroups? Are they available for the appropriate time periods? Is it possible to obtain data at the right level of analysis (e.g., individual student versus school)? Do different databases feeding into the study contain comparable variables? Are they coded the same way?

If extant databases are used, the researcher may need to ask if the database is sufficiently complete to support the research. Are all variables of interest recorded in it? If an interrupted time series design is contemplated, the researcher may need to make sure that it is possible to obtain enough observations prior to the intervention in question, and that there has been consistency in data reporting throughout the analytic time frame.

☐ *Types of Data Collection Instruments*

Observational Recording Forms

Observational recording forms are guides to be used in the requesting and documenting of information. The subjects may be events, actions, or circumstances, whether live or re-created through discussions or review of written documentation. Observational recording forms are needed when there is substantial information to be collected through observational means or when there are multiple data collectors. When the study will employ multiple data collectors, creating a recording guide can help the researcher make sure that all areas have been covered, and can eliminate the need for recontacting research participants. Also, when there are multiple data collectors, the use of a recording form provides necessary structure to the data collection process, thereby ensuring that all collectors are following similar procedures and employing similar criteria in choosing to include or exclude information.

Tests

In applied studies, researchers are more likely to make use of existing instruments to measure knowledge or performance than to develop new ones. Whether choosing to use a test "off the shelf" or to capitalize on an existing database that includes such data, it is very important that the researcher be thoroughly familiar with the content of the instrument, its scoring, the literature on its creation and norming, and any ongoing controversies about its accuracy.

Data Extraction Forms/Formats

Frequent reliance on administrative records and documents is a major factor underlying the use of this type of data collection. Whether obtaining information from manual case records or computerized data tapes, the researcher needs to screen the data source for the key variables and record them into the research database.

A data extraction form may be a manual coding sheet for recording information out of a paper file folder, or the data collector may use a portable computer to enter information directly into a preformatted research database.

Even when the original source is computerized, the researcher will still need to create a data extraction format. The format should identify the relevant variables on the computerized file and include a program to extract the appropriate information into the research file. In circumstances where there are multiple sources of data (e.g., monthly welfare caseload data tapes), it may be necessary to apply these procedures to multiple data sources, using another program to merge the information into the appropriate format for analysis.

Structured Interview Guides

Whenever a research project requires that the same information items be obtained from multiple individuals, it is desirable for the researcher to create a structured interview guide. The need for structured data collection processes becomes even greater when multiple data collectors are being used (see Fowler, Chapter 12, this volume, on standardized survey interviewing).

A structured interview guide may begin with an explanation of the purpose of the interview and then proceed to a set of sequenced inquiries designed to collect information about attitudes, opinions, memories of events, characteristics, and circumstances. The questions may be about the respondents themselves or about activities occurring in their environment (e.g., individual dietary habits, program activities, world events). The guide itself typically is structured to interact with the individual's responses, branching from one area to the next based on the individual's previous answer. There also are instances in which semistructured or even unstructured interviews may be appropriate. These approaches are generally appropriate for the conduct of descriptive, exploratory research in a new area of inquiry.

Mail and Telephone Surveys

Mail and telephone surveys are used when the researcher needs to obtain the same information from large numbers of respondents. There are many parallels between these methods and structured in-person interview data collection, with the key difference being the mode of data collection. In Chapter 15 of this volume, Lavrakas describes telephone survey methods, including issues of sampling and selection of respondents and supervision of interviewers. In Chapter 14, Mangione provides more detail on the use of mail surveys.

■ *Resource Planning*

Before making final decisions about the specific design to use and the type of data collection procedures to employ, the investigator must take into account the resources available and the limitations of those resources. Resource planning is an integral part of the iterative Stage II planning activities (see Figure 1.2). Resources important to consider are the following:

- *Data:* What are the sources of information needed and how will they be obtained?
- *Time:* How much time is required to conduct the entire research project and its elements?
- *Personnel:* How many researchers are needed and what are their skills?
- *Money:* How much money is needed to implement the research and in what categories?

☐ *Data as a Resource*

The most important resource for any research project consists of the data used to answer the research question. Data for research can be obtained primarily in two ways: from original data collected by the investigator and from existing data. We discuss below in turn the issues associated with primary data collection and the issues involved in the use of secondary data.

Primary Data Collection

There are five major issues the researcher needs to consider in planning for primary data collection: site selection, authorization, the data collection process, accessibility, and other support needed.

Site selection. Applied research and basic research differ on a number of dimensions, as discussed earlier, but probably the most salient difference is in the location of the research. The setting has a clear impact on the research, not only in defining the population studied, but also in the researcher's formulation of the research question addressed, the research design implemented, the measures used, and the inferences that can be drawn from the study. The setting can also determine whether there are enough research participants available.

Deciding on the appropriate number and selection of sites is an integral part of the design/data collection decision, and there often is no single correct answer. Is it best to choose "typical" sites, a "range" of sites, "representative" sites, the "best" site, or the "worst" site? There are always more salient variables for site selection than resources for study execution, and no matter what criteria are used, research critics will claim that other important variables (or other more important variables) were omitted. For this reason, we recommend that the researcher make decisions regarding site selection in close coordination with the research client and/or advisory group. In general, it is also better to concentrate on as few sites as are required, rather than stretching the time and management efforts of the research team across too many locations.

The distinction between "frontstage" and "backstage" made by Goffman (1959) also helps distinguish settings. Frontstage activities are available to anyone, whereas backstage entrance is limited. Thus in a trial, the actions that take place in the courtroom constitute frontstage activity, open to anyone who can obtain a seat. Entrance to the judge's chambers is more limited, presence during lawyer-client conferences is even more restricted, and the observation of jury deliberations is impossible. The researcher needs to assess the openness of the setting before taking the next step: seeking authorization for the research.

Authorization. Even totally open and visible settings usually require some degree of authorization for data collection. Public space may not be as totally available to the researcher as it may seem. For example, it is a good idea to notify authorities if a research team is going to be present in some public setting for an extended period of time. Although the team members' presence may not be illegal and no permission is required for them to conduct observations or interviews, residents of the area may become suspicious and call the police.

If the setting is a closed one, the researcher will be required to obtain the permission of the individuals who control or believe they control access. If there are a number of sites that are eligible for participation and they are within one organization, then it behooves the researcher to explore the independence of these sites from the parent organization. For example, in planning a study of bystander reactions to staged shoplifting, researchers had to obtain the cooperation of the supermarket in which the crime was to be staged (Bickman, 1984; Bickman & Rosenbaum, 1977). They had the choice of contacting the headquarters of the company or approaching the supermarket manager for permission to conduct the study. If they approached the main office first and were refused permission, then the project could not be implemented. However, if one local manager refused, the researchers could approach another one. The researchers elected to approach first a local manager, who informed them he could not participate without approval from his company's headquarters. The manager, however, was persuaded to provide a supporting letter to accompany the researchers' request for permission. The researchers' personal visit to the company's head of security finally helped obtain the necessary cooperation.

The planner needs to know not only at which level of the organization to negotiate, but also which individuals to approach. Again, this will take some intelligence gathering. Personal contacts help, because authorities are usually more likely to meet and be cooperative with the researcher if he or she is recommended by someone they know and trust. Thus the investigator should search for some connection to the organization. If the planner is at a university, then it is possible that someone on the board of trustees is an officer of the organization. If so, contact with the university's development office is advisable. It is advisable for the researcher to obtain advance recommendations from credible sources and hence to avoid approaching an organization cold.

Permission from a central authority does not necessarily imply cooperation from the sites needed for data collection. Nowhere is this more evident than in state/county working relationships. Often central approval will be required just for the researcher to approach local sites. However, the investigator should not assume that central approval guarantees cooperation from those lower down on the organization's hierarchy; this belief can lead the investigator to behave in an insensitive manner. Those at the upper levels of an organization tend to believe they have more power than they actually wield. A wise investigator will put a great deal of effort into obtaining cooperation at the local level, where he or she will find the individuals who feel they control that environment and with whom he or she will be interacting during the data collection phase.

Some closed organizations have procedures that must be followed before they can issue permission to conduct research in their settings (e.g., prisons and schools). Confidentiality and informed consent are usually significant issues for any organization. Will participants be identified or identifiable? How will the data be protected from unauthorized access? Will competitors learn something about the organization from this research that will put it at a disadvantage? Will individuals in the organization be put in any jeopardy by the project? The researcher needs to resolve such issues before approaching an organization for permission.

Organizations that have experience with research usually have standard procedures for working with researchers. For example, school systems typically have standard forms for researchers to complete and deadlines by which these forms must be submitted. These organizations understand the importance of research and are accustomed to dealing with investigators. In contrast, other organizations may not be familiar with applied research. Most for-profit corporations fall into this category, as do many small nonprofit organizations. In dealing with such groups, the investigator will first have to convince the authorities that research, in general, is a good idea, and that their organization will gain something from their participation. In some cases, the researcher may also have to obtain the support of staff within the organizations participating if they are needed to collect data or to obtain access to research participants. In conducting research on programs for homeless families, for example, researchers often have to convince program staff that the research will be worthwhile, will not place the families in the position of "guinea pigs," and will treat the families with respect and dignity. Most important, an organization's decision makers must be convinced that the organization will not be taking a significant risk in participating in the study. The planner must be prepared to present a strong case for why a non-research-oriented organization should want to involve itself in a research project.

Finally, any agreement between the researcher and the organization should be in writing. This may take the form of an informal letter addressed to the organization's project liaison officer (there should be one) for the research. The letter should describe the procedures that will take place and indicate the dates that the investigator will be on-site. The agreement should be detailed and should include how the organization will cooperate with the research.

Data collection process. The primary purpose of obtaining access to a site is to be able to collect data from or about people. The researcher should not assume that having access ensures that the target subjects will agree to participate in the study. Moreover, the researcher should be skeptical regarding assurances from management concerning others' willingness to participate in a study. In a review of 30 randomized studies in drug abuse, Dennis (1990) found that 54% seriously underestimated the client flow by an average of 37%. Realistic and accurate participant estimates are necessary for the researcher to allocate resources and to ensure sufficient statistical power. Many funding agencies require power analyses as part of submitted grant proposals. These power analyses should be supported by evidence that the number of cases used in these analyses are valid estimates.

A planner can try to avoid shortfalls in the number of cases or subjects needed by conducting a small pilot study (Boruch & Wothke, 1985). In a pilot study, the researcher can verify enrollment and attendance data as well as willingness to participate. In cases where potential subjects enter into some program or institution, it will be important to verify the actual subject flow (e.g., number per week). Related to the number of participants is the assurance that the research design can be successfully implemented. Randomized designs are especially vulnerable to implementation problems. It is easy to promise that there will be no new taxes, that the check is in the mail, and that a randomized experiment will be conducted—but it is often difficult to deliver on these promises. In an applied setting, the investigator should obtain agreement from authorities in writing that they will cooperate in the conduct of the study. This agreement must be detailed and procedurally oriented, and should clearly specify the responsibilities of the researcher and those who control the setting.

The ability to implement the research depends on the ability of the investigator to carry out the planned data collection procedures. A written plan for data collection is critical to success, but it does not guarantee effective implementation. A pilot study or walk-through of the procedure is necessary to determine if it is feasible. In this procedure, the investigator needs to consider both accessibility and other support.

Accessibility. There are a large number of seemingly unimportant details that can damage a research project if they are ignored. Will the research participants have the means to travel to the site? Is there sufficient public transportation? If not, will the investigator arrange for transportation? If the study is going to use an organization's space for data collection, will the investigator need a key? Is there anyone else who may use the space? Who controls scheduling and room assignments? Has this person been notified? For example, a researcher about to collect posttest data in a classroom should ensure that he or she will not be asked to vacate the space before data collection is completed.

Other support. Are the lighting and sound sufficient for the study? If the study requires the use of electrical equipment, will there be sufficient electrical outlets? Will the equipment's cords reach the outlets, or should the researcher bring extension cords? Do the participants need food or drink? Space is a precious commodity in many institutions; the researcher should never assume that the research project will have sufficient space.

Secondary Data Analysis

The use of existing data, compared with collecting primary data, has the advantage of lower costs and time savings, but it may also entail managing a large amount of flawed and/or inappropriate data. In some cases, these data exist in formats designed for research purposes; for example, there are a number of secondary data sources developed by university consortia, or by federal agencies such as the Bureau of the Census. Other kinds of data exist as administrative records (e.g., mental health agency records) that were not designed to answer research questions.

In the planning process, the investigator must establish with some confidence that the records to be used contain the information required for the study. Sampling the records will not only provide the researcher with an indication of their content, it will give him or her an idea of their quality. It is frequently the case that clinical or administrative records are not suitable for research purposes. The planner must also have some confidence in the quality of the records. Are the records complete? Why were the data originally collected? The database may serve some hidden political purpose that could induce systematic distortions. What procedures are used to deal with missing data? Are the same procedures used for all variables or only selected variables? Do the computerized records bear a close resemblance to the original records (if available)? Are some data items periodically updated or purged from the computer file? How were the data collected and entered, and by whom? What quality control and verification checks are used? To assess the quality of the database, the planner should interview the data collectors and others experienced with the data, observe the data entry process, and compare written records to the computerized version. Conducting an analysis of administrative records seems easy only if it is not done carefully.

The investigator should not assume that the level of effort needed to process extant data will be small or even moderate. Data sets may be exceedingly complex, with changes occurring in data fields and documentation over time. Moreover, if the researcher is interested in matching cases across existing data sets (as in tracking service use across multiple county databases), he or she will need to ensure that identification fields are available in each data set to match individuals' records. Often matching alone can take a considerable amount of time and resources.

Finally, once the researcher has judged the administrative records or other database to be of sufficient quality for the study, he or she must then go through the necessary procedures to obtain the data. In addition to determining the procedures for extracting and physically transferring the data, the investigator also must demonstrate how the confidentiality of the records will be protected.

☐ *Time as a Resource*

Time takes on two important dimensions in the planning of applied research: calendar time and clock time. Calendar time is the total amount of time available for a project, and it varies across projects.

Time and the Research Question

The calendar time allotted for a study should be related to the research questions. Is the phenomenon under study something that lasts for a long period, or does it exist only briefly? Does the phenomenon under study occur in cycles? Is the time allocated to data collection sufficient?

Time and Data Collection

The second way in which the researcher needs to consider time is in terms of the actual or real clock time needed to accomplish particular tasks. For example, the event that is being studied might exist infrequently and only for a short period of time, thus a long period of calendar time might need to be devoted to the project, but only a short period of clock time for data collection. Having established the time estimates, the investigator needs to estimate how long actual data collection will take. In computing this estimate, the researcher should consider how long it will take to recruit study participants and to gain both cooperation and access. The researcher should also attempt to estimate attrition or dropout from the study. If high attrition is predicted, then more time is needed for data collection for the data to have sufficient statistical power. Thus, in computing the time needed, the investigator should have an accurate and comprehensive picture of the environment in which the study will be conducted.

Time Budget

In planning to use any resource, the researcher should create a budget that describes how the resource will be allocated. Both calendar and clock time need to be budgeted. To budget calendar time, the researcher must know the duration of the entire project. In applied research, the duration typically is set at the start of the project, and the investigator then tailors the research to fit the length of time available. There may be little flexibility in total calendar time on some projects. Funded research projects usually operate on a calendar basis; that is, projects are funded for specific periods of time. Investigators must plan what can be accomplished within the time available.

The second time budget a researcher must create concerns clock time. How much actual time will it take to develop a questionnaire or to interview all the participants? It is important for the investigator to decide what units of time (e.g., hours, days, months) will be used in the budget. That is, what is the smallest unit of analysis of the research process that will be useful in calculating how much time it will take to complete the research project? To answer this question, we now turn to the concept of tasks.

Tasks and Time

To "task out" a research project, the planner must list all the significant activities (tasks) that must be performed to complete the project. The tasks in a project budget serve a purpose similar to that of the expense categories—rent, utilities, food, and so on—used in planning a personal financial budget. When listing all of these expense items, one makes implicit decisions concerning the level of refinement that will be used. Major categories (such as utilities) are usually divided into finer subcategories. The degree of refinement in a research project task budget depends on how carefully the investigator needs to manage resources.

To construct a time budget, the investigator needs to list all the tasks that must be accomplished during the research project. Typically, these can be grouped into a number of major categories. The first category usually encompasses conceptual development. This includes literature reviews and thinking and talking about the problem to be investigated. Time needs to be allocated also for consulting with experts in areas where investigators need additional advice. The literature reviews could be categorized into a number of steps, ranging from conducting computerized searches to writing a summary of the findings.

The second phase found in most projects is instrument development and refinement. Regardless of whether the investigator plans to do intensive face-to-face interviewing, self-administered questionnaires, or observation, he or she needs to allocate time to search for, adapt, or develop relevant instruments used to collect data. The researcher also needs to allocate time for pilot testing of the instruments. Pilot testing should never be left out of any project. Typically, a pilot test will reveal "new" flaws that were not noted by members of the research team in previous applications of the instrument. If the data collection approach involves extracting information from administrative records, the researcher should pilot test the training planned for data extractors as well as the data coding process. Checks should be included for accuracy and consistency across coders.

When external validity or generalization is a major concern, the researcher will need to take special care in planning the construction of the sample. The sampling procedure describes the potential subjects and how they will be selected to participate in the study. This procedure may be very complex, depending upon the type of sampling plan adopted. (For excellent descriptions of sampling methods, see Henry, 1990.)

The next phase of research is usually the data collection. The investigator needs to determine how long it will take to gain access to the records, as well as how long it will take to extract the data from the records. It is important not only that the researcher ascertain how long it will take to collect the data from the records, but that he or she discover whether information assumed to be found in those records is there. If the researcher is planning to conduct a survey, the procedure for estimating the length of time needed for this process could be extensive. Fowler (1993; see also Chapter 12, this volume) describes the steps involved in conducting a survey. These include developing the instrument, recruiting and training interviewers, sampling, and the actual collection of the data. Telephone interviews require some special techniques that are described in detail by Lavrakas (1993; see also Chapter 15, this volume).

The next phase usually associated with any research project is data analysis. Whether the investigator is using qualitative or quantitative methods, time must be allocated for the analysis of data. Analysis includes not only statistical testing using a computer, but also the preparation of the data for computer analysis. Steps in this process include "cleaning" the data (i.e., making certain that the responses are readable and unambiguous for data entry personnel), physically entering the data, and checking for the internal consistency of the data. Once the data are clean, the first step in quantitative analysis is the production of descriptive statistics such as frequencies, means, standard deviations, and measures of skewness. More complex studies may require researchers to conduct inferential statistical tests.

Finally, time needs to be allocated for communicating the results. An applied research project almost always requires a final report, usually a lengthy, detailed analysis. Within the report itself, the researcher should take the time needed to communicate the data to the audience at the right level. In particular, visual displays often can communicate even the most complex findings in a more straightforward manner than prose. In Chapter 18 of this volume, Henry outlines the various types of graphical displays possible, categorizing them according to the purposes they serve and the types of data they display.

Because most people will not read the entire report, it is critical that the researcher include a two- or three-page executive summary that succinctly and clearly summarizes the main findings. The executive summary should focus on the findings, presenting them as the highlights of the study. No matter how much effort and innovation went into data collection, those procedures are of interest primarily to other researchers, not to typical sponsors of applied research or other stakeholders. The best the researcher can hope to accomplish with these latter audiences is to educate them about the limitations of the findings based on the specific methods used.

The investigator should allocate time not just for producing a report, but also for verbally communicating study findings to sponsors and perhaps to other key audiences. Moreover, if the investigator desires to have the results of the study utilized, it is likely that he or she needs to allocate time to work with the sponsor and other organizations in interpreting and applying the findings of the study. This last utilization-oriented perspective is often not included by researchers planning their time budgets.

Time Estimates

Once the researcher has described all the tasks and subtasks, the next part of the planning process is to estimate how long it will take to complete each task. One way to approach this problem is to reduce each task to its smallest unit. For example, in the data collection phase, an estimate of the total amount of interviewing time is needed. The simplest way to estimate this total is to calculate how long each interview should take. Pilot data are critical for helping the researcher to develop accurate estimates.

The clock-time budget indicates only how long it will take to complete each task. What this budget does not tell the researcher is the sequencing and the real calendar time needed for conducting the research. Calendar time can be calculated from clock-time estimates, but the investigator needs to make certain other assumptions as well. For example, if the study uses interviewers to collect data and 200 hours of interviewing time are required, the length of calendar time needed will depend on several factors. Most clearly, the number of interviewers will be a critical factor. One interviewer will take a minimum of 200 hours to complete this task, whereas 200 interviewers could do it in one hour. However, the larger number of interviewers may create a need for other mechanisms to be put into place (e.g., interviewer supervision and monitoring) as well as create concerns regarding the quality of the data. Thus the researcher needs to specify the staffing levels and research team skills required for the project. This is the next kind of budget that needs to be developed.

□   *Personnel as a Resource*

Skills Budget

Once the investigator has described the tasks that need to be accomplished, the next step is to decide what kinds of people are needed to carry out those tasks. What characteristics are needed for a trained observer or an interviewer? What are the requirements for a supervisor? To answer these questions, the investigator should complete a skills matrix that describes the requisite skills needed for the tasks and attaches names or positions of the research team to each cluster of skills. Typically, a single individual does not possess all the requisite skills, so a team will need to be developed for the research project. In Chapter 13 of this volume, van Kammen and Stouthamer-Loeber describe the requirements for a research team in conducting large-scale surveys.

In addition to specific research tasks, the investigator needs to consider management of the project. This function should be allocated to every research project. Someone will have to manage the various parts of the project to make sure that they are working together and that the schedule is being met.

Person Loading

Once the tasks are specified and the amount of time required to complete each task is estimated, the investigator must assign these tasks to individuals. The assignment plan is described by a person-loading table that shows how much time each person is supposed to work on each task.

At some point in the planning process, the researcher needs to return to real, or calendar, time, because the project will be conducted under real time constraints. Thus the tasking chart, or Gantt chart, needs to be superimposed on a calendar. This chart simply shows the tasks on the left-hand side and the months of the study period at the top. Bars show the length of calendar time allocated for the completion of specific subtasks. The Gantt chart shows not only how long each task takes, but also the approximate relationship in calendar time between tasks. Although inexact, this chart can show the precedence of research tasks. One of the key relationships and assumptions made in producing a plan is that no individual will work more than 40 hours a week. Thus the person-loading chart needs to be checked against the Gantt chart to make sure that tasks can be completed by those individuals assigned to them within the periods specified in the Gantt chart. Very reasonably priced computer programs that can run on microcomputers are available to help the planner do these calculations and draw the appropriate charts.

☐ *Financial Resources*

Usually, the biggest part of any research project's financial budget is consumed by personnel—research staff. Social science research, especially applied social science, is very labor-intensive. Moreover, the labor of some individuals can be very costly. To produce a budget based on predicted costs, the investigator needs to follow a few simple steps.

Based on the person-loading chart, the investigator can compute total personnel costs for the project by multiplying the hours allocated to various individuals by their hourly costs.

The investigator should compute personnel costs for each task. In addition, if the project will take place over a period of years, the planner will need to provide for salary increases in the estimates. Hourly cost typically includes salary and fringe benefits and may also include overhead costs. (In some instances, personnel costs need to be calculated by some other time dimensions, such as daily or yearly rates; similarly, project costs may need to be broken down by month or some time frame other than year.)

After the budget has been calculated, the investigator may be faced with a total cost that is not reasonable for the project, either because the sponsor does not have those funds available or because the bidding for the project is very competitive. If this occurs, the investigator has a number of alternatives available. The most reasonable alternative is to eliminate some tasks or reduce the scope of some. The investigator needs to use ingenuity to try to devise not only a valid, reliable, and sensitive project, but one that is efficient as well.

The financial budget, as well as the time budget, should force the investigator to realize the trade-offs that are involved in applied research. Should the investigator use a longer instrument, at a higher cost, or collect fewer data from more subjects? Should the subscales on an instrument be longer, and thus more reliable, or should more domains be covered, with each domain composed of fewer items and thus less reliable? Should emphasis be placed on representative sampling as opposed to a purposive sampling procedure? Should the researcher use multiple data collection techniques, such as observation and interviewing, or should the research plan include only one technique, with more data collected by that procedure? These and other such questions are ones that any research planner faces. However, when a researcher is under strict time and cost limitations, the salience of these alternatives is very high.

■ *Making Trade-Offs and Testing Feasibility*

Before making a firm go/no-go decision, it is worthwhile for the researcher to take the time to assess the strengths and weaknesses of the proposed approach and decide whether it is logistically feasible. This section returns to a discussion of the iterative process that researchers typically use as they assess and refine the initial design approach. Two major activities take place: (a) identifying and deciding on design trade-offs and (b) testing the feasibility of the proposed design. These activities almost always occur simultaneously. The results may require the researcher to reconsider the potential design approach or even to return to the client to renegotiate the study questions.

☐   *Making Design Trade-Offs*

Examples of areas where design trade-offs often occur include external generalizability of study results, conclusiveness of findings, precision of estimates, and comprehensiveness of measurement. Trade-offs are often forced by external limitations in dollar and staff resources, staff skills, time, and the quality of available data.

Generalizability

Generalizability refers to the extent to which research findings can be credibly applied to a wider setting than the research setting. For example, if one wants to describe the methods used in vocational computer training programs, one might decide to study a local high school, an entire community (including both high schools and vocational education agencies and institutions), or schools across the nation. These choices vary widely with respect to the resources required and the effort that must be devoted to constructing sampling frames. The trade-offs here are ones of both resources and time. Local information can be obtained much more inexpensively and quickly than can information about a larger area; however, one will not know whether the results obtained are representative of the methods used in other high schools or used nationally.

Generalizability can also involve time dimensions, as well as geographic and population dimensions. Moreover, generalizability decisions need to have considerable stakeholder involvement. Stakeholders need to have a clear understanding of the generalizability boundaries at the initiation of the study.

Conclusiveness of Findings

One of the key questions the researcher must address is how conclusive the study must be. Research is often categorized as to whether it is exploratory or confirmatory in nature. An exploratory study might seek only to identify the dimensions of a problem—for example, the types of drug abuse commonly found in a high school population. More is demanded from a confirmatory study. In this case, the researcher and client have a hypothesis to test—for example, among high school students use of marijuana is twice as likely as abuse of cocaine or heroin. In this example, it would be necessary to measure with confidence the rates of drug abuse for a variety of drugs and to test the observed differences in rate of use.

Precision of Estimates

In choosing design approaches, it is essential that the researcher have an idea of how small a difference or effect it is important to be able to detect for an evaluation or how precise a sample to draw for a survey. This decision drives the choice of sample sizes and sensitivity of instrumentation, and thus affects the resources that must be allocated to the study.

Sampling error in survey research poses a similar issue. The more precise the estimate required, the greater the amount of resources needed to conduct a survey. If a political candidate feels that he or she will win by a landslide, then fewer resources are required to conduct a political poll than if the race is going to be close and the candidate requires more precision or certainty concerning the outcome as predicted by a survey.

Comprehensiveness of Measurement

The last area of choice involves the comprehensiveness of measurement used in the study. It is usually desirable to use multiple methods or multiple measures in a study, for this allows the researcher to look for consistency in results, thereby increasing confidence in findings. However, multiple measures and methods can sometimes be very expensive and potentially prohibitive. Thus researchers frequently make trade-offs between resources and comprehensiveness in designing measurement and data collection approaches.

Choosing the most appropriate strategy involves making trade-offs between the level of detail that can be obtained and the resources available. Calendar time to execute the study also may be relevant. Within the measurement area, the researcher often will have to make a decision about breadth of measurement versus depth of measurement. Here the choice is whether to cover a larger number of constructs, each with a brief instrument, or to study fewer constructs with longer and usually more sensitive instrumentation. Some trade-off between comprehensiveness (breadth) and depth is almost always made in research. Thus, within fixed resources, a decision to increase external validity by broadening the sample frame may require a reduction in resources in other aspects of the design. The researcher needs to consider which aspects of the research process require the most resources.

☐ *Feasibility Testing of the Research Design/Plan*

Once the researcher has tentatively selected a research design, he or she must determine whether the design is feasible. Areas to be tested for feasibility include the assessment of any secondary data, pilot tests of data collection procedures and instruments, and pilot tests of the design itself (e.g., construction of sampling frames, data collection procedures, and other study procedures). Additionally, efforts may be needed to explore the likelihood of potential confounding factors—that is, whether external events are likely to distort study results or whether the study procedures themselves may create unintended effects. The process of feasibility testing may take as little as a few hours or may involve a trial run of all study procedures in a real-world setting and could last several weeks or months.

The premise of feasibility testing is that, although sometimes time-consuming, it can greatly improve the likelihood of success or, alternatively, can prevent resources from being wasted on research that has no chance of answering the posed questions. A no-go decision does not represent a failure on the part of the researcher, but rather an opportunity to improve on the design or research procedures, and ultimately results in better research and hopefully better research utilization. A go decision reinforces the confidence of the researcher and others in the utility of expending resources to conduct the study.

Once the researcher has appropriately balanced any design trade-offs and determined the feasibility of the research plan, he or she should hold final discussions with the research client to confirm the proposed approach. If the client's agreement is obtained, the research planning phase is complete. If agreement is not forthcoming, the process may start again, with a change in research scope (questions) or methods.

■ *Conclusion*

The key to conducting a sound applied research study is planning. In this chapter, we have described a variety of steps that can be taken in the planning stage to bolster a study and increase its potential for successful implementation. We hope that these steps will help you to conduct applied research that is credible, feasible, and useful.

■ *References*

Bickman, L. (1984). Bystander intervention in crimes: Theory, research and applications. In J. Karylowski, J. Rekowsky, E. Staub, & D. Bar-Tal (Eds.), *Development and maintenance of prosocial behavior: International perspectives.* New York: Plenum.

Bickman, L. (1985). Randomized experiments in education: Implementations lessons. In R. F. Boruch (Ed.), *Randomized field experiments* (pp. 39-53). San Francisco: Jossey-Bass.

Bickman, L. (1987). The functions of program theory. In L. Bickman (Ed.), *Using program theory in evaluation* (pp. 5-18). San Francisco: Jossey-Bass.

Bickman, L. (1989). Barriers to the use of program theory: The theory-driven perspective. *Evaluation and Program Planning, 12,* 387-390.

Bickman, L. (Ed.). (1990). *Advances in program theory.* San Francisco: Jossey-Bass.

Bickman, L., & Rog, D. J. (1986). Stakeholder assessment in early intervention projects. In L. Bickman & D. Weatherford (Eds.), *Evaluating early childhood intervention programs.* Austin, TX: Pro-Ed.

Bickman, L., & Rosenbaum, D. (1977). Crime reporting as a function of bystander encouragement, surveillance, and credibility. *Journal of Personality and Social Psychology, 35,* 577-586.

Boruch, R. F., & Wothke, W. (Eds.). (1985). *Randomization and field experimentation.* San Francisco: Jossey-Bass.

Chen, H., & Rossi, P. H. (Eds.). (1992). *Using theory to improve program and policy evaluations.* Westport, CT: Greenwood.

Cochran, N. (1978). Grandma Moses and the "corruption" of data. *Evaluation Quarterly, 2,* 363-373.

Cook, T. D., & Campbell, D. T. (1979). *Quasi-experimentation: Design and analysis issues for field settings.* Chicago: Rand McNally.

Dennis, M. L. (1990). Assessing the validity of randomized field experiments: An example from drug treatment research. *Evaluation Review, 14,* 347-373.

Fowler, F. J., Jr. (1993). *Survey research methods* (2nd ed.). Newbury Park, CA: Sage.

Goffman, E. (1959). *The presentation of self in everyday life.* Garden City, NY: Doubleday.

Henry, G. T. (1990). *Practical sampling.* Newbury Park, CA: Sage.

Lavrakas, P. J. (1993). *Telephone survey methods: Sampling, selection, and supervision* (2nd ed.). Newbury Park, CA: Sage.

Lipsey, M. W. (1990). *Design sensitivity: Statistical power for experimental research.* Newbury Park, CA: Sage.

Rog, D. J. (1994). Expanding the boundaries of evaluation: Strategies for refining and evaluating ill-defined interventions. In S. L. Friedman & H. C. Haywood (Eds.), *Developmental follow-up: Concepts, genres, domains, and methods* (pp. 139-154). New York: Academic Press.

Rog, D. J., & Huebner, R. (1992). Using research and theory in developing innovative programs for homeless individuals. In H. Chen & P. H. Rossi (Eds.), *Using theory to improve program and policy evaluations* (pp. 129-144). Westport, CT: Greenwood.

Stewart, D. W., & Kamins, M. A. (1993). *Secondary research: Information sources and methods* (2nd ed.). Newbury Park, CA: Sage.

Wholey, J. S. (1987). Evaluability assessment: Developing program theory. In L. Bickman (Ed.), *Using program theory in evaluation* (pp. 77-92). San Francisco: Jossey-Bass.

2

Design Sensitivity

Statistical Power for Applied Experimental Research

Mark W. Lipsey

Applied experimental research investigates the effects of deliberate intervention in situations of practical importance. A psychotherapist, for instance, might study the efficacy of systematic desensitization for reducing the symptoms of snake phobia; a school might evaluate the success of a drug education program; or a policy maker might ask for evidence that altering the tax rate on gasoline will discourage consumption. The basic elements of experimental research are well-known: selection of subjects and assignment of them to experimental and control conditions, preferably using a random procedure; application of the intervention of interest to the experimental group but not to the control group; monitoring of the research situation to ensure that there are no differences between the experimental and control conditions other than the intervention; measurement of selected outcomes for both groups; and statistical analysis to determine if the groups differ on those dependent variable measures. To ensure that the conclusions about intervention effects drawn from experimental design are correct, the design must have both sensitivity and validity. *Sensitivity* refers to the likelihood that an effect, if present, will be detected. *Validity* refers to the likelihood that what is detected is, in fact, the effect of interest. This chapter is about the problem of sensitivity (for discussion of the problem of validity, see Chapter 7 of this volume, by Reichardt and Mark.)

Sensitivity in intervention research is thus the ability to detect a difference between the experimental and control conditions on some outcome of interest. If the research has been designed to be valid, that difference will represent the effect of the intervention under investigation. What, then, determines our ability to detect it? Answering this question requires that we specify what is meant by *detecting a difference* in experimental research. Following current convention, we will take this to mean that statistical criteria are used to reject the null hypothesis of no difference between the mean on the relevant outcome measure observed on the sample of persons in the experimental condition and the mean observed on the sample in the control condition. In particular, we conclude that there is an effect if an appropriate statistical test reaches statistical significance.

My goal in this chapter is to help researchers to "tune" experimental design to maximize sensitivity. However, before I can offer a close examination of the practical issues related to design sensitivity, I need to present a refined framework for describing and assessing the desired result—a high probability of detecting a given magnitude of effect if it exists. This brings us to the topic of *statistical power,* the concept that will provide the idiom for my discussion of design sensitivity.

■ *The Statistical Power Framework*

In the final analysis, applied experimental research comes down to just that: analysis (data analysis, that is). After all the planning, implementation, and paperwork, the researcher is left with a set of numbers that carry the information about measured differences between the experimental conditions and upon which the crucial tests of statistical significance are conducted. There are four possible scenarios for this testing: There either *is* or *is not* a real (population) experimental versus control difference, and, for each case, the statistical test on the sample data either *is* or *is not* significant. The various combinations can be depicted in a 2×2 table along with the associated probabilities, as shown in Table 2.1. Finding statistical significance when, in fact, there is no effect is known as Type I error; the Greek letter α is used to represent the probability of that happening. Failure to find statistical significance when, in fact, there is an effect is known as Type II error; the Greek letter β is used to represent that probability. Most important, *statistical power* is the probability $(1 - \beta)$ that statistical significance will be attained *given* that there really is an intervention effect. This is the probability that must be maximized for a research design to be sensitive to actual intervention effects.

Note that α and β in Table 2.1 are statements of *conditional* probabilities. They are of the following form: *If* the null hypothesis is true (false), *then* the probability of an erroneous statistical conclusion is α (β). Thus when the null

Table 2.1 The Possibilities of Error in Statistical Significance Testing of Treatment (T) Versus Control (C) Group Differences

	Population Circumstances	
Conclusion from statistical test on sample data	T and C Differ	T and C Do Not Differ
Significant difference (reject null hypothesis)	Correct conclusion Probability = $1 - \beta$ (power)	Type I error Probability = α
No significant difference (fail to reject null hypothesis)	Type II error Probability = β	Correct conclusion Probability = $1 - \alpha$

hypothesis is true, the probability of a statistical conclusion error is held to 5% by the convention of $\alpha = .05$. When the null hypothesis is false (i.e., there is a real effect), however, the probability of error is β, and β can be quite large. If we want to design experimental research in which statistical significance is found when the intervention has a real effect, therefore, we must design for a low β error, that is, for high statistical power $(1 - \beta)$.

An important question at this juncture concerns what criterion level of statistical power the researcher should strive for—that is, what level of risk for Type II error is acceptable? By convention, researchers generally set $\alpha = .05$ as the maximum acceptable probability of a Type I error. There is no analogous convention for β. Cohen (1977, 1988) suggests $\beta = .20$ as a reasonable value for general use (more specifically, he suggests that power, equal to $1 - \beta$, be at least .80). This suggestion represents a judgment that Type I error is four times as serious as Type II error. This position may not be defensible for many areas of applied research, where a null statistical result for a genuinely effective intervention may represent a great loss of valuable practical knowledge.

A more reasoned approach would be to analyze explicitly the cost-risk issues that apply to the particular research circumstances at hand (more on this later). At the first level of analysis, the researcher might compare the relative seriousness of Type I and Type II errors. If they are judged to be equally serious, the risk of each should be kept comparable; that is, alpha should equal beta. Alternatively, if one is judged to be more serious than the other, it should be held to a stricter standard even at the expense of relaxing the other. If a convention must be adopted, it may be wise to assume that, for intervention research of potential practical value, Type II error is at least as important as Type I error. In this case we would set $\beta = .05$, as is usually done for α, and thus attempt to design research with power $(1 - \beta)$ equal to .95.

☐ *Determinants of Statistical Power*

There are four factors that determine statistical power: sample size, alpha level, statistical test, and effect size.

Sample size. Statistical significance testing is concerned with sampling error, the expectable discrepancies between sample values and the corresponding population value for a given sample statistic such as a difference between means. Because sampling error is smaller for large samples, real differences between means are less likely to be obscured by such error and statistical power is greater.

Alpha level. The level set for alpha influences the likelihood of statistical significance—larger alpha makes significance easier to attain than does smaller alpha. When the null hypothesis is false, therefore, statistical power increases as alpha increases.

Statistical test. Because investigation of statistical significance is made within the framework of a particular statistical test, the test itself is one of the factors determining statistical power.

Effect size. If there is some real difference between the experimental conditions, the size of this difference will have an important influence on the likelihood of attaining statistical significance. The larger the effect, the more probable is statistical significance and the greater the statistical power. For a given dependent measure, effect size can be thought of simply as the difference between the means of the experimental versus control *populations*. In this form, however, its magnitude is partly a function of how the dependent measure is scaled. For most purposes, therefore, it is preferable to use an effect size formulation that standardizes differences between means by dividing by the standard deviation to adjust for arbitrary units of measurement. The effect size for a given difference between means, therefore, can be represented as follows:

$$ES = \frac{\mu_e - \mu_c}{\sigma}$$

where μ_e and μ_c are the respective means for the experimental and control populations and σ is their common standard deviation. This version of the effect size index was popularized by Cohen (1977, 1988) for purposes of statistical power analysis and is widely used in meta-analysis to represent the magnitude of intervention effects (Cooper & Hedges, 1994). By convention, *ES* is computed so that positive values indicate a "better" outcome for the experimental group than for the control group and negative values indicate a "better" outcome for the control group.

For all but very esoteric applications, the most practical way actually to determine the numerical values for statistical power is to use precomputed tables. Particularly complete and usable reference works of statistical power tables have been published by Cohen (1977, 1988). Other general reference works along similar lines include those of Owen (1962, 1965) and Kraemer and Thiemann (1987). There are also several computer programs on the market for conducting statistical power calculations, such as nQuery Advisor (from Statistical Solutions, Boston), Stat-Power 2, and Statistical Power Analysis (both from Lawrence Erlbaum, Hillsdale, New Jersey). The reader should turn to sources such as these for information on determining statistical power beyond the few illustrative cases presented in this chapter.

Figure 2.1 presents a statistical power chart for one of the more common situations. This chart assumes (a) that the statistical test used is a *t* test, one-way ANOVA, or other parametric test in this same family (more on this later) and (b) that the conventional $\alpha = .05$ level is used as the criterion for statistical significance. Given these circumstances, this chart shows the relationships among power $(1 - \beta)$, effect size (*ES*), and sample size (*n* for each group) plotted on sideways log-log paper, which makes it easier to read values for the upper power levels and the lower sample sizes. (Similar charts for other alpha levels can be found in Lipsey, 1990.) Figure 2.1 shows, for instance, that if we have an experiment with 40 subjects in each of the experimental and control groups, the power to detect an effect size of .80 (.8 standard deviations difference between experimental and control group means) is about .94 (i.e., given a population *ES* = .80 and group *n* = 40, statistical significance would be expected 94% of the time at the $\alpha = .05$ level with a *t* test or one-way ANOVA).

■ Optimizing Statistical Power

To maximize the sensitivity of experimental research for detecting intervention effects using conventional criteria of statistical significance, the researcher must maximize statistical power. In the remainder of this chapter, I examine each of the determinants of statistical power and discuss how it can be manipulated to enhance power. The objective of this discussion is to provide the researcher with the conceptual tools to design experimental research with the greatest possible sensitivity to intervention effects given the resources available. Moreover, in those cases where an appropriately high level of statistical power cannot be attained, these same concepts can be used to analyze the limitations of the research design and guard against misinterpretation.

□ Sample Size

The relationship between sample size and statistical power is so close that most textbooks that discuss power at all do so in terms of determining the

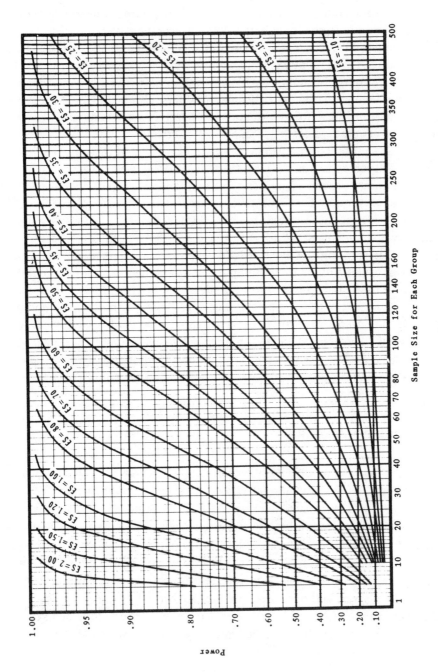

Figure 2.1. Power Chart for $\alpha = .05$, Two-Tailed, or $\alpha = .025$, One-Tailed

sample size necessary to attain a desired power level. A look at Figure 2.1 makes clear why sample size warrants so much attention. Virtually any desired level of power for detecting any given effect size can be attained by making the samples large enough.

The difficulty that the relationship between sample size and statistical power poses for intervention research is that the availability of subjects is often quite limited. The researcher can increase power considerably by parading a larger number of subjects through the study, but there must be subjects ready to march before this becomes a practical strategy. In practical intervention situations, there may be relatively few persons appropriate for the intervention; or, if there are enough appropriate persons, there may be limits on the facilities for treating them. If facilities are adequate, there may be few who will volunteer or whom program personnel are willing to assign; or, if assigned, few may sustain their participation until the study is complete. The challenge for the intervention researcher, therefore, is often one of keeping power at an adequate level with quite modest sample sizes. If modest sample sizes in fact generally provided adequate power, this particular challenge would not be very demanding. Unfortunately, they do not.

Suppose, for instance, that we set $ES = .20$ as the minimal effect size level that we would want an intervention study to detect reliably. An effect size of .20 is equivalent to a 22% improvement in the success rate for the experimental group (more on this later). It is also the level representing the first quintile in the effect size distribution derived from meta-analyses of psychological, behavioral, and educational intervention research (Figure 2.2, presented later). Absent other considerations, therefore, $ES = .20$ is a reasonable minimal effect size level to ask research to detect—it is large enough to potentially represent an effect of practical significance, but not so small as to represent an extreme outcome for intervention research.

If we calculate the sample size needed to yield a power level of .95 ($\beta = \alpha = .05$), we find that the experimental and control group must each have a minimum of about 650 subjects, for a total of about 1,300 in both groups (see Figure 2.1). The mean sample size found by Lipsey, Crosse, Dunkle, Pollard, and Stobart (1985) in a collection of published intervention studies was about 40 in each experimental group, that is, a total of 80 in both the experimental and control groups. Other reviews of intervention research have shown similar patterns (Kroll & Chase, 1975; Mazen, Graf, Kellogg, & Hemmasi, 1987; Ottenbacher, 1982; Reed & Slaichert, 1981). Thus if we want to increase the power for detecting $ES = .20$ through sample size alone, we must increase the number of subjects approximately 1600% over the average in present practice in order to attain a power level that makes Type II error as small as the conventional limit on Type I error. Even attaining the much more modest .80 power level suggested as a minimum by Cohen would require a sample size of about 400 per experimental group, a tenfold increase over the mean for present practice.

Thus, although increased sample size is an effective means to increase statistical power and should be used whenever feasible, cost and availability of subjects may restrict the researcher's ability to use this approach. It is important, therefore, that the researcher be aware of alternative routes to increasing statistical power. The remainder of this chapter discusses some of these alternate routes.

□ *Alpha Level*

Alpha is conventionally set at .05 for statistical significance testing and, on the surface, may seem to be the one straightforward and unproblematic element of statistical power for the intervention researcher. That impression is misleading. An alpha of .05 corresponds to a .95 probability of a correct statistical conclusion only when the null hypothesis is true. However, a relatively conservative alpha makes statistical significance harder to attain when the null hypothesis is false and, therefore, decreases the statistical power. Conversely, relaxing the alpha level required for statistical significance increases power. The problem is that this reduction in the probability of a Type II error comes at the expense of an increased probability of a Type I error. This means that the researcher cannot simply raise alpha until adequate power is attained but, rather, must find some appropriate balance between alpha and beta. Both Type I error (α) and Type II error (β) generally have important implications in the investigation of intervention effects. Type I error can mean that an ineffective or innocuous intervention is judged beneficial or, possibly, harmful, whereas Type II error can permit a truly effective intervention (or a truly harmful one) to go undiscovered. Useful perspectives on how to think about this balancing act can be found in the works of Brown (1983), Cascio and Zedeck (1983), Nagel and Neef (1977), and Schneider and Darcy (1984). In summary form, the advice of these authors is to consider the following points in setting error risk levels.

Prior probability. Because the null hypothesis is either true or false, only one type of inferential error is possible in a given study—Type I for a true null hypothesis and Type II for a false null hypothesis. The problem, of course, is that we do not know if the null hypothesis is true or false and thus do not know which type of error is relevant to our situation. However, when there is evidence that makes one alternative more likely, the associated error should be given more importance. If, for example, prior research tends to show an intervention effect, the researcher should be especially concerned about protection against Type II error and should set beta accordingly.

Directionality of significance testing. A significance test of a one-tailed hypothesis (e.g., that the experimental group mean is superior to the control group) conducted at a given alpha level has higher power (smaller beta) than a two-tailed test at the same alpha (e.g., that the experimental group is either superior *or* inferior to control). In applied intervention research, concern often centers on one direction of effects, for instance, whether a new intervention is better than an existing one. In these situations it is reasonable to argue that one-tailed tests are justified and that using two-tailed tests amounts to inappropriate restriction of the alpha level.

Relative costs and benefits. Perhaps the most important aspect of error risk in intervention research has to do with the consequences of error. Rarely will the costs of each type of error be the same, nor will the benefits of each type of correct inference be the same. Sometimes intervention effects and their absence can be interpreted directly in terms of dollars saved or spent, lives saved or lost, and the like. In such cases the optimal relationship between alpha and beta error risk should be worked out according to their relative costs and benefits. When the consequences of Type I and Type II error cannot be specified in such definite terms, the researcher may still be able to rely on some judgment about the relative seriousness of the risks. He or she might approach this by asking those familiar with the intervention circumstances to rate the error risks and the degree of certainty they feel is minimal for the conclusions of the research. For instance, such questioning may reveal that knowledgeable persons feel, on average, that a 95% probability of detecting a meaningful effect is minimal and that Type II error is three times as serious as Type I. This indicates that beta should be set at .05 and alpha at .15. Nagel and Neef (1977) provide a useful decision theory approach to this judgment process that has the advantage of requiring relatively simple judgments from those whose views are relevant to the research context.

If some rational analysis of the consequences of error is not feasible, it may be necessary to resort to a convention (such as $\alpha = .05$) as a default alternative. For practical intervention research, the situation is generally one in which *both* types of error are serious. Under these circumstances, the most straightforward approach is to set alpha risk and beta risk equal unless there is a clear reason to do otherwise. If we hold to the usual convention that alpha should be .05, therefore, we should design research so that beta will also be .05. If such high standards are not practical, then both alpha and beta should be relaxed to some less stringent level—for example, .10 or even .20.

To provide some framework for consideration of the design issues related to the criterion levels of alpha and beta set by the researcher, Table 2.2 shows the required sample size per group for the basic two-group experimental design at various effect sizes under various equal levels of alpha (two-tailed) and beta. It is noteworthy that maintaining relatively low levels of alpha and beta risk (e.g., .05 or below) requires either rather large effect sizes or rather large sample sizes. Moreover, relaxing alpha levels does not generally yield dramatic increases in statistical power for the most difficult to detect effect sizes. Manipulation of other aspects of the power function, such as those described

Table 2.2 Approximate Sample Size for Each Group Needed to Attain Various
Equal Levels of Alpha and Beta for a Range of Effect Sizes

	Level of Alpha and Beta ($\alpha = \beta$)			
Effect Size	*.20*	*.10*	*.05*	*.01*
.10	900	1,715	2,600	4,810
.20	225	430	650	1,200
.30	100	190	290	535
.40	60	110	165	300
.50	35	70	105	195
.60	25	50	75	135
.70	20	35	55	100
.80	15	30	45	75
.90	10	25	35	60
1.00	10	20	30	50

below, will usually be more productive for the researcher seeking to detect potentially modest effects with modest sample sizes.

☐ *Statistical Test*

Consider the prototypical experimental design in which one experimental group is compared with one control group. The statistical tests for analyzing this design are among the most familiar: *t* test, one-way analysis of variance, chi-square, and so forth. These tests use an "error term" based on the within-group variability in the sample data to assess the likelihood that the mean difference between the groups could result from sampling error. To the extent that within-group variability can be eliminated, minimized, or somehow offset, intervention research will be more powerful—that is, more sensitive to true effects if they are present.

Two aspects of the statistical test are paramount in this regard. First, for a given set of experimental versus control group data, different tests may have different formulations of the sampling error estimate and the critical test values needed for significance. For instance, nonparametric tests, those that use only rank order or categorical information from dependent variable scores, generally have less inherent power than do parametric tests, which use scores representing degrees of the variable along some continuum.

The second and most important aspect of a statistical test that is relevant to power is the way it partitions sampling error and which components of that error variance are used in the significance test. It is often the case in intervention research that a certain amount of the variability on a given dependent measure is associated with subject characteristics that are not likely to change as a result of intervention. If certain factors extraneous to the intervention issues contribute substantially to the population variability on the dependent measure of interest, the variability resulting from those factors can be removed from the estimate of sampling error against which differences between experimental and control means are tested.

A simple example might best illustrate the issue. Suppose that men and women, on average, differ greatly in the amount of weight they can lift. Suppose further that we want to assess the effects of an exercise regimen that was expected to increase muscular strength. Forming experimental and control groups by simple random sampling of the undifferentiated population would mean that part of the luck of the draw—that is, sampling error—would be the chance proportions of men and women that end up in each experimental group and, additionally, would mean that part of the population variability would be the natural differences between men and women. This source of variability may well be judged irrelevant to an assessment of the intervention effect—that intervention may rightfully be judged effective if it increases the strength of women relative to the natural variability in women's strength and that of men relative to the natural variability in men's strength. The corresponding sampling procedure is not simple random sampling but stratified random sampling, drawing women and men separately from their respective populations.

All statistical significance tests assess effects relative to an estimate of sampling error, but they may make different assumptions about the nature of the sampling and, hence, the magnitude of the sampling error. The challenge to the intervention effectiveness researcher is to identify the measurable extraneous factors that contribute to population variability and then use a sampling strategy and corresponding statistical test that assess intervention effects against an appropriate estimate of sampling error. Where there are important extraneous factors that correlate with the dependent variable (and there almost always are), using a statistical significance test that partitions them out of the error term can greatly increase statistical power. With this in mind, I review below some of the more useful of the variance control statistical designs with regard to their influence on power.

Analysis of Covariance

One of the most useful of the variance control designs for intervention research is the one-way analysis of covariance (ANCOVA). Functionally, the ANCOVA is like the simple one-way analysis of variance (ANOVA), except that the dependent variable variance that is correlated with a covariate variable (or linear combination of covariate variables) is removed from the error term used for significance testing. For example, a researcher with a reading achievement test as a dependent variable may wish to remove the component of performance associated with IQ before comparing the experimental and control groups. IQ is a stable individual differences variable that may well be viewed as nuisance variance that is correlated with reading scores but may not be especially relevant to the impact of the program upon those scores.

It is convenient to think of the influence of variance control statistical designs upon statistical power as a matter of adjusting the effect size in the power relationship. Recall that *ES,* as it is used in statistical power determination, is defined as $(\mu_e - \mu_c)/\sigma$, where σ is the pooled within-groups standard deviation. For assessing the power of variance control designs, we adjust this *ES* to create a new value that is the one that is operative for statistical power determination. For the analysis of covariance statistical design, the operative *ES* for power determination is as follows:

$$ES_{ac} = \frac{\mu_e - \mu_c}{\sigma\sqrt{1 - r_{dc}^2}}$$

where ES_{ac} is the effect size formulation for the one-way analysis of covariance; μ_e and μ_c are the means for the experimental and control populations, respectively; σ is the common standard deviation; and r_{dc} is the correlation between the dependent variable and the covariate. As this formula shows, the operative effect size for power determination using ANCOVA is inflated by a factor of $1/\sqrt{1 - r^2}$, which multiplies *ES* by 1.15 when $r = .50$ and 2.29 when $r = .90$. Thus when the correlation of the covariate(s) with the dependent variable is substantial, the effect of ANCOVA on statistical power can be equivalent to more than doubling the operative effect size. Examination of Figure 2.1 reveals that such an increase in the operative effect size can greatly enhance power at any given sample size.

An especially useful application of ANCOVA in intervention research is when both pretest and posttest values on the dependent measure are available. In many cases of experimental research, preexisting individual differences on the characteristic that intervention is intended to change will not constitute an appropriate standard for judging intervention effects. Of more relevance will be the size of the intervention effect relative to the dispersion of scores for subjects that began at the same initial or baseline level on that characteristic. In such situations, a pretest measure is an obvious candidate for use as a covariate in ANCOVA. Because pretest-posttest correlations are generally high, often approaching the test-retest reliability of the measure, the pretest as a covariate can dramatically increase the operative effect size in statistical power. Indeed, ANCOVA with the pretest as the covariate is so powerful and so readily attainable in most instances of intervention research that it should be taken as the standard to be used routinely unless there are good reasons to the contrary.

ANOVA With a Blocking Factor

In this design subjects are first categorized into blocks, that is, groups of subjects that are similar to each other on some characteristic related to the dependent variable. For example, to use gender as a blocking variable, one would first divide subjects into males and females, then assign some males to the experimental group and the rest to the control group and, separately, assign some females to experimental and the rest to control.

In the blocked design the overall variance on the dependent measure can be viewed as the sum of two components: the within-blocks variance and the between-blocks variance. Enhanced statistical power is gained in this design because it removes the contribution of the between-blocks variance from the error term against which effects are tested. As in the ANCOVA case, this influence on power can be represented in terms of an adjusted effect size. If we let PV_b equal the proportion of the total dependent variable variance represented by the difference among blocks, a researcher can calculate the operative ES for this case as follows:

$$ES_{ab} = \frac{\mu_e - \mu_c}{\sigma\sqrt{1 - PV_b}}$$

where ES_{ab} is the effect size formulation for the blocked one-way analysis of variance, σ is the pooled within-groups standard deviation (as in the unadjusted ES), and PV_b is σ_b^2/σ^2, with σ_b^2 the between-blocks variance and σ^2 the common variance of the experimental and control populations.

The researcher, therefore, can estimate PV_b, the between-blocks variance, as a proportion of the common (or pooled) variance within experimental groups and use it to adjust the effect size estimate in such a way as to yield the operative effect size associated with the statistical power of this design. If, for instance, the blocking factor accounts for as much as half of the common variance, the operative ES increases by more than 40%, with a correspondingly large increase in power.

Paired Subjects or Repeated Measures Designs

An important variant on the *t* test and one-way ANOVA is the case where the two samples being compared are not independent but, instead, consist of observations that are paired in some way such that members of each pair are more similar than the members of different pairs. The most familiar case is the pre-post or repeated measures design in which each subject serves as his or her own control. Each pair of observations thus consists of the value of the dependent variable at Time 1 (pretest) and at Time 2 (posttest) for a particular subject. An analogous case occurs when two different subjects are represented in each pair, but, prior to the experiment, they are matched on some relevant characteristic or set of characteristics. One subject from each pair is then assigned to the experimental group and the other to the control group. To the extent that the chosen matching variables are related to the dependent variable at issue, subjects within these pairs will have more similar values on the dependent variable than will unpaired subjects.

In both these cases, the net result is that the *t* test or *F* test is based on an error term that is reduced in proportion to the strength of the correlation (r_{ec}) between the paired values (assuming, as is likely, that the correlation is positive). Correspondingly, the denominator of the effect size index decreases and the operative effect size for statistical power increases. The adjusted *ES* for paired observation designs thus is as follows:

$$ES_{ap} = \frac{\mu_e - \mu_c}{\sigma\sqrt{1 - r_{ec}}},$$

where ES_{ap} is the effect size formulation for the correlated *t* test or one-way ANOVA with paired observations; μ_e and μ_c are the means for the experimental and control populations, respectively; σ is the common standard deviation of the two populations; and r_{ec} is the correlation between the paired values in those populations. As in the other variance control statistical designs, the operative effect size for statistical power purposes is inflated to the extent that there is a correlation (r_{ec}) between the paired values with a consequent increase in power.

Power Advantages of Variance Control Designs

The variance control statistical designs described above all have the effect of reducing the denominator of the effect size index and, hence, increasing the operative effect size that determines statistical power. Depending upon the amount of variance controlled in these designs, the multiplier effect on the effect size can be quite considerable. Table 2.3 summarizes that multiplier effect for different proportions of the within-groups variance associated with the control variable. Although the effects are modest when the control variable accounts for a small proportion of the dependent variable variance, they are quite considerable for higher proportions. For instance, when the control variable accounts for as much as 75% of the variance, the operative effect size is double what it would be without the control variable. Reference back to Figure 2.1, the statistical power chart, will reveal that a doubling of the effect size has a major effect on statistical power. Careful use of variance control designs, therefore, is one important tactic the intervention researcher can use to increase statistical power dramatically without requiring additional subjects in the samples.

☐ Effect Size

The effect size parameter in statistical power can be thought of as a signal-to-noise ratio. The signal is the difference between experimental and control population means on the dependent measure (the *ES* numerator, $\mu_e - \mu_c$). The noise is the within-groups variability on that dependent measure (the *ES* denominator, σ). Effect size and, hence, statistical power is large when the signal-to-noise ratio is high, that is, when the *ES* numerator is large relative to

Table 2.3 Multiplier by Which *ES* Increases When a Blocking Variable, Covariate, or Paired Subjects Design Is Used to Reduce Within-Groups Variance

Proportion of Variance Associated With Control Variable[a]	*Multiplier for ES Increase*
.05	1.03
.10	1.05
.15	1.08
.20	1.12
.25	1.15
.30	1.20
.35	1.24
.40	1.29
.45	1.35
.50	1.41
.55	1.49
.60	1.58
.65	1.69
.70	1.83
.75	2.00
.80	2.24
.85	2.58
.90	3.16
.95	4.47
.99	10.00

a. PV_b for blocked ANOVA; r^2 for ANCOVA; r for paired subjects (assumed positive).

the *ES* denominator. In the preceding subsection, we saw that variance control statistical designs increase statistical power by removing some portion of nuisance variance from the *ES* denominator and making the operative *ES* for statistical power purposes proportionately larger. Here we will look at some other approaches to increasing the signal-to-noise ratio as represented in the effect size.

Dependent Measures

The dependent measures in intervention research yield the set of numerical values upon which statistical significance testing is performed. Each measure chosen for a study constitutes a sort of listening station for certain effects expected to result from the intervention. If the listening station is in the wrong place or is unresponsive to effects when they are present, nothing will be heard. To optimize the signal-to-noise ratio represented in the effect size, the ideal measure for intervention effects is one that is maximally responsive to any change the intervention brings about (making a large *ES* numerator) and minimally responsive to anything else (making a small *ES* denominator). In particular, three aspects of outcome measurement have direct consequences for the magnitude of the effect size parameter and, therefore, statistical power: (a) validity for measuring change, (b) reliability, and (c) discrimination of individual differences among subjects.

Validity for change. For a measure to respond to the signal, that is, to intervention effects, it must, of course, have validity for measuring the characteristic the intervention is expected to change (Cleary, Linn, & Walster, 1970). But validity alone is not sufficient to make a measure responsive to intervention effects. What is required is validity for *change.* A measure can be a valid indicator of a characteristic but still not be a valid indicator of change on that characteristic. Validity for change means that the measure shows an observable difference when there is, in fact, a change on the characteristic measured that is of sufficient magnitude to be interesting in the context of application.

There are various ways in which a measure can lack validity for change. For one, it may be scaled in units that are too gross to detect the change. A measure of mortality (death rate), for instance, is a valid indicator of health status but is insensitive to variations in how sick people are. Graduated measures, those that range over some continuum, are generally more sensitive to change than are categorical measures, because the latter record change only between categories, not within them. The number of readmissions to a mental hospital, for example, constitutes a continuum that can differentiate one readmission from many. This continuum is often represented categorically as "readmitted" versus "not readmitted," however, with a consequent loss of sensitivity to change and statistical power (Cohen, 1983).

Another way in which a measure may lack validity for measuring change is by having a floor or ceiling that limits downward or upward response. A high school-level mathematics achievement test might be quite unresponsive to improvements in Albert Einstein's understanding of mathematics—he would most likely score at the top of the scale with or without such improvements. Also, a measure may be specifically designed to cancel out certain types of change, as when scores on IQ tests are scaled by age norms to adjust away age differences in ability to answer the items correctly.

In short, measures that are valid for change will respond when intervention alters the characteristic of interest and, therefore, will differentiate an experimental group from a control group. The stronger this differentiation, the greater the contrast between the group means will be and, correspondingly, the larger the effect size.

Reliability. Turning now to the noise in the signal detection analogy, we must consider variance in the dependent measure scores that may obscure any signal due to intervention effects. Random error variance—that is, unreliability in the measure—is obviously such a noise (Cleary & Linn, 1969; Subkoviak & Levin, 1977). Unreliability represents fluctuations in the measure that are unrelated to the characteristic being measured, including intervention effects on that characteristic. Some measurement error is intrinsic—it follows from the properties of the measure. Self-administered questionnaires, for instance, are influenced by fluctuations in respondents' attention, motivation, comprehension, and so forth. Some measurement error is procedural—it results from inconsistent or inappropriate application of the measure. Raters who must report on an observed characteristic, for instance, may not be trained to use the same standards for their judgment, or the conditions of measurement may vary for different subjects in ways that influence their responses.

Also included in measurement error is systematic but irrelevant variation—response of the measure to characteristics other than the one of interest. When these other characteristics vary differently from the one being measured, they introduce noise into a measure. For example, frequency of arrest, which may be used to assess the effects of intervention for juvenile delinquency, indexes police behavior (e.g., patrol and arrest practices) as well as the criminal behavior of the juveniles. Measures with lower measurement error will yield less variation in the distribution of scores for subjects within experimental groups. Because within-groups variance is the basis for the denominator of the *ES* ratio, less measurement error makes that denominator smaller and the overall *ES* larger.

Discrimination of individual differences. Another source of systematic but often irrelevant variation that is especially important in intervention effectiveness research has to do with relatively stable individual differences on the characteristic measured. When a measure is able to discriminate strongly among subjects, the variance of its distribution of scores is increased. This variation does not represent error, as subjects may truly differ, but it nonetheless contributes to the noise variance that can obscure intervention effects. In a reading improvement program, for example, the primary interest is whether each individual involved shows improvement in reading level, irrespective of his or her initial reading level, reading aptitude, and so forth. If the measure selected is responsive to such other differences, the variability may be so great as to overshadow any gains from the program.

Where psychological and educational effects of intervention are at issue, an important distinction is between "psychometric" measures, designed primarily to discriminate individual differences, and "edumetric" measures, designed primarily to detect change (Carver, 1974). Psychometric measures are those developed using techniques that spread out the scores of respondents; IQ tests, aptitude tests, personality tests, and other such standardized tests would generally be psychometric measures. By comparison, edumetric measures are those developed through the sampling of some defined content domain that represents the new responses subjects are expected to acquire as a result of intervention. Mastery tests, such as those an elementary school teacher would give students to determine whether they have learned to do long division, are examples of edumetric tests.

Because they are keyed specifically to the sets of responses expected to result from intervention, edumetric tests, or measures constructed along similar lines, are more sensitive than psychometric tests to the changes induced by intervention and less sensitive to preexisting individual differences. To the extent that any measure reflects less heterogeneity among subjects, within-group variability on that measure is smaller. That, in turn, results in a smaller denominator for the *ES* ratio and a corresponding increase in statistical power.

The Independent Variable

The independent variable in intervention research is defined by the experimental conditions to which subjects are exposed. The general relationship between the independent variable and statistical power is readily apparent. For an effective intervention, the stronger it is relative to the control condition, the larger the measured effect should be. Larger effects, in turn, increase the probability of attainment of statistical significance and, hence, statistical power. Conversely, anything that degrades the intervention (or upgrades the control condition) will decrease the measured effect and, with it, statistical power.

Dose response. Experimental design is based on the premise that intervention levels can be made to vary and that different levels might result in different responses. Generally speaking, the "stronger" the intervention, the larger the response should be. One way to attain a large effect size, therefore, is to design intervention research with the strongest possible dose of the intervention represented in the experimental condition. If the intervention is effective, the larger effect size resulting from a stronger dose will increase statistical power for detecting the effect.

Optimizing the strength of the intervention operationalized in research requires some basis for judging what might constitute the optimal configuration for producing the expected effects. There may be insufficient research directly on the intervention under study (else why do the research?), but there may be other sources of information that can be used to select an intervention sufficiently strong to have potentially detectable effects. One source, for example, is the experience and intuition of practitioners in the domain where the intervention, or variants, is applied. Practitioners' judgments of the strength and likelihood of effects from various operationalizations of the intervention may help guide the researcher in selecting one worth consideration.

Variable delivery of the intervention. The integrity of an intervention is the degree to which it is delivered as planned and, in particular, the degree to which it is delivered in a uniform manner in the right amounts to the right subjects at the right time (Yeaton & Sechrest, 1981). At one end of the continuum, we might consider the case of intervention research conducted under tightly controlled clinical or laboratory conditions in which delivery can be regulated very closely.

Under these conditions, we would expect a high degree of intervention integrity, that is, delivery of a constant, appropriate dose to each subject.

Intervention research, however, cannot always be conducted under such carefully regulated circumstances. It must often be done in the field with voluntary subjects whose compliance with the intervention regimen is difficult to ensure. Moreover, the interventions of interest are often not those for which dosage is easily determined and monitored, nor are they necessarily delivered uniformly. The result is that the subjects in an experimental group may receive widely different amounts and even kinds of intervention (e.g., different mixes of components). If subjects' responses to intervention vary with its amount and kind, then it follows that variation in the intervention will generate additional variation in dependent variable scores.

When statistical analysis is done comparing experimental and control groups, all that registers as an intervention effect is the difference between the experimental group's mean response and the control group's mean response. If there is variation around those means, it goes into the within-groups variance of the effect size denominator, making the overall *ES* smaller. Maintaining a uniform application of experimental and control conditions is the best way to prevent this problem. One useful safeguard is for the researcher actually to measure the amount of intervention received by each subject in the experimental and control conditions. This technique yields information about how much variability there actually was and generates a covariate that may permit some statistical adjustment of any unwanted variability.

Control group contrast. Not all aspects of the relationship between the independent variable and the effect size have to do primarily with the intervention. The choice of a control condition also plays an important role. The contrast between the experimental and control means can be heightened or diminished by the choice of a control condition that is more or less different from the experimental condition in its expected effects upon the dependent measure.

Generally, the sharpest contrast can be expected when the control group receives no intervention or any other attention. For some situations, however, this type of control may be very unrepresentative of subjects' experiences in nonexperimental conditions or may be unethical. This occurs particularly for problems that do not normally go unattended—severe illness, for example. In such situations, other forms of control groups are often used. The "treatment as usual" control, for instance, uses a control group that receives the usual services in comparison to an experimental group that receives innovative services. Or a placebo control might be used in which the control group receives attention similar to that received by the experimental group but without the specific active ingredient that is presumed to be the basis of the intervention's efficacy. Finally, the intervention of interest may simply be compared with some alternative intervention, for example, traditional psychotherapy compared with behavior modification as treatment for phobias. Usually in such circumstances one of these interventions is considered an innovation and the other the traditional service.

The types of control conditions described above are listed in approximate order according to the magnitude of the contrast they would generally be expected to show when compared with an effective intervention. The researcher's choice of a control group, therefore, will influence the size of the potential contrast and hence of the potential effect size that appears in a study. Selection of the control group likely to show the greatest contrast from among those appropriate to the research issues can thus have an important bearing on the statistical power of the design.

■ *Design Strategy to Enhance Power*

Perhaps the most important point to be gleaned from the above discussion of the factors that determine statistical power is that each of them can be manipulated to increase power. A research design that is sensitive to intervention effects, therefore, is achieved through the integration of decisions about all of these factors in a way that is appropriate and practical for the particular research circumstances. This requires awareness of statistical power issues during the planning phase of a study, incorporation of procedures to enhance power in the design, and an analysis and interpretation of study results that reflects statistical power considerations.

The general strategy for optimizing power in intervention research necessarily begins with a decision about the minimum effect size the research should be designed to detect reliably. This should be set as a threshold value such that below that level, intervention effects are considered too small to be important, but above that level they are potentially meaningful and thus should be detected by the research. It is at this point that the researcher must consider what experimental versus control contrast will be represented in that effect size. This requires decisions about the "dosage" for the intervention, the nature of the control group (no treatment, placebo, service as usual, and so on), the character of the dependent variable(s) (e.g., psychometric versus edumetric), and the other matters raised above in the discussion of effect size.

Given decisions on these points, the researcher must then decide what numerical value of the effect size under the planned research circumstances represents a meaningful minimum to be detected. This usually involves a complex judgment regarding the practical meaning of effects within the particular intervention context. The next section provides some suggestions for framing this issue. For now, suppose that a threshold value has been set: Say that $ES = .20$ is judged the smallest effect size the research should reliably detect. The next question is how reliably the researcher wishes to be able to detect that value— that is, what level of statistical power is desired. If the desired power is .80, for instance, statistically significant results would be found 80% of the time an effect of .20 was actually present in the populations sampled for the research, and null results would occur 20% of the time despite the population effect. If greater reliability is desired, a higher level of power must be set. Setting the desired power level, of course, is equivalent to setting the beta level for risk of Type II error. Alpha level for Type I error should also be set at this time, using some rational approach to weighing the risks of Type I versus Type II error, as discussed earlier.

With a threshold effect size value and a desired power level in hand, the researcher is ready to address the question of how actually to attain that power level in the research design. At this juncture it is wise to consider what variance control statistics might be used. These can generally be applied at low cost and with only a little extra effort to collect data on appropriate covariate or blocking variables. Using the formulas and discussion provided above in the subsection on the statistical test, the researcher can estimate the operative effect size with a variance control design and determine how much larger it will be than the original threshold value. With an ANCOVA design using the pretest as a covariate, for instance, the pretest-posttest correlation might be expected to be at least .80, increasing the operative effect size from the original .20 to a value of .33 (see Table 2.2).

With an operative effect size and a desired power level now established, the researcher is ready to turn to the question of the size of the sample in each experimental group. This is simply a matter of looking up the appropriate value using a statistical power chart or computer program. If the result is a sample size the researcher can achieve, then all is well.

If the required sample size is larger than can be attained, however, it is back to the drawing board for the researcher. The options at this point are limited. First, of course, the researcher may revisit previous decisions and further tune the design—for example, enhancing the experimental versus control contrast, improving the sensitivity of the dependent measure, or applying a stronger variance control design. If this is not possible or not sufficient, all that remains is the possibility of relaxing one or more of the parameters of the study. Alpha or beta levels, or both, might be relaxed, for instance. Because this increases the risk of a false statistical conclusion in the research, and because alpha levels particularly are governed by strong conventions, this must obviously be done with caution. Alternatively, the threshold effect size the research can reliably detect may be increased. This amounts to reducing the likelihood that effects already determined potentially meaningful will be detected.

Despite best efforts, the researcher may have to proceed with an underpowered design. Such a design may be useful for detecting relatively large effects but may have little chance of detecting smaller, but still meaningful, effects. Under these circumstances, the researcher should take responsibility for communicating the limitations of the research along with its results. To do otherwise encourages misinterpretation of statistically null results as findings of "no effect" when there is a reasonable probability of an actual effect that the research was simply incapable of detecting.

As is apparent in the above discussion, designing research sensitive to intervention effects depends heavily on an advance specification of the magnitude of statistical effect that represents the threshold for what is important or meaningful in the intervention context. In the next section, I discuss some of the ways in which researchers can approach this judgment.

■ *What Effect Size Is Worth Detecting?*

Various frameworks can be constructed to support reasonable judgment about the minimal effect size an intervention study should be designed to detect. That judgment, in turn, will permit the researcher to consider statistical power in a systematic, and not just intuitive, manner during the design phase of the research. Also, given a framework for judgment about effect size, the researcher can more readily interpret the statistical results of intervention research after it is completed. I review below three frameworks for judging effect size: the actuarial approach, the statistical translation approach, and the criterion group contrast approach.

□ *The Actuarial Approach*

If enough research exists similar to that of interest, the researcher can use the results of those other studies to create an actuarial base for effect sizes. He or she can then use the distribution of such effect size estimates as a basis for judging the likelihood that the research being planned will produce effects of specified size. For example, a study could reliably detect 80% of the likely effects if it is designed to have sufficient power for the effect size at the 20th percentile of the effect size distribution.

Other than the problem of finding sufficient research literature to draw upon, the major difficulty with the actuarial approach is the need to extract effect size estimates from studies that typically do not report their results in those terms. This, however, is exactly the problem faced in meta-analysis, when a researcher attempts to obtain effect size estimates for each of a defined set of studies and do higher-order analysis on them. Books and articles on meta-analysis techniques contain detailed information about how to estimate effect sizes from the statistics provided in study reports (see, e.g., Glass, McGaw, & Smith, 1981; Holmes, 1984; Rosenthal, 1984).

A researcher can obtain a very general picture of the range and magnitude of effect size estimates in intervention research by examining a number of meta-analyses simultaneously. Lipsey and Wilson (1993) report the distribution of effect sizes from more than 300 meta-analyses of research on psychological, behavioral, and educational research. That distribution had a median effect size of .44, with the 20th percentile at .24 and the 80th percentile at .68. These values might be compared with the rule of thumb for effect size suggested by Cohen (1977, 1988), who reports that across a wide range of social science research, $ES = .20$ could be judged a "small" effect, .50 as "medium," and .80 as "large."

☐ *The Statistical Translation Approach*

Expressing effect size in standard deviation units has the advantage of staying close to the terms in statistical significance testing and thus facilitates statistical power analysis. However, that formulation has the disadvantage that in many intervention domains there is little basis for intuition about the practical meaning of a standard deviation's worth of difference between experimental groups. One approach to this situation is to translate the effect size index (ES) from standard deviation units to some alternate form that is easier to assess.

Perhaps the easiest translation is simply to express the effect size in the units of the dependent measure of interest. The ES index, recall, is the difference between the means of the experimental groups divided by the pooled standard deviation. Previous research, norms for standardized tests, or pilot research is often capable of providing a reasonable value for the relevant standard deviation. With that value in hand, the researcher can convert to the metric of the specific variable any level of ES he or she is considering. For example, if the dependent variable is a standardized reading achievement test for which the norms indicate a standard deviation of 15 points, the researcher can think of $ES = .50$ as 7.5 points on that test. In context, it may be easier to judge the practical magnitude of 7.5 points on a familiar test than .50 standard deviations.

Sometimes what we want to know about the magnitude of an effect is best expressed in terms of the proportion of people who attained a given level of benefit as a result of intervention. One attractive way to depict effect size, therefore, is in terms of the proportion of the experimental group, in comparison to the control group, elevated over some success threshold by the intervention. This requires, of course, that the researcher be able to set some reasonable criterion for success on the dependent variable, but even a relatively arbitrary threshold can be used to illustrate the magnitude of the difference between experimental and control groups.

One general approach to expressing effect size in success rate terms is to set the mean of the control group distribution as the success threshold value. With symmetrical normal distributions, 50% of the control group will be below that point and 50% will be above. These proportions can be compared with those of the experimental group distribution below and above the same point for any given difference between the two distributions in standard deviation units. Figure 2.2 depicts the relationship for an effect size of $ES = .50$. In this case, 70% of the experimental group is above the mean of the control group, or, in failure rate terms, only 30% of the treated group is below the control group mean. There are various ways to construct indices of the overlap between

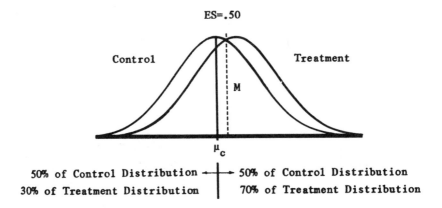

50% of Control Distribution ◄──┼──► 50% of Control Distribution
30% of Treatment Distribution │ 70% of Treatment Distribution

Figure 2.2. Depiction of the Percentage of the Treatment Distribution Above the Success Threshold Set at the Mean of the Control Distribution

distributions to represent effect size. This particular one corresponds to Cohen's (1977) *U3* measure (p. 21).

A variation on the percentage overlap index has been offered by Rosenthal and Rubin (1982), who used it to construct something they call a "binomial effect size display" (BESD). They suggest that the success threshold be presumed to be at the grand median for the conjoint control and experimental distribution (line M in Figure 2.2). Though use of the grand median as a success threshold is somewhat arbitrary, it confers a particular advantage on the BESD. With normal distributions, the difference between the "success" proportions of the experimental and control groups has a simple relationship to the effect size expressed in correlational terms. In particular, when we express effect size as a correlation (r), the value of that correlation corresponds to the difference between the proportions of the respective distributions that are above the grand median success threshold. Effect size in standard deviation units can easily be converted into the equivalent correlation using the following formula:

$$r = ES/\sqrt{ES^2 + 4} .$$

For example, if the correlation between the independent variable and the dependent variable is .24, then the difference between the success proportions of the groups is .24, evenly divided around the .50 point, that is, $.50 \pm .12$, or 38% success in the control group, 62% in the experimental group. More generally, the distribution with the lower mean will have $.50 - (r/2)$ of its cases above the grand median success threshold, and the distribution with the greater mean will have $.50 + (r/2)$ of its cases above that threshold. For convenience, Table 2.4 presents the BESD terms for a range of *ES* and *r* values as well as Cohen's *U3* index, described above.

Table 2.4 Effect Size Equivalents for *ES*, *PV*, *r*, *U3*, and BESD

ES	PV (r²)	r	U3: % of T Above $\overline{X}_c$	BESD C Versus T Success Rates		BESD C Versus T Differential
0.1	.002	.05	54	.47	.52	.05
0.2	.01	.10	58	.45	.55	.10
0.3	.02	.15	62	.42	.57	.15
0.4	.04	.20	66	.40	.60	.20
0.5	.06	.24	69	.38	.62	.24
0.6	.08	.29	73	.35	.64	.29
0.7	.11	.33	76	.33	.66	.33
0.8	.14	.37	79	.31	.68	.37
0.9	.17	.41	82	.29	.70	.41
1.0	.20	.45	84	.27	.72	.45
1.1	.23	.48	86	.26	.74	.48
1.2	.26	.51	88	.24	.75	.51
1.3	.30	.54	90	.23	.77	.54
1.4	.33	.57	92	.21	.78	.57
1.5	.36	.60	93	.20	.80	.60
1.6	.39	.62	95	.19	.81	.62
1.7	.42	.65	96	.17	.82	.65
1.8	.45	.67	96	.16	.83	.67
1.9	.47	.69	97	.15	.84	.69
2.0	.50	.71	98	.14	.85	.71
2.1	.52	.72	98	.14	.86	.72
2.2	.55	.74	99	.13	.87	.74
2.3	.57	.75	99	.12	.87	.75
2.4	.59	.77	99	.11	.88	.77
2.5	.61	.78	99	.11	.89	.78
2.6	.63	.79	99	.10	.89	.79
2.7	.65	.80	99	.10	.90	.80
2.8	.66	.81	99	.09	.90	.81
2.9	.68	.82	99	.09	.91	.82
3.0	.69	.83	99	.08	.91	.83

The most striking thing about the BESD and the *U3* representations of the effect size is the different impression they give of the potential practical significance of a given effect from that of the standard deviation expression. For example, an effect size of one-fifth of a standard deviation (*ES* = .20) corresponds to a BESD success rate differential of .10, that is, 10 percentage points between the experimental and control group success rates (55% versus 45%).

A success increase of 10 percentage points on a control group baseline of 45% represents a 22% improvement in the success rate (10/45). Viewed in these terms, the same intervention effect that may appear rather trivial in standard deviation units now looks potentially meaningful.

☐ *The Criterion Contrast Approach*

Although actuarial and statistical translation approaches to assessing effect size may be useful for many purposes, they are generally somewhat removed from the specific context of any given intervention study. Often, the best answer to the question of what effect size has practical significance is one that is closely tied to the particular problems, populations, and measures relevant to the intervention under investigation. For example, if we could identify and measure a naturally occurring effect in the intervention context whose practical significance is easily recognized, it could be used as a criterion value or benchmark against which any expected or obtained intervention effect could be compared. What is required in the criterion group contrast approach is that some such comparison be identified and represented as a statistical effect size on the dependent measure relevant to intervention research.

The criterion group contrast approach is best explained by example. Consider a community mental health center in which prospective patients receive a routine diagnostic intake interview and are sorted into those judged to need, say, inpatient therapy versus outpatient therapy. This practice embodies a discrimination of more serious from less serious cases and the "size" of the difference between the severity of the symptoms for these two groups would be well understood at the practical level by those involved in community mental health settings. If we administer a functional status measure that is of interest as an outcome variable for both these groups, we could represent the difference between them as an effect size, that is, the difference between their means on that measure divided by the pooled standard deviations. Though this effect size does not represent the effects of intervention, we can nonetheless think of it in comparison with an intervention effect. That is, how successful would we judge a treatment to be that, when applied to clients as severe as the inpatient group, left them with scores similar to those of the outpatient group? Such an effect may well be judged to be of practical significance and would have recognized meaning in the treatment context. Real or anticipated intervention effects can thus be compared with this criterion contrast value as a way of judging their practical significance.

Reasonable criterion comparisons are often surprisingly easy to find in applied settings. All one needs to create a criterion contrast are, first, two groups whose difference on the variable of interest is easily recognized and, second, the results of measurement on that variable. It is also desirable to use groups that resemble, as much as possible, those samples likely to be used in any actual intervention research. Some of the possibilities for criterion contrasts that frequently occur in practical settings include the following:

1. Eligible versus ineligible applicants for service where eligibility is determined primarily on the basis of judged need or severity. For example, a contrast on economic status might compare those who do not qualify for food stamps with those who do.

2. Sorting of intervention recipients into different service or diagnostic categories based on the severity of the problems to be treated. For example, a contrast on literacy might compare those adult education students enrolled in remedial reading classes with those enrolled in other kinds of classes.

3. Categories of termination status after intervention. For example, a contrast on functional status measures might compare those patients judged by physical therapists to have had successful outcomes with those judged to have had unsuccessful outcomes.

4. Comparison of "normal" subjects with those who have the target problem. For example, a contrast on delinquent behavior could compare the frequency of self-reported delinquency for a sample of males arrested by the police with that of similar-age males from a general high school sample.

5. Maturational differences and/or those occurring with usual service. For example, a contrast on mathematics achievement might compare the achievement test scores of third graders with those of fifth graders.

■ *Conclusion*

Attaining adequate statistical power in intervention research is not an easy matter. The basic dilemma is that high power requires a large effect size, a large sample size, or both. Despite their potential practical significance, however, the interventions of interest all too often produce modest statistical effects, and the samples upon which they can be studied are often of limited size. Intervention researchers need to learn to live responsibly with this problem. The most important elements of a coping strategy are recognizing the predicament and attempting to overcome it in every possible way during the design phase of a study. The keys to designing sensitive intervention research are an understanding of the factors that influence statistical power and the adroit application of that understanding to the planning and implementation of each study undertaken. As an aid to recall and application, Table 2.5 lists the factors discussed in this chapter that play a role in the statistical power of experimental research (along with other factors discussed in Lipsey, 1990).

Table 2.5 Factors That Work to Increase Statistical Power in Treatment Effectiveness Research

Independent variable

Strong treatment, high dosage in the treatment condition (1, 2, **7**)

Untreated or low-dosage control condition for high contrast with treatment (7)

Treatment integrity; uniform application of treatment to recipients (1, 2, **7**)

Control group integrity; uniform control conditions for recipients (1, 2, **7**)

Subjects

Large sample size in each experimental condition (1, 2, 4, **6**)

Increased numbers in one condition when fixed sample size in other (6)

Deploying limited subjects into few rather than many experimental groups (6)

Little initial heterogeneity on dependent variable (1, 2, **5**)

Measurement or variance control of subject heterogeneity (1, 4, **5**, **6**)

Uniform response of subjects to treatment (1, 6, **7**)

Differential subject response accounted for statistically (interactions) (6)

Dependent variables

Validity for measuring characteristic expected to change (1, 2, **5**, 7)

Validity, sensitivity for change on characteristic measured (1, 2, **5**)

Fine-grained units of measurement rather than coarse or categorical (1, 2, **5**)

No floor or ceiling effects in the range of expected response (1, 2, **5**)

Mastery or criterion-oriented rather than individual differences measures (2, **5**)

Inherent reliability in measure; unresponsiveness to irrelevant factors (1, 2, **5**)

Consistency in measurement procedures (1, 2, **5**)

Aggregation of unreliable measures (5)

Timing of measurement to coincide with peak response to treatment (1, **7**)

Measurement of more proximal effects rather than more distal ones (7)

Statistical analysis

Larger alpha for significance testing (2, 4, **6**)

One-tailed directional tests rather than two-tailed nondirectional ones (1, 2, 4, **6**)

Significance tests for graduated scores, not ordinal or categorical (1, 2, **5**)

Statistical variance control; blocking, pairing, ANCOVA, interactions (1, 2, 4, 5, **6**)

NOTE: Numbers in parentheses indicate chapters in Lipsey (1990) where the particular topics are discussed. Bold numbers indicate chapters with the most extensive discussions of given topics.

■ References

Brown, G. W. (1983). Errors, Type I and II. *American Journal of Disorders in Childhood, 137,* 586-591.

Carver, R. P. (1974). Two dimensions of tests: Psychometric and edumetric. *American Psychologist, 29,* 512-518.

Cascio, W. F., & Zedeck, S. (1983). Open a new window in rational research planning: Adjust alpha to maximize statistical power. *Personnel Psychology, 36,* 517-526.

Cleary, T. A., & Linn, R. L. (1969). Error of measurement and the power of a statistical test. *British Journal of Mathematical and Statistical Psychology, 22,* 49-55.

Cleary, T. A., Linn, R. L., & Walster, G. W. (1970). Effect of reliability and validity on power of statistical tests. In E. F. Borgatta & G. W. Bohrnstedt (Eds.), *Sociological methodology* (pp. 130-138). San Francisco: Jossey-Bass.

Cohen, J. (1977). *Statistical power analysis for the behavioral sciences* (rev. ed.). New York: Academic Press.

Cohen, J. (1983). The cost of dichotomization. *Applied Psychological Measurement, 7,* 249-253.

Cohen, J. (1988). *Statistical power analysis for the behavioral sciences* (2nd ed.). Hillsdale, NJ: Lawrence Erlbaum.

Cooper, H., & Hedges, L. V. (Eds.). (1994). *The handbook of research synthesis.* New York: Russell Sage Foundation.

Glass, G. V, McGaw, B., & Smith, M. L. (1981). *Meta-analysis in social research.* Beverly Hills, CA: Sage.

Holmes, C. T. (1984). Effect size estimation in meta-analysis. *Journal of Experimental Education, 52,* 106-109.

Kraemer, H. C., & Thiemann, S. (1987). *How many subjects? Statistical power analysis in research.* Newbury Park, CA: Sage.

Kroll, R. M., & Chase, L. J. (1975). Communication disorders: A power analytic assessment of recent research. *Journal of Communication Disorders, 8,* 237-247.

Lipsey, M. W. (1990). *Design sensitivity: Statistical power for experimental research.* Newbury Park, CA: Sage.

Lipsey, M. W., Crosse, S., Dunkle, J., Pollard, J., & Stobart, G. (1985). Evaluation: The state of the art and the sorry state of the science. *New Directions for Program Evaluation, 27,* 7-28.

Lipsey, M. W., & Wilson, D. B. (1993). The efficacy of psychological, educational, and behavioral treatment: Confirmation from meta-analysis. *American Psychologist, 48,* 1181-1209.

Mazen, A. M., Graf, L. A., Kellogg, C. E., & Hemmasi, M. (1987). Statistical power in contemporary management research. *Academy of Management Journal, 30,* 369-380.

Nagel, S. S., & Neef, M. (1977). Determining an optimum level of statistical significance. In M. Guttentag & S. Saar (Eds.), *Evaluation studies review annual* (Vol. 2, pp. 146-158). Beverly Hills, CA: Sage.

Ottenbacher, K. (1982). Statistical power and research in occupational therapy. *Occupational Therapy Journal of Research, 2,* 13-25.

Owen, D. B. (1962). *Handbook of statistical tables.* Reading, MA: Addison-Wesley.

Owen, D. B. (1965). The power of Student's t-test. *Journal of the American Statistical Association, 60,* 320-333.

Reed, J. F., & Slaichert, W. (1981). Statistical proof in inconclusive "negative" trials. *Archives of Internal Medicine, 141,* 1307-1310.

Rosenthal, R. (1984). *Meta-analytic procedures for social research.* Beverly Hills, CA: Sage.

Rosenthal, R., & Rubin, D. B. (1982). A simple, general purpose display of magnitude of experimental effect. *Journal of Educational Psychology, 74,* 166-169.

Schneider, A. L., & Darcy, R. E. (1984). Policy implications of using significance tests in evaluation research. *Evaluation Review, 8,* 573-582.

Subkoviak, M. J., & Levin, J. R. (1977). Fallibility of measurement and the power of a statistical test. *Journal of Educational Measurement, 14,* 47-52.

Yeaton, W. H., & Sechrest, L. (1981). Critical dimensions in the choice and maintenance of successful treatments: Strength, integrity, and effectiveness. *Journal of Consulting and Clinical Psychology, 49,* 156-167.

3

Designing a Qualitative Study

Joseph A. Maxwell

Contrary to what you may have heard,
qualitative research designs do exist.
—Miles and Huberman
Qualitative Data Analysis, 1994

As the above quote suggests, "qualitative research design" has often been treated as an oxymoron. One reason for this is that the dominant, quantitatively oriented models of research design presented in textbooks fit poorly with the ways that most qualitative researchers go about their work (Lincoln & Guba, 1985). These models usually treat "design" in one of two ways. Some take designs to be fixed, standard arrangements of research conditions and methods that have their own coherence and logic, as possible answers to the question, What research design are you using? For example, a randomized, double-blind experiment is one research design; an interrupted time series design is another. Qualitative research lacks any such elaborate typology into which studies can be pigeonholed.

Other models present design as a logical progression of stages or tasks, from problem formulation to the generation of conclusions or theory, that are necessary in planning or carrying out a study. Although some versions of this approach are circular or iterative (see, for example, Bickman, Rog, & Hedrick, Chapter 1, this volume), so that later steps connect back to earlier ones, all such models are linear in the sense that they are made up of one-directional sequences of steps that represent what is seen as the optimal order for conceptualizing or conducting the different components or activities of a study.

This view of design does not adequately represent the logic and process of qualitative research. In a qualitative study, the activities of collecting and analyzing data, developing and modifying theory, elaborating or refocusing the research questions, and identifying and dealing with validity threats are usually going on more or less simultaneously, each influencing all of the others. In addition, the researcher may need to reconsider or modify any design decision during the study in response to new developments or to changes in some other aspect of the design. Grady and Wallston (1988) argue that applied research in general requires a flexible, nonsequential approach and "an entirely different model of the research process than the traditional one offered in most textbooks" (p. 10).

This does not mean that qualitative research lacks design; as Yin (1994) says, "Every type of empirical research has an implicit, if not explicit, research design" (p. 19). Qualitative research simply requires a broader and less restrictive concept of "design" than the traditional ones described above. Thus Becker, Geer, Hughes, and Strauss (1961), authors of a classic qualitative study of medical students, begin their chapter titled "Design of the Study" by stating:

> In one sense, our study had no design. That is, we had no well-worked-out set of hypotheses to be tested, no data-gathering instruments purposely designed to secure information relevant to these hypotheses, no set of analytic procedures specified in advance. Insofar as the term "design" implies these features of elaborate prior planning, our study had none.
>
> If we take the idea of design in a larger and looser sense, using it to identify those elements of order, system, and consistency our procedures did exhibit, our study had a design. We can say what this was by describing our original view of the problem, our theoretical and methodological commitments, and the way these affected our research and were affected by it as we proceeded. (p. 17)

For these reasons, the model of design that I present here, which I call an *interactive* model, consists of the components of a research study and the ways in which these components may affect and be affected by one another. It does not presuppose any particular order for these components, or any necessary directionality of influence; as with qualitative research in general, "it depends." One of my goals in this chapter is to try to point out the things that I think these influences depend *on*.

The model thus resembles the more general definition of *design* employed outside of research: "an underlying scheme that governs functioning, developing, or unfolding" and "the arrangement of elements or details in a product or work of art" (*Merriam-Webster's Collegiate Dictionary,* 1993). A good design, one in which the components work harmoniously together, promotes efficient and successful functioning; a flawed design leads to poor operation or failure.

This model has five components, each of which addresses a different set of issues that are essential to the coherence of your study:

1. *Purposes:* What are the ultimate goals of this study? What issues is it intended to illuminate, and what practices will it influence? Why do you want to conduct it, and why should we care about the results? Why is the study worth doing?

2. *Conceptual context:* What do you think is going on with the things you plan to study? What theories, findings, and conceptual frameworks relating to these will guide or inform your study, and what literature, preliminary research, and personal experience will you draw on? This component of the design contains the *theory* that you already have or are developing about the setting or issues that you are studying.

3. *Research questions:* What, specifically, do you want to understand by doing this study? What do you *not* know about the things you are studying that you want to learn? What questions will your research attempt to answer, and how are these questions related to one another?

4. *Methods:* What will you actually do in conducting this study? What approaches and techniques will you use to collect and analyze your data, and how do these constitute an integrated strategy?

5. *Validity:* How might you be wrong? What are the plausible alternative explanations and validity threats to the potential conclusions of your study, and how will you deal with these? Why should we believe your results?

These components are not radically different from the ones presented in many other discussions of qualitative or applied research design (e.g., LeCompte & Preissle, 1993; Lincoln & Guba, 1985; Miles & Huberman, 1994; Robson, 1993). What is distinctive in this model are the relationships among the components. The components form an integrated and interacting whole, with each component closely tied to several others, rather than being linked in a linear or cyclic sequence. The lines between the components in Figure 3.1 represent two-way connections of influence or implication. Although there are also connections other than those emphasized here (for example, between purposes and methods, and between conceptual context and validity), those shown in the figure are usually the most important.

The upper triangle of this model should be a closely integrated unit. Your research questions should have a clear relationship to the purposes of your study, and should be informed by what is already known about the things you are studying and the theoretical tools that can be applied to these. In addition, the purposes of the study should be informed both by current theory and knowledge and by what questions you can actually answer, and your choices of relevant theory and knowledge depend on the purposes and questions.

Similarly, the bottom triangle of the model should also be closely integrated. The methods you use must enable you to answer your research questions, and also to deal with plausible validity threats to these answers. The questions, in turn, need to be framed so as to take the feasibility of the methods

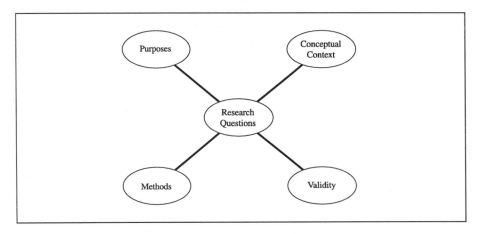

Figure 3.1. An Interactive Model of Research Design

and the seriousness of particular validity threats into account; in addition, the plausibility and relevance of particular validity threats depend on the questions and methods chosen. The research questions are the center or hub of the model; they connect the other four components into a coherent whole, and need to inform, and be responsive to, all of the other components.

There are many other factors besides these five components that should influence the design of your study; these include your research abilities, the available resources, perceived problems, ethical standards, the research setting, and the data and preliminary conclusions of the study. In my view, these are not part of the *design* of a study; rather, they either belong to the *environment* within which the research and its design exist or are *products* of the research. Figure 3.2 presents some of the environmental factors that can influence the design and conduct of a study.

I do not believe that there is one right model for qualitative or applied research design. However, I think that the model I present here is a useful one, for three main reasons:

1. It explicitly identifies as *components* of design the key issues about which decisions need to be made. These issues are therefore less likely to be ignored, and can be dealt with in a systematic manner.

2. It emphasizes the *interactive* nature of design decisions in qualitative and applied research, and the multiple connections among the design components.

3. It provides a model for the structure of a *proposal* for a qualitative study, one that clearly communicates and justifies the major design decisions and the connections among these (see Maxwell, 1996a).

Because a design for your study always exists, explicitly or implicitly, it is important to *make* this design explicit, to get it out in the open, where its strengths, limitations, and implications can be clearly understood. In the re-

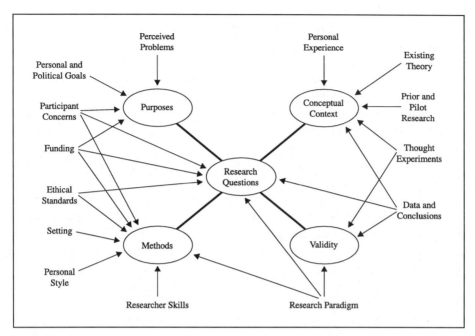

Figure 3.2. Contextual Factors Influencing Research Design

mainder of this chapter, I present the main design issues involved in each of the five components of my model, and the implications of each component for the others. I do not discuss in detail how to actually *do* qualitative research, or deal in depth with the theoretical and philosophical views that have informed this approach. For additional guidance on these topics, see the contributions of Fetterman (Chapter 16) and Stewart and Shamdasani (Chapter 17) to this handbook; the more extensive treatments by Patton (1990), Eisner and Peshkin (1990), LeCompte and Preissle (1993), Glesne and Peshkin (1992), Weiss (1994), Miles and Huberman (1994), and Wolcott (1995); and the encyclopedic handbooks edited by LeCompte, Millroy, and Preissle (1992) and by Denzin and Lincoln (1994). My focus here is on how to design a qualitative study that arrives at valid conclusions and successfully and efficiently achieves its goals.

■ *Purposes: Why Are You Doing This Study?*

Without a clear sense of the purposes of your research, you are apt to lose your focus and spend your time and effort doing things that won't contribute to these purposes. (I use *purpose* here in a broad sense, to include motives, desires, and goals—anything that leads you to do the study or that you hope to accomplish by doing it.) Your purposes help to guide your other design decisions, to ensure that your study is worth doing, that you get out of it what you want.

It is useful to distinguish among three kinds of purposes for doing a study: personal purposes, practical purposes, and research purposes. Personal purposes are those that motivate *you* to do this study; they can include a desire to change some existing situation, a curiosity about a specific phenomenon or event, or simply the need to advance your career. These personal purposes often overlap with your practical or research purposes, but they may also include deeply rooted individual desires and needs that bear little relationship to your "official" reasons for doing the study.

It is important that you recognize and take account of the personal purposes that drive and inform your research. Eradicating or submerging your personal goals and concerns is impossible, and attempting to do so is unnecessary. What *is* necessary, in qualitative design, is that you be *aware* of these concerns and how they may be shaping your research, and that you think about how best to deal with their consequences. To the extent that your design decisions and data analyses are based on personal desires and you have *not* made a careful assessment of the implications of these for your methods and results, you are in danger of arriving at invalid conclusions.

However, your personal reasons for wanting to conduct a study, and the experiences and perspectives in which these are grounded, are not simply a source of "bias" (see the later discussion of this issue in the section on validity); they can also provide you with a valuable source of insight, theory, and data about the phenomena you are studying (Marshall & Rossman, 1995, pp. 17-22; Strauss & Corbin, 1990, pp. 42-43). This source is discussed in the next section, in the subsection on experiential knowledge.

One personal purpose in particular that deserves thought is your motivation for choosing a qualitative approach. Qualitative research is *not* easier than quantitative research, and seeking to avoid statistics bears little relationship to having the personal interests and skills required for the conduct of qualitative inquiry (Locke, Spirduso, & Silverman, 1993, pp. 107-110). Your reasons for adopting a qualitative approach need to be compatible with your other purposes, your research questions, and the requirements of carrying out qualitative research.

Besides your personal purposes, there are two other, more public kinds of purposes that I want to distinguish and discuss: practical purposes (including administrative or policy purposes) and research purposes. Practical purposes are focused on *accomplishing* something—meeting some need, changing some situation, or achieving some goal. Research purposes, on the other hand, are focused on *understanding* something, gaining some insight into what is going on and why it is happening. Although applied research design places much more emphasis on practical purposes than does basic research, you still need to address the issue of what you want to *understand* by doing the study, and how this understanding will contribute to your accomplishing your practical purposes. (The issue of what you want to understand is discussed in more detail below, in the section on research questions.)

There are five particular research purposes for which qualitative studies are especially useful:

1. Understanding the *meaning*, for participants in the study, of the events, situations, and actions they are involved with, and of the accounts that they give of their lives and experiences. In a qualitative study, you are interested not only in the physical events and behavior taking place, but also in how the participants in your study make sense of these, and how their understandings influence their behavior. The perspectives on events and actions held by the people involved in them are not simply their accounts of these events and actions, to be assessed in terms of truth or falsity; they are *part of* the reality that you are trying to understand (Maxwell, 1992; Menzel, 1978). This focus on meaning is central to what is known as the "interpretive" approach to social science (Bredo & Feinberg, 1982; Geertz, 1973; Rabinow & Sullivan, 1979).

2. Understanding the particular *context* within which the participants act, and the influence this context has on their actions. Qualitative researchers typically study a relatively small number of individuals or situations and preserve the individuality of each of these in their analyses, rather than collecting data from large samples and aggregating the data across individuals or situations. Thus they are able to understand how events, actions, and meanings are shaped by the unique circumstances in which these occur.

3. Identifying unanticipated phenomena and influences, and generating new, "grounded" theories about the latter. Qualitative research has long been used for this purpose by survey and experimental researchers, who often conduct "exploratory" qualitative studies to help them design their questionnaires and identify variables for experimental investigation. Although qualitative research is not restricted to this exploratory role, it is still an important strength of qualitative methods.

4. Understanding the *processes* by which events and actions take place. Although qualitative research is not unconcerned with outcomes, a major strength of qualitative studies is their ability to get at the processes that lead to these outcomes, processes that experimental and survey research are often poor at identifying (Britan, 1978; Patton, 1990, pp. 94ff.).

5. Developing causal explanations. The traditional view that qualitative research cannot identify causal relationships has long been disputed by some qualitative researchers (Britan, 1978; Denzin, 1978), and both qualitative and quantitative researchers are increasingly accepting the legitimacy of using qualitative methods for causal inference (e.g., Cook & Shadish, 1985; Erickson, 1986/1990, p. 82; Maxwell, 1996b; Miles & Huberman, 1994, pp. 144-148; Mohr, 1995, pp. 261-273, 1996; Rossi & Berk, 1991, p. 226; Sayer, 1992). Deriving causal explanations from a qualitative study is not an easy or straightforward task, but qualitative research is no different from quantitative research in this respect. Both approaches need to identify and deal with the plausible validity threats to any proposed causal explanation, as discussed below.

These research purposes, and the inductive, open-ended strategy that they require, give qualitative research an advantage in addressing numerous practical purposes, including the following.

Generating results and theories that are understandable and experientially credible, both to the people being studied and to others (Bolster, 1983). Although quantitative data may have greater credibility for some purposes and audiences, the specific detail and personal immediacy of qualitative data can lead to their greater influence in other situations. For example, I was involved in one evaluation, of how teaching rounds in one hospital department could be improved, that relied primarily on participant observation of rounds and open-ended interviews with staff physicians and residents (Maxwell, Cohen, & Reinhard, 1983). The evaluation led to decisive departmental action, in part because department members felt that the report, which contained detailed descriptions of activities during rounds and numerous quotes from interviews to support the analysis of the problems with rounds, "told it like it really was" rather than simply presented numbers and generalizations to back up its recommendations.

Conducting formative studies, ones that are intended to help improve existing practice rather than simply to determine the outcomes of the program or practice being studied (Scriven, 1967, 1991). In such studies, which are particularly useful for applied research, it is more important to understand the *process* by which things happen in a particular situation than to measure outcomes rigorously or to compare a given situation with others.

Engaging in collaborative, action, or "empowerment" research with practitioners or research participants (e.g., Cousins & Earl, 1995; Fetterman, Kaftarian, & Wandersman, 1996; Oja & Smulyan, 1989; Whyte, 1991). The focus of qualitative research on particular contexts and their meaning for the participants in these contexts, and on the processes occurring in these contexts, makes it especially suitable for collaborations with practitioners or with members of the community being studied (Patton, 1990, pp. 129-130; Reason, 1994).

A useful way of sorting out and formulating the purposes of your study is to write memos in which you reflect on your goals and motives, as well as the implications of these for your design decisions (for more information on such memos, see Maxwell, 1996a; Mills, 1959, pp. 197-198; Strauss & Corbin, 1990, chap. 12). I regularly use such memos as assignments in my methods courses; one doctoral student, Isabel Londoño, said that "writing memos for classes was key, having to put things to paper," in figuring out her purposes in choosing a dissertation topic (see Maxwell, 1996a, pp. 22-23).

■ *Conceptual Context: What Do You Think Is Going On?*

The conceptual context of your study is the system of concepts, assumptions, expectations, beliefs, and theories that supports and informs your research. This context, or a diagrammatic representation of it, is often called a "conceptual framework" (Hedrick, Bickman, & Rog, 1993, p. 19; Miles & Huberman, 1994; Robson, 1993). Miles and Huberman (1994) state that a conceptual framework "explains, either graphically or in narrative form, the main things to be studied—the key factors, concepts, or variables—and the presumed relationships among them" (p. 18).

Thus your conceptual context is a formulation of what you think is *going on* with the phenomena you are studying—a tentative *theory* of what is happening. Theory provides a model or map of *why* the world is the way it is (Strauss, 1995). It is a simplification of the world, but a simplification aimed at clarifying and explaining some aspect of how it works. It is not simply a "framework," although it can provide that, but a *story* about what you think is happening and why. A useful theory is one that tells an enlightening story about some phenomenon, one that gives you new insights and broadens your understanding of that phenomenon. The function of theory in your design is to inform the rest of the design—to help you to assess your purposes, develop and select realistic and relevant research questions and methods, and identify potential validity threats to your conclusions.

Some writers label this part of a research design or proposal as the "literature review." This can be a dangerously misleading term, for three reasons. First, it can lead you to focus narrowly on "literature," ignoring other conceptual resources that may be of equal or greater importance for your study, including your own experience. Second, it tends to generate a strategy of "covering the field" rather than focusing specifically on those studies and theories that are particularly *relevant* to your research. Third, it can make you think that your task is simply descriptive—to tell what previous researchers have found or what theories have been proposed. In developing a conceptual context, your purpose is not only descriptive, but also critical; you need to treat "the literature" not as an *authority* to be deferred to, but as a useful but fallible source of *ideas* about what's going on, and to attempt to see alternative ways of framing the issues.

Another way of putting this is that the conceptual context for your research study is something that is *constructed,* not found. It incorporates pieces that are borrowed from elsewhere, but the structure, the overall coherence, is something that *you* build, not something that exists ready-made. Becker (1986, pp. 141ff.) systematically develops the idea that prior work provides *modules* that you can use in building your conceptual context, modules that you need to examine critically to make sure they work effectively with the rest of your design. There are four main sources for these modules: your own experiential knowledge, existing theory and research, pilot and exploratory studies, and thought experiments.

☐ *Experiential Knowledge*

Traditionally, what you bring to the research from your background and identity has been treated as "bias," something whose influence needs to be *eliminated* from the design, rather than a valuable component of it. However, the explicit incorporation of your identity and experience (what Strauss, 1987, calls "experiential data") in your research has recently gained much wider theoretical and philosophical support (e.g., Berg & Smith, 1988; Jansen & Peshkin, 1992). Using this experience in your research can provide you with a major source of insights, hypotheses, and validity checks. For example, Grady and Wallston (1988, p. 41) describe how one health care researcher used insights from her own experience to design a study of why many women don't do breast self-examination.

This is not a license to impose your assumptions and values uncritically on the research. Reason (1988) uses the term "critical subjectivity" to refer to "a quality of awareness in which we do not suppress our primary experience; nor do we allow ourselves to be swept away and overwhelmed by it; rather we raise it to consciousness and use it as part of the inquiry process" (p. 12). However, there are few well-developed and explicit strategies for doing this. One technique that I use in my qualitative methods course and in my own research is what I call a "researcher experience memo"; I have given suggestions for this elsewhere (Maxwell, 1996a). Basically, this involves reflecting on, and writing down, the different aspects of your experience and identity that are potentially relevant to your study. Doing this can generate unexpected insights and connections, as well as create a valuable record of these.

☐ *Existing Theory and Research*

The second major source of modules for your conceptual context is existing theory and research. This can be found not only in published work, but in unpublished papers and dissertations, in conference presentations, and in the heads of active researchers in your field (Locke et al., 1993, pp. 48-49).

Using existing theory in qualitative research has both advantages and dangers. A useful theory helps you to organize what you see. Particular pieces of data that otherwise might seem unconnected or irrelevant to one another or to your research questions can be related if you can fit them into the theory. A useful theory also illuminates what you are seeing in your research. It draws your attention to particular events or phenomena, and sheds light on relationships that might otherwise go unnoticed or misunderstood.

However, Becker (1986) warns that the existing literature, and the assumptions embedded in it, can deform the way you frame your research, causing you to overlook important ways of conceptualizing your study or key implications of your results. The literature has the advantage of what he calls "ideological hegemony," making it difficult for you to see any phenomenon in ways that are different from those that are prevalent in the literature. Trying to fit your insights into this established framework can deform your argument, weakening its logic and making it harder for you to see what this new way of framing the phenomenon might contribute. Becker describes how existing theory and perspectives deformed his early research on marijuana use, leading him to focus on the dominant question in the literature and to ignore the most interesting implications and possibilities of his study.

Becker (1986) argues that there is no way to be sure when the established approach is wrong or misleading or when your alternative is superior. All you can do is try to identify the ideological component of the established approach, and see what happens when you abandon these assumptions. He asserts that "a serious scholar ought routinely to inspect competing ways of talking about the same subject matter," and warns, "Use the literature, don't let it use you" (p. 149; see also Mills, 1959).

A review of relevant prior research can serve several other purposes in your design besides providing you with existing theory (see Strauss, 1987, pp. 48-56). First, you can use it to develop a justification for your study—to show how your work will address an important need or unanswered question (Marshall & Rossman, 1995, pp. 22-26). Second, it can inform your decisions about methods, suggesting alternative approaches or revealing potential problems with your plans. Third, it can be a source of *data* that you can use to test or modify your theories. You can see if existing theory, the results of your pilot research, or your experiential understanding is supported or challenged by previous studies. Finally, you can use prior research to help you *generate* theory. For example, I have used a wide range of empirical studies, as well as modules derived from existing theory, to develop a radically different theory of the relationships among diversity, social solidarity, and community from that prevalent in the literature (Maxwell, in press), and I am currently applying this theory in an attempt to explain the success of a systemic educational reform initiative in a multiracial and multiethnic urban school district.

☐ *Pilot and Exploratory Studies*

Pilot studies serve some of the same functions as prior research, but they can be focused more precisely on your own concerns and theories. You can design pilot studies specifically to test your ideas or methods and explore their implications, or to inductively develop *grounded* theory. One particular use that pilot studies have in qualitative research is to generate an understanding of the concepts and theories held by the people you are studying—what I have called "interpretation" (Maxwell, 1992). This is not simply a source of additional concepts for your theory; instead, it provides you with an understanding of the *meaning* that these phenomena and events have for the actors who are involved in them, and the perspectives that inform their actions. In a qualitative study, these meanings and perspectives should constitute an important focus of your theory; as discussed earlier, they are one of the things your theory is *about,* not simply a source of theoretical insights and building blocks for the latter.

☐ *Thought Experiments*

Thought experiments have a long and respected tradition in the physical sciences (much of Einstein's work was based on thought experiments), but have received little attention in discussions of research design, particularly qualitative research design. Thought experiments draw on both theory and experience to answer "what if" questions, to seek out the logical implications of various properties of the phenomena you want to study. They can be used both to test your current theory for logical problems and to generate new theoretical insights. They encourage creativity and a sense of exploration, and can help you to make explicit the experiential knowledge that you already possess. Finally, they are easy to do, once you develop the skill. Valuable discussions of thought experiments in the social sciences are presented by Mills (1959) and Lave and March (1975).

Experience, prior theory and research, pilot studies, and thought experiments are the four major sources of the conceptual context for your study. The ways in which you can put together a useful and valid conceptual context from these sources are particular to each study, and not something for which any cookbook exists. The main thing to keep in mind is the need for integration of these components with one another, and with your purposes and research questions. A particularly valuable tool for generating and understanding these connections in your research is a technique known as concept mapping (Novak & Gowin, 1984); I have provided guidance for using concept maps in qualitative research design elsewhere (Maxwell, 1996a).

■ Research Questions: What Do You Want to Understand?

Your research questions—what you specifically want to understand by doing your study—are at the heart of your research design. They are the one component that directly connects to all of the other components of the design. More than any other aspect of your design, your research questions will have an influence on, and should be responsive to, every other part of your study.

This is different from seeing research questions as the starting point or primary determinant of the design. Models of design that place the formulation of research questions at the beginning of the design process, and that see these questions as determining the other aspects of the design, don't do justice to the interactive and inductive nature of qualitative research. The research questions in a qualitative study should not be formulated in detail until the purposes and context (and sometimes general aspects of the sampling and data collection) of the design are clarified, and should remain sensitive and adaptable to the implications of other parts of the design. Often you will need to do a significant part of the research before it is clear to you what specific research questions it makes sense to try to answer.

This does not mean that qualitative researchers should, or usually do, begin studies with *no* questions, simply going into the field with "open minds" and seeing what is there to be investigated. Every researcher begins with a substantial base of experience and theoretical knowledge, and these inevitably generate certain questions about the phenomena studied. These initial questions frame the study in important ways, influence decisions about methods, and are one basis for further focusing and development of more specific questions. However, these specific questions are generally the *result* of an interactive design process, rather than the starting point for that process. For example, Suman Bhattacharjea (1994; see Maxwell, 1996a, p. 50) spent a year doing field research on women's roles in a Pakistani educational district office before she was able to focus on two specific research questions and submit her dissertation proposal; at that point, she had also developed several hypotheses as tentative answers to these questions.

☐ *The Functions of Research Questions*

In your research design, the research questions serve two main functions: to help you to focus the study (the questions' relationship to your purposes and conceptual context) and to give you guidance for how to conduct it (their relationship to methods and validity). A design in which the research questions are too general or too diffuse creates difficulties both for conducting the study—in knowing what site or informants to choose, what data to collect, and how to analyze these data—and for clearly connecting what you learn to your purposes and existing knowledge (Miles & Huberman, 1994, pp. 22-25). Research questions that are precisely framed too early in the study, on the other hand, may lead you to overlook areas of theory or prior experience that are relevant to your understanding of what is going on, or cause you to pay too little attention to a wide range of data early in the study, data that can reveal important and unanticipated phenomena and relationships.

A third problem is that you may be smuggling unexamined assumptions into the research questions themselves, imposing a conceptual framework that doesn't fit the reality you are studying. A research question such as "How do teachers deal with the experience of isolation from their colleagues in their classrooms?" assumes that teachers *do* experience such isolation. Such an assumption needs to be carefully examined and justified, and without this justification it might be better to frame such a question as a tentative subquestion to broader questions about the nature of classroom teachers' experience of their work and their relations with colleagues.

For all of these reasons, there is real danger to your study if you do not carefully formulate your research questions in connection with the other components of your design. Your research questions need to take account of what you want to accomplish by doing the study (your purposes), and of what is already known about the things you want to study and your tentative theories about these phenomena (your conceptual context). There is no reason to pose research questions for which the answers are already available, that don't clearly connect to what you think is actually going on, or that would have no direct relevance to your goals in doing the research.

Likewise, your research questions need to be ones that are answerable by the kind of study you can actually conduct. There is no value to posing questions that no feasible study could answer, either because the data that could answer them could not be obtained or because any conclusions you might draw from these data would be subject to serious validity threats.

A common problem in the development of research questions is confusion between research issues (what you want to *understand* by doing the study) and practical issues (what you want to *accomplish*). Your research questions need to *connect* clearly to your practical concerns, but in general an empirical study cannot directly answer practical questions such as, "How can I improve this program?" or "What is the best way to increase medical students' knowledge of science?" In order to address such practical questions, you need to focus on what you don't *understand* about the phenomena you are studying, and to investigate what is really going on with these phenomena. For example, the practical goal of Martha Regan-Smith's (1992) dissertation research was to improve the teaching of the basic sciences in medical school (see Maxwell, 1996a, pp. 116ff.). However, her research questions focused not on this goal, but on what exceptional teachers in her school did that helped students to learn science—something she had realized that she didn't know, and that ought to have important implications for how to improve such teaching overall. Unless you frame research questions that your study can clearly address, you run the risk of either designing a study with unanswerable questions or smuggling your goals into the answers to the questions themselves, destroying the credibility of your study.

A second confusion, one that can create problems for interview studies, is that between research questions and interview questions. Your research questions identify the things that you want to understand; your interview questions generate the data that you need to understand these things. This distinction is discussed in more detail below, in the section on methods.

There are three issues that you should keep in mind in formulating research questions for applied social research. First, research questions may legitimately be framed in particular as well as general terms. There is a strong tendency in basic research to state research questions in general terms, such as, "How do students deal with racial and ethnic difference in multiracial schools?" and then to "operationalize" these questions by selecting a particular sample or site. This tendency can be counterproductive when the purpose of your study is to understand and improve some particular program, situation, or practice. In applied research, it is often more appropriate to formulate research questions in particular terms, such as, "How do students at North High School deal with racial and ethnic difference?"

Second, some researchers believe that questions should be stated in terms of what the respondents report or what can be directly observed, rather than in terms of inferred behavior, beliefs, or causal influences. This is what I call an instrumentalist or positivist, rather than a realist, approach to research questions (Maxwell, 1992; Norris, 1983). Instrumentalists formulate their questions in terms of observable or measurable data, and are suspicious of inferences to things that cannot be defined in terms of such data. For example, instrumentalists would reject a question such as, "How do exemplary teachers help medical students learn science?" and replace it with questions like "How do medical students *report that* exemplary teachers help them learn science?" or "How are exemplary teachers *observed to teach* basic science?"

Realists, in contrast, don't assume that research questions about feelings, beliefs, intentions, prior behavior, effects, and so on need to be reduced to, or reframed as, questions about the actual data that one uses. Instead, they treat their data as fallible *evidence* about these phenomena, to be used critically to develop and test ideas about what is going on (Campbell, 1988; Cook & Campbell, 1979; Maxwell, 1992).

The main risk of using instrumentalist questions is that you will lose sight of what you are really interested in, and define your study in ways that obscure the actual phenomena you want to investigate, ending up with a rigorous but uninteresting conclusion. As in the joke about the man who was looking for his keys under the streetlight (rather than where he dropped them) because the light was better there, you may never find what you started out to look for. An instrumentalist approach to your research questions may also make it more difficult for your study to address important purposes of your study directly, and can inhibit your theorizing about phenomena that are not directly observable.

My own preference is to use realist questions, and to address as systematically and rigorously as possible the validity threats that this approach involves. The seriousness of these validity threats (such as self-report bias) needs to be assessed in the context of a particular study; these threats are often not as serious as instrumentalists imply. There are also effective ways to address these threats in a qualitative design, which I discuss below in the section on validity. The risk of trivializing your study by restricting your questions to what can be directly observed is usually more serious than the risk of drawing invalid conclusions. As the statistician John Tukey (1962) put it, "Far better an approximate answer to the right question, which is often vague, than an exact answer to the wrong question, which can always be made precise" (p. 13).

One issue that is not entirely a matter of realism versus instrumentalism is whether research questions in interview studies should be framed in terms of the respondents' perceptions or beliefs rather than the actual state of affairs. You should base this decision not simply on the seriousness of the validity threats, but also on what you actually want to understand. In many qualitative studies, the real interest is in how participants make sense of what has happened, and how this perspective informs their actions, rather than determining precisely what took place.

Finally, many researchers (consciously or unconsciously) focus their questions on variance rather than process (Maxwell, 1996a; Mohr, 1982). Variance questions deal with difference and correlation; they often begin with "Is there," "Does," "How much," or "To what extent." For example, a variance approach to Martha Regan-Smith's (1992) study would ask questions like "Do exemplary medical school teachers differ from others in their teaching of basic science?" or "Is there a relationship between teachers' behavior and students' learning?" and attempt to measure these differences and relationships. Process questions, in contrast, focus on *how* and *why* things happen, rather than *whether* there is a particular difference or relationship or how much it is explained by other variables. Regan-Smith's actual questions focused on *how* these teachers helped students learn, that is, the process by which their teaching helped the students to learn.

In a qualitative study, it can be dangerous for you to frame your research questions in a way that focuses on differences and their explanation. This may lead you to begin thinking in variance terms, to try to identify the variables that will account for observed or hypothesized differences, and to overlook the real strength of a qualitative approach, which is in understanding the process by which phenomena take place. Variance questions are often best answered by quantitative approaches, which are powerful ways of determining *whether* a particular result is causally related to one or another variable, and to *what extent* these are related. However, qualitative research is often better at showing *how* this occurred. Variance questions are legitimate in qualitative research, but they are often best grounded in the answers to prior process questions.

Qualitative researchers thus tend to generate two kinds of questions that are much better suited to process theory than to variance theory: questions about the *meaning* of events and activities to the people involved in them and questions about the influence of the physical and social *context* on these events and activities. (See the earlier discussion of meaning and context as research purposes.) Because both of these types of questions involve situation-specific phenomena, they do not lend themselves to the kinds of comparison and control that variance theory requires. Instead, they generally involve an open-ended, inductive approach, in order to discover what these meanings and influences are, and *how* they are involved in these events and activities—an inherently processual orientation.

Developing relevant, focused, answerable research questions takes time; such questions cannot be thrown together quickly, nor in most studies can they be definitively formulated before data collection and analysis begin. Generating good questions requires that you pay attention not just to the questions themselves, but to their connections with all of the other design components: the purposes that answering the questions might serve, the implications for your questions of your conceptual context, the methods you could use to answer the questions, and the validity threats you will need to address. As is true with the other components of your design, writing memos about these issues is an extremely useful tool for developing your questions (Maxwell, 1996a, pp. 61-62).

■ *Methods: What Will You Actually Do?*

There is no "cookbook" for doing qualitative research. The appropriate answer to almost any question about the use of qualitative methods is "It depends." The value and feasibility of your research methods cannot be guaranteed by your adhering to methodological rules; rather, they depend on the specific setting and phenomena you are studying and the actual consequences of your strategy for studying it.

□ *Prestructuring a Qualitative Study*

One of the most important issues in designing a qualitative study is how much you should attempt to prestructure your methods. Structured approaches can help to ensure the comparability of data across sources and researchers, and are thus particularly useful in answering variance questions, questions that deal with *differences* between things and the explanation for these differences. Unstructured approaches, in contrast, allow the researcher to focus on the *particular* phenomena studied; they trade generalizability and comparability for internal validity and contextual understanding, and are particularly useful for understanding the processes that led to specific outcomes, what Huberman and Miles (1988) call "local causality." Sayer (1992, pp. 241ff.) refers to these two approaches as "extensive" and "intensive" research designs, respectively.

However, Miles and Huberman (1994) warn that

> highly inductive, loosely designed studies make good sense when experienced researchers have plenty of time and are exploring exotic cultures, understudied phenomena, or very complex social phenomena. But if you're new to qualitative studies and are looking at a better understood phenomenon within a familiar culture or subculture, a loose, inductive design is a waste of time. Months of fieldwork and voluminous case studies may yield only a few banalities. (p. 17)

They also point out that prestructuring reduces the amount of data that you have to deal with, functioning as a form of preanalysis that simplifies the analytic work required.

Unfortunately, most discussions of this issue treat prestructuring as a single dimension, and view it in terms of metaphors such as hard versus soft and tight versus loose. Such metaphors have powerful connotations (although they are different for different people) that can lead you to overlook or ignore the numerous ways in which studies can vary, not just in the *amount* of prestructuring, but in *how* prestructuring is used. For example, you could employ an extremely open approach to data collection, but use these data for a confirmatory test of explicit hypotheses based on a prior theory (e.g., Festinger, Riecker, & Schachter, 1956). In contrast, the approach often known as ethnoscience or cognitive anthropology (Werner & Schoepfle, 1987a, 1987b) employs highly structured data collection techniques, but interprets these data in a largely inductive manner, with very few preestablished categories. Thus the decision you face is not primarily *whether* or *to what extent* you prestructure your study, but *in what ways* you do this, and *why*.

Finally, it is worth keeping in mind that you can lay out a *tentative* plan for some aspects of your study in considerable detail, but leave open the possibility of substantially revising this if necessary. Emergent insights may require new sampling plans, different kinds of data, and different analytic strategies.

I distinguish four main components of qualitative methods:

1. The research relationship that you establish with those you study

2. Sampling: what times, settings, or individuals you select to observe or interview, and what other sources of information you decide to use

3. Data collection: how you gather the information you will use

4. Data analysis: what you do with this information in order to make sense of it

It is useful to think of all of these components as involving *design* decisions— key issues that you should consider in planning your study, and that you should rethink as you are engaged in it.

☐ *Negotiating a Research Relationship*

Your relationships with the people in your study can be complex and changeable, and these relationships will necessarily affect you as the "research instrument," as well as have implications for other components of your research design. My changing relationships with the people in the Inuit community in which I conducted my dissertation research (Maxwell, 1986) had a profound effect not only on my own state of mind, but on who I was able to interview, my opportunities for observation of social life, the quality of the data I collected, the research questions I was able to answer, and my ability to test my conclusions. The term *reflexivity* (Hammersley & Atkinson, 1983) is often used for this unavoidable mutual influence of the research participants and the researcher on each other.

There are also philosophical, ethical, and political issues that should inform the kind of relationship that you want to establish. In recent years, there has been a growing interest in alternatives to the traditional style of research, including participatory action research, collaborative research, feminist research, critical ethnography, and empowerment research (see Denzin & Lincoln, 1994; Fetterman et al., 1996; Oja & Smulyan, 1989; Whyte, 1991). Each of these modes of research involves different sorts of relationships between the researcher and the participants in the research, and has different implications for the rest of the research design.

Thus it is important that you think about the kinds of relationships you want to have with the people whom you study, and what you need to do to establish such relationships. I see these as *design decisions,* not simply as external factors that may affect your design. Although they are not completely under your control and cannot be defined precisely in advance, they are still matters that require systematic planning and reflection if your design is to be as coherent as possible.

☐ *Decisions About Sampling: Where, When, Who, and What*

Whenever you have a choice about when and where to observe, whom to talk to, or what information sources to focus on, you are faced with a sampling decision. Even a single case study involves a choice of this case rather than others, as well as requiring sampling decisions *within* the case itself. Miles and Huberman (1994, pp. 27-34) and LeCompte and Preissle (1993, pp. 56-85) provide valuable discussions of particular sampling issues; here, I want to talk more generally about the nature and purposes of sampling in qualitative research.

Works on quantitative research generally treat anything other than probability sampling as "convenience sampling," and strongly discourage the latter. For qualitative research, this ignores the fact that most sampling in qualitative research is neither probability sampling nor convenience sampling, but falls into a third category: purposeful sampling (Patton, 1990, pp. 169ff.). This is a strategy in which particular settings, persons, or events are deliberately selected for the important information they can provide that cannot be gotten as well from other choices.

There are several important uses for purposeful sampling. First, it can be used to achieve representativeness or typicality of the settings, individuals, or activities selected. A small sample that has been systematically selected for typicality and relative homogeneity provides far more confidence that the conclusions adequately represent the average members of the population than does a sample of the same size that incorporates substantial random or accidental variation. Second, purposeful sampling can be used to capture adequately the heterogeneity in the population. The goal here is to ensure that the conclusions adequately represent the entire *range* of variation, rather than only the typical members or some subset of this range. Third, a sample can be purposefully selected to allow for the examination of cases that are critical for the theories the study began with, or that have subsequently been developed. Finally, purposeful sampling can be used to establish particular comparisons to illuminate the reasons for differences between settings or individuals, a common strategy in multicase qualitative studies.

You should not make sampling decisions in isolation from the rest of your design. They should take into account your research relationship with study participants, the feasibility of data collection and analysis, and validity concerns, as well as your purposes and conceptual context. In addition, feasible sampling decisions often require considerable knowledge of the setting studied, and you will need to alter them as you learn more about what decisions will work best to give you the data you need.

□ *Decisions About Data Collection*

Most qualitative methods texts devote considerable space to the strengths and limitations of particular data collection methods (see particularly Bogdan & Biklen, 1992; Patton, 1990; Weiss, 1994), so I won't deal with these issues here. Instead, I want to address two key design issues in selecting and using data collection methods: the relationship between research questions and data collection methods, and the triangulation of different methods.

Although researchers often talk about "operationalizing" their research questions, or of "translating" the research questions into interview questions, this language is a vestigial remnant of logical positivism that bears little relationship to qualitative research practice. There is no way to convert research questions into useful methods decisions; your methods are the *means* to answering your research questions, not a logical transformation of the latter. Their selection depends not only on your research questions, but on the actual research situation and what will work most effectively in that situation to give you the data you need. For example, your interview questions should be judged not by whether they can be logically derived from your research questions, but by whether they provide the *data* that will contribute to answering these questions, an issue that may require pilot testing a variety of questions or actually conducting a significant part of the interviews. You need to anticipate, as best you can, how particular interview questions or other data collection strategies will actually work in practice. In addition, your interview questions and observational strategies will generally be far more focused, context-specific, and diverse than the broad, general research questions that define what you seek to understand in conducting the study. The development of a good data collection plan requires creativity and insight, not a mechanical translation of your research questions into methods.

In addition, qualitative studies generally rely on the integration of data from a variety of methods and sources of information, a general principle known as triangulation (Denzin, 1978). This reduces the risk that your conclusions will reflect only the systematic biases or limitations of a specific method, and allows you to gain a better assessment of the validity and generality of the explanations that you develop. Triangulation is also discussed below, in the section on validity.

☐ *Decisions About Data Analysis*

Analysis is often conceptually separated from design, especially by writers who see design as what happens *before* the data are actually collected. Here, I treat analysis as a part of design, and as something that must itself be designed. Every qualitative study requires decisions about how the analysis will be done, and these decisions should influence, and be influenced by, the rest of the design.

One of the most common problems qualitative researchers have is that they let their unanalyzed field notes and transcripts pile up, making the task of final analysis much more difficult and discouraging than it needs to be. In my dissertation research on Inuit kinship, if I had not analyzed my data as I collected it, I would have missed the insights that enabled me to collect many of the data I eventually used to support my conclusions. You should begin data analysis immediately after finishing the first interview or observation, and continue to analyze the data as long as you are working on the research. This allows you to progressively focus your interviews and observations, and to decide how to test your emerging conclusions.

Strategies for qualitative analysis fall into three main groups: categorizing strategies (such as coding and thematic analysis), contextualizing strategies (such as narrative analysis and individual case studies), and memos and displays. These strategies are discussed in more detail by Coffey and Atkinson (1996) and Dey (1993). These methods can, and generally should, be combined, but I will begin by discussing them separately.

The main categorizing strategy in qualitative research is coding. This is rather different from coding in quantitative research, which consists of applying a preestablished set of categories to the data according to explicit, unambiguous rules, with the primary goal being to generate frequency counts of the items in each category. In qualitative research, in contrast, the goal of coding is not to produce counts of things, but to "fracture" (Strauss, 1987, p. 29) the data and rearrange it into categories that facilitate comparison between things in the same category and between categories. These categories may be derived from existing theory, inductively generated during the research (the basis for what Glaser & Strauss, 1967, term "grounded theory"), or drawn from the categories of the people studied (what anthropologists call "emic" categories). Such categorizing makes it much easier for you to develop a general understanding of what is going on, to generate themes and theoretical concepts, and to organize and retrieve your data to test and support these general ideas. (An excellent practical source on coding is Bogdan & Biklen, 1992; for more elaborate treatment, see Dey, 1993.)

However, fracturing and categorizing your data can lead to the neglect of contextual relationships among these data, relationships based on contiguity rather than similarity (Maxwell & Miller, n.d.), and can create analytic blinders, preventing you from seeing alternative ways of understanding your data. Atkinson (1992) describes how his initial categorizing analysis of data on the teaching of general medicine affected his subsequent analysis of the teaching of surgery: "On rereading the surgery notes, I initially found it difficult to *escape* those categories I had initially established [for medicine]. Understandably, they furnished a powerful conceptual grid. . . . The notes as I confronted them had been fragmented into the constituent themes" (pp. 458-459).

What I call contextualizing strategies (Maxwell & Miller, n.d.) were developed in part to deal with these problems. Instead of fracturing the initial text into discrete elements and re-sorting it into categories, contextualizing analysis attempts to understand the data (usually, but not necessarily, an interview transcript or other textual material) in context, using various methods to identify the relationships among the different elements of the text. Such strategies include some forms of case studies (Patton, 1990), profiles (Seidman, 1991), some types of narrative analysis (Coffey & Atkinson, 1996), and ethnographic microanalysis (Erickson, 1992). What all of these strategies have in common is that they look for relationships that connect statements and events within a particular context into a coherent whole. Atkinson (1992) states:

> I am now much less inclined to fragment the notes into relatively small segments. Instead, I am just as interested in reading episodes and passages at greater length, with a correspondingly different attitude toward the act of reading and hence of analysis. Rather than constructing my account like a patchwork quilt, I feel more like working with the whole cloth. . . . To be more precise, what now concerns me is the nature of these products as *texts*. (p. 460)

The distinction between categorizing and contextualizing strategies has important implications for your research questions. A research question that asks about the way events in a specific context are connected cannot be answered by an exclusively categorizing analysis (Agar, 1991). Conversely, a question about similarities and differences across settings or individuals, or about general themes in your data, cannot be answered by an exclusively contextualizing analysis. Your analysis strategies have to be compatible with the questions you are asking. Both categorizing and contextualizing strategies are legitimate and valuable tools in qualitative analysis, and a study that relies on only one of these runs the risk of missing important insights.

The third category of analytic tools, memos and displays, is also a key part of qualitative analysis (Miles & Huberman, 1994, pp. 72-75; Strauss & Corbin, 1990, pp. 197-223). As discussed above, memos can perform functions not related to data analysis, such as reflection on methods, theory, or purposes. However, displays and memos are valuable *analytic* techniques for the same reasons they are useful for other purposes: They facilitate your thinking about relationships in your data and make your ideas and analyses visible and retrievable. You should write memos frequently while you are doing data analysis, in order to stimulate and capture your ideas about your data. Displays (Miles & Huberman, 1994), which include matrices or tables, networks or concept maps, and various other forms, also serve two other purposes: data reduction and the presentation of data or analysis in a form that allows you to see it as a whole.

There are now a substantial number of computer programs available for analyzing qualitative data and a number of recent books comparing and evaluating these (e.g., Tesch, 1990; Weitzman & Miles, 1995). Although none of these programs eliminates the need to read your data and create your own concepts and relationships, they can enormously simplify the task of coding and retrieving data in a large project. However, most of these programs are designed primarily for categorizing analysis, and may distort your analytic strategy toward such approaches. For example, one group of researchers, employing a widely used qualitative analysis program to analyze interviews with historians about how they worked, produced a report that identified common themes and provided examples of how individual historians talked about these, but completely failed to answer the funder's key questions, which had to do with how individual historians thought about the connections among these different issues in their own work (Agar, 1991). So-called hypertext programs (Coffey & Atkinson, 1996, pp. 181-186) allow you to create electronic links, representing any sort of connection you want, among data within a particular context, but the openness of such programs can make them difficult for less experienced researchers to use effectively. A few of the more structured programs, such as ATLAS/ti, enable you not only to create links among data chunks, codes, and memos, but also to display the resulting networks (Weitzman & Miles, 1995, pp. 222-224).

■ *Validity: How Might You Be Wrong?*

Quantitative and experimental researchers generally attempt to design, in advance, controls that will deal with both anticipated and unanticipated threats to validity. Qualitative researchers, on the other hand, rarely have the benefit of formal comparisons, sampling strategies, or statistical manipulations that "control for" the effect of particular variables, and must try to rule out most validity threats after the research has begun, using evidence collected during the research itself to make these "alternative hypotheses" implausible. This approach requires you to identify the *specific* threat in question and to develop ways to attempt to rule out that particular threat. It is clearly impossible to list here all, or even the most important, validity threats to the conclusions of a qualitative study, but I want to discuss two broad types of threats to validity that are often raised in relation to qualitative studies: researcher bias and the effect of the researcher on the setting or individuals studied, generally known as reactivity.

Bias refers to ways in which data collection or analysis are distorted by the researcher's theory, values, or preconceptions. It is clearly impossible to deal with these problems by eliminating these theories, preconceptions, or values, as discussed earlier. Nor is it usually appropriate to try to "standardize" the researcher to achieve reliability; in qualitative research, the main concern is not with eliminating *variance* between researchers in the values and expectations they bring to the study, but with understanding how a *particular* researcher's values influence the conduct and conclusions of the study. As one qualitative researcher, Fred Hess, has phrased it, validity in qualitative research is the result not of indifference, but of integrity (personal communication). Strategies that are useful in achieving this are discussed below (and in more detail in Maxwell, 1996a).

Reactivity is a second problem that is often raised about qualitative studies. The approach to reactivity of most quantitative research, of trying to "control for" the effect of the researcher, is appropriate to a "variance theory" perspective, in which the goal is to prevent researcher *variability* from being an unwanted cause of variability in the outcome variables. However, eliminating the *actual* influence of the researcher is impossible (Hammersley & Atkinson, 1983), and the goal in a qualitative study is not to eliminate this influence but to understand it and to use it productively.

For participant observation studies, reactivity is generally *not* as serious a validity threat as many people believe. Becker (1970, pp. 45ff.) points out that in natural settings, an observer is generally much less of an influence on participants' behavior than is the setting itself (though there are clearly exceptions to this, such as settings in which illegal behavior occurs). For all types of interviews, in contrast, the interviewer has a powerful and inescapable influence on the data collected; what the interviewee says is *always* a function of the interviewer and the interview situation (Briggs, 1986; Mishler, 1986). Although there are some things you can do to prevent the more undesirable consequences of this (such as avoiding leading questions), trying to "minimize" your effect on the interviewee is an impossible goal. As discussed above for "bias," what is important is to understand *how* you are influencing what the interviewee says, and how this affects the validity of the inferences you can draw from the interview.

☐ *Validity Tests: A Checklist*

I discuss below some of the most important strategies you can use in a qualitative study to deal with particular validity threats and thereby increase the credibility of your conclusions. Miles and Huberman (1994, pp. 262ff.) include a more extensive list, having some overlap with mine, and other lists are given by Becker (1970), Kidder (1981), Guba and Lincoln (1989), and Patton (1990). Most of these strategies operate primarily not by *verifying* your conclusions, but by *testing* the validity of your conclusions and the existence of potential threats to those conclusions (Campbell, 1988). The idea is to look for evidence that challenges your conclusion, or that makes the potential threat implausible.

The modus operandi approach. One strategy often used for testing explanations in qualitative research, which differs significantly from those prevalent in quantitative research, has been called the "modus operandi method" by Scriven (1974). It resembles the approach of a detective trying to solve a crime, an FAA inspector trying to determine the cause of an airplane crash, a physician attempting to diagnose a patient's illness, or a historian, geologist, or evolutionary biologist trying to account for a particular sequence of events. However, its logic has received little formal explication (recent exceptions are found in Gould, 1989; Maxwell, 1996b; Mohr, 1995; Ragin, 1987), and has not been clearly understood even by many qualitative researchers. Basically, rather than trying to deal with alternative possible causes or validity threats as *variables,* by either holding them constant or comparing the result of differences in their values in order to determine their effect, the modus operandi method deals with them as *events,* by searching for clues as to whether they took place and were involved in the outcome in question. Thus a researcher who is concerned about whether some of her interviews with teachers were being influenced by their principal's well-known views on the topics being investigated, rather than eliminating teachers with this principal from her sample or comparing interviews of teachers with different principals to detect this influence, would look for internal evidence of this influence in her interviews or other data, or would try to find ways of investigating this influence directly through her interviews.

Searching for discrepant evidence and negative cases. Looking for and analyzing discrepant data and negative cases is an important way of testing a proposed conclusion. There is a strong and often unconscious tendency for researchers to notice supporting instances and ignore ones that don't fit their preestablished conclusions (Miles & Huberman, 1994, p. 263; Shweder, 1980). Thus you need to develop explicit and systematic strategies for making sure that you don't overlook data that could point out flaws in your reasoning or conclusions. However, discrepant evidence can itself be flawed; you need to examine both the supporting and discrepant evidence to determine whether the conclusion in question is more plausible than the potential alternatives.

Triangulation. Triangulation, as discussed above, reduces the risk of systematic distortions inherent in the use of only one method, because no single method is completely free from all possible validity threats. The most extensive discussion of triangulation as a validity-testing strategy in qualitative research is offered by Fielding and Fielding (1986), who emphasize the fallibility of *any* particular method and the need to design triangulation strategies to deal with specific validity threats. For example, interviews, questionnaires, and documents may all be vulnerable to self-report bias or ideological distortion; effective triangulation would require an additional method that is *not* subject to this particular threat, though it might well have other threats that would be dealt with by the former methods.

Feedback. Soliciting feedback from others is an extremely useful strategy for identifying validity threats, your own biases and assumptions, and flaws in your logic or methods. You should try to get such feedback from a variety of people, both those familiar with the phenomena or settings you are studying and those who are strangers to them. These two groups of individuals will give you different sorts of comments, but both are valuable.

Member checks. One particular sort of feedback deserves special attention: the systematic solicitation of the views of participants in your study about your data and conclusions, a process known as "member checks" (Guba & Lincoln, 1989, pp. 238-241; Miles & Huberman, 1994, pp. 275-277). This is the single most important way of ruling out the possibility of your misinterpreting the meaning of what the participants say and the perspective they have on what is going on. However, it is important that you not assume that participants' reactions are themselves necessarily valid (Bloor, 1983); their responses should be taken simply as *evidence* regarding the validity of your account (see Hammersley & Atkinson, 1983).

Rich data. "Rich" data are data that are detailed and complete enough that they provide a full and revealing picture of what is going on. In interview studies, such data generally require verbatim transcripts of the interviews, rather than simply notes on what you noticed or felt was significant. For observation, rich data are the product of detailed, descriptive note taking about the specific, concrete events that you observe. Becker (1970, pp. 51ff.) argues that such data "counter the twin dangers of respondent duplicity and observer bias by making it difficult for respondents to produce data that uniformly support a mistaken conclusion, just as they make it difficult for the observer to restrict his observations so that he sees only what supports his prejudices and expectations" (p. 52). The key function of rich data is to provide a *test* of your developing theories, rather than simply a source of supporting instances.

Quasi-statistics. Many of the conclusions of qualitative studies have an implicit quantitative component. Any claim that a particular phenomenon is typical, rare, or prevalent in the setting or population studied is an inherently quantitative claim, and requires some quantitative support. Becker (1970, p. 31) has coined the term "quasi-statistics" to refer to the use of simple numerical results that can be readily derived from the data. Quasi-statistics not only allow you to test and support claims that are inherently quantitative, they also enable you to assess the *amount* of evidence in your data that bears on a particular conclusion or threat, such as how many discrepant instances exist and from how many different sources they were obtained. For example, Becker et al. (1961), in their study of medical students, present more than 50 tables and graphs of the amount and distribution of their observation and interview data to support their conclusions.

Comparison. Although explicit comparisons (such as control groups) for the purpose of assessing validity threats are mainly associated with quantitative, variance-theory research, there are valid uses for comparison in qualitative studies, particularly multisite studies (e.g., Miles & Huberman, 1994, p. 237). In addition, single case studies often incorporate implicit comparisons that contribute to the interpretability of the case. For example, Martha Regan-Smith (1992), in her "uncontrolled" study of how exemplary medical school teachers helped students learn, used both the existing literature on "typical" medical school teaching and her own extensive knowledge of this topic to determine what was distinctive about the teachers she studied. Furthermore, the students she interviewed explicitly contrasted these teachers with others whom they felt were not as helpful to them, explaining not only what the exemplary teachers did that increased their learning, but *why* this was helpful.

☐ *Generalization in Qualitative Research*

Qualitative researchers often study only a single setting or a small number of individuals or sites, using theoretical or purposeful rather than probability sampling, and rarely make explicit claims about the generalizability of their accounts. Indeed, the value of a qualitative study may depend on its *lack* of generalizability in the sense of being representative of a larger population; it may provide an account of a setting or population that is illuminating as an extreme case or "ideal type." Freidson (1975), for his study of social controls on work in a medical group practice, deliberately selected an atypical practice, one in which the physicians were better trained and more "progressive" than usual and that was structured precisely to deal with the problems he was studying. He argues that the documented failure of social controls in this case provides a far stronger argument for the generalizability of his conclusions than would the study of a "typical" practice.

The generalizability of qualitative studies is usually based not on explicit sampling of some defined population to which the results can be extended, but on the development of a theory that can be extended to other cases (Becker, 1991; Ragin, 1987; Yin, 1994). For this reason, Guba and Lincoln (1989) prefer to talk of "transferability" rather than "generalizability" in qualitative research. Hammersley (1992, pp. 189-191) and Weiss (1994, pp. 26-29) list a number of features that lend credibility to generalizations made from case studies or nonrandom samples, including respondents' own assessments of generalizability, the similarity of dynamics and constraints to other situations, the presumed depth or universality of the phenomenon studied, and corroboration from other studies. However, none of these permits the kind of precise extrapolation of results to defined populations that probability sampling allows.

■ *Conclusion*

Harry Wolcott (1990) provides a useful metaphor for research design: "Some of the best advice I've ever seen for writers happened to be included with the directions I found for assembling a new wheelbarrow: *Make sure all parts are properly in place before tightening*" (p. 47). Like a wheelbarrow, your research design not only needs to have all the required parts, it has to *work*—to function smoothly and accomplish its tasks. This requires attention to the connections among the different parts of the design—what I call *coherence*. There isn't One Right Way to create a coherent qualitative design; in this chapter I have tried to give you the tools that will enable you to put together *a* way that works for you and your research.

■ *References*

Agar, M. (1991). The right brain strikes back. In N. G. Fielding & R. M. Lee (Eds.), *Using computers in qualitative research* (pp. 181-194). Newbury Park, CA: Sage.

Atkinson, P. (1992). The ethnography of a medical setting: Reading, writing, and rhetoric. *Qualitative Health Research, 2,* 451-474.

Becker, H. S. (1970). *Sociological work: Method and substance.* New Brunswick, NJ: Transaction.

Becker, H. S. (1986). *Writing for social scientists: How to start and finish your thesis, book, or article.* Chicago: University of Chicago Press.

Becker, H. S. (1991). Generalizing from case studies. In E. W. Eisner & A. Peshkin (Eds.), *Qualitative inquiry in education: The continuing debate* (pp. 233-242). New York: Teachers College Press.

Becker, H. S., Geer, B., Hughes, E. C., & Strauss, A. L. (1961). *Boys in white: Student culture in medical school.* Chicago: University of Chicago Press.

Berg, D. N., & Smith, K. K. (Eds.). (1988). *The self in social inquiry: Researching methods.* Newbury Park, CA: Sage.

Bhattacharjea, S. (1994). *Reconciling "public" and "private": Women in the educational bureaucracy in "Sinjabistan" Province, Pakistan.* Unpublished doctoral dissertation, Harvard Graduate School of Education.

Bloor, M. J. (1983). Notes on member validation. In R. M. Emerson (Ed.), *Contemporary field research: A collection of readings* (pp. 156-172). Prospect Heights, IL: Waveland.

Bogdan, R. C., & Biklen, S. K. (1992). *Qualitative research for education: An introduction to theory and methods* (2nd ed.). Boston: Allyn & Bacon.

Bolster, A. S. (1983). Toward a more effective model of research on teaching. *Harvard Educational Review, 53,* 294-308.

Bredo, E., & Feinberg, W. (1982). *Knowledge and values in social and educational research*. Philadelphia: Temple University Press.

Briggs, C. L. (1986). *Learning how to ask: A sociolinguistic appraisal of the role of the interview in social science research*. Cambridge: Cambridge University Press.

Britan, G. M. (1978). Experimental and contextual models of program evaluation. *Evaluation and Program Planning, 1,* 229-234.

Campbell, D. T. (1988). *Methodology and epistemology for social science: Selected papers*. Chicago: University of Chicago Press.

Coffey, A., & Atkinson, P. (1996). *Making sense of qualitative data: Complementary research strategies*. Thousand Oaks, CA: Sage.

Cook, T. D., & Campbell, D. T. (1979). *Quasi-experimentation: Design and analysis issues for field settings*. Chicago: Rand McNally.

Cook, T. D., & Shadish, W. R. (1985). Program evaluation: The worldly science. *Annual Review of Psychology, 37,* 193-232.

Cousins, J. B., & Earl, L. M. (Eds.). (1995). *Participatory evaluation in education: Studies in evaluation use and organizational learning*. London: Falmer.

Denzin, N. K. (1978). *The research act* (2nd ed.). New York: McGraw-Hill.

Denzin, N. K., & Lincoln, Y. S. (1994). *Handbook of qualitative research*. Thousand Oaks, CA: Sage.

Dey, I. (1993). *Qualitative data analysis: A user-friendly guide for social scientists*. London: Routledge.

Eisner, E. W., & Peshkin, A. (Eds.). (1990). *Qualitative inquiry in education: The continuing debate*. New York: Teachers College Press.

Erickson, F. (1990). Qualitative methods. In *Research in teaching and learning* (Vol. 2, pp. 75-194). New York: Macmillan. (Reprinted from *Handbook of research on teaching,* 3rd ed., pp. 119-161, by M. C. Wittrock, Ed., 1986, New York: Macmillan)

Erickson, F. (1992). Ethnographic microanalysis of interaction. In M. D. LeCompte, W. L. Millroy, & J. Preissle (Eds.), *The handbook of qualitative research in education* (pp. 201-225). San Diego, CA: Academic Press.

Festinger, L., Riecker, H. W., & Schachter, S. (1956). *When prophecy fails*. Minneapolis: University of Minnesota Press.

Fetterman, D. M., Kaftarian, S. J., & Wandersman, A. (Eds.). (1996). *Empowerment evaluation: Knowledge and tools for self-assessment and accountability*. Thousand Oaks, CA: Sage.

Fielding, N. G., & Fielding, J. L. (1986). *Linking data*. Beverly Hills, CA: Sage.

Freidson, E. (1975). *Doctoring together: A study of professional social control*. Chicago: University of Chicago Press.

Geertz, C. (1973). *The interpretation of cultures: Selected essays*. New York: Basic Books.

Glaser, B. G., & Strauss, A. L. (1967). *The discovery of grounded theory: Strategies for qualitative research*. Chicago: Aldine.

Glesne, C., & Peshkin, A. (1992). *Becoming qualitative researchers: An introduction*. White Plains, NY: Longman.

Gould, S. J. (1989). *Wonderful life: The Burgess shale and the nature of history*. New York: W. W. Norton.

Grady, K. E., & Wallston, B. S. (1988). *Research in health care settings*. Newbury Park, CA: Sage.

Guba, E. G., & Lincoln, Y. S. (1989). *Fourth generation evaluation*. Newbury Park, CA: Sage.

Hammersley, M. (1992). *What's wrong with ethnography? Methodological explorations*. London: Routledge.

Hammersley, M., & Atkinson, P. (1983). *Ethnography: Principles in practice.* London: Tavistock.

Hedrick, T. E., Bickman, L., & Rog, D. J. (1993). *Applied research design: A practical guide.* Newbury Park, CA: Sage.

Huberman, A. M., & Miles, M. B. (1988). Assessing local causality in qualitative research. In D. N. Berg & K. K. Smith (Eds.), *The self in social inquiry: Researching methods* (pp. 351-381). Newbury Park, CA: Sage.

Jansen, G., & Peshkin, A. (1992). Subjectivity in qualitative research. In M. D. LeCompte, W. L. Millroy, & J. Preissle (Eds.), *The handbook of qualitative research in education* (pp. 681-725). San Diego, CA: Academic Press.

Kidder, L. H. (1981). Qualitative research and quasi-experimental frameworks. In M. B. Brewer & B. E. Collins (Eds.), *Scientific inquiry and the social sciences.* San Francisco: Jossey-Bass.

Lave, C. A., & March, J. G. (1975). *An introduction to models in the social sciences.* New York: Harper & Row.

LeCompte, M. D., Millroy, W. L., & Preissle, J. (Eds.). (1992). *The handbook of qualitative research in education.* San Diego, CA: Academic Press.

LeCompte, M. D., & Preissle, J., with Tesch, R. (1993). *Ethnography and qualitative design in educational research* (2nd ed.). San Diego: Academic Press,

Lincoln, Y. S., & Guba, E. G. (1985). *Naturalistic inquiry.* Beverly Hills, CA: Sage.

Locke, L., Spirduso, W. W., & Silverman, S. J. (1993). *Proposals that work* (3rd ed.). Newbury Park, CA: Sage.

Marshall, C., & Rossman, G. (1995). *Designing qualitative research* (2nd ed.). Thousand Oaks, CA: Sage.

Maxwell, J. A. (1986). *The conceptualization of kinship in an Inuit community.* Unpublished doctoral dissertation, University of Chicago.

Maxwell, J. A. (1992). Understanding and validity in qualitative research. *Harvard Educational Review, 62,* 279-300.

Maxwell, J. A. (1996a). *Qualitative research design: An interactive approach.* Thousand Oaks, CA: Sage.

Maxwell, J. A. (1996b). *Using qualitative research to develop causal explanations.* Paper presented to the Task Force on Evaluating New Educational Initiatives, Committee on Schooling and Children, Harvard University.

Maxwell, J. A. (in press). Diversity, solidarity, and community. *Educational Theory.*

Maxwell, J. A., Cohen, R. M., & Reinhard, J. D. (1983). A qualitative study of teaching rounds in a department of medicine. In *Proceedings of the Twenty-second Annual Conference on Research in Medical Education.* Washington, DC: Association of American Medical Colleges.

Maxwell, J. A., & Miller, B. A. (n.d.). Categorization and contextualization in qualitative data analysis. Unpublished paper.

Menzel, H. (1978). Meaning: Who needs it? In M. Brenner, P. Marsh, & M. Brenner (Eds.), *The social contexts of method.* New York: St. Martin's.

Merriam-Webster's Collegiate Dictionary (10th ed.). (1993). Springfield MA: Merriam-Webster.

Miles, M. B., & Huberman, A. M. (1994). *Qualitative data analysis: An expanded sourcebook* (2nd ed.). Thousand Oaks, CA: Sage.

Mills, C. W. (1959). *The sociological imagination.* New York: Oxford University Press.

Mishler, E. G. (1986). *Research interviewing: Context and narrative.* Cambridge, MA: Harvard University Press.

Mohr, L. (1982). *Explaining organizational behavior.* San Francisco: Jossey-Bass.

Mohr, L. (1995). *Impact analysis for program evaluation* (2nd ed.). Thousand Oaks, CA: Sage.

Mohr, L. (1996). *The causes of human behavior: Implications for theory and method in the social sciences.* Ann Arbor: University of Michigan Press.

Norris, S. P. (1983). The inconsistencies at the foundation of construct validation theory. In E. R. House (Ed.), *Philosophy of evaluation* (pp. 53-74). San Francisco: Jossey-Bass.

Novak, J. D., & Gowin, D. B. (1984). *Learning how to learn.* Cambridge: Cambridge University Press.

Oja, S. N., & Smulyan, L. (1989). *Collaborative action research: A developmental approach.* London: Falmer.

Patton, M. Q. (1990). *Qualitative evaluation and research methods* (2nd ed.). Newbury Park, CA: Sage.

Rabinow, P., & Sullivan, W. M. (1979). *Interpretive social science: A reader.* Berkeley: University of California Press.

Ragin, C. C. (1987). *The comparative method: Moving beyond qualitative and quantitative strategies.* Berkeley: University of California Press.

Reason, P. (1988). Introduction. In P. Reason (Ed.), *Human inquiry in action: Developments in new paradigm research* (pp. 1-17). Newbury Park, CA: Sage.

Reason, P. (1994). Three approaches to participative inquiry. In N. K. Denzin & Y. S. Lincoln (Eds.), *Handbook of qualitative research* (pp. 324-339). Thousand Oaks, CA: Sage.

Regan-Smith, M. G. (1992). *The teaching of basic science in medical school: The students' perspective.* Unpublished doctoral dissertation, Harvard Graduate School of Education.

Robson, C. (1993). *Real world research: A resource for social scientists and practitioner-researchers.* London: Blackwell.

Rossi, P. H., & Berk, R. A. (1991). A guide to evaluation research theory and practice. In A. Fisher, M. Pavlova, & V. Covello (Eds.), *Evaluation and effective risk communications: Workshop proceedings* (pp. 201-254). Washington, DC: Interagency Task Force on Environmental Cancer and Heart and Lung Disease.

Sayer, A. (1992). *Method in social science: A realist approach* (2nd ed.). London: Routledge.

Scriven, M. (1967). The methodology of evaluation. In R. E. Stake (Ed.), *Perspectives on curriculum evaluation* (pp. 39-83). Chicago: Rand McNally.

Scriven, M. (1974). Maximizing the power of causal investigations: The modus operandi method. In W. J. Popham (Ed.), *Evaluation in education: Current applications* (pp. 68-84). Berkeley, CA: McCutchan.

Scriven, M. (1991). Beyond formative and summative evaluation. In M. W. McLaughlin & D. C. Phillips (Eds.), *Evaluation and education at quarter century* (pp. 19-64). Chicago: National Society for the Study of Education.

Seidman, I. E. (1991). *Interviewing as qualitative research.* New York: Teachers College Press.

Shweder, R. A. (Ed.). (1980). *Fallible judgment in behavioral research.* San Francisco: Jossey-Bass.

Strauss, A. L. (1987). *Qualitative analysis for social scientists.* New York: Cambridge University Press.

Strauss, A. L. (1995). Notes on the nature and development of general theories. *Qualitative Inquiry, 1,* 7-18.

Strauss, A. L., & Corbin, J. (1990). *Basics of qualitative research: Grounded theory procedures and techniques.* Newbury Park, CA: Sage.

Tesch, R. (1990). *Qualitative research: Analysis types and software tools.* New York: Falmer.

Tukey, J. (1962). The future of data analysis. *Annals of Mathematical Statistics, 33,* 1-67.

Weiss, R. S. (1994). *Learning from strangers: The art and method of qualitative interviewing.* New York: Free Press.

Werner, O., & Schoepfle, G. M. (1987a). *Systematic fieldwork: Vol. 1. Foundations of ethnography and interviewing.* Newbury Park, CA: Sage.

Werner, O., & Schoepfle, G. M. (1987b). *Systematic fieldwork: Vol. 2. Ethnographic analysis and data management.* Newbury Park, CA: Sage.

Weitzman, E. A., & Miles, M. B. (1995). *Computer programs for qualitative data analysis.* Thousand Oaks, CA: Sage.

Whyte, W. F. (Ed.). (1991). *Participatory action research.* Newbury Park, CA: Sage.

Wolcott, H. F. (1990). *Writing up qualitative research.* Newbury Park, CA: Sage.

Wolcott, H. F. (1995). *The art of fieldwork.* Walnut Creek, CA: Altamira.

Yin, R. K. (1994). *Case study research: Design and methods* (2nd ed.). Thousand Oaks, CA: Sage.

4

Practical Sampling

Gary T. Henry

Researchers in the social and policy sciences are presented with a dilemma in the early stages of designing their studies. Researchers would like to be able to speak about entire populations of interest, such as adult residents of the United States or children enrolled in public preschool programs. However, time and costs permit them to collect data from only a limited number of population members. The researcher needs a bridge to connect the goals of the study with the practical considerations of conducting the research. Sampling methods, or the methods by which members of a population are selected for a study, provide that bridge.

For some studies, a formal structure is needed to produce results within precise tolerances. For example, to estimate the reading proficiency of fourth graders in each state, the sampling methods must be rigorously established and followed (Mullis, Dossey, & Phillips, 1993). In other cases, less formal structures will accomplish the study goals. In a recent evaluation of a program that provided funds for safety equipment in schools, for instance, 12 schools that varied in size, region, grade level, and amount of funds received were selected as cases for intensive data collection (Todd, Kellerman, Wald, Lipscomb, & Fajman, 1996). This chapter should make clear that the nature of the sampling method—the type of bridge constructed—depends on the goals and the practicalities of the research.

Sample design and execution require careful consideration of the goals of the research and the resources available to carry out the research. Throughout the process, sampling theory guides the trade-offs between the resources available and the accuracy and precision of the information. For example, a common trade-off pits choosing more cases for the original sample against intensively following up with sample members who do not respond to the original request.

Both require resources: one for contacting a larger sample of population members, the other for recontacting sample members who did not initially cooperate with the request for information. Allocating more resources to the attempt to collect data on more cases will draw down the amount available for implementing follow-up procedures that encourage greater rates of response. Sampling theory shows that a researcher can actually improve the overall quality of the data by selecting fewer cases for the sample and allocating more resources to carrying out procedures that increase the proportion of the sample from which data are received.

Throughout sample design and execution, researchers make trade-offs between cost, on one hand, and the accuracy or precision of the information, on the other. This chapter will help readers to understand the consequences of making one choice or another. The choices are ultimately made by the research team. The information provided here will allow the researchers as well as the consumers of study findings to assess the impacts of those choices on the quality of the findings. I begin with some definitions and basic sampling issues. Knowing the most basic issues of sampling leads to a consideration of the two basic types of sample designs, probability and nonprobability samples. These are the two types of structures, or bridges, to continue with the analogy, for connecting the sample results to the population of interest. The choice of one or the other will establish the limits on how the sample data can be used. Because the formal structure of probability samples is so much more extensive than that of nonprobability samples, I devote the remainder of the chapter to them. After a discussion of the types of errors arising in the sampling process that can affect the quality of data, I present in the final sections a guide for researchers who face more of the types of trade-offs introduced above.

■ *Basic Sampling Issues*

For purposes of this chapter, a *sample* is defined as a model of the population or a subset of the population that is used to gain information about the entire population. A good model produces good information about the population. Often, samples are described as being *representative* as a way of indicating that they are good models of given populations. Unfortunately, no standards exist for labeling samples as representative, the way they do for labeling certain foods as low-fat. Whether or not you agree with the criteria used to establish a food as low-fat, at least you are assured that the food has met that standard. The labeling of a sample as representative reflects a subjective judgment of the writer, no more and no less. One needs much more information to assess a sample.

Assessing a sample, whether we are formulating a design or reading study findings, requires that we address three issues: population definition, selection of the sample, and precision of the results. These issues can be formulated as questions:

1. Is the population from which the sample is drawn consistent with the population of interest for the study?

2. Have the methods for selecting subjects or units biased the sample?

3. Are the estimates or sample statistics sufficiently precise for the study purpose?

By providing a specific response to each of these questions, we have a framework for understanding how sampling contributes to the *total error* that is involved with any particular study. In some cases, not all population members are included in the list used to draw the sample, or others who are not in the population appear on the list, both of which make the list inconsistent with the population of interest. Bias arises both from the use of human judgment in decision making about which particular population members are included in the sample and in more inadvertent ways, such as from the use of a list on which some population members appear more than once. Finally, even when samples are selected without bias, there may not be enough cases selected to provide estimates that are sufficiently reliable for the study. Although the third question garners the greatest attention, the others are equally important. Of course, there are other sources of error in applied social research, but these three are central to sampling.

Researchers should strive to answer the three questions above when reporting results. The questions should be answered for the actual sample selected, not based on the sample design. The design reflects an intent that can be relatively simple—for example, "We will randomly sample public school students in Oklahoma." As always, however, it is the details of how the intent has been put into practice that are important. Were students from all grades sampled, or was the sampling limited to a few grades? Did the list include students in schools run by the Bureau of Indian Affairs or only those within the state school system? With the answers to the three general questions above, careful consumers of any study can make their own judgments about how good the sample is.

For the researcher, these three questions reflect a concern for how well the sample models the population, which is usually raised in the context of generalizability, or "external validity" (Bickman, Rog, & Hedrick, Chapter 1, this volume; Campbell & Stanley, 1963; Cook & Campbell, 1979). Cook and Campbell (1979) pose the central question of external validity by asking, "Given that there is probably a causal relationship . . . , how generalizable is this relationship across persons, settings, and times?" (p. 39).

Sampling issues also affect the statistical conclusion validity of a study, or the ability to conclude that a relationship or covariation exists (Cook & Campbell, 1979, p. 37). The most obvious impact of sampling on statistical conclusion validity relates to sample size. Usually, the conclusion about covariation rests on a statistical test that determines "whether the evidence [for the relationship] is convincing beyond a reasonable doubt" (Kraemer & Thiemann, 1987, p. 23). These tests are sensitive to both the size of a relationship and the size of the sample (Lipsey, 1990; see also Chapter 2, this volume). Small sample sizes may contribute to a conservative bias that favors not rejecting a null hypothesis when it is in fact false. Large samples may show statistically significant effects or covariations that have little practical significance. Whereas reliance on statistical tests of significance is a practice worth questioning for many reasons (Cohen, 1994), sampling and sample size are key considerations in the assessment of differences in effect sizes or the development of conclusions about covariation.

To enhance the validity and credibility of social research, probability samples, or random samples, are being used with increasing frequency. Probability samples are selected in such a way that every member of the population has a chance of being included in the sample. The researcher creates a probability sample by randomly choosing members of the population for the sample, thus eliminating human judgment in the selection process. This type of sampling has an extensive formal structure to guide the selection of members of the population and allows the researcher to make estimates of errors associated with the sampling process. Other types of samples impose less structure on the selection process, but incorporate human judgment in the selection of sample members. These samples can be lumped into the category of nonprobability samples. In the next section, I describe nonprobability samples and contrast them with probability samples. Following that, the remainder of the chapter deals exclusively with probability samples.

■ *Nonprobability Sampling*

Nonprobability samples are used for many research projects. These samples can be chosen for convenience or on the basis of systematically employed criteria. Nonprobability sampling actually comprises a collection of sampling approaches that have the distinguishing characteristic that subjective judgments play a role in sample selection. The selection methods for nonprobability samples contrast with the methods used for probability samples, which are selected by random mechanisms that assure selection independent of subjective judgments.

Six nonprobability sampling designs that are used frequently in social research are listed in Table 4.1, along with descriptions of their selection strategies (each of these designs is described more fully in Henry, 1990). Nonprobability samples are often used very effectively in qualitative research designs (see Maxwell, Chapter 3, this volume). To point out some of the implications of using nonprobability samples, I will consider briefly here one type, the con-

Table 4.1 Nonprobability Sample Designs

Type of Sampling	Selection Strategy
Convenience	Select cases based on their availability for the study.
Most similar/ dissimilar cases	Select cases that are judged to represent similar conditions or, alternatively, very different conditions.
Typical cases	Select cases that are known beforehand to be useful and not to be extreme.
Critical cases	Select cases that are key or essential for overall acceptance or assessment.
Snowball	Group members identify additional members to be included in sample.
Quota	Interviewers select sample that yields the same proportions as in the population on easily identified variables

venience sample. A convenience sample consists of a group of individuals who are readily available to participate in a study. For example, psychologists interested in the relationship between violence in movies and aggressive behaviors by the American public may use volunteers from an introductory psychology class in an experiment. The researchers may take measures of attitudes and behaviors relating to violence among their subjects, and then show them a movie containing graphic violence. Finally, the researchers take a second set of measures. This fits the schema of a simple pretest-posttest design, often used when issues of internal validity are paramount (see Bickman et al., Chapter 1, and Mark & Reichardt, Chapter 7, this volume).

To expose and then clarify a point of confusion that often arises in connection with research design, I will add a *randomly assigned control group* to this design. Before the treatment is given—in this case, before the movie is shown—each student is randomly assigned to one of two treatments, a movie with graphic violence and a movie without violence. *Random assignment* means that the students are assigned by some method that makes it equally likely that each student will be assigned to the treatment group (Boruch, Chapter 6, this volume). In this case, the design employs random assignment but convenience sampling. The strength of this design is in its ability to detect differences in the two groups that are attributable to the treatment, that is, watching a violent movie.

Although this type of design rates highly in isolating the effect of violent movies, the convenience sample restricts the external validity of the design. If we are interested in the effect of violent movies on the U.S. population, this study poses significant concern for external validity. Can the differences in these two groups be used to estimate the impact of violent movies on the U.S. population? Other conditions, such as age, may alter responses to seeing violent movies. The students in this sample are likely to be in their teens and early 20s, and their reactions to the violent movie may be different from the reactions of older adults. Applying the effects found in this study to the entire U.S. population is clearly inappropriate. The randomization or randomized assignment that was used increases the internal validity of a study; it should not be confused with random sampling. Random sampling is a probability sampling technique that increases external validity. Although studies can be designed to provide high levels of both internal validity and generalizability, most stress one over the other.

The effects of violent movies found in this example study are restricted to the particular sample in which those effects were found, because of the convenience sample that was used. These effects should not be generalized, or extrapolated, to other populations. In fact, this is a limitation associated with all nonprobability samples. A characteristic of all nonprobability samples, including the convenience sample in this example, is that human judgment is exercised in the selection of the sample. Because no theoretical basis exists for the selection process, there is no systematic way to relate the sample results to the population as a whole (Kalton, 1983, p. 7).

Perhaps the most famous example of the type of error that can arise in nonprobability sampling is that of the polls conducted concerning the presidential election of 1948. Three prominent polling firms, using the nonprobability technique called quota sampling, were convinced that Thomas Dewey would defeat Harry Truman by a significant margin. Truman actually received 50% of the population vote, compared with Dewey's 45%. The subjective bias of interviewers tilted toward the selection of more Republicans for interviews, even though the sample proportions matched the voting population proportions in terms of location, age, race, and economic status. The unintended bias affected the accuracy and credibility of the polls and caused polling firms to begin to use more costly probability samples, which are the focus of the remaining sections of this chapter.

■ *Probability Samples*

Probability samples have the distinguishing characteristic that each unit in the population has a known, nonzero probability of being selected for the sample. To have this characteristic, a sample must be selected through a random mechanism. Random selection mechanisms are independent means of selection that are free from human judgment and the other biases that can inadvertently undermine the independence of each selection.

Random selection mechanisms include a lottery-type procedure in which balls on which members of the population have been identified are selected from a well-mixed bowl of balls, a computer program that generates a random list of units from an automated listing of the population, and a random-digit dialing procedure that provides random lists of four digits matched with working telephone prefixes in the geographic area being sampled (see Lavrakas, Chapter 15, this volume, for an example). Random selection requires ensuring that the selection of any unit is not affected by the selection of any other unit. The procedure must be carefully designed and carried out to eliminate any potential human or inadvertent biases. Random selection is never arbitrary or haphazard (McKean, 1987).

The random selection process underlies the validity, credibility, and precision of sample data and statistics. The validity of the data affects the accuracy of inferring sample results to the population and drawing correct conclusions from the procedures used to establish covariation. Credibility, in large measure, rests on absence of bias in the sample selection process. Sampling theory provides the basis for actually calculating the precision of statistics for probability samples. Because sampling variability has an established relationship to several factors (including sample size and the variance), the precision for a specific sample can be planned in advance of conducting a study.

A distinct advantage of probability samples is that sampling theory provides the researcher with the means to decompose and in many cases calculate the probable error associated with any particular sample. One form of error is known as bias. *Bias,* in sampling, refers to systematic differences between the sample and the population that the sample represents. Bias can occur because the listing of the population that is used to draw the sample (sampling frame) is flawed or because the sampling methods cause some populations to be overrepresented in the sample. Bias is a direct threat to the external validity of the results.

The other form of error in probability samples, *sampling variability,* is the amount of variability surrounding any sample statistic that results from the fact that a random subset of cases is used to estimate population parameters. Because the sample is chosen at random from the population, different samples will yield somewhat different estimates of the population parameter. Sampling variability is the expected amount of variation in the sample statistic based on the variance of the variable and the size of the sample. Taken together, bias and sampling variability represent *total error* for the sample. Error can arise from other sources, as other contributors to this volume point out, but here the focus is on total error that arises from sampling. In the next section, I describe the sources of total error in some detail.

■ *Sources of Total Error in Sampling Design*

The researcher can achieve the goal of practical sampling design by minimizing the amount of total error in the sample selection to an acceptable level given the purpose and resources available for the research. *Total error* is de-

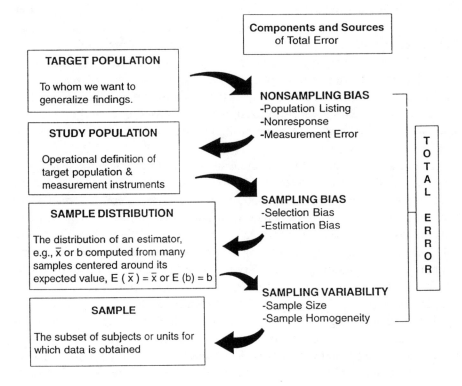

Figure 4.1. Decomposing Total Error

fined as the difference between the true population value for the target population and the estimate based on the sample data. Total error has three distinct components:

- *Nonsampling bias:* systematic error not related to sampling, such as differences in target and study populations or nonresponse
- *Sampling bias:* systematic error in the actual sampling that produces an overrepresentation of a portion of the study population, such as a sampling frame that lists some population members more than once
- *Sampling variability:* the fluctuation of sample estimates around the study population parameters that results from the random selection process

Each component generates concerns for the researcher, and all three sources of error should be explicitly considered in the design or critique of sampling methods. Each of the three components of total error and some examples of the sources of each are illustrated in Figure 4.1.

Because sample design takes place under resource constraints, decisions that allocate resources to reduce error from one component necessarily affect the resources available for reducing error from the other two components. Limited resources force the researcher to make trade-offs in reducing the components of total error. The researcher must be fully aware of the three components of error to make decisions based on the trade-offs to be considered in reducing total error. Below, I describe each of the three sources of error, and then return to the concept of total error for an example.

□ Nonsampling Bias

Nonsampling bias is the difference between the true target population value and the population value that would be obtained if the data collection operations were carried out on the entire population. Nonsampling bias results from decisions as well as implementation of decisions during data collection efforts that are not directly related to the selection of the sample. For example, the definition of the study population may exclude some members of the target population that the researcher would like to include in the study findings. Even if data were collected on the entire study population in this case, the findings would be biased because of the exclusion of some target population members. For example, using the telephone directory as the sampling frame would produce biased estimates of household characteristics due to unlisted numbers, new listings, and households without phones.

Differences in the true mean of the population and the survey population mean arise from several sources. A principal difference relevant to sample design is the difference between the target population and the study population. The target population is the group about which the researcher would like to make statements. The target population can be defined based on conditions and concerns that arise from the theory being tested or on concerns generated from the policy being examined. For instance, in a comprehensive needs assessment for homeless individuals, the target population should include all homeless individuals, whether served by current programs or not. On the other hand, an evaluation of the community mental health services provided to the homeless should include only homeless recipients of community mental health care. The target population for the needs assessment is more broadly defined and inclusive of all homeless.

Also, nonresponse creates nonsampling bias. Nonresponse results from the researcher's inability to contact certain members of the population or from the refusal of requests for data by some members. If nonresponse is truly random, it does not represent a bias, but this is frequently not the case and can never be assumed without further examination. More frequently, nonrespondents come from a definable subgroup of the population, and the omission of this subgroup from the data that are actually collected creates a bias in the results.

□ Sampling Bias

Sampling bias is the difference between the study population value and the expected value for the sample. The expected value of the mean is the average of the means obtained by repeating the sampling procedures on the study population. The expected value of the mean is equal to the study population value if the sampling and calculation procedures are unbiased.

Sampling bias can be subdivided into two components: selection bias and estimation bias. Selection bias occurs when not all members of the study population have an equal probability of selection. Estimation procedures can adjust for the unequal probabilities, when the probabilities of selection are known. The researcher makes adjustments by using weights to compensate for the unequal probabilities of selection.

An illustrative example of selection bias is a case in which a sample is selected from a study population list that contains duplicate entries for some members of the population. In the citizen survey example presented in Henry (1990), two lists are combined to form the study population list: state income tax returns and Medicaid-eligible clients. An individual appearing on both lists would have twice the likelihood of being selected for the sample. It is impossible from a practical standpoint to purge such a combined list of any duplicate listings. However, it is possible to adjust for the unequal probability of selection that arises.

To adjust for this unequal probability of selection, a weight (w) equal to the inverse of the ratio of the probability of selection of the unit to the probability of selection of units only listed once (r) should be applied in the estimation process:

$$w = 1/p = 1/2 = .5.$$

The probability of selection for this individual was twice the probability of selection for the members of the study population appearing on the list only once. Therefore, this type of individual would receive only one-half the weight of the other population members to compensate for the increased likelihood of appearing in the sample. The logic here is that those with double listings have been overrepresented by a factor of two in the sample and therefore must be given less weight individually to compensate.

Estimation bias occurs when the average calculated using an estimation technique on all possible simple random samples from a population does not equal the study population value. For example, the median is a biased estimate of the population mean. This is due to the fact that the expected value of the median of the sample means is not equal to the true study population mean. By using the weighted mean to compensate for selection bias as described above, the researcher can adjust the biased estimate for the bias in selection, thus canceling out the bias.

☐ *Sampling Variability*

The final component of total error in a sample is directly attributable to the fact that statistics from randomly selected samples will vary from one sample to the next due to chance. In any particular sample, some members of the study population will be included and others will be excluded, which produces this variation. Because statistics are not usually exactly equal to the study population value, it is useful to have an estimate of their likely proximity to the population value—in other words, their precision.

Sampling theory can be used to provide a formula to estimate the precision of any sample based on information available from the sample. Two factors influence sampling variability: the variability of the variable (standard deviation) and the size of the sample. Smaller standard deviations reduce the sampling error of the mean. The larger the sample, the smaller the standard deviation of the sampling distribution.

Because the standard deviation for the population can be estimated from the sample information and the sample size is known, a formula can be used to estimate the standard deviation of the sampling distribution, referred to hereafter as the standard error of the estimate, in this particular case, the standard error of the mean:

$$s_{\bar{x}} = s/(n)^{\frac{1}{2}};$$

$$s = [\Sigma(x_i - \bar{x})^2(n - 1)]^{\frac{1}{2}};$$

where $s_{\bar{x}}$ is the estimate of the standard error, s is the estimate of the standard deviation, n is the sample size, x_i is the sample observations, and $\bar{x}$ is the mean of the sample. Using this formula allows the researcher to estimate the standard error, the statistic that measures the final component of total error, based solely on information from the sample.

The standard error of the estimate is used to compute a confidence interval, or the range which is likely to include the true mean for the study population. The likelihood that the confidence interval contains the true mean is based on the t statistic chosen for the following formula:

$$CI = \bar{x} \pm t(s_{\bar{x}}).$$

The confidence interval is the most popular direct measure of the precision of the estimates. In most cases, the researcher should report the confidence interval along with the statistic to give the audience an understanding of the precision of the estimates.

Two more technical points are important for discussion here. First, probability sampling design discussions in this chapter assume that the sample would be selected without replacement; that is, once a unit has been randomly drawn from the population to appear in the sample, it is set aside and not eligible to be selected again. Sampling without replacement limits the cases available for selection as more are drawn from the population. If a sample is drawn from a finite population, sampling without replacement may cause a finite population correction factor (FPC) to be needed in the computation of the standard error of the estimate.

For the standard error of the mean, the formula using the FPC is

$$s_{\bar{x}} = (1 - n/N)^{1/2} s/(n)^{1/2}.$$

As a rule of thumb, the sample must contain more than 5% of the population to require the FPC. This is based on the fact that the finite population correction factor is so close to 1 when the sampling fraction is less than .05 that it does not appreciably affect the standard error calculation.

Second, standard error calculations are specific to the particular statistics being estimated. For example, the standard error for proportions is also commonly used:

$$s_p = [(pq)/n]^{1/2}.$$

Most statistics textbooks present formulas for the standard error of several estimators. Also, they are calculated for the statistic being used by almost any statistical software package. These formulas, like the formulas presented above, assume that a simple random sample design has been used to select the sample. Formulas must be adjusted for more complex sampling techniques (Henry, 1990).

One further note on terminology: The terms *sampling error* and *standard error* are used interchangeably in the literature. They are specific statistics that measure the more general concept of sampling variability. *Standard error,* however, is the preferred term. The common use of *sampling error* is unfortunate for two reasons. First, it implies an error in procedure rather than an unavoidable consequence of sampling. Second, the audience for a study could easily assume that sampling error is synonymous with total error concept, which could lead to the audience's ignoring other sources of error.

□ *Total Error*

Total error combines the three sources of error described above. Sample design is a conscious process of making trade-offs to minimize these three components of total error. Too frequently, reducing the standard error becomes the exclusive focus of sample design because it can be estimated. Because the two bias components cannot be calculated as readily, they are often given short shrift during the design process. When this occurs, sampling design is reduced to the calculation of sample size. However, failing to consider and to attempt to reduce all three components of total error sufficiently can lessen the validity and credibility of the study findings, as we will see in the example that follows.

For an evaluation of Georgia's prekindergarten program for 4-year-olds, my colleagues and I developed a complex sampling design that paid specific attention to the trade-offs posed by the three types of error. The purpose of the evaluation is to examine what type of program works best for which students, with an explicit concern for whether the program effects are enhanced or diminished by the types of educational programs the children receive after pre-kindergarten. The evaluation sponsors wanted the option to continue the study for a period of 16 years, essentially following the students into college or work at age 20. The issue of nonsampling bias was raised with respect to ensuring that the participants included in the study actually received the services of the program. We wished to sample at the beginning of the school year in order to obtain some preprogram measures of the cognitive, social, and motor skills of the 4-year-olds entering the program. However, early-year records are often incomplete due to the start-up of new classes to meet unanticipated demand (omissions) and can include students who are later withdrawn from the program (ineligibles). The trade-off between going into the field just as the program year was beginning to record data simultaneously with student entry into the program and waiting until enrollment changes had settled down somewhat led us to delay the initial data collection until later in the year. Also, we planned an end-of-year visit, to record the extent of the program completed by each student and rate the students' skills for a second time.

Another important aspect of this program is that it is the first statewide program to provide services for all 4-year-olds whose families wish to enroll them. The program is operated by private and public providers, each of which had to choose one of three established, developmentally appropriate curricula or submit its own curriculum for approval by a group of experts. Of the 3,037 classes offered in 1996-1997, local school systems provided 1,310 classes; the remainder were provided by private entities. The private sector provided a much larger percentage of the classes in the area around Atlanta than in other parts of the state. The Project High Scope curriculum dominated the local school programs; at the other end of the spectrum, the Montessori curriculum was in use in only 22 sites. The curricula in more than 2,000 sites were not listed in the available database at the time when the sample was to be drawn.

We elected to use a disproportionate stratified cluster sample approach in this case. This approach ensured that we could get a representation of the curricula that were relatively sparsely utilized for subpopulation analysis and maintain a large representation throughout the state's five regions. Table 4.2 shows the study population numbers and the sample sizes for each of the cells. I should highlight the column labeled "No Info." in this discussion. If we had included only those classes for which curriculum information was available, the omission on the other sites could have caused a significant nonsampling bias. Instead, we grouped these sites together and sampled from them using the overall sampling fraction as the guide for the number of units to sample. This serves as a reminder that we must be mindful of errors throughout the sampling process because errors can creep into the sampling design at any point. We oversampled from the less used curricula and, therefore, undersampled from the Project High Scope and no information groups. The trade-off between choosing an equal probability of selection sample, which is more simple to analyze, and choosing a disproportionate sample that would allow analysis of students served by each specific curriculum, but which is complex to analyze, went in favor of the latter.

Table 4.2   Population and Sample Information, Prekindergarten Example

Public School System

Region	Creative	High Scope	Montessori	Locally Developed	No Info.	Total Public
1	0 / 0	6 / 2	0 / 0	0 / 0	150 / 9	156 / 11
2	2 / 2	16 / 2	0 / 0	0 / 0	327 / 20	345 / 24
3	0 / 0	18 / 2	0 / 0	0 / 0	264 / 16	282 / 18
4	0 / 0	4 / 2	0 / 0	0 / 0	279 / 17	283 / 19
5	0 / 0	46 / 2	0 / 0	0 / 0	198 / 12	244 / 14
Total	2 / 2	90 / 10	0 / 0	0 / 0	1218 / 74	1310 / 86

Private Schools

Region	Creative	High Scope	Montessori	Locally Developed	No Info.	Total Private
1	9 / 2	32 / 2	1 / 1	5 / 5	97 / 6	144 / 16
2	122 / 10	233 / 12	15 / 6	126 / 15	653 / 41	1149 / 84
3	2 / 2	104 / 6	1 / 1	0 / 0	60 / 4	167 / 13
4	12 / 2	67 / 4	5 / 2	0 / 0	94 / 6	178 / 14
5	6 / 2	40 / 2	0 / 0	0 / 0	43 / 3	89 / 7
Total	151 / 18	476 / 26	22 / 10	131 / 20	947 / 60	1727 / 134

Public and Private

Region	Total
1	300 / 27
2	1494 / 108
3	449 / 31
4	461 / 33
5	333 / 21
Total	3037 / 220

Finally, we began to consider the overall sampling variability that we could tolerate in the design. We had to plan for the 16-year duration of the study and expected significant attrition among the students we would be able to follow over the entire time period. We expected that we could tolerate plus or minus 5 percentage points in the estimates of the population that finished high school or attended college, two important measures of educational attainment. Using the formula derived from the formula for standard errors of proportions, we decided on a sample of size of approximately 800 in 16 years. Using a rate of attrition of 10% per year, a conservative estimate of loss due to mobility and dropout, we determined that the study should begin with approximately 4,000 students. Because the study would involve travel to the sites for observations and a number of teacher interviews and ratings, we elected to trade off lower sampling errors that would result from sampling students directly for the easier-to-administer sampling of classes. To obtain 4,000 students, we divided by the average number of students per class, 18.4, and decided that 220 classes would provide a sufficient sample to meet the sampling variability requirements.

From this example, we can see that total error is important to decision making in every sample design. As noted above, the first component, non-sampling bias, is the difference between the true mean of the target population and the observed mean of the study population. Nonsampling bias includes differences arising from the definition of the population as well as errors attributable to instrumentation problems and field operations. The example shows that issues of nonsampling bias do not stop once the sampling frame is chosen. Omissions from the frame, ineligibles in the sample, and nonresponse can crop up throughout the process.

Sampling bias, the second component, is the difference between the observed mean of the study population and the mean of the sampling distribution, $E(\bar{x})$. Differences here are due to bias in selection or bias in the estimation process. We deliberately created a sampling bias in the example, but will be able to correct for the bias by weighting the observations during analysis. This is the easiest form of sampling bias to correct for. Inadvertent bias is much more difficult.

Finally, sampling variability is the difference between the mean of the sampling distribution and its sample estimate, $\bar{x}$ in this case. As the example indicates, the number of cases originally selected can be reduced by factors such as attrition and, in other cases, noncooperation. These must be planned for to the extent possible, or the study results will not be as precise as the sample design anticipated. Obviously, the consideration of total error in a sample is very complex. The next section walks through the practical sample design framework, providing concrete steps that lead to a careful consideration of total error throughout the phases of the design.

■ *Practical Sampling Design Framework*

The framework for practical sampling design is a heuristic tool for researchers and members of the audience for research findings to use in sample design as well as critique. The framework is, in essence, a series of choices that must be made, with each choice having implications for the validity and integrity of the study. My purpose in providing the framework here is to help researchers and consumers of research structure their thinking about design choices and the effects of their choices on total error.

The framework includes three phases of the overall design of the research project, which have been further subdivided into 14 questions (see Table 4.3).

Table 4.3   Questions for Sample Design

Presampling choices

    What is the nature of the study—exploratory, descriptive, or analytic?

    What are the variables of greatest interest?

    What is the target population for the study?

    Are subpopulations or special groups important for the study?

    How will the data be collected?

    Is sampling appropriate?

Sampling choices

    What listing of the target population can be used for the sampling frame?

    What is the precision needed for the study?

    What types of sampling techniques will be used?

    Will the probability of selection be equal or unequal?

    How many units will be selected for the sample?

Postsampling choices

    How can the impact of nonresponse be evaluated?

    Is it necessary to weight the sample data?

    What are the standard errors and related confidence intervals for the study
       estimates?

Although answers to all the questions have direct impacts on the sampling design, the focus of this chapter is specifically on sampling choices. More detail on the implications of various responses to all of the questions, as well as four detailed examples that illustrate how choices were actually made in four sample designs, is provided in Henry (1990). In addition, other chapters in this handbook provide discussion of the other issues. In the next few sections, all 14 questions will be explicated, but more detail will be provided for sampling choices.

■ *Presampling Choices*

☐ *What Is the Nature of the Study—Exploratory, Descriptive, or Analytic?*

Establishing the primary purpose of the study is one of the most important steps in the entire research process (see Bickman et al., Chapter 1, this volume). Exploratory research is generally conducted to provide an orientation or familiarization with the topic under study. It serves to enlighten the researcher about salient issues, helps focus future research on important variables, and generates hypotheses to be tested. Descriptive research is the core of many survey research projects in which estimates of population characteristics, attributes, or attitudes are study objectives (see Fowler, Chapter 12, and Lavrakas, Chapter 15, this volume). Analytic research examines expected relationships between groups and/or relationships between variables. In practice, many studies attempt both descriptive and analytic tasks, which means priorities are needed.

Exploratory research is often a preliminary activity leading to a more rigorous descriptive or analytic study. The sampling approach is quite reasonably limited by resource and time constraints placed on exploratory studies. Preferred sampling methods include those that ensure a wide range of groups are covered in the study rather than those that reduce error, because estimates, such as averages and proportions, are not reasonable study products. Sample designs that ensure coverage of a wide range of groups or, said another way, intentionally heterogeneous samples are purposeful quota samples or small stratified samples. This strategy reduces the potential problem of a confounding relationship between the sample and the existence of an effect.

Both descriptive and analytic studies are concerned with reducing total error. Although they have similar objectives for reducing both types of bias, the sampling variability component of total error is quite different. For descriptive studies, the focus is on the precision needed for estimates. For analytic studies, the most significant concern is whether the sample will be powerful enough to allow the researcher to detect an effect given the expected effect size. This is done through a power test (see Lipsey, Chapter 2, this volume). Analytic and descriptive studies will be the focus in the responses to the remaining questions.

☐ *What Are the Variables of Greatest Interest?*

Selecting variables and estimating their variability is an important precursor to the sampling design. Studies often have multiple purposes. The researcher may envision including many tables in the write-up or using several statistical tools to examine expected relationships. Choosing the variable of greatest interest is a matter of setting priorities. Usually, the most central dependent variable in a study will be the one of greatest interest. The variables of greatest interest are then used in the determination of sample size later on in the design process.

☐ *What Is the Target Population for the Study?*

The target population for a study is the group about which the researcher would like to speak. The population can be individuals (residents of North Carolina or homeless in Los Angeles), groups of individuals (households in Richmond or schools in Wisconsin), or other elements (invoices, state-owned cars, schools, or dwelling units).

Two types of populations characterize most social and policy research. The first is known as a *general population,* usually defined as adult (18 or older) residents of a specific geographic area, such as a county or state. State and national polls often use general population sampling frames; evaluation research has not used general population surveys extensively (Henry, 1996).

In contrast, *special populations* are more narrowly defined by the research purpose and questions. African American voters or clients of the child support system are special populations. In both cases, specific time frames for membership in the population, geographic location, age, and other criteria are often used in the definition and should be specified. A clear definition and rationale will be important when the choice of sampling frame or list of the target population comes up later.

☐ *Are Subpopulations or Special Groups Important for the Study?*

Often a researcher will choose to focus on a part of the target population for additional analysis. For example, households headed by single, working females were of particular interest to some scientists examining the impact of income maintenance experiments (Skidmore, 1983). When subgroups are important focal points for analysis, sampling choices, such as sample size and sampling technique, must recognize this. A sample designed without taking the subpopulation into account can yield too few of the subpopulation members in the sample for reliable analysis. Increasing the overall sample size or disproportionately increasing the subgroup sample, if it can be identified before sampling, are potential remedies.

☐ *How Will the Data Be Collected?*

Certain sampling choices can be used only in conjunction with specific data collection choices. For example, random-digit dialing, a technique that generates a probability sample of households with working phones, is an option when interviews are to be conducted over the phone (see Lavrakas, Chapter 15, this volume). A probability sample of dwelling units is useful mainly for studies in which on-site fieldwork, usually in the form of personal interviews, is to be used. The collection of data from administrative records or mailed questionnaires also poses specific sampling concerns. For example, mailed questionnaires can have a high proportion of nonrespondents in some populations (see Mangione, Chapter 14, this volume). Nonresponse affects sampling variability and is likely to cause nonsampling bias if the sample members who choose not to respond are different from those who do. In making a decision about sample size, which comes a bit later in these questions, the researcher should factor nonresponse into the final calculation. Because the sampling error depends on the number who actually respond, not the number surveyed, it is common to divide the desired sample size by the proportion expected to respond. For example, a desired sample size of 500 with an expected response rate of .80 will require an initial sample size of 625. If an alternative method of administering the instrument will reduce response rates, it will increase the sample size required for the same number of completes.

☐ *Is Sampling Appropriate?*

The decision to sample should be made deliberatively. Sampling is generally required to meet resource constraints. Because of resource constraints operating on a study, in many cases sampling will produce more accurate results than a population or census-type study. Often, resources for studies of entire populations are consumed by attempts to contact all population members. Response to the first contact is often less than 50%, causing substantial nonsampling bias. Sampling the population would require fewer resources for the initial contacts and would allow the investment of more resources in follow-up activities designed to increase responses, paying dividends in lowering nonsampling bias. Even when automated databases that contain all members of the population are being used, sampling can improve the accuracy of results. Missing data are a frequent problem with automated databases. Missing data are another form of nonresponse bias, because the data missing cannot be assumed to be random. The cost of collecting or supplementing information in the database will be less for the sample than for the entire population, in nearly every case.

On the other hand, small populations and use of the information in the political environment may weigh against sampling. For studies that may affect funding allocations or when there is expert knowledge of specific cases that may appear to be "unusual" or "atypical," the use of a sample can affect the credibility of a study. Credibility is vital when study results are used to inform decisions. Because decisions often determine winners and losers, credibility rather than validity may be the criterion on which the use of the findings turns.

■ **Sampling Choices**

☐ *What Listing of the Target Population Can Be Used for the Sampling Frame?*

The sampling frame, or the list from which the sample is selected, provides the definition of the study population. Differences between the target population and the sampling frame constitute a significant part of nonsampling bias. The sampling frame is the operational definition of the population, the group about which the researchers *can* reasonably speak.

For general population surveys, it is nearly impossible to obtain an accurate listing of the target population. A telephone directory would seem to be a likely explicit sampling frame for a study of the population in a community. However, it suffers from all four flaws that are commonplace in sampling frames:

- *Omissions:* target population units missing from the frame (example: new listings and unlisted numbers)
- *Duplications:* units listed more than once in the frame (example: households listed under multiple names)
- *Ineligibles:* units not in the target population (example: households recently moved out of the area)
- *Cluster lists:* groupings of units listed in the frame (example: households, not individuals, listed)

The most difficult flaw to overcome is the omission of part of the target population from the sampling frame. This can lead to a bias that cannot be estimated for the sample data. An alternative would be to use additional listings that include omitted population members to formulate a combination frame, or to choose a technique that does not require a frame, such as random-digit dialing instead of the phone book.

Duplications, or multiple listings of the same unit, increase the probability of selection for these units. Unchecked duplications result in sampling bias. For random-digit dialing, households with two or more phones are analogous to duplications. In some cases, researchers can address duplications by removing them from the list before sampling. In other cases, weights can be calculated based on the number of duplications for each case in the sample (Henry, 1990) and used to adjust estimates.

Ineligibles occur when cases that are not members of the target population appear on the sampling list. When ineligibles can be screened from the list or from the sample, the only concerns are the cost of screening and the reduction of the expected sample size. The cost of screening for a telephone survey includes making contact with someone in the household to determine eligibility. This can require several phone calls and can become quite costly, especially when the proportion of ineligibles is large. In addition to screening, the sample size may have to be increased so that sampling errors will not increase due to the screening.

Cluster listings are caused by sampling frames that include groups of units that are to be analyzed, rather than the units themselves. Many general population surveys, such as random-digit dialing telephone surveys, actually sample households. Listings for special population surveys may also contain multiple units. For example, welfare rolls may actually be listings of cases that include all members of affected families. The primary issue for sampling is the selection of the unit or units from the cluster listing. In most cases, information is sought only from one individual per cluster listing. If the selection of the individual is done randomly, a correction may be needed to compensate for the probability of selection if the clusters are unequal in size. To return to the telephone survey example, a member of a household with four adults is half as likely to be selected out of that household as is a member of a household with two adults. If the selection is not done randomly, a systematic bias may be introduced.

□ *What Is the Precision Needed for the Study?*

Precision, for descriptive studies, refers to the size of the confidence interval that is drawn around the sample mean or proportion estimates. The level of precision required relates directly to the purpose for which the study results will be used. A confidence interval of ±5% may be completely satisfactory for a planning study, but entirely too large for setting a candidate's campaign strategy.

Precision requirements are used in the calculations of efficient sample sizes. The objective of the researcher is to produce estimates within the limits of a specified confidence band. Sample size is a principal means by which the researcher can achieve this objective. But the efficiency of the sampling techniques can have considerable impact on the amount of sampling error and the estimate of desired sample size. These factors are combined in the calculation of sample size, discussed below.

□ *What Types of Sampling Techniques Will Be Used?*

The five probability sampling techniques are simple random sampling, systematic sampling, stratified sampling, cluster sampling, and multistage sampling. The choice of a technique will depend on several factors, including availability of an adequate sampling frame, the cost of travel for data collection, and the availability of prior information about target population. However, the choices do not end with the selection of a technique.

Choices branch off independently for each technique. If stratified sampling is chosen, how many strata should be used? If cluster sampling is chosen, how should the clusters be defined? For multistage samples, can the researcher better reduce sampling variability by selecting more of the primary sampling units with fewer secondary units for each primary unit or by selecting fewer primary units with more secondary units for each primary unit? Table 4.4 presents the definitions of all five types of sampling techniques, as well as their requirements and benefits.

□ *Will the Probability of Selection Be Equal or Unequal?*

Choices about the probability of selection will also affect sampling bias. For simple random sampling, the probability of selecting any individual unit is equal to the sampling fraction or the proportion of the population selected for the sample (n/N). The probability of selecting any unit is equal to the probability of selecting any other unit. For stratified sampling, the probability of selection for any unit is the sampling fraction for the stratum in which the unit is placed. Probabilities using a stratified sampling technique can be either equal or unequal. If subpopulations are a focus of the analysis or some strata are known to have much higher variability for important variables, a disproportionate sampling strategy should be considered, which would result in unequal probability of selection. Equal probability of selection techniques (proportionate selection

Table 4.4 Probability Sampling Techniques

	Simple Random	Systematic	Stratified	Cluster	Multistage (two stage)
Definition	Equal probability of selection sample where n units are drawn from population list.	Equal probability of selection sample where a random start is chosen and every unit that falls at a certain interval from the first unit is selected.	Either equal or unequal probability of selection sample where population is divided into strata (or groups) and a simple random sample of each stratum is selected.	Clusters that contain members of the study population are selected by a simple random sample and all members of the selected clusters are included in the study.	First, clusters of study population members are sampled, then study population members are selected by random sampling.
Requirements	List of study population	List of physical representation of study population	List of study population divided into strata	List of clusters	List of primary sampling units
	Count of study population (N)	Approximate count of study population (N)	Count for each stratum	All members of study population in one and only one cluster	List of members for selected primary sampling units
	Sample size (n)	Sample size (n)	Sample size for each stratum	Count of clusters (C)	Count of primary sampling units
	Random selection mechanism	Sampling interval ($I = N/n$)	Random selection used in each stratum	Approximate size of clusters (N_c)	Number of primary sampling units to be selected
		Random start ($I \leq R \leq I$)		Number of clusters to be sampled (c)	Number of members to be selected from primary sampling units
				Random selection mechanism	Random selection mechanism for primary sampling units and members
Benefits	Easy to administer	Easy to administer in field, physical listing, such as files or invoices, may be more available than list	Reduces standard error	List of study population unnecessary	All benefits for cluster, plus may reduce standard error
	Self-weighting		Disproportionate stratifications can be used to increase sample size of subpopulations	Limits costs associated with travel or approvals from all clusters	Most complex but often most efficient and flexible
	Standard error calculation is automatic in most software			Clusters can be stratified for efficiency	

in each stratum) should be considered the default strategy. Why? A sample with equal probability of selection is termed a self-weighting sample, indicating that no weights are needed to adjust for unequal probabilities. Unequal probabilities of selection indicate bias and require weights to adjust for unequal probabilities. The benefits of disproportionate stratification must outweigh the costs of weighting the data for analysis.

☐ *How Many Units Will Be Selected for the Sample?*

The topic of the estimation of efficient sample size is a reasonable place to begin a discussion of sample size. For this chapter, efficient sample size is described for descriptive studies. In descriptive studies, the question posed is, What sample size will produce estimates that are precise enough to be useful, given the sampling technique? Precision, from the sampling perspective, is a function of the confidence interval, which is influenced primarily by three variables: the standard deviation of the variable of interest, the sample size, and level of confidence required (represented by the t statistic). To a lesser extent, it can be influenced by sampling fraction as a result of the finite population correction. The researcher directly controls only the sample size; to produce an estimate from the sample that is precise enough for the study objectives, the researcher can adjust the sample size. But increasing the sample size means increasing the cost of data collection. Trade-offs between precision and cost are inherent at this juncture.

For a descriptive study, assuming a simple random sample, the sample size calculation is done using the following formulas:

$$n' = s^2/(te/t)^2;$$

$$n = n'/(1 + f);$$

where n' is the sample size computed in the first step, s is the estimate of the standard deviation, te is the tolerable error, t is the t value for the desired probability level, n is the efficient sample size using the finite population correction error factor, and f is the sampling.

The most difficult piece of information to obtain for these formulas, considering it is used prior to conducting the actual data collection, is the estimate of the standard deviation. A number of options are available, including prior studies, small pilot studies, and estimates using the range.

Although the sample size is the principal means for influencing the precision of the estimate once the design is set, an iterative process can be used to examine the impact on efficient sample size when altering the design, especially the sampling technique. Stratification or the selection of more primary sampling units in multistage sampling can improve the efficiency of the design. Of course, these adjustments are also likely to increase costs, but perhaps less than increasing the sample size would.

In addition, other sample size considerations should be brought to bear at this point. For example, will the number of members of subpopulations that are to be described be sufficient in the design using the efficient sample size? Determining the sample size is generally an iterative process. The researcher must consider and analyze numerous factors that may alter earlier choices. It is important for the researcher to review the proposed alternatives carefully in terms of total error, changes in the study population definition from using different sampling frames, ability to meet the study objectives, time, and cost.

■ *Postsampling Choices*

☐ *How Can the Impact of Nonresponse Be Evaluated?*

Nonresponse is the lack of valid responses from some members of the sample. Nonresponse can occur when a respondent refuses to answer a particular question or refuses to participate in the survey, or when a respondent cannot be contacted. If the nonresponding portion of the population is reduced, the nonsampling bias is reduced (Kalton, 1983). Fowler (1993; see also Chapter 12, this volume) discusses several ways of reducing nonresponse. It is often necessary for the researcher to evaluate the impact of nonresponse by conducting special studies of the nonrespondents, comparing the sample characteristics with known population parameters, or examining various weighting schemes (Henry, 1990; see also Braverman, 1996; Couper & Groves, 1996; Krosnick, Narayan, & Smith, 1996).

☐ *Is It Necessary to Weight the Sample Data?*

Weighting is usually required to compensate for sampling bias when unequal probabilities result from the researcher's sampling choices. Unequal probabilities of selection can occur inadvertently, as with duplicates on the sampling frame or cluster listing. They can also arise from deliberate choices, such as disproportionate stratification. Generally, weights should be applied in all these cases. (For a discussion of the calculation of appropriate weights, see Henry, 1990.)

☐ *What Are the Standard Errors and Related Confidence Intervals for the Study Estimates?*

The precision of the estimates and the sensitivity of hypothesis tests are determined by the standard errors. It is important to know that the sampling error formulas are different for the different sampling techniques. Formulas for calculating the standard error of the mean calculation for simple random samples were presented earlier in the chapter. Other sampling techniques require modifications to the formula and can be found in Henry (1990), Kalton (1983), Sudman (1976), and Kish (1965).

However, some general guidance can be provided. Stratification lowers the sampling error, all other things held constant. Sampling error can be further lowered when larger sampling fractions are allocated to strata that have the highest standard deviations. Cluster sampling has the opposite impact on sampling error. This occurs because the number of independent choices is the number of clusters in cluster sampling, not the number of units finally selected. The effect is reduced when clusters are internally heterogeneous on the important study variables (large standard deviations within the clusters) or cluster means do not vary. Sampling variability can often be reduced by stratification of the clusters before selection. This means that the clusters must be placed into strata before selection, and the variables used to define the strata must be available for all clusters. This was the strategy used in the prekindergarten evaluation example discussed above. The sampling unit was classes, and the classes were stratified and selected disproportionately. This type of design generally results in standard errors very close to those associated with simple random samples.

■ Summary

The challenge of sampling lies in making trade-offs to reduce total error while keeping study goals and resources in mind. The researcher must act to make choices throughout the sampling process to reduce error, but reducing the error associated with one choice can increase errors from other sources. Faced with this complex, multidimensional challenge, the researcher must concentrate on reducing total error. Error can arise systematically from bias or can occur due to random fluctuation inherent in sampling. Error cannot be eliminated entirely. Reducing error is the practical objective, and this can be achieved through careful design.

■ References

Braverman, M. T. (1996). Survey use in evaluation. *New Directions in Evaluation, 71,* 3-15.

Campbell, D. T., & Stanley, J. C. (1963). *Experimental and quasi-experimental designs for research.* Chicago: Rand McNally.

Cohen, J. (1994). The earth is round. *American Psychologist, 49,* 997-1003.

Cook, T. D., & Campbell, D. T. (1979). *Quasi-experimentation: Design and analysis issues for field settings.* Chicago: Rand McNally.

Couper, M. P., & Groves, R. M. (1996). Household-level determinants of survey nonresponse. In M. T. Braverman & J. K. Slaters (Eds.), *Advances in survey research* (pp. 63-79). San Francisco: Jossey-Bass.

Fowler, F. J., Jr. (1993). *Survey research methods* (2nd ed.). Newbury Park, CA: Sage.

Henry, G. T. (1990). *Practical sampling.* Newbury Park, CA: Sage.

Henry, G. T. (1996). Does the public have a role in evaluation? Surveys and democratic discourse. *New Directions in Evaluation, 71,* 85-90.

Kalton, G. (1983). *Introduction to survey sampling.* Beverly Hills, CA: Sage.

Kish, L. (1965). *Survey sampling.* New York: John Wiley.

Kraemer, C. H., & Thiemann, S. (1987). *How many subjects? Statistical power analysis in research.* Newbury Park, CA: Sage.

Krosnick, J. A., Narayan, S., & Smith, W. R. (1996). Satisficing in surveys: Initial evidence. In M. T. Braverman & J. K. Slaters (Eds.), *Advances in survey research* (pp. 29-44). San Francisco: Jossey-Bass.

Lipsey, M. W. (1990). *Design sensitivity: Statistical power for experimental research.* Newbury Park, CA: Sage.

Mullis, I. U. S., Dossey, J. A., & Phillips, G. W. (1993). *NAEP 1992 mathematics report card for the nation and the states.* Washington, DC: U.S. Department of Education.

McKean, K. (1987, January). The orderly pursuit of pure disorder. *Discover,* 72-81.

Skidmore, F. (1983). *Overview of the Seattle-Denver Income Maintenance Experiment: Final report.* Washington, DC: Government Printing Office.

Sudman, S. (1976). *Applied sampling.* New York: Academic Press.

Todd, K. H., Kellerman, A. L., Wald, M., Lipscomb, L., & Fajman, N. (1996, October). *An evaluation of lottery expenditures for public school safety in Georgia.* Paper presented to the Council for School Performance.

5

Planning Ethically Responsible Research

Joan E. Sieber

Applied researchers examine issues that directly affect people's lives—issues such as education, health, work, finances, and access to government benefits. Ethical applied researchers recognize the interests of all parties concerned in an issue, and plan research so that those interests are respected. Needless to say, there is a practical as well as a moral point to this. Unless all parties concerned are recognized, it is likely that the research questions will be inappropriately specified, and that the findings may have limited usefulness. Therefore, unethical applied researchers are likely to harm themselves and their research as well as those they study.

This chapter focuses on research planning and ethical problem solving, not on details of federal or state law governing human research, or on preparing research protocols for institutional review boards (IRBs). Readers may wish to contact the Office for Protection from Research Risk for the current federal regulations governing human research. Details on approaches to compliance with various aspects of federal law, and how to write a research protocol in compliance with IRB and federal requirements, are presented in *Planning Ethically Responsible Research* (Sieber, 1992) in the Applied Social Research Methods Series published by Sage Publications. Each reader's own IRB can provide information on its specific requirements.

■ *An Introduction to Planning*

The purpose of this section is to illustrate that ethical planning is integral to the research topic and to the process of research design and planning. The

127

ethics of social research is about creating a mutually respectful, win-win relationship in which participants are pleased to respond candidly, valid results are obtained, and the community considers the conclusions constructive. This requires more than goodwill or adherence to laws governing research. It requires investigation into the perspectives and cultures of the participants and their community early in the process of research design, so that their needs and interests can be understood and appropriately served.

In contrast, a researcher who does not investigate the perspective of the participants and plan accordingly may leave the research setting in pandemonium. The ensuing turmoil may harm all of the individuals and institutions involved, as illustrated by the following example, adapted from an actual study.

A researcher sought to gather information that would help local schools meet the needs of children of Hispanic migrant farmworkers. He called on families at their homes to ask them, in his halting Spanish, to sign a consent statement and to respond to his interview questions. Most of the families seemed not to be at home, and none acknowledged having children. Many farmworkers are undocumented aliens, and they assumed that the researcher was connected with the U.S. Immigration and Naturalization Service (INS). News of his arrival spread quickly, and families responded accordingly—by fleeing the scene.

A better scientist would have understood that community-based research cannot be planned or conducted unilaterally. He or she would have enlisted the help of community leaders in formulating the research procedures. Steps would have been taken to understand and allay respondents' real and imagined fears; perhaps the researcher would have obtained a certificate of confidentiality from the Office for Protection from Research Risk to prevent subpoena of the data by the INS or other authorities. Members of the community would have been employed and trained to conduct the interviews. Effective communication and informed consent would have occurred informally, through a correctly informed community grapevine. The researcher would have developed the formal consent statement with the help of community leaders and would have communicated its contents to the largely illiterate community at an enjoyable meeting, perhaps a picnic provided by the researcher. The researcher would have learned what respondents would like to receive in return for their participation, and likely would have arranged a mutually rewarding relationship so that he or she would have been welcome to create an ongoing research and development program for the community. Such enlightened, ethical research practices make for successful science, yet many researchers have been trained to focus narrowly on their research agendas and to ignore the perceptions and expectations of their participants and of society at large. When one is narrowly focused on completing a research project, it is easy to overlook some of the interests and perspectives of the subjects and of society at large. Insensitive researchers become part of the stimulus array; participants respond accordingly.

Ethical research practice entails skillful planning and management of communication, reduction of risk, and creation of benefits, as these issues pertain to the stakeholders in the research. *Stakeholders* include any persons who have interests in the research. Especially in field research, it is important that researchers try to identify all stakeholders early in the planning process. These might include the participants and their families, guardians, employers, institutions, and community; the researchers and their institutions and funders; and, depending on the nature and scope of the research, social advocates and the mass media.

Stakeholders are not just those whom the researcher wishes to consult. They are also those who expect the researcher to consult them. For example, a researcher investigating the effects on learning of extensive parental involvement in the classroom readily perceives that parents, teachers, and school administrators are stakeholders who should be involved. But what of the teachers' union? What of the clique of parents who are known to be suspicious of any new approaches to education? If the interests of potential stakeholders are not considered at the outset, the chances for successful completion of the research may be diminished. Identifying all significant stakeholders and their interests in the research may require the researcher to conduct considerable ethnographic inquiry, networking, and consultation, and to do so with cultural sensitivity.

☐ *Institutional Review Boards*

The early integration of ethical concerns with methodological and procedural planning is likely to satisfy the requirements of an institutional review board, thus writing the IRB protocol is largely a matter of reporting what has already been arranged. If the IRB is ill informed and proposes inappropriate procedures (such as the requirement of signed consent when this would jeopardize participants, as discussed below), the researcher can capably defend the appropriate procedures. The steps required to complete and defend the protocol are described elsewhere (see Sieber, 1992). Before leaving the topic of protocols, however, it is important to note the protections they offer to the researcher.

The protocol has legal status as a "control document." It is the paper trail showing that the research is acceptable to a legally constituted board of reviewers. Should anyone raise questions about the project, the approved protocol shows that the project is of sufficient value to justify any risks involved. Hence the protocol must reflect what is actually done in the research. Once the IRB has approved a protocol for a particular project, the investigator must follow that procedure, have any desired changes approved by the IRB, or risk disaster—such as the following:

> Dr. Knowall interviewed schoolchildren about their understanding of right and wrong. A parent who gave permission for his child to participate in the research later felt that the project sought to change his child's religious beliefs. He called the newspaper, the ACLU, the mayor, the school board, the governor, and others to complain that Dr. Knowall's research violated the separation of church and

state. The university, required to respond, proffered the approved protocol, which should have been powerful evidence in any legal proceeding that the project was socially and legally acceptable—except for one thing: The researcher had slipped in a few questions about religion after receiving IRB approval. The researcher found himself in serious trouble, and without enthusiastic backing from his institution.

We turn now to three major aspects of ethical problem solving: consent (including debriefing and deception), privacy/confidentiality, and risk/benefit planning.

■ *Voluntary Informed Consent*

The consent statement should explain the research to be undertaken and should fulfill legal requirements (see Sieber, 1992, chaps. 2-4). It should be simple and friendly in tone, and should translate a scientific proposal into simple, everyday language, omitting details that are unimportant to the subjects, but including details that are important to them. The researcher needs to learn what is important to the subjects and how to express that in ways they understand. The consent statement should be free of jargon and legalese.

Voluntary informed consent is not simply a consent form. It goes beyond the statement that is prepared and administered in the so-called consent procedure. It is an ongoing, two-way communication process between research participants and the investigator, as well as a specific agreement about the conditions of the research participation. Often, questions and concerns occur to the participants only after the research is well under way. Sometimes it is only then that meaningful communication and informed consent can occur. If the researcher is not open to continuing two-way communication, participants may become uncooperative and drop out of the study.

Voluntary means without threat or undue inducement. When consent statements are presented as a plea for help or when people are rushed into decisions, they may agree to participate even though they would rather not. They are then likely to show up late, fail to appear, or fail to give the research their full attention. To avoid this, the researcher should urge each subject to make the decision that best serves his or her own interests. Also, the researcher should not tie participation to other things, such as obtaining benefits of some kind (e.g., health services), especially if participants are indigent or otherwise vulnerable to coercion.

Informed means knowing what a reasonable person in the same situation would want to know before giving consent. Mostly, people want to know what they are likely to experience. If the procedure is unusual or complicated, a videotape of the procedure may be more informative than a verbal description.

Although the competence to understand and make decisions about research participation is conceptually distinct from voluntariness, these qualities become blurred in the case of some populations. Children, retarded adults, the poorly educated, and prisoners, for instance, may not understand their right to refuse to participate in research when asked by someone of apparent authority. They may also fail to grasp details relevant to their decision. The researcher may resolve this problem by appointing an advocate for the research subject, in addition to obtaining the subject's assent. For example, children cannot legally consent to participate in research, but they can "assent" to participate, and must be given veto power over adults who give permission for them to participate (see Sieber, 1992, chap. 10).

Consent means explicit agreement to participate. Competence to consent or assent and voluntariness are affected by the way the decision is presented (Melton & Stanley, 1991). An individual's understanding of the consent statement and acceptance of his or her status as an autonomous decision maker will be most powerfully influenced not by what the individual is told, but by how he or she is engaged in the communication. There are many aspects of the investigator's speech and behavior that communicate information to subjects. Body language, friendliness, a respectful attitude, and genuine empathy for the role of the subject are among the factors that may speak louder than words. To illustrate, imagine a potential subject who is waiting to participate in a study:

Scenario 1: The scientist arrives late, wearing a rumpled lab coat, and props himself in the doorway. He ascertains that the subject is indeed the person whose name is on his list. He reads the consent information without looking at the subject. The subject tries to discuss the information with the researcher, who seems not to hear. He reads off the possible risks. The nonverbal communication that has occurred is powerful. The subject feels resentful and suppresses an urge to storm out. What has been communicated most clearly is that the investigator does not care about the subject. The subject is sophisticated and recognizes that the researcher is immature, preoccupied, and lacking in social skills, yet he feels devalued. He silently succumbs to the pressures of this unequal status relationship to do "the right thing"; he signs the consent form amid a rush of unpleasant emotions.

Scenario 2: The subject enters the anteroom and meets a researcher who is well-groomed, stands straight and relaxed, and invites the subject to sit down with him. The researcher's eye contact,[1] easy and relaxed approach, warm but professional manner, voice, breathing, and a host of other cues convey that he is comfortable communicating with the subject. He is friendly and direct as he describes the study. Through eye contact, he ascertains that the subject understands what he has said. He invites questions and responds thoughtfully to comments, questions, and concerns. When the subject raises scientific questions about the study (no matter how naive), the scientist welcomes the subject's interest in the project and enters into a brief discussion, treating the subject as a respected peer. Finally, the researcher indicates that there is a formal consent form to be signed and shows the subject that the consent form covers the issues they have discussed. He mentions that it is important that people not feel pressured to participate, but rather should participate only if they really want to. The subject signs the form and receives a copy of the form to keep.

Though the consent forms in these two cases may have been identical, only the second scenario exemplifies adequate, respectful informed consent. The second researcher was respectful and responsive; he facilitated adequate decision making. Congruence, rapport, and trust were essential ingredients of his success.

Congruence of verbal and body language. The researcher in Scenario 1 was incongruent; his words said one thing, but his actions said the opposite. The congruent researcher in Scenario 2 used vocabulary that the research participant easily understood, spoke in gentle, direct tones, breathed deeply and calmly, and stood or sat straight and relaxed. To communicate congruently, one's mind must be relatively clear of distracting thoughts.

Rapport. When consent procedures must be administered to many participants, the process can turn into a singsong routine delivered without a feeling of commitment. The researcher's friendly greeting, openness, positive body language, and willingness to hear what each subject has to say or to ask about the study are crucial to establishing rapport.

Trust. If participants believe that the investigator may not understand or care about them, there will not be the sense of partnership needed to carry out the study satisfactorily. The issue of trust is particularly important when the investigator has higher status than the subjects or is from a different ethnic group. It is useful for the researcher to ask members of the subject population to examine the research procedures to make sure they are respectful, acceptable, and understandable to the target population.

There are many ways to build respect, rapport, and trust, as the following examples illustrate:

Example 1: A Caucasian anthropologist sought to interview families in San Francisco's Chinatown to determine what kinds of foods they eat, how their eating habits have changed since they immigrated here, and what incidence of cancer has been experienced in their families. She employed several Chinese American women to learn whether her interview questions were appropriate and to translate them into Mandarin and Cantonese. The research assistants worked on the basis of their personal knowledge of the language and culture of Chinatown, then tested their procedures on pilot subjects. There was confusion among pilot subjects about the names of some Chinese vegetables; the researchers devised pictures of those vegetables so that subjects could confirm which ones they meant. The Chinese American research assistants rewrote the questions and the consent statement until they were appropriate for the population that was to be interviewed, and then conducted the interviews. Their appearance, language, and cultural background engendered a level of trust, mutual respect, and communication that the researcher herself could not have created.

Example 2: A researcher studying safe-sex knowledge and behavior of gay men identified legitimate leaders in the local gay community—gay physicians and other leaders concerned about the health and welfare of their community. He worked with them to develop a useful survey, an acceptable sampling and recruitment procedure, and ways to let the community know what safeguards to confidentiality were built into the study and what benefits from the study would flow back to the participating community.

Example 3: A researcher studying infant nutrition offered to share data with the host community for its own policy-making purposes (e.g., Pelto, 1988). The community leaders were invited to request that any items of interest to them be added to a survey, and they were then assisted with analyses and interpretations of the data. The result was a collaborative effort to achieve a shared goal—improved health and nutrition in that community.

There are many ways to enhance communication, rapport, respect, and trust, and to increase the benefits to subjects of a research project, depending on the particular setting and circumstances. When planning research, especially in a field setting, it is useful for researchers to conduct focus groups from the target population, to consult with community gatekeepers, or to consult with pilot subjects to learn how they are likely to react to the various possible research procedures and how to make the research most beneficial and acceptable to them. In some cases this consultation should extend to stakeholders and community representatives who should have a part in the research planning. The rewards to the researcher for this effort include greater ease of recruiting cooperative participants, a research design that will work, and a community that evinces goodwill.

In summary, it is important for the researcher to determine what the concerns of the subject population actually are. Pilot subjects from the research population, as well as other stakeholders, should have the procedure explained to them and should be asked to try to imagine what concerns people would have about participating in the study. Often some of these concerns turn out to be very different from those the researcher would imagine, and they are likely to affect the outcome of the research if they are not resolved, as illustrated by the following case of misinformed consent:

A Ph.D. student interviewed elderly persons living in a publicly supported geriatric center on their perceptions of the center. At the time of the research, city budget cuts were occurring; rumors were rampant that eligibility criteria would change and many current residents would be evicted. Mrs. B, an amputee, was fearful that she would be moved if she were perceived as incompetent. After she signed the informed consent form the researcher asked her several questions:

Researcher:	"Can you recite the alphabet?"
Mrs. B:	"Backwards or forwards?" (Seeking to demonstrate her intellectual competence.)
Researcher:	"How do you like the service here?"
Mrs. B:	"Oh it's great!" (She constantly complained to her family about the poor service and bad food.)
Researcher:	"How do you like the food here?"
Mrs. B:	"It's delicious."

Mrs. B's anxiety was rising, and midway through the questioning she asked the student, "Did I pass the test?"

Researcher:	"What test?"
Mrs. B:	"The one for whether I can stay in the hospital."
Researcher:	"I'm not working for the hospital."

Mrs. B spun her chair around and wheeled herself away. (Fisher & Rosendahl, 1990, pp. 47-48)

Should consent be obtained in writing? Signed (or documented) consent proves that consent was obtained, and probably does more to protect the institution than to protect the subjects. Most IRBs require signed consent for most kinds of research, except in the following situations (as specified in the federal regulations): (a) when signed consent is offensive to subjects or inconvenient and subjects can easily refuse (e.g., by hanging up on a phone interviewer or by throwing out a survey received in the mail), and (b) when signed consent would jeopardize the well-being of subjects. If the research focuses on illegal or stigmatized aspects of the subjects, for example, it is not in their best interest for the researcher to have a record of their identities.

However, just because signed consent is not required does not mean that consent is not necessary. Consent is necessary, and a copy of the consent statement may be given to the subject; only the signed agreement to participate is waived in such a situation.

☐ *Debriefing*

The benefits of research include its educational or therapeutic value for participants. Debriefing provides an appropriate time for the researcher to consolidate the educational and therapeutic value of the research to subjects through appropriate conversation and handouts. The researcher can provide rich educational material immediately, based on the literature that forms the foundation of the research. Debriefing also offers an opportunity for the researcher to learn about subjects' perceptions of the research: Why did they respond as they did—especially those whose responses were unusual? How do their views of the usefulness of the findings comport with those of the researcher? Typically, the interpretation and application of findings are strengthened by researchers' thoughtful discussions with participants. Many a perceptive researcher has learned more from the debriefing process than the data alone could ever reveal.

Debriefing should be a two-way street: Subjects deserve an opportunity to ask questions and express reactions, as well as a few minutes in which to interact with a truly appreciative investigator. The researcher should be listening.

☐ *Deception*

In deception research, the researcher studies reactions of subjects who are purposely led to have false beliefs or assumptions. This is generally unacceptable in applied research, but consent to concealment may be defensible when it is the only viable way (a) to achieve stimulus control or random assignment, (b) to study responses to low-frequency events (e.g., fights, fainting), (c) to obtain valid data without serious risk to subjects, or (d) to obtain information that would otherwise be unobtainable because of subjects' defensiveness, embarrassment, or fear of reprisal. An indefensible rationale for deception is to trick people into research participation that they would find unacceptable if they correctly understood it. If it is to be acceptable at all, deception research should not involve people in ways that members of the subject population would find unacceptable.

There are three kinds of deception that involve consent and concealment, respecting subjects' right of self-determination:

1. *Informed consent to participate in one of various conditions:* The various conditions to which subjects may be assigned are clearly described to subjects ahead of time. For example, most studies employing placebos use this consent approach. Subjects know that they cannot be told the particular conditions to which they will be assigned, as this knowledge would affect their responses. Complete debriefing is given afterward. Subjects who do not wish to participate under these conditions may decline to participate.

2. *Consent to deception:* Subjects are told that there may be misleading aspects of the study that will not be explained to them until after they have participated. A full debriefing is given as promised.

3. *Consent to waive the right to be informed:* Subjects waive the right to be informed and are not explicitly forewarned of the possibility of deception. They receive a full debriefing afterward.

■ *Privacy, Confidentiality, and Anonymity*

Privacy refers to persons' interest in controlling the access of others to themselves. *Confidentiality* is an extension of the concept of privacy; it concerns data (records about the person, e.g., notes, a videotape of the person) and agreement as to how the data are to be handled in keeping with the subjects' interest in controlling the access of others to information about themselves. The confidentiality agreement is handled in the informed consent, which states what may be done with information the subject conveys to the researcher. The terms of the confidentiality agreement need to be tailored to the particular situation. *Anonymity* means that the names and other unique identifiers (e.g., social security number, address) of subjects are never attached to the data or known to the researcher.

☐ *Privacy*

What one person considers private, another may not. We certainly know when our own privacy has been invaded, but do we know when another person's privacy is likely to be invaded? How can investigators protect subjects from the pain of having their privacy violated? How can investigators guard the integrity of their research against the lies and subterfuges that subjects will employ to hide some private truths or to guard against intrusions? Promises of confidentiality and the gathering of anonymous data may solve some of these problems.

The need to protect their privacy—that is, subjects' degree of control of the access that others have to them and to information about them—affects individuals' willingness to participate in research and to give honest responses. An understanding of the privacy concerns of potential subjects enables the researcher to communicate an awareness of, and respect for, those concerns, and to protect subjects from invasion of their privacy. Because privacy issues are often subtle and researchers may not understand them, appropriate awareness and safeguards may be omitted, with unfortunate results. Following are some examples.

A researcher interviews uneducated families about their attitudes concerning AIDS. Unknown to the researcher, these people consider it immoral, and sacrilegious, even to talk about homosexuality or AIDS. Most pretend not to understand his questions.

A researcher gets access to medical records, discovers which persons have asthma, and contacts them directly to ask them to participate in research on coping strategies of asthmatics. "How did you get my name?" "What are you doing with my medical records?" were the thoughts, if not the actual questions, of most of those called. Most refused to participate. The researcher should have asked physicians to send their asthmatic patients a letter (drafted and paid for by the researcher) asking if they would be interested in participating in the research, and saying that, if so, the physician would release their names to the researcher.

A researcher interviews children about their moral beliefs. Believing that the children would want privacy, he interviews 5-year-olds alone. However, the children are sufficiently afraid to be alone with the researcher that they do not respond as well as they would have if their mothers had been present. Recognizing his error, the researcher then makes sure that subjects from the next group, 8-year-olds, are accompanied by their mothers. However, the 8-year-olds have entered that stage of development in which some privacy from parents is important. Consequently, they do not answer all of the questions honestly. This researcher should have invested time in better scholarship into the development of privacy needs in children (see Thompson, 1991).

A researcher decides to use telephone interviews to learn about the health histories of lower-class older people, as the phone typically offers greater privacy than face-to-face interviews. She fails to recognize, however, that poor elderly people rarely live alone or have privacy from their families when they use the phone, and many keep health secrets from their families.

In each of the above cases, the researcher has been insensitive to privacy issues idiosyncratic to the research population, and has not addressed the problems these issues pose for the research. Had the researcher consulted with the psychological literature, community gatekeepers, consumers of the research, or others familiar with the research population, he or she might have identified these problems and solved them in the design stage. Most of the topics that interest social scientists concern somewhat private or personal matters. Yet most topics, however private, can be effectively and responsibly researched if researchers employ appropriate sensitivity and safeguards.

Do subjects have a right to privacy? The right to privacy from research inquiry is protected by the right to refuse to participate in research. An investigator is free to do research on consenting subjects or on publicly available information, including unobtrusive observation of people in public places. May researchers videotape or photograph the behavior of people in public without consent? If they do so, they should heed rules of common courtesy and should be sensitive to local norms. Intimate acts, such as goodbyes at airports, should be regarded as private, though done in public.

Constitutional and federal laws have little to say directly about privacy and social research. The only definitive federal privacy laws governing social research are the following: the so-called Buckley Amendment, which prohibits access to children's school records without parental consent; the Hatch Act, which prohibits asking children questions about religion, sex, or family life without parental permission; and the National Research Act, which requires parental permission for research on children (see Stanley & Sieber, 1991). Recent legislative initiatives have sought to eliminate all forms of passive consent by parents and to require that all instructional materials to be used in connection with any survey be available for inspection by the parents or guardians of the children. Moreover, these requirements would pertain to any school receiving federal monies. Because such stringent requirements for parental consent reduce the possibility of valid sampling, much debate has surrounded these legislative initiatives. In the current legislative and political environment, researchers would be well-advised to consult their IRBs and relevant school administrators at the outset when planning research on schoolchildren. Local norms as well as federal and state laws must be considered.

Tort law provides a mechanism through which persons might take action against an investigator alleged to have invaded their privacy. In such an action, the law defines privacy in relation to other interests. It expects behavioral scientists to be sensitive to persons' claims to privacy, but recognizes that claims to privacy must sometimes yield to competing claims. Any subject may file a suit against a researcher for "invasion of privacy," but courts of law are sensitive to the value of research as well as the value of privacy.

Important protections against such a suit are adequate informed consent statements signed by all participants, as well as parental permission for research participation by children. Persons other than research participants, however, may feel their privacy has been invaded by the research. For example, family members of research participants may feel that the investigation probes into their affairs. If the research is socially important and validly designed, if the researcher has taken reasonable precautions to respect the privacy needs of typical subjects and others associated with the research, and if the project has been approved by an IRB, such a suit is likely to be dismissed. But what exactly is this privacy about which researchers need to be so careful?

☐ *A Behavioral Definition of Privacy*

As a behavioral phenomenon, privacy concerns certain needs to establish personal boundaries; these needs seem to be basic and universal, but they are manifested differently depending on learning and on cultural and developmental factors (see Laufer & Wolfe, 1977, for a complete discussion of these factors as they relate to privacy). Privacy does not simply mean being left alone. Some people have too little opportunity to share their lives with others, or to bask in public attention. When treated respectfully, many are pleased when an investigator is interested in hearing about their personal lives. Because of this desire on the part of lonely people for understanding and attention, competent survey investigators often have more difficulty exiting people's homes than entering.

Desire for unusual personal boundaries was found by Klockars (1974), a criminologist, when he undertook a case study of a well-known "fence." The fence was an elderly pawnshop owner who had stolen vast amounts earlier in his life. Klockars told the fence that he would like to document the details of his career, as the world has little biographical information about the lives of famous thieves. Naturally, Klockars offered to change names and other identifying features of the account to ensure the informant's anonymity. The fence, however, wanted to go down in history and make his grandchildren proud of him. He offered to tell all, but only provided that Klockars use the fence's real name and address and publish the entire account in a book. This was done, and the aging fence proudly decorated his pawnshop with clippings from the book. (Thus confidentiality does not always involve a promise not to reveal the identity of research participants; rather, it entails whatever promise is mutually acceptable to researcher and participant. Klockars agreed to reveal the identity of the fence.)

Privacy may also be invaded when people are given unwanted information. A researcher may breach a subject's privacy by showing him pornography, or by requiring him to listen to more about some other person's sex life than he cares to hear. Privacy is also invaded when people are deprived of their normal flow of information, as when nonconsenting subjects (who do not realize they are participating in a study) are deprived of information they ordinarily would use to make important decisions.

Many claims to privacy are also claims to autonomy. For example, subjects' privacy and autonomy are violated when their self-report data on marijuana use become the basis for their arrest, when IQ data are disclosed to schoolteachers who would use it to track students, or when organizational research data disclosed to managers become the basis for firing or transferring employees. The most dramatic cases in which invasion of privacy results in lowered autonomy are those in which something is done to an individual's thought processes—the most private part of a person—through behavior control techniques such as psychopharmacology.

☐ *Privacy and Informed Consent*

A research experience regarded by some as a delightful opportunity for self-disclosure may constitute an unbearable invasion of privacy for others. Informed consent provides the researcher with an important way to respect these individual differences. The investigator specifies the kinds of things that will occur in the study, the kinds of information that will be sought and given, and the procedures that will be used to assure anonymity or confidentiality. The subject can then decide whether or not to participate under those conditions. A person who considers a given research procedure an invasion of privacy can simply decline to participate.

However, informed consent is not the entire solution. A researcher who is insensitive to the privacy needs of members of the research population may be unprepared to offer the forms of respect and protection they want.

☐ *Gaining Sensitivity to Privacy Interests of Subjects*

Although there is no way for researchers to be sure of the privacy interests of all members of a research population, they can learn how typical members would feel. If the typical member considers the research activity an invasion of privacy, the data are likely to be badly flawed. Evasion, lying, and dropping out of the study are likely to occur, and those who answer honestly will worry about the consequences.

To learn about the privacy interests of a particular population, the researcher can (a) ask someone who knows that population (e.g., ask teachers and parents about the privacy interests of their children; ask a psychotherapist about the privacy interests of abused children; ask a social worker about the privacy interests of low socioeconomic-status parents), (b) ask a researcher who works with that population, and (c) ask members of the population what they think other people in their group might consider private in relation to the intended study.

☐ *"Brokered" Data*

The term *broker* refers to any person who works in some trusted capacity with a population to which the researcher does not have access, and who obtains data from that population for the researcher. For example, a broker may be a psychotherapist or a physician who asks patients if they will provide data for important research being conducted elsewhere. A broker may serve other functions in addition to gathering data for the researcher, as discussed below.

"Broker-sanitized" responses. Potential subjects may be concerned that some aspects of their responses will enable the investigator to deduce their identities. For example, if a survey is sent to organization leaders in various parts of the country, a postmark on an envelope might enable someone to deduce the identity of some respondents. To prevent this, a mutually agreeable third party may receive all of the responses, remove and destroy the envelopes, and then send the responses to the investigator.

Brokers and aliases. Sometimes lists of potential respondents are unavailable directly to the researcher. For example, the researcher wishing to study the attitudes of psychiatric patients at various stages of their therapy may not be privy to their names. Rather, the individuals' treating psychiatrists may agree to serve as brokers. The psychiatrists then obtain the informed consent of their patients and periodically gather data from those who consent. Each patient is given an alias. Each time data are gathered, the psychiatrist refers to a list for the alias, substitutes it for the patient's real name, and transmits the completed questionnaire back to the researcher.

Additional roles for brokers. A broker may (a) examine responses for information that might permit deductive disclosure of the identity of the respondent and remove that information, (b) add information (e.g., a professional evaluation of the respondent), or (c) check responses for accuracy or completeness.

There should be some quid pro quo between researcher and broker. Perhaps the broker may be paid for his or her time, or the researcher may make a contribution to the broker's organization.

□ *Confidentiality*

The confidentiality agreement between researcher and participant is part of the informed consent agreement. For example, a confidentiality agreement such as the following might be included in a consent letter from a researcher seeking to interview families in counseling:

> To protect your privacy, the following measures will ensure that others do not learn your identity or what you tell me:
>
> 1. No names will be used in transcribing from the audiotape, or in writing up the case study. Each person will be assigned a letter name as follows: M for mother, F for father, MS1 for male first sibling, and so on.
>
> 2. All identifying characteristics, such as occupation, city, and ethnic background, will be changed.
>
> 3. The audiotapes will be reviewed only in my home (and in the office of my thesis adviser). The tapes and notes will be destroyed after my report of this research has been accepted for publication.
>
> 4. What is discussed during our session will be kept confidential, with two exceptions: I am compelled by law to inform an appropriate other person if I hear and believe that you are in danger of hurting yourself or someone else, or if there is reasonable suspicion that a child, elder, or dependent adult has been abused.[2]

Noteworthy characteristics of this agreement are that it (a) recognizes the privacy of some of the information likely to be conveyed, (b) states what steps will be taken to ensure that others are not privy to the identity of subjects or to identifiable details about individuals, and (c) states legal limitations to the assurance of confidentiality.

□ *Why Is Confidentiality an Issue in Research?*

Participants will not and should not share highly personal information with a researcher unless they are certain that their data will be kept from falling into the wrong hands, such as those who would gossip, blackmail, take adverse personnel action against the subjects, or subpoena the data.

The researcher must employ adequate safeguards of confidentiality, and these should be described in specific terms in the consent statement. Many people, especially members of minority populations (Turner, 1982), doubt such promises unless the details are spelled out clearly. Alternatively, the researcher could gather the data anonymously—that is, without gathering any unique identifiers such as subjects' names, social security numbers, or driver's license numbers. When designing the research, the researcher should decide whether the data can be gathered anonymously. Four major reasons for gathering unique identifiers are as follows:

1. They make it possible for the researcher to recontact subjects if their data indicate that they need help or information.

2. They make it possible for the researcher to link data sets from the same individuals. (This problem might be solved with code names.)

3. They allow the researcher to mail results to the subjects. (This problem can be solved by having subjects address envelopes to themselves, which are then stored apart from the data. After the results are mailed out, no record of the names of subjects remains in the researcher's hands.)

4. They make it possible for the researcher to screen a large sample on some measures in order to identify a low-base-rate sample (e.g., families in which there are twins or triplets).

Note that for the first two reasons, the issue is whether to have names associated with subjects' data; for the next reason, the issue is whether to have names on file at all. In the fourth case, identifiers may be expunged from the succeeding study as soon as those data are gathered. If the data can be gathered anonymously, subjects will be more forthcoming, and the researcher will be relieved of some responsibilities connected with assuring confidentiality. If the research cannot be done anonymously, the researcher must consider procedural, statistical, and legal methods for assuring confidentiality. Readers who want to investigate methods beyond those presented here are referred to Boruch and Cecil's *Assuring the Confidentiality of Social Research Data* (1979).

☐ *Some Procedural Approaches to Assuring Confidentiality or Anonymity*

Certain procedural approaches eliminate or minimize the link between the identifiers and the data, and may be appropriate, depending on whether the research is cross-sectional, longitudinal, or experimental.

Cross-Sectional Research

In cross-sectional research, where unique identifiers are needed, they might be constructed identifiers, such as initials, date of birth, or the last four digits of a phone number. If there is no need to link individual data gathered at one time to data gathered at another, some simple methods of preventing disclosure of unique identifiers in cross-sectional research are as follows:

- *Anonymity:* The researcher has no record of the identity of the respondents. For example, respondents mail back their questionnaires or hand them back in a group, without names or other unique identifiers.

- *Temporarily identified responses:* It is sometimes important to ensure that only the appropriate persons have responded and that their responses are complete. After the researcher checks the names against a list or makes sure responses are complete, the names are destroyed.

- *Separately identified responses:* In mail surveys, it is sometimes necessary to know who has responded and who has not. To accomplish this with an anonymous survey, the researcher may ask each respondent to mail back the completed survey anonymously and to mail separately a postcard with his or her name on it. This method enables the researcher to check off those who have responded and to send another wave of questionnaires to those who have not.

Any of these three methods can be put to corrupt use if the researcher is so inclined. Because people are sensitive to corrupt practices, the honest researcher must demonstrate integrity. The researcher's good name and that of the research institution may reduce the suspicion of potential respondents.

Longitudinal Research

In a longitudinal study, the researcher must somehow link together the various responses of particular persons over time. A common way to accomplish this is to have each subject use an easily remembered code, such as his or her mother's birth date, as an alias. The researcher makes sure there are no duplicate aliases. The adequacy of this method depends upon subjects' ability to remember their aliases—inner-city drug addicts are an example of a population in which subjects may not remember. In cases where a subject's mistakenly using the wrong alias might seriously affect the research or the subject (e.g., the subject gets back the wrong HIV test result), this method of linking data would clearly be inappropriate.

☐ Interfile Linkage

Sometimes a researcher wants to link research records on persons with some other independently stored records on those same persons (exact matching), or on persons who are similar on some attributes (statistical matching). A researcher can link files without disclosing the identity of the individuals by constructing identifications based on the files, such as a combination of letters from the individual's name, his or her date of birth and gender, and the last four digits of the person's social security number.

Another approach to interfile linkage would be through use of a broker, who would perform the linkage without disclosing the identity of the individuals. An example would be court-mandated research on the relationship between academic accomplishment and subsequent arrest records of juveniles who have been sentenced to one of three experimental rehabilitation programs. The court may be unwilling to grant a researcher access to the records involved, but may be willing to arrange for a clerk at the court to gather all of the relevant data on each subject, remove identifiers, and give the anonymous files to the researcher. The obvious advantages of exact matching are the ability to obtain data that would be difficult or impossible to obtain otherwise and the ability to construct a longitudinal file.

Statistical matching enables the researcher to create matched comparison groups. An example of statistical matching would be if each boy having a certain test profile were matched with a girl having a similar test profile. Statistical matching may also permit imputation—estimation of the values of missing data—by revealing how similar persons would answer given items. Interfile linkage entails a complex set of techniques, the details of which are beyond the purview of this chapter. The interested reader is referred to Campbell, Boruch, Schwartz, and Steinberg (1977) and to Cox and Boruch (1986).

□ *Statistical Strategies for Assuring Confidentiality*

It is folly to ask respondents directly whether they have engaged in illegal behavior—for example, if they have used cocaine, beat their children, or cheated on their taxes. Methods of randomized response, or error inoculation, provide a strategy for asking questions in such a way that no one can know who has given incriminating responses, but the researcher can determine the proportion of respondents who have given the incriminating response. In the simplest variant of this strategy, the researcher gives each subject a die to roll before answering a yes/no question. The respondent might be instructed to answer untruthfully if the die comes up, say, two. Otherwise, he is to answer truthfully. The respondent rolls the die, does not let the researcher see how the die comes up, and gives his answer according to instructions. The researcher knows that one response in six is false, and computes the true percentage of persons who acknowledge actual incriminating behavior. There are many variations on this method, and the details of computing the proportion of true incriminating responses are fairly involved. Interested readers should see Boruch and Cecil (1979, 1982) or Fox and Tracy (1986) for more on this method.

□ *Certificates of Confidentiality*

Under certain circumstances, priests, physicians, and lawyers may not be required to reveal to a court of law the identities of their clients or sources of information. This privilege does not extend to researchers. Prosecutors, grand juries, legislative bodies, civil litigants, and administrative agencies can use their subpoena powers to compel disclosure of confidential research information. What is to protect research from this intrusion? Anonymous data, aliases, colleagues in foreign countries to whom sensitive data can be mailed as soon as it is gathered, and statistical strategies are not always satisfactory solutions.

The most effective and yet underutilized protection against subpoena is the certificate of confidentiality.

In 1988, the U.S. Congress enacted a law providing for an apparently absolute researcher-participant privilege when it is covered by a certificate of confidentiality issued by the Department of Health and Human Services. The provisions of this relatively new law authorize

> persons engaged in biomedical, behavioral, clinical or other research (including research on the use and effect of alcohol and other psychoactive drugs) to protect the privacy of individuals who are the subject of such research by withholding from all persons not connected with the conduct of such research the names, or other identifying characteristics, of such individuals. Persons so authorized to protect the privacy of such individuals may not be compelled in any Federal, State, or local civil, criminal administrative, legislative, or other proceedings to identify such individuals. (Public Health Service Act, 301[d], 42 U.S.C. 242a)

Certificates of confidentiality are granted on request for any bona fide research project of a sensitive nature, in which protection of confidentiality is judged necessary to achieve the research objectives. The research need not be funded by or otherwise connected with any federal agency. Some government funders also issue certificates of confidentiality to their grantees upon request. Persons interested in learning more about certificates of confidentiality are referred to the Office for Protection from Research Risk, National Institutes of Health (phone [301] 496-8101) or to the Office of Health Planning and Evaluation, Office of the Assistant Secretary of Health (phone [301] 472-7911).

☐ *Confidentiality and Consent*

An adequate consent statement shows the subject that the researcher has conducted a thorough analysis of the risks to confidentiality and has acted with the well-being of the subject foremost in mind. The consent statement must specify any promises of confidentiality that the researcher cannot make. Typically, these have to do with reporting laws pertaining to child abuse, child molestation, and threats of harm to self and others. Reporting laws vary from state to state, so the researcher should be familiar with the laws in the state where the research is to be conducted. Thus the consent statement warns the subject not to reveal certain kinds of information to the researcher. A skilled researcher can establish rapport and convince subjects to reveal almost anything, including things the researcher may not want to be responsible for knowing.

There are many ways in which confidentiality might be discussed in a consent statement. A few examples follow:

> ***Example 1:*** To protect your privacy, this research is conducted anonymously. No record of your participation will be kept. Do not sign this consent or put your name on the survey.

Example 2: This is an anonymous study of teacher attitudes and achievements. No names of people, schools, or districts will be gathered. The results will be reported in the form of statistical summaries of group results.

Example 3: The data will be anonymous. You are asked to write your name on the cover sheet because it is essential that I make sure your responses are complete. As soon as you hand in your questionnaire, I will check your responses for completeness and ask you to complete any incomplete items. I will then tear off and destroy the cover sheet. There will be no way anyone else can associate your name with your data.

Example 4: This survey is anonymous. Please complete it, and return it unsigned in the enclosed, postage-paid envelope. At the same time, please return the postcard bearing your name. That way we will know you responded, but we will not know which survey is yours.

Example 5: This anonymous study of persons who have decided to be tested for HIV infection is being conducted by Dr. John Smith at Newton University. Because we do not want to intrude on your privacy in any way, Dr. Sam Jones at the AIDS Testing Center has agreed to ask you if you would be willing to respond to this survey. Please look it over. If you think you would be willing to respond, take it home, answer the questions, and mail it back to me in the attached, stamped, self-addressed envelope. If you are interested in knowing the results of the study, please write to me at the above address, or stop by the AIDS Testing Center and ask for a copy of the results, which will be available after May 1.

Example 6: Because this is a study in which we hope to track your progress in coping with an incurable disease and your responses to psychotherapy designed to help you in that effort, we will need to interview you every 2 months and match your new interview data with your prior data. To keep your file strictly anonymous, we need to give you an alias. Think of one or more code names you might like to use. Make sure it is a name you will remember, such as the name of a close high school friend, a pet, or a favorite movie star. You will need to check with the researcher to make sure that no other participant has chosen the same name. The name you choose will be the only name that is ever associated with your file. We will be unable to contact you, so we hope you will be sure to keep in touch with us. If you decide to drop out of the study, we would be grateful if you would let us know.

Example 7: In this study, I will examine the relationship between your child's SAT scores and his attitude toward specific areas of study. We respect the privacy of your child. If you give me permission to do so, I will ask your child to fill out an attitude survey. I will then give that survey to the school secretary, who will write your child's SAT subscores on it, and erase your child's name from it. That way, I will have attitude and SAT data for each child, but will not know the name of any child. The data will then be statistically analyzed and reported as group data.

These are merely examples. The researcher needs to give careful consideration to the content and wording of each consent statement.

☐ *Data Sharing*

If research is published, the investigator is accountable for the results, and is normally required to keep the data for 5 to 10 years. The editor of the publication in which the research is reported may ask to see the raw data to check its veracity. Some funders require that the documented data be archived in user-friendly form, and made available to other scientists. Data sharing, if done with due respect for confidentiality, is regarded positively by most subjects, who like to think of their data as a contribution to science and available to other legitimate scientists to examine, critique, and build upon. When data are shared via a public archive, the researcher must ensure that all identifiers are removed and there is no way for anyone to deduce subjects' identities.

A variety of techniques have been developed to transform raw data into a form that prevents deductive disclosure. Variables or cases with easily identifiable characteristics are removed. Random error can be implanted into the data, introducing enough noise to foil attempts at deductive disclosure, but not enough to obscure conclusions. Microaggregation creates synthetic individuals; instead of releasing the individual data on 2,000 participants in a study of small business owners, one might group the data into 500 sets of 4 subjects each, and release average data on every variable for each set, along with the within-variance data. Outside users could do secondary analyses on the data from these 500 synthetic small business owners. For details, see Gates (1988), Kim (1986), Duncan and Lambert (1987), and Boruch and Cecil (1979).

■ Recognizing Elements of Research Risk

Risk assessment is not intuitively easy. Most investigators are sensitive only to the risks they have already encountered and may fail to assess major risks in new settings. The goal of this brief section is to help researchers recognize kinds and sources of risk.

Kinds of risk. Risk, or the possibility of some harm, loss, or damage, may involve mere inconvenience (e.g., boredom, frustration, time wasting), physical risk (e.g., injury), psychological risk (e.g., insult, depression, upset), social risk (e.g., embarrassment, rejection), economic risk (e.g., loss of job, money, credit), or legal risk (e.g., arrest, fine, subpoena).

What aspect of research creates risk? Risk may arise from (a) the theory, which may become publicized and may blame the victim or create wrong ideas; (b) the research process; (c) the institutional setting in which the research occurs, which may be coercive in connection with the research; and (d) the uses of the research findings.

Who is vulnerable? Some persons may be more vulnerable than others. In particular, the researcher should be sensitive to the vulnerability of (a) those whose lives are visible or public, (b) those lacking resources or autonomy, (c) those who are scapegoated or targets of prejudice, (d) those who are weakened or institutionalized, (e) those who cannot speak for themselves, (f) those engaged in illegal activities, and (g) those damaged by the revelations of research participants (e.g., family members).

How can these guidelines be used? The researcher should brainstorm with colleagues, gatekeepers, community members, and others who understand the risks in the setting. The researcher should also be aware of his or her own biases, and of alternative points of view; of the assumptions underlying the research theories and methods, and of the limitations of the findings; and of how the media and opinion leaders may translate the researcher's statements into flashy and dangerous generalizations.

■ *Maximizing the Benefits of Research*

When researchers vaguely promise benefit to science and society, they approach being silly. These are the least probable of good outcomes. Researchers typically overlook the more likely and more immediate benefits that are the precursors of social and scientific benefit. Some of the most immediate benefits are those to subjects and—in the case of some community-based research—to their communities. These are not only easy to bring about, but are also owed, and may facilitate future research access to that population. The intermediate benefits—to the researcher, the research institution, and the funder, if any—are ones that any talented investigator with an ongoing research program can produce in some measure. It is upon these immediate and intermediate goals or benefits that any ultimate scientific and social benefits are likely to be based.

For example, a researcher started an externally funded school-based experiment with instructional methods designed to improve the performance of students identified as learning disabled. Each method was designed to develop diagnostic and teaching procedures that could ultimately be used by school personnel. The researcher began by discussing her intervention and research plans with school administrators, teachers, parents, and students, and asking them to describe problems with which they would like to have assistance. Where feasible, she made slight alterations in her program to accommodate their wishes. She integrated the research program with a graduate course so that her students received extensive training in the conduct of research in the school setting, under her rigorous supervision.

She provided the school faculty with materials on learning disabilities, and gave bag-lunch workshops and presentations on her project. She worked with teachers who were interested in trying her approaches in their classrooms, urging them to adapt and modify her approaches as they deemed appropriate, and asked that they let her know the outcomes. Together, the researcher and the teachers pilot tested adaptations of the methods concurrently with the formal experiments. All learning disabled children who participated received special recognition and learned how to assist other students with similar problems. Two newspaper articles about the program brought favorable publicity to the researcher, the school, and the researcher's university. This recognition further increased the already high morale of students, teachers, and the researcher.

Of the six procedures examined, only two showed significant long-term gains on standardized tests of learning. However, the teachers who had gotten involved with pilot testing of variations on the treatments were highly enthusiastic about the success of these variations. When renewal of funding was sought, the funder was dissatisfied with the formal findings, but impressed that the school district and the university, together, had offered to provide in-kind matching funds. The school administrators wrote a glowing testimony to the promise of the new pilot procedures and of the overall approach, and the funder supported the project for a second year. The results of the second year, based on modified procedures, were much stronger. Given the structure that had been created, it was easy for the researcher to document the entire procedure on videotape and to disseminate it widely. The funder provided seed money to permit the researcher, her graduate students, and the teachers who had collaborated on pilot testing to start a national-level traveling workshop, which quickly became self-supporting. This additional support provided summer salary to the researcher, to teachers, and to graduate students for several years.

This tale of providing benefits to the many stakeholders in the research process is not strictly relevant to all research. Not every researcher does field research designed to benefit a community. In some settings, too much missionary zeal to include others in "helping" may expose some subjects to serious risk, such as breach of confidentiality. Also, not all research is funded or involves student assistants. Many researchers engage in simple, unfunded, unassisted, one-time laboratory studies to test theory. Even in such uncomplicated research, however, any benefit to the institution (e.g., a Science Day research demonstration) may favorably influence the institution to provide resources for future research, and efforts to benefit subjects will be repaid with their cooperation and respect.

Significant contributions to science and society are not the results of one-shot activities. Rather, such contributions typically arise from a series of competently designed research or intervention efforts, which themselves are possible only because the researcher has developed appropriate institutional or community infrastructures and has disseminated the findings in a timely and

Table 5.1 Benefit Table of a Hypothetical Learning Research Project

Benefit	Subjects	Community	Researcher	Institution	Funder	Science	Society
Relationships	respect of researcher	ties to university site	future access to community	improved town-gown relationships	ties with a successful project	ideas shared with other scientists	access to a new specialist
Knowledge/ education	informative debriefing	understanding of relevant learning problems	knowledge	improved graduate research	outstanding final report	national symposium	media presentation
Material resources	workbook	books	grant support	videotapes of research	instructional materials	refereed publications	useful popular literature
Training opportunity	tutoring skills	trained practitioners	greater research expertise	student training program	model project for future grant applicants	workshop at national meetings	training for practitioners nationally
Do good/earn esteem	esteem of peers	local enthusiasm for project	professional respect	esteem of community	satisfaction of funder overseers	recognition of scientific contribution	greater respect for science
Empowerment	earn leadership status	prestige from the program	national reputation with funder	good reputation	congressional increase in funding	increased prestige of discipline	increased power to help people
Scientific/clinical success	improved learning ability	effective program	leadership opportunities in national program	headquarters for national teacher program	proven success of funded treatment	improved training via workshops	nationally successful programs

effective way. Benefit to society also depends on widespread implementation, which, in turn, depends on the goodwill, support, and collective wisdom of many specific individuals, including politicians, funders, other professionals, and community leaders. Thus the successful contributor to science and society is a builder of many benefits and a provider of those benefits to various constituencies, even if the conduct of the research, per se, is a solo operation.

As shown in Table 5.1, research benefits may be divided into seven (nonexclusive) categories, ranging from those that are relatively easy to provide through those that are extremely difficult. These seven kinds of benefits, in turn, might accrue to any of seven kinds of recipients—subjects, communities, investigators, research institutions, funders, science, and society in general. The seven categories of benefit are described below as they might pertain to a community that is the site of field research:

- *Valuable relationships:* The community establishes ties with helping institutions and funders.

- *Knowledge or education:* The community develops a better understanding of its own problems.

- *Material resources:* The community makes use of research materials, equipment, and funding.

- *Training, employment, opportunity for advancement:* Community members receive training and continue to serve as professionals or paraprofessionals within the ongoing project.

- *Opportunity to do good and to receive the esteem of others:* The community learns how to serve its members better.

- *Empowerment* (personal, political, and so on): The community uses findings for policy purposes and gains favorable attention from the press, politicians, and others.

- *Scientific/clinical outcomes:* The community provides treatment to its members (assuming that the research or intervention is successful).

Note that even if the experiment or intervention yields disappointing results, all but the last benefit might be available to the community, as well as to individual subjects. Let us now consider the seven kinds of beneficiaries.

The *subjects* may enjoy such benefits as the respect of the researcher, an interesting debriefing, money, treatment, or future opportunities for advancement. The *community or institution* that provides the setting for the field research may include the subjects' homes, neighborhood, clinic, workplace, or recreation center. A community includes its members, gatekeepers, leaders, staff, professionals, clientele, and peers or family of the subjects. Benefits to the community are similar to those for the subjects. Sometimes community members also serve as research assistants and so would receive benefits associated with those of the next category of recipients as well.

The *researcher,* as well as research assistants and others who are associated with the project, may gain valuable relationships, knowledge, expertise, access to funding, scientific recognition, and so on, if the research is competently conducted, and especially if it produces the desired result or some other dramatic outcome. By creating these benefits for him- or herself and other members of the research team, the investigator gains the credibility needed to go forward with a research program and to exert a significant influence upon science and society.

The *research institution* may benefit along with the researcher. Institutional benefits are likely to be described as good university-community relations, educational leadership, funding of overhead costs and equipment, and a good scientific reputation for scientists, funders, government, and the scientific establishment. Such benefits increase a university's willingness to provide the kinds of support (e.g., space, clerical assistance, small grants, equipment, matching funds) that enable the researcher to move the research program forward with a minimum of chaos.

The *funder* is vital to the success of a major research program, and hopes to receive benefits such as the following, if only the researcher remembers to provide them: ties to a good project and its constituents, well-written intellectual products promptly and effectively disseminated, good publicity, evidence of useful outcomes, good ideas to share with other scientists, and good impressions made on politicians and others who have power to reward the funder. Such benefits make a funder proud to have funded the project, eager to advertise it, and favorably disposed to funding future research of that investigator.

Science refers to the disciplines involved, to the scientists within them, their scientific societies, and their publications. Benefits to science parallel benefits to funders, and depend on the importance, rigor, and productivity of the research. Development of useful insights and methods may serve science, even in the absence of findings that might benefit society. Initial papers and symposia give way to publications and invited addresses. Others evaluate, replicate, promote, and build upon the work, thus earning it a place in the realm of scientific ideas. A single publication upon which no one builds is hardly a contribution to science.

Society, including the target population from which subjects were sampled and to which the results are to be generalized, is the one group that benefits only when the hoped-for scientific outcome occurs and is generalizable to other settings. This represents the most advanced developmental stage of any given research project. By the time benefits of this magnitude have accrued, the researcher or others have already adapted and implemented the idea broadly in society. The idea has begun to take on a life of its own, to be modified to a variety of uses, and to be adapted, used, and even claimed by many others.

The conjunction of the seven kinds of benefits and seven kinds of beneficiaries described above yields a 49-cell table that is useful in research planning. This table suggests that turning a research idea into a scientific and social contribution requires that benefits be developed at each stage of the process. It is useful for the researcher to design a tentative table of benefits as the basic research idea and design are being formulated and to continue planning the benefits as the project proceeds. Many valuable benefits may be easily incorporated, provided the researcher is attuned to opportunities for doing so.

■ *Research on Children and Adolescents*

As a research population, minors are special in several respects: (a) They have limited psychological, as well as legal, capacity to give informed consent; (b) they may be cognitively, socially, and emotionally immature; (c) there are external constraints on their self-determination and independent decision making; (d) they have unequal power in relation to authorities, such as parents, teachers, and researchers; (e) their parents and certain institutions, as well as the youngsters themselves, have an interest in their research participation, and (f) national priorities for research on children and adolescents include research on drug use, the problems of runaways, pregnancy among teenagers, and other sensitive topics, compounding the ethical and legal problems surrounding research on minors.

Federal and state laws governing research respond to these characteristics of youngsters by requiring that they have special protections and that parental rights be respected. See Areen (1991) for discussion of federal and state laws governing research on minors. The law also expects social scientists to respond to these characteristics using knowledge of human development to reduce risk and vulnerability. See Thompson (1991) for discussion of developmental aspects of vulnerability to research risk.

Even quite young children should be given an opportunity to assent (to decide for themselves) to participate in research. The assent procedure should be tailored to the cognitive and social/emotional level of the child (see Tymchuk, 1991). Both child assent and parent/guardian permission are required, and either child or parent/guardian may veto the child's participation in research. Parental or guardian permission may be waived only in some low-risk research that could not be conducted otherwise, or when a parent or guardian is not situated to act in the minor's best interests (see Sieber, 1992, pp. 112-114). Yet who is best able to judge the vulnerabilities of children and the conditions under which their well-being is best safeguarded in research?

In consequence of the tendency of troubled youngsters to defy their parents or to run away, the law recognizes that parental consent may be waived by an IRB under certain circumstances. In most cases, such research is conducted within an institution such as an HIV testing site, an abortion clinic, a youth detention center, a shelter for runaway children, or a drug treatment center. The problems of obtaining meaningful consent are manifold. These problems have been discussed extensively by Grisso (1991), who focuses on issues surrounding waiver of parental permission, and by Rotheram-Borus and Koopman (1991), who are concerned primarily with consent issues in their research and treatment of runaway gay and sexually active youth, whose relationships with their parents are often marked by secrecy, conflict, and long absences. The following list summarizes some of their main points:

1. The youngster is unlikely to believe that the research is independent of the institution or that he or she may decline to participate with impunity.

2. The youngster is unlikely to believe promises of confidentiality, especially when he or she is in trouble with his or her parents and other authorities.

3. Issues of privacy, which are normally salient for adolescents, are likely to be even more heightened for this population.

4. Maltreated youngsters are likely to experience the research as more stressful than are normal children. If the researcher effectively establishes rapport, the youngster may reach out for help; the researcher must be prepared to respond helpfully.

The complexities of research on children are significant, and space constraints precludes their treatment here. The reader is referred to Sieber (1992, chap. 10) and to Stanley and Sieber (1991) for comprehensive discussion of these issues.

■ *Vulnerable Populations*

In this chapter I have emphasized sensitivity to the needs of vulnerable research populations. The problem is only partly one of lack of understanding and empathy. Even a researcher who has been a member of the vulnerable population to be studied (e.g., the researcher of homeless people who has, herself, been homeless; the researcher of victims of domestic violence who was once a victim of domestic violence) may not be able to empathize with the current concerns of members of that population, and will not automatically be trusted, for the researcher is no longer an insider to that population. Moreover, the researcher may be unaware of current regulations governing research on that population.

Most of the social research that is regarded as high priority by funders and society today is concerned with vulnerable populations—drug abusers, runaways, prostitutes, persons with AIDS, victims of violence, and so on. All that I have said so far about communication, risk/benefit assessment, and privacy/confidentiality is doubly important for vulnerable populations. Furthermore, members of many stigmatized and fearful populations are especially unwilling to be candid with researchers who are interested primarily in discovering scientific truth, rather than helping the individuals being studied. Contrary to the usual scientific directive to be objective, the researcher who investigates the lives of runaways, prostitutes, or victims of domestic violence or spousal rape must be an advocate for those studied in order to gain their trust and cooperation, and must relate in a personal and caring manner if candor and participation are to be forthcoming from members of the research population. However, the devil is in the details. General prescriptions pale alongside of accounts of ethical issues in specific contexts. Each vulnerable research population has its own special set of fears, its own reasons for mistrusting scientists, and its own culture, which outsiders can scarcely imagine.

Researchers working among vulnerable populations must become scholars of those populations' cultures, ethnographers of the communities in which the research is to occur. Obviously, such details are far beyond the purview of this chapter. Interested readers are referred to Renzetti and Lee's *Researching Sensitive Topics* (1993) for further discussion.

■ Notes

1. The researcher should be aware that the significance of eye contact varies with culture. Direct eye contact conveys honesty in some cultures, whereas in others it is construed as a sign of disrespect.

2. This example, adapted from a statement developed by David H. Ruja, is discussed in Gil (1986).

■ References

Areen, J. (1991). Legal constraints on research with children. In B. Stanley & J. E. Sieber (Eds.), *The ethics of research on children and adolescents* (pp. 7-28). Newbury Park, CA: Sage.

Boruch R. F., & Cecil, J. S. (1979). *Assuring the confidentiality of social research data.* Philadelphia: University of Pennsylvania Press.

Boruch R. F., & Cecil, J. S. (1982). Statistical strategies for preserving privacy in direct inquiry. In J. E. Sieber (Ed.), *The ethics of social research: Surveys and experiments* (pp. 208-232). New York: Springer-Verlag.

Campbell, D. T., Boruch, R. F., Schwartz, R. D., & Steinberg, J. (1977). Confidentiality-preserving modes of access to files and to interfile exchange for useful statistical analysis. *Evaluation Quarterly, 1,* 269-300.

Cox, L. H., & Boruch, R. F. (1986). Emerging policy issues in record linkage and privacy. In *Proceedings of the International Statistical Institute* (pp. 9.2.1-9.2.116). Amsterdam: International Statistical Institute.

Duncan, G., & Lambert, D. (1987). The risk of disclosure for microdata. In U.S. Bureau of the Census, *Proceedings of the Third Annual Research Conference.* Washington, DC: Government Printing Office.

Fisher, C. B., & Rosendahl, S. A. (1990). Psychological risks and remedies of research participation. In C. G. Fisher & W. W. Tryon (Eds.), *Ethics in applied developmental psychology: Emerging issues in an emerging field* (pp. 43-59). Norwood, NJ: Ablex.

Fox, J. A., & Tracy, P. E. (1986). *Randomized response: A method for sensitive surveys.* Beverly Hills, CA: Sage.

Gates, G. W. (1988, August). *Census Bureau microdata: Providing useful research data while protecting the anonymity of respondents.* Paper presented at the annual meeting of the American Statistical Association, New Orleans.

Gil, E. (1986). *The California child abuse reporting law: Issues and answers for professionals* (Publication No. 132). Sacramento: California Department of Social Services, Office of Child Abuse Prevention.

Grisso, T. (1991). Minors' assent to behavioral research without parental consent. In B. Stanley & J. E. Sieber (Eds.), *The ethics of research on children and adolescents* (pp. 109-127). Newbury Park, CA: Sage.

Kim, J. (1986). A method for limiting disclosure in microdata based on random noise and transformation. In *Proceedings of the Survey Methodology Research Section* (pp. 370-374). Washington, DC: American Statistical Association.

Klockars, C. B. (1974). *The professional fence.* New York: Free Press.

Laufer, R. S., & Wolfe, M. (1977). Privacy as a concept and a social issue: A multidimensional developmental theory. *Journal of Social Issues, 33,* 44-87.

Melton, G. B., & Stanley, B. H. (1991). Research involving special populations. In B. H. Stanley, J. E. Sieber, & G. B. Melton (Eds.), *Psychology and research ethics* (pp. 177-202). Lincoln: University of Nebraska Press.

Pelto, P. J. (1988). [Informal remarks]. In J. E. Sieber (Ed.), *Proceedings of a conference on sharing social research data, February 18-20, 1988, National Science Foundation/American Association for the Advancement of Science, Washington DC.* Unpublished manuscript.

Renzetti, C. M., & Lee, R. M. (Eds.). (1993). *Researching sensitive topics.* Newbury Park, CA: Sage.

Rotheram-Borus, M. J., & Koopman, C. (1991). Protecting children's rights in AIDS research. In B. Stanley & J. E. Sieber (Eds.), *The ethics of research on children and adolescents* (pp. 143-161). Newbury Park, CA: Sage.

Sieber, J. E. (1992). *Planning ethically responsible research: A guide for students and internal review boards.* Newbury Park, CA: Sage.

Stanley, B., & Sieber, J. E. (Eds.). (1991). *The ethics of research on children and adolescents.* Newbury Park, CA: Sage.

Thompson, R. A. (1991). Developmental changes in research risk and benefit: A changing calculus of concerns. In B. Stanley & J. E. Sieber (Eds.), *The ethics of research on children and adolescents* (pp. 31-64). Newbury Park, CA: Sage.

Turner, A. G. (1982). What subjects of survey research believe about confidentiality. In J. E. Sieber (Ed.), *The ethics of social research: Surveys and experiments* (pp. 151-166). New York: Springer-Verlag.

Tymchuk, A. J. (1991). Assent processes. In B. Stanley & J. E. Sieber (Eds.), *The ethics of social research on children and adolescents* (pp. 128-140). Newbury Park, CA: Sage.

Part II

Applied Research Framework

███████████████

*I*n this section of the handbook we move from the broader design and planning issues raised in Part I to more specific research designs and approaches. In Part I, the contributors noted the unique characteristics of applied research and discussed issues such as sampling, statistical power, and ethics. In Part II, the focus narrows to particular types of designs, including experimental and quasi-experimental designs, case studies, needs analysis, cost-effectiveness evaluation, and research synthesis.

In Chapter 6, Boruch focuses on one type of design, the randomized experiment. The randomized study is considered the gold standard for studying interventions, both in applied settings and in more basic research settings. Boruch provides justifications for this widespread belief, noting the investigations that have demonstrated the relative strengths of randomized studies over quasi-experiments. However, implementing a randomized design in a field setting is difficult. Through the use of multiple examples, Boruch describes some of the best ways to implement this design. He notes the need to conduct pipeline studies, as well as the need for careful attention to the ethical concerns raised by randomized experiments. Boruch also discusses the management requirements of a randomized design and issues concerning the reporting of results.

Although randomized experiments represent the gold standard, it is not always possible to conduct such research. In Chapter 7, Reichardt and Mark move us from

Handbook
of Applied
Social
Research
Methods

158

the simpler, but elegant, randomized design to discussion of quasi-experiments. They reconceptualize the traditional ways of thinking about the several forms of validity. Their approach clarifies many of the problems of previous schemes for describing the variety of quasi-experiments. Chapter 7 can serve as a guide for researchers who want to avoid some of the difficulties in planning quasi-experiments and interpreting their results.

Experiments and quasi-experiments are designed to answer questions of a causal nature, but they often are not able to provide detailed explanations as to how and why an intervention was successful. As Yin describes in Chapter 8, case study research offers investigators the ability to explore these questions. Yin provides an overview of the steps involved in designing, conducting, and analyzing case studies, particularly explanatory case studies, and offers a perspective based on a natural science orientation to inquiry. He stresses the key concept of triangulation, or following converging lines of evidence from different sources of the evidence being sought to establish a fact. Yin disavows the notion that case study research is synonymous with qualitative research only, and outlines a variety of quantitative and qualitative data methods and sources that can be used in case studies. He outlines six key sources of evidence: documentation, archival records, interviews, direct observations, participant observations, and physical artifacts.

An underlying theme of Chapter 8 is the importance of theory in all aspects of case study research—developing the design, conducting the analyses, and writing the reports. Yin introduces logic models and discusses them as a key analytic strategy, stipulating a chain of events over time, displaying the causal relationship among independent, intervening, and dependent variables.

One strength of Yin's chapter is that he includes discussion of some of the practical features involved in case study research. In particular, he provides details on the skills needed to conduct the research and offers guidelines for organizing data, creating a database, synthesizing and analyzing the data, and writing the report.

In Chapter 9, McKillip focuses on the areas of applied research most often referred to as needs assessment. He describes several techniques for conducting needs analyses aimed at informing the most common struggles faced by policy makers and others: how to allocate scarce resources and develop programs and policies that are appropriately targeted. McKillip outlines the steps to be taken in both identifying and assessing needs. As he illustrates, needs analysis is an area that draws upon a range of methods (e.g., survey research, secondary analysis, qualitative methods) and necessitates the researcher's constant communication with decision makers and other key stakeholders. In particular, he highlights how values, always a part of applied research, are particularly salient in needs analysis and become an explicit part of the process.

In applied research, the question of interest is typically not only, "Did the intervention work?" but, "At what cost?" In Chapter 10, Yates provides a comprehensive framework that integrates costs and cost-effectiveness and incorporates many of the aspects of design and analysis introduced in earlier chapters. Yates calls his model CPPO, which stands for cost → procedure → process →

outcome analysis. To evaluate an intervention fully, according to Yates, the researcher needs to know the budget limits of what are acceptable costs, the effectiveness or outcomes of the intervention, and the intervention's cost-effectiveness. In his framework, Yates includes factors that may moderate an intervention's effectiveness, such as client and community characteristics as well as client processes that are hypothesized to be affected by the program and the actual program procedures.

As we noted in our introduction, a major theme of this handbook is the importance of accumulating knowledge in substantive areas so as to make possible more definitive answers to key questions. Do we have the tools and methods in applied research to pull together the vast number of studies that have been completed? In Chapter 11, Cooper and Lindsay summarize techniques developed in the past 20 years to produce quantitative summaries of often hundreds of studies. Although most of these techniques have been developed recently, the authors note that the first meta-analysis was actually published in 1904.

The development of meta-analysis has not been without controversy, and Cooper and Lindsay review many of the problems with early approaches. Strategies for combining studies, determining what statistics to use, how to treat poor-quality studies, and decision rules about inclusion of studies have all been widely debated. Cooper and Lindsay describe how these issues have been addressed. In addition, they describe several ways to interpret effect sizes, which is a common outcome of meta-analysis. Finally, the meta-analyst interested in applications needs to communicate the results not only to the research community but to the policy community.

6

Randomized Controlled Experiments for Evaluation and Planning

Robert F. Boruch

Suppose you were asked to determine the effectiveness of a new police strategy to reduce domestic violence. The strategy involves arresting individuals for misdemeanor assault as opposed to conventional handling of the offense—that is, restoring order and leaving the premises. A study of the topic would require comparing the recidivism rates of individuals who were arrested against the recidivism rates of those who were not. The study's object is to establish whether arresting an offender reduces subsequent violence.

In an uncontrolled or observational study, particular police officers will prefer to arrest some offenders and not to arrest others. This *selection factor,* born of officers' preferences, leads to two offender groups that are likely to differ systematically in ways that are observable. Arrestees may, for instance, have a higher unemployment rate. The groups may also differ in unobservable ways. For instance, offenders who were not arrested may have lied to police officers about their employment status so as to generate sympathy. They may have talked about the dispute in a way that produced a more lenient treatment by the police officer. These factors are arguably relevant to the outcome of primary interest, recidivism. Still other selection factors may depend on the officers' moods, the offenders' demeanors, the number of calls that are backlogged, and so on.

The differences between the groups that evolve from natural processes, rather than a controlled study, will then be inextricably tangled with the actual effect of arrest on recidivism, if indeed there is an effect. A simple difference in recidivism between the two groups, one composed of individuals who were arrested and one composed of those who were not, will not then register the effect of arrest alone. It will reflect the effect of arrest and the combined effect of all selection factors: police officers' preferences, unmeasured motivational differences among offenders, and so on. As a consequence, the estimate of the effect of arrest based on a simple difference in the recidivism rate between the groups is equivocal at best. It may also be misleading.

Recidivism in the arrested group, for instance, may be higher, making it appear that arrest increases assaults, when, in fact, arrest has had no effect. It is the selection factors that produce the difference. Thus a simple observational study of arrested and nonarrested offenders, which merely compares recidivism rates after the police encounter, will yield a result that cannot be interpreted easily.

Eliminating the selection factors in evaluations that are designed to estimate the relative effectiveness of alternative approaches to reducing the incidence of violence is difficult. This same difficulty affects nonrandomized studies, based on passive surveys for instance, that purport to assess the impact of human resources training programs, health care systems, compensatory education efforts, and innovation in civil and criminal justice. It also affects studies that purport to match individuals in each group to the extent that matching is imperfect or incomplete in ways that are unknown or unknowable.

That many applied research and evaluation projects cannot take selection factors into account does not mean such studies are useless. It does imply that, where appropriate and feasible, researchers ought to exploit sturdy methods for estimating the relative effects of initiatives, methods that are not vulnerable to selection problems and do not lead to estimates that are equivocal or biased in unknown ways. The approach covered here, randomized field experiments, is less vulnerable to such problems. The text is based on Boruch (1997).

■ *Randomized Controlled Experiments*

In the simplest randomized experiment, individuals are randomly assigned to one of two or more treatment groups. The groups so composed are, roughly speaking, equivalent. They do not differ systematically.

The various treatments that are applied to each group may eventually produce a difference in the state of each group, the experiment being designed so as to discern such a difference. In the Spouse Assault Replication Program (SARP), for instance, adult offenders were randomly assigned either to be arrested on a misdemeanor assault charge or to a treatment where the dispute was mediated. In this latter "control" condition, police left the scene after restoring order. The object was to learn whether recidivism would differ depending on how individuals in each group were treated. Arrest was expected by some victims' advocates and theorists to decrease recidivism.

In more complex experiments, a sample of individuals or institutions may be matched first, then randomly assigned to treatment groups. Matching and other strategies that are discussed later usually enhance the statistical power of the experiment. That is, treatment effects are rendered more detectable in an experiment that employs matching, or blocking, or other precision-enhancement tactics. Regardless of these tactics, the randomization assures that unknown influences on behavior are equalized across the treatment groups regardless of the effectiveness of matching.

Entire institutions or jurisdictions may be randomly assigned to different regimens in large-scale experiments. For instance, a sample of 20 police departments might be split randomly in half, one group being assigned to a new communications system and the remaining group using conventional systems, all in the interest of estimating the new system's effect on police response time relative to the existing systems. Sample size is an issue in such designs; it is discussed below.

The first of two principal benefits of randomized tests is that they permit fair comparison. Estimates of the relative differences among the treatments being compared will be unbiased. That is, the estimates will not be tangled with competing explanations of what caused the difference in observed outcome. This is because the groups being compared will not differ systematically on account of the random allocation. The virtue of a comparison that leads to clearly interpretable results was recognized more than a century ago by Jastrow and Pierce in psychophysical laboratory experiments (see Stigler, 1978). It is a virtue that has become valuable in planning and evaluating programs in the social arena, to judge from increased use of the method in policy research.

The second benefit is a statistical statement of the researcher's confidence in the results of the experiment. This depends on recognizing that the experiment's results are subject to ordinary variability in human behavior and that this variability needs to be taken into account. The ability to make such a statement is important on scientific grounds. We know that we will err, at times, in judging a treatment's effectiveness simply because ordinary chance variability in human behavior (and institutional behavior) can be substantial. Understanding the character of the random error and delimiting its magnitude is then important. The construction of formal statistical tests about the relative differences among treatments in a randomized experiment, based on the randomization procedure, is attributable to Sir Ronald Fisher (1935) and to colleagues such as Kempthorne (1952).

■ *Distinctions*

Randomized experiments are distinguished from observational studies, in which there is an interest in establishing cause-effect relations but no opportunity to assign individuals to alternative treatments in accord with a randomization plan (Cochran, 1983; Rosenbaum, 1995). Such studies are often based on survey samples and depend on specialized methods for constructing comparison groups and estimates of treatment differences.

Observational studies can and often do produce high-quality descriptive data on the state of individuals or groups. They cannot always sustain defensible analyses of the relative effects of different treatments, although they are often employed to this end. Statistical advances in the theory and practice of designing better observational studies, and in analyzing resultant data and potential biases in estimated treatment effects, are covered by Rosenbaum (1995).

Randomized field tests are also different from quasi-experiments. Quasi-experiments have the object of estimating the relative effectiveness of different treatments that have a common aim, just as randomized experiments and observational studies do, but they depend on methods other than randomization to rule out competing explanations or treatment differences that may be uncovered, or to recognize bias in estimates of a difference. In some respects, quasi-experiments function to approximate the results of randomized field tests (Campbell & Stanley, 1966; Cochran, 1983; Cook & Campbell, 1979).

A variety of important statistical approaches have been invented to try to isolate the effects of treatments in analyses of observational surveys and quasi-experiments. They attempt to recognize all the variables that may influence outcomes, including selection factors, to measure them, to separate the treatment effects from other factors, and to estimate these effects. Recent advances in this arena fall under the rubric of *structural models, selection models,* and *propensity scores.* Antecedents and augmentations to these approaches include covariance analysis and matching methods. Such techniques are reviewed in Coyle, Boruch, and Turner (1991) in the context of testing AIDS prevention programs and in Chapter 7 of this volume. Rosenbaum's (1995) handling of related matters is deeper and more technical.

These approaches have been useful in science and policy research partly because it is not always possible or desirable to employ randomized experiments in comparing different policies, programs, or practices. The nonrandomized approaches can also be useful in conjunction with randomized tests for a variety of reasons. A randomized test, for instance, may be undertaken with a modest sample of individuals to evaluate a set of practices; a quasi-experimental framework might be used simultaneously with a large sample to try to estimate the effect of a policy from which the sample is drawn (e.g., Boruch, 1994; U.S. General Accounting Office, 1992, 1994).

In this chapter, the phrase *randomized experiment* will be used interchangeably with other terms that have roughly the same meaning and are common in different research literatures. These terms include *randomized test* and *randomized social experiments,* used frequently during the 1970s and 1980s. They also include *randomized clinical trials,* a phrase often used to describe the same design for evaluating the relative effectiveness of medical or pharmaceutical treatments (Friedman, Furberg, & DeMets, 1985; Meinert, 1986).

■ *Illustrative Experiments From Different Fields*

Some of the examples that follow concern small but important components of larger programs, such as efforts to enhance the well-being of maltreated children who are associated with a preschool center. Others involve comparative tests that are national in scope. The illustrations from Boruch (1997), help to clarify the character and scope of contemporary randomized field tests.

☐ *Education*

In education as in other arenas, researchers may randomly allocate individuals, institutions, and other entities to different treatments in order to produce good estimates of the treatments' relative effectiveness. The choice of the experiment's *unit* of assignment depends on the nature of the treatment and on whether the units can be regarded as statistically independent. For instance, entire schools have been randomly assigned to alternative regimens in studies designed to determine whether intensive schoolwide campaigns could delay or prevent youngsters' use of tobacco, alcohol, and drugs (e.g., Ellickson & Bell, 1990). Classrooms have been allocated randomly to different classroom teacher-based approaches to enhancing children's cognitive achievement (Porter, 1988). In one of the most important experiments on class size to date, students and teachers were randomly assigned to small classes or to regular classes in Tennessee (Finn & Achilles, 1990). The weight of evidence in this experiment, incidentally, leads to the conclusion that small classes have an effect that is remarkable and, moreover, sustained over time (see Mosteller, Light, & Sachs, 1995, and references therein).

At least a few randomized tests have focused on innovations at each level of education. They have been mounted at the preschool level to learn whether early educational enrichment programs would lead to enhanced academic achievement of economically deprived children (Barnett, 1985). Because the relative impact of magnet schools is hard to estimate, Crain, Heebner, and Si (1992) analyzed data from New York City's Career Magnet schools, to which a sample of eighth-grade students were assigned randomly, to learn whether the schools did in fact reduce the likelihood of dropout and increase reading achievement levels. At the high school level, multisite randomized tests have been undertaken to assess dropout prevention programs (Dynarski, Gleason, Rangarajan, & Wood, 1995; U.S. Department of Education, 1991a) and the effects of Upward Bound programs on level of education and achievement (U.S. Department of Education, 1991b). There have been experiments at the college level to test programs that were thought to enhance the performance of high-risk students, to increase comprehension to improve the efficiency of instruction, and to achieve other goals (e.g., Light, Singer, & Willett, 1990).

☐ *Employment and Training*

The Rockefeller Foundation has supported randomized controlled field tests of integrated education and employment programs under its Female Single Parent Program. The objective was to understand whether a program involving a constellation of child care, job skills training, general education, and coun-seling would enhance the economic well-being of single mothers with low education and low employment skills (Cottingham, 1991; Rockefeller Foundation, 1988).

The field tests were mounted in collaboration with community-based organizations. Each involved randomly assigning eligible women to either the new integrated program or a control group whose members had access to employment, training, and other services that were generally available in the community. The collaborating organizations employed randomized experiments to assure that the evidence from the evaluation could withstand harsh criticism in scientific and public policy forums.

The experiments eliminated the problem of creaming—that is, selecting superior applicants in the interest of making a human resources training program look good. This selection factor was chronic in evaluations of employment programs of the 1960s and 1970s. Further, the randomization helped to avoid a major problem encountered in earlier attempts to evaluate such programs. That is, it is difficult or impossible to disentangle the average effect of a new program from the characteristics of individuals who elect (or do not elect) to enter a new program, another selection factor, unless a controlled experiment is done.

Related large-scale examples include multistate evaluations of work-welfare initiatives (Gueron & Pauly, 1991; Hollister, Kemper, & Maynard, 1984) and regional tests of new programs designed to retrain and employ workers displaced from their jobs by technology and competition (Bloom, 1990). These studies form part of a substantial effort to generate good evidence for labor policy and administration.

☐ *Tax Administration*

The interests of the U.S. Internal Revenue Service (IRS) and of tax agencies in other countries lie partly in understanding how citizens can be encouraged to pay the proper amount of taxes. For example, delinquent taxpayers identified by the IRS have been randomly assigned to different encouragement strategies, then tracked to determine which strategies yielded the best returns on investment. One set of strategies focused on varying the characteristics of letters to tax delinquents; the letters varied in frequency and in the severity of their tone (Perng, 1985). Other experiments have been undertaken to determine how tax forms may be simplified and how taxpayer errors might be reduced through various alterations in tax forms (e.g., Roth, Scholz, & Witte, 1989).

Such research extends a remarkable early experiment by Schwartz and Orleans (1967) to learn how people might be persuaded to report certain taxable income more thoroughly. This study compared the relative effectiveness of appeals to moral conscience, threats of legal action, and provision of information about the socially embarrassing consequences of failure to report the income. Which strategy worked best depended on income level. Appeals to conscience produced better reporting among low-income individuals, and the possibility of social sanction affected those with higher incomes. This study was small, and it is not clear whether similar results would be found in other settings.

Random allocation of taxpayers to the various treatment groups assures that the groups are equivalent apart from enhanced differences that can be taken into account. For instance, if the contents of letters sent to delinquent taxpayers in the Perng (1985) study had been determined by individual IRS staff members, the effect of factors such as frequency and severity of the letters would have been inextricably mixed with the effect of the staffers' preferences, that is, a selection factor. Developing a defensible estimate of the relative effectiveness of letter strategies independent of such preferences would arguably have been impossible.

□ *Civil and Criminal Justice*

The Minneapolis Domestic Violence Experiment was designed to determine how misdemeanor domestic violence cases could be best handled by police officers (Sherman & Berk, 1984). Within the limits set by the police departments involved and by legal counsel, such cases were randomly allocated to one of three different police handling tactics: arrest of the offender, mediation of the dispute, or immediate temporary separation of the offender and victim. The object was to determine which of these treatments produced the lowest level of subsequent domestic violence in these households.

The credibility of the Minneapolis results depended heavily on the random allocation of cases assigned to treatment. That is, the cases in each treatment group were statistically equivalent on account of the random assignment. Competing explanations that were common in earlier nonrandomized studies could then be ruled out, including differential police preferences for one or another way to handle particular violence complaints. The Minneapolis experiment helped to inform a 15-year debate on handling such cases in that arresting an offender was found to work better than other strategies tested. Similar experiments were later undertaken in the SARP by six other police departments to determine whether arrest would prove more effective in other cities and to test other methods of reducing violence (Garner, Fagen, & Maxwell, 1995; Reiss & Boruch, 1991).

There have been two substantial reviews of randomized field experiments in civil and criminal justice. Dennis (1988) analyzed the factors that influenced the quality of 40 studies undertaken in the United States. His dissertation updated Farrington's (1983) examination of the rationale, conduct, and results of randomized experiments in Europe and North America. The range of treatments whose effectiveness has been evaluated in controlled tests is, to judge from each review, remarkable. They have included appeals processes in civil court, telephone-based appeals hearings, victim restitution plans, jail time for offenders, diversion from arrest, arrest versus mediation, juvenile diversion and family systems intervention, probation rules, bail procedures, work-release programs for prisoners, and sanctions that involve community service rather than incarceration.

☐ *Mental Health*

The National Institute of Mental Health has supported a variety of multisite experiments aimed at increasing understanding of the effectiveness of different approaches to mental illness. One such trial involved the random assignment of people who were seriously depressed from a pool of volunteer patients to one of three promising treatment approaches: a specialized brief form of cognitive behavior therapy, pharmacotherapy with clinical management, and placebo with clinical management. The object was to estimate the relative effectiveness of treatments so as to assure that estimates would not be systematically contaminated by unknowable extraneous influences such as physician or patient preferences and beliefs (Collins & Elkin, 1985). The groups being compared were statistically equivalent prior to treatment by virtue of randomization.

More recent experiments have been mounted, for example, to produce unbiased estimates of the relative effectiveness of consumer case managers (Solomon & Draine, 1993) and programs for mentally ill individuals released from jail (Solomon & Draine, 1995).

☐ *Abused and Neglected Children*

One object of research concerning abused and neglected children is to determine how to enhance positive behaviors of withdrawn, maltreated preschool children. A randomized field test was undertaken by Fantuzzo et al. (1988) to evaluate the effectiveness of an innovative approach to this problem. The new approach involved having highly interactive and resilient preschoolers play with their maltreated peers. The program essentially involved children in initiating activity and sharing during play periods with children who had been withdrawn and timid.

The field test compared the withdrawn children who were randomly assigned to this approach against children who had been randomly assigned to specialized adult-based activity. The results from blind on-site observations and school records showed remarkable increases in positive behaviors and decreases in problem behaviors among the withdrawn children who were engaged by their peers. The initial study was small. Larger-scale tests were undertaken by Fantuzzo and his colleagues in Head Start centers in Philadelphia partly on the basis of the results of the initial effort.

A different stream of controlled experiments has been undertaken to understand how to prevent out-of-home placement of neglected and abused children. In Illinois, for instance, the studies involve randomly assigning children at risk of foster care to either the conventional placement route, which includes foster care, or a special Family First program, which leaves the child with the parents but provides intensive services from counselors and family caseworkers. Related research has been undertaken by other agencies involved in child care in California, Utah, Washington, New York, New Jersey, and Michigan. Schuerman, Rzepnicki, and Littell (1994), who investigated the Illinois experiment, found that the program was actually targeted at low-risk, rather than high-risk, families, virtually guaranteeing that no treatment differences would appear. The need to produce good evidence in this arena is driven partly by political and professional interest in learning whether foster care can be avoided.

☐ *Nutrition*

The U.S. Department of Agriculture's Food and Nutrition Service is responsible each year for a $12 billion food stamp program, a $4 billion school lunch program, and a $2 billion food program for women, infants, and children. Each program directs attention to individuals who are economically vulnerable and, on this account, also likely to be nutritionally at risk; the poor, including infants, often do not have an adequate diet.

Evaluation and policy analysis units at the Food and Nutrition Service have mounted randomized controlled tests of different approaches to improving service since the early 1980s. Among these have been multisite experiments that compare strategies for securing employment for food stamp recipients who would otherwise be unemployed. The objective has been to understand which of more than a dozen strategies work, and in what sense, to increase the recipients' earnings and reduce their dependence on the food stamp program (Wargo, 1989).

☐ *Health Care Research*

The Robert Wood Johnson Foundation and the U.S. Department of Health and Human Services' Division of Nursing have supported randomized experiments to assess safety, efficacy, and cost savings of various nursing care interventions. For instance, Brooten et al. (1986) conducted a randomized clinical trial of early hospital discharge and home follow-up nursing intervention for very low birth-weight infants. The low birth-weight infants (weighing 1,500 grams or less) were randomly assigned to either a control group of infants discharged to the nursery with a discharge weight of 2,200 grams or the experimental group of infants, who were discharged with a mean discharge date of 11 days earlier, weighed less than 2,200 grams, and were 2 weeks younger. Both parent groups received support and instruction from the nurses regarding the infants' care following hospitalization, and received follow-up home visits and daily on-call availability by a nurse specialist for 18 months. The study reported no differences in the numbers of rehospitalizations, acute care visits, and mental or physical measurements of growth.

O'Sullivan and Jacobsen (1992) tested the effectiveness of a special health care intervention on more than 200 black adolescent mothers and their infants. All of the mothers were 17 years old or younger, unwed, and on Medicaid. They were randomly assigned either to a control group that received routine well-baby care or to a treatment group that received routine care plus rigorous follow-up care by a nurse practitioner. The follow-up treatment included planning for the mother's return to school, education in the use of family planning methods, and extra health teaching. Most of the mothers were located for the 18-month follow-up interview, at which point the repeat pregnancy rate was 12% in the experimental group compared with 28% in the control group. Infants in the experimental group were twice as likely to be fully immunized as were the infants in the control group after 12 months. Mothers in the experimental group were less likely to use the emergency room than were mothers in the control group. The implication drawn was that comprehensive health care programs initiated by nurse practitioners can effect better health outcomes for mothers and infants in special need of services.

■ *Elements of a Randomized Experiment*

The broad elements of a randomized test for learning what works better are discussed briefly in this section. The description is based mainly on controlled field tests sponsored by the National Institute of Justice on police handling of domestic violence: the Spouse Assault Replication Program. Other substantive examples, such as tests of employment and training, and education projects, are used to reiterate the fundamental character of the elements (details are given in Boruch, 1997). In general, the elements of a randomized field experiment are as follows:

- The questions and the role of theory
- Assuring ethical propriety
- The experiment's design
- Management
- The analysis and reporting of the results

□ *The Questions and the Role of Theory*

Put bluntly, the questions best addressed by a randomized controlled experiment are as follows: What works better? For whom? And for how long? The primary question must, of course, be framed more specifically for the particular study. Secondary questions are often important for science or policy, and their lower priority needs to be made plain.

In the Spouse Assault Replication Program, for example, the *primary* question was: Does arrest for the misdemeanor domestic violence lead to lower recidivism relative to conventional police handling of such cases? The question was determined by the sponsoring agency, the National Institute of Justice, based on earlier policy research.

The primary question was also based partly on theory. At least one criminological theory, for example, holds that arrest has a specific deterrent effect on the individual who is arrested. The rationale for the question was based on the need to understand whether arrest is more effective in a variety of settings than conventional police attempts to restore order and mediate domestic disputes. The primary outcome variable of interest in all cases was recidivism— that is, a subsequent assault event involving the same couple.

Secondary questions were also posed by principal investigators in each site in which the experiments were run. Omaha's Police Department, for example, examined the question of how to handle cases in which the alleged offender was not present when police arrived (Dunford, Huizinga, & Elliott, 1990). In collaboration with researchers at the University of Colorado, police designed a randomized test to understand whether issuing warrants on offenders who were "gone on arrival" resulted in a lower recidivism rate for these individuals, relative to the usual practice. Warrants are not issued in many jurisdictions when the alleged offender in a misdemeanor domestic case is gone on arrival.

The technology of controlled experiments, when applied well, yields the least ambiguous evidence possible on the question, What works better? It is not designed to address other questions that are often no less important, such as, What is the nature and scope of the problem? and What programs are planned and actually put in place?

Answers to these latter questions are prerequisite to the design of a good experiment. For instance, understanding the incidence of domestic cases in various neighborhoods of a police jurisdiction is in itself important. The evidence comes from police records or surveys prior to an experiment. Studies of this sort fall under the rubric of needs assessment surveys, in the vernacular of evaluation research. Learning that there are a variety of existing victim services apart from police and learning about how they work are often essential to a researcher's designing field tests of new approaches and interpreting the results of an experiment on the treatments. Applied social research and evaluation research on how alternative treatment programs work, for example, have often taken the form of case studies, process evaluation, implementation studies, or formative evaluation, in the context of a randomized experiment or otherwise.

Theory

Contemporary books on the design of experiments (apart from Boruch, 1997) do not handle the substantive theory underlying the treatments. Nonetheless, the topic of theory must be addressed.

A theory (or several theories) should drive the selection of treatments. For example, the choice of "arrest" versus "mediation" treatments in the Spouse Assault Replication Program had its origins in the theory that arrest has an individual-specific deterrence effect, in contrast to the general deterrence that might be caused by a communitywide violence prevention program.

Theory must drive the identification of the units of allocation in a field experiment. See my later remarks in this chapter about programs directed toward individuals, psychotherapy, or case management in mental health, and programs directed toward reducing health risks more broadly—school-based substance abuse programs, for instance. Each kind of program is influenced by ideas, or theory, that specify who or what should be the target of the program and, by implication, the unit of allocation in a randomized controlled experiment. Statistical theory has a role here also inasmuch as most simple approaches to analysis depend on the assumption that the units of allocation and analysis in the experiment are independent (Mosteller, 1986).

Theory, implicit or explicit, also drives the choice of outcome variables to be measured. In the SARP, for example, measurement focused on individuals' subsequent domestic violence, rather than on (say) attitudes toward women or petty theft convictions. This was based on specific deterrence theory. In their experiments on class size, Finn and Achilles (1990) measured student achievement based on theory and earlier research about whether and how class size could influence a child's academic performance.

Well-articulated theory also helps to determine whether context variables need to be measured. For instance, most experiments on new employment and training programs attend to measuring the local job market in which the program is deployed. This is based on rudimentary theory of demand and supply of workers. Knowing that there are no jobs available in an area, for example, is important for understanding the results of an experiment that compares wage rates of participants in a new training programs against wages of those involved in ordinarily available community employment and training programs.

Finally, substantive theory may also drive how one interprets a simple comparison of the outcomes of two programs, deeper analyses based on data from the experiment at hand, and broader analyses of the experiment in view of research in the topical area generally. Rossi and Freeman's (1993) discussion of different kinds of hypothesis bearing on evaluation of a program is the broadest we have seen on the topic. The implications of their discussion are that we ought to have a theory (an enlarged hypothesis or hypothesis system) that addresses people and programs in the field, a theory about the treatments in the experiment given the field theory, and a theory about what would happen if the results of the experiment were exploited to change things in the field.

Suffice it to say that comparing two groups in a controlled randomized experiment is a simple objective, misleadingly so. Recent experience suggests that the design of future experiments will be, and should be, sensitive to theory, however rudimentary this theory may be. Regardless of the adjective *rudimentary,* the theory ought to be explicit. It is up to the experiment's design team to draw that theory into the open with delicacy and with a sense of our ignorance.

□ *Assuring Ethical Propriety*

Whether an experiment is ethical depends on a variety of criteria. The medical, social, and behavioral sciences and education have been vigorous in producing ethical guidelines for research and monitoring adherence to them. Two kinds of standards are relevant.

The first set of standards, developed by the Federal Judicial Center (1983), involves general appraisal of the ethical propriety of randomized tests. The FJC's threshold conditions for deciding whether an experiment ought to be considered involve addressing the following questions:

- Is there need for improvement?
- Is the effectiveness of proposed improvements uncertain?
- Will a randomized experiment yield more defensible evidence than alternatives?
- Will the results be used?
- Will the rights of participants be protected?

Affirmative responses to all these questions invite serious consideration of a randomized experiment.

The second set of standards relevant to the behavioral and social sciences is that enunciated by the institutional review board (IRB). In any institution receiving federal research funds, an IRB is responsible for reviewing the ethical propriety of research, including field experiments. The principal investigator for an experiment is responsible for presenting the field test's design to the IRB. The responsibility for capitalizing on the IRB's counsel and tailoring the design to meet good ethical standards is also the principal investigator's.

In the SARP, for instance, discussions of each of the Federal Judicial Center's threshold questions were undertaken in effect by the National Institute of Justice and its advisers and at the local level, for example, by the Milwaukee City Council, the Milwaukee Police Department, and the city's various advocacy groups. An independent IRB also reviewed the experiment's design in accordance with the federal legal requirement to do so. The principal investigator has the responsibility to explain matters to each group, and to develop a design that meets local concerns about the ethical appropriateness of the experiment.

Sieber (1992; see also Chapter 5, this volume) provides general guidance for meeting ethical standards in social research; Silverman (1989) does so in context of medical clinical trials. Scholarly discussions of ethical issues appear in Stanley and Sieber (1992) and are also regularly published in professional journals that bear on applied social and psychological research and educational research.

□ *The Experiment's Design*

The design of a controlled randomized field experiment involves the following elements:

- Specifying the population and units of randomization
- Sampling method and sample size
- Interventions and methods for their observation
- The method of random assignment and checks on its integrity
- The response or outcome variables and their measurement
- Analysis and reporting

Each of these topics is considered below.

Population, Power, and the Pipeline

The majority of contemporary field experiments undertaken in the United States focus on individuals as the unit of allocation to treatments and analysis. Consequently, in this chapter I stress how researchers can engage individuals in experiments. Institutions or other entities also are at times allocated randomly to different regimens. Schools have been randomly assigned to substance use prevention programs and to control conditions. The policy justification for doing so is that treatments are delivered at the entity level. The statistical justification lies in the assumption underlying analysis that units are independent; students within classrooms or even schools are not clearly independent of one another with respect to response to treatment. See Coyle et al. (1991) and Boruch (1994) for brief illustrations of the use of entities as the unit in experiments and Ellickson and Bell (1990) for a report on a relevant large-scale study. Identifying the appropriate unit of allocation is linked naturally to the task of identifying the appropriate target population of units.

In experiments in criminal justice, medicine, employment and training, and other areas, the *target population* depends heavily on the specification of eligibility criteria for the individuals (or entities) who are expected to benefit from the treatments being compared. The SARP, for instance, included only adults in the sample partly because handling juvenile offenders would have entailed different legal procedures and, in any case, they were less relevant to domestic violence policy than were adults. Similarly, police had to establish the existence of probable cause evidence to believe that a misdemeanor crime had been committed for a case to be eligible, the arrest treatment being irrelevant to noncriminal events (Garner et al., 1995).

Eligibility criteria that are used in evaluating employment and training programs or services in the child abuse and neglect area are also often specified on the basis of relevant law and regulation. At times, the specification, or the theory implicit in the criteria, is found to be weak once the experiment is done. Schuerman et al. (1994), for instance, discovered that the main eligibility standard for Family First programs in Illinois, a child's "imminent risk of placement" into a foster home, was of dubious value in identifying such children in experiments on services.

Not all eligible target units will be reached, of course. Some assailants who might otherwise have been eligible in SARP may not have been engaged in the experiment simply because police were not called to the scene. Similarly, children at "imminent risk" may not be entrained in the child neglect system at all. In such experiments and others, it is important for researchers to anticipate these de facto exclusions, possibly through pipeline studies of the sort described below.

Eligibility and exclusionary criteria, then, substantially define the target population. And this in turn helps to characterize the experiment's generalizability (considered later in this chapter). The criteria also influence the statistical power of the experiment through their effect on producing a heterogeneous or homogeneous sample and their restriction of sample size. It is to this topic that we turn next, emphasizing sample size issues.

Statistical power refers to the experiment's capacity to detect treatment differences. The power is calculable, and should be calculated prior to the experiment given and assumptions about what differences are worth detecting, characteristics of the formal statistical tests used in assessing differences, and certain features of the experiment, such as sample size.

Each of the experiments referenced in this chapter was preceded by statistical power calculation to assure that, among other things, sample sizes were adequate. For example, each SARP experiment was designed around the idea that a 10-15% difference in recidivism rate was important to discern, with a probability of at least 85%, using simple chi-square statistical tests at an alpha level of .05. Developing power calculations, in this and other cases, is relatively easy with personal-computer-based software such as Ex-Sample (Idea Works, 1993) and that described by Borenstein and Cohen (1990). Lipsey (1990), Kraemer and Thiemann (1987), and Cohen (1992) cover this general topic in different but interesting ways (see also Lipsey, Chapter 2, this volume).

A *pipeline study* directs attention to how, why, when, and how many individuals may be entrained in the experiment. In a sense, it characterizes the eligible and ineligible target population over time. It helps to anticipate the sample size and statistical power that can be achieved. Further, a pipeline study enhances understanding of the institutional processes in which treatments can be deployed and the social contexts in which this happens.

Each of the SARP investigators developed such a study prior to the experiment. In most, the following events and the numbers attached to each was the evidential base: total police calls received, cases dispatched on call, cases dispatched as domestic violence cases, domestic cases that were found on site actually to be domestic violence cases, and domestic cases in which eligibility requirements were met. In one site over a 2-year period, for example, nearly 550,000 calls were dispatched; 48,000 of these were initially dispatched as domestic cases. Of these, only about 2,400 were actually domestic disputes and met eligibility requirements. That is, the cases that involved persons in spouselike relationships, in which there were grounds for believing that misdemeanor assault had occurred, and so on, were far fewer than those initially designated as "domestic" by police dispatchers.

Research akin to pipeline studies has been run at times in other areas of applied social research. Schuerman et al. (1994) collected information on more than 6,000 families involved in the Family First child abuse/neglect program in Illinois, and in anticipation of experiments on the program itself. Early precedents also lie in the Seattle and Denver Income Maintenance Experiments. Each household's consent to participate in the study had to be elicited and represented in a small but notable restriction of the flow of households into the experiment (Murarka & Spiegelman, 1978).

Population, power, and pipeline are intimately related to one another in field experiments. Considering them together in the study's design is then essential. Where this planning is inadequate or based on wrong assumptions, and especially when early stages of the experiment show that the flow of cases into the experiment is sparse, drastic change may be warranted. Such changes might include extending the time frame for the experiment, so as to accumulate more cases. This tactic was employed in the SARP experiments and the Rockefeller Foundation's studies of programs for single female parents (Burghardt & Gordon, 1990; Cottingham, 1991), among others. Intensifying outreach efforts so as to identify and better engage target cases is another common tactic for assuring adequate sample size. It was employed in the Rockefeller studies (Boruch, Dennis, & Carter, 1988), and can be regarded as a treatment program element that is manipulatable (Leviton & Schuh, 1991).

The Treatments

Treatments here means the programs or projects, program components, or program variations whose relative effectiveness is of primary interest. That said, it is obvious that the researcher ought to know what activities characterize each program being compared, how they are supposed to work, and how he or she can verify that they occur.

In the SARP experiments, for instance, the two interventions to which individuals were randomly assigned included arrest and mediation. That an arrest occurred when it was supposed to occur was determined by reliance on police reports. Deeper understanding of what "arrest" means is not so easy if one recognizes that the process may involve an offender's spending 2 hours at the police station in some jurisdictions and more than a few hours in an unpleasant holding tank in other jurisdictions.

New treatment programs are, of course, not always delivered as they are supposed to be. In the SARP, establishing that people who should have been arrested were actually arrested was important. Consequently, these experiments involved careful attention to departures from the treatments assigned. Similarly, fertility control devices designed to reduce birthrates have not been distributed to potential users. Human resources training projects have not been put into place, in the sense that appropriate staff have not been hired. Drug regimens have been prescribed for tests, but individuals assigned to a drug do not always comply with the regimen.

Understanding how to assure that treatments are delivered properly falls under the rubric of compliance research in drug trials and some medical experiments. In small experiments, the research team usually develops "manipulation checks." In medium- to large-scale studies, where program staff, rather than experimenters, are responsible for treatment delivery, the topic is usually handled through program guidelines, training sessions, briefings, and the like.

In most applied social research, the "control" condition is *not* one in which any treatment is absent. Rather, the label usually denotes a condition in which conventional or customary treatment is delivered. This being the case, the composition of the control group must be measured and understood as that of the new treatment group is. For instance, the mediation control condition in the SARP involved an array of ordinary police practices during an encounter. The police officers may issue verbal warnings, tell the offender to leave the premises, restore order in the sense of quieting the disputants or defusing an argument, or any combination of these.

Similarly, experiments on classroom size have included a control condition in which classrooms are of customary large size, with observations being made on what happens in these as on what happens in smaller classrooms. Well-done employment and training experiments verify that the new program is not delivered to control group members and, moreover, document processes and events in the latter as in the new treatment conditions.

The point is that interventions including control conditions need to be understood. Absent such understanding, a field experiment is useless at best. With such understanding, clear statements of what works, or what works better, are far more likely.

Random Assignment

Basic advice on how to assign individuals or entities randomly to treatments is readily available in textbooks on experiments and in documentation for statistical software packages. Researchers must also recognize the realities of field conditions, beyond these sources of counsel. Inept or subverted assignments are, for example, distinct possibilities. Berk, Smyth, and Sherman (1988) discuss this matter in the context of the Minneapolis Domestic Violence Experiment. See Conner (1977) and Silverman (1989) for earlier illustrations, and Boruch (1997) for more recent ones.

Current good practice focuses on *who* controls the assignment procedure, when the procedure is employed, and *how* it is structured. Any choice is driven by standards that demand that the assignment cannot be anticipated (and therefore subverted), cannot be subverted post facto, and cannot be manipulated apart from the control exercised by a blind assignment process. As a practical matter, the standard also precludes processes that produce clumps of assignments that are nonrandom, such as coin flips and card deck selections.

Contemporary experiments then employ a centralized procedure that assures control and independence of treatment delivery. Experiments in New York City's magnet schools, for instance, used an independent agent, the Educational Testing Service, to generate random assignments blindly and to record the assignment of each student to the special school versus a conventional one (Crain et al., 1992). The SARP experiments employed a similar strategy. Each site created a central entity to generate random assignments to treatments independent of street officers and others involved in cases. Officers radioed the entity for the assignment of each case and proceeded with treatment, to the extent possible, based on the call.

The timing of the assignment is important in at least one respect. A long interval between assignment and actual delivery of treatment can engender the problem that assigned individuals disappear, engage alternative treatments, and so on. For example, individuals assigned to one of two different employment programs may, if engagement in the program is delayed, seek other options. The experiment then is undermined. A similar problem can occur in tests of other kinds of programs, in rehabilitation, medical services, and civil justice. The implication is that assignment should take place as close as possible to the point of entry to treatment.

The random assignment process must be structured so as to meet the demands of the experiment's design and field conditions. The individual's or entity's eligibility for treatment, for instance, must usually be determined prior to assignment, otherwise there may be considerable wastage of effort. Moreover, individuals may have to be grouped on the basis of demographic characteristics *prior* to their assignments. This is partly to meet the constraints of (say) a randomized block design and partly to address volatile field issues. For example, one may group four individuals into two groups consisting of two individuals each, one group containing two African Americans and the second containing two Hispanics. The randomization process then involves assigning one African American to one of the treatments and the second individual to the remaining one. The randomization of Hispanics is done separately, within the Hispanic stratum. This approach assures that chance-based imbalances will not occur. That is, one will not encounter a string of Hispanics being assigned to one treatment rather than another. This in turn avoids local quarrels about favoritism. It also enhances the power of the experiment to the extent that ethnic or racial characteristics influence individuals' responses to the treatments; that is, interaction and blocking variables are taken into account.

Simple allocations of one unit to treatment A, a second unit to treatment B, a third to treatment C, and so on are common. Good reasons for departing from this simple 1:1 allocation scheme often appear in the field. The demand for one treatment may be strong, and the supply of eligible candidates for all treatments may be ample. This scenario justifies consideration of allocating in a (say) 2:1 ratio in a two-treatment experiment. Allocation ratios different from 1:1 are of course legitimate and, more important, may resolve local constraints.

They can do so without appreciably affecting the statistical power of the experiment if the basic sample sizes are adequate.

A final aspect of the structuring of the random assignment, and the experiment's design more generally, involves a small sample size. Experiments that involve organizations or communities, for example, as the primary unit of random assignment and analysis can often engage far fewer than 100 entities. Some experiments that focus on individuals as the unit must also contend with small sample size, for example, local tests of treatments for those who attempt suicide, sexually abuse children, or avoid paying certain taxes.

Regardless of what the unit of allocation is, a small sample presents special problems. A simple randomization scheme may by chance result in obviously imbalanced assignment; for example, four impoverished schools may be assigned to one health program and four affluent schools assigned to a second. The approaches recommended by Cox (1958) are sensible and endorsed here. First, if it is possible to match or block prior to randomization, this ought to be done. Second, where "unpleasant" random allocations appear, they ought to be abandoned and the units rerandomized. This strategy is sensible on scientific grounds. Third, one can catalog all possible random allocations that are possible, eliminate those that arguably would produce peculiarly uninterpretable results, and then choose randomly from the remaining set of arrangements. Ellickson and Bell (1990) did so, to good effect, in experiments that were designed to determine whether certain substance abuse programs, mounted at the school level and using the school as the unit of allocation and analysis, worked. Mosteller (1986) also has recognized the issue; he presents fine illustrations and provides the opportunity to think further on this topic.

Observation and Measurement

The targets for observation in experiments include response (outcome) variables, treatment variables, baseline information, context, cost, and "missingness." Theory about how treatments are supposed to work, and for whom, is essential to specifying what variables are to be observed. In rehabilitation programs, for instance, rudimentary theory suggests that certain outcomes, such as functional level, are influenced by certain kinds and duration of treatments (e.g., sheltered long-term workshops versus conventional approaches). These are also affected by contextual factors, such as living arrangements and family, and may depend on pretreatment condition (baseline) of the individuals who are engaged in the treatments (e.g., Lipsey, 1993). Each variable must then be measured; each engenders choices about how to measure.

The basis for choosing a measure of the response variables and others lies partly in the variables' theoretical relevance to treatments. It lies also in conventional criteria such as the reliability and validity of the observational method and how these might vary over time and across treatment groups. In the SARP, for example, both victim interviews and police arrest records were used to measure recidivism, partly because both could be construed as relevant to treatments and because they arguably differed in validity and reliability. Descriptions of how measurement quality differs over time and across groups in an experiment are given by Aiken and West (1990) and Cook and Campbell (1979), among others.

Learning about how well response variables are measured in experiments at times involves qualitative observation. "Ride alongs" with police officers, for instance, were done routinely in the SARP. They illuminated what the variable called "arrest" meant, and how the manner of arrest varied despite the singularity implied by the word *arrest.* Similarly, the variable called "employment," although easily measurable in one sense in human resource experiments, can arguably be understood more fully with qualitative observation. Indeed, recent experiments on Residential Job Corps depend partly on ethnographic work for this and other reasons.

In principle, nothing prevents researchers from obtaining different kinds of information on outcomes and the processes that underlie experiments. Contemporary experiments often include both quantitative and qualitative approaches. See Maxwell (Chapter 3, this volume) for a related but different perspective, and Miles and Huberman (1994) more generally. Lavrakas's work on telephone surveys (see Chapter 15, this volume) has been consistently attentive to understanding how to elicit information better, based on both qualitative and quantitative indicators.

The frequency and periodicity of measurement of each treatment group is important to the extent that theory suggests that treatment differences decay or appear late, or that responses to one treatment are more rapid than responses to another. No consolidated handling of this matter is available yet for social experiments. Contemporary experience, however, suggests that continuous monitoring is warranted in police experiments and school dropout studies, where specialized analytic methods such as event history analysis can be exploited. Further, one ought to expect decay in relative differences of earlier programs over time, and so multiple posttest measures are warranted. See, for instance, St. Pierre, Swartz, Murray, Deck, and Nickel (1995) on Even Start programs for impoverished families.

Once said, it is obvious that the treatments that were assigned randomly and those actually delivered ought to be observed. The simplest observation is a count, of course. But measures on at least two deeper levels are commonly made to inform policy and science on the character of the treatments. At the study level, the counts on departures from randomization are, as a matter of good practice, augmented by qualitative and often numerical information on them. In the SARP, for instance, departures were monitored and counted at each site to assure proper execution of the basic experiment's design and to learn about how departures occurred through qualitative interviews with police officers. At the treatment provider level, measures may be simple—for example, establishing how many police officers in the SARP contributed how many eligible cases and with what rate of compliance with assigned treatments. In large education and employment experiments, measures are often more elaborate, attending to duration, character, and intensity of training and support services, and to staff responsible for them. See, for example, St. Pierre et al. (1995) and Gueron and Pauly (1991) and references therein.

The function of baseline measures in experiments is to assure that treatments are delivered to the right target individuals, to enhance the interpretability of the experiments, and to increase the statistical power of analysis. Each function is critical and requires a slightly different use of the data. For example, eligibility standards in the SARP focused attention on adults as assailants, and the variable called adulthood was then not used in any statistical analysis. Because prior arrest record was deemed important to understanding whether arrest versus other treatments affected offenders differentially, police records were obtained and used in analyses that took interactions into account.

Consider next the observation of context. In training and employment programs that attempt to enhance participants' wage rates, it seems sensible to obtain data on the local job market. This is done in some experiments to understand whether indeed certain programs have an opportunity to exercise an effect. The measurement of job markets, of course, may also be integrated with employment program operations. Studies of programs designed to prevent school dropout or to reduce recidivism of former offenders might also, on theoretical grounds, attend to job markets, though it is not yet common practice to do so.

Here, as in measuring response and treatment variables, qualitative observations can be helpful in understanding the settings in which the experiments are taking place. Patton (1990) and Yin (1989), among others, provide general counsel on studying context, but a good integration of this approach with the design of experiments is not yet available.

Understanding what to measure about context depends partly on expectations and on theory. Exploiting the data in experiments well depends on the researcher's obtaining information across multiple sites. The state of the art in this respect appears primitive, because multisite experiments are infrequent and the theory on what contextual variables to measure is crude.

In some areas of social experiments, measurement of costs is customary and often intensive. Most studies of employment and training programs, for example, address cost seriously, as in the Rockefeller Foundation's experiments on programs for single parents (Burghardt & Gordon, 1990; Cottingham, 1991) and work-welfare projects (e.g., Gueron & Pauly, 1991; Hollister et al., 1984). But producing good estimates of costs requires resources, including expertise, that are not always available in other sectors. No experiments in the SARP, for instance, focused measurement attention on cost; the focus was on the treatments' effectiveness. This is despite the fact that the treatments being tested, arresting an offender versus separating the couple for a time period (treatments), arguably differ in their costs to the service provider (police), to the victim and offender, and to society. Guidelines on measuring different kinds of costs are available in textbooks on evaluation (see, e.g., Rossi & Freeman,

1993). Illustrations are contained in such texts, in reports of the kind cited earlier, and in monographs on cost-effectiveness analysis (e.g., Gramlich, 1990).

Missingness here refers to failures to obtain data on who was assigned to and received what treatments, on what the outcome or response to treatment was for each individual or unit, and on baseline characteristics of each participant. A missing data registry, a compilation of what data are missing from whom at what level of measurement, is not yet a formal part of a measurement system in many social experiments. The need for such registries is evident. The rate of follow-up on victims in ambitious police experiments such as SARP, for example, does not exceed 80%. On the other hand, follow-up based on police records is nearly perfect. Understanding the missingness rate and especially how the rate may differ among treatments (and can be affected by treatments) is obviously valuable for the study at hand and for designing better studies. Understanding *why* data are missed is no less important, but the relevant state of the art in the experiments in contrast to national surveys is not well developed. This presents an opportunity for able new experimenters and qualitative researchers to go beyond precedent.

Management

Three features of the management of experiments are important in executing field tests. The first involves identifying and recruiting partners who are competent. Some arrangements in the SARP experiments, for instance, involved joint efforts between a police department and a private research group. In Milwaukee, this partnership included the Milwaukee Police Department and the Crime Control Institute of Washington, D.C. The Omaha Police Department and the Behavioral Research Institute at the University of Colorado joined in Omaha's experiment. The types of arrangements possible are numerous, but developing linkages that are productive between practitioners and researchers is not easy.

A second feature that is important in medium- and larger-scale efforts is the formation of advisory groups. Researchers may choose a committee to help assure that the experiment is run well locally. Or they may construct committees that help to address technical issues, or political ones, or both, that assist in meeting naive as well as informed attempts to attack a fragile but important effort to get evidence. In some of the SARP sites, for example, representatives of community groups such as victims' advocates for the local police department and social services agencies advised and facilitated the experiment's emplacement. In multisite, large-scale evaluations, an oversight group may be formed by the experiments' sponsor (Reiss & Boruch 1991).

Third and most obviously, experiments depend on good planning and management of the tasks that they engender. No texts on this topic exist; however, fine descriptions appear at times in reports issued by experiment teams. See, for instance, Sherman, Schmidt, and Rogan (1992) on managing the Milwaukee SARP and Dolittle and Traeger (1990) on the massive Job Training Partnership Act study. Occasionally, advice based on the experience of able managers of evaluation research can also be found. Hedrick, Bickman, and Rog (1993), for instance, counsel applied researchers in how to think about resources, data, time, personnel, and money in planning applied social research and assuring that it is done well. Their advice is pertinent to the running of field experiments of the kind described here and ought to be exploited.

Understanding what tasks need to be done, by whom, when, and how is basic to management in this arena as in others. The tasks fall to both sponsor and experiment team at times, for example, in clarifying the role of each and in developing partnerships and advisory groups. Part of the experiment team's responsibilities include scouting and recruitment of sites for the experiment, for not all sites will be appropriate, on account of small sample size for instance, or willingness to cooperate in an experiment. The tasks include outreach within a site by the experiment team or program staff to identify and screen individuals who are eligible to participate in the experiment. Contact with individuals must be maintained over time, of course, requiring forward and backward tracing and contact maintenance methods of the kinds used in the Perry Preschool Experiments over a 20-year period (Schweinhart, Barnes, & Weikert, 1993), among others. Interviews are usually done, and this must often be coupled to separate related efforts to capitalize on administrative record systems. In the SARP, for example, the researchers accessed police records to learn about offenders' arrests following treatment and also sought victim reports through interviews. Treatments must be randomly allocated, and so, as suggested earlier, this activity must be handled so as to insulate it from field staff. And, of course, management requires attention to treatment delivery. Although responsibility for this usually lies with program staff, as in human resources training and work-welfare experiments, the burden may be borne by the experiment team in smaller-scale studies such as the SARP. In the latter case, for instance, police departments and experiment staff shared the responsibility for assuring that cases that were supposed to involve arrest and other treatments did indeed do so.

Analysis

Contemporary experiments usually involve at least four classes of analyses. The first class focuses on quality assurance. It entails developing information on which treatments were assigned to whom and which treatments were actually received by whom, and analyses of departures from the random assignment. Each experiment in the SARP, for instance, engaged these tasks to assure that the experiments were executed as designed and to assess the frequency and severity of departures from design during the study and at its conclusion. Quality assurance also usually entails examination of baseline (pretreatment) data to establish that indeed the randomized groups do not differ systematically prior to treatment. Presenting tables on the matter in final reports is typical. See, for example, Schuerman et al. (1994) on Families First programs, Solomon and

Draine (1993) on the treatment of individuals released from jails who are mentally ill, and Dunford et al. (1990) on the Omaha Domestic Violence Experiment. Quality assurance may also include side studies on measurement and preliminary core analysis that precedes the final core analysis.

Core analysis usually refers to the basic comparisons among treatments that were planned prior to the experiment. The fundamental theme underlying the core analysis is to "analyze them as you have randomized them." That is, the groups that are randomly assigned to each treatment are compared regardless of which treatment was actually received. At this level of analysis, departures from assignment then are ignored.

This approach is justified on statistical grounds, notably, the theory underlying formal test of hypotheses and the logic of comparing equivalent groups. It also has a policy justification: Under real field conditions, one can often expect departures from an assigned treatment. In the Spouse Assault Replication Program, for instance, some individuals who were assigned to a mediation treatment then became obstreperous and were then arrested; arrest was a second randomized treatment. Such departures occur normally in field settings. Comparing randomly assigned groups regardless of actual treatment delivered recognizes that a reality of core analysis is basic in medical and clinical trials (e.g., Friedman et al., 1985; Meinert, 1986) as in the social and behavioral sciences (Riecken et al., 1974).

The product of the core analysis is an estimate of relative treatment difference, addressing the question, What works for whom? and a statistical statement of confidence in the result, based on randomized groups. Where departures from random assignment are substantial, the researcher has to decide whether any core analysis is warranted and indeed whether the experiment has been executed at all. The experiment or core analysis or both may have to be aborted. If information on the origins or process of departures has been generated, as it should be, the researcher may design and execute a better experiment. This sequence of failure and trying again is a part of science generally, of course, not just applied social science. See, for instance, Silverman's (1989) descriptions of research on retrolental fibroplasia, covering blindness of premature infants as a function of enriched oxygen environments.

Levels of analysis that are deeper than "core" are often warranted on account of the complexity of the phenomenon under study or on account of serious unanticipated problems in the study's execution. For example, finding "no differences" among treatments may be a consequence of using treatments that were far less different than the researcher anticipated, inadequate sample size (i.e., low statistical power), or unreliable or invalid measures of the outcomes for each group. The matter is understudied, but good counsel has been developed by Yeaton and Sechrest (1986, 1987) and Julnes and Mohr (1989). The special case of experiments that are designed to establish the equivalence of treatment regimens is handled by Rogers, Howard, and Vessey (1993) in the context of psychological therapies.

A final class of analysis in experiments, one that demands more development, directs attention to how the current experiment's results relate to other similar studies and other populations to which one might wish to generalize. Exploring how a given study fits into the larger scientific literature on related studies is often difficult. One disciplined approach to the task lies in exploiting the practice underlying high-quality meta-analyses. That is, the researcher does a conscientious accounting for each study of who or what was the target (eligibility for treatments, target samples and population), what variables were measured and how, the character of the treatments and control conditions, how the specific experiment was designed, and so on. For example, the U.S. General Accounting Office (1994) formalized such an approach to understand the relative effectiveness of mastectomy and lumpectomy on 5-year survival rates of breast cancer victims. See Lipsey (1992, 1993) in the juvenile delinquency arena, Light and Pillemer (1984) in education, Cordray and Fischer (1994), and the U.S. General Accounting Office (1992, 1994) more generally on the topic of synthesizing the results of studies. Each contains implications for understanding how to view the experiments at hand against earlier work.

Reporting

The topic of "reporting" an experiment has an uneven history across the academic disciplines. The medical sciences have led the way in developing standards for reporting (e.g., Chalmers et al., 1981). In the social sciences, no similar standards have been produced, partly because randomized experiments have become a standard for evidence more recently than in the medical sector. Evaluation researchers who undertake experiments cut across disciplines. They must then recognize various standards and the influences on them.

The fundamental issues in reporting, to judge from contemporary experiments, are as follows:

- *To whom* should information about the experiment be reported?
- *How* should the information be reported?
- *In what form* should the information be reported?

To whom information should be reported usually depends on who sponsored the study and on the legal responsibilities of the sponsor and the experimenter. In the United States, executing an experiment is often a matter of contract between a government agency and the contractor or between a private foundation and a contractor. For instance, the U.S. Department of Education engaged a private contractor to undertake controlled experiments on dropout prevention (Dynarski et al., 1995). The Social Security Administration engaged Abt Associates to study various ways to enhance the productivity of physically and emotionally disabled individuals. In each case, the experimenter's responsibility, as contractor, was to report to the sponsor of the study. Where resources and opportunity are ample, the researcher may also have a responsibility to report to those who oversee the direct sponsor, such as the U.S. Congress or a state legislature.

When the experiment is sponsored by a grant from a private or public foundation, the reporting requirement is less restrictive. Most such arrangements recognize the independence of the principal investigator. Each SARP research team that received a federal grant (not a contract) to study the effects of different approaches to police handling of domestic violence did not legally have to report first to the grant agency, the National Institute of Justice. In this case, grantees issued press releases and reports on their work without intensive prior vetting by NIJ and to good effect (e.g., Sherman & Cohn, 1989).

When and what information on an experiment should be reported is determined partly by the sponsor. A government agency can, and should, require reports from a contractor on progress at specified times. Government or private foundations avoid distracting grantees with report requirements for grants. Generally, contract-sponsored experimenters are required to report in accord with provisions of the contract. Regardless of the financial arrangement, contemporary good practice entails reporting on all elements of the experiment, including its justification, authorization, purpose, statistical design, and analysis of results.

In the best of reports, problems in executing the design or in analysis are handled, sponsorship and potential conflicts of interest are acknowledged, and idiosyncratic ethical, legal, or methodological problems are discussed. Ideally, parts of the reports on such issues may be published in research journals. Dennis (1990), for instance, provides a detailed accounting of methodological problems encountered in experiments on drug abuse treatment programs undertaken by the Research Triangle Institute. His description of validity problems and ways to handle them builds on the contributions of Cook and Campbell (1979), among others, to understanding of the evidential and judgmental basis for conclusions. No formal standards have been promulgated for the content of reports on social experiments, but Boruch (1997) provides a checklist based on contemporary good practice. This list is similar to one prepared for reports on clinical trials in medicine issued by the Standards of Reporting Trials Group (1994).

The forms in which reports are issued are determined by agencies that sponsor contracts and sometimes by those that make grants. The fundamental forms include (a) prose reports accompanied by numerical tables and charts and (b) public use of data sets that permit verification and reanalyses. For instance, the National Institute of Justice asked that each SARP grantee provide both kinds of information for the NIJ within a few months of the grant period's end.

Thoughtful experimenters and sponsors of experiments have, at times, tried to enlarge on the form of reporting. Metzger (1993) and his colleagues have, for example, produced videotapes to assure that individuals who were eligible for HIV vaccine trials were well-informed about their options. The

Rockefeller Foundation (1988, 1990) produced videotapes on the foundation's experiments on programs for single female parents, apparently to good effect. Contemporary experiments will doubtless depend on a variety of channels for sharing information. Little research has been conducted on new vehicles for reporting on experiments, such as the World Wide Web.

■ *Concluding Remarks*

During the 1960s, when Donald T. Campbell developed his prescient essays on the experimenting society, fewer than 100 formal field experiments had been mounted to test domestic programs. The large number of randomized experiments undertaken since then is countable, but not without substantial effort. Building durable or even reliable temporary knowledge in the social sciences lies partly in this activity. It helps us to transcend debates about quality of evidence and, instead, to grapple with social choices based on good evidence. In the absence of controlled experiments on policy and programs, we will, in Walter Lippman's (1933) words, leave matters to the unwise ". . . those who bring nothing constructive to the process, and who greatly imperil the future . . . by leaving great questions to be fought out by ignorant change on the one hand, and ignorant opposition to change on the other."

■ *References*

Aiken, L. S., & West, S. G. (1990). Invalidity of true experiments: Self-report pretest bias. *Evaluation Review, 14,* 374-390.

Barnett, W. S. (1985). Benefit-cost analysis of the Perry Preschool program and its long-term effects. *Educational Evaluation and Policy Analysis, 7,* 333-342.

Berk, R. A., Smyth, G. K., & Sherman, L. W. (1988). When random assignment fails: Some lessons from the Minneapolis Spouse Abuse Experiment. *Journal of Quantitative Criminology, 4,* 209-223.

Bloom, H. S. (1990). *Back to work: Testing reemployment services for displaced workers.* Kalamazoo, MI: W. E. Upjohn Institute for Employment Research.

Borenstein, M., & Cohen, J. (1990). *Statistical power analysis.* Hillsdale, NJ: Lawrence Erlbaum.

Boruch, R. F. (1994). The future of controlled randomized experiments: A briefing. *Evaluation Practice, 15,* 265-274.

Boruch, R. F. (1997). *Randomized controlled experiments for planning and evaluation: A practical guide.* Thousand Oaks, CA: Sage.

Boruch, R. F., Dennis, M., & Carter, K. (1988). Lessons from the Rockefeller Foundation's experiments on the Minority Female Single Parent Program. *Evaluation Review, 12,* 396-426.

Brooten, D., Savitri, K., Brown, L., Butts, P., Finkler, S., Bakewell-Sachs, S., Gibbons, A., & Delivoria-Papadopolous, M. (1986). A randomized clinical trial of early hospital discharge and home follow-up of very low birth weight infants. *New England Journal of Medicine, 315,* 934-939.

Burghardt, J., & Gordon, A. (1990). *More jobs and higher pay: How an integrated program compares with traditional programs.* New York: Rockefeller Foundation.

Campbell, D. T., & Stanley, J. C. (1966). *Experimental and quasi-experimental designs for research.* Chicago: Rand McNally.

Chalmers, T. C., Smith, H., Blackburn, B., Silverman, B., Schroeder, B., Reitman, D., & Ambroz, A. (1981). A method for assessing the quality of a randomized controlled trial. *Controlled Clinical Trials, 2*(1), 31-50.

Cochran, W. G. (1983). *Planning and analysis of observational studies* (L. E. Moses & F. Mosteller, Eds.). New York: John Wiley.

Cohen, J. (1992). A power primer. *Psychological Bulletin, 112,* 155-159.

Collins, J. F., & Elkin, I. (1985). Randomization in the NIMH treatment of depression collaborative research program. *New Directions for Program Evaluation, 28,* 27-38.

Conner, R. F. (1977). Selecting a control group: An analysis of the randomization process in twelve social reform programs. *Evaluation Quarterly, 1,* 195-243.

Cook, T. D., & Campbell, D. T. (1979). *Quasi-experimentation: Design and analysis issues for field settings.* Chicago: Rand McNally.

Cordray, D. S., & Fischer, R. L. (1994). Synthesizing evaluation findings. In J. S. Wholey, H. H. Hatry, & K. Newcomer (Eds.), *Handbook of practical program evaluation* (pp. 198-231). San Francisco: Jossey-Bass.

Cottingham, P. H. (1991). Unexpected lessons: Evaluation of job training programs for single mothers. In R. S. Turpin & J. N. Sinacore (Eds.), *Multi-site evaluation* (pp. 59-70). San Francisco: Jossey-Bass.

Cox, D. R. (1958). *Planning of experiments.* New York: John Wiley.

Coyle, S. L., Boruch, R. F., & Turner, C. F. (Eds.). (1991). *Evaluating AIDS prevention programs.* Washington, DC: National Academy of Sciences Press.

Crain, R. L., Heebner, A. L., & Si, Y. (1992). *The effectiveness of New York City's career magnet schools: An evaluation of ninth grade performance using an experimental design.* Berkeley, CA: National Center for Research in Vocational Education.

Dennis, M. L. (1988). *Implementing randomized field experiments: An analysis of criminal and civil justice research.* Unpublished Ph.D. dissertation, Northwestern University, Department of Psychology.

Dennis, M. L. (1990). Assessing the validity of randomized field experiments: An example from drug abuse treatment research. *Evaluation Review, 14,* 347-373.

Dolittle, F., & Traeger, L. (1990). *Implementing the national JTPA study.* New York: Manpower Demonstration Research Corporation.

Dunford, F. W., Huizinga, D., & Elliott, D. S. (1990). The Omaha Domestic Violence Experiment. *Criminology, 28,* 183-206.

Dynarski, M., Gleason, P., Rangarajan, A., & Wood, R. (1995). *Impacts of dropout prevention programs.* Princeton, NJ: Mathematica Policy Research.

Ellickson, P. L., & Bell, R. M. (1990). Drug prevention in junior high: A multi-site longitudinal test. *Science, 247,* 1299-1306.

Fantuzzo, J. F., Jurecic, L., Stovall, A., Hightower, A. D., Goins, C., & Schachtel, D. (1988). Effects of adult and peer social initiations on the social behavior of withdrawn, maltreated preschool children. *Journal of Consulting and Clinical Psychology, 56*(1), 34-39.

Farrington, D. P. (1983). Randomized experiments on crime and justice. *Crime and Justice: Annual Review of Research, 4,* 257-308.

Federal Judicial Center. (1983). *Social experimentation and the law.* Washington, DC: Author.

Finn, J. D., & Achilles, C. M. (1990). Answers and questions about class size: A statewide experiment. *American Education Research Journal, 27,* 557-576.

Fisher, R. A. (1935). *The design of experiments.* Edinburgh: Oliver & Boyd.

Friedman, L. M., Furberg, C. D., & DeMets, D. L. (1985). *Fundamentals of clinical trials.* Boston: John Wright.

Garner, J., Fagen, J., & Maxwell, C. (1995). Published findings from the Spouse Assault Replication Program: A critical review. *Journal of Quantitative Criminology, 11*(1), 3-28.

Gramlich, E. M. (1990). *Guide to benefit cost analysis.* Englewood Cliffs, NJ: Prentice Hall.

Gueron, J. M., & Nathan, R. (1985). The MDRC Work/Welfare Project: Objectives, status, and significance. *Policy Studies Review, 4*(3).

Gueron, J. M., & Pauly, E. (1991). *From welfare to work.* New York: Russell Sage Foundation.

Hedrick, T. E., Bickman, L., & Rog, D. J. (1993). *Applied research design: A practical guide.* Newbury Park, CA: Sage.

Hollister, R. G., Kemper, P., & Maynard, R. (1984). *The National Supported Work Program.* Madison: University of Wisconsin Press.

Julnes, G., & Mohr, L. B. (1989). Analysis of no-difference findings in evaluation research. *Evaluation Review, 13,* 628-655.

Idea Works, Inc. (1993). *Ex-Sample (Statistical Power Software).* Columbia, MO: Author.

Kempthorne, O. (1952). *The design and analysis of experiments.* New York: John Wiley.

Kraemer, H. C., & Thiemann, S. (1987). *How many subjects? Statistical power analysis in research.* Newbury Park, CA: Sage.

Leviton, L., & Schuh, R. (1991). Evaluation of outreach as a project element. *Evaluation Review, 15,* 533-554.

Light, R. J., & Pillemer, D. B. (1984). *Summing up: The science of reviewing research.* Cambridge, MA: Harvard University Press.

Light, R. J., Singer, J. D., & Willett, J. B. (1990). *By design: Planning research on higher education.* Cambridge MA: Harvard University Press.

Lippman, W. (1933, 1963) The Savannal speech. In C. Rossiter & J. Lare (Eds.), *The essential Lippman.* New York: Random House.

Lipsey, M. W. (1990). *Design sensitivity: Statistical power for experimental design.* Newbury Park, CA: Sage.

Lipsey, M. W. (1992). Juvenile delinquency treatment: A meta-analysis inquiry into the variability of effects. In T. D. Cook, H. M. Cooper, D. S. Cordray, H. Hartmann, L. V. Hedges, R. J. Light, T. Louis, & F. Mosteller, *Meta-analysis for explanation: A casebook* (pp. 83-127). New York: Russell Sage Foundation.

Lipsey, M. W. (1993). Theory as method: Small theories of treatments. In L. B. Sechrest & A. G. Scott (Eds.), *Understanding causes and generalizing about them* (pp. 5-38). San Francisco: Jossey-Bass.

Meinert, C. L. (1986). *Clinical trials: Design, conduct, and analysis.* New York: Oxford University Press.

Metzger, D. (1993). *Trials on trial* [Videotape]. Philadelphia: University of Pennsylvania/VAMC Center for Studies of Addiction.

Miles, M. B., & Huberman, A. M. (1994). *Qualitative data analysis: An expanded sourcebook* (2nd ed.). Thousand Oaks, CA: Sage.

Mosteller, F. (1986). Errors: Nonsampling errors. In W. H. Kruskal & J. M. Tanur (Eds), *International encyclopedia of statistics* (Vol. 1, pp. 208-229). New York: Free Press.

Mosteller, F., Light, R. J., & Sachs, J. (1995). *Sustained inquiry in education: Lessons from ability grouping and class size.* Cambridge, MA: Harvard University, Center for Evaluation of the Program on Initiatives for Children.

Murarka, B. A., & Spiegelman, R. G. (1978). *Sample selection in the Seattle and Denver Income Maintenance Experiment* (SRI Technical Memorandum No. 1). Menlo Park, CA: SRI International.

O'Sullivan, A., & Jacobsen, B. S. (1992). A randomized trial of a health care program for first-time adolescent mothers and their infants. *Nursing Research, 41,* 210-215.

Patton, M. Q. (1990). *Qualitative evaluation and research methods* (2nd ed.). Newbury Park, CA: Sage.

Perng, S. S. (1985). The Accounts Receivable Treatments Study. In R. F. Boruch & W. Wothke (Eds.), *Randomization and field experimentation* (pp. 55-62). San Francisco: Jossey-Bass.

Porter, A. C. (1988). Comparative experimental methods in educational research. In R. M. Jaeger (Ed.), *Complementary methods for research in education* (pp. 391-417). Washington, DC: American Educational Research Association.

Reiss, A. J., & Boruch, R. F. (1991). The program review team approach to multi-site experiments: The Spouse Assault Replication Program. In R. S. Turpin & J. N. Sinacore (Eds.), *Multi-site evaluation* (pp. 33-44). San Francisco: Jossey-Bass.

Riecken, H. W., Boruch, R. F., Campbell, D. T., Caplan, N., Glennau, T. K., Pratt, J. W., Rees, A., & Williams, W. W. (1974). *Social experimentation: A method for planning and evaluating social programs.* New York: Academic Press.

Rockefeller Foundation. (1988). *Irrefutable evidence: Lessons from research funded by the Rockefeller Foundation* [Videotape]. New York: Author.

Rockefeller Foundation. (1990). *Into the working world* [Videotape]. New York: Author.

Rogers, J. L., Howard, K. I., & Vessey, J. T. (1993). Using significance tests to evaluate equivalence between two experimental groups. *Psychological Bulletin, 113,* 553-565.

Rosenbaum, P. R. (1995). *Observational studies.* New York: Springer-Verlag.

Rossi, P. H., & Freeman, H. F. (1993). *Evaluation: A systematic approach* (5th ed.). Newbury Park, CA: Sage Publications.

Roth, J. A., Scholz, J. T., & Witte, A. D. (Eds.). (1989). *Paying taxes: An agenda for compliance research* (Report of the Panel on Research on Tax Compliance Behavior National Academy of Sciences). Philadelphia: University of Pennsylvania.

St. Pierre, R., Swartz, J., Murray, S., Deck, D., & Nickel, P. (1995). *National evaluation of Even Start family literacy program* (USDE Contract LC 90062001). Cambridge, MA: Abt Associates.

Schuerman, J. R., Rzepnicki, T. L., & Littell, J. (1994). *Putting families first: An experiment in family preservation.* New York: Aldine de Gruyter.

Schwartz, R. D., & Orleans, S. (1967). On legal sanctions. *University of Chicago Law Review, 34*(274), 282-300.

Schweinhart, L. J., Barnes, H. V., & Weikert, D. P. (1993). *Significant benefits: The High/Scope Perry Preschool Study through age 27.* Ypsilanti, MI: High/Scope Press.

Sherman, L. W., & Berk, R. A. (1984). The specific deterrent effects of arrest for domestic assault. *American Sociological Review, 49,* 261-272.

Sherman, L. W., & Cohn, L. (1989). The impact of research on legal policy: The Minneapolis Domestic Violence Experiment. *Law and Society Review, 23,* 117-144.

Sherman, L. W., Schmidt, J. D., & Rogan, D. P. (1992). *Policing domestic violence: Experiments and dilemmas.* New York: Free Press.

Sieber, J. E. (1992). *Planning ethically responsible research: A guide for students and internal review boards.* Newbury Park, CA: Sage.

Silverman, W. A. (1989). *Human experimentation.* New York: Oxford University Press.

Solomon, P., & Draine, J. (1993). The efficacy of a consumer case management team: Two year outcomes of a randomized trial. *Journal of Mental Health Administration, 22*(2), 135-146.

Solomon, P., & Draine, J. (1995). One-year outcome of a randomized trial of case management with seriously mentally ill clients leaving jail. *Evaluation Review, 19,* 256-273.

Standards of Reporting Trials Group. (1994). A proposal for structural reporting of randomized clinical trials. *Journal of the American Medical Association, 272,* 1926-1931.

Stanley, B., & Sieber, J. E. (Eds.). (1992). *Social research on children and adolescents: Ethical issues.* Newbury Park, CA: Sage.

Stigler, S. M. (1978). Mathematical statistics in the early states. *Annals of Statistics, 6,* 239-265.

U.S. Department of Education, Planning and Evaluation Service. (1991a). *Request for proposals: Evaluation of Upward Bound programs.* Washington. DC: Government Printing Office.

U.S. Department of Education, Planning and Evaluation Service. (1991b, February 4). School dropout demonstration assistance program: Notice inviting applications for new awards for fiscal year FY 1991 (CFDA No. 84.201). *Federal Register, 56,* 4364-4369.

U.S. General Accounting Office. (1992). *Cross-design synthesis: A new strategy for medical effectiveness research* (Publication No. GAO/PEMD-92-18). Washington, DC: Government Printing Office.

U.S. General Accounting Office. (1994). *Breast conservation versus mastectomy: Patient survival in day to day medical practice and in randomized studies* (Publication No. PEMD-95-9). Washington, DC: Government Printing Office.

Wargo, M. J. (1989). Characteristics of successful program evaluation. In J. S. Wholey & K. E. Newcomb (Eds.), *Improving government performance: Evaluation strategies for strengthening public agencies and programs* (pp. 71-82). San Francisco: Jossey-Bass.

Yeaton, W. H., & Sechrest, L. (1987). No difference research. *New Directions for Program Evaluation, 34,* 67-82.

Yeaton, W. H., & Sechrest, L. (1986). Use and misuse of no difference findings in eliminating threats to validity. *Evaluation Review, 10,* 836-852.

Yin, R. M. (1989). *Case study research design and methods.* Newbury Park, CA: Sage.

7

Quasi-experimentation

Charles S. Reichardt
Melvin M. Mark

Applied social science researchers are often interested in assessing the effects of treatments. For example, program evaluators have estimated the effects of television shows, drug abuse interventions, and human resources training programs, to name just a few of the types of treatments that have been of interest. Randomized experiments and quasi-experiments are two research designs that are used to assess the effects of treatments. In both randomized experiments and quasi-experiments, comparisons are drawn between what happens when a treatment is present and what happens when no treatment (or an alternative treatment) is present. The difference between these two design types is that in a randomized experiment, a random process determines who receives the treatment and who receives the no-treatment or alternative treatment condition, whereas in a quasi-experiment, assignment to treatment conditions is determined nonrandomly.

In this chapter we focus on quasi-experiments, explicating four prototypical quasi-experimental designs: before-after, interrupted time series, regression-discontinuity, and nonequivalent group designs. For purposes of comparison, we also briefly discuss randomized experiments.

■ Threats to Validity

The size of a treatment effect depends on five factors: the cause, the recipients, the setting, the time, and the outcome variable. Consider each of these five factors in turn. First, the size of the treatment effect depends on the treatment or cause. For example, the effect of taking an aspirin is different from the effect of taking an antihistamine, and the effect of taking one aspirin tablet is different from the effect of taking two. Second, the size of the treatment effect depends upon the recipients, that is, on who receives the treatment. For example, the effect of aspirin can differ across people, reducing headache pain in most but perhaps increasing headache pain in those allergic to aspirin. Third, the size of the treatment effect depends on the setting. For example, the effect of aspirin on headache pain can depend on the surrounding environment, perhaps having little effect in a noisy bar but a large effect in a quiet seaside cottage. Fourth, the size of the treatment effect depends on the time between when the treatment is administered and when the effect is assessed. For example, aspirin takes time to have any effect on headache pain, then the effect increases, and then the effect subsequently decreases over time. Fifth, the size of the treatment effect depends on the outcome variable. For example, aspirin can affect headache pain and the risk of a heart attack, but has little or no effect on visual acuity and weight loss.

To designate the treatment effect that is being assessed, a researcher specifies or labels the five factors described above. However, the researcher could misspecify or mislabel any of these five factors. For example, imagine that a researcher estimates the effect of a treatment by comparing those who volunteer for the treatment with those who refuse to take the treatment. Further, suppose the researcher concludes that observed differences in outcome are due to the treatment, whereas the observed differences in outcome are really due to initial differences between volunteers and nonvolunteers—differences that would have been present even if the two groups of individuals had received the same treatment. In this case the researcher has misspecified or mislabeled the cause of the effect: The effect is due not to the treatment, as the researcher concludes, but to initial differences between the treatment groups. In analogous ways, a researcher may also mislabel the setting, recipients, time, and/or outcome variable.

That an alternative label for one of the five factors might be correct threatens the validity of the label that has been given. For this reason, an alternative label is called a *threat to validity.* In the preceding example, the presence of initial differences between the treatment groups is a threat to validity because these initial differences could account for the treatment effect but were ignored in the label that was given by the researcher. Threats to validity are also called *rival hypotheses* or *alternative explanations,* because a threat to validity provides an alternative way to account for an effect. One of the major tasks of the researcher in estimating treatment effects is to recognize and cope with threats to validity.

In their pioneering work on quasi-experiments, Campbell and Stanley (1963, 1966) codified two types of threats to validity, internal and external. Cook and Campbell (1975, 1979) have expanded the list into five categories of threats: internal validity, construct validity of the cause, construct validity of the effect, external validity, and statistical conclusion validity. Cook and Campbell's five types of validity threats concern mislabelings of the five factors of an effect; however, the mapping from the five types of threats to the five factors is not one-to-one but somewhat more complicated (Mark, 1986). As we shall see, internal validity and construct validity of the cause are both mislabelings of the cause. Construct validity of the effect is a mislabeling of the outcome variable. External validity is a mislabeling of the recipients, setting, or time. Statistical conclusion validity is a mislabeling of the uncertainty that exists about an estimate of a treatment effect. We describe each of these five types of threats to validity further below.

☐ *Internal Validity*

The effect of Treatment A, compared with Treatment B, is the difference between (a) the outcome that would have arisen at Time 2 if Treatment A had been administered at Time 1 and (b) the outcome that would have arisen at Time 2 if Treatment B had been administered at Time 1 instead but (c) everything else at Time 1 had been the same. The effect of Treatment A compared with no treatment is defined in the same way, but with "no treatment" replacing "Treatment B" in the definition. For example, the effect that aspirin, compared with no aspirin, has on headache pain is the difference between (a) the headache pain that would have been present if aspirin had been taken some time earlier and (b) the headache pain that would have been present if no aspirin had been taken at the earlier time but (c) everything else had been the same initially. This comparison, between what would subsequently happen if a treatment had been given earlier and what would subsequently happen if either no treatment or an alternative treatment had been given earlier, but where everything else had initially been the same, is called the *ideal comparison.*

Unfortunately, the ideal comparison cannot be obtained in practice. This is because *everything else* cannot be the same if a treatment is to be administered in one condition and not administered in the other (or if a treatment is to be administered in one condition and an alternative treatment is to be administered in the other). Something else must differ at the time the different treatments are introduced. For example, a researcher could compare (a) headache pain in a group of individuals who earlier had taken aspirin with (b) headache pain in a group of individuals who earlier had not taken aspirin. But in this case, not only are the treatments different in the two conditions, but the individuals receiving the treatments are different as well. Alternatively, a researcher could compare headache pain in a group of individuals before taking aspirin with headache pain in that same group of individuals after taking aspirin. Although this comparison holds the individuals constant across the treatment conditions, time and changes that would occur over time even in the absence of a treatment effect are not held constant.

Obtaining the ideal comparison would require the researcher to have the ability to travel backward in time. Given this ability, the researcher could administer the treatment and measure the outcome variable at some later time. Then the researcher could go back in time so as to start over again, with everything returned to the same initial state except that no treatment (or an alternative treatment) would be administered and the outcome variable would again be measured at the same later time. In theory, this could produce the ideal comparison—but time travel is of course impossible in practice, so the ideal comparison is also impossible.

An advantage of the ideal comparison is that any difference between the treatment conditions at Time 2 could be due *only* to the treatment differences that were introduced at Time 1, because everything else would have been the same. In contrast, in any comparison that can be obtained in practice, a difference between the treatment conditions at Time 2 could be due either to the treatment differences that were introduced at Time 1 or to the other differences that existed between the treatment conditions, or to both. If a researcher concludes that an outcome difference is due to a difference in treatments when the outcome difference is at least partly due to other things that varied across the treatment conditions, he or she is making a mistake. In particular, the researcher would be mislabeling the cause of the effect. The sources of such mislabelings (i.e., the other things, besides the treatments, that vary across the treatment conditions) are called *threats to internal validity.*

For example, suppose a researcher compares two groups of individuals, one of which received aspirin and the other of which received no analgesic. Further suppose that the two groups of individuals differed in the degree of headache pain they felt at the start of the study and, as a result, would have differed in the degree of headache pain they felt at the end of the study even if they had both received the same treatment. Then, if the researcher concludes that the observed difference in headache pain at the end of the study was due to the effect of the aspirin, he or she has mislabeled the cause of the observed difference. The observed difference was due not only to any effect of the aspirin, but also to initial differences between the groups. In this example, the initial group differences, also called initial selection differences, are a threat to internal validity.

Because the ideal comparison is unattainable, threats to internal validity are always present. That is, any comparison used to estimate an effect in practice will necessarily differ from the ideal comparison, and all such differences are potential threats to internal validity. If threats to internal validity are ignored, the cause of the effect could be mislabeled. Different threats to internal validity arise in different types of comparisons. Therefore, we explicate specific threats to internal validity when we discuss different design options.

☐ *Construct Validity of the Cause*

As just described, a threat to internal validity is a mislabeling of the cause of an effect. A threat to the construct validity of the cause is also a mislabeling of the cause of an effect. But although they both involve mislabelings of the cause, the two types of threats to validity come about in different ways. As described above, a threat to internal validity is a mislabeling of the cause that arises because the comparison used in practice differs from the ideal but unattainable comparison. Another way of saying this is that threats to internal validity cannot arise in the ideal comparison. In contrast, a threat to the construct validity of the cause is a mislabeling of the cause that could arise even in the ideal comparison.

A threat to the construct validity of the cause arises if a researcher labels the treatment in terms of one theoretical construct when in fact a different theoretical construct is responsible for the effect. For example, a threat to the construct validity of the cause would be present if the researcher concludes that an effect was due to dissonance arousal when the true theoretical construct causing the effect was negative incentive. A threat to the construct validity of the cause would also be present if an investigator concludes that ingesting small amounts of a food additive caused cancer, when in fact ingesting only excessively large amounts of the additive caused cancer. A threat to the construct validity of the cause would arise if a researcher concludes that a social program was ineffective, but the program was not implemented with sufficient strength and integrity to provide a fair test. These examples all illustrate threats to the construct validity of the cause rather than threats to internal validity, because the threat could arise in either a practical or an ideal comparison.

☐ *Construct Validity of the Effect*

Threats to the construct validity of the effect involve a mislabeling of the outcome variable. For example, suppose an educational program improves reading ability but not mathematical ability. Further, suppose that because the research participants can read faster, they do better on a timed mathematics test. Then a conclusion that the program improves mathematical *ability* would be incorrect because the program, through its effect on reading, improved only mathematical *performance* and not underlying ability. In this case, the outcome variable has been mislabeled and the mislabeling is a threat to the construct validity of the effect.

For another example, suppose a researcher studies the effects that a treatment has on the number of punches a child inflicts on an inflatable clown doll. Further, suppose the researcher interprets the number of punches as a measure of aggression and, therefore, concludes that the treatment influences aggression. Finally, suppose that punching the doll really reflects only creative play, modeling of behavior, or guessing of the research hypothesis and attempting to please the experimenter. In this case, the outcome variable would be mislabeled, and the alternative labels would be threats to the construct validity of the effect. Other possible sources of threats to the construct validity of the effect include demand characteristics, response sets, approval seeking, social desirability, evaluation apprehension, direction of wording effects, yea-saying, order effects, and halo effects.

☐ *External Validity*

Threats to external validity concern the mislabeling of the recipients, setting, or time of an effect. For example, Faludi (1991) describes a study that concludes that "women between the ages of thirty-one and thirty-five . . . [have] a nearly 40 percent chance of being infertile" (p. 27). Yet the study's conclusions are based on a sample of women who were seeking to get pregnant by artificial insemination, and there are important differences between women who seek to get pregnant this way and other women. Artificial insemination, it has been estimated, is only one-fourth as likely to lead to pregnancy as is having intercourse regularly. Because the study's conclusions were applied to all women, but the results held true only for a relatively small subclass of women (those seeking pregnancy through artificial insemination), external validity was threatened: The recipients were mislabeled.

In his classic studies of obedience, Milgram (1965) demonstrated that subjects will comply with requests to administer electric shocks to others even when the shocks appear to cause great pain. Critics were quick to argue that Milgram mislabeled the setting of the effect because he implied that his results held beyond the university laboratory environment in which they were obtained. To counter this threat to external validity, Milgram subsequently obtained the same effects in other settings outside the university laboratory.

Threats to external validity can also arise through mislabelings of time. For example, antibiotics lose their effectiveness when bacteria mutate, just as DDT lost its effectiveness as an insecticide over time as insects developed resistance to it. Similarly, advertising campaigns can become boring and therefore less effective over time. The time or time lag of an effect would be mislabeled if, in any of these cases, incorrect conclusions were drawn about how the effect varied or did not vary over time.

☐ *Statistical Conclusion Validity*

Threats to statistical conclusion validity concern the mislabeling of the degree of uncertainty in an estimate of a treatment effect. The size of a treatment effect can seldom, if ever, be calculated exactly. As a result, a researcher cannot be confident that a treatment effect is equal to a precise point value. Instead, researchers can credibly conclude only that a treatment effect lies within a range of values. For example, a confidence interval is a range of values that takes account of uncertainty due to random sampling variability. A hypothesis test is a related way to account for uncertainty due to random sampling variability. In the same vein, Reichardt and Gollob (1987) introduce the notion of a plausibility bracket to take account of other sources of uncertainty besides random sampling variability.

Both a confidence interval and a plausibility bracket provide a range of estimates and a statement of the probability that the given range includes the true size of the treatment effect. If the probability is misspecified for the given range of estimates, the mislabeling is a threat to statistical conclusion validity.

Sources of threats to statistical conclusion validity include, among others, violations of the assumptions of statistical procedures and data fishing.

□   *Other Criticisms*

"Validity" is equivalent to truth. A conclusion is valid if it is true; otherwise it is invalid. As a result, a threat to validity is a criticism that a conclusion is incorrect. Of course, a conclusion can be criticized on many grounds other than that it is incorrect. In this subsection, we consider two additional criticisms involving uncertainty and irrelevance.

A conclusion can be valid and still be criticized as too uncertain. For example, if you want to know whether you should carry an umbrella tomorrow, a prediction that the chance of rain is between 0 and 100% is not wrong, but it is too uncertain to be of any use. In estimating an effect, uncertainty is represented by the width of the range of estimates within which the treatment effect lies with a specified probability. If this interval is too wide for the consumer's purposes, the conclusion can be criticized as being too uncertain. For example, a study could be correct when it concludes that the probability is .95 that a treatment to improve Scholastic Aptitude Test (SAT) scores has an average effect of between −200 and +300 points, but this interval is too wide to tell whether the course is likely to be helpful or harmful, much less to tell whether the course is worth the expense. In terms of statistical significance tests, the criticism of too much uncertainty raises the issue of power. Sources of uncertainty that increase the width of the interval of estimates of a treatment effect and reduce power in a statistical test include the unreliability of the outcome variable and heterogeneity in the respondents, the settings, the time lags, or the implementation of the treatment.

Note that statistical conclusion validity is concerned with whether the degree of uncertainty, whatever its magnitude, is labeled correctly, whereas the criticism of uncertainty is concerned with whether the magnitude of uncertainty is too large to be useful, but not with whether it is correctly labeled. In essence, criticisms of invalidity are concerned with bias, whereas criticisms of uncertainty are concerned with precision and power. Being able to bracket the size of an effect correctly is important but not sufficient. It is also important to be able to produce a narrow bracket for a specified probability.

A conclusion can also be criticized because it is irrelevant. The criticism of irrelevance is conceptually independent of both invalidity and uncertainty. For example, makers of one brand of mouthwash advertise that their product kills germs. But most people use a mouthwash to reduce bad breath, and bad breath is rarely caused by germs. The advertising claim is not incorrect, nor is it necessarily too uncertain, but it is (or should be) irrelevant to most consumers. Similarly, suppose an effect is different in the laboratory from in a field setting, that a laboratory study is conducted and the researcher correctly labels the results as applying only to the laboratory. In this case, the conclusion may well be both correct and sufficiently precise, but it will not be relevant to a practitioner who wishes to know the size of the effect in a field setting rather than in the laboratory.

In designing a study, analyzing the data, and interpreting the results, the researcher should try to determine which criticisms are most important and credible, and then try to take these criticisms into account. Which criticisms are most important and credible will vary with the research design. This is especially true with threats to internal validity. For this reason, in the ensuing discussion of design options we focus mostly on threats to internal validity.

■ *Before-After Designs*

In 1955, 324 people died in automobile accidents in the state of Connecticut (Campbell & Ross, 1968). At the end of 1955, penalties for speeding were stiffened in that state. In 1956, Connecticut traffic fatalities were only 284. By comparing the number of traffic fatalities before the speeding crackdown with the number of traffic fatalities after the crackdown, the governor of Connecticut concluded that the state's crackdown on speeding saved 40 lives, which represents a 12% reduction in fatalities.

The preceding example illustrates a before-after, or pretest-posttest, design. In a before-after design, the effect of a treatment is estimated by comparing (a) what happened before the treatment was implemented with (b) what happened after the treatment was implemented. Such a design can be schematically represented as follows:

Before Observation → Treatment → After Observation

Or, in even simpler notation, if O represents an observation and X represents a treatment, and assuming time runs from left to right, then a before-after design can be diagrammed as

O X O

Although before-after designs are easily implemented and therefore widely used, a variety of threats to internal validity can arise, resulting in mislabeling of the cause of the observed difference between the before and after observations. We describe some of the most common threats to internal validity below.

□ *History*

History refers to specific events, other than the intended treatment, that occurred between the before and after observations and that could cause changes in the outcome of interest. Consider, for example, several historical events that might have produced a decrease in traffic fatalities between 1955 and 1956, if they had occurred early in 1956: a particularly gruesome and well-published traffic accident that led people to drive more carefully; the closing or repair of a particularly dangerous road; a change in the drinking laws, such as an increase in the drinking age; or new safety legislation, such as a law requiring the use of seat belts.

☐ *Maturation*

Maturation refers to processes that occur over time within study participants, such as growing older, becoming hungrier, growing more fatigued, and growing wiser. The threat of maturation is different from the threat of history in that maturation involves relatively continuous processes emanating naturally from within study participants, whereas history involves more discrete, external events. In the Connecticut crackdown on speeding, maturation would be a threat to internal validity, for example, if the reduction in traffic fatalities came about in part due to the aging of a relatively young driving population.

☐ *Testing*

The threat of *testing* is introduced when the very act of taking a test (or recording an observation) alters the results of a later test (or later observation). For example, individuals unfamiliar with tests such as the SAT may score higher on a second taking of the test than on the first, simply because they have become more familiar with the test format. In the Connecticut crackdown on speeding, the recorded death rate in 1955 serves as the "before" observation. Testing would be a threat to internal validity if, for example, publicity about the high death rate in 1955 lowered the death rate in 1956, without any effect of the crackdown on speeding.

☐ *Instrumentation*

Instrumentation is a threat to internal validity when an apparent effect is the result of a change in a measuring instrument. One way for instrumentation to arise is through changes in calibration. For example, the national average of SAT scores rose sharply in 1995 when the test format was changed (Stecklow, 1995), and failure to account for this recalibration could lead a school district to reach erroneous conclusions about the effects of a new program or policy that was introduced at the same time. Instrumentation can also occur because of changes in the definition of an outcome variable, as illustrated by Paulos (1988): "Government employment figures jumped significantly in 1983, reflecting nothing more than a decision to count the military among the employed. Similarly, heterosexual AIDS cases rose dramatically when the Haitian category was absorbed into the heterosexual category" (pp. 124-125). And instrumentation can arise as a threat to validity because of changes in the procedures or standards of those who record the observations, as would arise if observers' standards for what constitutes aggressive behavior were to change over time.

Instrumentation would have been a threat to internal validity in the Connecticut study, for example, if in 1955 the definition of a traffic fatality included both individuals who died at the scene of an accident and those who died later in a hospital, whereas in 1956 the definition was changed to include only those individuals who died at the scene of the accident.

☐ *Regression Toward the Mean*

Regression toward the mean is a threat to internal validity that occurs most strongly when the "before" observation is either substantially higher or lower than average. In this case, the "after" observation tends to return to a more average or "normal" level, resulting in a difference between the before and after observations that is not due to the treatment. For example, the crackdown on speeding in Connecticut was imposed at the end of 1955, in part precisely because the number of traffic fatalities in 1955 was at a record high compared with previous years. As a result, traffic fatalities in 1956 were likely to be closer to the average than in 1955 even without a crackdown on speeding. The same effect is often called *spontaneous remission* in medical treatments or psychotherapy. That is, people often seek out treatment when their physical or emotional conditions are at a low ebb, and, because many conditions get better on their own, patients often improve without any intervention.

☐ *Attrition or Experimental Mortality*

Attrition, or *experimental mortality,* refers to the loss of participants in a study. Such a loss can create a difference in a before-after comparison. For example, the average test scores of college seniors tend to be higher than the average test scores of college freshmen simply because poor-performing students are more likely than high-performing students to drop out of school. Attrition would have been a threat to internal validity in the crackdown-on-speeding study if, having heard about the crackdown, reckless drivers chose to drive more in surrounding states, thereby removing from the highways a relatively accident-prone segment of the population.

☐ *Conclusions*

The before-after design is easy to implement, and so is often used. Under ideal circumstances, before-after designs can be implemented so that serious threats to validity are avoided and, therefore, so that conclusions are credible. The plausibility of threats to validity depends not only on the research design, but also on the particular content and context. For example, a threat to internal validity due to history is relatively unlikely to arise in a study of the learning of nonsense syllables. But in most circumstances, one or more of the threats to internal validity described above are likely to be sufficiently plausible and

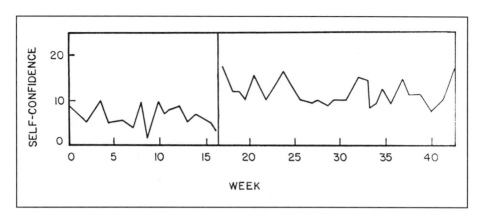

Figure 7.1. Weekly Self-Confidence Levels Both Before and After an Outward Bound Experience

SOURCE: Adapted from Smith et al. (1976) and from G. V Glass, "Quasi-experiments: The Case of Interrupted Time Series," in R. M. Jaeger (Ed.), *Complementary Methods for Research in Education* (Washington, DC: American Educational Research Association, 1988), p. 454. Copyright 1988 by the American Educational Research Association. Adapted by permission of the publisher.

sufficiently large in size that little can be learned about the size of the treatment effect using a before-after design. Consequently, it is worthwhile for researchers to consider ways to improve upon the elementary before-after design.

Interrupted Time Series Designs

The Outward Bound program offers physical and interpersonal challenges for its youthful participants to confront in the wilderness. In their study of Outward Bound, Smith, Gabriel, Schoot, and Padia (1976) assessed the effects of the program on a number of outcomes, including self-confidence. Each week, the researchers sent a questionnaire that assessed self-confidence to a random sample of the approximately 200 study participants. This weekly assessment was made for 16 weeks before the treatment. The 200 individuals then participated in a 3-week Outward Bound program and the weekly assessments continued for several months afterward. The results are presented in Figure 7.1. The vertical line after week 15 indicates when the Outward Program began. Notice the apparent increase in the posttreatment assessments of self-confidence, relative to the pretreatment assessments. This jump in self-confidence, which occurs at the time of the treatment, appears to be an effect of the Outward Bound program.

The comparison used in the preceding example is called an interrupted time series (ITS) design. Using the X and O notation introduced previously, a simple interrupted time series design can be represented in the following fashion:

O   O   O   OXO   O   O   O

In this design, a series of observations is collected over a period of time, a treatment is introduced, and then another series of observations is collected. In essence, the trend in the pretreatment observations is estimated and projected forward in time so as to provide an assessment of how the data would have appeared if there had been no treatment. In other words, the projected trend is compared with the actual trend in the posttreatment observations, and the difference between the projected and actual trends is used to estimate the effect of the treatment. For example, the abrupt and positive "interruption" in the time series of observations that occurs in Figure 7.1 at the time of the treatment suggests that the treatment had an abrupt and positive effect.

☐ *The Temporal Pattern of an Effect*

Effects can follow different patterns over time. Figure 7.2 gives examples of just a few possible patterns that a treatment effect could follow over time. In Figure 7.2, the small arrow in each time series indicates when the treatment was implemented. For simplicity, the trend in the time series before the intervention is smooth and level. As shown in Figure 7.2, a treatment could change the level, the slope, or both the level and the slope of the observations. A treatment effect could also be either immediate or delayed, and could also be either permanent or temporary.

The level of confidence that should be placed in the results of an interrupted time series design often depends on the pattern of a treatment's effect over time. For example, if an effect is delayed rather than immediate, less confidence is generally warranted unless the length of the delay is clearly predicted. The longer the delay between the start of a treatment and the start of the effect, the more opportunity there is for a threat to validity due to history to arise.

In addition, one can often have more confidence in an estimate of a treatment effect when the effect is abrupt (i.e., causes a change in level) than when the effect is gradual (i.e., causes a change in slope). This is because with a gradual effect, it is more difficult to be convinced that the data pattern is not just a curvilinear trend that would have arisen even if there had been no treatment.

☐ *More Complex ITS Designs: Adding Either a
Control Time Series or Multiple Treatment Interventions*

Regardless of the time course of the effect, the credibility of an estimate of a treatment effect depends on one's confidence that the projection of the trend in the pretreatment data into the future accurately reflects the data pattern that would arise in the absence of a treatment. Foreshadowing later comments, it is often possible to reduce uncertainty about the projected trend, and thereby reduce uncertainty about the estimate of the treatment effect, by adding a con-

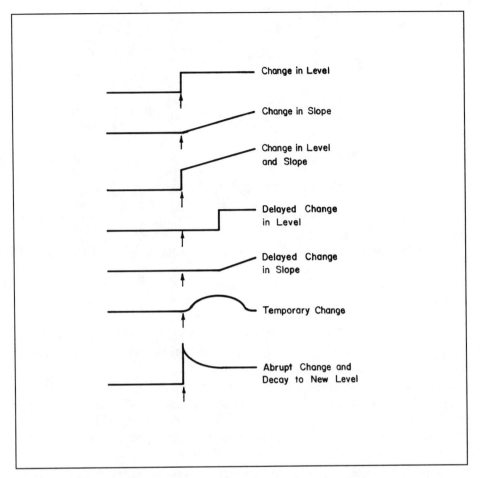

Figure 7.2. Possible Patterns That a Treatment Effect Could Follow Over Time
SOURCE: Adapted from Reichardt (1992) by permission. Original copyright © held by Praeger, an imprint of Greenwood Publishing Group, Inc.

trol time series. An ITS design with a control time series can be represented diagrammatically as follows:

$$O \quad O \quad O \quad OXO \quad O \quad O \quad O$$
$$- - - - - - - - - - - - - - -$$
$$O \quad O \quad O \quad O \quad O \quad O \quad O \quad O$$

The top line of Os represents the data from the experimental subjects who receive the treatment, whereas the bottom line of Os represents the data from the control subjects who do not receive the treatment. The broken line indicates that the two time series of observations did not come from randomly assigned groups. Ideally, the control time series would be affected by everything that affects the experimental time series, except for the treatment. To the extent this

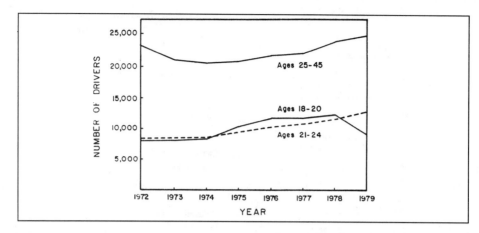

Figure 7.3. The Number of Drivers Involved in Crashes While Drinking, Plotted Yearly Both Before and After the Legal Drinking Age Was Raised in 1979 from 18 to 21

SOURCE: Adapted from Wagenaar (1981) by permission.

is the case, the control series increases one's knowledge of how the experimental series would behave in the absence of a treatment, and thereby increases one's confidence in the estimate of the treatment effect.

For example, Wagenaar (1981, 1986) was interested in the effect that an increase in the drinking age had on traffic accidents. In 1979, the drinking age in Michigan was raised from 18 to 21. To assess the effect of this change, Wagenaar (1981) plotted one experimental time series (for the number of drivers 18-20 years old who were involved in a crash) and two control series (for the number of drivers 21-24 or 25-45 years old who were involved in crashes). These time series are reproduced in Figure 7.3. A drop in fatalities occurred in 1979 only for the experimental time series—that is, only for the data from the 18- to 20-year-old drivers. The two control series add to our confidence that the dip in the experimental series is an effect of the treatment, and not due to other effects that would be shared with the control series, such as changes in the severity of weather patterns or changes in the price of gasoline (which could alter the number of miles people drive).

Other design elaborations can also be useful. When the treatment's effects are transitory (meaning they disappear when the treatment is removed), one useful option is to introduce and remove the treatment repeatedly. Such a design is diagrammatically depicted as follows:

O O O X O O O –X O O O X O O O –X O O O

where X indicates the treatment was introduced and –X indicates that the treatment was removed. For example, Schnelle et al. (1978) estimated the effects of police helicopter surveillance, as an adjunct to patrol car surveillance, on the frequency of home burglaries. As the time series in Figure 7.4 reveals, a

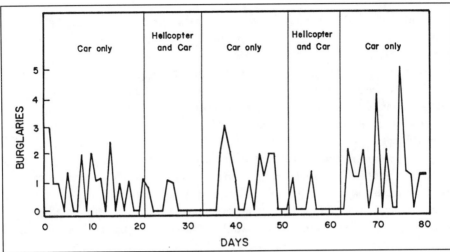

Figure 7.4. The Number of Home Burglaries When Either Police Cars or Both Police Cars and Helicopters Patrolled the Neighborhood

SOURCE: Adapted from Schnelle et al. (1978, p. 15) by permission.

baseline of observations was established with patrol car surveillance alone. Helicopter surveillance was then added, whereupon the frequency of burglaries decreased. Then helicopter surveillance was removed, whereupon the frequency of burglaries increased. Helicopter surveillance was once again reintroduced, and the frequency of burglaries again decreased, and so on.

☐ *Threats to Internal Validity*

In the preceding section on before-after designs, we introduced six threats to internal validity. Interrupted time series designs often provide a credible means of addressing these six threats.

Maturation is a threat to internal validity in the before-after design. In the interrupted time series design, the researcher estimates the pattern of maturation from the trend in the pretreatment observations. To the extent the pretreatment trend in the data can be correctly modeled and projected into the future, maturation is removed as a threat to internal validity. For example, if maturation follows a curvilinear path, the effects of maturation will be removed if the proper curvilinear model is fit to the pretreatment data and projected into the future. Adding a control time series can help in modeling the pretreatment trend and projecting it into the future.

The researcher can also use pretreatment observations to assess the likely degree of *regression toward the mean* and thereby take its biasing effects into account. In particular, the series of pretreatment observations makes it possible to tell if the observations immediately prior to the treatment are unusually high or low and, if so, to remove the validity threat by assessing the "normal" or average level to which the posttreatment observations should regress, something a simple before-after design does not allow. Again, a control time series can also help.

Testing is a threat to internal validity in the before-after design, but it is less likely to be a threat to the interrupted time series design. With observations being repeated over time before the intervention, testing effects are likely to diminish over time, and are unlikely to be powerful at the time the treatment is introduced.

Instrumentation can be a threat to validity in interrupted time series designs if the intervention is associated with changes in the way observations are defined or recorded. For example, estimating the effects of changes in sexual assault laws with an interrupted time series design can be complicated by corresponding changes in the way sexual assaults are defined (Marsh, 1985). Either a control series or careful analysis of record-keeping procedures may be necessary to determine the plausibility of such threats.

History effects are as likely in interrupted time series designs as in before-after designs, if the interval between observations is the same. However, history will generally be less plausible the shorter the time interval between observations, and sometimes time series designs will have shorter intervals. In addition, history will often be less plausible with an immediate than with a delayed effect. Further, a control time series can be used to take account of the validity threat of history to the extent the control time series is affected by the same history effects. In this case, the treatment effect is estimated as the size of the change in the experimental series after the treatment is introduced, minus the size of the change in the control series at the same point in time. The researcher can also greatly lessen the threat of history by elaborating the experimental time series so that the treatment is introduced, removed, then introduced again, and so on. To the extent history effects are unlikely to have the same pattern of decreases and increases, history becomes an implausible threat to internal validity in such a "multiple-intervention" design.

Finally, *attrition* can be a threat to validity in the ITS design just as in the before-after design. If the amount of attrition follows a relatively smooth and continuous pattern, the researcher can take the effect of attrition into account in much the same way he or she can take maturation into account, by modeling the trend in the pretreatment observations. However, if attrition is induced by the treatment itself, taking account of this threat to validity may require either a control time series that directly assesses the number of subjects who contribute to each observation or a multiple-intervention ITS design, where the treatment is repeatedly removed and reintroduced.

In short, elaborating a before-after design into an interrupted time series design can help to make threats to internal validity less plausible. Additional elaborations, such as adding a control time series or removing and repeating the treatment in a multiple-intervention design, often further reduce the plausibility of threats to internal validity.

□ *Statistical Analysis*

Within a time series of observations, data points that are adjacent in time are likely to be more similar than data points that are far apart in time. This pattern of similarity, called *autocorrelation,* violates the assumptions of typical regression analysis, which uses ordinary least squares (OLS) and otherwise would seem to be the obvious choice for analyzing data from an interrupted time series design. Although autocorrelation does not bias the estimate of the treatment effect in OLS regression, it does bias the estimate of the standard error, which invalidates both hypothesis tests and confidence intervals. This makes autocorrelation a threat to statistical conclusion validity.

At least three alternative analysis strategies are available for dealing with the threat of autocorrelation. To distinguish among the three strategies, we take note of two factors: *observations,* which refers to the number of repeated data points (e.g., how many months of monthly data), and *units,* which is the number of individuals or groups of individuals upon which separate time series of observations are available (e.g., if a separate time series of observations is collected on each of 10 individuals, there are 10 units, but if a single time series of observations is collected for a city, then there is only one unit, regardless of the population of the city). Interrupted time series designs require multiple observations but can have any number of units. Designs with both multiple units and multiple observations are sometimes called pooled cross-sectional and time series designs (Dielman, 1983, 1989).

An ITS design with only a single unit can be analyzed with autoregressive integrated moving average (ARIMA) models, though the number of observations must be relatively large, perhaps as large as 50 to 100 time points (Box & Jenkins, 1970; Box & Tiao, 1975; Glass, Willson, & Gottman, 1975; McCain & McCleary, 1979; McCleary & Hay, 1980). If there is more than one unit, an ARIMA model could be applied separately to each. In this case, the ARIMA approach allows the shape of the treatment effect and the autocorrelation structure to vary across the units. However, the ARIMA approach requires that, within any one unit, the autocorrelation structure is constant across time.

In contrast, the multivariate analysis of variance (MANOVA) approach allows the correlation structure to vary across time periods (Algina & Swaminathan, 1979; Swaminathan & Algina, 1977). But the MANOVA approach requires the autocorrelation structure and the shape of the treatment effect to be the same for all units within an experimental or control condition. In addition, the MANOVA approach requires that the number of units be substantially larger than the number of observations, though the number of observations can be quite small.

The hierarchical linear modeling (HLM) approach requires that the number of units be substantially greater than one, but the number of units need not be greater than the number of observations (Bryk & Raudenbush, 1987, 1992; Raudenbush, 1988; Raudenbush & Bryk, 1986). With the HLM approach, different models of the treatment effect can be fit to each unit and differences in the effects of the treatment across units can readily be assessed.

☐   *Conclusions*

In the interrupted time series design, a series of observations is collected over time both before and after a treatment is implemented. The trend in the pretreatment observations is projected forward in time and compared with the trend in the posttreatment observations. Differences between these two trends are used to estimate the treatment effect. The ITS design is often most credible when the effect of the treatment is relatively immediate and abrupt. Some of the advantages of the interrupted time series design are that it (a) can be used to assess the effects of the treatment on a single individual (or a single aggregated unit, such as a city), (b) can estimate the pattern of the treatment effect over time, and (c) can be implemented without the treatment's being withheld from anyone. The researcher can often strengthen the design by removing and then repeating the treatment at different points in time, adding a control time series, or both.

■ *Between-Group Designs*

In both the before-after and the interrupted time series designs, the researcher estimates the treatment effect by comparing the same individuals at different points in time, before and after the treatment. The other primary means of estimating a treatment effect (which we have illustrated in the discussion of a control time series) is by comparing different groups of individuals at the same time. Designs of this nature are called between-group designs.

In the simplest between-group design, individuals (or other experimental units) are categorized into two groups, and one group receives the treatment (the treatment group) while the other does not (the control or comparison group). Later, after the treatment has been given time to have its presumed effect, the members of both groups are assessed on an outcome measure. The difference between the groups on the outcome variable is used to estimate the size of the treatment effect.

Research participants can be categorized or assigned to groups in three basic ways, each of which produces a different between-group design and demands a different approach to take account of the most obvious threat to internal validity in between-group designs: *initial selection differences.* The threat of initial selection differences involves the possibility that, because different groups of individuals are being compared, differences between the treatment group and the control (or comparison) group on the outcome measure are due to initial differences between the groups rather than to the treatment effect. We describe below the three between-group designs and the corresponding means of addressing the threat of initial selection differences. The first between-group design to be discussed is the randomized experiment. The other two between-group designs are both quasi-experiments.

□ *The Randomized Experiment*

In a between-group randomized experiment, individuals are randomly assigned to treatment conditions. Random assignment removes any bias due to initial selection differences. It does not, however, remove *all* initial selection differences. With random assignment, the treatment groups still differ initially so that, even in the absence of a treatment effect, the mean posttest difference between the two groups is unlikely to be exactly zero. But with random assignment, initial selection differences between the groups are completely random. As a result, the classical statistical procedures of confidence intervals and hypothesis tests can well model and thereby take into account the random selection differences that exist.

Given the way the effects of random selection differences can be removed statistically, an estimate of the treatment effect that is unbiased by initial selection differences can be obtained in a randomized experiment with or without a pretest measurement. In other words, a simple two-group randomized experiment could take either of two forms:

$$
\begin{array}{ccc}
R & X & O \\
R & & O
\end{array}
$$

or

$$
\begin{array}{ccc}
R & O\ X & O \\
R & O & O
\end{array}
$$

where the R denotes random assignment to the groups. Even though a pretest is not required in a randomized experiment (as in the first design diagrammed above), there can be at least four significant advantages to having a pretest measure (as in the second design diagrammed above):

1. Pretests can increase the power and precision of the analysis, with more benefit the higher the absolute value of the correlation between the pretest and posttest.

2. Randomization is not always easy to implement and sometimes is corrupted (Boruch & Wothke, 1985; Braucht & Reichardt, 1993; Conner, 1977), and pretests can help the researcher to assess both the likelihood that the randomization procedure was compromised and the damage done by such corruption.

3. Differential attrition across the treatment groups can introduce bias into a randomized experiment, and pretests can enable the researcher to address this bias.

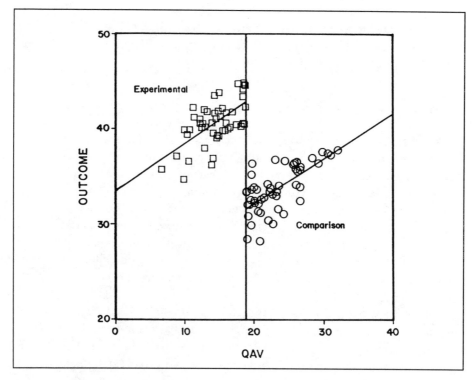

Figure 7.5. Hypothetical Data From a Regression-Discontinuity Design With a
Positive Treatment Effect

SOURCE: Adapted from Reichardt & Bormann (1994).

4. The effect of the treatment can vary across individuals with different characteristics, and the inclusion of one or more pretests allows the researcher to
estimate the size of these interactions of the treatment with individual characteristics.

☐ *The Regression-Discontinuity Design*

In the regression-discontinuity design, participants are assigned to treatment groups based on their scores on a measure called the quantitative assignment variable, or QAV. The participants who score above a specified cutoff
value on the QAV are assigned to one treatment group, and the subjects who
score below the cutoff value are assigned to the other group. (With more than
two treatment groups, more than one cutoff value would be used.) Following
assignment to the treatment groups, those in the experimental group receive
the treatment, and all participants are subsequently assessed on the outcome
measure. For example, in using a regression-discontinuity design to examine
the effect of a job layoff on plant workers, Mark and Mellor (1991) used the
number of years worked in the plant as the QAV. All those who had 19 or fewer
years of seniority were laid off; those with 20 or more years were not laid off.

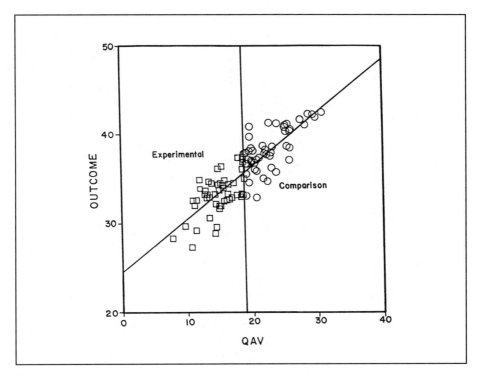

Figure 7.6. Hypothetical Data From a Regression-Discontinuity Design With No
Treatment Effect
SOURCE: Adapted from Reichardt & Bormann (1994).

To estimate the treatment effect in a regression-discontinuity design, a regression line is fit separately to the data in each treatment group. Then the treatment effect is estimated as the difference, or discontinuity, between the regression lines in the two groups. For example, Figure 7.5 presents hypothetical data depicting a positive treatment effect. In Figure 7.5, the QAV is plotted along the horizontal axis and the outcome measure is plotted along the vertical axis. The vertical line in the figure marks the cutoff value on the QAV. The squares denote the scores of subjects in the experimental group and the circles denote the scores of subjects in the control group. Separate regression lines for the regression of the outcome scores on the QAVs are drawn for each group. In this case, the treatment is estimated to have a positive effect because the regression line in the experimental group is displaced vertically above the regression line in the control group. In particular, the estimate of the treatment effect is equal to the size of the vertical displacement between these two regression lines.

In contrast to Figure 7.5, Figure 7.6 presents hypothetical data in which the treatment is estimated to have no effect. The lack of a treatment effect is revealed by the fact that neither regression line is displaced vertically relative to the other.

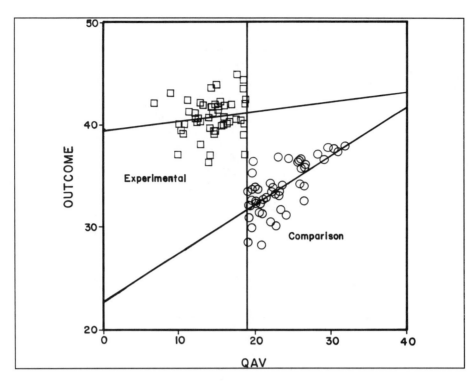

Figure 7.7. Hypothetical Data From a Regression-Discontinuity Design With a
Treatment-by-QAV Interaction

SOURCE: Adapted from Reichardt & Bormann (1994).

Figure 7.7 presents hypothetical data in which the size of the treatment
effect varies across the QAV. For subjects with lower scores on the QAV, the
treatment effect is relatively large. This is revealed by the relatively large vertical displacement between the two regression lines at low scores on the QAV.
Conversely, for subjects with higher scores on the QAV, the treatment effect
is relatively small, as indicated by the smaller vertical displacement between
the two regression lines at high scores on the QAV. In other words, there is an
interaction between the treatment and the QAV.

When interactions are present, researchers can generally place more confidence in the treatment effect estimate at the cutoff value than at any other
point along the QAV. In estimating the size of the treatment effect at any other
score, the researcher must extrapolate one of the regression lines into a region
where there are no data. For example, to estimate the size of the treatment effect
at a low score on the QAV in Figure 7.7, the researcher has to extrapolate the
regression line from the control group below the cutoff value, where there are
no control group data. In contrast, when the treatment effect is estimated right
at the cutoff value, extrapolation is kept to a minimum.

Nonetheless, if the size of the treatment effect varies along the QAV, as in
Figure 7.7, the interaction between the treatment and the QAV needs to be
taken into account in the regression lines that are fit to the data. Otherwise, the

estimate of the main effect of the treatment is likely to be biased. Similarly, if the regression slopes in either of the treatment groups are curvilinear, the regression lines that are fit to the data need to model this curvilinearity properly. Otherwise, estimates of both the main and interaction effects are likely to be biased. In other words, interactions and curvilinearity are threats to the internal validity of the regression-discontinuity design. Trochim (1984) and Reichardt, Trochim, and Cappelleri (1995) discuss procedures for modeling interactions and curvilinearity, and for performing the regression analysis in general.

The higher the correlation between the QAV and the outcome variable, the greater the precision or power of the statistical analysis. In general, a QAV that is operationally identical to the outcome variable has the highest correlation with the outcome measure. However, the QAV can be any quantitative variable on which a numerical cutoff value can be used to assign recipients to conditions.

☐ *The Nonequivalent Group Design*

In nonequivalent group designs, either subjects are self-selected into the different treatment groups or others, such as program administrators or researchers, assign subjects to the different treatment groups in some other non-random fashion. A simple posttest-only nonequivalent group design results if two groups are observed only after the treatment has been administered. Such a design can be represented as follows:

$$X \quad O$$
$$\text{-----}$$
$$O$$

where the broken line denotes that the groups are nonequivalent, which simply means that group assignment was not random. In general, the threat of initial selection differences will create great uncertainty about the size of the treatment effect in this version of the nonequivalent group design.

In a more prototypical nonequivalent group design, the groups are observed on both a pretest and a posttest. Diagrammatically, this before-after nonequivalent group design is as follows:

$$O \quad X \quad O$$
$$\text{-------}$$
$$O \qquad O$$

where the dashed line again denotes nonequivalent groups. With this design, the researcher can use the pretest to try to take account of initial selection differences, a task that can be approached in several different ways through different statistical analyses (Reichardt, 1979).

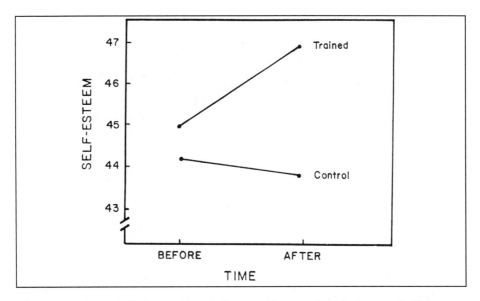

Figure 7.8. Mean Self-Esteem Scores for Two Groups of Little League Ballplayers Both Before and After the Coaches of One of the Groups Received Training to Improve Players' Self-Esteem

SOURCE: Adapted from Figure 1 (p. 606) in F. L. Smoll, R. R. Smith, N. P. Barnett, & J. J. Everett, "Enhancement of Children's Self-Esteem Through Social Support Training for Youth Sport Coaches," *Journal of Applied Psychology,* 1993, *78,* 602-610. Copyright 1993 by the American Psychological Association. Adapted with permission.

First, gain score analysis focuses on the average pretest-to-posttest gain in each group. In particular, the difference between the two groups in the average pretest-posttest gain is the estimate of the treatment effect. That is, the treatment effect is estimated by how much more or less the treatment group gained on average compared with the control group. Because it focuses on the change between the pretest and posttest, the gain score analysis is sensible only if the two measures are operationally identical.

Gain score analysis controls for simple main effects of initial selection differences. For example, imagine that the treatment group begins 15 points higher than the control group at the pretest, and would remain 15 points ahead at the posttest except for the effect of the treatment. In this case, gain score analysis would perfectly adjust for the effect of the initial selection difference. But the analysis does not control for interactions, such as a selection-by-maturation interaction, whereby one of the groups improves faster than the other group even in the absence of a treatment effect.

The credibility of gain score analysis often depends on the pattern of the results (Cook & Campbell, 1979). For example, Smoll, Smith, Barnett, and Everett (1993) used a nonequivalent group design to compare one group of Little League coaches who were given training to increase their ballplayers' self-esteem and another group of coaches who were not given this training. The self-esteem of the ballplayers in both groups was assessed both before and after

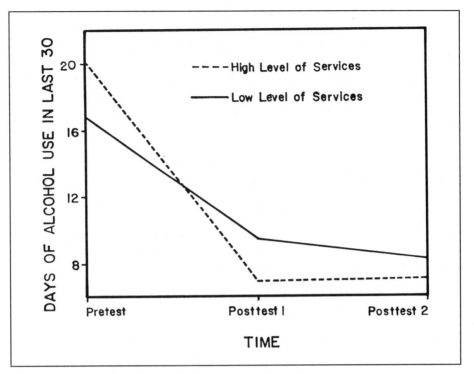

Figure 7.9. Number of Days of Alcohol Use Both Before and After Two Groups of Homeless Individuals Received Different Amounts of Substance Abuse Treatment
SOURCE: Adapted from Braucht et al. (1995, p. 103) by permission.

the treatment. The pattern of results, which is displayed in Figure 7.8, is less plausibly explained by most threats to validity than by a treatment effect. This is partly because the group difference on the pretest is small and partly because the self-esteem in the control group gets worse over time, whereas the self-esteem in the experimental group improves.

A crossover (or X-shaped) interaction is also a pattern of outcomes that can often be plausibly interpreted as a treatment effect. For example, Braucht et al. (1995) examined the effects of a continuum of services on the use of alcohol by homeless substance abusers. As Figure 7.9 reveals, those who received more services used more alcohol at the time of the pretest than those who received fewer services, but this difference is reversed at the two posttest times. Such a crossover interaction usually cannot be interpreted as due to any of the most common threats to the internal validity of the gain score analysis, such as selection-by-maturation effects and differential regression toward the mean.

An alternative analytic procedure is the analysis of covariance (ANCOVA), which controls statistically for initial selection differences. In essence, ANCOVA statistically matches individuals in the two treatment groups on their pretest scores, and uses the average difference between the matched groups on the posttest to estimate the treatment effect. Measurement error in the pretest scores will introduce bias into the ANCOVA's estimate of the treatment effect, because the statistical adjustment would not control for the true initial differences. The researcher can address this bias by obtaining parallel pretest measures and using a latent variable approach to ANCOVA (Magidson & Sorbom, 1982; Sorbom, 1978). Bias will also arise unless the statistical model includes all the variables that both affect the outcome variable and account for initial selection differences. Typically, there will be fewer such variables when the pretest is operationally identical to the posttest. But there is seldom any way to be confident that all such variables have been appropriately included in the analysis. So the possibility of bias due to initial selection differences usually remains.

More complex analysis strategies for coping with initial selection differences are also available. Interested readers are referred to Reichardt (1979), Rindskopf (1986), and Rosenbaum (1995).

☐ *Other Threats to Internal Validity in Between-Group Designs*

In addition to initial selection differences, other threats to the internal validity of between-group designs are also possible. The five additional threats described next were first emphasized by Cook and Campbell (1979).

First, *compensatory equalization of treatments* is a threat to internal validity that arises when, external to the study, alternative treatments are given to the control group to make up for the absence of the experimental treatment that is being given only to the experimental group. Second, *compensatory rivalry,* also known as the John Henry effect, can arise when control group members are aware of the treatment given to the experimental group and respond with increased competition in an effort to do just as well as the experimental group in spite of not receiving the experimental treatment (just as the mythical John Henry increased his efforts in a competition against technological innovation). Researchers can attempt to avoid this threat by trying to curtail both awareness of and expectations about the presumed benefits of the experimental treatment. Third, *resentful demoralization* is a potential threat when the treatment under study is sufficiently attractive that being assigned to the control group is aversive. In this case, the control participants might be demoralized because they were not given the desirable treatment, and this demoralization might affect their performance on the outcome variable so as to bias the results of the study. Researchers sometimes avoid this source of bias either by promising to give the same treatment to the control participants after the study is completed or by providing services to the control group that are equally attractive but not directed to the same outcomes as the experimental treatment. Fourth, *diffusion or imitation of the treatment* can occur if the control participants learn about and adopt the same treatment that is given to the experimental participants. This threat to internal validity is especially likely to arise when the experimental and control participants are in close proximity and the treatment involves a practice that can easily be imitated. Fifth, *local history* arises when historical conditions, other than the intended treatment, differ across the treatment groups. The obvious solution is for the researcher to try to treat the two groups as similarly as possible except for the intended treatments and, in the case of the nonequivalent group design, to select groups that share, as much as possible, the same historical conditions.

These five threats are threats to internal validity because they could not arise in the ideal comparison. For example, four of the five threats can arise only when study participants (or outside observers) are aware of both of the study conditions and see them as differentially desirable. But neither study participants nor outside observers could be aware of both conditions if, after implementing one, we could travel back in time before implementing the other.

☐ *Comparisons Among the Three Between-Group Designs*

Taking account of initial selection differences. In terms of taking account of initial selection differences, the randomized experiment is generally more credible than the regression-discontinuity design, which in turn is generally more credible than the nonequivalent group design. Unlike the randomized experiment, the regression-discontinuity design must correctly model any curvilinearity in the relationship between the outcome variable and the QAV as well as any interaction between the treatment and the QAV, if unbiased estimates of the treatment effect are to be obtained. Unbiased estimates in the nonequivalent group design impose even more stringent requirements on the analysis, though the data provide even less guidance in satisfying these requirements. In fact, a number of authors have warned against being overly confident about the feasibility of removing biases due to initial selection differences in the nonequivalent group design. For example, Lord (1967) notes, "With the data usually available for such studies, there simply is no logical or statistical procedure that can be counted on to make allowances for uncontrolled preexisting differences between groups" (p. 305). And there is ever-growing evidence of biases in nonequivalent group designs due to initial selection differences that were not adequately taken into account (e.g., Bunker, Barnes, & Mosteller, 1977; Chalmers, Celano, Sacks, & Smith, 1983; Director, 1979; Gilbert, Light, & Mosteller, 1975; Sacks, Chalmers, & Smith, 1982).

If the nonequivalent group design is the strongest design that can reasonably be implemented, it is generally desirable to make the treatment groups as similar as possible at the start. Often initial similarity can be maximized by using cohorts (see Cook & Campbell, 1979). In addition, it is also generally desirable to make the treatment effect as large as possible so as to overwhelm the effects of initial selection differences. In any case, the researcher should pay particular attention to the effects of initial selection differences when analyzing the data and interpreting the results from nonequivalent group designs.

Precision and power. Even if biases due to initial selection differences are completely removed, estimates of the size of the treatment effect are more precise and statistical tests of the treatment effect are more powerful in the randomized experiment than in either the regression-discontinuity design or the nonequivalent group design. For example, to have the same precision and power as the randomized experiment, the regression-discontinuity design must have at least 2.7 times as many subjects (Goldberger, 1972).

Threats to internal validity other than initial selection differences. In practice, randomized experiments and regression-discontinuity designs are more likely than nonequivalent group designs to focus attention on who gets and who does not get the experimental treatment. As a result, randomized experiments and regression-discontinuity designs are probably more likely than nonequivalent group designs to suffer from the threats to internal validity, such as compensatory rivalry, that result from participants' awareness of both conditions in a study. For example, there is good evidence that resentful demoralization is more likely to arise when assignment to treatments is random than when subjects self-select their own treatment conditions (Fetterman, 1982; Lam, Hartwell, & Jekel, 1994).

Practical and ethical considerations. Not surprisingly, the nonequivalent group design is the easiest of the three between-group designs to implement. The regression-discontinuity design is particularly well suited to settings where the treatment is assigned on the basis of need or merit, and need or merit can be quantified (e.g., Thistlethwaite & Campbell, 1960). The regression-discontinuity design would likely be used more often if it were more widely recognized as a viable option. Interestingly, the design was independently invented by Thistlethwaite and Campbell (1960; Campbell & Stanley, 1963, 1966), Goldberger (1972), and Cain (1975), with the later two inventors apparently unaware of the design's prior genesis.

The randomized experiment is often the most difficult of the three designs to implement because of resistance from service providers and because of ethical concerns about intentionally withholding potentially beneficial treatments. A variety of strategies have been devised to overcome these types of obstacles (Cook & Campbell, 1979). When withholding the treatment from a control group seems unethical, the treatment can be given to the control group after the study is completed. Alternatively, the researcher could compare alternative treatments, rather than treatment and no-treatment conditions, so that no subject is denied services. Or a treatment can be implemented in varying doses with the recognition that a less intensive dose may be just as effective while also being easier and less costly. When demand is greater than supply or when the treatment cannot be delivered to all who desire it, researchers might stress that random assignment is the fairest means of dispensing the scarce resource. In addition, researchers can argue that it is unethical to implement a weak design and thereby obtain biased results that could prolong the use of treatments that appear effective but are not (Rosenthal, 1994). In this regard, many treatments thought to be helpful have later been proved to be harmful, and many treatments thought to be harmful have later been proved to be helpful (Goodwin & Goodwin, 1984).

■ *The Logic of Ruling Out Threats to Validity*

A researcher can rule out threats to validity by (a) thinking through the implications of the treatment so as to discover ones that conflict with implications of the threat to validity and (b) obtaining data to see whether it is the implications of the treatment or of the validity threat that hold true. In other words, when a comparison is susceptible to a threat to validity, the researcher can assess the plausibility of the threat by adding a comparison that puts the treatment and the alternative explanation into competition. We call this process *competitive elaboration.*

Many of the design features previously discussed in this chapter operate by competitive elaboration. For example, competitive elaboration explains how a control time series can rule out history effects in an interrupted time series design. Consider the data from Wagenaar (1981, 1986), shown previously in Figure 7.3. The experimental time series (from ages 18-20) and the two control time series (from ages 21-24 and 25-45) should share many of the same history effects. So to the extent history effects are a threat to validity, one would predict similar patterns of change in the control and experimental series at the point the treatment is introduced. In contrast, if the treatment is effective, one would predict a different pattern of change for the experimental and control series after the treatment is introduced, because the treatment should affect only the experimental series. Because the pattern across time in the experimental and control series in Figure 7.3 is similar before the treatment is introduced but quite different afterward, the difference is more plausibly attributed to the effect of the treatment than to history effects.

Discovering implications of the treatment that conflict with implications of the threat to validity, and therefore that can be put into competition, requires thinking through how the effect of the treatment and how the effect of the threat to validity should be expected to differ across the five factors of an effect. In other words, to discover conflicting implications of the treatment and of threats to validity, one thinks of how the effects of each might differ across causes, recipients, settings, times, and outcome variables, as illustrated below.

☐ *Differential Effects Across Different Causes*

Azar (1994) describes a study by Dr. Sarah Leibowitz of Rockefeller University that examined the effect of galantin on fat ingestion. After galantin was injected into the paraventricular nucleus (PVN) of their brains, normal rats gained weight. But instead of an effect of galantin, the gain could have been due to the trauma of the injection. This threat to validity was effectively ruled out through the injection into the PVN of some rats of a substance that *blocks* galantin production, which subsequently caused a reduction in body weight. In short, different treatments would produce opposite effects, whereas the threat to validity would produce the same effect. That opposite effects were observed suggests the different treatments, rather than the threat to validity, were responsible.

Conversely, a report by Obmascik (1989) sheds doubt on a suspected treatment effect because outcomes did not vary with exposure to differing levels of the treatment. In particular, elevated cancer rates in a city were initially blamed on pollution from a neighboring arsenal. But other communities that received even more pollution from the arsenal did not have elevated cancer rates.

☐ *Differential Effects Across Different Recipients*

In the study by Wagenaar (1981, 1986), whose results are depicted in Figure 7.3, the experimental and control time series came from two different types of subjects. The treatment (an increase in the drinking age from 18 to 21) was expected to have an impact on the experimental group of 18-20-year-olds, but not on the control groups of 21-24- and 25-45-year-olds. On the other hand, threats to validity such as history effects, instrumentation, and testing were expected to have similar effects across these three different age groups. Therefore, the different pattern of outcomes across the different recipients in the experimental and the control groups was evidence in support of a treatment effect.

Glass (1988) suggested a similar strategy to assess whether a drop in enrollment in Denver public schools following court-ordered desegregation in 1969 was due to (a) white flight to the suburbs or (b) some other cause, such as a general population decline. Specifically, Glass suggested drawing comparisons across different recipients, for example, comparing enrollment declines across different racial groups. If white flight was the cause, one would expect greater declines among Caucasians than among members of other racial groups. Glass also suggested comparing enrollment declines across different socioeconomic levels (perhaps assessed by using data available for different census tracts). If white flight was the cause, one would expect greater enrollment declines among wealthier families, who could more easily afford to relocate. In contrast, the alternative explanation of a general decline in the population would predict no differential pattern of effects in either of these two comparisons (also see Underwood, 1975).

☐ *Differential Effects Across Different Settings*

Anderson (1989) examined the effect that a Scottish law mandating the use of seat belts by those riding in the front seats of cars would have on traffic injuries. A time series of the number of injuries to front-seat automobile occupants showed a dramatic decline after the law was enacted in 1983. Separate control time series plotting the number of injuries to pedestrians, rear-seat passengers, and occupants in four-wheel and other vehicles showed no corresponding declines. Thus an effect was found in precisely the setting where an effect would be expected (that is, in the front seat of cars) because this was the setting in which seat belt use was mandated, but not in other settings that would have shared the influence of most threats to validity but not the treatment effect.

□   *Differential Effects Across Different Times*

Ross, Campbell, and Glass (1970) examined the effects a 1967 crackdown on drunken driving had on traffic fatalities. The crackdown took place in Britain, where much drinking occurs in pubs and where regulations dictate when pubs can be open. A time series of the number of casualties that occurred during the hours when pubs were open (including weekend nights) showed a dramatic decline following the crackdown. In contrast, a time series of the number of casualties that occurred during the hours when pubs were closed (including commuting hours) showed no corresponding decline after the crackdown. In this way, a differential pattern of effects at different times supported the attribution of an effect to the crackdown rather than to threats to validity such as changes in weather patterns, in the safety of cars, and the like.

□   *Differential Effects Across Different Outcome Variables*

As noted previously, the data in Figure 7.9 come from a study by Braucht et al. (1995) of the effects of a treatment for substance abuse among the homeless. As shown in Figure 7.9, those who used more alcohol at the pretest received more services and subsequently exhibited less alcohol use after treatment, relative to those who used less alcohol at the start. The results are consistent with the notion that service providers recognized that individuals with initially higher alcohol use needed more services, and that these services reduced alcohol use. This pattern of results cannot plausibly be explained by threats to validity such as regression toward the mean, testing, and maturation. However, it could be argued that the pattern of results arose not because of the effectiveness of the treatment, but because of differences in motivation. That is, perhaps those who used alcohol more at the pretest both received more services and changed more because of their greater motivation, and this greater motivation, rather than the treatment, produced the crossover interaction in the data. If this motivation hypothesis is correct, one would expect measures of other outcomes to show much the same pattern of improvement as the measure of alcohol use. For example, the homeless individuals under study initially had relatively poor relationships with other members of their families. Those homeless individuals who were most motivated to get their lives back in order would be expected not only to reduce their drinking but also to begin to repair their relationships with their families. On the other hand, if the treatment was responsible for the reduction in alcohol use, one would not expect similar patterns of change in family relationships because the treatment was focused on the former outcome but not the latter. The results showed no corresponding change in family relationships, in support of the hypothesis that the treatment was effective.

■ *Conclusions*

A variety of designs are available for estimating the effects of a treatment. No single design type is always best. The choice among designs depends on the circumstances of a study, particularly on how well potential threats to validity and other criticisms can be avoided under the given circumstance. For this reason, researchers would be well-advised to consider a variety of designs before making their final choices. Researchers should evaluate each design relative to the potential validity threats that are likely to be most plausible in their specific research contexts.

Researchers should also be mindful that they can rule out threats to validity by adding comparisons that put the treatment and threat into direct competition. Sometimes researchers can add such a comparison simply by disaggregating data that have already been collected. For example, in the British Breathalyser study, the researchers ruled out threats to validity by disaggregating the available data into times when pubs were open and times when they were closed (Ross et al., 1970). In other cases, researchers must plan ahead of time the additional comparisons needed to evaluate threats to validity. For example, in the study of the effects of galantin on weight gain, the researchers had to plan explicitly, before the data were collected, the comparison that assessed the effects of the substance that blocked the uptake of galantin (Azar, 1994).

At its best, quasi-experimentation is not simply a matter of picking a prototypical design out of a book. Rather, considerable intellectual challenge is encountered in recognizing potential threats to validity and elaborating design comparisons so as to minimize uncertainty about the size of the treatment effect.

Regardless of the chosen design and the elaborateness of comparisons, however, some uncertainty about the size of treatment effects will always remain. It is impossible to rule out completely all threats to validity. Ultimately, researchers must rely on accumulating evidence across multiple designs and the corresponding multiple estimates of effects. Usually this accumulation is accomplished across research projects, but sometimes wise and adequately funded researchers are able to implement multiple designs and produce multiple estimates in a single research project. For example, the project reported by Lipsey, Cordray, and Berger (1981) is exemplary in a number of ways, not the least of which is that their evaluation of the effects of juvenile diversion programs on criminal recidivism incorporated multiple comparisons, including an interrupted time series design, nonequivalent group design, randomized experiment, and regression-discontinuity design. The convergence of estimates across these designs enabled a more confident conclusion than would have been warranted based on any one of the designs alone.

■ *References*

Algina, J., & Swaminathan, H. (1979). Alternatives to Simonton's analyses of the interrupted and multiple-group time-series designs. *Psychological Bulletin, 86,* 919-926.

Anderson, A. J. B. (1989). *Interpreting data: A first course in statistics.* London: Chapman & Hall.

Azar, B. (1994, November). Eating fat: Why does the brain say, "Ahhh"? *APA Monitor,* p. 20.

Boruch, R. F., & Wothke, W. (1985). Seven kinds of randomization plans for designing field experiments. In R. F. Boruch & W. Wothke (Eds.), *Randomization and field experimentation* (pp. 95-113). San Francisco: Jossey-Bass.

Box, G. E. P., & Jenkins, G. M. (1970). *Time-series analysis: Forecasting and control.* San Francisco: Holden-Day.

Box, G. E. P., & Tiao, G. C. (1975). Intervention analysis with applications to economic and environmental problems. *Journal of the American Statistical Association, 70,* 70-92.

Braucht, G. N., & Reichardt, C. S. (1993). A computerized approach to trickle-process, random assignment. *Evaluation Review, 17,* 79-90.

Braucht, G. N., Reichardt, C. S., Geissler, L. J., Bormann, C. A., Kwiatkowski, C. F., & Kirby, M. W., Jr. (1995). Effective services for homeless substance abusers. *Journal of Addictive Diseases, 14,* 87-109.

Bryk, A. S., & Raudenbush, S. W. (1987). Application of hierarchical linear models to assessing change. *Psychological Bulletin, 101,* 147-158.

Bryk, A. S., & Raudenbush, S. W. (1992). *Hierarchical linear models: Applications and data analysis methods.* Newbury Park, CA: Sage.

Bunker, J. P., Barnes, B. A., & Mosteller, F. (Eds.). (1977). *Costs, risks, and benefits of surgery.* New York: Oxford University Press.

Cain, G. G. (1975). Regression and selection models to improve nonexperimental comparisons. In C. A. Bennett & A. A. Lumsdaine (Eds.), *Evaluation and experiment: Some critical issues in assessing social programs* (pp. 297-317). New York: Academic Press.

Campbell, D. T., & Ross, H. L. (1968). The Connecticut crackdown on speeding: Time-series data in quasi-experimental analysis. *Law and Society Review, 3,* 33-53.

Campbell, D. T., & Stanley, J. C. (1963). Experimental and quasi-experimental designs for research on teaching. In N. L. Gage (Ed.), *Handbook of research on teaching.* Chicago: Rand McNally.

Campbell, D. T., & Stanley, J. C. (1966). *Experimental and quasi-experimental designs for research.* Chicago: Rand McNally.

Chalmers, T. C., Celano, P., Sacks, H., & Smith, H. (1983). Bias in treatment assignment in controlled clinical trials. *New England Journal of Medicine, 309,* 1358-1361.

Conner, R. F. (1977). Selecting a control group: An analysis of the randomization process in twelve social reform programs. *Evaluation Quarterly, 1,* 195-243.

Cook, T. D., & Campbell, D. T. (1975). The design and conduct of quasi-experiments and true experiments in field settings. In M. D. Dunnette (Ed.), *Handbook of industrial and organizational research* (pp. 223-326). New York: Rand McNally.

Cook, T. D., & Campbell, D. T. (1979). *Quasi-experimentation: Design and analysis issues for field settings.* Chicago: Rand McNally.

Dielman, T. E. (1983). Pooled cross-sectional and time series data: A survey of current statistical methodology. *American Statistician, 37,* 111-122.

Dielman, T. E. (1989). *Pooled cross-sectional and time series data analysis.* New York: Marcel Dekker.

Director, S.M. (1979). Underadjustment bias in the evaluation of manpower training. *Evaluation Quarterly, 3,* 190-218.

Faludi, S. (1991). *Backlash: The undeclared war against American Women.* New York: Crown.

Fetterman, D. M. (1982). Ibsen's baths: Reactivity and insensitivity. *Educational Evaluation and Policy Analysis, 4,* 261-279.

Gilbert, J. P., Light, R. J., & Mosteller, F. (1975). Assessing social innovation: An empirical base for policy. In C. A. Bennett & A. A. Lumsdaine (Eds.), *Evaluation and experiment: Some critical issues in assessing social programs* (pp. 39-193). New York: Academic Press.

Glass, G. V (1988). Quasi-experiments: The case of interrupted time series. In R. M. Jaeger (Ed.), *Complementary methods for research in education* (pp. 445-464). Washington, DC: American Educational Research Association.

Glass, G. V, Willson, V. L., & Gottman, J. M. (1975). *Design and analysis of time-series experiments.* Boulder: Colorado Associated University Press.

Goldberger, A. S. (1972). *Selection bias in evaluating treatment effects: Some formal illustrations* (Discussion Paper 123-72). Madison: University of Wisconsin, Institute for Research on Poverty.

Goodwin, J. S., & Goodwin, J. M. (1984). The tomato effect: Rejection of highly efficacious therapies. *Journal of the American Medical Association, 251,* 2387-2390.

Lam, J. A., Hartwell, S. W., & Jekel, J. F. (1994). "I prayed real hard, so I know I'll get in": Living with randomization. In K. J. Conrad (Ed.), *Critically evaluating the role of experiments* (pp. 55-66). San Francisco: Jossey-Bass.

Lipsey, M. W., Cordray, D. S., & Berger, D. E. (1981). Evaluation of a juvenile diversion program: Using multiple lines of evidence. *Evaluation Review, 5,* 283-306.

Lord, F. M. (1967). A paradox in the interpretation of group comparisons. *Psychological Bulletin, 68,* 304-305.

Magidson, J., & Sorbom, D. (1982). Adjusting for confounding factors in quasi-experiments: Another reanalysis of the Westinghouse Head Start evaluation. *Educational Evaluation and Policy Analysis, 4,* 321-329.

Mark, M. M. (1986). Validity typologies and the logic and practice of quasi-experimentation. In W. M. K. Trochim (Ed.), *Advances in quasi-experimental design and analysis* (pp. 47-66). San Francisco: Jossey-Bass.

Mark, M. M., & Mellor, S. (1991). The effect of the self-relevance of an event on hindsight bias: The foreseeability of a layoff. *Journal of Applied Psychology, 76,* 569-577.

Marsh, J. C. (1985). Obstacles and opportunities in the use of research on rape legislation. In R. L. Shotland & M. M. Mark (Eds.), *Social science and social policy* (pp. 295-310). Beverly Hills, CA: Sage.

McCain, L. J., & McCleary, R. (1979). The statistical analysis of simple interrupted time-series quasi-experiments. In T. D. Cook & D. T. Campbell, *Quasi-experimentation: Design and analysis issues for field settings* (pp. 233-293). Chicago: Rand McNally.

McCleary, R, & Hay, R. A., Jr. (1980). *Applied time series analysis for the social sciences.* Beverly Hills, CA: Sage.

Milgram, S. (1965). Some conditions of obedience and disobedience to authority. *Human Relations, 18,* 55-76.

Obmascik, M. (1989, December 12). State cancer study triggers dispute. *Denver Post,* pp. 1B, 8B.

Paulos, J. A. (1988). *Innumeracy: Mathematical illiteracy and its consequences.* New York: Hill & Wang.

Raudenbush, S. W. (1988). Educational applications of hierarchical linear models: A review. *Journal of Educational Statistics, 13,* 85-116.

Raudenbush, S. W., & Bryk, A. S. (1986). A hierarchical model for studying school effects. *Sociology of Education, 59,* 1-17.

Reichardt, C. S. (1979). The statistical analysis of data from nonequivalent group designs. In T. D. Cook & D. T. Campbell, *Quasi-experimentation: Design and analysis issues for field settings* (pp. 147-205). Chicago: Rand McNally.

Reichardt, C. S. (1992). Estimating the effects of community prevention trials: Alternative designs and methods. In H. D. Holder & J. M. Howard (Eds.), *Community prevention trials for alcohol problems: Methodological issues* (pp. 137-158). Westport, CT: Praeger, an imprint of Greenwood Publishing Group, Inc.

Reichardt, C. S., & Bormann, C. A. (1994). Using regression models to estimate program effects. In Wholey, J. S., Hatry, H. P., & Newcomer, K. E. (Eds.), *Handbook of practical program evaluation.* (pp. 417-455). San Francisco: Jossey-Bass.

Reichardt, C. S., & Gollob, H. F. (1987). Taking uncertainty into account when estimating effects. In M. M. Mark & R. L. Shotland (Eds.), *Multiple methods in program evaluation* (pp. 7-22). San Francisco: Jossey-Bass.

Reichardt, C. S., Trochim, W. M. K., & Cappelleri, J. C. (1995). Reports of the death of regression-discontinuity analysis are greatly exaggerated. *Evaluation Review, 19,* 39-63.

Rindskopf, D. (1986). New developments in selection modeling for quasi-experimentation. In W. M. K. Trochim (Ed.), *Advances in quasi-experimental design and analysis* (pp. 79-89). San Francisco: Jossey-Bass.

Rosenbaum, P. R. (1995). *Observational studies.* New York: Springer-Verlag.

Rosenthal, R. (1994). Science and ethics in conducting, analyzing, and reporting psychological research. *Psychological Science, 5,* 127-134.

Ross, H. L., Campbell, D. T., & Glass, G. V (1970). Determining the social effects of a legal reform: The British "Breathalyser" crackdown of 1967. *American Behavioral Scientist, 13,* 493-509.

Sacks, H., Chalmers, T. C., & Smith, H. (1982). Randomized versus historical controls for clinical trials. *American Journal of Medicine, 72,* 233-240.

Schnelle, J. F., Kirchner, R. E., Macrae, J. W., McNees, M. P., Eck, R. H., Snodgrass, S., Casey, J. D., & Uselton, P. H., Jr. (1978). Police evaluation research: An experimental and cost-benefit analysis of a helicopter patrol in a high-crime area. *Journal of Applied Behavior Analysis, 11,* 11-21.

Smith, M. L., Gabriel, R., Schoot, J., & Padia, W. L. (1976). Evaluation of the effects of Outward Bound. In G. V Glass (Ed.), *Evaluation studies review annual* (Vol. 1, pp. 400-421). Beverly Hills, CA: Sage.

Smoll, F. L., Smith, R. R., Barnett, N. P., & Everett, J. J. (1993). Enhancement of children's self-esteem through social support training for youth sport coaches. *Journal of Applied Psychology, 78,* 602-610.

Sorbom, D. (1978). An alternative methodology for analysis of covariance. *Psychometrika, 43,* 381-396.

Stecklow, S. (1995, August 24). SAT scores rise strongly after test is overhauled. *Wall Street Journal,* pp. B1, B11.

Swaminathan, H., & Algina, J. (1977). Analysis of quasi-experimental time-series data. *Multivariate Behavioral Research, 12,* 111-131.

Thistlethwaite, D. L., & Campbell, D. T. (1960). Regression-discontinuity analysis: An alternative to the ex-post-facto experiment. *Journal of Educational Psychology, 51,* 309-317.

Trochim, W. M. K. (1984). *Research designs for program evaluation: The regression-discontinuity approach.* Beverly Hills, CA: Sage.

Underwood, B. J. (1975). Individual differences as a crucible in theory construction. *American Psychologist, 30,* 128-134.

Wagenaar, A. C. (1981). Effects of the raised legal drinking age on motor vehicle accidents in Michigan. *HSRI Research Review, 11*(4), 1-8.

Wagenaar, A. C. (1986). Preventing highway crashes by raising the legal minimum age for drinking: The Michigan experience 6 years later. *Journal of Safety Research, 17,* 101-109.

8

The Abridged Version of Case Study Research

Design and Method

Robert K. Yin

■ *Purpose*

This chapter is intended to provide an overview of more thorough treatments of case study research (Yin, 1994a; see also Yin, 1993). The chapter also includes new material on one especially important but still emerging aspect of case study research—the development and usefulness of logic models. This chapter serves as a refresher for those of you who are already familiar with case study research, as well as a starting point for those who may be considering case studies for research for the first time. It summarizes the basic tools, warns about major pitfalls, and previews ongoing attempts to advance the state of the art. In this sense, the chapter also is a springboard for eventually turning (or returning) to the fuller texts upon which much of it is based.

Case study research is a complex and multifaceted topic. A brief chapter cannot cover the material in depth and is likely to leave many loose ends. Thus the chapter emphasizes the core processes in case study research. As an initial orientation, you should be warned that the chapter caters to those who want (a) to use empirical methods (i.e., collect evidence) as part of a case study and (b) to emulate procedures from the physical and biological (otherwise known as "natural") sciences in pursuing inquiry. Among the working assumptions are that investigators can ideally establish the "facts" of a case objectively, that theory-driven inquiries are to be preferred, and that multiple-case studies are best designed around the same "replication" logic that underlies the design of multiple scientific experiments. The emulation of these and other features from natural science methods does not mean that case study research represents a natural science—only that the more the emulation, the greater the confidence in the results from a positivist perspective. One result of this perspective is that a case study inquiry may be defined as a technically distinctive situation in which there will be many more variables of interest than data points.

As with the texts from which it is drawn, this chapter also gives greater emphasis to the research design phase in doing case study research (compared with data collection, analysis, or composition). This phase has traditionally received insufficient attention, yet it is the most critical phase of case study research. In contrast, much other work exists on both data collection and research composition. As for case study data analysis, the unfortunate commentary is that formal procedures are still relatively undeveloped, but this chapter offers a start. As a final note, the chapter emphasizes here explanatory and not descriptive or exploratory case studies. (Works cited within this chapter using italicized authors' names are illustrative case studies.)

■ *Starting a Case Study*

Starting a case study requires three ingredients. The first is the capability to deal with a diversity of evidence. The second is the ability to articulate research questions and theoretical propositions. The third is the production of a research design. However, although these processes will be described in linear fashion for convenience's sake, you should always remember that doing case study research truly involves continued interactions among design, data collection, and analysis (see Maxwell, Chapter 3, this volume).

☐ *Be Expert at Handling Different Types of Evidence*

The most important element for doing case studies is the researcher's ability to handle a variety of evidence derived from diverse data collection techniques. Some persons, due to their training or preference, can comfortably deal only with a single type of evidence—such as interview data from a survey or experimental data from a laboratory. Such persons will interpret and use alternative techniques only within the implicit confines of their favored technique. In contrast, if you are to do case studies, you must recognize a broad range of types of evidence and be able to use each type to the best of the current state of the art. This means that a good case study investigator will continue to monitor methodological developments for many techniques. Table 8.1 lists the six types of evidence most commonly used in case study research; these are described more fully below, in the section on data collection. At a minimum, you should be able to handle this entire array and should have had some formal research training or experience with each of these kinds of evidence. (If you

Table 8.1   Six Sources of Evidence: Strengths and Weaknesses

Sources of Evidence	Strengths	Weaknesses
Documentation	Stable—can be reviewed repeatedly	Retrievability—can be low
	Unobtrusive—not created as a result of the case study	Access—may be deliberately blocked
	Exact—contains exact names, references, and details of an event	Biased selectivity, if collection is incomplete
	Broad coverage—long span of time, many events, and many settings	Reporting bias—reflects (unknown) bias of author
Archival records	Same as above for documentation	Same as above for documentation
	Precise and quantitative	Accessibility due to privacy reasons
Interviews	Targeted—focuses directly on case study topic	Bias due to poorly constructed questions
	Insightful—provides perceived causal inferences	Response bias
		Inaccuracies due to poor recall
		Reflexivity—interviewee gives what interviewer wants to hear
Direct observations	Reality—covers events in real time	Time-consuming
	Contextual—covers context of event	Selectivity—unless broad coverage
		Reflexivity—event may proceed differently because it is being observed
		Cost—hours needed by human observers
Participant observation	Same as above for direct observations	Same as above for direct observations
	Insightful into interpersonal behavior and motives	Bias due to investigator's manipulation of events
Physical artifacts	Insightful into cultural features	Selectivity
	Insightful into technical operations	Availability

SOURCE: Yin (1994a).

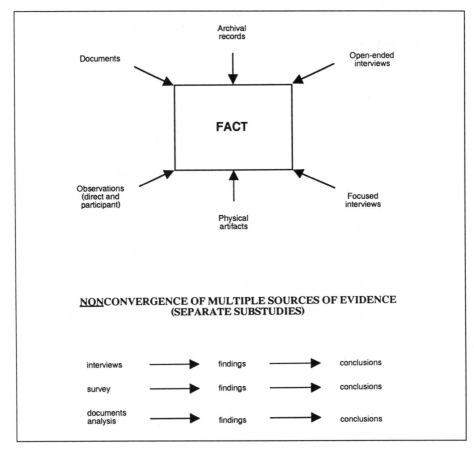

Figure 8.1. Convergence of Multiple Sources of Evidence (Single Study)
SOURCE: COSMOS Corporation.

have not had such opportunities, reading separate methodological texts—each specializing in one of these types of evidence—would be a good idea.)

☐   *Seek Converging Lines of Evidence*

What is to be done with this array of evidence also is extremely important. Your case study must use the evidence in a converging manner—to define the "facts" of the case, as illustrated in the top half of Figure 8.1. For instance, your case study might focus on the leadership patterns within a community partnership. How partnership decisions are made, and by whom (potentially reflected by documents), should be corroborated by interviews with partnership members as well as direct observations of interpersonal interactions—all converging on the identification of the actual leaders of the partnership. The methodological goal is to apply the concept of *triangulation* (the use of this concept is exactly analogous to its use in geometry and the defining of a point in space with three vectors). Using the concept for the case study method, a robust fact may be considered to have been established if evidence from three (or more) different sources all coincides. To get such convergence, you must ask the same questions of the different sources of evidence.

Such convergence is to be contrasted with a totally different strategy—the separation of each type of evidence into a substudy, as illustrated in the bottom half of Figure 8.1. For instance, what was thought to be a multiple-case study of 10 schools was based on surveys and observations at the schools, but the survey data were compiled across all schools (as one substudy) and then the observational data were compiled across all schools (as another substudy). The different sources of evidence were not directly compared *within* a given school. The result was a study consisting of two substudies (one based on surveys and the other on observation), with a comparison of the findings from the two substudies, but this was not a multiple-case study.

In summary, when you use a diverse array of evidence to converge on the facts of a case study, you have begun to satisfy one aspect of the basic definition of case studies—reliance on "multiple sources of evidence" (Yin, 1994a, p. 13).

□ *Articulate Your Research Questions Carefully*

Given your ability to use multiple data collection techniques, the direction and design of your case study derive wholly from your research questions and your articulation of the theoretical propositions related to these questions. Sometimes, careful deliberation will reveal that the case study method is not best suited to answer your research question. As a general matter, the more your question seeks to explain *how* and *why* events occur, the more the case study method will be relevant. In contrast, the more the question requires the enumeration of events (as in questions starting with "How many . . . "), the more other methods are likely to be relevant.

An excellent example is the central set of questions underlying Graham *Allison*'s (1971) well-known case study of the Cuban missile crisis of 1962:

- Why did the Soviet Union place strategic offensive missiles in Cuba?
- Why did the United States respond with a naval quarantine of Soviet shipments to Cuba?
- Why were the missiles withdrawn?

The articulation and selection of these questions is not to be taken lightly. Their identification is already an important accomplishment in doing case studies. In Allison's study, the questions also reflected some mystery. For example, the historical fact is that the United States did indeed respond to the placement of the offensive missiles (in Cuba) with a naval quarantine. But, as Allison quickly points out, the illogic is that a quarantine would have had no effect on the missiles that were already in Cuba.

Especially for *explanatory* case studies, the appropriate theoretical propositions extend this principle even further. The theoretical propositions made at the outset of the research could specify a complete and logical (but hypothesized) series of causal events, connecting variables and constructs—or, in the words of Sutton and Staw (1995), "a story about why acts, events, structure, and thoughts occur" (p. 378). The more your initial research questions and ensuing theoretical propositions are constructed along these lines, the greater the likelihood that your case study will yield fruitful results.

□ *Develop Theory to Help Design Your Case Study*

Theory development is essential for designing your case study. An example might be a case study on the implementation of a new management information system (MIS). The simplest ingredient of a theory is a proposition such as the following: "The case study will show *why* implementation only succeeded when the organization was able to re-structure itself, and not just overlay the new MIS on the old organizational structure" (*Markus,* 1983; emphasis added). The statement presents the nutshell of a theory of MIS implementation—that is, that organizational restructuring is needed to make MIS implementation work.

Using the same case, an additional ingredient might be the following proposition: "The case study will also show why the simple replacement of key persons was not sufficient for successful implementation" (*Markus,* 1983). This second statement presents the nutshell of a *rival* theory—that is, that MIS implementation fails because of the resistance to change or lack of training on the part of individual people, and that the replacement of such people is the only requirement for implementation to succeed. You can see that, as these two theoretical propositions are elaborated in their hypothesized form, the ideas will increasingly point to the relevant data that need to be collected to compare the propositions. Thus stating the theoretical propositions will help you to design the entire case study.

Rival theories. Extremely important in the preceding example is the concept of rival theories, which also can take the form of rival hypotheses or rival explanations (or alternative explanations). Quasi-experimental research pays considerable attention to these rivals under the rubric of "threats to validity" (e.g., Campbell & Stanley, 1963, p. 5). For a case study, identifying such rivals goes beyond worrying about artifacts or threats to become part of the theoretical foundation for the study. Thus use of rivals not only strengthens the research design but also sharpens theoretical thinking. Within a single case, theory can even be "tested" if there are rivals (e.g., *Allison,* 1971; *Gross, Giacquinta, & Bernstein,* 1971); across multiple cases, having rivals will help to identify the most desirable collection of cases (discussed further below).

Unfortunately, existing texts rarely give guidance on how to develop such rivals. The most common rival theory has been the null hypothesis. A null hypothesis is simply the absence of the target hypothesis. However, for doing case studies, the best rival is not simply the absence of the target theory or hypothesis, because such a rival would not be particularly helpful in pointing to the contrary data collection. Instead, the best rival would be a rival *theory*, an attempt to explain the same outcome with a different substantive theory than that of the target theory. If you have rival theories in this sense, you can collect data to test both theories.

Developing theory for your case study. Your theoretical propositions need not reflect grand theory in social science, nor are you asked to be a masterful theoretician. Rather, the simple goal is to have a sufficient blueprint for your study, and this requires theoretical propositions. Then, the complete research design will provide surprisingly strong guidance as you determine what data to collect and the strategies to use in analyzing the data. For this reason, theory development is an essential step in doing case studies.

To overcome barriers in theory development, you should try to prepare for your case study by doing such things as reviewing the literature related to your study, discussing your ideas with colleagues or teachers, and asking yourself challenging questions about what you are studying, why you are proposing to do the study, and what you hope to learn as a result. The most useful outcome of your efforts will be your ability to cover these topics in plain English, without resorting to social science jargon. A useful tool for theory development, which I will describe later in this chapter, is a logic model.

☐ *Distinguish Among Explanatory, Descriptive, and Exploratory Case Studies*

The preceding theoretical propositions have highlighted situations where "how" or "why" questions are the driving force. The completed case study driven by such questions is likely to be an explanatory case study. However, you may alternatively be interested in descriptive or exploratory questions, resulting in descriptive or exploratory case studies. In this respect, case studies are like other methods, each of which can have explanatory, descriptive, or exploratory versions. In this discussion, the traditional notion that the case study is the exploratory phase for other methods (consider, for instance, that there can be both exploratory surveys and exploratory experiments) is rejected.

Descriptive case studies. Concerning descriptive case studies, you should be warned strongly to avoid trying to use the case study method so that you can "describe everything." Although ethnographic efforts can lead to case studies with "thick description," in fact all description is selective. To think that a case study can cover everything is to overlook this inevitable selectivity and also leads to an impossible undertaking. Instead, you should focus on such questions as (a) the purpose of the descriptive effort, (b) the full but realistic range of topics that might be considered a "complete" description of what is to be studied, and (c) the likely topic(s) that will be the essence of the description (e.g., *Lynd & Lynd,* 1929; *Whyte,* 1955). Good answers to these questions, including the rationales underlying your answers, will help you go a long way toward developing the needed theoretical base (descriptive topics)—and research design—for your study. Without this guidance, you risk either trying to do too much (and still being unknowingly selective) or having your descriptive case study be an incomplete rendition of what you are studying.

Exploratory case studies. When the available literature or existing knowledge base is poor, offering no clues for conceptual frameworks or notable propositions, a new empirical study is likely to assume the characteristic of being an *exploratory* study. You also may be in an exploratory phase because you are trying some methodological innovations. In either of these situations, however, your case study should still start with some theoretical propositions. The propositions in this situation assume a "meta" posture, defining (a) what is to be explored, (b) the purpose of the exploration, and (c) the criteria by which the exploration will be judged to have been successful.

Possibly the major problem with exploratory case studies is that the data collected during the pilot phase are then also used as part of the ensuing "real" study. An extremely important quality control procedure is to avoid this practice. Exploratory case studies (like exploratory studies using other methods) are undertaken because of some uncertainty about a major aspect of a "real" study—the research questions to be studied, the hypotheses of study, the data collection methods, access to the data, or the data analysis methods. Once the uncertainty is investigated and resolved, the pilot or exploratory phase should be considered completed. Now, you are ready to start the "real" study—from scratch.

■ *Designing a Case Study*

A design is the logical sequence that connects the empirical data to a study's initial research questions and, ultimately, to its conclusions. Colloquially, a research design is *an action plan for getting from here to there,* where *here* may be defined as the initial set of questions to be answered and *there* is some set of conclusions (answers) about these questions. Between here and there may be a number of major steps, including data collection and data analysis. Figure 8.2 presents the entire set of processes. Note that a research design is much more than a work plan. The main purpose of the design is to help you avoid the situation in which the evidence does not address the initial research questions. In this sense, a research design deals with a *logical* problem and not a *logistical* problem.

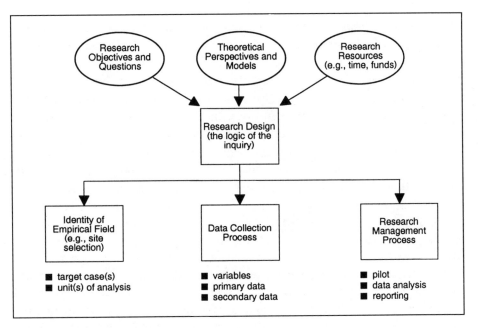

Figure 8.2. The Central Function of a Research Design
SOURCE: F. Borum (personal communication, 1991).

By already having developed your research questions and theoretical propositions, you will have started your case study design. Now let these questions and propositions help you make the following specific choices.

☐ *Define Your Unit(s) of Analysis*

Your unit of analysis is your basic definition of the "case." In the classic case study, an individual person is the subject of study and therefore the primary unit of analysis. More commonly in recent research, however, case studies have been about such units as (a) groups of persons or organizations, (b) key decisions, (c) public programs, or (d) organizational change. In each situation, the corresponding unit of analysis is different (the group, the decision, the program, or the change). The importance of defining a unit of analysis is great: Without a good definition, you will not know how to limit the boundaries of your study.

Phenomenon and context. Do not expect your case study ever to be rigidly delimited, however. In fact, another key part of defining a case study is that it permits research when the boundary between the "case" (the phenomenon being studied—or the unit of analysis) and its context is not clearly evident (Yin, 1994a, p. 13). A strong advantage of the case study method in the first place is its ability to deal with contextual conditions, and the reality of many social phenomena is that phenomenon and context are indeed not precisely distinguishable. To take a simple example, if a case study is about a group, group member-ships often change over time, and the case study could be carried out even though the identification of those within the group (the "case") and outside the group (a contextual condition) is unstable. Other examples are more complicated. Any-one studying decision making knows that when, where, and how a decision is made (the "case") can occur diffusely with regard to time, space, and process (contextual conditions). One of the advantages of the case study method is that it allows you to start an investigation without knowing precisely the boundaries of the case, and even to discover telling insights into the ways that decisions are made—because initially contextual conditions may turn out to be key parts of the decision-making process and therefore later become part of the "case."

Once you have established the general definition of the case, other clarifi-cations in the unit of analysis become important, and you need to operationalize them. In so doing, you develop a case study design that helps you to clarify data collection and analysis priorities. For instance, if the case is about public services in a specific geographic area, you need to make decisions about the specific public services to be studied, as well as the time span to be included in the case study. The decisions will reflect both theoretical priorities and con-siderations of practicality and feasibility, such as the resources available to do the study (refer again to Figure 8.2 and note how these prior topics both feed into the research design). When you consider and answer these and similar types of questions, you are in the process of designing your case study, but the result also will be an articulation of the specific data to be collected and their purpose.

Embedded units of analysis. As an added complication, your case study may have a main unit of analysis and also one or more subunits of analyses within the main unit. For instance, a case study may be about a neighborhood (main unit) but may also have important questions or propositions requiring the col-lection of data from the residents (subunits) within the neighborhood. The major conclusions would still be about the single neighborhood, but there might be secondary conclusions about the residents and their behavior or perceptions.

Overall, a case study with only a main unit of analysis may be considered a *holistic* case study; one with a main unit and subunits of analyses requires data collection and analysis at each level, and may be considered an *embedded* case study. Distinctive in this regard is the possibility that the data collection for the subunits of analysis might even involve a survey or the use of extensive economic or archival data. The completed case study could then be based on highly quantitative data and analysis at the subunit level and highly qualitative data at the level of the main unit of analysis. In this sense, the entire case study would be both quantitative and qualitative. For this reason, another traditional belief that is rejected here is the notion that doing case study research is syn-onymous with doing qualitative research only. (This issue is discussed further below, in the section on data collection.)

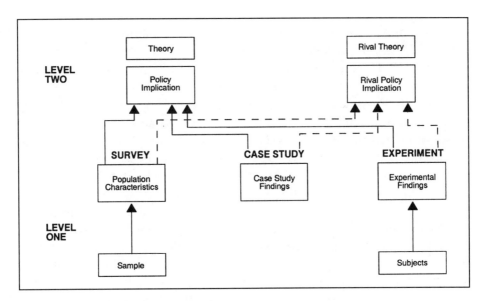

Figure 8.3. Making Inferences: Two Levels
SOURCE: COSMOS Corporation.

☐ *Distinguish Between Single- and Multiple-Case Studies*

A case study may be about a single case or about multiple cases. For instance, you can examine and "test" theoretical propositions with a single case if you define both your target propositions and rival propositions ahead of time. The single case would then be the opportunity, carried out fairly, to collect data to substantiate or challenge either set of propositions.

Generalizing from single-case studies. Even your single case can enable you to generalize to other cases that represent similar theoretical conditions. In fact, the classic single-case studies are classic in part because of their broad implications or generalizability—even though only single cases were the subjects of study. In other words, generalizing from case studies is not a matter of *statistical generalization* (generalizing from a sample to a universe) but a matter of *analytic generalization* (using single or multiple cases to illustrate, represent, or generalize to a theory). Figure 8.3 illustrates the contrast between the two types of generalization. Surveys and experiments, for instance, both involve statistical generalization from a sample (or subjects) to a universe (Level 1 inference), but both also involve analytic generalization from single study to theory (Level 2 inference). Case studies involve only analytic generalizations (Level 2 only).

Replication logic for multiple-case studies. The benefit of multiple-case studies is that they strengthen or broaden the analytic generalizations, in a manner similar to the role of multiple experiments in comparison to the single experiment. Analytic generalizations may be strengthened because the multiple cases were designed to "replicate" each other—producing corroboratory evidence from two or more cases (*literal replication*). Alternatively, generalizations may be broadened because the multiple cases were designed to cover different theoretical conditions, producing contrasting results, but for predictable reasons (*theoretical replication*). The appropriate multiple-case study design can do both. Thus the ability to design and conduct 6 to 10 case studies is analogous to the ability to conduct 6 to 10 experiments on a related topic: A few cases (two or three) would be literal replications, whereas a few others (four to six) might be designed to pursue two different patterns of theoretical replications.

An excellent, simple example of this replication pattern is provided by a multiple-case study consisting of only two cases: the aeronautics industry and the microelectronics industry (*Hooks,* 1990). The two industries contrasted strongly in that, historically, one (aeronautics) received much more in federal subsidies to support its development and maturation than the other (microelectronics). Yet the researcher's closer investigation of these two industries revealed significant participation in both industries on the part of U.S. Defense Department procurement policies. The conclusion was that, although the two industries represented classically different situations (theoretical replication), their common defense experience nevertheless helped both to grow. The important public policy conclusion from both cases was that U.S. Defense Department policy can have industrial development impacts that are often unappreciated in typical comparisons of U.S. and Japanese government support of business as it affects international competitiveness. A more elaborate multiple-case design might have included several cases in each of the two categories (highly subsidized or not highly subsidized). If the same results were found, the evidence would have been even stronger regarding the main conclusion than with the original two cases (there would have been literal replications within a set of theoretical replications).

The replication approach to case studies combines the theory development stage with case selection. Within each individual case study, the data should converge on why a particular theoretical proposition was supported or disconfirmed, preferably with the specification of rival theories; across cases, the variety of situations would indicate the extent of the replication logic, and why certain cases were predicted to have certain results, whereas other (deliberately contrary) cases were predicted to have contrasting results.

Defining the number of cases in a multiple-case study. When you are using a multiple-case design, a further question you will encounter has to do with the number of cases deemed necessary or sufficient for your study. However, because traditional sampling logic should not be used, the typical criteria regarding sample size also are irrelevant. Instead, you should think of this decision as a

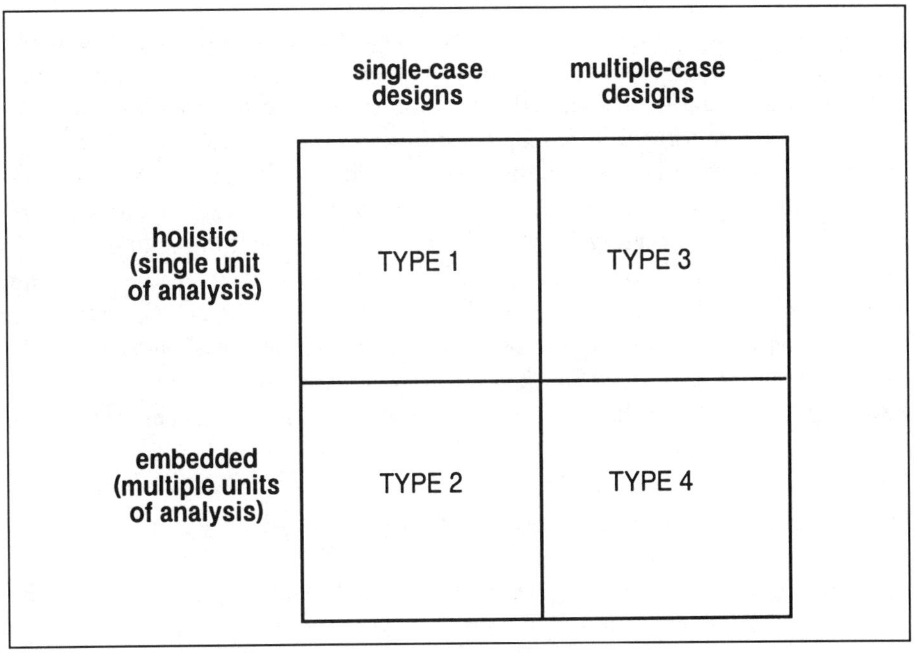

	single-case designs	multiple-case designs
holistic (single unit of analysis)	TYPE 1	TYPE 3
embedded (multiple units of analysis)	TYPE 2	TYPE 4

Figure 8.4. Basic Types of Designs for Case Studies
SOURCE: COSMOS Corporation.

reflection of the number of case replications—both literal and theoretical—that you would like to have in your study. In making this decision, an appropriate analogy from statistical studies is the selection of the criterion for establishing levels of significance. Much as the choice of "$p < .05$" or "$p < .01$" is not derived from any formula but is a matter of discretionary, judgmental choice, your selection of the number of replications depends upon the certainty you want to have about your multiple-case results (greater certainty lies with larger numbers of cases). For example, you may want to settle for two or three literal replications when the rival theories are grossly different and the issue at hand does not demand an excessive degree of certainty. However, if your rivals have subtle differences or if you want a high degree of certainty, you may press for five, six, or more replications.

Four types of basic case study designs. The fact that a design calls for multiple-case studies does not eliminate the distinction, described earlier, between holistic and embedded case studies. Both single- and multiple-case studies may be either holistic or embedded, depending upon the type of phenomenon being studied. This 2×2 combination therefore produces four possible types of basic case study designs (see Figure 8.4).

The following is an example of the most complicated of the four types: a multiple-case study with embedded units of analysis. This study was concerned with the delivery of services by different community mental health centers (*Larsen,* 1982). Each center (the main unit of analysis) was rightfully the topic of a case study; the theoretical framework dictated that nine such centers be included as cases, three to replicate a direct result (literal replications) and six others to deal with contrasting conditions (theoretical replications). In all nine centers, an embedded design also was used because surveys of the centers' clients (the subunit of analysis) were conducted. However, the results of each survey were *not* pooled across centers. Rather, the survey data were part of the findings and conclusions for each individual center, or case. These data were highly quantitative, focusing on the attitudes and behaviors of individual clients, and the data were used along with archival information and interviews of center staff to interpret the success and operations of the given center.

☐   *Continually Judge the Quality of Your Case Study Design*

Four tests have commonly been used to establish the quality of any empirical social research: whether a study has (a) construct validity, (b) internal validity, (c) external validity, and (d) reliability (Kidder & Judd, 1986, pp. 26-29). Because case studies are one form of such empirical research, the four tests also are relevant to case study research. The important challenge is to define the specific case study tactics that deal with each test. A further revelation is that these tactics do not all occur at the outset of the case study, as precautionary measures. Rather, the tactics occur throughout the case study process—during design of the study, collection of data, data analysis, and reporting of the results. You will increase the quality of your case study tremendously, and overcome traditional criticisms of the weaknesses of case study research, by using these tactics.

Table 8.2 lists 11 recommended tactics covering the four tests, also indicating the phase of research in which each tactic might most likely occur (some tactics will occur during more than one phase). For instance, a major tactic during the research design phase is the use of rival theories in single-case studies (whether the single-case studies are part of a multiple-case study or not) and a replication logic in multiple-case studies. The other tactics occur during other phases of the research process; these will be referenced back to Table 8.2 when discussed later in the chapter.

Thus, working on your case study design is an ongoing process. In contrast, in the past, "doing" case studies has been taken as synonymous with collecting case study data. This is because the traditional view of case study research was that you could go into the field with minimal preparation and then "tell it like it is." Yet above I have described critical topics in case study design. By following these design procedures, you have already been "doing" your case study. Data collection must be considered only another phase in doing case study research.

Table 8.2   Case Study Tactics for Four Design Tests

Tests	Case Study Tactic	Phase of Research in Which Tactic Occurs[a]
Construct validity	Use multiple sources of evidence.	Data collection
	Establish chain of evidence.	Data collection
	Have key informants review draft case study report.	Composition
Internal validity	Do pattern matching.	Data analysis
	Do explanation building.	Data analysis
	Do time series analysis.	Data analysis
	Do logic models.	Data analysis
External validity	Use rival theories within single cases.	Research design
	Use replication logic in multiple-case studies.	Research design
Reliability	Use case study protocol.	Data collection
	Develop case study database.	Data collection

SOURCE: Revised from Yin (1994a).

a. Some tactics can occur during more than one phase of research.

■ *Preparing to Collect Case Study Data*

Even after you have substantially articulated your case study design, other preparation is still needed before data collection can proceed. General preparation is related to the desired skills of the case study investigator; specific preparation is related to the specific case study data collection to be undertaken. Only with such preparation can actual data collection be done well.

□ *Develop the Desired Investigative Skills*

Five investigative skills are especially important for doing good case study research. Unfortunately, no tests exist to determine the extent to which you or others have such skills, and no certification process exists for determining who might be qualified to do such research. However, it is highly likely that different persons have the five skills to varying degrees. Further, these skills are sufficiently demanding that successful case study data collection will usually be done by seasoned investigators, not research assistants—a pattern different from that found in experimental or survey research.

Question asking. An inquiring mind is a major prerequisite *during* data collection, not just before or after the activity. Data collection follows a formal plan, but the specific information that may be relevant to a case study is not readily predictable. Like a detective, as you do your fieldwork, you must constantly ask yourself why events appear to have happened or be happening. When you are able to ask good questions, you will be mentally and emotionally exhausted at the end of a day in the field. This is far different from the experience of collecting experimental or survey data, in which a person may become physically exhausted but has been mentally untested after a day of data collection.

Listening. Listening in case study data collection is not limited to the aural modality; it includes observing and sensing more generally. Being a good listener means being able to assimilate large amounts of new information without bias. Whether conducting an interview or reviewing a document, the good investigator constantly asks whether there is any important message between the lines; any inferences, of course, need to be corroborated by other sources of information, but important insights may be gained this way. Poor listeners may not even realize that there can be information between the lines.

Adaptiveness and flexibility. Very few case studies will end up going exactly as planned. The skilled investigator must remember the original purpose of the investigation and then must be willing to change procedures or plans if unanticipated events occur. For instance, throughout case study data collection, you should be conducting preliminary data analysis. If the analysis points to the potential need to change subsequent data collection activities, you must have the adaptiveness and flexibility to entertain such a change.

Grasp of the issues being studied. Case study research, unlike other methods, requires an understanding or grasp of the issues being studied on the part of the members of the data collection team (in other methods, it may be preferable for the data collection team members to have little such understanding). Case study data collection is not merely a matter of *recording* the data in a mechanical fashion, as it is in other types of research. You must be able to interpret the information as it is being collected and to know immediately, for instance, if several sources of information contradict one another and lead to the need for additional evidence. Much as in good detective work, the best grasp of the issues being studied involves a "theory" of what occurred, and why, regarding the topic of the case study.

Lack of bias. All of the preceding conditions will be negated if you seek to use a case study only to substantiate your preconceived positions. One test of your possible bias is the degree to which you are open to contrary findings. For example, researchers studying "nonprofit" organizations may be surprised to find that many of these organizations have entrepreneurial and capitalistic motives. Test your own tolerance of contrary findings by reporting your preliminary results to some colleagues. Inevitably, good colleagues offer alternative explanations that require your further investigation.

☐ *Design and Develop Specific Training*

Any given case study requires specific training for the investigators involved. Befitting the need for experienced investigators with knowledge of the case study subject, this training should assume the character of a seminar rather than a mechanistic review of field procedures. That is, the training is likely to be dominated by reading, discussion, and homework on the substance of the case study. This kind of training is especially important for multiple-case studies in which multiple investigators are needed because the data need to be collected simultaneously or within a short time span. The goal of the training is to have all investigators develop a shared understanding of the basic concepts, terminology, and issues relevant to the study. The understanding must be sufficiently deep that each investigator can spontaneously frame substantive questions—even a whole line of inquiry—for any given field situation. Preferably, the training continues until the lines of inquiry among different investigators have become extremely similar.

The training also may reveal problems that you need to address. These can include flaws in the research design, incompatibilities within the case study team, and unrealistic deadlines or expectations. Regardless of the types of problems revealed, you should be glad they have been identified during training. You should rectify whatever you can at this stage.

■ Collecting Case Study Data

As noted previously, case studies can involve both quantitative (numeric) and qualitative (nonnumeric) data. For instance, a relevant place for quantitative data in a case study may be in enumerating the outcomes of a particular intervention; the qualitative data might then demonstrate a particularly compelling explanation for the outcomes. The skills needed for assembling and analyzing quantitative data may differ considerably from those for qualitative data, and for this as well as deeper philosophical reasons, quantitative and qualitative strategies have frequently been pitted against each other (Yin, 1994b). However, the most desirable case studies are likely to use both types; thus the four procedures described next are intended to cover both quantitative and qualitative evidence.

☐ *Design and Use a Case Study Protocol*

Using a formal case study protocol is one of the most important tactics for upholding the quality of case study research—mainly the reliability of the research (refer back to Table 8.2). The protocol is more than an instrument containing the study questions; it also contains the procedures and general rules to be followed in data collection. Having a protocol is desirable under all circumstances, but it is essential if you are using a multiple-case design.

A good protocol will not only delineate the case study questions but also clarify how these questions might be reframed in the field. There are actually multiple levels of questions (Yin, 1994a, p. 71), and the most important lesson for the present discussion is that the case study research questions are not necessarily the same questions one might ask in the field. Rather, a case study protocol and its basic questions are considered the "agenda" of the case study investigator; in the collection of data, the questions asked of any given field informant or in the review of any given document might deviate from the original case study questions to an unrecognizable degree—again, this is not unlike the work of a detective.

A good protocol also should include the preliminary thinking about the final case study report(s). Thinking ahead to your reporting needs is generally missing from case study plans, and the recommended thinking again reflects the benefits from a nonlinear approach to the design and conduct of case study research. One reason for thinking about the report is that case study reports do not necessarily suit (or are not constrained by) journal formats, which dominate the publications based on other research methods. Thus anticipation of reporting expectations and topics—and the extent and quality of the desired documentation—will go a long way toward helping you to define realistic and still targeted case study research studies. As a whole, the development and review of the entire case study protocol should occur as part of the case study training and pilot testing.

☐ *Collect Evidence From Multiple Sources*

This chapter began by noting the requirement that potential investigators be able to handle skillfully the full variety of evidence in social science, listing six types of evidence as discussed next (refer back to Table 8.1).

Documentation. Except for studies of preliterate societies (increasingly rare), documentary information is likely to be relevant to every case study. Documents are not necessarily accurate or unbiased. You need to use them carefully, and not accept them as literal recordings of events that have taken place. Nevertheless, documents are extremely important for corroborating and augmenting evidence from other sources. The importance of documents ranges from their helping you to spell names and titles correctly to their providing inferential evidence about substantive events, corroborating information from other sources.

Archival records. Archival records mainly take the form of computerized and quantitative data files—service records, organizational records, lists, surveys done by others, and other data files. Unlike documentary evidence, the relevance of archival records will vary from case study to case study. When you deem archival records to be relevant, you must be careful to ascertain the conditions under which the records were produced and their accuracy. For instance, service records that note the times the material in them was recorded may actually reflect the times particular service workers were available to do the recording, not necessarily the times of the events.

Interviews. Most commonly, case study interviews are of an open-ended nature. The more this is true, the more case study respondents should be considered informants, and not respondents. Regardless of the design of a case study, interview data must be understood as *verbal reports* only. From such a perspective, reported attitudes and perceptions might be considered definitive (only the informant is the authoritative source for this type of information), but reported behaviors still need to be corroborated by other types of evidence (e.g., documents) before the information should be accepted as valid.

Direct observation. By making a field visit to a case study site, you create the opportunity for direct observation. The usefulness of such observation is inversely dependent on the degree to which the phenomena of interest are historical; the more historical, the less useful are any contemporary observations. To increase the reliability of observational evidence, a common procedure is to have more than a single observer, whether formal or casual observations are the desired result. Thus, when resources permit, case studies involving site visits should have multiple investigators.

Participant observation. Participant observation is a special mode of research investigation in which the research investigator actively participates in the social situations he or she is simultaneously observing. The technique has been used most frequently in anthropological studies of different cultural groups and provides unusual opportunities for collecting case study data—primarily for collecting data about "private" situations that are not amenable to other types of data collection (e.g., illegal immigration, membership in closed or secretive groups, and informal participation in group behavior). From these perspectives, one of the most notable participant observation studies was a case study of how a bill was passed by the U.S. Congress (*Redman,* 1973). This case study provides insight into the daily operations of the Congress and is an excellent example of participant observation in a contemporary setting, covering subtle legislative strategies, the overlooked roles of committee clerks and lobbyists, and informal interaction between the legislative and executive branches of government during the development of new legislation.

Physical artifacts. Historians and anthropologists specialize in identifying and using physical artifacts (e.g., technological devices, tools or instruments, works of art) as evidence. The value of such artifacts is usually underestimated in most contemporary case studies. However, attending to status symbols to confirm status relationships within an organization, using computer printouts to confirm work that is claimed to have been done on the computer, and accounting for the physical layout or location of offices as an implicit function of the offices' "distance" from key affairs all illustrate the relevance of physical artifacts for case study research in contemporary settings.

☐   *Create a Case Study Database*

Once you have completed data collection, you need to organize, quickly and efficiently, the accumulated case study evidence. Traditionally, this step has not received attention in discussions of case study research, because the thinking has been that once the data are collected, the next step is "writing the case up." However, such practice is not acceptable, as it leads immediately to another long-standing criticism of case study research—that evidence is presented selectively because of inevitable confusion between the data and interpretation of the data.

Creating a case study database is a formal way to organize your evidence. The database should exist independent of any subsequent case study report, just as survey databases exist independent of any survey report. Further, a case study database is not merely a collection of field notes and the other materials collected in the field. This database should include new narrative, written to the files, that organizes and cites (through footnotes) the fieldwork and field materials.

One way of organizing the narrative is to follow the sequence of topics or questions in the case study protocol. If the protocol has been designed properly, it consists of a series of questions or topics that reflect your substantive agenda. This same agenda then becomes an excellent structure for organizing the case study database, which can now consist of (your own) open-ended answers to the questions in the case study protocol. Creating your database therefore forces you to organize all of your evidence into topics that reflect your case study design and inquiry, thus yielding two extremely important benefits: (a) The composition of your case study report is made considerably easier, and (b) the thorough use of your evidence in covering any given topic reduces your need to go back continually to sift through the evidence. Naturally, constructing a good database takes time and effort, and you should not expect that you will use all of the assembled topics in your later report (not all of the data in a survey database are necessarily used in survey reports either).

Important throughout this process is that you synthesize the evidence from multiple sources, where different sources address the same question or topic. A serious mistake would be to construct a database that keeps the various sources of evidence segregated (e.g., summarizing the information from the interview notes only, and then summarizing the information from the documentary sources only, and so on). Again, if there are multiple investigators working together, you must organize the effort to keep the integration of all evidence at this topical level (not just at the end of the analytic process) as the highest priority (as opposed to assigning one person to do the notes and another to do the documentation). When properly done, the case study database therefore constitutes one of the 11 previously cited tactics (return again to Table 8.2) for assuring the quality of your research.

During this process of constructing the case study database, you should be prepared to find important insights into your data. This is a stage where new categories may emerge, following the lessons of grounded theory (Strauss & Corbin, 1990). Whether the categories are old or new, you should also think about using "word tables" and other displays as part of your database. Word tables contain words (or concepts) rather than numbers, but otherwise perform the same function as numeric tables. A word table is a way of organizing qualitative data, whereas a numeric table is a way of organizing quantitative data. Further, although other investigators have offered contrary advice, the creation of the database is not dependent upon rewriting, editing, or polishing the interview notes or other raw materials themselves. Synthesis across sources of evidence is the main function of the database, with the result being new narrative or new tabulations based on the synthesis.

"Playing with the data" and creating a case study database are invaluable preludes to further case study analysis. However, you should not believe (as implied by some qualitative methods texts) that this is the complete analysis process. I will offer more on case study analysis later in this chapter.

☐ *Maintain a Chain of Evidence*

The data collection phase is the occasion for you to practice another of the 11 previously cited tactics (see Table 8.2)—maintaining a chain of evidence. The principle is based on a similar practice used in criminological investigations: A line of evidence should be traceable from initial research questions to ultimate case study conclusions. As with criminological evidence, the process should be tight enough so that, figuratively speaking, evidence presented in "court"—the case study report—is assuredly the same evidence that was collected at the scene of the "crime" during the data collection process. Conversely, no original evidence should have been lost, through carelessness or bias, and therefore fail to receive appropriate attention in consideration of the "facts" of a case.

To understand how a chain of evidence is maintained in case study research, imagine the following scenario. You have read the conclusions in a case study report, want to know more about the derivation of the conclusions, and are tracing the research process backward. First, the report itself should make sufficient citation to the relevant portions of the case study database, by citing documents, interviews, and observations. Second, the database, upon inspection, should reveal the actual evidence and also indicate the circumstances under which the evidence was collected—for example, the times and places of interviews. Third, these circumstances should be consistent with the specific procedures and questions contained in the case study protocol, to show that the data collection accurately followed the protocol. Finally, the protocol should link directly back to the initial study questions. In the aggregate, you should therefore be able to move from one portion of the case study research process to another, with clear references to methodological procedures and the resulting evidence. This is the ultimate chain of evidence that is desired.

■ *Analyzing Case Study Data*

In an important sense, case study investigators practice "analysis" during data collection (see Maxwell, Chapter 3, this volume). Case study data collection is flexible, permitting you to pursue new leads as a result of just having found something out by perusing a document or interviewing a person. Thus triangulating evidence—or getting the evidence to converge on a set of case study facts—is already an analytic process, and it occurs throughout data collection. Further, you should be concerned with how you will do your case study analysis even as you consider your research design.

In another sense, the major case study analysis occurs after data collection has been completed. Now you are ready to review all your evidence, and your analysis activities will consist of inspecting, categorizing, tabulating, recombining, or otherwise manipulating the amassed evidence—to address the initial propositions of your study.

This section discusses the latter type of analyzing, plans for which ideally should have been developed as part of the case study protocol. At the same time, analyzing case study evidence is especially difficult, compared with other methods, because the strategies and techniques have not been well developed. Therefore, a serious threat to your entire study is that you may get stalled at the analysis stage. There have been numerous situations in which amassed case study data have consumed a lot of file space but have gone ignored month after month because the investigator did not know what to do with the evidence. Because of this problem, the experienced case study investigator is likely to have great advantages over the novice at the analytic stage. If you are a novice, you should overcompensate for this stage by overpreparing, and as much ahead of time as possible. However, the major problem is that there are few fixed formulas or cookbooks to guide you in this process. What you must rely on are (a) your own style of rigorous thinking, along with (b) the sufficient presentation of evidence and (c) careful consideration of alternative interpretations.

☐ *Follow a General Analytic Strategy*

You are best off if you have a general analytic strategy, even if such a strategy emerges only after you have started your analyses and "played with the data." Playing with the data may include categorizing, summarizing, condensing, or recombining the data (Strauss & Corbin, 1990)—much as survey researchers might produce scales or clusters of variables.

The first and preferred strategy, detailed further below, is to follow the theoretical propositions that led to the case study. The second general strategy is to develop a descriptive framework for organizing the case study. As a brief reminder, the main goal of this second strategy is to have a descriptive framework that covers the topic being studied in some comprehensive, yet not redundant, way. However, you should not think that the descriptive strategy is necessarily easily concocted. In a deep sense, what constitutes the complete but parsimonious description of a phenomenon also assumes an implicit theory of what the phenomenon is.

As for the first strategy—following the theoretical propositions that led to the case study in the first place—four specific modes of analysis may be considered as options. Three of them are described next; the fourth (developing logic models) is given special attention. All of them are among the 11 tactics intended to improve the quality of your research, in this case by addressing issues of internal validity (see Figure 8.4).

☐ *Consider Three Different Modes of Analysis*

Pattern matching. One of the most desirable modes of analysis is to compare an empirically based pattern with a predicted one. If the case study is an explanatory one, the patterns may be related to the dependent or the independent variables of study (or both). The dependent variables pattern is derived from one of the more potent quasi-experimental research designs—the "nonequivalent, dependent variables design" (Cook & Campbell, 1979, p. 118). According to this design, a study may have multiple dependent variables—that is, a variety of outcomes. If, for each outcome, the initially predicted values have been confirmed, and at the same time alternative patterns from rival predictions have not been confirmed, strong causal inferences can be made.

At this point in the state of the art, the actual pattern-matching procedure involves no precise comparisons. Whether you are predicting a pattern of nonequivalent dependent variables, a pattern based on rival explanations reflected by different independent variables, or a simple pattern, the fundamental comparison between the predicted and actual pattern may involve no quantitative or statistical criteria. This lack of precision can allow for interpretive discretion on the part of the investigator, who may be overly restrictive in claiming a pattern to have been violated or overly lenient in deciding that a pattern has been matched. Until further advances are made, you are cautioned to combat these conditions by not postulating very subtle patterns. The main objective would be to do case studies in which the outcomes are likely to lead to gross matches or mismatches, so that the pattern-matching results are less debatable.

Explanation building. The mode of explanation building also is relevant mainly to explanatory case studies, although a similar procedure has commonly been cited as part of a hypothesis-generating process for exploratory case studies (Glaser & Strauss, 1967).

To "explain" a phenomenon is to stipulate a set of causal links about it. In the explanation-building mode, you may begin by taking the data you have collected for a single case and attempting to see whether they converge over a logical sequence of events (chronologically) that appears to explain your case's outcomes. If you have been doing a multiple-case study that was designed to produce a series of direct replications, the tentative explanation then becomes the hypothesized set of events that you should seek in analyzing the data from the second case study. The data from the second case may confirm or disconfirm the hypothesized set—or cause you to alter the original explanation. If you alter that explanation, you may return to the first case study to see whether its data will support the altered version as much as the original version. Once this is done, you may then proceed to analyze the data from your third case study in a similar manner, and so on. Overall, the explanation-building process across all of your case studies constitutes your "cross-case analysis" (you should note how this rendition of cross-case analysis differs dramatically from "counting" across cases, which is usually not a good strategy at all).

The most desired form of explanation building again includes your entertaining other plausible or rival explanations. Again, too, this analytic mode is difficult to implement and will favor experienced investigators over novices. As the iterative process progresses, for instance, one danger is that the explanation that is being built has drifted undesirably from the original topic of interest. Constant references to the original purpose of the inquiry and possible alternative explanations will help to reduce this problem.

Time series analysis. A third analytic mode is to conduct a time series analysis, directly analogous to the time series analysis conducted in experiments and quasi-experiments. Compared to the more general pattern-matching analysis, a time series mode can be much simpler in one sense: In time series, there may be only a single dependent or independent variable. When a large number of data points is relevant and available, statistical tests can even be used to analyze the data. Alternatively, time series analyses also can benefit if there are a wide variety of data, all with their own markers over time. Tracking a case study of neighborhood change, for instance, might be done through the analysis of changes in multiple indicators (e.g., housing condition, service delivery, resident turnover, and neighborhood economic conditions) over time.

As with the other two analytic modes, the stipulation of rival (and therefore contrasting) time series patterns, followed by the empirical "testing" of these rivals, will strengthen any use of time series analysis. This is what Campbell (1969) did in his now famous study of the Connecticut speed limit law.

☐ *Develop and Use Logic Models, Especially for Case Study Evaluations*

A logic model combines pattern matching and time series analysis. The model deliberately stipulates a complex chain of events (pattern) over time (time series), covering the causal relationship among independent, intervening, and dependent variables. This fourth analytic strategy has become extremely useful for doing case study evaluations, but also can be used for case study research.

For evaluation, the logic model is initially created during the design phase of the research. The intervention (public program) being evaluated is supposed to produce a certain outcome. However, most interventions are complex chains of events: Initial activities have their own immediate outcomes, which in turn produce some intermediate outcome, which in turn produce final or ultimate outcomes. The strength of the logic model is its requirement of an explicit conceptualization of the chain of events, sufficiently detailed that operational measures can be envisaged for each step in the chain. This conceptualization actually reflects the "theory" of the intervention. Then, the data collection is designed to include coverage of the operational measures. For every measure, a key component is marking the calendar time of the event, so that chronologies are usually an essential aspect of logic model data. Finally, the findings from the data are compared to the original logic model in a pattern-matching mode, to determine the viability of the original conceptualization.

Figures 8.5 and 8.6 provide examples of two logic models, reflecting two diverse circumstances. The first, Figure 8.5, tracks the possible steps that could be taken by a single youth, ending with an undesirable result—becoming part of a violent, drug-dealing gang (see Steps 6 and 7 in the figure) and committing a gang-related offense (Step 8). The logic model therefore illustrates a tool that could be used in case study research, not just evaluation. However, this first logic model also suggests 11 places at which different public policy interventions can and have been designed to intervene in the overall path taken by the youth, to avoid or "prevent" the undesirable result (see the key at the bottom of the figure). In this sense, the logic model also is a comprehensive framework for depicting possible prevention strategies and the beginning of concomitant evaluation designs—which was the main motive for creating the logic model in the first place.

The second logic model (Figure 8.6) is an increasingly common type of logic model used in case study evaluations. The model is more strictly a

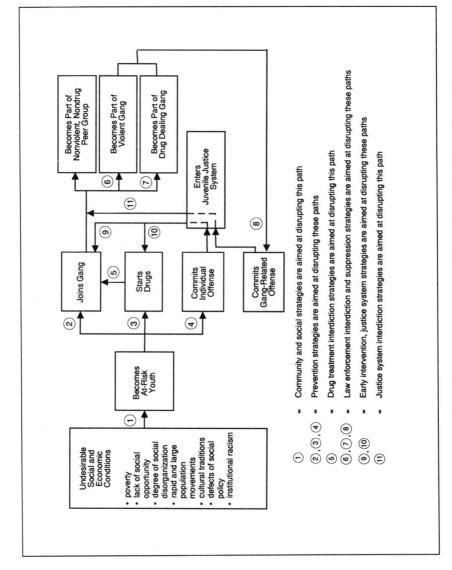

Figure 8.5. Illustrative Analytic Framework for Gang-Related Drug Prevention
SOURCE: Yin (1993).

"program" logic model (Wholey, 1979), depicting the presumed course of events influenced by an intervention (the brokerage and technical assistance services shown in Boxes 2 and 3). The evaluation and pattern-matching design calls for data collection about each box, ultimately confirming whether the intervention produced a series of desired outcomes culminating in changed business performance and public benefits (Boxes 8, 9, 10, and 11). Distinctive about this logic model is that it has a place for two sets of rival explanations (Boxes 12 and 13), reflecting that the same outcomes might have occurred due to conditions other than the brokerage and technical assistance services. The complete data collection therefore includes collecting evidence about the possibility of these rivals, enabling the evaluation to strengthen or challenge the attribution of outcomes back to the intervention.

Work with logic models has become increasingly common during the past few years. However, there is a long way to go before they can be made into more mechanized analytic strategies. An important gap, for instance, is the way that the "arrows" in the logic models are to be operationalized, and how these arrows actually represent key substantive processes unrecognized by most current logic models. Without further elucidation of the arrows, the "pattern" of the logic models is still a sequential pattern of boxes and therefore correlated stages over time, but may not be a complete explanation of how outcomes are actually produced. Further work on this and related problems is currently under way (Yin & Chavis, 1996).

☐ *Press for a High-Quality Analysis*

Carrying out the analysis phase of case study research is still a primitive art. Given this problem, you must make sure that your analysis is of the highest quality. This will be more likely to be the case if you follow four principles (Yin, 1994b). First, show that you examined and entertained all the relevant evidence, in an exhaustive manner. Second, include the major rival interpretations, and use your evidence to address these rivals. Third, focus on the most significant research questions that initially led to your case study, to show that your analysis did not merely follow the path of least resistance. Fourth, compare your analytic procedures and findings to as much prior research as possible, to show that you have tried hard to build on research rather than reinvent it.

■ *Reporting Case Studies*

To create your case study report, you must be good at composing, not just able to put up with it. As difficult as case study design and analysis might be, the compositional phase of case study research also puts great demands on an

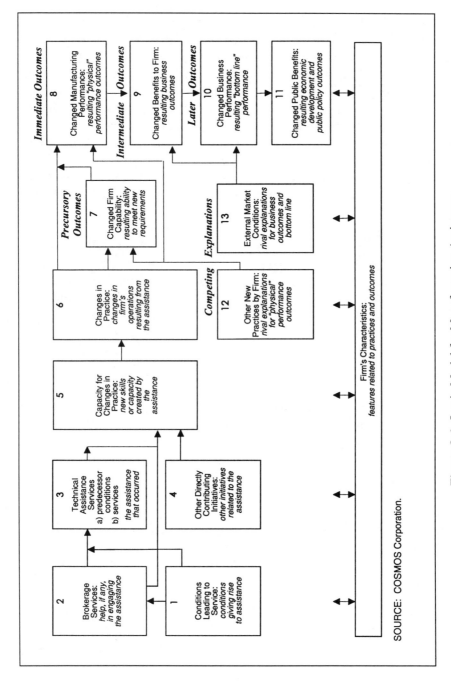

Figure 8.6. Logic Model for Manufacturing Assistance
SOURCE: COSMOS Corporation.

SOURCE: COSMOS Corporation.

256

investigator. This is because the case study "report" does not follow any stereo-typical form, such as that of a journal article in psychology. Also, the case study report need not be limited to the written mode, but can appear as an oral presentation or even a videotape.

Unfortunately, few people are forewarned about this problem that lies at the end of designing and doing a case study. In contrast, the smart investigator will give explicit attention to the compositional phase throughout the earlier phases of the case study, and will actually have begun composing the report even before data collection and analysis have been completed. For instance, the development of the case study protocol and the case study database are important, early junctures when you can devote serious thought to your antici-pated case study report. Your successful completion of your case study report will require you to overcome all of the known barriers that constitute "writers' cramps," as well as to identify and communicate with your report's audience, processes given ample attention elsewhere. Thus the remaining pages focus on two salient features of case study reports: composing a compelling report and aiming for an exemplary study.

☐ *Compose a Compelling Report*

Your case study report can assume several different forms, reflecting the desired logical structure of your case and how you decide to present individual cases when you are doing a multiple-case study.

Illustrative structures for case study compositions. The chapters, sections, subtopics, and other components of your report must be organized in some way—this constitutes your report's structure. Attending to such a structure has become increasingly common in social science writing, with the most common form being the recommended "hourglass" shape of reports for empirical studies (the text starts broadly, with the issues being studied, then narrows to the meth-ods and data in the study, and then broadens again at the end to cover the inter-pretations, conclusions, and implications of the findings). For case studies, this hourglass shape will work, but it may not be the best way of presenting your material. Therefore, you may want to think about the following six other possi-ble structures (and you are certainly welcome to develop others).

The first is a straightforward, linear-analytic structure, presenting the re-search questions, methods, findings, and interpretations—similar to the hour-glass form. The second is a comparative structure, in which the same case study in its entirety is repeated two or more times, but each time from a different theoretical angle that interprets the database in a different manner and illus-trates the empirical "testing" of the theoretical angle (e.g., *Allison,* 1971). Third would be a chronological structure, which might track the decision-making process, for instance, over time (e.g., *Pressman & Wildavsky,* 1973). Fourth is a theory-building structure, directly reflecting, for instance, the explanation-building process that might have been your analytic strategy. The fifth structure, which might be considered a "suspense" structure, is especially suited to explanatory case studies—the findings or outcome data are presented first, and the remainder of the report is devoted to building and considering alternative explanations for these findings or outcomes. The sixth structure has no particular logical sequence, but covers the presumed core topics related to the subject of study. For instance, the main descriptive components of a descriptive case study might be the topics of separate chapters (e.g., *Lynd & Lynd,* 1929).

Presentation of individual cases in a multiple-case study. Regardless of the structure you choose, you also have another option when doing a multiple-case study: whether to present the individual case studies in their entirety, in summary fashion or as part of word tables only, or not at all. There are existing models reflecting all of these combinations, and you should examine illustrative reports (many are cited in Yin, 1994a) to understand fully the consequences and implications of selecting any one.

Review by original informants. Whatever the compositional structure, an extremely important quality control tactic is to have your draft report reviewed not only by peers but also by the participants and informants in the case. Such a review is more than a matter of professional courtesy; it represents an essential way of corroborating facts and evidence presented in your report. Thus this procedure is considered one of the 11 tactics you should follow to improve the quality of your case study research (refer back to Table 8.2).

☐   *Aim for an Exemplary Case Study*

An exemplary case study goes beyond all of the methodological procedures highlighted throughout this chapter. If you want to aim high, to produce an exemplary case study, consider the following advice.

First, choose a significant topic. You will be spending a lot of effort on your case study, and you should use your knowledge of existing literature and opportunities to select a significant topic that deserves your work. Second, make sure your case study is "complete," from both theoretical and evidentiary perspectives. One way of knowing that your case might be complete is the absence of artifactual conditions—that you had to end your research, for instance, because time or resources expired. Third, consider alternative perspectives, if not actual rival conditions, in interpreting your research, even if it is a descriptive or exploratory case study. Fourth, display sufficient evidence, defined as the critical evidence a reader would need to reach (or refute) the same conclusions that you have reached in your report. Finally, compose your report in an engaging manner. One way of being engaging, in addition to using good writing style, is to convey enthusiasm and excitement about your work. You should believe that your study contains earth-shattering conclusions.

Allison, G. T. (1971). *Essence of decision: Explaining the Cuban missile crisis.* Boston: Little, Brown.

Borum, Finn (1990). Personal communication. Copenhagen, Denmark: Copenhagen Business School.

Campbell, D. T. (1969). Reforms as experiments. *American Psychologist, 24,* 409-429.

Campbell, D. T., & Stanley, J. C. (1963). *Experimental and quasi-experimental designs for research.* Chicago: Rand McNally.

Cook, T. D., & Campbell, D. T. (1979). *Quasi-experimentation: Design and analysis issues for field settings.* Chicago: Rand McNally.

Glaser, B. G., & Strauss, A. L. (1967). *The discovery of grounded theory: Strategies for qualitative research.* Chicago: Aldine.

Gross, N., Giacquinta, J. B., & Bernstein, M. (1971). *Implementing organizational innovations.* New York: Basic Books.

Hooks, G. (1990). The rise of the Pentagon and U.S. state building: The defense program as industrial policy. *American Journal of Sociology, 96,* 358-404.

Kidder, L., & Judd, C. M. (1986). *Research methods in social relations* (5th ed.). New York: Holt, Rinehart & Winston.

Larsen, J. (1982). *Use of knowledge in mental health services.* Palo Alto, CA: American Institutes for Research.

Lynd, R. S., & Lynd, H. M. (1929). *Middletown: A study in American culture.* New York: Harcourt, Brace.

Markus, M. L. (1983). Power, politics, and MIS implementation. *Communications of the ACM, 26,* 430-444.

Pressman, J. L., & Wildavsky, A. (1973). *Implementation: How great expectations in Washington are dashed in Oakland.* Berkeley: University of California Press.

Redman, E. (1973). *The dance of legislation.* New York: Simon & Schuster.

Strauss, A. L., & Corbin, J. (1990). *Basics of qualitative research: Grounded theory procedures and techniques.* Newbury Park, CA: Sage.

Sutton, R. I., & Staw, B. M. (1995). What theory is *not. Administrative Science Quarterly, 40,* 371-384.

Wholey, J. S. (1979). *Evaluation: Promise and performance.* Washington, DC: Urban Institute.

Whyte, W. F. (1955). *Street corner society: The social structure of an Italian slum* (2nd ed.). Chicago: University of Chicago Press.

Yin, R. K. (1993). *Applications of case study research.* Newbury Park, CA: Sage.

Yin, R. K. (1994a). *Case study research: Design and methods* (2nd ed.). Thousand Oaks, CA: Sage.

Yin, R. K. (1994b). Evaluation: A singular craft. In C. S. Reichardt & S. F. Rallis (Eds.), *The qualitative-quantitative debate: New perspectives* (pp. 71-84). San Francisco: Jossey-Bass.

Yin, R. K., & Chavis, D. M. (1996). *Developing evaluative explanations of how and why community partnerships work in substance abuse prevention.* Unpublished manuscript, COSMOS Corporation, Bethesda, MD.

9

Need Analysis
Process and Techniques

Jack McKillip

In this chapter, I define *need* and describe the process of need analysis, including need identification and need assessment. I then detail data-gathering techniques of resource inventories, secondary analysis, surveys, and group processes, and describe their uses for need identification. Finally, I describe both qualitative and quantitative techniques for information integration in need assessment.

■ *Need Analysis Process*

Need analysis is a decision-aiding tool used for resource allocation, program planning, and program development in the fields of health, education, and the human services. It rests on the optimistic assumption that planned programming can alleviate distress and aid growth. Need analysis has two primary components: *need identification* and *need assessment.* For need identification, information is gathered on those in need, their environments, problems confronting them, and solutions to these problems. For need assessment, this information is synthesized, ordering options for the originating decision.

One distinguishing characteristic of need analysis is that it ties programming to the *circumstances and status of those in need* rather than of service providers, funders, or scholars. The concerns of members of these latter groups are more directly addressed by strategic planning, cost-benefit analysis, or program evaluation. A second characteristic of need analysis is that it assembles decision-aiding information using social science methodologies that seek to *minimize and make explicit the biases and values* that inevitably affect public agency programming decisions. It is this at least prima facie objectivity that may be the primary motivator for needs assessment. Third, need analysis focuses on groups rather than individuals, partly because the decisions that utilize need analyses have a public policy orientation and partly because the methodologies used usually are not sensitive enough for use in individual-level decisions.

□ *Definition of Need*

The first difficulties confronting need analysis arise from ambiguity surrounding the term *need*. Among its many uses (Taylor, 1959), the two most relevant involve *instrumentality* and *moral concern*.

The instrumental nature of a need statement consists in a factual assertion of a means-ends relationship:

X needs Y for W.

Y, what is needed, is a means to achieving some goal state, W, for X (e.g., Frankfurt, 1984). Instrumental need statements suggest but do not impel action. Because needs are instrumental statements, they are open to empirical investigation and verification.

A sense of moral concern often is attached to a need statement and thus does guide or compel action (e.g., Becker, 1973). Some writers base this obligatory facet of need statements on a restriction of the goals states (Ws) that need statements may legitimately include, so-called fundamental needs. Thomson (1987) and Scriven (1991), restrict the goals of need statements to avoiding "harm" or "unsatisfactory states." Ramsay (1992) wants to limit the goals to "health or survival." For these writers, needs are based in human nature and thus have a universal quality that is not conditioned on characteristics of those in need or those making the need statement. An advantage of this restrictive definition of need is that it avoids the current confusion of needs with wants or preferences (Witkin, 1994). As Scriven and Roth (1978) point out, just because one wants something or is willing to spend money on it does not indicate that one needs the thing.

Basing the directive nature of need statements on fundamental or universal goals must be rejected on two grounds. First, the restriction of legitimate goals to "fundamentals" only postpones ambiguity, it does not lessen it (Hare, 1963). What is harmful or healthy is no less open to debate than what is needed.[1] Second, in practice, need analyses are not restricted to avoiding unsatisfactory states or promoting survival. Need analyses recommend actions (Ys) that involve such nonfundamental goals (Ws) as "wellness," "job improvement," and "growth." In practice, need statements cannot be restricted to universals but must be allowed to be conditional on the place and station of those who might possess the needs.

An alternative, and preferred, basis for the directive nature of need statements comes from the consensus-building and verifiable nature of the need analysis process itself. Need analyses compel action because they are *not* based simply on preferences or the personal judgments of an individual. They compel action when based on a participatory and explicit study of problems, solutions, and payoffs.

In the context of need analysis, a need is a *value judgment* that some *group* has a *problem* that can be *solved*. There are four key terms in this definition. Recognition of need involves a narrowing of focus by an observer, a choice among possible goal states (W in the assertion above). This choice represents a preference or *value judgment* that may be independent of its instrumental or verifiable nature.

A need is possessed by a particular *group* of people in a certain set of circumstances (the target group, or Xs). A description of the target population and its environment is an important part of need analysis. Note that the target population may not agree with the need statement. An observer may judge another's state of affairs to be inadequate, even though there is no personal experience of dissatisfaction.

A *problem* is an inadequate outcome, an outcome that violates expectations of what the group's experiences could be. Children may read below grade level or seniors may miss medical appointments. There are many sources of expectations (Bradshaw, 1972), including (a) expert or service provider opinions about what a group's outcomes or services ought to be, such as standards of the Joint Committee on the Accreditation of Health Care Organizations (JCAH), called *normative need*; (b) the target group's preferences for outcomes or services, perhaps from a survey or in focus groups, called *felt need*; (c) the target group's behaviors that respond to the problem, such as actual service utilization or waiting lists, called *expressed need*; and (d) outcome or service usage of groups apparently similar to the target groups, called *comparative need*. Problems can also be identified if a group possesses characteristics that predict poor outcomes, characteristics called *at-risk* indicators. Lack of computer training may predict future unemployment. Finally, a problem may be dormant because a solution or service is in place; this is called a *maintenance need* (Scriven & Roth, 1978). Maintenance needs are often discovered only after a service is withdrawn, such as the need for medical coverage revealed when a person on welfare takes an entry-level job that lacks such coverage and Medicaid eligibility is withdrawn.

Solutions are the instrumental part of a need statement (Ys in the assertion above). They point to what should be done to solve the problem. A solution may be a pullout remedial reading program for children below grade level, or an agency van that can transport seniors who have no access to regular transportation to medical appointments. Adequately analyzed, solutions have three components: (a) efficacy information, or evidence that the solution will solve the problem (see also Cooper & Lindsay, Chapter 11, this volume); (b) feasibility information, or estimates of cost, infrastructure, and personnel needed to mount the solution (see also Yates, Chapter 10, this volume); and (c) utilization information, or evidence that the target group will use or adopt the solution. Solutions are less easily identified than problems, in part because only modest investments have been made in program evaluation and these undertakings usually are narrowly focused on specific situations.

It is part of received wisdom among planners and social activists that the definition of a problem in need analysis greatly influences the solution adopted for it (e.g., Kidder & Fine, 1986). There has been amazingly little research on this notion. McKillip and Kinkner (1991) found that varying whether a problem was attributed to structural or personal factors affected observers' willingness to a endorse a risky programming solution. Alternately, strategic planners often work from the opposite direction, examining the solutions that an agency can provide and seeking means of framing the problems to fit these available solutions.

☐ *Steps in Need Analysis*

1. Identification of users and uses. The first step for need analysis, like that for all decision-aiding processes, is to identify the users and uses of the analysis. The users of the analysis are those who will act on the basis of the analysis and audiences who may be affected by it. The involvement of both groups will usually facilitate the analysis and implementation of its recommendations. Knowing the uses of the need analysis helps the researcher to focus on the problems and solutions that can be entertained, but also may limit the problems and the solutions identified in Step 3, below.

2. Description of the target population and service environment. The second step in need analysis is to describe the target population and the existing service environment. Geographic dispersion, transportation, demographic characteristics (including strengths) of the target population, eligibility restrictions, and service capacity are important. Social indicators are often used to describe the target population either directly or by projection. Resource inventories detailing services available can identify gaps in services and complementary and competing programs. Comparison of those who use services with the target population can reveal unmet needs or barriers to solution implementation.

3. Need identification. The third step is to identify need. Here problems of the target population(s) and possible solutions are described. Usually, more than one source of information is used. Identification should include information on expectations for outcomes, on current outcomes, and on the efficacy, feasibility, and utilization of solutions. Social indicators, surveys, community forums, and direct observations are frequently used.

4. Need assessment. Once problems and solutions have been identified, this information is integrated to produce recommendations for action. Both quantitative and qualitative integration algorithms can be used. The more explicit and open the process, the greater the likelihood that results will be accepted and implemented.

5. Communication. Finally, the results of a need identification must be communicated to decision makers, users, and other relevant audiences. The effort that goes into communication should equal that given the other steps of the need analysis. This step is discussed in depth in McKillip (1987) and will not be covered in this chapter (see also Henry, Chapter 18, this volume).

In practice, need analysis is an iterative and satisficing process: The cycle of decision, data gathering, analysis, and integration repeats until further cycles are judged unnecessary. Although this description implies an orderly and incremental process, this rarely happens. Questions are raised about potential problems and/or solutions; information is gathered and evaluated. Analysis leads to further questions, data gathering, and evaluation. The process ends when those engaged are satisfied that additional information would not be worth the cost of gathering and analyzing it.

■ *Techniques for Need Analysis*

This section is devoted to discussion of data-gathering and integration techniques frequently used in need analysis. First I present the steps for implementing the techniques, and then discuss the uses of the technique for need analysis.

☐ *Resource Inventory*

Procedure

A resource inventory is a compilation and analysis of (usually) services available to one or more target groups, often in a specific geographic region. Information is gathered from service providers, either by survey or personal interview, in answer to these questions: (a) *Who is providing services?* including agency/company name, address, phone number, hours of operation, and possibly number of staff and qualifications; (b) *What services are provided?* including types of services and capacity; and (c) *Who receives services?* including eligibility, ages, and client types. It is important that services, capacity,

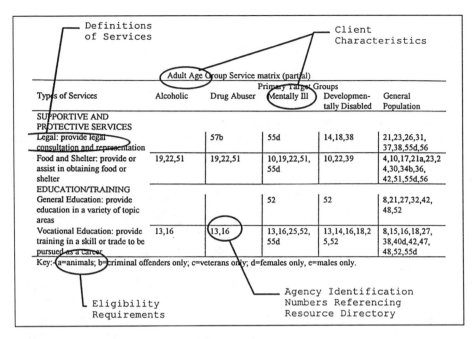

Figure 9.1. Example of Human Services Resource Inventory
SOURCE: Adapted from Fitzgerald and Cutler (1983).

and client categories be clearly defined in the inventory questionnaire, for consistency in responding among service providers. Snowball sampling techniques are useful for identifying service providers to include in the resource inventory; it is especially useful to ask agencies to report where their referrals come from and to what other agencies they make referrals.

Information gathered in response to the above questions can easily be compiled into two types of documents: (a) a directory of resources, which is useful to a wide range of human service agencies, schools, and service providers, often useful enough to warrant their participation; and (b) a resource matrix that arrays services by client characteristics. The directory lists agency contact persons, addresses, and phone numbers for easy access and referrals. The matrix cells are filled with identifiers for agencies that provide the particular services-client combinations, with notes indicating eligibility or other restrictive requirements. Figure 9.1 presents an example of a page from a resource matrix (Fitzgerald & Cutler, 1983). Resource inventories have been widely used for natural resource and other planning areas (Bureau of Land Management, 1990; National Park Service, 1995).

Use in Need Identification

Resource inventories (matrices) have several uses. First, the systematic mapping of services available points to gaps and to widely available services, and may identify services that planners were not aware of. Resource inventories are particularly appropriate for agencies such as United Way, that fund a wide range of services in specified geographic areas.

The utility of resource matrices for need analysis depends on meaningful selection of (a) service typologies such as the United Way's UWASIS (Sumariwalla, 1976) or those in JCAH and the Commission on Accreditation of Rehabilitation Facilities's accreditation standards,[2] and (b) client typology, such as diagnosis or psychosocial functioning level. Fitzgerald and Cutler's (1983) resource inventory examined 27 services from five categories available to five diagnostic and three age groupings of clients.

Alone, empty cells in Figure 9.1 do not indicate need and well-populated cells do not indicate duplication. Combined with other need identification information on the number in the target population who would benefit from a given service, such judgments may be appropriate. A frequent occurrence is that although services are available (a cell is not empty), eligibility restrictions or cultural barriers limit accessibility (see Table 9.1 and related discussion).

Resource inventories are not restricted to enumeration and analyses of services available to a target population, but can be expanded to include other assets and strengths of the target group and its geographic location.

☐ *Secondary Data Analysis*

Government agencies, businesses, funding sources, and academic scholars have assembled large sets of quantitative information that can be accessed in hard copy or in machine-readable form for use in need analysis (McKillip & Stephenson, 1992). Bronfenbrenner's (1996) recent work provides a useful compilation and example of the use of secondary data sources for policy considerations.

Sources of Secondary Data

U.S. Census.[3] Every 10 years, the U.S. Bureau of the Census conducts a nationwide census of population and housing. Basic demographic (e.g., age, race, gender) and housing (e.g., number of rooms, rent) characteristics are enumerated for the entire population. Additional social and economic characteristics (e.g., education, labor force participation) and more detailed housing characteristics (e.g., mobility) are surveyed among a sample of the population. Much of this information is available in book form for large geographic areas (e.g., Metropolitan Statistical Areas) and political units (e.g., states, counties). More detailed information that can be aggregated as required is available on CD-ROMs that are accessible by personal computer. The Census Bureau also has developed a topical integrated geographic encoding and referencing system that maps every inch of the United States in a manner that allows easy collation with census data. The combination of mapping and census information can be used to locate precisely current or potential clients in an agency's catchment area.

Other data archives. In addition to the decennial census, the U.S. government collects and compiles a wide range of information relevant to need analysis that is available through publications or easily accessible databases. Excellent starting points for identifying this information are the *Statistical Abstract of the United States,* the *State and Metropolitan Area Data Book,* and the *County and City Data Book.* All are published in book form and are also available on CD-ROM; the first two appear yearly and the third appears in years ending in 3 and 8. Aside from this wealth of substantive material, the sources of all are referenced. Many of these data archives are available through the National Technical Information Service.[4]

The U.S. government collects a wide range of health statistics.[5] Among the most relevant to need assessment is the National Vital Statistics System for information on births, deaths, marriages, and divorces; the National Health Interview Survey for information on illness, injuries, impairments, and use of health resources; the National Health and Nutrition Examination Survey for objective information on nutritional status, health, and health behavior; and the National Medical Care Expenditure Survey, which covers utilization and expenditures on health resources. The most important survey of mental health is the NIMH-sponsored Epidemiological Catchment Area study (ECA; Robins & Regier, 1991).

Additional data archives are available at the University of Michigan's Inter-University Consortium for Political and Social Research, at Princeton's Office of Population Research, and from private vendors, such as Sociometrics[6] that maintain pregnancy and family data archives. A good source of state, local, and business data is the *Statistical Reference Index* (Congressional Information Service, 1994).

Service utilization. In addition to national information such as the National Medical Care Expenditure Survey, local-agency-based information on characteristics of service users and services received is very important for need analysis. Such information should include (a) unduplicated client demographics, including place of residence; (b) services provided; and (c) referral sources.

Use in Need Analysis

Target population description. In order to set the context for a need analysis, service planners should study and describe both the service environment (resource inventory) and the target population. A target population description seeks to enumerate and describe all people who are eligible to be served by an agency or service. Characteristics should include these important demographic characteristics: age, income, gender, ethnicity, and place of residence. Service planners will particularly benefit from a geographic display of the residences of the eligible target population. Such a display is relatively easily accomplished with the aid of geographic information software.[7]

Synthetic estimation. Often, descriptive or other information is available only for a population larger than or otherwise different from the target population. For example, statistics may be available on pregnancy rates for the United States as a whole or for particular states, but not for a county or a university student body. Sometimes it is appropriate to extrapolate to the target population directly from the larger or different (reference) population. For example, the ECA study indicates that 15.4% of adults suffer from a mental disorder in any month (one-month prevalence; Regier et al., 1988). Because such data are not available for Jackson County, Illinois,[8] the ECA national percentage could be used to estimate the monthly prevalence by multiplying it by the adult population of the county. The result is a monthly prevalence estimate of 7,618 mentally ill adults ($49,467 \times .154$).

The appropriateness of direct extrapolation for a reference population may be contested because a target population differs from it in important ways. Synthetic estimation can be used (a) with the assumption that differences between the target and the reference populations are due to differences in stable demographic characteristics, and (b) if reference population statistics are available for demographic subgroups. For example, it might be assumed that Jackson County differs from the ECA sites because the county has a higher proportion of young males than the reference population due to college enrollment. Figure 9.2 illustrates the use of synthetic estimation to derive a monthly prevalence for mental illness, for substance abuse, and for cognitive impairment for Jackson County from ECA data. Synthetic estimates were 2.4% higher than direct extrapolation for mental illness, 24.7% higher for substance abuse cases, and 6.1% lower for cases of cognitive impairment. These differences reflect the higher proportion of young adults, especially young males, in the Jackson County population than found at the ECA sites.

Client analysis. Client analysis involves comparison of those receiving services (clients) with the target population that is eligible for or in need of those services. Comparative under- or overuse of services is then studied in combination with a resource inventory and other information for barriers to use of current services or for indications of unmet need. The definition of the target population is important. Some programs are aimed at the entire population of a given area, others only at those at risk for developing a specific problem, and others only at those currently with the problem. Client analysis is illustrated in Figure 9.3 for a college alcohol program.

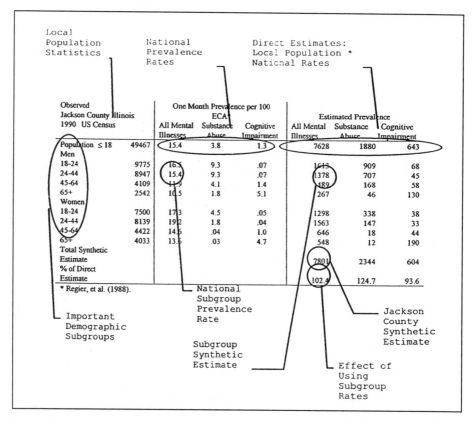

Figure 9.2. Use of Synthetic Estimation

These steps are followed:

1. *Identify important subgroups of client and/or target population.* The subgroups used should be meaningful locally and to funding sources. In Figure 9.3 the important subgroups are gender and academic class. The client population is users of a campus alcohol counseling program and the target population is alternately the general student body and the population of binge drinkers on campus (e.g., Presley, Meilman, & Lyerla, 1993).

2. *For each subgroup, compute the proportion in the target population and the proportion of clients.* These percentages are computed in the middle panel of Figure 9.3.

3. *Compare proportions.* The first column in the third panel of Figure 9.3 assumes that client characteristics should reflect total population characteristics: members of each subgroup should be *equally likely* to use the service of the college alcohol program. Potential unmet needs are indicated if the proportion in the total population is greater than the proportion in the client population. Relative underuse and potential unmet need are indicated by a negative value. As illustrated in Figure 9.3, freshman and sophomore males and freshman and senior women constitute groups with potential unmet need.

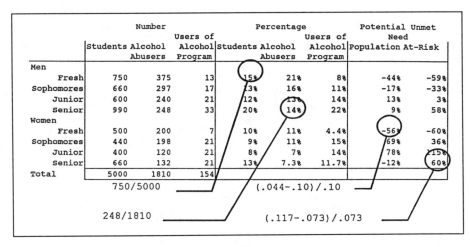

Figure 9.3. Client Analysis for Potential Unmet Need

An alternate assumption is that subgroups should use services according to their membership in an *at-risk* population (here, alcohol abusers). For example, because male freshmen are more likely to abuse alcohol than are others on campus, this group should be more likely to use alcohol program services. This assumption is used in the final column of Figure 9.3. Potential unmet needs are indicated if the proportion in the at-risk population is greater than the proportion in the client population. Relative underuse and potential unmet need are indicated by a negative value. As illustrated in Figure 9.3, freshman and sophomore males and freshman women, but *not* senior women, are groups with potential unmet need.

4. *Examine whether relative underuse indicates unmet need.* Underuse may indicate the absence of a problem, barriers to use of current services, or the alternative and, perhaps, preferred alternative sources of treatment. Barriers can be lack of service availability, lack of client or gatekeeper awareness, service unacceptability, and service inaccessibility. Table 9.1 presents the information needed to examine each type of barrier and a possible source of this information.

Direct and at-risk indicators. Social indicators have been widely used in need analysis, especially in mental health need analysis (Goldsmith, Lin, Bell, & Jackson, 1988). Census-derived indicators usually are taken as indirect, or at-risk, indicators of need. Direct indicators of poor outcomes are usually specifically developed for epidemiological studies. Both are used in aggregate, although there has been little research on their validity. Ciarlo, Tweed, Shern, Kirkpatrick, and Sachs-Ericsson's (1992) pioneering work on the validity of direct indicators of poor mental health shows that they are only weakly related to actual use of services. The researchers related a *DSM-III*-based diagnostic interview and self-report measures of dysfunction in daily living and of depression to use of mental health services. Their results indicate that only 8% of those given a psychiatric diagnosis, 9% of those with dysfunction, and 10% of those depressed had used mental health services within the month of measurement.

Table 9.1 Barriers to Service Use

Barrier	Information Needed	Source
Availability	Are there eligibility restrictions on current services? Does service system have capacity for additional clients?	Resource inventory
Awareness	Is client subgroup or usual subgroup of gatekeepers aware of service? Can client subgroup recognize problem symptoms?	Survey of population subgroup of gatekeepers
Acceptability	Are client subgroup members satisfied with services, setting, staff, convenience?	Survey of client subgroup
Accessibility	How easy is it to use service? Is it accessible to the handicapped or those with childcare needs?	Examination of usual travel time, waiting time, cost and payment schedules; callback interviews with those missing appointments

□ *Surveys*

Survey methodology has been widely adopted as a technique of need identification (Witkin, 1994). Specifics of sample selection and standardized interviewing are discussed at length elsewhere in this volume (see Henry, Chapter 4; Fowler, Chapter 12; Mangione, Chapter 14; and Lavrakas, Chapter 15); I will discuss the use of various types of surveys in need analysis.

Compared with secondary data analysis, surveys present a challenge to need analysis because they involve direct contact with potential service users and providers. Studying a problem or potential service can itself create the expectation among those studied that action will be taken to address the problem and implement the service. This expectation may generate support for implementation of the results of a need analysis, but it may also generate pressure on the direction of the recommendations or skepticism at the lack of follow through.

Use in Need Analysis

Key informants. Key informants are opportunistically connected individuals with the knowledge and ability to report on community needs. Key informants are lawyers, judges, physicians, ministers, minority group leaders, and service providers who are aware of the needs and services perceived as important by a community. Key informant surveys are quick and relatively inexpensive to conduct. They are particularly useful when the problems investigated are rare and when issues of acceptability of a service are raised. Because key informants are important members of their communities, surveying them may affect community support for program changes. On the negative side, key informants may have an organizational perspective on community needs and may be biased toward the activities in which they themselves are involved. Key informant reports often overestimate problems facing the target population and underestimate the population's willingness to participate in programming.

Client satisfaction. Surveys of consumer or client preferences and satisfaction are common in the human services and education. They bring an essential perspective to need analysis and serve to counter the absence of market mechanisms for evaluation and planning of services. Clients use services, and utilization is often a bottom line for program planning.

Several aspects of client surveys are important. Some question the ability of many clients, such as students or mental health patients, to make valid discriminations about programming. Client preferences are often affected by clients' lack of experience with alternatives or shorter horizon for outcomes than is optimal. Second, careful development research on client satisfaction measures has routinely resulted in scales that measure only gross satisfaction or dissatisfaction. Judgments of components of programs are highly correlated with overall judgments. A related issue is that client satisfaction ratings are invariably positive. In an examination of 26 consumer satisfaction studies in mental health, Lebow (1982) found that between 70% and 90% satisfaction was typical, and that a median of 49% of respondents were "very satisfied." A fourth concern with client surveys has to do with sampling bias. Because clients, by definition, are aware of an available and accessible program, they may be different from those who are impeded from program use by various barriers. Consumers who respond to the survey may not represent all consumers, but rather may oversample the more satisfied. Finally, especially when distributed at the time of service use, consumer surveys are potentially reactive. Respondents say what they think their teachers or therapists want to hear. Studies of client satisfaction have shown a lack of relationship to more rigorously defined measures of client outcome (Williams, 1994).

McKillip, Moirs, and Cervenka (1992) suggest that standardized client satisfaction questions be supplemented by direct, open-ended solicitation of reasons for dissatisfaction, even from generally satisfied clients. They found that critical comments were judged to be the most useful information for program planning and improvement.

Training surveys. Planning for training and continuing education is a primary need analysis activity (Queeney, 1995). Surveys of experts, supervisors,

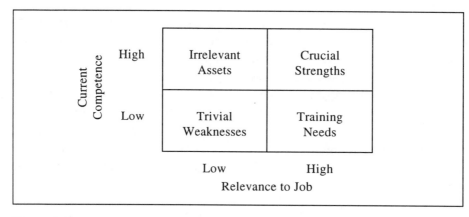

Figure 9.4. Use of Relevance and Competence Ratings for Training Need Identification

and/or potential trainees are common and focus on two components of training need: the *competence* or ability of individuals to perform a task and the *relevancy* or importance of a skill or ability for the job role (Alberty & Mihalik, 1989). A training need survey includes these steps:

1. A list of potential training topics is developed. This list may come from the work of a small committee of experts, such as supervisors, or may be the result of a task analysis for the job.

2. A survey is developed that asks respondents to rate each potential training topic on the level of competence of current job holders and on the relevance of the training topic to the job. Respondents may be experts, supervisors, or potential trainees themselves.

3. Training topics that get below a midpoint rating (mean, median) on current competence and above-average ratings in relevance to the job are identified as training needs. This is the lower right-hand quadrant of Figure 9.4. Queeney (1995) reports that professionals' self-reports of training needs tend to understate the need for refresher or remedial workshops (crucial strengths in Figure 9.4) and overstate the need for training on new technologies or new procedures (training needs in Figure 9.4).

☐ *Group Procedures*

Perhaps the simplest method of need analysis is to assemble groups of experts and concerned citizens and charge them with identifying the needs of a population. Using the members' knowledge and experience with the population and awareness of services currently available, a need analysis committee can identify and rank problems and their solutions. Such a straightforward approach is often unsuccessful, however, in part because of inadequacies of unstructured group processes (Gillette, McCollom, & Janis, 1990).

Structured groups provide a supplement and an alternative to traditional survey techniques. I will review three here. *Focus groups* are widely used in marketing to explore consumers' reactions to products and packaging. This technique is discussed in depth elsewhere in this volume (see Stewart & Shamdasani, Chapter 17), so I will comment only on its use in need analysis. *Nominal groups* provide a highly structured but interactive way to generate and evaluate ideas. They are useful for identifying problems of a target population and generating solutions. *Community forums and public hearings* are the data collection methods of choice in the political arena. They are useful when public display is critical to the acceptance of the results of a need analysis.

Group techniques engender participant enthusiasm and expectations about future action, especially community and public hearings. Resultant enthusiasm and expectations may politicize or disappoint participants and complicate as well as advance the planning process.

Procedures

Nominal groups. Delbecq (1986) developed the nominal group technique to allow for idea generation and evaluation while avoiding typical problems of unstructured group dynamics: A few higher-status members do most of the talking, idea evaluation discourages idea generation, and the group strays from its agenda. In contrast, the result of the nominal group is a priority ranking of answers to various need analysis questions derived from the active input of all participants.

Nominal group sessions generally last between 2 and 4 hours. The technique requires a room large enough to hold all participants and a nonparticipating group leader, a table for every 6-9 participants, a flip pad for each table, and paper or index cards. The steps for running a nominal group are as follows:

1. Develop questions for participants, requiring that they generate problem dimensions or differentiated solutions. For example, What factors account for a high rate of teenage pregnancy in an area? What alternatives are available for promoting responsible student alcohol use?

2. Select participants from among those who can contribute to answering the questions that have been developed. Representatives of different perspectives should be included in the total group and in the subgroups of 6-9 members at each table. Identify a leader at each table who will direct but not participate in that group.

3. After assembling the subgroups and describing the full procedure to all participants, have each participant answer the first question by writing individual alternatives on index cards. Do not permit discussion at this step.

4. Record the ideas generated on a flip chart, each with an identifying letter, in round-robin fashion. Have each participant present one idea in turn until all ideas have been listed. As you fill pages on the chart, display them on the walls around the room. Do not allow discussion.

5. Explain and clarify, but do not criticize, each idea. Allow consensus collapsing or grouping of ideas. No more than 25% of the time allowed for the entire process should be expended on this step.

6. Have each group member privately rank the top ideas on index cards (e.g., the top five), using the ideas' identifying letters. Collate the responses on these cards and then record the popularity of each idea on the pages of the flip chart.

7. Hold a brief clarifying discussion; surprise rankings may be due to group members' misunderstanding of some ideas.

8. Have each member again privately rank the top ideas, and combine the rankings from the subgroups for an overall tally.

The cycle of Steps 1-8 is repeated for each of the need analysis questions.

Public hearings. Public hearings are an investigative and evaluative tool. Members of a committee hear testimony from selected witnesses, raise questions, cross-examine witnesses, and issue a summary report. "Blue-ribbon" committees can increase the public credibility of a need analysis and calm concern over its implications, at least in the short run. I have presented the following steps for public hearings in earlier work (McKillip, 1987):

1. The parent body (e.g., a United Way board) outlines the charge to the committee, selects committee members, appoints a chairperson, and identifies counsel and other professional support staff. The inclusion of representatives of affected groups as well as experts from outside the management structure will increase credibility.

2. In line with the committee's charge, committee members and support staff prepare background work, brief other committee members, and identify witnesses.

3. The committee plans the hearing, including notifying witnesses and informing them about the rules of operation.

4. The chairperson conducts the hearing, including examination of witnesses. Credibility is in large part dependent on the seriousness of the hearing and the attention, reflected in questions, paid to the witnesses.

5. The chairperson and counsel draft a report that is reviewed by other committee members. The final report is submitted to the parent body.

Community forums. A less expensive but more public approach than the public hearing is a community forum or town meeting. A typical forum involves an evening meeting in a politically neutral auditorium. Concerned members of the community address need analysis issues such as desirability of a particular type of programming. Wide advertising is important to the success of a community forum, as are established ground rules about the length and content of public statements. Rules, such as a 3-minute limit on statements, should be made explicit at the beginning of the forum and enforced by the leader. The purpose of the forum should be made clear by banners and should be reiterated frequently by the leader. Follow-up mailings thanking those who attended and summarizing the results (especially future actions) of the forum are important. A sign-up sheet for collecting the names and addresses of participants will ease this task and provide the basis of assembling a network of interested community members and activists.

Use in Need Analysis

Focus groups. Focus groups let participants react to problem dimensions or the acceptability and accessibility of proposed solutions in a nonstructured environment. Participants can be clients, target population members, or service providers, although subgroups need to be kept separate (Buttram, 1990). A focus group is a particularly attractive source of information when those identifying and assessing needs are not themselves members of or knowledgeable about the target population. Focus groups allow planners to hear and see the target population. The power of focus groups is based on the intense involvement between moderator and subjects (Krueger, 1994).

The immediacy and vividness of participants' answers to questions may create problems for need analysis. Focus group participants are usually selected because of homogeneity. If the target population is relatively homogeneous in problems or in reactions to solutions, focus group data will give inexpensive and useful insights into program development and planning. If the target group is not homogeneous, focus groups by themselves create a false sense of understanding of needs. In addition, inexperienced observers may be affected by what is called an availability heuristic—a tendency for vivid or concrete anecdotes to be given more credibility than more somber but firmly based evidence (Tversky & Kahneman, 1974).

Nominal groups. Nominal groups separate idea generation from idea evaluation, while developing an easily summarized ranking of the ideas brought forth. Clients, key informants, staff members, or service providers can easily be assembled in nominal groups to identify problems or to propose solutions. Because of the structure of participation, status hierarchies that might stifle interactions within or among members of some groups are less worrisome for nominal groups.

Several parts of the nominal group process are easily summarized and useful for planning. The lists of ideas that are generated in the process are available on the flip chart pages. These can be codified, compared between groups, and subjected to further analyses (e.g., clustering). The ranking of ideas that results from participants' votes similarly can be used to prioritize needs, problems, or solutions. On the downside, because nominal groups are highly structured, participants are sometimes dissatisfied with the extent or the quality of opportunities for expression.

Public hearings and community forums. Because need analysis often takes place in a politicized atmosphere and depends on consensus among diverse groups, public hearings and community forums are often appropriate. Both provide the opportunity for participation and input from many audiences. Both help identify groups in the community that are supportive of or antagonistic toward proposed solutions to community problems. Both can contribute to broader public acceptance of need analysis recommendations. Both also have drawbacks.

Public hearings can take on a confrontational nature in which advocacy groups vie for political attention rather than try to build consensus (Vining, 1992). In addition, although open to broad-based participation, actual participants often are not representative of the populations for which they seek to speak (Mater, 1984). Community forums share these shortcomings, although they tend to be less severe. Forums should be used more to build support for ideas than to gather information. A forum can be useful if a cross-section of the community is involved, if an experienced leader is available, and if the purpose of the forum is made clear.

☐ *Information Integration*

The result of a need identification is a set of need statements, each with supporting information gathered from various data sources. The supporting information may include several indicators of target group outcomes along with information on solution feasibility, efficacy, and probable utilization. This information may be displayed in a matrix similar to that in Figure 9.5.

Need analysis should not end with an assembly of a list of needs or problems. To be most helpful in decision making, need analysis requires integration of need identification information. This is the task of need assessment. Information integration is fairly simple if, as is too often the case (Witkin, 1994), need identification relies on a single data source. Complications arise when multiple data sources are used to identify needs. No need or problem is dominant—that is, highest—on all data sources. In this case, the choice among needs involves trade-offs—the need or needs selected for intervention will be lower on some dimension than those not selected.

Although the need for systematic means for information integration has been obvious for some time (Kimmel, 1977; Shapek, 1975), the topic has been studiously avoided in much of the literature. Below, I review several techniques for integrating information from a need identification matrix such as that shown in Figure 9.5.

Qualitative Integration Rules

Pruning. For this rule, data sources or need indicators are first ordered from the most to the least important and are considered in this order. First, need statements that are low on the most important dimension are eliminated. For

| | Need Indicators/Data Sources | | | | | |
| | Secondary Data Sources | | Survey Results | | Solution Information | |
Need Statements	SI[1]	SI[2]	Key Informants[3]	Clients[4]	Feasibility[5]	Efficacy[6]
Group A needs X to R	.23	.52	6.2	4.3	.35	.24
Group A needs Y to S	.15	.63	6.5	5.4	.78	.35
Group B needs Z to T	.36	.23	4.8	5.2	.13	.62
Group D needs X to T	.08	.84	5.9	6.3	.54	.14

Figure 9.5. A Fictional Need Identification Matrix

NOTE: Cells contain information gathered as part of need identification.

1. Proportion of group currently using services.
2. Proportion of group with at-risk characteristic.
3. Rating of need on scale from low (1) to high (7).
4. Rating of need on scale from low (1) to high (7).
5. Proportion in top five, from service provider nominal group process.
6. Average impact in literature, effect size.

the example in Figure 9.5, if acceptability to clients is seen as very important (column 4), the first need statement should be dropped. Next, among those need statements that remain, those low on the second most important dimension are eliminated. This procedure is followed until the need statements to be implemented remain.

Minimum criterion analysis. For this rule, a minimally acceptable level is identified for each need indicator. Only those need statements that are above the minimal level on all indicators are considered. For example, in Figure 9.5, if a solution must have at least moderate probability of being implemented (e.g., .5), then the first and the third need statements should be dropped.

Balance sheet method.[9] Information on each need statement is examined for each need indicator and assigned either a plus sign, indicating strong evidence of need, or a minus sign, indicating weak evidence of need. Need statements are then eliminated from consideration or retained based on the patterns of pluses and minuses.

Quantitative Integration Rules

Rank orders. For each need indicator (column) separately, all need statements are ranked from highest to lowest. The highest-ranked statement is the one whose information indicates the greatest need. In Figure 9.5, this statement could be given the value of 4. Information on the lowest-ranked statements indicates the least need and receives the value of 1. Ties receive the same rank. After need statements are ranked on all need indicators, ranks can be added or averaged. Statements with the highest overall rank reveal the greatest overall need.

Standardization. If the need information is itself quantitative, values can be standardized within each indicator and then added or averaged, as with the ranks above. Two standardization procedures are popular. A Z-score transformation changes original need indicators' values using this formula:

$$Z_{score} = \frac{\text{Original Value} - \text{Mean of Column}}{\text{Standard Deviation of Column}}$$

Z scores have certain desirable statistical properties and can then be added or averaged across need indicators.[10] Z scores have the drawback that they are not easily interpreted by the statistically unsophisticated. In Figure 9.5, the Z score for the first need statement on the first need indicator (first row, first column) is

$$\frac{23 - .21}{.11} = .24.$$

A zero-one normalization sets the value of the lowest-ranked need statement on each need indicator to zero and the value of the highest-ranked need statement to one. Intermediate need statement values are transformed using this formula:

$$\text{Normalized}_{score} = \frac{\text{Original Value} - \text{Lowest Column Value}}{\text{Highest Column Value} - \text{Lowest Column Value}}$$

Normalized scores can also be added or averaged over need indicators (columns), as with Z scores. In Figure 9.5, the normalized score for the first need statement on the first need indicator (first row, first column) is

$$\frac{.23 - .08}{.36 - .08} = .54.$$

Weighting by importance. One drawback of simply adding or averaging transformed need indicators is that aggregation assumes that all indicators are equally important for the decision and to all decision makers. This may rarely be the case. In earlier work, I have suggested the following magnitude procedure

	Need Indicators/Data Sources					
	Secondary Data Sources		Survey Results			
Weight Calculations	SI	SI	Key Informants	Clients	Feasibility	Efficacy
Rank on Importance (Step 1)	6	2	1	5	4	3
Magnitude Estimation (Step 2-4)	45	15	10	40	35	25
Importance (Step 5)	.29	.09	.06	.24	.21	.15

Figure 9.6. Example of Calculation of Importance Weights for Example in Figure 9.5

for developing weights to reflect the importance of need indicators to the decision or to individual decision makers or audiences (McKillip, 1987):

1. Considering the highest and lowest values that actually occur on each of the need indicators, rank the need indicators from the least to the most important. This step is illustrated by the first row of Figure 9.6.

2. Assign the importance value of 10 to the least important need indicator.

3. Compare the two least important indicators. Assign an importance value to the second indicator that reflects how much more important it is than the least important one. For example, an importance value of 15 indicates that it is 50% more important. A value of 10 indicates that it is of equal importance.

4. Repeat Step 3 for each pair of need indicators, moving from least to most important (e.g., 7 versus 6, 6 versus 5, 5 versus 4). Consistency checks are advisable and revisions are common. Steps 2 to 4 are illustrated in the second row of Figure 9.6.

5. Compute an importance weight for each need indicator by dividing its final importance value by the sum of all importance values (e.g., 170 in Figure 9.6). Importance weights now sum to 1.0. The value of each weight indicates how much of the decision depends on the particular indicator. This step is illustrated in the third row of Figure 9.6.

When aggregating across need indicators, one first multiplies standardized values by each indicator's importance weight. The sum of these products presents an interval measure of each need statement. Values can be compared between decision makers. The entire procedure is easily implemented on a computer spreadsheet program such as Excel or Lotus 123. This and alternative procedures are discussed in detail in Pitz and McKillip (1984).

■ *Summary and Conclusions*

Need analysis is one place applied researchers meet the rough-and-tumble world of competing demands for and justifications of actions. Need analysis is wading into a white-water stream compared to basic research's stroll in a park. However, with the competing pressures comes the opportunity for researchers to help identify and have an impact on issues that are of concern to and can benefit the general public.

Need analysis is also challenging because it calls for several different technical and interpersonal skills. The analyst or technical consultant must know about secondary data analysis, survey research, qualitative interviewing, and group process. I have not discussed here the issue of which mixture of techniques is appropriate and feasible for any analysis; I address this topic at length in McKillip (1987).

Finally, need analysis is an area where communication with decision makers and other audiences is more important than is typical for basic research. Information sought and compiled should be communicated forthrightly and regularly. In addition, the value choices that are constantly part of the need analysis should be made with input and attention from all concerned.

■ *Notes*

1. This argument reaches back at least to Plato, with the dispute between Socrates and Glaucon on the relative merits of a healthy city versus a city on fire (Plato, 1968, pp. 372-373).

2. The Internet home page address of the Joint Committee on Accreditation of Health Care Organizations is http://www.jcaho.org; the home page address for the Commission on Accreditation of Rehabilitation Facilities is http://www.carf.org.

3. The U.S. Census Bureau's Internet home page address is http://www.census.gov.

4. The Internet home page address of the National Technical Information Service is http://www. fedworld.gov/ntis.

5. The Internet home page address of the National Center for Health Statistics is http://www.cdc.gov/nchswww/nchshome.htm.

6. The Internet home page address of the Inter-University Consortium for Political and Social Research is http://www.icpsr.umich.edu; the address for the Office of Population Research is http://opr.princeton/edu; and the address for Sociometrics is http://www.socio.com.

7. The Internet home page address for the National Center for Geographic Information and Analysis is http://www.ncgia.ucsb.edu. Home pages for two widely used GIS programs, Mapinfo and Maptitude, can be found at http://www.mapinfo.com and http://www.caliper.com/mtover.htm, respectively.

8. Jackson County is the home of Southern Illinois University at Carbondale.

9. Development of this method is attributed to Benjamin Franklin.

10. Z scores preserve interval information in the original need indicator metric. By contrast, ranks are only ordinal measures.

■ References

Alberty, S., & Mihalik, B. J. (1989). The use of importance performance analysis as an evaluative technique in adult education. *Evaluation Review, 13,* 33-44.

Becker, L. C. (1973). *On justifying moral judgments.* London: Routledge & Kegan Paul.

Bradshaw, J. (1972). The concept of social need. *New Society, 30,* 640-643.

Bronfenbrenner, U. (1996). *The state of Americans: This generation and the next.* New York: Free Press.

Bureau of Land Management. (1990). *Cultural resources inventory general guidelines* (4th ed., rev.). Washington, DC: U.S. Department of the Interior.

Buttram, J. L. (1990). Focus groups: A starting point for need assessment. *Evaluation Practice, 11,* 207-212.

Ciarlo, J. A., Tweed, D. L., Shern, D. L., Kirkpatrick, L. A., & Sachs-Ericsson, N. (1992). I. Validation of indirect methods to estimate need for mental health services. *Evaluation and Program Planning, 15,* 115-131.

Congressional Information Service. (1994). *Statistical reference index.* Washington, DC: Author.

Delbecq, A. L. (1986). *Group techniques for program planning: A guide to nominal group and Delphi processes.* Middleton, WI: Green Briar.

Fitzgerald, C. T., & Cutler, W. (1983). *Resource inventory and directory of services for Jackson County, Illinois.* Carbondale: Southern Illinois University, Applied Research Consultants.

Frankfurt, H. (1984). Necessity and desire. *Philosophy and Phenomenological Research, 45,* 1-13.

Gillette, J., McCollom, M., & Janis, I. (Eds.). (1990). *Groups in context: A new perspective on group dynamics.* Reading, MA: Addison-Wesley.

Goldsmith, H. F., Lin, E., Bell, R. A., & Jackson, D. J. (Eds.). (1988). *Needs assessment: Its future* (DHHS Publication No. ADM 88-1550). Washington, DC: Government Printing Office.

Hare, R. M. (1963). *Freedom and reason.* Oxford: Oxford University Press.

Kidder, L. H., & Fine, M. (1986). Making sense of injustice: Social explanations, social action, and the role of the social scientist. In E. Seidman & J. Rappaport (Eds.), *Redefining social problems* (pp. 49-64). New York: Plenum.

Kimmel, W. (1977). *Needs assessment: A critical perspective.* Washington DC: U.S. Department of Health, Education and Welfare, Office of Program Systems.

Krueger, R. A. (1994). *Focus groups: A practical guide for applied research* (2nd ed.). Thousand Oaks, CA: Sage.

Lebow, J. (1982). Consumer satisfaction with mental health treatment. *Psychological Bulletin, 91,* 244-259.

Mater, J. (1984). *Public hearings, procedures and strategies.* Englewood Cliffs, NJ: Prentice Hall.

McKillip, J. (1987). *Need analysis: Tools for the human services and education.* Newbury Park, CA: Sage.

McKillip, J., & Kinkner, T.L. (1991). *Performance deficit and solution selection: Problem explanation and framing effects.* Paper presented at the annual meeting of the American Evaluation Association, Chicago.

McKillip, J., Moirs, K., & Cervenka, C. (1992). Asking open-ended consumer questions to aid program planning. *Evaluation and Program Planning, 15,* 1-6.

McKillip, J., & Stephenson, H. (1992). Using government information and other archives. In A. Vaux, M. S. Stockdale, & M. J. Schwerin (Eds.), *Independent consulting for evaluators* (pp. 127-140). Newbury Park, CA: Sage.

National Park Service. (1995). *Natural resource inventory and monitoring in national parks.* Washington, DC: U.S. Department of the Interior.

Pitz, G. F., & McKillip, J. (1984). *Decision analysis for program evaluators.* Beverly Hills, CA: Sage.

Plato. (1968). *The Republic of Plato* (A. Bloom, Trans.). New York: Stephoni.

Presley, C. A., Meilman, P. W., & Lyerla, R. (1993). *Alcohol and drugs on American college campuses* (Vol. 1). Carbondale: Illinois Core Institute, Center for Alcohol and Other Drug Studies.

Queeney, D. S. (1995). *Assessing needs in continuing education: An essential tool for quality improvement.* San Francisco: Jossey-Bass.

Ramsay, M. (1992). *Human needs and the market.* Aldershot, England: Avebury.

Regier, D. A., Boyd, J. H., Burke, J. D., Rae, D. S., Myers, J. K. Kramer, M., Robbins, L. N., George, L. K., Karno, M., & Locke, B. Z. (1988). One month prevalence of mental disorders in the United States. *Archives of General Psychiatry, 45,* 977-986.

Robins, L. N., & Regier, D. A. (1991). *Psychiatric disorders in America: The Epidemiologic Catchment Area Study.* New York: Free Press.

Scriven, M. (1991). *Evaluative thesaurus* (Vol. 4). Newbury Park, CA: Sage.

Scriven, M., & Roth, J. (1978). Needs assessment: Concept and practice. *New Directions for Program Evaluation, 1,* 1-11.

Shapek, R. A. (1975). Problems and deficiencies in the needs assessment process. *Public Administration Review, 35,* 754-758.

Sumariwalla, R. D. (1976). *UWASIS II: A taxonomy of social goals and human service programs.* Alexandria, VA: United Way of America.

Taylor, P. (1959). "Need" statements. *Analysis, 19*(5), 106-111.

Thomson, G. (1987). *Needs.* London: Routledge & Kegan Paul.

Tversky, A., & Kahneman, D. (1974). Judgment under uncertainty: Heuristics and biases. *Science, 185,* 1124-1131.

Vining, J. (1992). Environmental emotions and decisions: A comparison of responses and expectations for forest managers, and environmental group, and the public. *Environment and Behavior, 24,* 3-34.

Williams, B. (1994). Patient satisfaction: A valid concept? *Social Science and Medicine, 38,* 509-516.

Witkin, R. B. (1994). Needs assessment since 1981: The state of the practice. *Evaluation Practice, 15,* 17-27.

10

Formative Evaluation of Costs, Cost-Effectiveness, and Cost-Benefit

Toward Cost → Procedure → Process → Outcome Analysis

Brian T. Yates

■ *Why Neither Effectiveness nor Cost Is Enough*

Versions of the following tale are acted out daily as the terms *cost-effectiveness* and *cost-benefit* are dropped into discussions about whether to fund different human services:

> Three decision makers met to decide which of three programs to fund. Each presented a graph of carefully collected and analyzed data.
>
> The first decision maker said, "Program A should be funded because it was significantly more effective than Programs B or C, as shown in my graph (Figure 10.1a)."
>
> The second decision maker said, "No, my data show that Program C should be funded. It is significantly less expensive than Programs A or B, as shown in my graph (Figure 10.1b)."
>
> The third decision maker asserted, "Neither Program A nor C should be funded, as shown by my graph, which includes both your cost and your outcome

AUTHOR'S NOTE: Correspondence should be sent to Brian T. Yates, Department of Psychology, American University, Washington, DC 20016-8062. Phone and voice mail, (202) 885-1727; fax, (202) 885-1023; e-mail, BYates@American.edu or BrianYates@msn.com.

data (Figure 10.1c). According to budget limits, the highly effective Program A costs too much to be feasible. This budget constraint is represented by the vertical dashed line in my graph. According to quality standards, inexpensive Program C does not qualify for funding. Its effectiveness is below the minimum deemed acceptable by community and client representatives. This effectiveness constraint is represented by the horizontal line of long and short dashes. Only Program B is feasible and, therefore, it is the only program that can be funded."

Finally, a seasoned program evaluator noted, "All three graphs are correct. Figure 10.1a accurately represents the effectiveness of the three programs, but shows what happens when costs are ignored: They not only do not appear on the graph, but they do not enter into decision making at all. The first decision maker assumes that costs did not matter or were basically the same for Programs A, B, and C—a position shown more transparently by graphing effectiveness against cost (Figure 10.1d). This figure is obviously incorrect: Figure 10.1c shows that costs do indeed differ among the programs. The second decision maker assumed that outcomes did not matter, or basically were the same for the three programs. This position is presented in Figure 10.1e and also is clearly incorrect; outcomes do differ among the programs, again as shown in Figure 10.1c."

The moral of this story, of course, is that neither the evaluation of costs to the exclusion of outcomes nor the evaluation of outcomes to the exclusion of costs provides a complete picture of the effects of delivering human services. Only including data on costs and outcomes will begin to do that, and even more information—such as budget constraints and minimum acceptable levels of outcome—is needed (Yates, 1994). There are many ways to combine data on costs, outcomes, and other aspects of human services to evaluate and decide how to improve those services.

■ *Classic Cost-Effectiveness and Cost-Benefit Analysis*

Measuring and analyzing data on costs and outcomes of alternative programs form the essence of cost-effectiveness analysis and cost-benefit analysis. Classic cost-effectiveness analysis (CEA) compares costs to outcomes as they are typically measured in human services and social sciences—for example, "improved functioning," "quality-adjusted life years added" (see Levin, 1980; Yates & Newman, 1980a, 1980b). Classic cost-benefit analysis (CBA) compares costs to program outcomes that are measured in the same units as costs. For CBA, outcomes can be measured as costs offset or as benefits produced (see Thompson, 1980). Cost offsets are funds that other agencies or individuals did not have to spend because of what a program accomplished. Examples of cost offsets are decreased welfare payments to persons who gain employment and reduced future health care costs caused by reduced client need for health care (see Friedman, Sobel, Myers, Caudill, & Benson, 1995; Jones & Vischi, 1979; Yates, 1980b, 1984). Benefits produced are resources actually generated

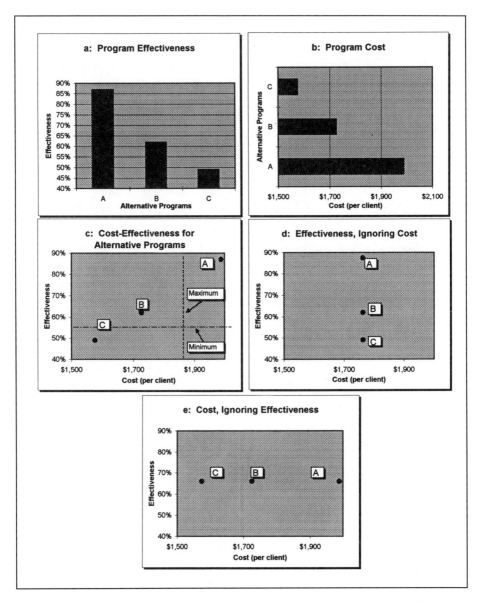

Figure 10.1. Graphs of Outcomes, Costs, and Cost → Outcome Relationships for Three Alternative Human Service Programs

by a program, such as the net income that an individual receives from employment or the taxes paid by an employed individual (see Friedman et al., 1995; Yates, 1985).

CEA and CBA can compare costs and outcomes separately, or cost and outcome data can be combined to form single indices such as ratios (Yates, 1985). Ratios of cost divided by effectiveness can be meaningful by themselves—for example, cost per life saved, cost per drug abuser prevented, or cost per pound of weight lost (e.g., Yates, 1978). Ratios of benefits divided by costs are especially appealing in their apparent simplicity and ease of use (see also Yates, 1987). If benefits exceed costs, the program appears to be beneficial and should be funded. If benefits do not exceed costs, the program apparently is a poor investment. Given the severity of limits on funds for human services, however, it usually is impossible to fund all programs that yield greater benefits than costs. In the making of funding decisions, ratios of benefit to cost end up being compared for different programs, as do ratios of cost to effectiveness.

■ *Comparing Costs and Outcomes Separately for Different Programs*

Considering costs and outcomes separately may generate more useful decisions, in that less information is discarded and constraints on costs and outcomes can be incorporated into the decision directly. Programs that exceed budget limits or that do not exceed minimum standards for outcomes will have to be excluded. For the remaining programs, it will have to be decided whether it is better to sponsor the least costly program that achieves the minimum allowable outcomes or to sponsor the program that achieves the highest effectiveness or most benefits within budget limits. Often a sort of dynamic decision making occurs at this point, with some interest groups raising the criterion for minimum acceptable outcome while other interest groups lower the maximum allowable cost.

Next, data on outcomes are analyzed statistically to find which of the remaining programs generate significantly better outcomes. Data on the cost of those programs for each client also can be analyzed statistically to find the program that requires the smallest amount of funds. (Statistical analyses of costs are often possible because costs can vary between clients according to client participation and the types and amounts of services used to help the client.) If one of these programs is both significantly more effective and significantly less costly than the others, it is funded. Similarly, if none of the programs in this group differ significantly on cost but one program is superior to the others in outcome, it is chosen. If none of the programs differ in outcomes but one costs less than the others, it is chosen.

Naturally, it is possible that several programs will be better than the others on outcomes or costs, but will not differ significantly among themselves. Each of these programs could be funded temporarily to see which might replicate or improve its cost $\rightarrow$ outcome performance. Unfortunately, it also may be the case that dividing funds among the more cost-effective or cost-beneficial programs could cause each to be so underfunded that it would generate less desirable cost $\rightarrow$ outcome relationships. In such instances, possible actions would be to combine program operations and to find alternative public or private sources of funding.

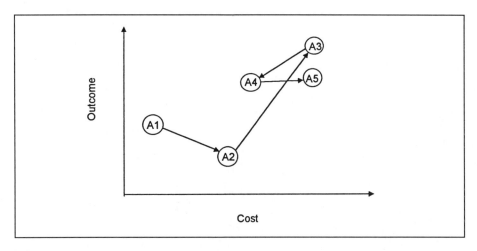

Figure 10.2. Changes in the Cost → Outcome Relationship for One Program (A)
Over Successive Quarters

NOTE: For example, A1 denotes the cost and outcome coordinates for January, February, and March
combined; A2 denotes the cost and outcome coordinates for April, May, and June combined; and so on.

■ *Graphing Cost → Outcome Functions for Service Procedures*

☐ *Cost → Outcome Graphs*

To enable decision makers to understand more fully the complex situation
of funding levels and cost → outcome relationships, the functional *relationship*
of costs to outcomes can be studied for different levels of funding. How outcomes vary as a function of costs may become clear if outcomes and costs for
one program are graphed over a period during which the program fluctuates in
funding or in other factors that determine expenditures. Figure 10.2 illustrates
how costs and outcomes might vary for a single program (A) over time. The
cost → outcome relationship for the first quarter (January, February, and
March) of Program A is indicated by A1 in the figure, the cost → outcome
relationship for the second quarter of Program A is indicated by A2, and so on.
Note that a return in Quarter 5 to the same level of funding as received in
Quarter 3 does not generate exactly the same outcome. This minor variation in
the cost → outcome relationship is common; it may be the result of error in
measurement, or of a change in factors that moderate the cost → outcome
relationship (e.g., use of more expensive personnel).

Naturally, the apparent pattern of cost → outcome relationships shown in
a graph may reflect influences of variables other than expenditures. It may be
more useful to find programs similar to those being considered for funding,
and to graph cost and outcome data for them as well. This sort of graph is shown
in Figure 10.3 for three programs (A, B, and C) for five quarters (A1, B1, C1
representing Quarter 1 performance, A2, B2, C2 representing Quarter 2 performance, and so on). The natural variation in levels of expenditure that may

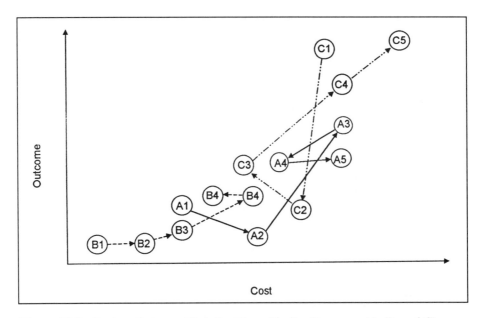

Figure 10.3. Cost → Outcome Plots for Three Similar Programs (A, B, and C)
Over Successive Quarters

exist for these programs may allow decision makers to predict how the outcomes of a similar program might change if funding is increased or decreased.

Factors external to the system may be responsible for some of the variation
in outcome and cost, potentially preventing discernment of the actual cost →
outcome relationship. For reasons unrelated to outcomes, some program sites
may require that personnel be paid more, and office space also may cost more.
It might be hoped that focusing on cost → outcome relationships inside a program might better reveal the nature of the cost → outcome function for the
program, but that too can be problematic. Figure 10.4 is a three-dimensional
graph showing the cost of producing change in the GAS (Global Assessment
Scale)—a measure of functioning for clients beginning treatment at different
levels of functioning (Spitzer, Gibbon, & Endicott, 1975). Generally, the
smaller changes, often beginning at the lowest levels of functioning, require
more expenditures of resources. The highest "peaks" of cost in Figure 10.4 are
located above the rows that correspond to the intersections of the lowest levels
of functioning before and after treatment. The lowest levels of cost in Figure
10.4 are located above cells that represent the highest levels of functioning
posttreatment and substantially lower levels of functioning pretreatment. This
unexpected, almost inverse relationship between outcome and cost is likely a
function of the humane orientation of the program manager and practitioners,
who devote additional service resources to clients who begin treatment at low
levels of functioning and who do not respond to the commonly prescribed
amount of treatment.

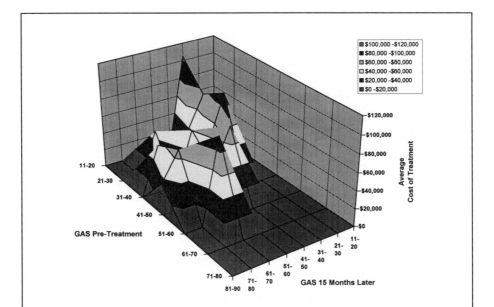

Figure 10.4. Three-Dimensional Graph of Cost → Outcome Relationships Within
One Program for Clients Beginning Treatment at Different Levels of Functioning
(as Measured by the Global Assessment Scale)
SOURCE: Yates (1996).

☐   *Cost → Procedure → Outcome Graphs*

As some of the preceding figures suggest, it often is possible to find meaningful relationships between costs and outcomes by graphing costs and outcomes of alternative programs. Figure 10.5, for instance, shows the costs and
outcomes expected for individual clients receiving different obesity treatments.
The circles indicate experts' estimates of the probable long-term effectiveness
and probable cost of each of several competing weight loss procedures. On
either side of the circle representing a weight loss procedure, horizontal lines
ending in arrowheads indicate the "best case" and "worst case" scenarios for
the cost of the technique. Vertical bars emerging from the same circle, also
ending in arrowheads, represent the "worst case" and "best case" scenarios for
the effectiveness of the technique. Taken as a whole, these data points suggest
that there is a logarithmic relationship between the cost and effectiveness of
obesity treatments. That is, a major increment in effectiveness seems to require
more money than the previous increment in effectiveness.

This cost → outcome function, known as diminishing returns on investment, is only one of many types of cost → outcome relationships that may be
found in human services. Cost → outcome graphs for some programs illustrate
the effects of economies of scale, providing treatment of the same effectiveness
for lower cost when more clients are treated—up to a point. It is possible to

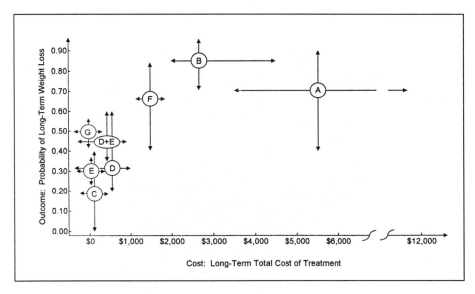

Figure 10.5. Cost → Outcome Relationships for Alternative Obesity Treatment
Programs
SOURCE: Adapted from Yates (1978).

find that point of optimal cost-effectiveness by graphing costs and outcomes
for a range of client loads, as shown in Figure 10.6. Different client loads per
counselor are indicated by the numbers within the squares shown in the cost
→ outcome graph. Note that there is a range of client loads (from five to eight
clients per counselor) that maintains relatively high effectiveness in this type
of service setting. Adding more clients to the counselors' load continues to
reduce the cost per client, but at the price of reduced effectiveness. Lines describing constraints on effectiveness and cost could be superimposed on a
graph such as this, as they were on Figure 10.1c earlier, to facilitate decisions
about the client load that is most cost-effective.

Better service technologies are, essentially, procedures that generate better
outcomes for a cost similar to or less than competing procedures. Research
often shows which of several procedures are more effective, but research also
measuring the costs of those procedures is rarer. Typically, it is assumed that
the cost of different procedures examined in clinical trials is the same. This is
not always true. In a field study of the effectiveness of psychodynamic versus
behavioral therapy, Sloane, Staples, Cristol, Yorkston, and Whipple (1975)
found that psychodynamic and behavioral therapies were comparable in effectiveness, but that behavioral therapy often required fewer sessions and was,
presumably, somewhat lower in cost. Even an inverse relationship between the
effectiveness and cost may be found for different procedures, as shown in Figure 10.7. In their comparison of the effectiveness of treatment procedures for
severe snake phobia, Bandura, Blanchard, and Ritter (1969) found that participant modeling was 90% effective in eliminating the phobia, whereas symbolic
modeling and systematic desensitization procedures were only 33% and 25%

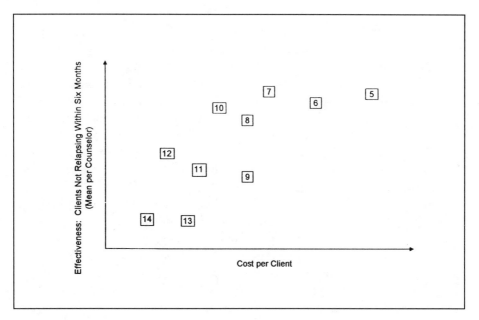

Figure 10.6. Graph of Cost → Outcome of a Service for Different Loads of Clients Per Service Provider

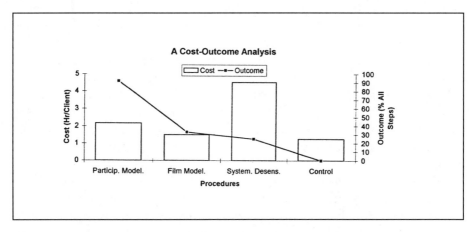

Figure 10.7. Inverse Relationship Between Effectiveness and Cost
SOURCE: Yates (1996).

effective, respectively. In addition, Bandura et al. report that participant modeling required only 2.17 hours on the average, whereas symbolic modeling required an average 2.77 hours and systematic desensitization cost an average 4.55 hours (see Yates, 1995).

More effective means for delivering the same basic service procedures also can result in better cost → outcome relationships. For example, Siegert and Yates (1980) provided the same child-management training to parents through individual in-office sessions, or through group meetings in an office, or through

meetings with individual parents in their homes. Parents were randomly assigned to one of these three delivery systems or to a waiting-list condition that
met for the same amount of time as the group condition and that completed the
same outcome and cost measures. The outcomes resulting from using the three
delivery systems for child-management training were not significantly different from each other, and were significantly superior to outcomes experienced
by the control condition. The costs of the three delivery systems differed markedly. The group in-office and individual in-home delivery procedures were
substantially less expensive than the individual in-office procedure for delivering the same treatment procedures.

The figures presented above compare cost → outcome relationships for
different service programs, service procedures, and methods of delivering
those procedures. Simple visual inspection of these graphs often uncovers the
programs or the service or delivery procedures that would generate the best
cost → outcome relationships. Essentially, these graphs portray cost → *procedure* → outcome relationships. (*Procedure* is used here to denote specific procedures of treatment and other services, amalgams of those procedures in service programs, or methods of delivering those procedures, depending on the
level of specificity and the focus of analysis.) The question for most social
service researchers is, Which procedures (broadly defined) generate the best
cost → outcome relationship, or what is the best cost → procedure → outcome
relationship possible within budget constraints and surpassing minimum outcome criteria?

Often there are simply a number of commonly accepted procedures to be
examined. There may, for instance, be only a few ways that a particular psychological, social, or medical problem can be addressed. Social scientists, however, may have theories suggesting which procedures should generate the best
outcomes. These theories may be based in psychology, sociology, anthropology, medicine, or related disciplines. Some of these procedures may have been
implemented only partially in the past, or may not have gained acceptance
among practitioners. It can be useful, especially when accepted procedures
generate minimally acceptable outcomes, to consider these theories and to
develop new procedures that correspond to hypothesized relationships to
outcomes.

■ *Incorporating Psychological and Other Processes Into Cost-Outcome Analysis*

Most theories in the social sciences hypothesize psychological, social, biological, or other processes that moderate the relationship between service procedures and service outcomes. Typically, these biopsychosocial processes occur in the personal environment of the individual client—often "inside the
skin"—and thus cannot be directly observed. To the extent that processes in-

tervening between procedures and outcomes can be measured, social scientists can incorporate them into analyses of cost → outcome relationships. For example, self-efficacy expectancies appear to be important moderators of the effects of pain management programs (see Bandura, Cioffi, Taylor, & Brouillard, 1988). Also, a complex web of expectancies and other cognitive social learning processes seem to determine whether women conduct breast self-examination (BSE) regularly (see Miller, Shoda, & Hurley, 1996). Miller et al. (1996) also show how interventions that change several of these processes can increase BSE (see also Champion & Scott, 1993; Glanz, Lewis, & Rimer, 1990; Rippetoe & Rogers, 1987.

As many readers realize, the word *processes* frequently has been used in the evaluation literature to denote what is done in the program—that is, what I have termed *procedures* in this chapter. To me, however, the word *processes* connotes actions that cannot be directly observed. I reserve the word *processes* for those psychological, biological, and, to a lesser extent, social activities that are important, unobservable determinants of outcomes (e.g., DiClemente, 1993). Observable activities conducted by service agents are, in this nomenclature, *procedures*. Procedures are directly observable—and directly measurable. To say that processes are unobservable is not, by the way, to imply that they are unmeasurable. Processes, or immediate signs of the occurrence of processes, usually can be measured with some degree of certainty. Considerable research in psychology, in particular, has focused on obtaining reliable and valid measures of psychological and social processes. Neuropsychologists and others have developed reliable and valid measures of a variety of biological processes, too.

■ *Toward Cost → Procedure → Process → Outcome Analysis*

A complete analysis of how costs are related to outcomes may benefit from inclusion of the key procedures and processes that moderate relationships between outcomes and costs. Because most procedures are designed to affect specific processes inside the individual or in the individual's personal life, these analyses can be depicted as cost → procedure → process → outcome analyses, or CPPOA (Yates, 1994, 1995, 1996). As more social scientists aspire not just to choose among alternative programs, but to improve systematically the delivery of services within one program or a set of programs, learning more about the "active ingredients" of a program will become a more common endeavor. Most scientists, service providers, decision makers, community representatives, and clients acknowledge that a human service system is more than its outputs (outcomes), and that it also is more than its inputs (resources, valued as costs). What goes on in the service system—what transforms professionals' time and talents, and the more mundane resources of meeting rooms and the rest, into alleviated human suffering and magnified human potential—is perhaps as important to know as it is difficult to measure. What professionals do when in contact with clients, and what changes result in the behavior, thoughts, feelings, and even biology of clients, is crucial to understand. It can be relatively easy to judge which program has the best outcomes, or the lowest costs. It is somewhat more challenging to discover which program has the lowest cost within budget limits and at least the mandated level of effectiveness. It is still more difficult to know whether these relationships between cost and outcome measures will hold when the scale of program implementation is changed. It often seems impossible, however, to know what the service provider is doing, objectively, and what the provider is trying to accomplish in altering the clients' internal and external environments.

The challenging task before the social scientist who wishes to contribute to the comprehensive understanding and management of the service system is not just to measure its present costs and outcomes, but also to know and quantify the service procedures used and the psychological and other processes engendered by those procedures. For example, Figure 10.8 lists costs, procedures, processes, and outcomes that might be assessed for a CPPOA of a sexually transmitted disease (STD) or HIV risk reduction program.

Even then, however, the task is not complete. Assessing costs, procedures, processes, and outcomes is one thing. Analyzing costs, procedures, processes, and outcomes means more than just measuring these variables. Comprehending the relationships that exist among costs, procedures, processes, and outcomes means knowing with some degree of certainty (a) how changes in costs would affect the professionals' procedures, (b) how these changes in procedures would affect the positive changes that are supposed to occur in clients' processes as a result of the procedures, and (c) how the alterations in process direction will influence the observable, final outcomes of the program. This degree of comprehension may require detailed understanding and statistical testing of each major cost → procedure → process → outcome (CPPO) relationship posited. Graphs can be used, but they may become encumbered by a large number of symbols, line variations, and axes indicating different costs, procedures, processes, and outcomes. Flowcharts sometimes provide better pictures of CPPO relationships. Figure 10.9 shows the paths through resources, procedures, processes, and outcomes that might be identified as the crucial ones to yield the desired reduction in new STD cases at a cost below the budget limit for resource expenditures. In this figure, all resources are related to all procedures, because each procedure takes some amount of each resource to execute. The exact amount can be indicated by attaching a number to each resource → procedure link. Moving from the left to the right of the figure, only those procedure → process and process → outcome links that were significant are shown. (This is a hypothetical illustration; CPPOAs using actual data are provided in Yates, 1995, 1996; Yates, Besteman, Filipczak, Greenfield, & De Smet, 1994, 1997.)

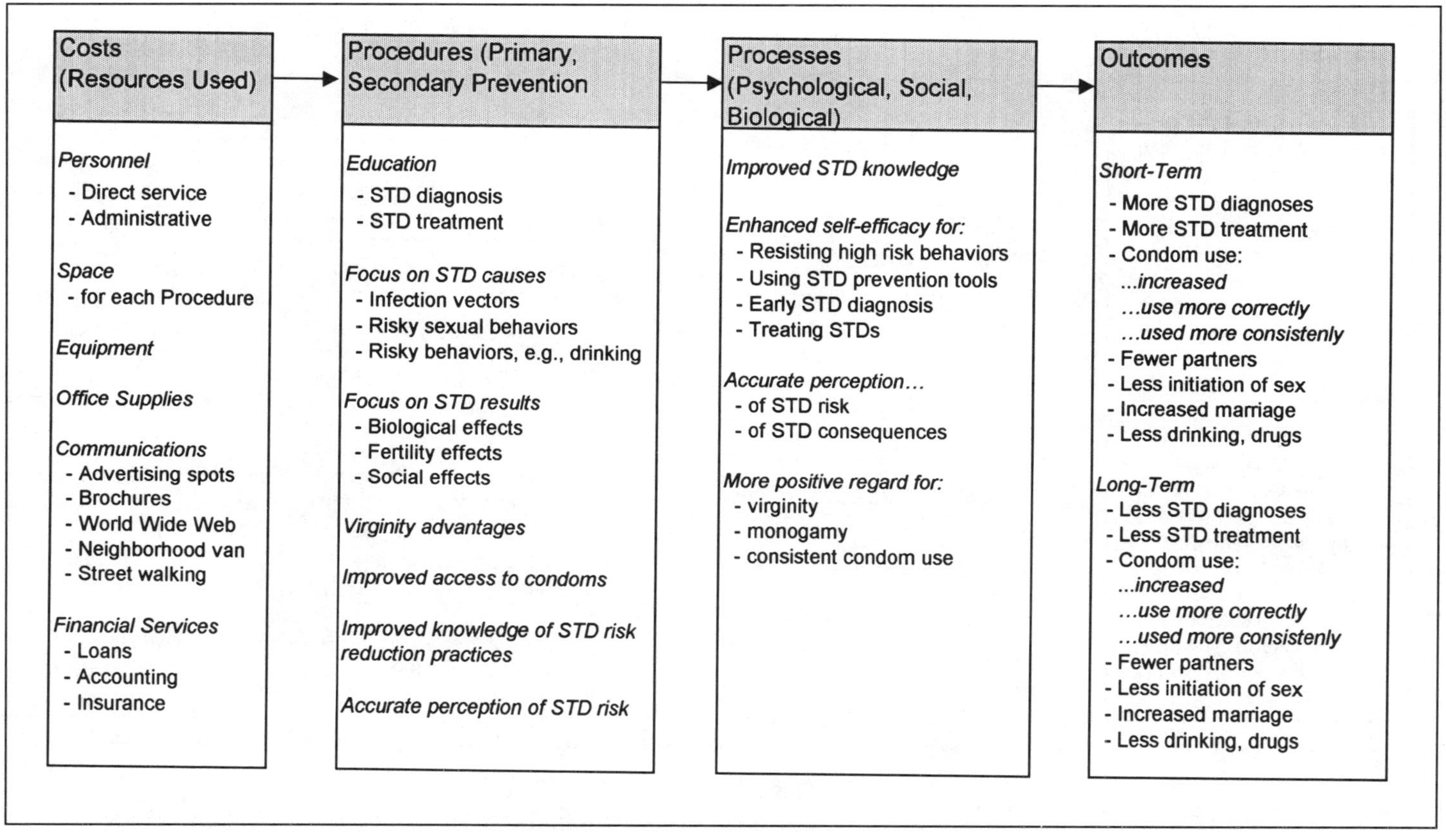

Figure 10.8. Costs, Procedures, Processes, and Outcomes to Be Assessed for Cost → Procedure → Process → Outcome Analysis of an STD and HIV Risk Reduction Program

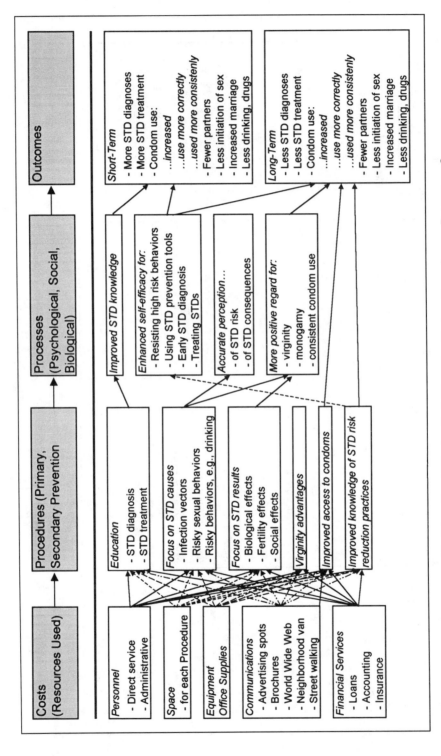

Figure 10.9. The Most Cost-Effective Path Through a Cost → Procedure → Process → Outcome Analysis Matrix for STD and HIV Risk Reduction

Measuring and Analyzing Costs, Procedures, Processes, Outcomes, and Contextual Moderators

In this section I discuss several issues in the assessment and analysis of costs, procedures, processes, outcomes, relationships among these four categories of variables, and the influence of other factors on these CPPO relationships. A more complete, comprehensive discussion of measurement and analysis methods for each category is provided in Yates (1996).

☐ Assessing Costs: The Value of Resources Used

Costs are the most commonly hidden criterion in social science research in general and program evaluation in particular. The time, energy, space, equipment, supplies, and other resources consumed to provide a service are rarely acknowledged and seldom measured, but are required in some measure for the service to operate at all. Services cannot be offered without some resources being expended. The personnel may be volunteers, the space may be donated, and the equipment, supplies, communications, and fiscal arrangements may be borrowed from funded programs, but resources are being used nonetheless that likely could have been put to other purposes. These *opportunity* costs can and need to be measured with the same diligence shown in the measurement of outcomes. As service procedures become increasingly effective, it may be costs that distinguish among them more than effectiveness. For example, whereas Hayashida et al. (1989) found no systematic, significant differences in the effectiveness of out- versus inpatient detoxification treatment, the costs of outpatient treatment were considerably less than the costs of inpatient treatment.

Despite their importance, costs typically are not measured or reported at all (Yates, 1994). When costs are mentioned, it is usually in passing. A single datum is provided, in most cases, with a brief explanation of how it was obtained. More frequently, costs are not measured quantitatively but are judged to differ between alternative programs or specific procedures in a direction and amount that is "obvious." Group treatment often is assumed, for example, to be less expensive per client than individual treatment (e.g., Webster-Stratton, 1989) without detailed cost assessment. Also, the cost of outpatient care is assumed to be far less than the cost of inpatient care, for example, at least from the perspective of most providers and most third-party funders. The cost of outpatient care may be far more than the cost of inpatient care, however, for those who will live with the patient and find that their private lives and employment are severely curtailed by the demands of outpatient treatment. McGuire (1991) found that care of schizophrenics at home required almost twice the resources as care in a public facility. The $cost_{home}/cost_{public\ facility}$ ratio was \$15,160/\$7,647, or 1.98, including both monetary outlays and the value of time devoted by the family to treatment-related activities. Similarly, Siegert and Yates (1980) found that different perspectives on cost could result in different choices of methods for delivering the same service procedures. Different perspectives on cost, particularly the "cash" or operations perspective, can generate substantially different estimates of the value of resources necessary for treatment procedures. Yates, Haven, and Thoresen (1979), for example, found that personnel costs for a residential treatment program for preadolescent youth cost $7,988 per month from the operations perspective but $27,112 per month from a comprehensive perspective that included the monetary value of services provided by undergraduate and graduate interns.

Another reason researchers may not consider costs to be as important to measure as outcomes is that whereas separate measures of outcomes usually are available for each client who receives a service, cost data often are made available to researchers only for the program as a whole. At best, cost data are made available for different budget categories and years. Not being able to analyze cost data separately for each client leaves researchers in the difficult position of not being able to use their favorite data-analytic techniques, such as analysis of variance. There are two ways to deal with this problem so as to obtain the cost of serving each individual client. First, however, a different conceptualization of cost may be necessary.

The "cost" of a product or service often is thought of as the amount of money billed to the client or a third party. A definition of cost that facilitates the acceptability as well as the performance of CEA and CBA is "the types and values of resources used in providing the service." Applying a resource to conduct a procedure is an observable event and, therefore, is potentially as measurable as any outcome. Few researchers would assume that the same outcomes are attained for each client; costs also should not be assumed to be identical for each client. Researchers are reluctant to measure outcomes with a single, summary variable. They should be similarly reluctant to measure costs with a single summary variable such as "total cost." Both monodimensional misconceptualizations ignore the multidimensional nature of outcomes—and of costs.

The time devoted to direct service by staff, and even by clients and their families and friends, can and needs to be measured separately for each client. The space used to provide services also can and needs to be measured, and separately for each client. Other resources used in direct service, from phones to travel to medicines, can be assessed per client as well. Finally, time spent by staff in meetings, and all other resources consumed by the service system (including administrators' time and office space), can be distributed across clients in proportion to each client use of direct service resources (e.g., counselor time, space, medication). (Yates, 1996, provides measures and detailed descriptions of procedures for assessing direct costs and allocating indirect costs across clients.) These costs can be assessed for sample periods or sample clients rather than continuously for all clients, at the risk of criticism for having a sample biased to show lower-than-average costs, and for being unable to generalize cost findings to all clients.

If outcome and cost data already have been collected, and cost data are not collected at the same level of detail as outcome data, reasonably valid estimates of the cost of treating each client still may be possible. If there is any variation in the amount of services received by different clients, just dividing the total cost by the number of clients clearly provides a poor estimate of the cost per client. A somewhat better estimate adjusts the average cost for differences between clients in program procedures received. The approximate costs of services provided for each client often can be deduced if data are available on the degree that clients participated in, or were provided with, the service. For example, if one client attended all 20 sessions of a substance abuse prevention program and another client attended only 10 sessions, the first client could be said to have consumed 20 sessions of the total of 30 sessions actually delivered by the program (if the program had only two clients). The first client could be said to have consumed 20/30, or 66.7%, of total direct service resources. The second client consumed 33.3% of total direct service resources. If the total cost of the service was $1,000, the cost of service to the first client would be $667 and the cost of service to the second client would be $333. The same basic cost calculation procedure can be followed for 2, 22, or 22,000 clients.

If different clients receive different mixtures of service procedures, and if those procedures involve resources of different types or values, additional adjustments can be made to the average cost per client. Suppose, for instance, that one client receives 10 individual sessions and 5 group sessions and another client receives 5 individual sessions and 5 group sessions. Also suppose that, compared to a group session, each individual session requires about four times the value of personnel, spatial, and other resources. A little algebra will suffice to show how the total cost figure should be divided among these clients. First, if group sessions cost X dollars each, then individual sessions cost $4 \times X$ each. Furthermore, the direct cost of treatment for the first client is $10 \times$ (the cost of individual sessions) + $5 \times$ (the cost of group sessions), or $[10 \times (4 \times X)] + (5 \times X) = 40X + 5X = 45X$. Similarly, the direct cost of treatment for the second client is $5 \times$ (the cost of individual sessions) + $5 \times$ (the cost of group sessions), or $[5 \times (4 \times X)] + (5 \times X) = 20X + 5X = 25X$. Supposing for simplicity that these are the only two clients in the program, the distribution of total program costs between these two clients would be their share of the total cost—that is, their cost divided by the total cost. For the first client that would be $45X/(45X + 25X) = 45X/70X$. The X cancels out in this ratio, naturally, leaving 45/70 or .64 (64%). By the same reasoning, the share of total program cost for the second client would be 25/70 or .36 (36%). One does not need to know the actual cost of group sessions to arrive at this estimate. Again, the same basic procedure could be followed to distribute a summary program cost among many clients.

As with the assessment of outcomes, there are several nuances in the assessment of costs. Just as the amount of time required for outcomes to transpire affects their value, so does delaying costs affect their value. Achieving positive outcomes quickly, and delaying negative outcomes such as relapse, results in more positive overall assessments of outcome. Spending fewer funds initially and more funds later also results in lower overall cost assessments. A reasonably simple calculation of the *present value* of an expense adjusts for how far in the future an expenditure is required (see Yates, 1996). Similarly, cost assessments also may need to be adjusted for temporal distortions (e.g., inflation) in cost assessments that are introduced by variations in the value of cost measurement units.

Costs vary as a function of many aspects of the service system, which also may be responsible for some researchers' apparent disdain for including costs in their battery of measures. It can be argued, however, that outcomes are similarly sensitive to the particulars of the situation that services are delivered in, and to the persons who execute and receive different service procedures. The cost of delivering standardized procedures can vary as a function of the specific delivery system for those procedures (e.g., individual versus group versus telephone versus video contacts with clients). Because many social service systems have considerable overhead and fixed costs (e.g., office leases that must be paid regardless of the number of clients served), cost per client can vary as a direct function of client load. Fewer clients may result in higher costs per client, for example.

Also, services just established may cost more per client than services that have operated stably for several years. Although it may be possible to spread out start-up costs over several years of operation, the early months and years of operation may be more costly due renovation expenses, equipment purchases, lease deposits, and the training of new personnel. Although researchers may be tempted to ignore these and other start-up costs, they are true expenses that can result in higher charges than would be made by an established service system. Depending on one's perspective, these costs can be included in the first months or first year of operation, or they can be distributed over a multiyear period. The latter strategy of cost assessment resembles the payment of loans taken out to open a service, in which case interest payments should be included when start-up costs are spread out over multiple years.

A variety of similar issues emerge in cost assessments, but these actually differ little from questions that can be asked about program effectiveness or benefit. The effectiveness of a program also may vary as a function of whether it is just starting out or has operated for years. Client load also can produce decrements in outcome, as overworked staff can readily attest.

☐ *When Costs Are Everything, and Outcomes Are Ignored*

Costs are not always ignored, of course. Sometimes they are all that is measured, or that is considered important in decisions about whether programs should continue or end. Although social scientists often act as if costs are too banal a measure to include in their battery of measures, third-party funders in public and private sectors may consider only costs while dismissing reports of effectiveness as biased, unreliable, insubstantial, or too technical. I have heard government decision makers ecstatically relate findings that one mode of delivering services for youth at risk (i.e., foster care and the delivery of social services to youth remaining with their parents) was substantially less expensive than another mode of delivering similar services (i.e., residential programs for youth). They made no mention of any possible differences in the outcomes of these services, such as improved social skills, continued education, reduction of risk for criminal behavior, and mental and physical health. The only criterion that seemed to enter into these funders' decision making was cost.

Intense focus on costs at the expense of outcomes is a choice that can be understood in several ways. Perhaps decision makers always consider costs and outcomes—but not necessarily (or at least exclusively) the costs and outcomes measured by social scientists. Possibly outcomes such as expected reactions of constituents and lobbyists to funding "home care" rather than "institutionalization" are weighted more than outcomes commonly endorsed by service providers and clients, such as risk reduction and better psychological status. To get the attention of government decision makers in the past, social activists have emphasized publicity and protest. Social scientists might emphasize outcomes such as estimated cost savings (Friedman et al., 1995) and "hard" measures such as percentage not receded within the first 24 months following program completion.

Even these outcome measures do not have great credence with some potential funders, however. For one thing, the outcomes of social services typically are probabilistic rather than certain. So many factors not controlled by a human service program can affect the client that positive outcomes cannot be guaranteed, and, sometimes, negative outcomes cannot be prevented. Moreover, unless sponsored and conducted by independent parties, research on the effectiveness and benefits of alternative programs is as suspect in the minds of some decision makers as a soap manufacturer's comparison of the effectiveness of its product versus a competitor's. The weighting of cost variables as more important than outcome variables thus may have its origins in experience. Differences in the funding requested by alternative programs are as clear and verifiable as dollar figures on "best and final" bids made in response to requests for contracts. Differences in the effectiveness of alternative programs usually are difficult to measure with the same certainty, and, in any case, will occur long after funds are allocated (and probably after the next election is held).

□ *Outcomes: The Result of Processes Altered by Procedures Made Possible by Resource Expenditures*

Despite these potential biases against measures of outcomes, they remain important to assess. If outcomes are not measured, the findings certainly cannot be used in decision making. What will be used is either the assumption of equivalence of outcomes or potentially inaccurate and even biased impressions of outcomes of alternative programs. Most of the methodology of social science, and especially program evaluation, has been devoted to measuring the outcomes of large programs and, occasionally, specific procedures for social services (e.g., Kazdin, 1992; Posavac & Carey, 1989). Space cannot be spent here reviewing these methods (see, however, Yates, 1996); researchers should, however, be aware of how these measures of general and specific effects of social services can be transformed into measures of the monetary *benefits* of those services.

Just as the effectiveness of services can be measured in terms of positive events made more likely and negative events made less likely, so can the monetary benefits of services be measured as income produced or expenditures avoided (see Thompson, 1980; e.g., Yates, 1986). Human services that help clients stay employed longer, or help clients become more productive in their current jobs, may eventually generate positive monetary flow for both clients (see French, Zarkin, Hubbard, & Rachal, 1991) and governments that can receive taxes from the clients. Human services of many sorts also are likely to help clients function better socially and to improve clients' physical and mental health (e.g., Smith, Glass, & Miller, 1980). These outcomes may result in substantial reductions in the use of other human services in the long run, although there may be a short-term increase in use of services to remedy existing problems. The long-term benefits in income generated and costs saved can be estimated from improvement on short-term measures, based on research into these relationships.

The probabilistic nature of human service outcomes means that monetary benefits as well as improved functioning will vary between clients. Not all clients will demonstrate the same income increments or reduced use of other human services. It is tempting to treat monetary measures of outcome as if they were as certain as the costs recorded for efforts to achieve those outcomes. Unfortunately, decision makers have to be given estimates not only of the likely effectiveness and benefits of the service, but of the variability they can expect in effectiveness and benefits. Best- and worst-case scenarios, as well as most-likely estimates, are one way to depict variability in outcome. When calculating ratios of cost to effectiveness or benefits to costs, and when graphing or otherwise analyzing these same relationships, the researcher can either calculate the ratios and graphs for each client or compute them using worst- as well as best-case and most-likely estimates. The result will be not a single "bottom line," but rather a "bottom range."

☐ *Procedures: What Service Systems Do With Clients*

Collecting data on the procedures received by clients can be as simple as recording the program or treatment condition to which clients have been assigned, or as complex as measuring the number of sessions attended and the degree of participation by each client. Recording the initial set of program procedures to which the client is assigned assumes that the client (and direct service providers) complied with the initial assignment. This may be neither correct nor desirable. In some areas of human need, service procedure assignments need to change when better information about the client's capabilities and problems arrives (typically several weeks or months after the client has begun receiving services). Service procedures also may have to be adapted to clients' progress and in response to major events in clients' lives.

Careful tracking of procedures administered to clients usually involves record keeping by direct service providers. These data often serve multiple purposes, making them important but difficult to collect. Information on the specific services provided to different clients may determine the cost assigned to the services received for each client, as described above. Service providers (e.g., therapists) have been known to underreport procedures administered to particular clients because they wish to keep procedures received by clients confidential, or may seek to reduce costs billed to clients. Other direct service providers may simply resist what they perceive to be unethical intrusions of service administrators or third-party funders into the confidential provider-client relationship. Providers may also see the additional "paperwork" involved in recording the procedures used for each client every day as a burden that should not be borne because it does not benefit the client directly. A variety of methods can be used to minimize the cost to practitioners of collecting these data (see Yates, 1996). The process also can be made rewarding; incentives can be offered to practitioners for recording direct services rendered (e.g., Yates, Yokley, & Thomas, 1994).

☐ *Processes: What Happens or Changes Inside Clients*

Processes might seem formidable to measure, given that many cannot be observed directly. Most biological, psychological, and other social science research, however, is devoted to studying processes, what affects those processes, and what outcomes those processes may produce. For example, the considerable research literature on depression (e.g., Haaga, Dyck, & Ernst, 1991) is replete with references to unobservable psychological processes such as cognitive self-statements, expectancies, attributions, beliefs, and self-regulatory strategies (see Mischel, 1973). These are all processes, and are especially interesting to psychologists and other social scientists because they are potentially modifiable by specific procedures common in some therapies. Basic research in psychology and other social sciences usually examines process → outcome relationships in some form. Applied research sometimes manipulates specific procedures and examines outcomes while ignoring potential mediating processes, in what might be characterized as *procedure* → outcome research (see Yates, 1995). The amount of service procedure administered may be correlated with the outcomes produced, yielding evidence for the importance of particular procedures in achieving targeted outcomes (e.g., Howard, Kopta, Krause, & Orlinsky, 1986).

If the outcomes of these procedures are examined for possible moderation by psychological or similar processes, the research might be termed *procedure* → process → outcome research. Much of the clinical psychology literature, for example, collects, analyzes, and reports data on relationships among procedures, processes, and outcomes. Experimental designs may be used to improve the plausibility of inferences about relationships between procedures and processes, and between procedures and outcomes (e.g., Kazdin, 1992). Potentially, the only major difference between these studies and CPPOA is the incorporation of carefully collected data for each subject on the types and values of resources consumed in treatment.

☐ *Context as Moderator of CPPO Links*

The *context* in which resources are expended, procedures are enacted, processes are encouraged, and outcomes are achieved can be a strong exogenous determinant of the resources, procedures, processes, and outcomes of a service system, and of the relationships possible among all four sets of variables. Consider, for example, the possible effects of client gender, age, cultural background, and other characteristics on biopsychosocial processes that need to be modified to achieve outcomes such as improved self-image or better employment. Each of these client attributes can indicate the existence of additional resources, procedures, and processes external to the service system. These exogenous contextual determinants of CPPO variables and CPPO relationships may or may not be within the ability of the service system to influence.

Examples of contextual processes that potentially mediate outcomes are "demographic" variables. These may appear to moderate procedures, such as substance abuse prevention programs, and outcomes of those programs, but these contextual variables can be more accurately conceptualized as stand-ins for social, psychological, or biological processes that really determine outcomes (and that may or may not be addressed by program procedures). For example, parents' level of education has been found to moderate adolescent substance use, but this variable appears to be only a surrogate for the actual moderating processes, that is, parental support, academic competence, behavioral skills, negative life events, and friends' substance use (Wills, McNamara, & Vaccaro, 1995). Similarly, although income is directly related to the probability of successful smoking cessation (Kaplan, 1994, p. 125), it is unlikely that being able to spend more money directly helps people quit smoking. Rather, biopsychosocial processes that decrease the likelihood of relapse to smoking probably correlate with income. Wealthier individuals, for example, may experience fewer of the interpersonal stressors that may make relapse more likely (Marlatt & Gordon, 1980) and may have higher self-efficacy for self-management. Another of the critical contextual variables that may alter CPPO relationships are the particular clients receiving the service. What clients bring with them, from self-control strategies to biological addictions and illnesses, may interact with service procedures to make the targeted processes more or less likely to occur.

In addition to processes and costs, the procedures that a service system can use are a function of the specific professional and community contexts in which the service seeks to function. Some professional climates dictate to a minor or major degree the types of therapy and other procedures that can and cannot be used in a service system. Analytic therapy, for example, is encouraged in some service systems and forbidden in others.

The culture of the community in which the service system operates can also limit the procedures that can be considered and the outcomes that can be included in service planning (see Heller et al., 1984). Communities that integrate a particular religion into all aspects of living may not allow procedures that are forbidden by that religion. For example, in some communities, service programs to reduce new cases of HIV and sexually transmitted diseases may be able to implement procedures including leaflets, school assemblies, newspaper and television advertisements, and park rallies that target the short-term outcomes of abstinence, low-risk sex, protected intercourse, longer sequential monogamous relationships, and monogamous marriage as means of attaining the long-term outcomes of reducing the spread of HIV and STDs. In other communities, only leaflet procedures and information on the outcomes of abstinence and monogamous lifelong marriage can be considered.

In addition, maintenance of long-term outcomes is arguably a function not only of the processes, procedures, and costs of the service system but also of the client's social, political, and economic environments. Enduring, positive outcomes are most likely when clients' family and peer groups support achievement and maintenance of program outcomes. Returning to school is a more difficult goal, for example, when family and friends literally profit from a client's choice to drop out of school to deal drugs full-time. This may require continuation of crucial service procedures by persons allied with the program in the community, rather than by agents in the service system. Maintenance and relapse prevention seem to be particularly important contextual determinants for preventing a return to substance abuse, depression, and a host of other common targets of human services.

There is a context that permeates not costs, not procedures, and not processes or outcomes, but the relationships possible among these components. The ways in which biopsychosocial processes determine changes in client functioning are not arbitrary but are trusted to reflect rather immutable principles studied by neurophysiologists, psychologists, sociologists, and other social scientists. Similarly, what procedures do to existing processes within the client, and what old processes are eliminated and new processes are begun, reflects principles that are inherent in the reality in which services are provided. Discovering and clarifying these principles of process $\rightarrow$ outcome relationships constitute, of course, the essence of most research in the social sciences.

Relationships possible between costs and procedures also are determined by the economic and political contexts in which services are provided. In some areas, some procedures are simply not possible because the professionals necessary to carry out those procedures will not work for the money offered. This may be a function of local supply-and-demand economics. In other instances, licensing regulations constrain providers to have certain minimal degrees and certain professional certifications before performing procedures such as psychotherapy or administering medication. The economic environment of service provision determines the types and amounts of resources that can be used to make service procedures happen in the first place. Economic and political processes also determine the maximum amount of each type of resources that is available to use in a human service. Resource constraints are a reflection of the context in which resources are sought.

■ *Operations Research: A Future for Cost-Effectiveness and Cost-Benefit Analysis*

I began this chapter with a brief description of alternative mathematical and graphic analyses of costs $\rightarrow$ outcome relationships. I then explored the complexities of assessing costs and noted the importance of including data on procedures and hypothesized mediating processes. I have discussed the ways in which the context of service delivery moderates relationships among costs, procedures, processes, and outcomes. What remains to be addressed is how data from these many sets of variables can be analyzed to yield useful recommendations about how to maximize the outcome of human services within cost constraints, or how to minimize the costs of achieving set outcomes.

As I have detailed elsewhere, the field of *operations research* provides several potentially useful models for optimizing cost-effectiveness and cost-benefit in mental health and other human services (Yates, 1980a). As illustrated in the last chapter of Yates (1996), the mathematical technique of *linear programming* can incorporate data on costs of specific service procedures, relationships between the procedures and biopsychosocial processes, and the links between changes in those processes and achievement of outcomes, to find the combination of procedures that maximizes outcomes within cost constraints. Widely available computer spreadsheet software (e.g., Microsoft Excel) can perform this linear programming rapidly on most computer hardware. Similar procedures can be used within the linear programming model to minimize costs of achieving outcome standards. Related models and analytic techniques developed by operations researchers can find the least expensive path through complex networks of resources that make accessible other resources ($resource_1 \rightarrow resource_2$ linkages), procedures that lead to other procedures ($procedure_1 \rightarrow procedure_2$ links), processes that lead to other processes ($process_1 \rightarrow process_2$ links), and short-term outcomes that make possible long-term outcomes ($outcome_1 \rightarrow outcome_2$ links; see Yates, 1980a, 1995).

What is necessary for these operations research techniques to be applied is identification of the many possible links among resources, procedures, processes, and outcomes that are strong enough to "work" for most clients. Theory can guide this identification process, but statistical testing through path analysis may be the best way to find the cost $\rightarrow$ procedure, procedure $\rightarrow$ process,

process → outcome, and other (e.g., context-moderated) links that should be represented in linear programming and other operations research analyses. Traditional manipulative and correlational research designs have become highly developed means of exploring the many possible relationships among service procedures, outcomes, and potential moderating biopsychosocial processes, and of choosing the relationships that are worthy of the designation "significant." From factorial designs and multivariate analysis of variance (Cohen & Cohen, 1993) to structural equation modeling and path analysis (Jöreskog & Sörbom, 1989), methods of testing the statistical significance of possible procedure → process → outcome links have been refined and made readily accessible to most researchers through inexpensive menu-driven computer software. The relative strengths of these relationships also can be ascertained, although the clinical or social significance of each procedure → outcome link remains challenging to quantify (see Kazdin, 1992).

Clearly, quantitative methods and analytic procedures are necessary to represent the complex relationships among resources, procedures, processes, outcomes, and their contexts, and to manipulate models of these relationships to generate solutions that optimize cost-effectiveness and cost-benefit. Seasoned managers of human service systems may understand many of these relationships based on years of experience, however, and may be able to make decisions that rival the ones recommended by quantitative means. Testing the differences between managers' and cost-outcome analysts' solutions for cost-effectiveness and cost-benefit problems could be a worthwhile endeavor.

Ultimately, it may be found that the detailed data collection and analytic techniques recommended here and in some portions of Yates (1980b) are too costly for the increment in decision-making wisdom that they generate over managers' recommendations. Hopefully, of course, the additional clarity and completeness of understanding that is encouraged when a researcher is trying to quantify a program's costs, procedures, processes, outcomes, and key CPPO relationships will foster better decisions even without full-fledged statistical analyses and linear programming. The process of developing a quantitative, or even a qualitative, model of the resources, procedures, processes, and outcomes for a human service system may facilitate understanding of cost-effectiveness and cost-benefit issues by administrators, practitioners, funders, and members of the community served.

■ *Using CPPOA Concepts to Understand Problems in Health Services Systems*

I opened this chapter with a hypothetical tale; I close it with a true story. This story, reported in the *Washington Post,* illustrates how the concepts of CPPOA may facilitate understanding, if not solution, of problems in optimizing the cost-effectiveness and cost-benefit of human services.

The delivery of medical services has increased in cost over the past century so that it now consumes more than 14% of the gross domestic product of the United States (Frank, 1993; Frank & VandenBos, 1994). Americans have sought, and in many cases have even required, medical services almost regardless of cost. Essentially, we have sought the most effective services regardless of cost—the same basic selection procedure advocated by the first decision maker in the fable that began this chapter. There was no real constraint on cost (except what the market would bear), so only quality (and quantity) of service mattered. This drove up quality, quantity, and cost.

In the last half of the 20th century, we have recognized that this choice was in error in several respects. Partially in an effort to address this problem, legal impediments to alternatives to one-on-one delivery of medical services were mitigated or removed. Of the new medical service delivery systems sanctioned in the United States, health maintenance organizations (HMOs) were perhaps the most popular. The impetus for the rise of HMOs included reduction of costs and improvement of quality through the pooling of both patient and physician resources. A low fixed fee would be paid monthly by clients whether they used medical services a little or a lot, thus providing clients with insurance against ruinous bills in the case of serious medical problems. Providers would receive a regular income from a known client base.

There are many other potential benefits for clients and providers, and some pitfalls, but a primary benefit that contributed to the explosive growth of HMOs and similar medical service delivery systems has been their use by small and large businesses. Medical benefits required in some states and demanded by employers in other states often can be met at relatively low cost when employees are signed up with an HMO. According to Segal (1996), many companies choose the HMOs they will offer to their employees strictly according to cost. The quality of each HMO was recently rated by an independent firm (the National Committee for Quality Assurance, or NCQA) as (a) full accreditation, (b) 1-year accreditation, (c) provisional accreditation, or (d) accreditation denied. Of 208 HMOs reviewed to date, 35% are fully accredited, 40% have 1-year accreditation, 11% have provisional accreditation, and 14% were denied accreditation.

NCQA findings are published in several printed forms and are made available 24 hours a day through the Internet. A World Wide Web site (http://WWW.NCQA.org) lists the accreditation, along with information on how the accreditation was determined, for each health service system both on-line through a simple search engine and via downloading. Despite the accessibility of this information in print and electronic media, many companies and individuals ignore the accreditations and instead choose HMO-like organizations that are simply the least expensive. So many employers chose these low-cost health care organizations in 1995 that one grew by 25% that year alone—even though it had been denied accreditation by NCQA. This is, of course, the sort of selection advocated by the decision maker who is cost-conscious and outcome-"unconscious": Essentially there is no minimum constraint on quality of service, so only the cost criterion affects decisions about service selection.

Some Fortune 500 firms have made the sort of decision recommended in the tale that started this chapter: They selected HMOs that exhibited basic levels of quality and maintained relatively low cost. These were the better decisions, although they still were not ideal. For one thing, the criteria that NCQA used to determine accreditation do not appear to be outcomes. NCQA instead seems to judge health care organizations according to how closely their service procedures adhere to professionally accepted standards and how high in quality their resources are (e.g., place and duration of physicians' training). Outcomes of medical services reflected in morbidity and mortality rates for common procedures are not ascertained, although client satisfaction is slated to be an accreditation criterion in the future.

Even these shortcomings may be understood better through the application of CPPOA concepts. It might be maintained, for example, that health service outcomes such as reduced morbidity and mortality simply cannot be measured or separated from factors exogenous to service system. Also, reputation, severity of patient dysfunction, and outcome may be confounded so that patients with the worst problems seek services from institutions with the best reputations. This would likely reduce the positiveness of outcomes of even the best service system. The success of other organizations in assessing outcomes of medical services, however, argues otherwise. For example, in the mid-1980s *Washingtonian Magazine* measured and reported quantitative data on successes, failures, and even death rates for a variety of specific medical problems at local hospitals and clinics. In additional, HealthPartners of Minneapolis-St. Paul has made available to patients, through more than 200 computer kiosks, detailed information on procedures, some processes, and a form of short-term outcomes (i.e., patient feedback) on approximately 4,500 physicians (Jossi, 1996). Even less objective outcomes of health services can be measured with reliability and validity, as illustrated by the detailed findings of *Consumer Reports* regarding the effectiveness of mental health services (see Seligman, 1995). The success of these journalistic endeavors in measuring health service outcomes suggests that the costs of assessing CPPO variables are not prohibitive. Hopefully, the competitive environment emerging in health care services will encourage this sort of third-party assessment and analysis of costs, procedures, processes, and outcomes. This information may not only be useful for consumers who need to make decisions, but may encourage service organizations to analyze and optimize their cost-effectiveness and cost-benefit.

■ References

Bandura, A., Blanchard, E. B., & Ritter, B. (1969). Relative efficacy of desensitization and modeling approaches for inducing behavioral, affective, and attitudinal changes. *Journal of Personality and Social Psychology, 13,* 173-199.

Bandura, A., Cioffi, D., Taylor, C. B., & Brouillard, M. E. (1988). Perceived self-efficacy in coping with cognitive stressors and opioid activation. *Journal of Personality and Social Psychology, 55,* 479-488.

Champion, V., & Scott, C. (1993). Effects of a procedural/belief intervention on breast self-examination performance. *Research in Nursing and Health, 16,* 163-170.

Cohen, J., & Cohen, P. (1993). *Applied multiple regression/correlation analysis for the behavioral sciences* (2nd ed.). Hillsdale, NJ: Lawrence Erlbaum.

DiClemente, C. C. (1993). Changing addictive behaviors: A process perspective. *Current Directions in Psychological Science, 2,* 101-106.

Frank, R. G. (1993). Health care reform: An introduction. *American Psychologist, 48,* 258-260.

Frank, R. G., & VandenBos, G. R. (1994). Health care reform: The 1993-1994 evolution. *American Psychologist, 49,* 851-854.

French, M. T., Zarkin, G. A., Hubbard, R. L., & Rachal, J. V. (1991). The impact of time in treatment on the employment and earnings of drug abusers. *American Journal of Public Health, 81,* 904-907.

Friedman, R., Sobel, D., Myers, P., Caudill, M., & Benson, H. (1995). Behavioral medicine, clinical psychology, and cost offset. *Health Psychology, 14,* 509-518.

Glanz, K., Lewis, F. M., & Rimer, B. (Eds.). (1990). *Health behavior and health education: Theory, research, and practice.* San Francisco: Jossey-Bass.

Haaga, D. A. F., Dyck, M. J., & Ernst, D. (1991). Empirical status of cognitive theory of depression. *Psychological Bulletin, 110,* 215-236.

Hayashida, M., Alterman, A. I., McLellan, A. T., O'Brien, C. P., Purtill, J. J., Volpicelli, J. R., Raphaelson, A. H., & Hall, C. P. (1989). Comparative effectiveness and costs of inpatient and outpatient detoxification of patients with mild-to-moderate alcohol withdrawal syndrome. *New England Journal of Medicine, 320,* 358-365.

Heller, K., Price, R. H., Reinharz, S., Riger, S., Wandersman, A., & D'Aunno, T. A. (1984). *Psychology and community change: Challenges of the future* (2nd ed.). Pacific Grove, CA: Brooks/Cole.

Howard, K. I., Kopta, S. M., Krause, M. S., & Orlinsky, D. E. (1986). The dose-effect relationship in psychotherapy. *American Psychologist, 41,* 159-164.

Jones, K., & Vischi, T. (1979, December). Impact of alcohol, drug abuse, and mental health treatment on medical care utilization [Special supplement]. *Medical Care.*

Jöreskog, K. G., & Sörbom, D. (1989). *LISREL 7: A guide to the program and applications* (2nd ed.). Chicago: SPSS.

Jossi, F. (1996). Easy way to find a doctor. *Wired, 4*(1), 54, 56.

Kaplan, G. (1994). Reflections on present and future research on bio-behavioral risk factors. In S. Blumenthal, K. Matthews, & S. Weiss (Eds.), *New research frontiers in behavioral medicine: Proceedings of the National Conference.* Washington, DC: National Institute of Health Publications.

Kazdin, A. E. (1992). *Research design in clinical psychology* (2nd ed.). New York: Macmillan.

Levin, H. M. (1980). *Cost-effectiveness: A primer.* Beverly Hills, CA: Sage.

Marlatt, G. A., & Gordon, J. R. (1980). Determinants of relapse: Implications for the maintenance of behavior change. In P. O. Davidson & S. M. Davidson (Eds.), *Behavioral medicine: Changing health life-styles.* New York: Brunner/Mazel.

McGuire, T. G. (1991). Measuring the economic costs of schizophrenia. *Schizophrenia Bulletin, 17,* 375-394.

Miller, S. M., Shoda, Y., & Hurley, K. (1996). Applying cognitive-social theory to health-protective behavior: Breast self-examination in cancer screening. *Psychological Bulletin, 119,* 70-94.

Mischel, W. (1973). Toward a cognitive social learning reconceptualization of personality. *Psychological Review, 80,* 252-283.

Posavac, E. J., & Carey, R. G. (1989). *Program evaluation: Methods and case studies* (3rd ed.). Englewood Cliffs, NJ: Prentice Hall.

Rippetoe, P., & Rogers, R. (1987). Effects of components of protection-motivation theory on adaptive and maladaptive coping with a health threat. *Journal of Personality and Social Psychology, 52,* 596-604.

Segal, D. (1996, 19 January). HMOs: How much, not how well. *Washington Post,* pp. F1, F3.

Seligman, M. E. P. (1995). The effectiveness of psychotherapy: The Consumer Reports study. *American Psychologist, 50,* 965-974.

Siegert, F. A., & Yates, B. T. (1980). Cost-effectiveness of individual in-office, individual in-home, and group delivery systems for behavioral child-management. *Evaluation and the Health Professions, 3,* 123-152.

Sloane, R. B., Staples, F. R., Cristol, A. H., Yorkston, N. J., & Whipple, K. (1975). *Psychotherapy versus behavior therapy.* Cambridge, MA: Harvard University Press.

Smith, M. L., Glass, G. V, & Miller, T. I. (1980). *The benefits of psychotherapy.* Baltimore: Johns Hopkins University Press.

Spitzer, R. L., Gibbon, M., & Endicott, J. (1975). Global assessment scale. In W. A. Hargreaves, C. C. Attkisson, L. M. Siegel, M. H. McIntyre, & J. E. Sorensen (Eds.), *Resource materials for community mental health program evaluation* (Publication No. ADM 76-291). Rockville, MD: U.S. Department of Health, Education and Welfare, National Institute of Mental Health.

Thompson, M. S. (1980). *Benefit-cost analysis for program evaluation.* Beverly Hills, CA: Sage.

Webster-Stratton, C. (1989). Systematic comparison of consumer satisfaction of three cost-effective parent training programs for conduct problem children. *Behavior Therapy, 20,* 103-116.

Wills, T. A., McNamara, G., & Vaccaro, D. (1995). Parental education related to adolescent stress-coping and substance use: Development of a mediational model. *Health Psychology, 14,* 464-478.

Yates, B. T. (1978). Improving the cost-effectiveness of obesity programs: Reducing the cost per pound. *International Journal of Obesity, 2,* 249-266.

Yates, B. T. (1980a). *Improving effectiveness and reducing costs in mental health.* Springfield, IL: Charles C Thomas.

Yates, B. T. (1980b). The theory and practice of cost-utility, cost-effectiveness, and cost-benefit analysis in behavioral medicine: Toward delivering more health care for less money. In J. Ferguson & C. B. Taylor (Eds.), *The comprehensive handbook of behavioral medicine* (Vol. 3, pp. 165-205). New York: SP Medical & Scientific.

Yates, B. T. (1984). How psychology can improve the effectiveness and reduce the costs of health services. *Psychotherapy, 21,* 439-451.

Yates, B. T. (1985). Cost-effectiveness analysis and cost-benefit analysis: An introduction. *Behavior Assessment, 7,* 207-234.

Yates, B. T. (1986). Economics of suicide: Toward cost-effectiveness and cost-benefit analysis of suicide prevention. In R. Cross (Ed.), *Non-natural death: Coming to terms with suicide, euthanasia, withholding or withdrawing treatment* (pp. 65-76). Denver: Rose Medical Center.

Yates, B. T. (1987). Cognitive vs. diet vs. exercise components in obesity bibliotherapy: Effectiveness as a function of psychological benefits versus psychological costs. *Southern Psychologist, 3,* 35-40.

Yates, B. T. (1994). Toward the incorporation of costs, cost-effectiveness analysis, and cost-benefit analysis into clinical research. *Journal of Consulting and Clinical Psychology, 62,* 729-736.

Yates, B. T. (1995). Cost-effectiveness analysis, cost-benefit analysis, and beyond: Evolving models for the scientist-manager-practitioner. *Clinical Psychology: Science and Practice, 2,* 385-398.

Yates, B. T. (1996). *Analyzing costs, procedures, processes, and outcomes in human services.* Thousand Oaks, CA: Sage.

Yates, B. T., Besteman, K. J., Filipczak, J., Greenfield, L., & De Smet, A. (1994). *Resource → procedure → process → outcome analysis (CPPOA): Preliminary findings of cost-effectiveness analysis of methadone maintenance program.* Abstract of paper presented at the meeting of the College on Problems of Drug Dependence, Palm Beach, FL.

Yates, B. T., Besteman, K. J., Filipczak, J., Greenfield, L., & De Smet, A. (1997). *Using resource procedure process outcome analysis to optimize the cost-effectiveness of a substance abuse treatment.* Manuscript in preparation, American University, Washington, DC.

Yates, B. T., Haven, W. G., & Thoresen, C. E. (1979). Cost-effectiveness analysis at Learning House: How much change for how much money? In J. S. Stumphauzer (Ed.), *Progress in behavior therapy with delinquents.* Springfield, IL: Charles C Thomas.

Yates, B. T., & Newman, F. L. (1980a). Approaches to cost-effectiveness analysis and cost-benefit analysis of psychotherapy. In G. VandenBos (Ed.), *Psychotherapy: Practice, research, policy* (pp. 103-162). Beverly Hills, CA: Sage.

Yates, B. T., & Newman, F. L. (1980b). Findings of cost-effectiveness and cost-benefit analyses of psychotherapy. In G. VandenBos (Ed.), *Psychotherapy: Practice, research, policy* (pp. 163-185). Beverly Hills, CA: Sage.

Yates, B. T., Yokley, J. M., & Thomas, J. V. (1994). Cost-benefit analysis of six alternative payment incentives for child therapists. *Journal of Consulting and Clinical Psychology, 62,* 627-635.

11

Research Synthesis
and Meta-analysis

Harris M. Cooper
James J. Lindsay

Social scientists rely more on research syntheses today than at any other time in history. Meta-analysis, a set of procedures for summarizing the quantitative results from multiple studies, has greatly improved the quality of research syntheses. We begin this chapter with a brief history of meta-analysis and research synthesis. We then describe the different stages of a rigorous research synthesis. Next, we outline a set of generally useful meta-analytic techniques, and follow this with a discussion of some of the difficult decisions that research synthesists face in carrying out a meta-analysis. We conclude with an examination of some broader issues concerning criteria for evaluating the quality of knowledge syntheses in general and meta-analyses in particular.

A general theme of the chapter is that social scientists who are conducting research syntheses need to think about what distinguishes good reviews from bad reviews. This kind of effort is crucial for assessing the value of existing research syntheses and for promoting high-quality research synthesis in the future.

AUTHORS' NOTE: Portions of this chapter appeared originally in H. M. Cooper, "Meta-analysis and the Integrative Research Review," in C. Hendrick and M. S. Clark (Eds.), *Research Methods in Personality and Social Psychology* (Sage Publications, 1990), and H. M. Cooper and N. Dorr, "Conducting a Meta-analysis," in F. T. L. Leong and J. T. Austin (Eds.), *The Psychology Research Handbook: A Guide for Graduate Students and Research Assistants* (Sage Publications, 1996). Also, portions of this chapter were presented at the National Conference on Research Synthesis: Social Science Informing Public Policy, June 21, 1994, Washington, DC.

■ *A Brief History of Research Synthesis and Meta-analysis*

In 1904, Karl Pearson published what is believed to be the first meta-analysis. Having been asked to review the evidence on a vaccine against typhoid, Pearson gathered data from 11 relevant studies, and for each study he calculated a recently developed statistic called the correlation coefficient. He averaged these measures of the treatment's effect across two groups of studies distinguished by the nature of their outcome variable. Based on the average correlations, Pearson concluded that other vaccines were more effective.

In 1932, Ronald Fisher, in his classic text *Statistical Methods for Research Workers,* noted, "It sometimes happens that although few or [no statistical tests] can be claimed individually as significant, yet the aggregate gives an impression that the probabilities are lower than would have been obtained by chance" (p. 99). Fisher then presented a technique for combining the *p* values that came from statistically independent tests of the same hypothesis. His work would be followed by more than a dozen papers published prior to 1960 on the same topic (see Olkin, 1990).

This early development of procedures for statistically combining results of independent studies went largely unused. However, beginning in the 1960s, social science research experienced a period of rapid growth. By the mid-1970s, when Robert Rosenthal and Donald Rubin undertook a review of research studying the effects of interpersonal expectations on behavior, they found 345 studies that pertained to their hypothesis (Rosenthal & Rubin, 1978). Almost simultaneously, Gene Glass and Mary Lee Smith were conducting a review of the relation between class size and academic achievement (Glass & Smith, 1979). They found 725 estimates of the relation, based on data from nearly 900,000 students. Smith and Glass (1977) also gathered assessments of the effectiveness of psychotherapy; this literature revealed 833 tests of the treatment. Likewise, John Hunter and Frank Schmidt uncovered 866 comparisons of the differential validity of employment tests for black and white workers (Hunter, Schmidt, & Hunter, 1979).

Each of these research teams realized that for some topic areas, prodigious amounts of empirical evidence had been amassed on why people act and feel the way they do and on the effectiveness of psychological, social, educational, and medical interventions. These researchers concluded that the traditional research synthesis simply would not suffice. Largely independently, the three research teams rediscovered and reinvented Pearson's and Fisher's solutions to their problem.

In discussing his solution, Glass (1976) coined the term *meta-analysis* to stand for "the statistical analysis of a large collection of analysis results from individual studies for purposes of integrating the findings" (p. 3). Shortly thereafter, other proponents of meta-analysis demonstrated that traditional review procedures led to inaccurate or imprecise characterizations of the literature, even when the size of the literature was relatively small (Cooper, 1979; Cooper & Rosenthal, 1980).

The first half of the 1980s witnessed the appearance of five books devoted primarily to meta-analytic methods. The first, by Glass, McGaw, and Smith (1981) presented meta-analysis as a new application of analysis of variance and multiple regression procedures, with effect sizes treated as the dependent variable. In 1982, Hunter, Schmidt, and Jackson introduced meta-analytic procedures that focused on (a) comparing the observed variation in study outcomes to that expected by chance and (b) correcting observed correlations and their variance for known sources of bias (e.g., sampling error, range restrictions, unreliability of measurements).

Rosenthal (1984) presented a compendium of meta-analytic methods covering, among other topics, the combining of significance levels, effect size estimation, and the analysis of variation in effect sizes. Rosenthal's procedures for testing moderators of effect size estimates were not based on traditional inferential statistics, but on a new set of techniques involving assumptions tailored specifically for the analysis of study outcomes.

Another text that appeared in 1984 also helped elevate the research review to a more rigorous level. Light and Pillemer (1984) focused on the use of research synthesis to help decision making in the social policy domain. Their approach placed special emphasis on the importance of meshing both numbers and narrative for the effective interpretation and communication of synthesis results.

Finally, in 1985, with the publication of *Statistical Methods for Meta-Analysis,* Hedges and Olkin helped to elevate the quantitative synthesis of research to an independent specialty within the statistical sciences. This book, summarizing and expanding nearly a decade of programmatic developments by the authors, not only covered the widest array of meta-analytic procedures but also established their legitimacy by presenting rigorous statistical proofs.

Meta-analysis did not go uncriticized. Some critics opposed quantitative synthesis, using arguments similar to those used to oppose primary data analysis (Barber, 1978; Mansfield & Bussey, 1977). Others linked meta-analysis with more general reviewing procedures that are inappropriate, but not necessarily related to the use of statistics in reviews. We address several of these issues later in this chapter.

Since the mid-1980s, several other books have appeared on meta-analysis. Some of these treat the topic generally (e.g., Cooper, 1989b; Hunter & Schmidt, 1990; Wolf, 1986), some treat it from the perspective of particular research design conceptualizations (e.g., Eddy, Hassleblad, & Schachter, 1992; Mullen, 1989), some are tied to particular software packages (e.g., Johnson, 1989), and some look to the future of research synthesis as a scientific endeavor (e.g., Cook et al., 1992; Wachter & Straf, 1990).

During and after the years that the works mentioned above were appearing, literally thousands of meta-analyses were published. The use of meta-analysis spread from psychology and education through many disciplines, especially social policy analysis (Light, 1983) and the medical sciences (see Lewin, 1996). Greenberg and Folger (1988) stated that "if the current interest in meta-analysis is any indication, then meta-analysis is here to stay" (p. 191). In 1994, the first edition of *Handbook of Research Synthesis* was published (Cooper & Hedges, 1994).

☐ *Research Synthesis as a Scientific Process*

Several early attempts that framed the integrative research review in the terms of a scientific process occurred independent of the meta-analysis movement. In 1971, Feldman published an article titled "Using the Work of Others: Some Observations on Reviewing and Integrating," in which he wrote, "Systematically reviewing and integrating . . . the literature of a field may be considered a type of research in its own right—one using a characteristic set of research techniques and methods" (p. 86).

In the same year, Light and Smith (1971) presented a "cluster approach" to research synthesis that was meant to redress some of the deficiencies in the existing strategies. They argued that if treated properly, the variation in outcomes among related studies could be a valuable source of information, rather than a source of consternation, as it appeared to be when treated with traditional reviewing methods.

Three years later, Taveggia (1974) struck a complementary theme:

> A methodological principle overlooked by [reviewers] . . . is that research results are probabilistic . . . they may have occurred simply by chance. It also follows that, if a large enough number of researches has been done on a particular topic, chance alone dictates that studies will exist that report inconsistent and contradictory findings! Thus, what appears to be contradictory may simply be the positive and negative details of a distribution of findings. (pp. 397-398)

Taveggia described six common problems in literature reviews: selecting research; retrieving, indexing, and coding studies; analyzing the comparability of findings; accumulating comparable findings; analyzing the resulting distributions; and reporting the results.

Two articles that appeared in the *Review of Educational Research* in the early 1980s brought the meta-analytic and review-as-research perspectives together. First, Jackson (1980) proposed six reviewing tasks "analogous to those performed during primary research" (p. 441). Jackson portrayed the limitations of meta-analysis as well as its strengths. His article employed a sample of 36 review articles from prestigious social science periodicals to examine the methods used in syntheses of empirical research. His conclusion was that "relatively little thought has been given to the methods for doing integrative reviews" (p. 459).

Cooper (1982) took the analogy between research synthesis and primary research to its logical conclusion. He presented a five-stage model of the integrative review that viewed research synthesis as a data-gathering exercise and, as such, applied to it criteria similar to those employed to judge primary research. Similar to primary research, a research review involves problem formulation, data collection (the literature search), data evaluation, data analysis and interpretation (the meta-analysis), and public presentation. For each stage, Cooper codified the research question asked, its primary function in the review, and the procedural differences that might cause variation in reviews' conclusions. In addition, Cooper applied the notion of threats to inferential validity—introduced by Campbell and Stanley (1966; also see Cook & Campbell, 1979) for evaluating the utility of primary research designs—to research synthesis. He identified numerous threats to validity associated with reviewing procedures that might undermine the trustworthiness of a research synthesis's findings. He also suggested that other threats might exist and that any particular review's validity could be threatened by consistent deficiencies in the set of studies that formed its database.

Table 11.1 presents Cooper's (1982) conceptualization of the research synthesis process. In the next section, we describe briefly the critical decisions that characterize each stage.

■ *The Stages of Research Synthesis*

□ *The Problem Formulation Stage*

During problem formulation, the variables involved in an inquiry, whether it be primary research or a research synthesis, are defined two different ways: conceptually and operationally.

The first source of variation in reviewers' conclusions enters during concept identification. Two reviewers using an identical label for an abstract concept can employ different definitions or levels of abstraction. Each definition may contain some operations excluded by the other, or one reviewer's definition may completely contain the other. Let's take as an example the concept of homework. One reviewer may consider as homework only assignments meant to have students practice what they have learned in class, whereas another may includes assignments to visit museums or to watch certain television programs. In such a case, the second reviewer employs a broader conception of homework, and this review will likely contain more research than will that of the first reviewer.

Synthesists can also vary in the attention they pay to theoretical and methodological distinctions in the literature. This variation is caused by differences in the way operations are treated *after* the relevant research has been retrieved. Thus two reviewers who employ identical conceptual definitions of homework and who review the same set of studies can still reach decidedly different conclusions if one reviewer retrieved more information about the features of studies and recognized a relation between a study feature and outcome that the other reviewer did not test. One reviewer might discover that the outcomes of homework studies depended on whether textbook or teacher-developed tests were

Table 11.1 Research Synthesis Conceptualized as a Research Process

Stage Characteristics	Stage of Research				
	Problem Formulation	Data Collection	Data Evaluation	Analysis and Interpretation	Public Presentation
Research question asked	What evidence should be included in the review?	What procedures should be used to find relevant evidence?	What retrieved evidence should be included in the review?	What procedures should be used to make inferences about the literature as a whole?	What information should be included in the review report?
Primary function in review	Constructing definitions that distinguish relevant from irrelevant studies	Determining which sources of potentially relevant studies to examine	Applying criteria to separate "valid" from "invalid" studies	Synthesizing valid retrieved studies	Applying editorial criteria to separate important from unimportant information
Procedural differences that create variation in review conclusions	1. Differences in included operational definitions 2. Differences in operational detail	Differences in the research contained in sources of information	1. Differences in quality criteria 2. Differences in the influence of nonquality criteria	Differences in rules of inference	Differences in guidelines for editorial judgment
Sources of potential invalidity in review conclusions	1. Narrow concepts might make review conclusions less definitive and robust. 2. Superficial operational detail might obscure interacting variables.	1. Accessed studies might be qualitatively different from the target population of studies. 2. People sampled in accessible studies might be different from target population.	1. Nonquality factors might cause improper weighting of study. 2. Omissions in study reports might make conclusions unreliable.	1. Rules for distinguishing patterns from noise might be inappropriate. 2. Review-based evidence might be used to infer causality.	1. Omission of review procedures might make conclusions irreproducible. 2. Omissions of review findings and study procedures might make conclusions obsolete.

used to assess impact, whereas another reviewer never even coded studies based on this feature of the outcome measure.

Each difference in how a problem is formulated introduces a potential threat to the trustworthiness of a review's conclusions. First, reviewers who focus on very narrow conceptualizations provide little information about how many different contexts a finding applies to. Therefore, reviewers who employ broad conceptual definitions can *potentially* produce more valid conclusions than reviewers using narrow definitions. However, broad definitions can lead to the erroneous conclusion that research results are insensitive to variations in a study's context. We can assume, therefore, that synthesists who examine more operational details within their broader constructs will produce more trustworthy conclusions. These synthesists present more information about contextual variations that do and do not influence the review outcome.

☐ *The Literature Search Stage*

The decisions a reviewer makes during the literature search determine the nature of studies that will ultimately form the basis for conclusions. Identifying populations for research syntheses is complicated by the fact that reviews involve two targets. First, the reviewer wants the findings to reflect the results of *all previous research* on the problem. The reviewer can exert some control over whether this goal is achieved through his or her choice of information sources. Second, the reviewer hopes that the included studies will allow generalizations to the *individuals that interest researchers in the topic area*. The reviewer's influence is constrained at this point by the types of individuals who were sampled by the primary researchers. Thus a synthesis of the homework research first should include as many of the previous studies as the reviewer can find, and hopefully these studies will include all the types of students for whom homework is a relevant issue.

Some discrepancies in synthesis conclusions are created by differences in the sources reviewers use to retrieve studies, such as journal networks, reference databases, and personal communications. The studies available through different sources are often different from one another. The first concern with the literature search is that the synthesis may not include, and probably will not include, all studies pertinent to the topic of interest. A synthesist who has utilized the broadest sources of information is most likely to retrieve a set of results that resembles the entire population of previous research. However, methodologists do differ over how exhaustive a literature search needs to be, especially as it pertains to the inclusion of unpublished research. We take up this debate below.

Cooper (1987) conducted a survey that asked research synthesists what searching techniques they used in preparing their reports. Authors of 57 reviews in psychology and education were quizzed on 15 different searching strategies. On average, reviewers reported using between six and seven search techniques. The most frequently used technique, and the one yielding the most central references, was examination of past reviews. Computer searches of reference databases were viewed as most useful, and were used by a large number of reviewers.

The second concern that arises during the literature search is that the participants in the retrieved studies may not represent all people in the target population. For instance, it may be that little or no research has been conducted that examines the effects of homework on first- or second-grade students. The synthesist cannot be faulted for the existence of this threat *if* his or her retrieval procedures were exhaustive. However, reviewers who qualify conclusions with information about the kinds of people missing or overrepresented in studies probably run less risk of making overly broad generalizations.

☐ *The Data Evaluation Stage*

After the literature is collected, the synthesist makes critical judgments about the quality of individual studies. Each study is examined to determine whether it is contaminated by factors irrelevant to the problem under consideration.

Differences in reviews are created by differences in reviewers' criteria for evaluating the quality of research. Just how this evaluation ought to proceed is another source of disagreement among research synthesists that we will address more fully below. Relatedly, variation in conclusions is created when factors other than research quality affect reviewers' decisions, for example, the reputation or institution of the primary researchers, or the research findings. The use of any criteria other than methodological quality ought to be considered a threat to the validity of a research review (e.g., Mahoney, 1977).

A second threat to trustworthiness during research evaluation is completely beyond the control of the reviewer. This threat involves incomplete reporting by primary researchers. If a reviewer must estimate or omit what happened in these studies, wider confidence intervals must be placed around review conclusions. We will examine some solutions to the problem of missing data below.

☐ *The Analysis and Interpretation Stage*

During analysis and interpretation, the separate research reports collected by the reviewer are synthesized into a unified statement about the research problem. It is at this stage that the synthesist must decide whether or not to use meta-analysis. Review conclusions can differ because reviewers employ different analytic interpretation techniques. A systematic relation that cannot be distinguished from noise under one set of rules may be discernible under another set.

One source of concern during the analysis and interpretation of studies involves the rules of inference employed by a reviewer. In nonquantitative syntheses, it is difficult to gauge the appropriateness of inference rules because they are not very often made explicit. For meta-analyses, the suppositions of statistical tests are generally known, and some statistical biases in reviews can be removed. Regardless of the strategy used for analysis and interpretation, the possibility always exists that the reviewer has used an invalid rule for inferring a characteristic of the target population. For this reason, the number of primary studies available, the degree of statistical detail presented in research reports, and the frequency of methodological replications need to be assessed before determining whether to perform a meta-analysis.

A second concern involves the misinterpretation of review-based evidence as supporting statements about causality. For example, it might be that a study finding a larger-than-normal effect of homework on achievement was conducted at an upper-income school. However, it might also be the case, known or unknown to the reviewer, that this study used unusually long homework assignments. The reviewer cannot discern, therefore, which characteristic of the study, if either, produced the larger effect. Thus when different study characteristics are found associated with the effects of a treatment, the synthesist should recommend that future researchers examine these factors within a single experiment.

☐ *The Public Presentation Stage*

Finally, the production of a document describing the review is a task with important implications for the accumulation of knowledge. Two threats to validity accompany report writing. First, the omission of details about how the review was conducted reduces the possibility that others can replicate the conclusions. The second threat involves the omission of evidence that others find important. A synthesis will quickly become obsolete if it does not address the variables and relations that are (or will be) important to an area.

■ *The Elements of Meta-analysis*

Suppose a research synthesist is interested in whether fear-arousing advertisements can be used to persuade adolescents that smoking is bad. Suppose further that the (hypothetical) synthesist is able to locate eight studies, each of which examined the question of interest. Of these, six studies reported nonsignificant differences between attitudes of adolescents exposed and not exposed to fear-arousing ads and two reported significant differences indicating less favorable attitudes held by adolescent viewers. One was significant at $p < .05$ and one at $p < .02$ (both two-tailed). Can the synthesist reject the null hypothesis that the ads had no effect?

There are multiple methods the research synthesist could employ to answer this question. First, the synthesist could cull through the eight reports, isolate those studies that present results counter to his or her own position, discard these disconfirming studies due to methodological limitations, and present the remaining supportive studies as presenting the truth of the matter. Such a research synthesis would be viewed with extreme skepticism. It would contribute little to answering the question.

☐ *The Vote Count*

As an alternative procedure, the synthesist could take each report and place it into one of three piles: statistically significant findings that indicate the ads were effective, statistically significant findings that indicate the ads created more positive attitudes toward smoking (in this case this pile would have no studies), and nonsignificant findings that do not permit rejection of the hypothesis that the fear-arousing ads had no effect. The synthesist then would declare the largest pile the winner. In our example, the null hypothesis wins.

This vote count of significant findings has much intuitive appeal and has been used quite often. However, the strategy is unacceptably conservative. The problem is that chance alone should produce only about 5% of all reports falsely indicating that viewing the ads created more negative attitudes toward smoking. Therefore, depending on the number of studies, 10% or less of positive and statistically significant findings might indicate a real difference due to the ads. However, the vote-counting strategy requires that a minimum 34% of findings be positive and statistically significant before the hypothesis is ruled a winner. Thus the vote counting of significant findings could, and often does, lead to the suggested abandonment of hypotheses (and effective treatment programs) when, in fact, no such conclusion is warranted.

Hedges and Olkin (1980) describe a different way to perform vote counts in research synthesis. This procedure involves (a) counting the number of positive and negative results, regardless of significance, and (b) applying the sign test to determine if one direction appears in the literature more often than would be expected by chance. This vote-count method has the advantage of using all studies but suffers because it does not weight a study's contribution by its sample size. Thus a study with 100 participants is given weight equal to a study with 1,000 participants. Further, the revealed magnitude of the hypothesized relation (or impact of the treatment under evaluation) in each study is not considered—a study showing a small positive attitude change is given equal weight to a study showing a large negative attitude change. Still, the vote count of directional findings can be an informative complement to other meta-analytic procedures, and can even be used to generate an effect size estimate (see Bushman, 1994; Hedges & Olkin, 1985).

☐ *Combining Probabilities Across Studies*

Taking these shortcomings into account, the research synthesist might next consider combining the precise probabilities associated with the results of each study. Becker (1994; also see Rosenthal, 1984) has cataloged 16 methods for combining the results of inference tests so that an overall test of the null hypothesis can be obtained. All of the methods require that the statistical tests (a) relate to the same hypothesis, (b) are independent, and (c) meet the initial statistical assumptions made by the primary researchers.

Of the 16 methods, the most frequently applied is called the *method of adding Zs*. In its simplest form, the Adding Zs method involves summing Z score associated with *p* levels and dividing the sum by the square root of the number of inference tests. In the example of the eight studies of fear-arousing ads, the cumulative Z score is 1.69, *p* < .05 (one-tailed). Thus the null hypothesis is rejected.

The combining probabilities procedure overcomes the improper weighting problems of the vote count. However, it has severe limitations of its own. First, whereas the vote-count procedure is overly conservative, the combining probabilities procedure is extremely powerful. In fact, it is so powerful that, for hypotheses or treatments that have generated a large number of tests, rejecting the null hypothesis is so likely that it becomes a rather uninformative exercise. Further, the combined probability addresses the question of whether or not an effect exists; it gives no information on whether that effect is large or small, important or trivial. Therefore, the question of greatest importance is often not, Do fear-arousing ads create more negative attitudes toward smoking in adolescents, yes or no? Instead, the question should be, How much of an effect do fear-arousing ads have? The answer might be zero or it might be either a positive or negative value. Further, the research synthesist would want to ask, What factors influence the effect of fear-arousing ads? He or she realizes that the answer to this question could contribute to sound recommendations about how to both improve and target the smoking interventions.

Given these new questions, the synthesists would turn to the calculation of average effect sizes, much like Pearson's.

□ *Estimating Effect Sizes*

Cohen (1988) has defined an effect size as "the degree to which the phenomenon is present in the population, or the degree to which the null hypothesis is false" (pp. 9-10). In meta-analysis, effect sizes are (a) calculated for the outcomes of studies (or sometimes comparisons within studies), (b) averaged across studies to estimate general magnitudes of effect, and (c) compared between studies to discover if variations in study outcomes exist and, if so, what features of studies might account for them.

Although numerous estimates of effect size are available, two dominate the literature. The first, called the d-index by Cohen (1988; also see Hedges & Olkin, 1985; Rosenthal, 1994), is a scale-free measure of the separation between two group means. Calculating the d-index for any study involves dividing the difference between the two group means by either their average standard deviation or the standard deviation of the control group. For example, Cooper (1989a) examined the difference in academic achievement of students

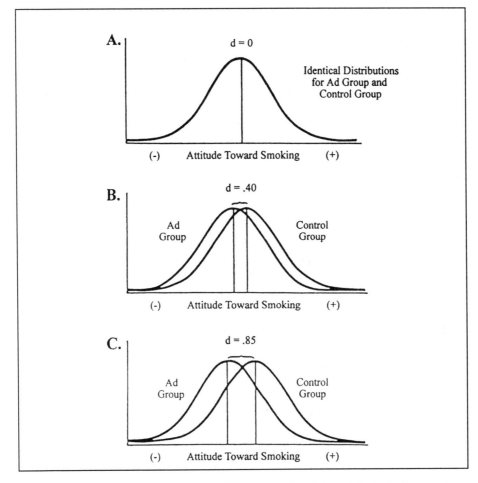

Figure 11.1. Three Relations Between Fear-Arousing Ads and Attitudes Toward Smoking Expressed by the d-index

who did and did not do homework. Across 20 studies, he found the average d-index was .21 favoring the homework doers. Thus the average academic achievement of students who did homework was .21 standard deviations above the average score of students who did not.

Figure 11.1 presents the d-indices associated with three hypothetical studies. In Figure 11.1A, the fear-arousing ad has no effect on adolescents' reported attitudes toward smoking, thus d = 0. In Figure 11.1B, the average adolescent viewing the ad has an attitude score that is four-tenths of a standard deviation less positive than the average adolescent not viewing the ad. Here d = .40. In Figure 11.1C, d = .85, indicating an even greater separation between the two group means.

The second effect size metric is the *r* index or correlation coefficient. It measures the degree of linear relation between two variables. For example, Cooper and Hazelrigg (1988) found eight studies that looked at whether an experimenter's need for social influence was correlated with the amount of biased responding the experimenter obtained from subjects. The average correlation for the eight studies was .15.

State-of-the-art meta-analytic procedures call for the weighting of effect sizes when they are averaged across studies. The reason is that studies yielding more precise estimates—that is, those with larger sample sizes—should contribute more to the combined result. Both Hedges and Olkin (1985) and Shadish and Haddock (1994) provide procedures for calculating the appropriate weights. Also, these authors describe how confidence intervals for effect sizes can be estimated. The confidence intervals can be used instead of the Adding Z scores method to test the null hypothesis that the difference between two means, or the size of a correlation, is zero (Hedges, Cooper, & Bushman, 1992).

□   *Examining Variance in Effect Sizes*

Another advantage of performing a statistical integration of research is that it allows the synthesist to test hypotheses about why the outcomes of studies differ. To continue with the fear-arousing ad example, the synthesist might calculate average d-indexes for subsets of studies, deciding that he or she wants different estimates based on certain characteristics of the data. For example, the reviewer might want to compare separate estimates for studies that use different outcomes, distinguishing between those that measured likelihood of smoking and those that measured attitude toward smoking. The reviewer might wish to compare the average effect sizes for different media formats, distinguishing print from video advertisements. The reviewer might want to look at whether advertisements are differentially effective for different types of adolescents, say males and females.

The ability to ask these questions about variables that moderate effects reveals one of the major contributions of research synthesis. Specifically, even if no individual study has compared different outcomes, media, or types of adolescents, by comparing results across studies the synthesist can give a first hint about whether these variables would be important to look at in future research and/or as guides to policy.

After calculating the average effect sizes for different subgroups of studies, the synthesist can statistically test whether these factors are reliably associated with different magnitudes of effect. This is sometimes called a *homogeneity analysis,* and it will likely provide the most interesting results of the research synthesis. Without the aid of statistics, the reviewer simply examines the differences in outcomes across studies, groups them informally by study features, and decides (based on an "interocular inference test") whether the feature is a significant predictor of variation in outcomes. At best, this method is imprecise. At worst, it leads to incorrect inferences.

In contrast, meta-analysis provides a formal means for testing whether different features of studies explain variation in their outcomes. Because effect sizes are imprecise, they will vary somewhat even if they all estimate the same underlying population value. Homogeneity analysis allows the synthesist to test whether sampling error alone accounts for this variation or whether features of studies, samples, treatment designs, or outcome measures also play a role. If reliable differences do exist, the average effect sizes corresponding to these differences will take on added meaning and will help the synthesist make policy recommendations.

Three statistical procedures for examining variation in effect sizes appear in the literature. The first approach applies standard inference tests, such as ANOVA or multiple regression. The effect size is used as the dependent variable and study features are used as independent or predictor variables. This approach has been criticized based on the questionable tenability of the underlying assumptions (see Hedges & Olkin, 1985).

The second approach compares the variation in obtained effect sizes with the variation expected due to sampling error (Hunter & Schmidt, 1990). This approach involves calculating not only the observed variance in effects but also the expected variance, given that all observed effects are estimating the same population value. This approach also can include adjustments to effect sizes to account for methodological artifacts.

The third approach, homogeneity analysis, provides the most complete guide to making inferences about a research literature. Analogous to ANOVA, studies can be grouped by features and the average effect sizes for groups can be tested for homogeneity. It is relatively simple to carry out a homogeneity analysis; formulas are described in Cooper (1989b), Cooper and Hedges (1994), Hedges and Olkin (1985), Rosenthal (1984), and Wolf (1986).

In sum, then, a generic meta-analysis might contain four separate sets of statistics: (a) a frequency analysis of positive and negative results and a sign test, (b) combinations of the *p* levels of independent inference tests, (c) estimates of average effect sizes with confidence intervals, and (d) homogeneity analyses examining study features that might influence study outcomes. The need for combined probabilities and sign tests diminishes as the body of literature grows or if the author provides confidence intervals around effect size estimates.

■ *Difficult Decisions in Research Synthesis*

When conducting primary research, investigators encounter decision points at which they have multiple choices about how to proceed. The same is true for reviewers conducting research syntheses. Some of these decisions will be easy to make, with choices being dictated by topic area considerations and the nature of the research base. Other decisions will be less clear. Four choice points have been generally perplexing for meta-analysts. One occurs during data collection, two during data evaluation, and one during data analysis. These involve (a) how exhaustive the literature search should be, (b) what rules should be used for including or excluding studies from reviews, (c) how to handle data missing from research reports, and (d) how to determine whether separate tests of hypotheses are actually independent of one another. In addition to these decisions, two other aspects of conducting meta-analyses confront research synthesists with complex issues, and therefore deserve special attention. These involve (a) how to interpret effect size estimates substantively and (b) how to synthesize data structures that go beyond estimates of simple bivariate relations.

☐ *Publish or Perish*

Research synthesists disagree about how exhaustive a literature search needs to be. Some reviewers go to great lengths to locate as much relevant material as possible; others are less thorough. Typically, disagreement centers on the importance of including unpublished research in reviews.

Those in favor of limiting syntheses to published material only argue that publication is an important screening device for maintaining quality control. Because published research has been reviewed for quality, it gives the best evidence available. Also, the inclusion of unpublished material typically does not change the conclusions drawn by reviewers. Therefore, the studies found in unpublished sources do not warrant the additional time and effort needed to obtain them.

Those who argue that research should not be judged based on publication status give three rationales. First, they dispute the claim that published research and unpublished research yield similar results; statistically significant results are more likely to be published (Begg, 1994). Second, even if publication status does relate to the quality of research, there will still be much overlap in the quality of published and unpublished studies. Superior studies sometimes are not submitted or are turned down for publication for other reasons. Inferior studies sometimes find their way into print. Application of the "publish or perish" rule may lead to the omission of numerous high-quality studies and will not ensure that only high-quality studies are included in the review. And finally, in a meta-analysis, both the reliability of effect size estimates, expressed through the size of confidence intervals, and tests for effect size moderators will depend on the amount of available data. Therefore, reviewers may unnecessarily impede their ability to make confident statistical inferences by excluding unpublished studies.

☐ *Judging the Quality of Primary Studies*

Another area of controversy in meta-analysis is related to the publication issue. All research reviewers agree that the quality of a study should dictate how heavily it is weighted when inferences based on a literature are drawn. However, there is disagreement about whether studies should be excluded from reviews entirely if they are flawed.

Proponents of excluding flawed studies often employ the "garbage in, garbage out" axiom (Eysenck, 1978). They argue that amassing numerous flawed studies cannot replace the need for better-designed ones. Others argue that reviewers should employ the principle of best evidence used in law. This principle argues that "the same evidence that would be essential in one case might be disregarded in another because in the second case there is better evidence available" (Slavin, 1986, p. 6). Thus a synthesist evaluates the entire literature and then bases decisions on only those studies that are highest in quality, even if these are not ideal.

Opponents of excluding studies contend that flawed studies can, in fact, accumulate to valid inferences. This might happen if the studies do not share the same design flaws but do come to the same result. Further, global decisions about what makes a study good or bad are fraught with difficulty. There is ample evidence that even the most sophisticated researchers can disagree about the dimensions that define quality and how these dimensions apply to particular studies (see Gottfredson, 1978). And finally, opponents of exclusion contend that the effect of research design on study outcomes is an empirical question. Rather than leaving studies out based on disputable, global judgments of rigor, the reviewer can examine the operational details of studies empirically for their relation to outcomes. Then, if studies with more desirable features produce results different from other studies, inferences about the literature can be adjusted accordingly.

☐   *How to Handle Missing Data*

Missing data constitute one of the most frustrating problems faced by research synthesists. Missing data can take two forms. First, the synthesist may miss entire research reports that are pertinent to the topic or that he or she knows about but cannot retrieve. The above discussion of publication bias is relevant to this issue. Second, there may be data missing from the reports themselves. Within a report, missing information might include (a) the magnitude of the effect size (because it is not reported and not enough information is given for the meta-analyst to calculate it) and/or (b) important study characteristics that might be tested as moderators of study outcomes. When data are missing, this can have a biasing effect on estimates of average effect sizes, on confidence intervals around estimates, and on comparisons between estimates.

Some strategies for handling missing data from reports are simple. They include omitting the cases with data missing from a given analysis or from the meta-analysis entirely. Alternatively, missing data points can be estimated using single-value imputation procedures. More complex methods involve the employment of maximum likelihood models. Details of these procedures are given in Piggott (1994).

Regardless of which method is employed, meta-analysts are obligated to discuss how many data were missing from their reports, how they handled the situation, and why they chose the methods they did. Finally, it is becoming increasingly common practice for meta-analysts with much missing data to conduct their analyses using more than one strategy and determining whether their findings are robust across different missing data assumptions (see Greenhouse & Iyengar, 1994).

☐ *Identifying Independent Hypothesis Tests*

Meta-analysts must make decisions concerning how to handle multiple effect sizes coming from the same study. These effect sizes may share method variance that makes them nonindependent data points. The problem is that the assumption that effects are independent underlies the meta-analysis procedures described above.

Sometimes a single study can contain multiple estimates of the same relation because (a) more than one measure of the same construct is used and the measures are analyzed separately or (b) results are reported separately for different samples of people. Taken a step further, a reviewer also might conclude that separate but related studies in the same report, or multiple reports from the same laboratory, are not independent.

Meta-analysts employ multiple approaches to handling nonindependent tests. Some reviewers treat each effect size as independent, regardless of the number that come from the same study. They assume that the effect of violating the independence assumption is not great. Others use the study as the unit of analysis. In this strategy, a mean or median result is calculated to represent the study. Still other meta-analysts advocate a shifting unit (Cooper, 1989b). Here, each study is allowed to contribute as many effects as there are categories in the given analysis, but effects within any category are averaged. Recently, application of generalized least squares regression has been suggested as a solution to the problem of nonindependence (Raudenbush, Becker, & Kalaian, 1988).

☐ *Guidelines for Interpreting the Magnitude of Effects*

Numerical estimates of effect are of little value unless they can be infused with substantive meaning. The first set of guidelines available to help interpret effect size was provided by Cohen (1988), who proposed effect size values "to serve as operational definitions of the qualitative adjectives 'small,' 'medium,' and 'large' " (p. 12). He recognized that judgments of "largeness" and "smallness" require comparison between the item under consideration and some other item, or contrasting element. Therefore, in operationally defining these adjectives, he compared different magnitudes of effect "with a subjective average of effect sizes as are encountered in the behavioral sciences" (p. 13).

Cohen defined a small effect as $d = .2$ or $r = .1$, which he said is representative of personality, social, and clinical psychology research. A large effect of $d = .8$ or $r = .5$ is more likely to be found in sociology, economics, and experimental or physiological psychology. According to Cohen, then, a social psychologist might interpret an effect size of $r = .1$ to be small when compared with all behavioral sciences but also about average when compared with other social psychological effects.

At the time Cohen offered his guidelines, holding an effect size up against a criterion as broad as "all behavioral sciences" might have been the best contrasting element available. Today, with so many meta-analytic estimates of effect at hand, such a comparison holds little information.

Cooper (1981) suggested an alternative to Cohen's benchmarks. Instead of a single set of criteria, multiple contrasting elements should be used as yardsticks to interpret effect sizes. These should include some that (a) are broader than the treatment or predictor variable under consideration (e.g., How does the effect of negative advertising on smoking compare with other influences on smoking, in general?), (b) are different from the treatment but within the same subclass (e.g., How does the effect of print ads compare with the effect of television ads?), and (c) share the same treatment or predictor but vary in outcome measure (e.g., Do ads affect attitudes more than behavioral intentions?). Cooper also suggested that effect sizes need to be interpreted in relation to the methodology used to generate them (e.g., the sensitivity of research designs, the trustworthiness of measures). A similar approach to interpretation of effect sizes is given by Lipsey (1990; see also Chapter 2, this volume).

Of course, judgments of "size" are not synonymous with judgments of "merit." The relative merit of different treatments or explanations involves components in addition to effect sizes. In applied settings involving treatment effects, most notable among these are (a) the cost of particular treatments and (b) the value placed on the changes the treatment is meant to create.

Levin and his colleagues have begun the task of establishing the relative cost-effectiveness of educational interventions (Levin, 1987; Levin, Glass, & Meister, 1987). They have compared the cost-effectiveness of computer-assisted instruction, cross-age tutoring, reductions in class size, and increases in daily instructional time. First, they established an estimate of the magnitude of effect of each intervention over a constant treatment duration. Then they calculated the cost per student of replicating each intervention. Finally, they established a cost-effectiveness ratio by calculating the effect size gain obtained for each $100 cost per student.

□ *Synthesis of Complex Forms of Data*

The statistical procedures for meta-analysis described above focus on integrating bivariate results from experimental and descriptive research. There exists a parallel set of synthesis procedures within applied psychology meant to help assess the generalizability of test validity (Schmidt & Hunter, 1977). Bushman, Cooper, and Lemke (1991) summarize techniques for the synthesis of factor analyses. Becker and Schram (1994; also see Becker, 1992) present some examples of how to synthesize correlation matrices so as to examine explanatory models.

Each of these techniques presents a unique set of problems, in regard to both the statistical theory needed to perform the integration and its practical application. For instance, present-day meta-analysts find incomplete and non-uniform standards of data reporting to be one of their most vexing problems. It is likely to be even more troublesome as the data to be synthesized become more complex.

■ *Judging the Quality of Research Syntheses and Meta-analyses*

Perhaps the most important and perplexing question stemming from the increased dependence on research syntheses concerns how to distinguish good reviews from bad ones. Some progress has been made toward applicable standards for quality judgments. For instance, the model of integrative reviewing as scientific research presented in Table 11.1 leads directly to several explicit questions about reviewing methods that relate to quality: (a) Do the operations appearing in the literature fit the reviewer's abstract definition? (b) Is enough attention paid to the methodological details of the primary studies? (c) Was the literature search thorough? (d) Were primary studies evaluated using explicit and consistent rules? (e) Were valid procedures used to combine the results of independent studies? Matt and Cook (1994) have expanded on this approach to assessing the validity of research synthesis conclusions.

Sacks, Berrier, Reitman, Ancona-Berk, and Chalmers (1987) used a related scheme to evaluate the quality of 86 meta-analyses in medicine. A checklist containing 23 items was divided into six general areas of meta-analysis methodology—meta-analysis design (e.g., protocol, literature search), similarity of the separate studies, control of bias, statistical analysis, sensitivity analysis (i.e., multiple tests of data using various assumptions), and application of results. Results indicated that only 28% of the meta-analyses addressed all six areas, whereas 59% addressed five of the six areas.

Several attempts have been made to pin down more general notions about how to determine the quality of reviews. These efforts have been both conceptual and empirical in nature. For example, Strike and Poser (1983) have proposed that a good synthesis, whether of empirical research or abstract ideas, requires both intellectual quality and utility. First, a synthesis should clarify and resolve rather than obscure inconsistencies within the material being synthesized. Second, a synthesis should result in a progressive problem shift, involving greater explanatory power, expanded scope of application, and increased capacity to pursue unsolved problems. Finally, a synthesis should demonstrate consistency, parsimony, and elegance. It should answer the questions asked; readers should finish the report with the sense that they got what they came for.

Cooper (1986) asked post-master's degree graduate students to read six reviews of school desegregation research that covered the same set of 19 studies.

He then asked the readers to judge the quality of the papers. Quality judgments were not strongly related to reviewers' or readers' positions on desegregation or their general political beliefs. Instead, judgments of quality were associated with readers' confidence in their interpretations of the review. Reviews seen as more interpretable were given higher quality ratings.

Cooper also asked the readers to provide open-ended comments on the papers. The comments mentioned (a) organization, (b) writing style, (c) clarity of focus, (d) use of citations, (e) attention to variable definitions, (f) attention to study methodology, and (g) manuscript preparation. Similar results were obtained by Becker (1991) in a study of editors of the *Psychological Bulletin* and the *Review of Educational Research.*

In sum, the general criteria that have been offered for good research reviewing range from the lofty pursuits of resolving conflict and stimulating progressive problem shifts to the mundane concerns of presenting material effectively. Social research methodologists need to continue to identify and systematize criteria for the evaluation of meta-analyses. This effort should guide and facilitate the generation of high-quality research syntheses in the future. As the role of reviews in our definition and acquisition of knowledge expands, the ability to distinguish good from bad reviews becomes more critical.

■ *References*

Barber, T. (1978). Expecting expectancy effects: Biased data analyses and failure to exclude alternative interpretations in experimenter expectancy research. *Behavioral and Brain Sciences, 3,* 388-390.

Becker, B. J. (1991). The quality and credibility of research reviews: What the editors say. *Personality and Social Psychology Bulletin, 17,* 267-272.

Becker, B. J. (1992). Models of science achievement: Factors affecting male and female performance in school science. In T. D. Cook, H. M. Cooper, D. S. Cordray, H. Hartmann, L. V. Hedges, R. J. Light, T. Louis, & F. Mosteller, *Meta-analysis for explanation: A casebook* (pp. 209-281). New York: Russell Sage Foundation.

Becker, B. J. (1994). Combining significance levels. In H. M. Cooper & L. V. Hedges (Eds.), *Handbook of research synthesis.* New York: Russell Sage Foundation.

Becker, B. J., & Schram, C. M. (1994). Examining explanatory models through research synthesis. In H. M. Cooper & L. V. Hedges (Eds.), *Handbook of research synthesis* (pp. 357-381). New York: Russell Sage Foundation.

Begg, C. B. (1994). Publication bias. In H. M. Cooper & L. V. Hedges (Eds.), *Handbook of research synthesis* (pp. 399-409). New York: Russell Sage Foundation.

Bushman, B. J. (1994). Vote-counting procedures in meta-analysis. In H. M. Cooper & L. V. Hedges (Eds.), *Handbook of research synthesis* (pp. 193-213). New York: Russell Sage Foundation.

Bushman, B. J., Cooper, H. M. & Lemke, K. M. (1991). Meta-analysis of factor analysis: An illustration using the Buss-Durkee Hostility Inventory. *Personality and Social Psychology Bulletin, 17,* 344-350.

Campbell, D. T., & Stanley, J. C. (1966). *Experimental and quasi-experimental designs for research.* Chicago: Rand McNally.

Cohen, J. (1988). *Statistical power analysis in the behavioral sciences.* Hillsdale, NJ: Lawrence Erlbaum.

Cook, T. D., & Campbell, D. T. (1979). *Quasi-experimentation: Design and analysis issues for field settings.* Chicago: Rand McNally.

Cook, T. D., Cooper, H. M., Cordray, D. S., Hartmann, H., Hedges, L. V., Light, R. J., Louis, T., & Mosteller, F. (1992). *Meta-analysis for explanation: A casebook.* New York: Russell Sage Foundation.

Cooper, H. M. (1979). Statistically combining independent studies: A meta-analysis of sex differences in conformity research. *Journal of Personality and Social Psychology, 37,* 131-146.

Cooper, H. M. (1981). On the effects of significance and the significance of effects. *Journal of Personality and Social Psychology, 41,* 1013-1018.

Cooper, H. M. (1982). Scientific guidelines for conducting integrative research reviews. *Review of Educational Research, 52,* 291-302.

Cooper, H. M. (1986). On the social psychology of using research reviews: The case of desegregation and black achievement. In R. S. Feldman (Ed.), *The social psychology of education* (pp. 341-363). Cambridge: Cambridge University Press.

Cooper, H. M. (1987). Literature searching strategies of integrative research reviewers: A first survey. *Knowledge: Creation, Diffusion, Utilization, 8,* 372-383.

Cooper, H. M. (1989a). *Homework.* White Plains, NY: Longman.

Cooper, H. M. (1989b). *Integrating research: A guide for literature reviews* (2nd ed.). Newbury Park, CA: Sage.

Cooper, H. M. (1990). Meta-analysis and the integrative research review. In C. Hendrick & M. S. Clark (Eds.), *Research methods in personality and social psychology* (pp. 142-163). Newbury Park, CA: Sage.

Cooper, H. M., & Dorr, N. (1996). Conducting a meta-analysis. In F. T. L. Leong & J. T. Austin (Eds.), *The psychology research handbook: A guide for graduate students and research assistants* (pp. 229-238). Thousand Oaks, CA: Sage.

Cooper, H. M., & Hazelrigg, P. (1988). Personality moderators of interpersonal expectancy effects: An integrative research review. *Journal of Personality and Social Psychology, 55,* 937-949.

Cooper, H. M., & Hedges, L. V. (Eds.). (1994). *Handbook of research synthesis.* New York: Russell Sage Foundation.

Cooper, H. M., & Rosenthal, R. (1980). Statistical versus traditional procedures for summarizing research findings. *Psychological Bulletin, 87,* 442-449.

Eddy, D. M., Hassleblad, V., & Schachter, R. (1992). *Meta-analysis by the confidence profile method.* New York: Academic Press.

Eysenck, H. (1978). An exercise in mega-silliness. *American Psychologist, 33,* 517.

Feldman, K. A. (1971). Using the work of others: Some observations on reviewing and integrating. *Sociology of Education, 4,* 86-102.

Fisher, R. A. (1932). *Statistical methods for research workers.* London: Oliver & Boyd.

Glass, G. V (1976). Primary, secondary, and meta-analysis of research. *Educational Researcher, 5,* 3-8.

Glass, G. V, McGaw, B., & Smith, M. L. (1981). *Meta-analysis in social research.* Beverly Hills, CA: Sage.

Glass, G. V, & Smith, M. L. (1979). Meta-analysis of research on class size and achievement. *Educational Evaluation and Policy Analysis, 1,* 2-16.

Gottfredson, G. (1978). Evaluating psychological research reports. *American Psychologist, 33,* 920-934.

Greenberg, J., & Folger, R. (1988). *Controversial issues in social research.* New York: Springer-Verlag.

Greenhouse, J. B., & Iyengar, S. (1994). Sensitivity analysis and diagnostics. In H. M. Cooper & L. V. Hedges (Eds.), *Handbook of research synthesis* (pp. 383-398). New York: Russell Sage Foundation.

Hedges, L. V., Cooper, H. M., & Bushman, B. J. (1992). Testing the null hypothesis in meta-analysis: A comparison of combined probability and confidence interval procedures. *Psychological Bulletin, 111,* 188-194.

Hedges, L. V., & Olkin, I. (1980). Vote-counting methods in research synthesis. *Psychological Bulletin, 88,* 359-369.

Hedges, L. V., & Olkin, I. (1985). *Statistical methods for meta-analysis.* Orlando, FL: Academic Press.

Hunter, J. E., & Schmidt, F. L. (1990). *Methods of meta-analysis: Correcting error and bias in research findings.* Newbury Park, CA: Sage.

Hunter, J. E., Schmidt, F. L., & Hunter, R. (1979). Differential validity of employment tests by race: A comprehensive review and analysis. *Psychological Bulletin, 86,* 721-735.

Hunter, J. E., Schmidt, F. L., & Jackson, G. B. (1982). *Meta-analysis: Cumulating research findings across studies.* Beverly Hills, CA: Sage.

Jackson, G. B. (1980). Methods for integrative reviews. *Review of Educational Research, 50,* 438-460.

Johnson, B. T. (1989). *DSTAT: Software for the meta-analytic review of research literatures.* Hillsdale, NJ: Lawrence Erlbaum.

Levin, H. M. (1987). Cost-benefit and cost-effectiveness analysis. *New Directions for Program Evaluation, 34,* 83-99.

Levin, H. M., Glass, G. V, & Meister, G. R. (1987). Cost-effectiveness of computer-assisted instruction. *Evaluation Review, 11,* 50-72.

Lewin, D. I. (1996). Meta-analysis: A new standard or clinical fool's gold? *Journal of NIH Research, 8,* 30-31.

Light, R. J. (Ed.). (1983). *Evaluation studies review annual* (Vol. 8). Beverly Hills, CA: Sage.

Light, R. J., & Pillemer, D. B. (1984). *Summing up: The science of research reviewing.* Cambridge, MA: Harvard University Press.

Light, R. J., & Smith, P. V. (1971). Accumulating evidence: Procedures for resolving contradictions among research studies. *Harvard Educational Review, 41,* 429-471.

Lipsey, M. W. (1990). *Design sensitivity: Statistical power for experimental research.* Newbury Park, CA: Sage.

Mahoney, M. (1977). Publication prejudice: An experimental study of confirmatory bias in the peer review system. *Cognitive Therapy and Research, 1,* 161-175.

Mansfield, R., & Bussey, T. (1977). Meta-analysis of research: A rejoinder to Glass. *Educational Researcher, 6,* 3.

Matt, G. E., & Cook, T. D. (1994). Threats to the validity of research syntheses. In H. M. Cooper & L. V. Hedges (Eds.), *Handbook of research synthesis* (pp. 503-520). New York: Russell Sage Foundation.

Mullen, B. (1989). *Advanced BASIC meta-analysis.* Hillsdale, NJ: Lawrence Erlbaum.

Olkin, I. (1990). History and goals. In K. W. Wachter & M. L. Straf (Eds.), *The future of meta-analysis* (pp. 3-10). New York: Russell Sage Foundation.

Pearson, K. (1904). Report on certain enteric fever inoculation statistics. *British Medical Journal, 3,* 1243-1246.

Piggott, T. D. (1994). Methods for handling missing data in research synthesis. In H. M. Cooper & L. V. Hedges (Eds.), *Handbook of research synthesis* (pp. 163-175). New York: Russell Sage Foundation.

Raudenbush, S. W., Becker, B. J., & Kalaian, H. (1988). Modeling multivariate effect sizes. *Psychological Bulletin, 103,* 111-120.

Rosenthal, R. (1984). *Meta-analytic procedures for social research*. Beverly Hills, CA: Sage.

Rosenthal, R. (1994). Parametric measures of effect size. In H. M. Cooper & L. V. Hedges (Eds.), *Handbook of research synthesis* (pp. 231-244). New York: Russell Sage Foundation.

Rosenthal, R., & Rubin, D. (1978). Interpersonal expectancy effects: The first 345 studies. *Behavioral and Brain Sciences, 3,* 377-415.

Sacks, H. S., Berrier, J., Reitman, D., Ancona-Berk, V. A., & Chalmers, T. C. (1987). Meta-analyses of randomized controlled trials. *New England Journal of Medicine, 316,* 450-455.

Schmidt, F. L., & Hunter, J. E. (1977). Development of a general solution to the problem of validity generalization. *Journal of Applied Psychology, 62,* 529-540.

Shadish, W. R., & Haddock, C. K. (1994). Combining estimates of effect size. In H. M. Cooper & L. V. Hedges (Eds.), *Handbook of research synthesis* (pp. 261-281). New York: Russell Sage Foundation.

Slavin, R. E. (1986). Best evidence synthesis: An alternative to meta-analytic and traditional reviews. *Educational Researcher, 15,* 5-11.

Smith, M. L., & Glass, G. V (1977). Meta-analysis of psychotherapy outcome studies. *American Psychologist, 32,* 752-760.

Strike, K., & Poser, G. (1983). Types of syntheses and their criteria. In S. Ward & L. Reed (Eds.), *Knowledge structure and use: Implications of synthesis and interpretation* (pp. 343-361). Philadelphia: Temple University Press.

Taveggia, T. C. (1974). Resolving research controversy through empirical cumulation: Toward reliable sociological knowledge. *Sociological Methods & Research, 2,* 395-407.

Wachter, K. W., & Straf, M. L. (Eds.). (1990). *The future of meta-analysis*. New York: Russell Sage Foundation.

Wolf, F. W. (1986). *Meta-analysis: Quantitative methods for research synthesis*. Beverly Hills, CA: Sage.

Practical Data Collection and Analysis Methods

In this section, we move from the concept of research design to a diversity of approaches to collecting, managing, and analyzing data. The first chapter in Part III concentrates on the art of designing good survey questions. Too often, the actual wording of survey questions is overlooked. Fowler, building on a wealth of survey experience, provides valuable information on how to ask questions in Chapter 12. Fowler places the design of questions within a total survey design framework that includes sampling, data collection techniques, interviewer training, and question construction.

Fowler offers five characteristics of a good question to help guide question construction. He anticipates some of the question design challenges a researcher might face and provides a number of tips and suggestions for tackling them. For example, he suggests some ways to reduce recall problems and how to obtain valid answers to sensitive questions that typically produce socially desirable responses. He also discusses practical decisions that need to be made, such as how many response categories to use in writing questions. Finally, because techniques alone cannot guarantee good questions, Fowler discusses three empirical approaches to producing better surveys. He briefly describes how focus groups, cognitive testing, and field pretesting are all useful in improving survey questions.

Chapters 13 through 15 describe three data collection approaches to collecting survey data—personal interviews, mail surveys, and telephone interviews. In

Chapter 13, van Kammen and Stouthamer-Loeber offer detailed guidance regarding the collection and management of personal interview data. As Bickman, Rog, and Hedrick stress in Chapter 1, van Kammen and Stouthamer-Loeber emphasize planning and management as key to a high-quality study. Without a management structure in place from the onset of a project, costly errors may be made, some of which may be irreversible. The authors first address the hiring of a research staff, with the goal of creating a team that has overlapping skills to ensure sufficient coverage of key research tasks. Among the key personnel in a survey study are the interviewers, and van Kammen and Stouthamer-Loeber describe strategies for training, selecting, supervising, and monitoring the work of interviewers to ensure a high-quality study. In addition, as a key interviewer responsibility is to obtain and retain participants in the study, they discuss strategies interviewers can use in approaching participants and obtaining informed consent; they also address compensating respondents for their participation. Finally, the authors describe procedures for the efficient collection and management of data. Among the procedures discussed are computerized tracking systems for data collection and strategies for preparing the data for computerization, including data checking, correcting errors, reconciling missing data, and developing a system for coding variables.

In Chapter 14, Mangione reviews the principles involved in conducting mail surveys. He begins with a discussion of when mail surveys may be the most appropriate data collection method, providing a list of the advantages of mail surveys as well as the situations in which the mail survey is the best method to use. One of the most commonly discussed weaknesses of mail surveys is poor response rate, and Mangione provides several concrete suggestions for how to improve response rates, including the type of letter to send, the use of return postage, and how to preserve confidentiality. He presents extensive discussion on how to remind people to return the survey and the use of incentives, and offers some surprising conclusions about how the length of a survey affects the return rate. He also makes several other practical suggestions with regard to such critical aspects as managing the survey process and how to improve the physical appearance of the survey instrument. Finally, Mangione reminds us that mail surveys need to follow good practice with regard to the wording of questions and sampling procedures, as discussed in the prior chapters by Fowler and Henry.

The third major survey approach involves the use of telephone interviews. In Chapter 15, Lavrakas provides a comprehensive overview of the design and implementation of telephone surveys. Similar to several other contributors to this handbook, Lavrakas takes what is called a total survey approach. This orientation recognizes that all aspects of research are interdependent and that weakness in any one area will affect the quality of the data collected. For example, the researcher may have done an excellent job in selecting the sample and constructing the interview, but if the interviewers are not properly trained and supervised, the data may not be of sufficient quality. Lavrakas takes the reader through the entire process of conducting telephone surveys, from sample selection to interviewer supervision, and shows how each of these steps is critical to the quality of the data collected.

The next two chapters focus on two qualitative data collection approaches common in applied social research. Ethnography, as Fetterman defines it in Chapter 16, is the art and science of describing a group or culture. He presents an overview of the concepts, methods, equipment, analysis, writing, and ethics involved in conducting ethnographic research. Like other contributors to this volume, Fetterman highlights the need for organization in research, but also notes the reality that much of what happens during the research will be unplanned and iterative. In ethnographic research in particular, the ethnographer is a human instrument who often is collecting and analyzing data simultaneously.

In Chapter 17, Stewart and Shamdasani describe the collection of information from focus groups, a technique that is being used with increasing frequency in applied research. A focus group is a group of 8 to 12 persons who meet for a session of approximately 2 hours to discuss the topic presented to them by the researcher. Although typically used in the early stages of research projects to help frame the focus of an effort or to formulate a more structured set of survey questions, focus groups have also been used in hypothesis testing.

Stewart and Shamdasani describe the theory underlying focus group research, provide an overview of how to conduct a focus group interview, and describe how to analyze the data collected. This chapter should help readers to decide whether the focus group approach would be useful for answering their research questions. The authors specify the steps that should be taken in forming a focus group and selecting a moderator, and provide several descriptions of how to analyze the data using both qualitative and quantitative approaches.

In the final chapter, Henry describes graphical displays as one mechanism for communicating quantitative data. He outlines the types of graphs that can be used, categorizing them by both purpose and functions. With respect to purpose, some graphs, such as trend lines, pie charts, and bar charts, are intended to summarize data and are used for descriptive purposes. More analytic graphs, such as bivariate plots, show the relationship between two variables. With respect to functions, graphs are generally designed to display parts of a whole, multiple units, trend or time series, or relations among variables. Bar charts and pie charts are common graphs for displaying parts of a whole, but studies have found that bars are better than pies for accuracy and processing time. Henry describes several types of graphs for displaying multiple units and multiple variables; the type of graph a researcher should use depends on the number of cases or units, whether individual cases are to be identified, the audience targeted for the graph, and the level at which the audience is to read the graph. Trend graphs have a measure of time on the horizontal axis and one or more dependent variables on the vertical axis. Finally, for all graphs, Henry discusses two key principles regarding the size of the graph: data density and distortion of effect size. Henry reviews key principles for preparing data to communicate the information accurately, avoiding ambiguity, enhancing clarity, and reaching the intended audience.

12

Design and Evaluation
of Survey Questions

Floyd J. Fowler, Jr.

The quality of data from a survey depends on the size and representativeness of the sample from which data are collected; the techniques used for collecting the data; the quality of the interviewing, if interviewers are used; and the extent to which the questions are good measures. Methodologists have a concept that they call *total survey design* (e.g., Groves, 1989). By that, they refer to the perspective of looking at all sources of error, not just a single source, when making survey design decisions. The quality of data from a survey is no better than the worst aspect of the methodology.

When Sudman and Bradburn (1974) looked at sources of error in surveys, they concluded that perhaps the major source of error in survey estimates was the design of survey questions. When Fowler and Mangione (1990) looked at strategies for reducing interviewer effects on data, they, too, concluded that question design was one of the most important roads to minimizing interviewer effects on data. Moreover, whereas the design of surveys often involves important trade-offs, improving the design and evaluation of survey questions is one of the least expensive components of the survey process. Compared with significantly increasing the size of a sample, or even the efforts required to improve response rates significantly, improving questions is very cost-effective. Thus, from the perspective of total survey design, investing in the design and evaluation of questions is a best buy, one of the endeavors that is most likely to yield results in the form of better, more error-free data.

■ *What Is a Good Question?*

A good question is one that produces answers that are reliable and valid measures of something we want to describe. *Reliability* is used here in the classic psychometric sense of the extent to which answers are consistent: When the state of what is being described is consistent, the answers are consistent as well (Nunnally, 1978). *Validity,* in turn, is the extent to which answers correspond to some hypothetical "true value" of what we are trying to describe or measure (Cronbach & Meehl, 1955).

There are five basic characteristics of questions and answers that are fundamental to a good measurement process:

1. Questions need to be consistently understood.

2. Questions need to be consistently administered or communicated to respondents.

3. What constitutes an adequate answer should be consistently communicated.

4. Unless measuring knowledge is the goal of the question, all respondents should have access to the information needed to answer the question accurately.

5. Respondents must be willing to provide the answers called for in the question.

A critical part of the science of survey research is the empirical evaluation of survey questions. Like measurement in all sciences, the quality of measurement in survey research varies. Good science entails attempting to minimize error and taking steps to measure the remaining error so that we know how good our data are and we can continue to improve our methods.

There are two types of question evaluation: those aimed at evaluating how well questions meet the five standards above, which can be thought of as process standards, and those aimed at assessing the validity of answers that result. In order to assess the extent to which questions meet process standards, we can take a number of possible steps. These include (a) focus group discussions; (b) cognitive interviews, in which people's comprehension of questions and how they go about answering questions is probed and evaluated; and (c) field pretests under realistic conditions. Each of these activities has strengths and limitations in terms of the kinds of information they provide about questions. However, in the past decade there has been growing appreciation of the importance of evaluating questions before using them in a research project, and a great deal has been learned about how to use these techniques to provide systematic information about questions.

I begin this chapter by describing what we know about how to design survey questions. The discussion is separated by whether the focus is on measuring objective facts or subjective states of respondents, such as knowledge, opinions, or feelings. The latter part of the chapter is devoted to the objective evaluation of survey questions. My overall goal in this chapter is to describe how to design survey questions that will be good measures.

Question Objectives

One of the hardest tasks for methodologists is to induce researchers, people who want to collect data, to define their objectives. The difference between a question objective and the question itself is a critical distinction. The objective defines the kind of information that is needed. Designing the particular question or questions to achieve the objective is an entirely different step. In fact, this chapter is basically about the process of going from a question objective to a set of words, a question, the answers to which will achieve that objective.

Sometimes the distance between the objective and the question is short:

Objective: Age

Possible Example 1: How old were you on your last birthday?

Possible Example 1a: On what date were you born?

The answer to either of these questions probably will meet this question objective most of the time. An ambiguity might be whether age is required to the exact year, or whether broad categories, or a rounded number, will suffice. Example 1 produces more ages rounded to 0 or 5. Example 1a may be less sensitive to answer than Example 1 for some people, because it does not require that the respondent explicitly state an age. There also may be some difference between the questions in how likely people are to err in their answers, due to recall or miscalculations. However, the relationship between the objective and the information asked for in the questions is close, and the two questions yield similar results.

Objective: Income

Possible Example 2: How much money do you make per month on your current job?

Possible Example 2a: How much money did you make in the last 12 months from paid jobs?

Possible Example 2b: What was the total income for you, and all family members living with you in your home, from jobs and from other sources during the last calendar year?

First, it should be noted that there are imperfections in each of these three questions. However, the key point is that each of the questions is a possible approach to meeting the objective as stated, but the results will be very different. Obviously, current salary or wage rate might be the best measure of the quality or status of the job a person holds. However, if the purpose of measuring income is to find out about the resources available to the person, income for the past year might be a more relevant and appropriate measure. Even more appropriate, because people tend to share in and benefit from income from other family members, the total family income from all people and all sources might have the most to do with how "well-off" the person is.

A good question objective has to be more specific than simply "income." More broadly, a question objective can be defined only within the context of an analysis plan, a clear view of how the information will be used to meet a set of overall research objectives. Measuring income is actually a way of measuring social status, resources, or quality of employment. It is necessary to be explicit about the question objective in order to choose a question.

It is good practice to produce a detailed list of question objectives and an analysis plan that outlines how the data will be used. An example of such a document is presented in Table 12.1. Let us now turn to some of the specific challenges for designing questions that meet research objectives.

■ *Questions to Gather Factual Data*

□ *Definition of Concepts and Terms*

One basic part of having people accurately report factual or objective information is ensuring that all respondents have the same understanding of what is to be reported, so that the researcher is sure that the same definitions have been used across all respondents. This is one of the most difficult tasks for the designer of survey questions, and failure to do it properly is a major source of error in survey research.

For example, respondents were asked how many days in the past week they had any butter to eat. Many people use the terms *butter* and *margarine* interchangeably, so respondents were inconsistent in whether they included or excluded margarine when they answered the question. When the question was rewritten to exclude margarine explicitly, 20% fewer people said they had had any "butter" to eat at all in the past week than was the case when the term was left undefined (Fowler, 1992).

There are two basic approaches to ensuring consistent understanding of terms:

1. The researcher can provide complete definitions so that all or most of the ambiguities about what is called for are resolved.

2. The respondents can be asked to provide all the information needed so that the researcher can properly classify events for them. In other words, rather than trying to communicate complex definitions to all respondents, if respondents report adequate information, the researcher can consistently apply complex criteria for counting during the coding or analysis phase of the project.

Certainly the most common way to write survey questions that are commonly understood is to build needed definitions into the questions.

Table 12.1 Example of an Outline of Survey Content and Question Objectives

---

Purpose of survey: Study correlates of use of medical care.

We think medical care is likely to be a function of the following:

Fiscal resources to afford medical care
Need for medical care
Access to medical care
Perception of value medical care

Within each of these categories, measurement objectives include the following:

Fiscal resources relevant to medical care:
Annual family income past year (all sources)
Liquid assets (savings, bank accounts)
Health insurance

Need for medical care:

Chronic health conditions that might require care
Onset of acute illness
Injuries
Age/gender (to match with appropriate routine tests and exams)

Access to medical care:

Regular provider or not
Perceived proximity of provider
Perceived ease of access
Perceived financial barriers

Perception of value of medical care:

When not ill (checkups, screenings, and the like)
For chronic conditions (not life threatening)
For acute conditions (self-limiting)

Use of medical care:

Visits to doctors
Other medical services (not M.D.)
Emergency room use
Hospitalizations

Example 3: In the past week, how many days did you eat any butter?

Problem: There are two potential ambiguities in this question. First, it has already been noted that whether the term *butter* includes margarine or not is ambiguous. Second, sometimes it has been found that the phrase *the past week* is ambiguous. It could mean the 7 days preceding the date of the interview, but it also could mean the most recent period stretching from Monday through Sunday (or Sunday through Saturday).

Possible solution 3a: In the past 7 days, not counting any margarine you may have eaten, how many days did you eat any butter?

Comment: The reworded question reduces ambiguity both about whether to include or exclude margarine and about the period that is to be covered.

Sometimes, the definitional problems are too complicated to be solved by simply changing a few words or adding a parenthetical phrase.

Example 4: What is your income?

Problem: As discussed above, there are numerous issues about how to calculate income. Among them are whether income is current or for some period of time in the past, whether it is only income earned from salaries and wages or includes income from other sources, and whether it is only the person's own income that is at issue or includes income of others in which the respondent might share.

Example 4a: Next we need to get an estimate of the total income for you and family members living with you during 1996. When you calculate income, we would like you to include what you and other family members living with you made from jobs and also any income that you or other family members may have had from other sources, such as rents, welfare payments, social security, pensions, or even interest from stocks, bonds, or savings. So, including income from all sources, before deductions for taxes, for you and for family members living with you, how much was your total family income in 1996?

Comment: This is a very complicated definition, but it is necessary because what the researcher wants to measure is a very complicated concept. However, even this complex definition avoids, or fails to address, some important issues. For example, what does the respondent do if household composition at the time of the interview is different from how it was during the reference period?

When the rules for counting events are quite complex, providing a comprehensive, complex definition probably is not the right answer. At the extreme, respondents may end up more confused and the results may actually be worse than if definitions were not provided. A different approach is probably needed.

One approach is to add some extra questions to cover commonly omitted kinds of events. For example, in response to the general question about visits to doctors, it has been found that receiving advice over the telephone from a physician, seeing nurses or assistants who work for a physician, and receiving services from physicians who are not always thought of as "medical doctors" (such as psychiatrists) often are left out. One solution is to ask a general question, and then ask some follow-up questions:

Example 5a: Other than the visits to doctors that you just mentioned, how many times in the past 12 months have you gotten medical advice from a physician over the telephone?

Example 5b: Other than what you've already mentioned, how many times in the past 12 months have you gotten medical services from a psychiatrist?

Using multiple questions to cover all aspects of what is to be reported, rather than trying to pack everything into a single definition, can be an effective way to simplify the reporting tasks for respondents. It is one of the easiest ways to make sure that commonly omitted types of events are included in the total count that is obtained. However, this approach can be pushed even further, in ways that may make for even better question design strategies.

Example 6: What kind of health insurance plan do you have: a staff model health maintenance organization, an IPA, PPO, or unrestricted fee-for-service health plan?

Comment: This may seem to be a ridiculous question; it is unreasonable to think that most people can make these distinctions among health insurance plans. The approach outlined above, of trying to communicate common definitions, would seem unlikely to succeed given the complexity of models of health insurance that exist in the United States in the late 20th century. However, there are some questions that people can answer that probably would enable researchers to classify the kind of health insurance plan to which most people belong.

Example 6a: In your health plan, can you initially go to any doctor you want, or can you go only to certain doctors or places for your health care?

Example 6b: [If from a specific list or group] Do the physicians you see only see people who are part of your plan, or do they see other kinds of patients too?

Example 6c: When you receive medical services under your plan, do you yourself always pay the same amount, no matter what the service, or does the amount you pay depend upon the service you receive?

Comment: Maybe the answers to these questions would not enable researchers to make all the distinctions they want to make. Moreover, there is a possibility that some people might not be able to answer some of these questions. However, respondents are much more likely to be able to answer these questions accurately than they are to learn the definitions of IPAs and HMOs. The general idea of asking people a series of questions they can answer, then attempting to apply more complex definitional strategies to classify the respondents and their experiences, is a sound way to solve many definitional problems.

Proper question design means making certain that the researcher and all respondents are using the same definitions when classifying people or counting events. In general, researchers have tended to solve the problem by telling respondents what definitions the researchers want to use and then asking the respondents to do the classification work. Although sometimes that may be the best way to solve the problem, good question design usually will make the task as simple as possible for respondents. It is a new extra step for most investigators to think about what information they need about people that would enable them (the researchers) to do the classification task. However, if investigators identify what simple, easy questions people can answer that will provide the basis for classification, on many occasions better measurement will occur.

☐ *Knowing and Remembering*

Once a question has been designed so that all respondents understand what is wanted, the next issue is whether or not respondents have the information needed to answer the question. There are three possible sources of problems:

1. The respondent may not have the information needed to answer the question.

2. The respondent may once have known the information, but may have difficulty recalling it.

3. For questions that require reporting events that occurred in a specific time period, respondents may recall that the events occurred, but have difficulty accurately placing them in the time frame called for in the question.

Lack of Knowledge

Often, the problem of asking people questions to which they do not know the answers is one of respondent selection rather than question design. Many surveys ask a specific member of a household to report information about other household members or about the household as a whole. When such designs are chosen, a critical issue is whether or not the information required is usually known to other household members or to the person who will be doing the reporting.

There is a large literature comparing self-reporting with proxy reporting (Cannell, Marquis, & Laurent, 1977; Clarridge & Massagli, 1989; Moore, 1988; Rodgers & Herzog, 1989). There are occasions when it appears that people can report as well for others as they do for themselves. However, unless questions pertain to relatively public events or characteristics, others will not know the answers. Across all topics, usually self-respondents are better reporters than proxy respondents.

There is another dimension to the topic of knowledge that more directly affects question design. Sometimes respondents have experiences or information related to a question, but do not have the information in the form the researcher wants it. A good example is a medical diagnosis. There is some evidence showing a lack of correspondence between the conditions patients say they have and the conditions recorded in medical records (Cannell, Fisher, & Bakker, 1965; Jabine, 1987; Madow, 1967). At least part of this mismatch results from patients' not being told how to name their conditions.

One critical part of the preliminary work a researcher must do in designing a survey instrument is to find out whether or not questions have been included to which some respondents do not know the answers. The limit of survey research is what people are able and willing to report. If a researcher wants to find out something that is not commonly known by respondents, the researcher must find another way to get the information.

Recall

Memory researchers tell us that few things, once directly experienced, are forgotten completely. The readiness with which information and experiences can be retrieved follows some fairly well-developed principles.

Some memories may be painful and subject to repression. However, that is not the issue for the sorts of things measured in most surveys. Rather, the three principles that probably are most relevant include the following (Cannell, Marquis, & Laurent, 1977; Eisenhower, Mathiowetz, & Morganstein, 1991):

1. The more recent the event, the more likely it is to be recalled.

2. The greater the impact or current salience of the event, the more likely it is to be recalled.

3. The more consistent an event was with the way the respondent thinks about things, the more likely it is to be recalled.

How does a researcher obtain accurate reporting in a survey? Obviously, one key issue is what the researcher chooses to ask about. If the researcher wants information about very small events that had minimal impact, it follows that it is not reasonable to expect respondents to report for a very long period. For example, when researchers want reporting about dietary intake or soft drink consumption, it has been found that even a 24-hour recall period can produce deterioration and reporting error due to recall. When people are asked to report their behavior over a week or two weeks, they resort to giving estimates of their average or typical behavior, rather than trying to remember (Blair & Burton, 1987). If a researcher wants accurate information about consumption, having respondents report for a very short period, such as a day (or even keep a diary), is probably the only way to get reasonably accurate answers (Smith, 1991).

A defining characteristic of most interviews is that they are quick question-and-answer experiences. Respondents' levels of motivation vary, but for the most part a survey is not an important event in a respondent's life. Hence, without special prodding, respondents are unlikely to invest a significant amount of effort in trying to reconstruct or recall the things the survey asks them to report (Cannell, Marquis, & Laurent, 1977). For these reasons, researchers have explored strategies for improving the quality of the recall performance of respondents.

One of the simplest ways to stimulate recall and reporting is to ask a long, rather than a short, question. This does not mean making questions more complex or convoluted; rather, adding some introductory material that prepares the respondent for the question has been shown to improve reporting (Cannell & Marquis, 1972). One reason may be simply that longer questions give respondents time to search their memories.

Two more direct strategies are used to improve recall. First, asking multiple questions improves the probability that an event will be recalled and reported

(Cannell, Marquis, & Laurent, 1977; Sudman & Bradburn, 1982). Second, stimulating associations likely to be tied to what the respondent is supposed to report, activating the cognitive and intellectual network in which a memory is likely to be embedded, is likely to improve recall as well (Eisenhower et al., 1991).

There are limits to what people are able to recall. If a question calls for information that most people cannot recall easily, the data will almost certainly suffer. However, even when the recall task is comparatively simple for most people, if getting an accurate count is important, asking multiple questions and developing questions that trigger associations that may aid recall are both effective strategies for improving the quality of the data.

Placing Events in Time

Many of the issues discussed above could reflect an interrelationship between recalling an event at all and placing it in time. If a survey is to be used to estimate the annual number of hospitalizations for a particular sample, people are asked what essentially is a two-part question: Have you been in the hospital recently, and how many times were you in the hospital in exactly the past 12 months?

There are two approaches researchers use to try to improve how well respondents place events in time:

1. They stimulate recall activities on the part of respondents to help them place events in time.

2. They design data collection procedures that generate boundaries for reporting periods.

In order to improve the ability of respondents to place events in time, the simplest step is to show respondents a calendar with the reference period outlined. In addition, respondents can be asked to recall what was going on and what kinds of things were happening in their lives at the time of the boundary of the reporting period. Filling in any life events, such as birthdays, can help to make the dates on the calendar more meaningful (e.g., Sudman, Finn, & Lannon, 1984).

A very different approach to improving the reporting of events in a time period is to create an actual boundary for respondents by conducting two or more interviews (Neter & Waksberg, 1964). During the initial interview, respondents are told that they are going to be asked about events and situations that happen during the period prior to the next interview. In the subsequent interview, they are then asked about what has happened between the time of the initial interview and the time of the second interview.

Obviously, such reinterview designs are much more expensive to implement than are one-time surveys. However, when accurate reporting of events in time is very important, they provide a strategy that improves the quality of data.

Finally, the technique of giving respondents a diary to keep should be mentioned. There are special challenges to getting people to maintain diaries. However, to obtain detailed information, such as on food consumption or small expenditures, for a short period of time, diaries are an option researchers should consider (Sudman & Bradburn, 1982; Sudman & Ferber, 1971).

☐ *The Form of an Answer*

Most questions specify the forms the answers are supposed to take. The form of the answer must fit the answer the respondent has to give.

> ***Example 7:*** In the past 30 days, were you able to climb a flight of stairs with no difficulty, with some difficulty, or were you not able to climb stairs at all?
>
> *Comment:* This question imposes an assumption: that the respondent's situation was stable for 30 days. For a study of patients with AIDS, my colleagues and I found that questions in this form did not fit the answers of respondents, because their symptoms (and ability to climb stairs) varied widely from day to day (Cleary, Fowler, Weissman, et al., 1993).

> ***Example 8:*** On days when you drink any alcohol at all, how many drinks do you usually have?
>
> *Comment:* Questions asking about "usual" behavior are common. However, they all impose the assumption of regularity on respondents. The question can accommodate some variability, but it is poorly suited to major variability. For example, if a respondent drinks much more on weekends than on weekdays, it is not clear at all how he or she should answer this question. Researchers need to scrutinize closely any questions using the term *usual* to make sure the answers fit the reality to be described.

> ***Example 9:*** How many miles are you from the nearest hospital?
>
> *Comment:* It is easy to imagine that a respondent might know the exact location of the nearest hospital, yet have a poor notion of the number of miles. Moreover, whereas miles may be a good measure of distance in a rural or suburban area, time via the likely mode of transportation might be a more appropriate metric for a city dweller and might provide the units in which respondents could answer most accurately.

Asking people questions to which they know the answers is important. However, it is easy to overlook the next essential step—giving respondents an answer task they can perform and that fits the true answer to the question.

☐ *Reducing the Effect of Social Desirability on Answers*

Studies of response accuracy suggest that there is a tendency among respondents to distort answers in ways that will make them look better or will avoid making them look bad. Locander, Sudman, and Bradburn (1976) found that convictions for drunken driving and experiences with bankruptcy were reported very poorly in surveys. Clearly, such events are significant enough that they are unlikely to have been forgotten; the explanation for poor reporting must be that people are reluctant to report such events about themselves. However, the effects of social desirability are much more pervasive than such extreme examples.

For example, when Cannell et al. (1965) coded the reasons for hospitalization by the likelihood that the condition leading to the hospitalization might be embarrassing or life threatening, they found that the hospitalizations associated with the most threatening conditions were significantly less likely to be reported in a health survey. Distortion can also produce overreporting. Anderson, Silver, and Abramson (1988) found notable overreporting of voting in elections.

Although *social desirability* has been used as a blanket term for these phenomena, there are probably several different forces operating to produce the response effects described above. First, there is no doubt some tendency for respondents to want to make themselves look good and avoid looking bad. In addition, sometimes surveys ask questions to which the answers could actually pose a threat to respondents. When surveys ask about illegal drug use, about drinking alcohol to excess, about the number of sexual partners people have had, the answers, if revealed, could expose respondents to divorce proceedings, loss of jobs, or even criminal prosecution. When the answer to a survey question poses such a risk for respondents, it is easy to understand why some respondents might prefer to distort their answers rather than take a chance on giving accurate answers, even if the risk of improper disclosure is deemed to be small.

Third, in a related but slightly different way, response distortion may come about because the literally accurate answer is not the way the respondent wants to think about him- or herself. When respondents distort answers about not drinking to excess or voting behavior, it may have as much to do with respondents' managing their own self-images as with their managing the images others have of them.

It is fundamental to understand that the problem is not "sensitive questions," but "sensitive answers." Questions tend to be categorized as sensitive if a yes answer is likely to be judged by society as undesirable behavior. However, for those for whom the answer is no, questions about any particular behavior are not sensitive. When Sudman and Bradburn (1982) asked respondents to rate questions with respect to sensitivity, the question rated highest concerned how often people masturbated. Presumably, this high rating stemmed from a combination of the facts that people felt that a positive answer was not consistent with the image they wanted to project and that it is a very prevalent behavior. Questions about drug use or drunken driving are not sensitive for people who do not use drugs or drive after drinking.

It also is important to remember that people vary in what they consider to be sensitive. For example, asking whether or not a person has a library card apparently is a fairly sensitive question; some people interpret a no answer as indicating something negative about themselves (Parry & Crossley, 1950). Library card ownership is considerably overreported.

Thinking broadly about the reasons for distorting answers leads to the notion that the whole interview experience should be set up in such a way as to minimize the forces on respondents to distort answers. Some of the steps affect data collection procedures, rather than question design per se.

With respect to data collection procedures, constructive steps to reduce the effects of these forces on answers include the following:

1. Ensure confidentiality of answers.

2, Emphasize through the introduction and in other ways the importance of the accuracy of answers (Cannell, Oksenberg, & Converse, 1977).

3. Use self-administration rather than interviewer administration, or have respondents enter their answers directly into a computer (Aquilino & Losciuto, 1990; Turner, Lessler, & Gfroerer, 1992).

In designing the questions themselves, constructive steps include the following:

1. Explain the purposes of questions so that respondents can see why they are appropriate.

2. Frame questions, and take care in wording, to reduce the extent to which respondents will perceive that particular answers will be interpreted in a negative or inaccurate light.

In extreme cases, having respondents answer in code or using random response techniques so that answers cannot be linked to individual respondents may reduce the effects of social desirability on answers (Fox & Tracy, 1986). Strategies such as random response techniques would be used only for a few key measurements that are thought to be extraordinarily sensitive. For example, if one wants estimates of the rate at which people have done something illegal, and those estimates are central to the purposes of the research, it might be worth investing 5 or 10 minutes of interviewing time to get two answers using random response. However, a well-designed self-administered strategy for data collection might be just as effective for improving the reporting of socially undesirable material.

For most research, the key messages here are that researchers should (a) ensure and communicate to respondents the confidentiality of answers, (b) make clear to respondents that being accurate is more important than self-image or rapport with the interviewer, and (c) design questions so as to minimize the likelihood that respondents will feel their answers will be put in negatively valued categories. These steps are likely to improve the quality of reporting in every area of a survey, not just those deemed to be particularly sensitive. Researchers never know when a question may cause a respondent some embarrassment or unease. A survey instrument should be designed to minimize the extent to which such feelings will affect answers to any question asked.

■ *Questions to Measure Subjective States*

A distinctive feature of the measurement of subjective states is that there are, in fact, no right or wrong answers to questions. "Rightness" implies the possibility of an objective standard against which to evaluate answers. Although we can assess the consistency of answers with other information, there is no direct way to know about people's subjective states independent of what they tell us.

This does not mean that there are no standards for questions designed to measure subjective states. The standards are basically the same as for questions about factual things: Questions should be understood consistently by all respondents so they are all answering the same question, and the response task, the way respondents are asked to answer the questions, should be one that respondents can do consistently and that provides meaningful information about what they have to say.

By far, the largest number of survey questions ask about respondents' perceptions or feelings about themselves or others. The basic task for the respondent on most questions in this category is to place answers on a continuum. Such questions all have the same basic framework, which consists of three components: (a) what is to be rated, (b) what dimension or continuum the rated object is to be placed on, and (c) the characteristics of the continuum that are offered to the respondent.

☐ *Defining What Is to Be Rated*

As with all survey questions, when researchers are designing questions to measure subjective states, it is important that they keep in mind that all respondents should be answering the same question.

> ***Example 10:*** In general, do you think government officials care about your interests a lot, some, only a little, or not at all?

"Government officials" are a very heterogeneous lot, and which government officials a respondent has in mind may affect how he or she answers the question. For example, people consistently rate local governments as more responsive than state and federal governments. Elected officials may not be rated the same as persons who have been appointed to positions in the executive branches of government. To the extent that people's answers vary based on the ways they interpret questions, a new source of error is introduced, and the answers will provide less than the best information on what the researchers are trying to measure.

> **Example 11:** Do you consider crime to be a big problem, some problem, or no problem at all?

Crime is also a heterogeneous category. Can people lump white-collar crime, drug dealing, and armed robbery into a single integrated whole? It would not be surprising for respondents to this question to key on different aspects of crime. Moreover, this particular question does not specify a locus for the problem: the neighborhood, the city, the state, the nation. The perspectives people take will affect their answers. People generally rate the crime problems in their own neighborhoods as less severe than average. To the extent that what is being rated can be specified more clearly, so that respondents do not vary in their interpretations of what they are rating, measurement will be better.

Seemingly small differences in wording can have big effects on answers (Schuman & Presser, 1981). Careful attention to wording is one key to good questions.

☐ *The Response Task*

Researchers have designed numerous strategies for evoking answers from respondents. The most common task for respondents is some variation of putting the object of the answer on a continuum.

The Rating Task

Figure 12.2 shows three different forms of a continuum with rankings from positive to negative. Such a continuum can be described to respondents in numerous ways, and there are numerous ways respondents can be asked to assign answers to positions on the continuum.

> **Example 12a:** Overall, how would rate your health—excellent, very good, good, fair, or poor?

> **Example 12b:** Consider a scale from 0 to 10, where 10 represents the best your health can be, where 0 represents the worst your health can be, and the numbers in between represent health states in between. What number would you give your health today?

> **Example 12c:** Overall, would you say you are in good health?

These three questions all ask the same thing; they differ only in the ways in which the respondents are asked to use the continuum.

When the goal is to have respondents place themselves or something else along a continuum, the researcher must make choices about the characteristics

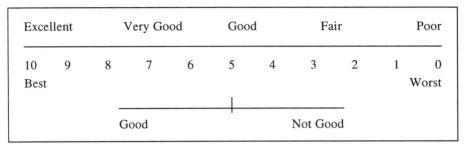

Figure 12.2. Some Examples of Forms for an Evaluative Continuum

of the scale or response task to be offered to respondents. Two key issues include (a) how many categories to offer and (b) whether to use scales defined by numbers or by adjectives. In general, the goal of any rating task is to provide the researcher with as much information as possible about where respondents stand compared with others. Consider a continuum from positive to negative and the results of a question such as the following:

> ***Example 13:*** In general, would you rate the job performance of the president as good or not so good?

Such a question divides respondents into two groups. That means that the information coming from this question is not very refined. Respondents who answer "good" are more positive than the people who say "not so good," but there is no information about the relative feelings of all the people who answer "good," even though there may be quite a bit of variation among them in the degree of positiveness they feel about the president's job performance.

There is another issue as well: the distribution of answers. In the above example, suppose most of the respondents answered the question in a particular way; for example, suppose 90% said the president is doing a "good" job. In that case, the value of the question is particularly minimal. The question gives meaningful information only for about 10% of the population, the 10% who responded "not good." For the 90% of the population that answered "good," absolutely nothing was learned about where they stand compared with others who gave the same answer.

This analysis suggests that there are two general principles for thinking about optimal categories for a response task. First, to the extent that valid information can be obtained, more categories are better than fewer categories. Second, generally speaking, an optimal set of categories along a continuum will maximize the extent to which people are distributed across the response categories.

Given these considerations, is there any limit to the number of categories that is useful? Is it always better to have more categories? There are at least two limiting factors to the principle that using more categories produces better measurement. First, there appear to be real limits to the extent to which people can use scales to provide meaningful information. Although the optimal number of categories on a scale may vary, in part with the dimension and in part based on the distribution of people or items rated, most studies have shown that little new valid information is provided by response tasks that provide more than 10 categories (Andrews, 1984). Beyond that, people seem not to provide new information; the variation that is added seems to be mainly a reflection of the different ways people use the scales. In fact, 5 to 7 categories are probably as many categories as most respondents can use meaningfully for most rating tasks.

A second issue has to do with ease of administration. If the survey instrument is being self-administered (with respondents reading the questions to themselves) or administered by an interviewer (who can hand respondents a list of the response categories), long lists of scale points do not pose any particular problem. However, when surveys are done on the telephone, it is necessary for respondents to retain all of the response options as the interviewer reads them in order to answer the question. There clearly are limits to peoples' abilities to retain complex lists of categories.

When long, complex scales are presented by telephone, sometimes it is found that this produces biases simply because respondents cannot remember the categories well. For example, there is some tendency for respondents to remember the first or the last categories better than some of those in the middle (Schwartz & Hippler, 1991). When questions are to be used on the telephone, researchers often prefer to use scales with only 3 or 4 response categories in order to ease the response task and ensure that respondents are aware of all the response alternatives when they answer questions.

Another decision is whether to use numerical or adjectival labels. The principal argument in favor of adjectival scales is that all of the points are more consistently calibrated by the use of words. The other side of the story is that it is difficult to think up adjectives for more than 5 or 6 points along most continua. When researchers have tried, some of the adjectival descriptions have sounded very close or similar to one another. It is virtually impossible to find a list of adjectives that will define a 10-point scale.

A related advantage of numbers is that a numerical 10-point scale is easy to remember and use. Thus, when doing telephone interviews, whereas it may be difficult to teach respondents 5 or 6 adjectives, it is comparatively easy to define a 10-point scale numerically. Hence using scales defined by numbers can increase the reliability of a rating task performed on the telephone, if numerous response alternatives are to be provided. Moreover, it may increase the comparability of measurement of subjective ratings across modes of data collection.

Finally, a problem in international research and increasingly in research in the United States is how to get consistent measurement of subjective states for different cultural groups. In particular, when scales are defined adjectivally, it has been found that it is virtually impossible to have exact translations across languages. Adjectival scaling tasks across languages are not comparable. Although it has not been documented, it seems reasonable that numerical scales could improve the comparability of data collected across languages.

Using an Agree-Disagree Format

In the preceding pages, I have discussed asking respondents to classify or rate something by putting it on a continuum, often choosing an adjective or number to place it on the scale. The same kind of tasks can be attacked using an agree-disagree format. The goal of such questions is basically the same as that of those discussed above: to order people along some continuum.

Example 14a: I like Ike.

Example 14b: My health is excellent.

Consider the continuum from positive to negative presented previously. Both of these statements can be reliably located at the positive end of a continuum, either feelings about former President Eisenhower or the rating of a person's health. Suppose a person is asked to agree or disagree with these statements. In essence, respondents are saying that their views lie at the generally positive end of the continuum within a reasonable distance of where they see the statements "I like Ike" or "My health is excellent" to be located.

Example 15a: I am sometimes depressed.

This statement lies somewhere between the statement "I am often depressed" and the statement "I am seldom or never depressed." If a respondent is asked to agree or disagree with such a statement, there is an interpretation problem if he or she disagrees. A person could disagree because "I am sometimes depressed" seems to understate the problem or because it seems to overstate the problem. As measurement, the results are unacceptable. To be able to interpret the answers, the researcher needs to choose a different point on the scale for the stem question:

Example 15b: I am usually depressed.

Example 15c: I am seldom depressed.

For measuring respondents' feelings about ideas or policies, questions in this form are difficult to avoid. I discuss such questions later in the chapter. However, if the goal is to have something rated or placed on a continuum, a more direct rating task will almost always accomplish the same thing better. We can ask people to agree or disagree with the statement "My health is excellent," but how much simpler, direct, and informative it is to ask, "How would you rate your health—excellent, very good, good, fair, or poor?"

Rank Ordering

There are occasions when researchers want respondents to compare objects on some dimension.

Example 16: Which candidate do you prefer?

Example 17: What do you consider to be the most important problem facing the city?

Example 18: Here are some factors some people consider when deciding where to live. Which is most important to you?

Proximity to work

Quality of schools

Parks

Safety

Access to shopping

Example 19: I'm going to read you a list of candidates. I want you to tell me which you consider to be the most liberal.

The basic question objectives can all be met through one of four tasks for respondents:

1. Respondents can be given a list of options and asked to rank order them from top to bottom on some continuum.

2. Respondents can be given a list of options and asked to name the most (second most, third most, and so on) extreme on the rating dimension.

3. Respondents can be asked to make a series of paired comparisons, ordering two options at a time.

4. Respondents can be given a list and asked to rate each one using some scale (rather than just putting them in order or picking one or more of the most extreme).

If there is a short list of options, Task 1 is not hard to do. However, as the list becomes longer, the task is harder, soon becoming impossible on the telephone, when respondents cannot see all the options. Task 2 is easier than Task 1 when the list is long (or even when the list is short). Often researchers are satisfied to know which are the one or two most important, rather than having a complete rank ordering. In that case, Task 2 is attractive. Psychometricians often like the paired comparison approach of Task 3, in which each alternative is compared with every other, one pair at a time. However, it is such a time-consuming and cumbersome way to create an ordered list that it is seldom used in general surveys.

Best of all may be Task 4. The task is probably easiest of all for respondents, regardless of data collection mode. Moreover, the rank ordering tasks

(Tasks 1 through 3) do not provide any information about where the items are located on the rating continuum. They could all be perceived as very high or very low—the rank order provides no information. Task 4 provides information about where the items are located on the rating scale. Although there can be ties, so ordering is not known perfectly, usually an aggregate order will result as well. For all these reasons, very often a series of ratings, rather than a rank order task, is the best way to achieve these objectives.

Narrative Answers

When the goal is to place answers on a continuum, allowing people to answer in their own words will not do. Consider a question such as the following:

Example 20: How is it going?

People can answer in all kinds of ways, Some will say "fine," some will say "great," some will say "not bad." If one were trying to order such comments, some ordinal properties would be clear. Those who say "terrible" would obviously be placed at a different point on a continuum from those who say "great." However, there is no way to order responses such as "not bad," "pretty good," "good enough," or "satisfactory."

In contrast, when the purpose of a question is to identify priorities or preferences among various items, there is a choice to be made between the following two approaches:

Example 21: What do you consider to be the most important problem facing your local city government today?

Example 21a: The following is a list of some of the problems that are facing your local city government. Which do you consider to be most important?
   a. Crime
   b. Tax rates
   c. Schools
   d. Trash collection

The open-ended approach has several advantages. It does not limit answers to those the researcher thought of, so there is opportunity to learn the unexpected. It also requires no visual aids, so it works on the telephone. On the other hand, the diversity of answers may make the results hard to analyze. The more focused the question and the clearer the kind of answer desired, the more analyzable the answers. Moreover, Schuman and Presser (1981) found that the answers are probably more reliable and valid when a list is provided than when the question is asked in open form. If the list of possible answers is not known or is very long, the open form may be the right approach. Although computer-assisted interviewing creates great pressure to use only fixed-response questions, respondents like to answer some questions in their own words. The measurement result may not be as easy to work with, but asking some questions to be answered in narrative form may be justified for that reason alone. However, if good measurement is the goal and the alternatives can be specified, providing respondents with a list and having them choose is usually best.

☐ *Measuring Responses to Ideas*

The tasks discussed in the preceding section all were geared to having respondents place something on a rating scale or order items on a scale. A large part of the survey research enterprise is focused on measuring people's responses to various ideas, analyses, or proposals. The content of such questions is as vast as the imagination of the survey research community. The common form of such questions is something like the following:

> *Example 22:* Do you favor or oppose the idea of sending U.S. bombers to attack Antarctica?

> *Example 23:* Higher taxes generally hurt the rich and benefit the poor. Do you agree or disagree?

> *Example 24:* In general, would you like to have more money spent on the parks and playgrounds in your neighborhood area or not?

An important distinction to be made in thinking about questions like these is the nature of the task confronting the respondent. In the examples given previously, respondents were asked to place themselves or others on some defined continuum. For example, they would be asked to rate their own health on a scale from excellent to poor or they would be asked to rate the job they thought that the president of the United States was doing from good to poor. The task posed by these questions, however, is somewhat different. Instead of being asked to place some object on a defined continuum, the respondent is asked to rate the distance between his or her own views or preferences and the idea expressed in the question.

> *Example 25a:* Do you favor or oppose gun control laws?

"Gun control laws" can mean many things. Such laws can cover a range of policies, including rules about who can buy guns, how long people have to wait to buy guns, and what kind of guns they can buy. A fundamental problem with questions such as this is that the meaning of what is being asked can be interpreted differently from respondent to respondent.

To the extent that researchers can minimize differences in interpretation of what questions mean, they can increase the validity of measurement. The goal is to have differences in answers reflect differences in where people stand on the issues, rather than differences in their interpretations of the questions.

Example 25b: Do you favor or oppose laws that would prevent people convicted of violent crimes from purchasing a handgun or pistol?

Obviously, this question addresses only one kind of gun control law. However, a question that is explicit about the policy that people are being asked about, that minimizes differences in interpretation about what the question means, should produce more valid measurement of where people stand.

It is very common to find multiple dimensions underlying questions posed in the agree-disagree format, or variations thereon. The following are examples cited by Robinson and Shaver (1973) that have this characteristic:

> *Example 26:* America is getting so far away from the true American way of life that force may be necessary to restore it.
>
> *Three issues:* How far America is from the true American way, whether or not the true American way should be restored, and whether or not force may be needed (or desirable) to restore it.
>
> *Example 27:* There is little use writing public officials because they often aren't really interested in the problems of the average man.
>
> *Two issues:* The value of writing officials and how interested officials are in the problems of the average man.

With respect to both of these questions, it is not possible to define what an "agree" or "disagree" answer actually means.

There are three common problems with questions in the agree-disagree form. First, many questions in this form do not produce interpretable answers, either because they are not on a clearly defined place on a continuum or because they reflect more than one dimension. Those problems can be solved through careful question design. However, two other problems—that these questions usually sort people into only two groups (agree or disagree) and that they often are cognitively complex—are more generic to the question form. Although it is possible to design good questions in this form, it often is possible to design a more direct rating task that will accomplish the same thing in a better way.

☐   *The Relativity of Answers About Subjective States*

The answers to questions about subjective states are always relative; they are never absolute. The kinds of statements that are justified based on answers to these kinds of questions are comparative. It is appropriate to say that Group A reports more positive feelings than Group B. It is appropriate to say that the population reports more positive feelings now than it did a year ago. It is not appropriate (at least not without some careful caveats) to say that people gave the president a positive rating, that they are satisfied with their schools, or that by and large they think their health is good.

One of the most common abuses of survey measurement is treating data collected using measures of subjective states, which are designed to produce ordinal measures, as if they had produced data with absolute meaning. When statements are made such as "Most people favor gun control," "Most people oppose abortion," and "Most people support the president," these statements should be viewed askance. All that happened in any of these cases was that a majority of respondents picked response alternatives to a particular question that the researcher chose to interpret as favorable or positive. That same group of people could be presented with different stimuli that apparently address the same topic that would produce different distributions and support very different statements.

■ *Some General Rules for Designing Good Survey Instruments*

In the preceding sections, I have discussed in some detail the problems associated with writing good survey questions and some general approaches to solving common problems. The following are some general principles that apply to all types of questions.

Principle 1: The strength of survey research is asking people about their firsthand experiences: what they have done, their current situations, their feelings and perceptions. Yet, surprisingly, a good bit of survey research is devoted to asking people questions to which most people do not have informed answers.

Principle 1a: Beware of asking about information that is only acquired second-hand.

Principle 1b: Beware of hypothetical questions.

Principle 1c: Beware of asking about perceptions of causality.

Principle 1d: Beware of asking about solutions to complex problems.

Principle 2: Questions should be asked one at a time.

Principle 2a: Avoid asking two questions at once.

Principle 2b: Avoid questions that impose unwarranted assumptions.

Principle 2c: Beware of questions that include hidden contingencies.

Principle 3: A survey question should be worded so that all respondents are answering the same question.

Principle 3a: To the extent possible, choose the words in questions so that all respondents understand their meaning and all respondents have the same sense of what the meaning is.

Principle 3b: To the extent that words or terms must be used that have meanings that are likely not to be shared, provide definitions to all respondents.

Principle 3c: The time period referred to by a question should be unambiguous.

Principle 3d: If what is to be covered is too complex to be included in a single question, ask multiple questions.

Principle 4: If a survey is to be interviewer administered, wording of the questions must constitute a complete and adequate script such that when the interviewer reads the question as worded, the respondent will be fully prepared to answer the question.

Principle 4a: If definitions are to be given, give them before the question itself is asked.

Principle 4b: A question should end with the question itself. If there are response alternatives, arrange the question so that they constitute the final part.

Principle 5: All respondents should understand the kind of answer that constitutes an adequate answer to a question.

Principle 5a: Avoid questions that begin with adverbs: how, when, where, why, to what extent. Such questions do not specify the terms of an adequate answer.

Principle 5b: Specify the number of responses to be given to questions for which more than one answer is possible.

Principle 6: Survey instruments should be designed so that the tasks of reading questions, following instructions, and recording answers are as easy as possible for interviewers and respondents.

■ *Presurvey Evaluation of Questions*

In recent years there has been increased attention given to the evaluation of survey questions from the cognitive and interactional perspectives. The basic idea is that before a question is asked in a full-scale survey, testing should be done to find out if respondents can understand it, if they can perform the tasks that it requires, and if the interviewers can and will read it as worded.

There are three main kinds of presurvey question evaluation activities: focus group discussions, intensive individual interviews (not replicating proposed survey procedures), and field pretesting (replicating to a reasonable extent procedures to be used in a proposed survey).

☐ *Focus Group Discussions*

In survey research, focus groups most often have been used to help define topics and research questions. However, focus groups also have a role to play in the question evaluation process. Using a focus group for the evaluation of proposed survey questions requires that there already be developed some clear ideas about what the proposed survey instrument will look like.

There are two main aspects of survey instrument design to which focus group discussions can contribute:

1. Helping to examine assumptions about the reality about which people will be asked.

2. Helping to evaluate assumptions about vocabulary, the way people understand terms or concepts that will be used in the survey instrument.

For example, researchers were planning a study of people's attendance at and participation in arts-related events and performances. A key part of the survey was to ask people how often they had attended certain kinds of performances. Several focus group discussions were conducted that were aimed at finding out what kinds of different arts-related activities people might think they should report and to examine the specific wording of proposed questions.

With respect to what counts, one key issue turned out to be the problem of incidental arts. If a person goes to dinner and there is a jazz pianist at the restaurant, does that count as attending a jazz performance? What about music heard at fairs or amusement parks? There was little question in people's minds about what counted if they bought a ticket and sat down for a program of music. However, art and music are present in many places in society, and clearly people did not know how to classify incidental exposure to various art performances and exhibits.

There are three basic topics of conversation in a focus group devoted to an interview schedule:

1. Do the questions appropriately cover what respondents are supposed to describe?

2. Are the response tasks that the questions will pose tasks that respondents are able and willing to perform?

3. Do the words or descriptions proposed in the questions convey consistent meaning, so that respondents have a common understanding of what question they are to answer?

Of course, a focus group discussion is only the beginning of the process. It helps lay out a range of problems that a good survey instrument will have to solve, and it guides the researcher in beginning to solve some vocabulary and conceptual problems. However, intensive individual interviews and field pretests are necessary to examine some aspects of survey questions that cannot be addressed in a focus group discussion.

☐ *Intensive Individual Interviews*

In the early 1980s, survey researchers and cognitive psychologists met to discuss their mutual interests. One key conclusion was that question testing should include procedures routinely used by cognitive psychologists to learn what respondents are thinking when they are trying to answer questions. Prior to that conference, researchers such as Belson (1981) had "debriefed" respondents about their understanding of questions. However, it probably is fair to trace the current interest in the cognitive laboratory interview to the impetus from the conference (Jabine, Straf, & Tanur, 1984) and to the pioneering work conducted at the National Center for Health Statistics (Lessler & Tourangeau, 1989).

Although cognitive or intensive interviews take several forms and shapes, there are some common elements that define them (Forsyth & Lessler, 1991):

1. The priority of the process is to find out how respondents understand questions and perform the response tasks; there is no particular effort to replicate the data collection procedures to be used in the full-scale survey.

2. Respondents often are brought into a special setting in which interviews can be recorded and observed; hence these are often referred to as "laboratory interviews."

3. Most critically, the basic protocol involves reading questions to respondents, having them answer the questions, and then using some strategy to find out what was going on in the respondents' minds during the question-and-answer process.

There are three common procedures for trying to monitor the cognitive processes of the respondent who is answering questions (Forsyth & Lessler, 1991): "think-aloud" interviews; asking probe or follow-up questions after each question, or short series of questions; and going through the questions twice, first having respondents answer them in the usual way, then returning to the questions and having a discussion with respondents about the response tasks.

Although the objectives and the products of these intensive interviews may seem similar to those of the focus groups, cognitive interviews are complementary to focus groups. The great advantage of focus groups is that they are efficient; the perceptions and experiences of seven or eight people can be garnered in an hour and a half. On the other hand, focus groups do not provide good tests of the specific wording of individual questions and how individuals actually answer specific questions. Focus groups attack these problems in a general way, whereas intensive individual interviews are designed to identify specific problems of comprehension and the response experience.

☐ *Field Pretesting*

There is a prototype of a traditional field pretest for interviewer-administered surveys. When a survey instrument is in near final form, experienced interviewers conduct 15 to 35 interviews with people similar to those who will be respondents in the planned survey. Data collection procedures are designed to be similar to those to be used in the planned survey, except that the people interviewed are likely to be chosen on the basis of convenience and availability, rather than according to some probability sampling strategy. Question evaluation from such a survey mainly comes from interviewers (Converse & Presser, 1986).

One limitation of traditional field pretests is that they do not provide much information about question comprehension or response difficulty (Presser, 1989). Cognitive interviews are supposed to fill that gap partially. However, there recently has been an effort to develop strategies for strengthening the traditional pretest as well. One of the most promising techniques is the systematic coding of interviewer and respondent behavior during the pretest interview (Fowler & Cannell, 1996; Oksenberg, Cannell, & Kalton, 1991).

The basic technique is straightforward. Pretest interviews are tape-recorded. This can be done in person or over the telephone. For telephone interviews, it is important to inform respondents explicitly that the interview is being taped and to get their permission for that, in order not to break any laws. It has been well established that respondents seldom decline to have interviews tape-recorded if the idea is properly presented (Fowler & Mangione, 1990). The recordings are then coded as an aid to evaluating questions.

The rationale behind coding the behavior in pretest interviews is as follows: When a survey interview is going perfectly, the interviewer will read the question exactly as written once, after which the respondent will give an answer that meets the question objectives. When there are deviations from this, the perfect question-and-answer process, it may be an indication of a question problem. The more often deviations occur, the more likely it is that there is a problem with the question.

It turns out that questions have reliable, predictable effects on the behavior of respondents and interviewers. In one study, the same survey instrument was pretested by two different survey organizations. The results of the behavior coding of the pretests were then compared, question by question. It was found that the rates at which three key behaviors occurred—reading questions exactly as worded, respondent requests for clarification, and respondents providing inadequate answers to questions—were highly and significantly correlated between the two pretests. Thus, regardless of who does the interviewing, the same questions are likely to produce misread questions, requests for clarification, and inadequate answers (Fowler & Cannell, 1996).

The product of the behavior coding is a simple distribution for each question. From the coding, the rate at which each of the behaviors occurred across all the pretest interviews is tabulated. The strengths of behavior coding results are that they are objective, systematic, replicable, and quantitative. Interviewers cannot have a real quantitative sense for how often they encounter respondents who have difficulty with questions. Indeed, interviewers are not even very good at identifying questions that they do not read exactly as written. Hence behavior coding adds considerably to the information researchers have about their questions.

The quantifiable nature of the results provides perspective by allowing comparison of how frequently problems occur across questions and across surveys. It also constitutes more credible evidence for researchers of the presence of a problem with a question. When interviewers say that they think respondents are having difficulty with a question, it is hard for researchers to know how much weight to give that perception. When the behavior coding shows that 25% of respondents asked for clarification before they answered a question, the evidence is clearer that something should be done.

□   *Summary*

A sensible protocol for the development of a survey instrument prior to virtually any substantial survey would include all of the steps outlined above: focus group discussions, intensive laboratory interviews, and field pretests with behavior coding. Moreover, in the ideal, at least two field pretests would be done, the second to make sure the problems identified in the first field pretest have been solved.

Arguments against this kind of question evaluation usually focus on time and money. Certainly the elapsed calendar time for the question design process will be longer if the researcher includes focus groups and cognitive interviews than if he or she does not; however, these processes can be carried out in a few weeks. The time implications of question testing have less to do with the amount of time it takes to gather information about the questions than with the time it takes to design new and better questions when problems are found. For almost any survey, experience shows that each of these steps yields information that will enable the researcher to design better questions.

■   *Evaluating the Validity of Questions*

Around 1970, Robinson and associates published critical evaluations of common survey measures of social psychological states and political attitudes (Robinson, Rusk, & Head, 1968; Robinson & Shaver, 1973). Those books gave embarrassing testimony to how little attention was given to the assessment of how well commonly used questions performed as measures.

Twenty years later, progress has been made. A recent book by Robinson, Shaver, and Wrightsman (1991) that covers ground similar to the earlier volumes finds many more standard measures that have been carefully evaluated. McDowell and Newell (1987) review common measures of health status and quality of life, and again find some encouraging trends with respect to the studies that have been done, particularly of more recently developed measures. A recent book by Stewart and Ware (1992) provides a kind of prototype for systematically developing measures of important health concepts.

Increasingly, the word is out that particularly when scales and indices are used, validation studies are necessary. On occasion, measures are referred to as if being "validated" were some absolute state, like beatification. Validity is the degree of correspondence between a measure and what is measured. Measures that can serve some purposes well are not necessarily good for other purposes. For example, some measurements that work well for group averages and to assess group effects are quite inadequate at an individual level (Ware, 1987). Validation studies for one population may not generalize to others (Kulka, Schlenger, Fairbank, et al., 1989).

The challenges are of two sorts. First, we need to continue to encourage researchers to evaluate the validity of their measurement procedures routinely from a variety of perspectives. Second, we particularly need to develop clear standards for what validation means for particular analytic purposes.

■ *Conclusion*

To return to the topic of total survey design, no matter how big and representative the sample, no matter now much money is spent on data collection and what the response rate is, the quality of the resulting data from a survey will be no better than the questions that are asked. Although we can certainly hope that the number and specificity of principles for good question design will grow with time, the principles outlined in this chapter constitute a good, systematic core of guidelines for writing good questions. In addition, whereas the development of evaluative procedures will also evolve with time, cognitive testing, good field pretests, and appropriate validating analyses provide scientific, replicable, and quantified standards by which the success of question design efforts can be measured.

A final word is in order about standards for survey questions. In fact, there are four kinds of standards for survey questions:

1. Are they measuring the right thing—that is, what is needed for an analysis?

2. Do they meet cognitive standards?

3. Do they meet psychometric standards?

4. Do they meet interactional standards (if they are to be interviewer administered)?

The first three kinds of standards have been the focus of this chapter. The fourth refers to the fact that an interview schedule is also a protocol for an interaction. It has been shown that the quality of measurement can be compromised by the way the questions affect the way interviewers and respondents interact (Schaeffer, 1991; Suchman & Jordan, 1990).

A tension is created because these standards are not necessarily positively related, and in fact can work against each other. For example, the easiest questions from a cognitive perspective may be weak psychometrically. One reason for weak survey questions is that researchers tend to one standard while neglecting the others. A real challenge is to design questions that meet all four of these kinds of standards.

That said, certainly the most important challenge is to induce researchers to evaluate questions routinely. Unfortunately, there is a long history of researchers designing questions in haphazard ways that do not meet adequate standards and have not even been well evaluated. Moreover, we have a large body of social and medical science, collected over the past 50 years, that includes some very bad questions. The case for holding on to the questions that have been used in the past, in order to track change or to compare new results with those from old studies, is not without merit. However, a scientific enterprise is probably ill served by repeated use of poor measures, no matter how rich their tradition. In the long run, science will be best served by the use of survey questions that have been carefully and systematically evaluated and that meet the standards enunciated here.

■ *References*

Anderson, B., Silver, B., & Abramson, P. (1988). The effects of race of the interviewer on measures of electoral participation by blacks. *Public Opinion Quarterly, 52,* 53-83.

Andrews, F. M. (1984). Construct validity and error components of survey measures: A structural modeling approach. *Public Opinion Quarterly, 48,* 409-422.

Aquilino, W. S., & Losciuto, L. A. (1990). Effects of interviewers on self-reported drug use. *Public Opinion Quarterly, 54,* 362-391.

Belson, W. A. (1981). *The design and understanding of survey questions.* London: Gower.

Blair, E., & Burton, S. (1987). Cognitive process used by survey respondents in answering behavioral frequency questions. *Journal of Consumer Research, 14,* 280-288.

Cannell, C. F., Fisher, G., & Bakker, T. (1965). Reporting of hospitalization in the health interview survey. In *Vital and health statistics* (Series 2, No. 6). Washington, DC: Government Printing Office.

Cannell, C. F., & Marquis, K. H. (1972). Reporting of health events in household interviews: Effects of reinforcement, question length and reinterviews. In *Vital and health statistics* (Series 2, No. 45). Washington, DC: Government Printing Office.

Cannell, C. F., Marquis, K. H., & Laurent, A. (1977). A summary of studies. In *Vital and health statistics* (Series 2, No. 69). Washington, DC: Government Printing Office.

Cannell, C. F., Oksenberg, L., & Converse, J. (1977). *Experiments in interviewing techniques: Field experiments in health reporting: 1971-1977.* Hyattsville, MD: National Center for Health Services Research.

Clarridge, B. R., & Massagli, M. P. (1989). The use of female spouse proxies in common symptom reporting. *Medical Care, 27,* 352-366.

Cleary, P. D., Fowler, F. J., Weissman, J., et al. (1993). Health-related quality of life in persons with acquired immune deficiency syndrome. *Medical Care, 31,* 569-580.

Converse, J. M., & Presser, S. (1986). *Survey questions: Handcrafting the standardized questionnaire.* Beverly Hills, CA: Sage.

Cronbach, L., & Meehl, P. (1955). Construct validity in psychological tests. *Psychological Bulletin, 52,* 281-302.

Eisenhower, D., Mathiowetz, N. A., & Morganstein, D. (1991). Recall error: Sources and bias reduction techniques. In P. N. Biemer, R. M. Groves, L. E. Lyberg, N. A. Mathiowetz, & S. Sudman (Eds.), *Measurement errors in surveys* (pp. 367-392). New York: John Wiley.

Forsyth, B. H., & Lessler, J. T. (1991). Cognitive laboratory methods: A taxonomy. In P. N. Biemer, R. M. Groves, L. E. Lyberg, N. A. Mathiowetz, & S. Sudman (Eds.), *Measurement errors in surveys* (pp. 393-418). New York: John Wiley.

Fowler, F. J., Jr. (1992). How unclear terms affect survey data. *Public Opinion Quarterly 56,* 218-231.

Fowler, F. J., Jr., & Cannell, C. F. (1996). Using behavioral coding to identify cognitive problems with survey questions. In N. Schwartz & S. Sudman (Eds.), *Answering questions* (pp. 15-36). San Francisco: Jossey-Bass.

Fowler, F. J., Jr., & Mangione, T. W. (1990). *Standardized survey interviewing: Minimizing interviewer-related error.* Newbury Park, CA: Sage.

Fox, J. A., & Tracy, P. E. (1986). *Randomized response: A method for sensitive surveys.* Beverly Hills, CA: Sage.

Groves, R. M. (1989). *Survey errors and survey costs.* New York: John Wiley.

Jabine, T. B. (1987). Reporting chronic conditions in the National Health Interview Survey: A review of tendencies from evaluation studies and methodological tests. In *Vital and health statistics* (Series 2, No. 105, DHHS Publication No. PHS 87-1397). Washington, DC: Government Printing Office.

Jabine, T. B., Straf, M. L., & Tanur, J. M. (1984). *Cognitive aspects of survey methodology: Building a bridge between disciplines.* Washington, DC: National Academic Press.

Kulka, R. A., Schlenger, W. E., Fairbank, J. A., et al. (1989). Validating questions against clinical evaluations: A recent example using diagnostic interview schedule-based and other measures of post-traumatic stress disorder. In F. J. Fowler, Jr. (Ed.), *Conference proceedings: Health survey research methods* (DHHS Publication No. PHS 89-3447) (pp. 27-34). Washington, DC: National Center for Health Services Research.

Lessler, J., & Tourangeau, R. (1989, May). Questionnaire design in the cognitive research laboratory. In *Vital and health statistics* (Series 6, No. 1). Washington, DC: Government Printing Office.

Locander, W., Sudman, S., & Bradburn, N. (1976). An investigation of interview method, threat and response distortion. *Journal of the American Statistical Association, 71,* 269-275.

Madow, W. (1967). Interview data on chronic conditions compared with information derived from medical records. In *Vital and health statistics* (Series 2, No. 23). Washington, DC: Government Printing Office.

McDowell, I., & Newell, C. (1987). *Measuring health: A guide to rating scales and questionnaires.* New York: Oxford University Press.

Moore, J. C. (1988). Self/proxy response status and survey response quality. *Journal of Official Statistics, 4,* 155-172.

Neter, J., & Waksberg, J. (1964). A study of response errors in expenditure data from household interviews. *Journal of the American Statistical Association, 59,* 18-55.

Nunnally, J. C. (1978). *Psychometric theory.* New York: McGraw-Hill.

Oksenberg, L., Cannell, C. F., & Kalton, G. (1991). New strategies for testing survey questions. *Journal of Official Statistics, 7,* 349-365.

Parry, H., & Crossley, H. (1950). Validity of responses to survey questions. *Public Opinion Quarterly, 14,* 61-80.

Presser, S. (1989). Pretesting: A neglected aspect of survey research. In F. J. Fowler, Jr. (Ed.), *Conference proceedings: Health survey research methods* (DHHS Publication No. PHS 89-3447) (pp. 35-38). Washington, DC: National Center for Health Services Research.

Robinson, J. P., Rusk, J. G., & Head, K. B. (1968). *Measures of political attitudes.* Ann Arbor, MI: Institute for Social Research, Survey Research Center.

Robinson, J. P., & Shaver, P. R. (1973). *Measures of social psychological attitudes* (rev. ed.). Ann Arbor, MI: Institute for Social Research, Survey Research Center.

Robinson, J. P., Shaver, P. R., & Wrightsman, L. S. (Eds.). (1991). *Measures of personality and social psychological attitudes* (Vol. 1). San Diego, CA: Academic Press.

Rodgers, W. L., & Herzog, A. R. (1989). The consequences of accepting proxy respondents on total survey error for elderly populations. In F. J. Fowler, Jr. (Ed.), *Conference proceedings: Health survey research methods* (DHHS Publication No. PHS 89-3447) (pp. 139-146). Washington, DC: National Center for Health Services Research.

Schaeffer, N. C. (1991). Interview: Conversation with a purpose or conversation? In P. N. Biemer, R. M. Groves, L. E. Lyberg, N. A. Mathiowetz, & S. Sudman (Eds.), *Measurement errors in surveys* (pp. 367-393). New York: John Wiley.

Schuman, H. H., & Presser, S. (1981). *Questions and answers in attitude surveys.* New York: Academic Press.

Schwartz, N., & Hippler, H. (1991). Response alternatives: The impact of their choice and presentation order. In P. N. Biemer, R. M. Groves, L. E. Lyberg, N. A. Mathiowetz, & S. Sudman (Eds.), *Measurement errors in surveys* (pp. 41-56). New York: John Wiley.

Smith, A. F. (1991). Cognitive processes in long-term dietary recall. In *Vital and health statistics* (Series 6, No. 4). Washington, DC: Government Printing Office.

Stewart, A. L., & Ware, J. E., Jr. (Eds.). (1992). *Measuring functioning and well-being: The medical outcomes study approach.* Durham, NC: Duke University Press.

Suchman, L., & Jordan, B. (1990). Interactional troubles in face-to-face survey interviews. *Journal of the American Statistical Association, 85,* 232-241.

Sudman, S., & Bradburn, N. (1974). *Response effects in surveys.* Chicago: Aldine.

Sudman, S., & Bradburn, N. (1982). *Asking questions.* San Francisco: Jossey-Bass.

Sudman, S., & Ferber, R. (1971). A comparison of alternative procedures for collecting consumer expenditure data for frequently purchased items. *Journal of Marketing Research, 11,* 128-135.

Sudman, S., Finn, A., & Lannon, L. (1984). The use of bounded recall procedures in single interviews. *Public Opinion Quarterly, 48,* 520-524.

Turner, C. F., Lessler, J. T., & Gfroerer, J. C. (1992). *Survey measurement of drug use: Methodological studies.* Washington, DC: U.S. Department of Health and Human Services, National Institute on Drug Abuse.

Ware, J. (1987). Standards for validating health measures: Definition and content. *Journal of Chronic Diseases, 40,* 473-480.

13

Practical Aspects of Interview Data Collection and Data Management

Welmoet Bok van Kammen
Magda Stouthamer-Loeber

Managing a large study requires practical skills and experience that are usually not acquired in graduate school or gained from conducting smaller, college-based studies. In addition, information on how to conduct studies is rarely found in articles published in the scientific journals to which social scientists turn for substantive information in their fields. Thus the "how to do it" part of conducting large studies is often learned the painful way, by trial and error, or transferred, like family lore, from one researcher to another in hints, bits of advice, and anecdotes.

Researchers have the responsibility to ensure that their studies are planned and executed as expertly as possible. Once a study is under way, errors in participant acquisition or data collection are not easy to fix and can seriously limit interpretation of the results. Therefore, to be successful, studies require careful planning of financial and human resources, well-prepared hiring and training strategies, and efficient data collection and data management procedures. Size and complexity do not change the tasks involved in conducting a study, but the larger the study, the more pressing the need for an informational structure that allows an overview of the research activities and progress.

Personnel management, budget management, and data quality control are the three core aspects of research studies that investigators need to cover to make their studies run well. First, project management mainly involves directing *people* and their job schedules. Job schedules are often interlocking, in that the timeline for one task determines when another task can be undertaken. The job of researcher resembles that of an air traffic controller, keeping an eye on the position and speed of a number of planes that need to be woven into an errorless pattern of timely landings and takeoffs.

Second, the *costs* of data collection and data management form a very large portion of the budget of most studies (Weinberg, 1983). Staying within the budget depends to a large extent on careful planning of the budget and the design of a study. However, even with the most careful planning, researchers must monitor expenditures constantly, and sometimes they will need to make creative adjustments midstream.

Third, the *quality* of the research can never be better than the quality of the data that are collected. This should be a foremost concern of the researcher and all staff members. Maintaining high-quality research requires constant vigilance at the level of sample selection, participant acquisition, data collection, data management, and analysis.

■ *Planning the Research Project*

The step-by-step planning of the actual execution of a study should take place at the time the study is conceptualized. Planning ensures that the study's goals, design, timeline, analyses, and budget are fully integrated and concordant with one another. Many early decisions are irreversible, and these will influence the future course of the study and the use of available funds. Needless to say, the researcher needs to make these decisions with care. In this section, we cover some of the topics related to planning.

Method of participant acquisition, sample size, and method of data collection. What participant selection criteria are necessary to address the questions contained in the goals of the study? Chapters 1 and 4 in this volume have covered design and sample selection, so we will not elaborate on this topic except to stress that the researcher must decide early in the process how the sample will be acquired, how large a sample to select, and how the data will be collected. These decisions will influence the timeline and budget, as well as the conclusions that can be drawn from the study.

Agency cooperation. Many studies require the cooperation of agencies such as hospitals, schools, or courts for researchers to gain access to participants or to acquire data on already existing samples. If agency cooperation is required, the researcher must not only secure it in advance but also clarify all details relative to obtaining access to records or to potential participants. The fact that potential participant groups or records exist does not mean that a researcher will automatically have access to them (Hedrick, Bickman, & Rog, 1993). The first hurdle is for the researcher to obtain formal permission to have access to potential participants or records. A prerequisite is that the researcher establish what the records contain; how current, accurate, and complete the information is; in what format the data are stored; and who will be allowed to extract them. It is necessary to have these details pinned down, preferably in writing, to prevent problems from surfacing when the work is about to begin (Ball & Brown, 1977).

Community contact. Should the community at large be informed about an upcoming study, should the researcher enlist the support of community leaders, and is it a good idea to form a community advisory board? It may seem to be good practice for the researcher to inform the community about an upcoming study and to invite input. However, by involving the community, the researcher creates a danger that he or she may fail to enlist uniform support and, instead, may create some opposition. For instance, some members of a community may feel strongly that a given topic is too sensitive or threatening, or that the group the members represent will be used for research purposes but will not benefit from the study or may be harmed by it. Thus the investigator needs to weigh the pros and cons of seeking community support carefully, because a wrong decision may fatally affect the study.

Coordination with other research groups. As part of the planning process, the researcher needs to find out what research is already ongoing or being developed that may impinge on the potential participant group necessary for the planned study. In general, it is not a good idea for researchers to use participants who are already participating in other studies, because the questions posed in one study may influence the answers given in another, and the timing of interviews may influence participation rates. In some cases, it may be possible for researchers to combine the protocols of several studies and design a single interview session for each participant. At other times, it may be necessary for them to divide the "turf" or make an agreement about a time schedule for competing studies. As a last resort, a researcher confronting such an issue may select another locale in which to conduct the study.

Preparation of consent forms. Federal and state laws require that investigators dealing with human subjects obtain a signed statement of informed consent from each participant before the research begins. Every research institution has an institutional review board (IRB) that is charged with protecting participants from undue research risks and with providing investigators with guidelines for writing consent forms in the required format and language (see Sieber, 1992). Because the start of the study is contingent on IRB approval of the research protocol and consent forms, the researcher needs to allow enough time between the formulation of the final protocol and the assessment of the first participant for this process to be completed successfully.

In-house data collection or contract with survey organization. Although our focus in this chapter is in-house data collection, we should note that researchers sometimes have reasons for deciding to contract out for data collection. It may be that specialized expertise (e.g., for household sampling) is not available within the research team, or that data collection will take place across the whole country and the researcher wants to make use of a network of interviewers affiliated with a survey organization. A researcher who feels that he or she does not have the expertise to manage a large data collection effort may prefer to contract that work out to specialists. Also, it takes time to set up a smooth-running field operation, whereas survey organizations usually have such infrastructure already in place. The drawback to contracting out data collection is that no matter how experienced and reputable the contractor, the researcher does not have direct control over the quality and completeness of the data and the well-being of the participants. Unless there is an independent quality control mechanism, the researcher has to rely on the contractor's word that the work is of high quality.

Key personnel and other staff issues. Before a researcher can start to think about personnel, he or she must have a clear picture of the flow of *tasks* that need to be completed during the course of the study. Once the researcher has an overview of the tasks, his or her next step is to combine the different tasks into staff positions and to organize the positions into some hierarchy for supervision and accountability. Some tasks may be ongoing, such as the work of a secretary or a data analyst, whereas others may be cyclical, such as interviewing and supervising interviewers. Some cyclical tasks can be combined into year-round positions, whereas for other tasks it is better to hire temporary staff. Although it is possible, and sometimes desirable, to make changes in the personnel structure once it has been set up, such changes are often disruptive and time-consuming. It is therefore important that the researcher design a workable personnel structure ahead of time that will distribute the tasks reasonably and comprehensively.

Interview locations. The choices of locations for conducting interviews are generally interview rooms in one location, interview rooms in several areas where participants are to be found, and the participants' homes. The first question the researcher should ask is whether a standardized setting is *required* because tests will be administered or because cumbersome or calibrated equipment is involved. Even if a standardized setting is not strictly necessary, there are advantages to conducting interviews in offices rather than in participants' homes. For example, interviewers will not have interference from telephone calls, television, relatives, and so on, and will not have to deal with such problems as inadequate lighting and lack of space. Also, interviewers will be more in control in the sense that participants will be guests and so may be less likely to be distracted or to engage in inappropriate behaviors. In addition, if interviewers do not have to go to participants' homes, they avoid possibly having to go to potentially dangerous neighborhoods. Against these advantages of office interviews, there is one major disadvantage: Many people do not mind participating in studies, but they may not be willing or able to travel from their homes to be interviewed.

Planning the interview format. Another decision the researcher needs to make early is how the data will be collected. Will the project use traditional paper-and-pencil booklets, machine-readable forms, or laptop computers? Naturally, this decision has effects on data entry staff, programming time, equipment, training of interviewers, and storage of interview materials.

Pretesting instruments and procedures. It is important for the researcher to know beforehand whether the study he or she is contemplating will, in all probability, be able to deliver the information the researcher is seeking, and will be able to do so within a certain budget and timeline. Thus the researcher needs to pretest any new instruments and procedures, including participant acquisition.

Planning for data entry and data management. Regardless of the mode of data collection, it is essential that the researcher plan how the data will be managed and analyzed if he or she does not want to end up with a large and costly mountain of undigested material. The researcher must make adequate provision in the budget for data management. Conventions for data reduction, data storage, and the creation and documentation of constructs require considerable planning and allocation of staff time. This is particularly important in studies where more than one person will be involved in the analysis of the data. Etiquette concerning the sharing of data with researchers in the group and outside the immediate study group is best organized beforehand (Sieber, 1991).

To summarize, the researcher needs to ensure that a certain amount of structure is in place right from the beginning, so that no fatal errors and not too many costly mistakes are made. The study's basic structure needs to be mostly correct from the start; from there on, the researcher can go about "beautifying" the study at a more leisurely pace.

■ *Hiring a Research Staff*

In the beginning of a research project, one of the first tasks the investigator must face is the hiring of competent staff. To make sure that all tasks are covered, the researcher needs to develop a personnel structure that includes all the data collection, data management, and data analysis tasks for each job, with workloads and reporting and supervisory responsibilities specified clearly. In planning the personnel structure, the researcher may want to consider building a research team with partly overlapping skills to ensure that any procedure that is crucial to the day-to-day operation of the project can be executed by more than one person. This will prevent the project from being crippled by the illness or other discontinuation of one employee.

Personnel department. In most cases, universities, hospitals, or research organizations are the official employers of the research staff, and the hiring process is regulated by a personnel department, which has a set of guidelines and rules. A good understanding of the hiring policies and the role and level of involvement of the institution's personnel department may greatly facilitate the researcher's hiring of project staff. For example, the researcher should be aware that he or she cannot ask certain questions when interviewing prospective employees and should know the selection criteria that can be used in the consideration of candidates. The researcher should also be informed about equal employment opportunity legislation before starting the hiring process. He or she should establish procedures to document hiring decisions, and should be aware of the length of time this documentation needs to be preserved.

Although it is time-consuming to do so, the researcher is usually well served by looking at all job applications, rather than having a personnel officer preselect candidates who meet the job specifications. Only the investigator has the overall picture of the different task skills required for the project, and he or she may be willing to compromise on some qualifications or to restructure some positions if a promising candidate with a good mixture of skills and experience applies.

Hiring interviewers. Although the investigator may be familiar with hiring secretaries or individuals to work on data analyses, he or she may be less familiar with hiring a team of data collectors. A good strategy for the researcher to follow is to hire interviewer supervisors first, so they can assist in the hiring process and in the training of interviewers. Interviewer supervisors should have past experience with interviewing in a research setting. They should be able to work in an organized and timely manner, have the ability to prioritize tasks, and know when to alert their superiors if they are falling behind. Supervisors are the main collectors and distributors of research materials. If they fall behind in their tasks, the rest of the research operation stagnates as well.

One of the first issues the researcher should consider when hiring interviewers is the number of interviewers needed to complete the study. This figure very much depends on the availability of participants. For instance, the time available to conduct interviews in participants' homes may be quite limited, because most interviews have to be done in the late afternoon and evening hours (Swires-Hennessy & Drake, 1992). Thus a greater number of interviewers may be needed. Also, the researcher needs to take a certain percentage of broken appointments into account when calculating the number of interviews each interviewer will be able to complete on the average.

It may seem a good idea for the researcher to hire full-time interviewers without any other work commitments, on the premise that they can devote all their time to the study. However, candidates with daytime employment but with sufficient time to work in the evenings and on weekends can be just as productive as candidates who have no other employment. If the institution allows it, the researcher may want to consider hiring interviewers who will be compensated per completed interview. If the remuneration also includes the average time and money incurred for traveling to and from interviews, this method greatly simplifies the monitoring of interviewing costs.

Most research organizations require that any interviewers they hire have at least a high school diploma and excellent reading and writing abilities (Fowler & Mangione, 1990). Field interviewers should be pleasant and streetwise individuals who are self-assured in dealing with others. They should be open-minded and able to keep their opinions to themselves. Interviewers should be self-starters, able to work independently and to follow instructions. Usually, the need for additional income is a good motivator for a productive interviewer. Although demographic similarities may have positive effects on the relationship between interviewer and respondent, studies show that concordance of demographic characteristics does not necessarily lead to better reporting (Davies & Baker, 1987; Groves, 1989; Weiss, 1968). For example, it may be important for a researcher to hire middle-aged female interviewers to solicit initial cooperation from women or retired people, who may be reluctant to let young male interviewers whom they do not know into their homes.

The researcher can make hiring a large number of interviewers less time-consuming by organizing group information sessions at which he or she provides an overview of the study, spells out requirements for the job, hands out application forms to be filled out, and collects résumés. Next, the researcher can conduct personal interviews with selected candidates, using a well-prepared script of questions to keep the evaluation process as consistent as possible. The researcher should use a large portion of the personal interview to obtain an idea of each applicant's interpersonal skills and to evaluate the manner in which he or she communicates. The researcher can test each candidate's flexibility and creativity by giving him or her some examples of problems that may arise in the field to see if the candidate can come up with solutions. It is important also for the researcher to ascertain whether candidates are available at times respondents want to be interviewed, and whether they are willing to do interviews wherever they need to be done. If the study deals with sensitive topics, it is important for the researcher to ascertain how applicants feel about asking participants questions related to these issues.

As part of the application process, each candidate should be required to conduct a mock interview with the recruiter, so that the recruiter can assess the candidate's ability to make appropriate eye contact with a respondent, to read questions exactly as stated, to follow skip patterns, and to record answers accurately. The mock interview also offers a good opportunity for the researcher to evaluate the candidate's voice quality.

Before making final selections, the researcher needs to check candidates' references. The researcher should avoid contacting personal references, and should concentrate instead on professional references. Although candidates' former or current employers listed as references may be unable to comment directly on the candidates' interviewing skills, they should be able to say something about their abilities to be self-starters, to take initiative, and to find creative solutions in difficult situations.

The researcher should always select more interviewers than it appears will be necessary to complete the study. Some candidates who are between jobs will keep searching for more permanent employment and may find other jobs by the time interviewer training begins; others will discover during training that they do not like the job, and still others will successfully finish training but for some reason will not be satisfactory interviewers. In our experience, not more than 20% of the original group of potential applicants who attended the initial information sessions will be left when data collection gets under way. Similar percentages have been observed by survey organizations using more traditional face-to-face hiring techniques (Davis & Smith, 1992).

Even after many years of hiring staff, many researchers still find it difficult to predict the productivity and tenacity of potential candidates. Thus, even if good hiring strategies are used, there will always be individuals for whom employment in a research project does not work out. It is therefore important that the researcher hire a few more interviewers than he or she thinks is strictly necessary, so that any unsatisfactory interviewers can be let go after the initial probationary period.

■ Interviewer Training

Although other members of the research team, such as coders and data cleaners, need training as well, in this chapter we focus exclusively on the training of interviewers. Training a group of interviewers is time-consuming and expensive, and, if not done well, it can have lasting negative consequences that are not always easily correctable. Successful training means that interviewers are fully capable of doing their job *before* they start to interview. In other words, their first interviews should be up to standard and of the same high quality as interviews done later in the assessment period.

Training schedule. To make sure that all training issues will be covered, the researcher should set aside sufficient time to plan every aspect of training. Without exception, attendance at all training sessions should be *mandatory* for interviewer trainees. Having to schedule additional training hours for people who have missed sessions is time-consuming and expensive. To avoid any problems with training hours, training dates should be established before the hiring process gets under way to eliminate prospective candidates whose other obligations will conflict with the training schedule.

The training sessions should be scheduled with long enough intervals between them to allow interviewers to absorb the materials that have been discussed in class. This strategy also gives staff members responsible for the training enough time to assess the progress of each trainee, to correct homework assignments, and, if necessary, to make adjustments to upcoming training sessions in order to address the needs of the interviewers more closely.

Role of the interviewer during training. No matter how many hours are invested in the training of interviewers, the instructions are of little use if the interviewers do not take the training seriously. Interviewers should be expected to read the training materials, prepare for what will be covered in each training session, arrive on time for all training sessions, participate in classroom exercises, and finish all homework assignments. At the end of training, the instructors should evaluate each interviewer to determine whether he or she is ready to go into the field. During training, instructors should maintain documentation that allows for the elimination of interviewers whose performance is not satisfactory.

Training curriculum. The development of a training curriculum is best achieved through the writing of a *comprehensive* manual. The manual should contain *all* the information that interviewers need to do their job. Besides general information about the study and instructions on how to interview, the manual should cover such issues as conditions of employment, legal and ethical aspects of the job, how to contact participants, and how to deal with refusals. A written policy statement that outlines the job requirements is helpful to ensure that every interviewer understands the obligations of employment. If interviewers are trained at different times or by different instructors, the manual ensures that everyone receives the same information and standardizes the way the study will be conducted.

Project regulations. The importance of adhering to the rules of the study cannot be emphasized enough during training, because one infraction can jeopardize the continuation of the entire study. Such rules include correctly explaining the study to participants and the proper administration of consent forms. Also, interviewers should carefully maintain the confidentiality of all the information they obtain from participants. Interviewers should not be permitted to tell funny stories, or horror stories, about participants just for amusement, even if names are omitted. Interviewers need clear guidelines on how to act in cases of actual or suspected child abuse or other potentially dangerous situations.

Except in life-threatening situations, the interviewer's task is to document carefully what he or she has observed and to report what has happened immediately to a supervisor, who will determine if further action needs to be taken.

Interviewer safety. Interviewers should be trained always to use common sense while they are in the field and to avoid exposing themselves unnecessarily to potentially dangerous situations. Most police departments have officers who are trained to talk about safety issues who can instruct interviewers on how to minimize their risks of being victimized.

Contact with participants. The initial interaction of the interviewer with a participant usually determines whether cooperation can be secured. If interviewers are instructed to have a positive attitude toward people, respondents will be more likely to agree to be interviewed. Not all participants in a study, however, will be equally easy to approach. Interviewers can be trained to deal with even the most difficult contacting situations through role playing that develops good listening skills, effective dialogue, correct eye contact, and appropriate body movement (Hornik, 1987).

Some interviewers rely heavily on the telephone, whereas others feel more comfortable contacting participants in person. However, from the potential participant's point of view, it is much easier to refuse on the telephone than in a face-to-face encounter. Thus, particularly on first contacts, interviewers should be trained to approach potential participants in person. Interviewers should be taught to discontinue a telephone approach to a potential participant when they sense the slightest reluctance on the other person's part. Interviewers should also be taught that when they encounter answering machines, they need to be prepared to leave clear and concise messages stating their names, affiliation, reason for calling, and how they can be reached.

Handling refusals. Interviewers should be trained to avoid outright refusals to participate. It is better to back off from trying to persuade a potential participant to do the interview, and thus keep the door open for another interviewer to try in the future, than to invite an outright refusal and lose any possibility of anyone's ever obtaining an interview. Reasons for refusals should be carefully documented to help other interviewers find the right strategies for contacting those persons again at a later date.

Preparing for the interview. Before conducting the interview, the interviewer must clearly explain the content and goals of the study, using terminology that the participant can understand, and obtain the participant's signature on the consent form. When setting up the appointment, the interviewer needs to specify the length of the interview and to make sure that the place where the interview will be conducted provides enough privacy for the participant to answer the questions freely. In the case of home interviews, a porch, the interviewer's car, and the neighborhood library may be good alternatives to dining and living rooms. It is also helpful if the interviewer explains the required answer format at the start of the interview.

Role of the interviewer. Interviewers should always maintain a professional relationship with interview participants. They should avoid either expressing opinions in response to participants' answers or making spontaneous comments. Interviewers should refrain from promoting certain causes, even if it is clear that a participant is in favor of them. They also should not allude to personal experiences or engage in business relations with participants. By the same token, interviewers should be taught how to ask participants to stop unacceptable behavior or, if necessary, how to interrupt the interview and leave.

Interviewing techniques. The uniformity of the data and the validity of the final results of the study depend primarily on the degree of standardization that is maintained in administration of the interviews. Interviewer instructors should be prepared to go through as many demonstrations and role-playing exercises as are necessary to teach interviewers that they must read the questions exactly as worded (see Fowler, Chapter 12, this volume) as well as such skills as the effective use of probing (see Lavrakas, Chapter 15, this volume). The key to good probing is for the interviewer to listen carefully to the participant's attempts to provide the appropriate response and to be able, without becoming directive, to zero in on the fitting answer. Open-ended questions often require probing. Instructors need to provide good examples of fitting answers to open-ended questions during training, so that interviewers know the kind of information that is sought and that can be coded later. Most "don't know" answers will require probing, but interviewers should learn to gauge when additional probing will lead to guesswork on the part of the participant or when the participant will be likely to come up with an answer just to please the interviewer.

Practice and observation interviews. Instructors should schedule several practice interviews for trainees in the office as well as observation interviews in the field before the trainees should be considered ready to interview participants. Because veteran interviewers are familiar with a study's questionnaires, they are the ideal mock participants for practice interviews, if they are available. They can give answers that create difficult skip patterns or that need to be probed, or set little traps for the new interviewers to resolve. In observation interviews, the trainees should be instructed to record the answers in the same way as the instructors, to make sure they are recording the answers correctly. Also, the trainees should be encouraged to mark questions or areas of the interview that they want to have clarified after the interview is completed. A performance checklist is a handy tool for standardizing the evaluation of practice and observation interviews and for documenting the trainees' progress.

Closing the interview. The interviewer should be trained to leave the participant with a positive feeling about the project. The last impression the participant has of the interviewer may determine how willing he or she will be to be interviewed again. Because the participant has just spent a sizable amount of time answering questions, some of them personal and of a sensitive nature, he or she should be given an opportunity to reflect on the interview, to ask questions, and to make comments. The interview booklet should provide a space for documenting the participant's observations about the interview, and these comments should be discussed with the supervisor later.

■ *Participant Acquisition and Retention*

Generally, people are willing to be interviewed, and consequently, acquiring and retaining participants is, for the most part, not difficult. However, contacting the *right* participants and acquiring *all* the targeted participants is not easy. Nor is it easy to retain all participants for follow-up. When potential participants are not included because of refusals or the inability to find them, the sample may be biased because different groups of people may have different likelihoods of refusing or of not being found (Bailar, 1989). The magnitude of the potential bias in sample acquisition is often difficult to evaluate because very little or no information may be available for the researcher to use in comparing participants with nonparticipants.

As with the initial loss of participants, the danger of attrition in later assessment waves is that the sample will become biased. Generally, studies have found that participants who live in disorganized families, who move often, who drink excessively, who use drugs, or who are engaged in criminal activities are less likely to be recaptured in follow-ups (Jessor & Jessor, 1977; Nurco, Robins, & O'Donnell 1977). In our experience, these participants are, indeed, more difficult to *locate,* but they are not more likely to *refuse.*

Reports of participation rates vary greatly among research surveys. Kalton (1983) mentions 70-75% participation rates for uncomplicated face-to-face interviews, with studies in cities having even lower response rates. According to Capaldi and Patterson (1987), private survey organizations report completion rates on general population surveys averaging 60-65%. However, with good planning and care it is possible to reach participation rates of *at least* 80%.

What can be expected in terms of the continued cooperation of participants in a follow-up study? Miller (1991) cites low figures for reinterview of around 67%, and states that young people, people in large cities, and less affluent individuals are more mobile, which may influence the ability of a research team to locate participants at follow-up. Other reviewers also mention relatively low reinterview rates (Capaldi & Patterson, 1987; Cordray & Polk, 1983; Menard, 1991). On the other hand, there are enough studies with retention rates in the high 80% to low 90% range to show that retention of participants is an appropriate expectation for well-conducted studies (Stouthamer-Loeber & van Kammen, 1995).

Maximizing participation and retention rates. Groves, Cialdini, and Couper (1992) have classified the factors that influence participation as follows. *Societal-level factors* are related to the social responsibility felt by the potential participant. Next are the *attributes of the study,* such as the topic, the length of the interview, interview location, the intrusiveness of the questions, and remuneration. Certain *characteristics of the potential participant* may also influence the participation rate, such as age, sex, and socioeconomic status. There are also temporary characteristics and circumstances that influence participation, such as worries, illnesses, disagreements in the household, or being very busy. Finally, there are *attributes of the interviewer.* The interviewer's sex, age, and/or race may interact with the participant's views, prejudices, and/or preferences. The way the interviewer looks, dresses, and speaks, and the way the interviewer tailors the introduction of the study to each individual, may be decisive.

Initial contact with participants. In their first contacts with potential participants, interviewers need to set the right tone by taking away fears, inspiring trust, and creating interest in taking part in the research project. This contact may be made in person, by telephone, or by mail. If possible, it is a good idea for the researcher to inform potential participants by mail that someone will be contacting them. Such a letter should be brief, relatively simple in language, and written on official letterhead. It should cover the goal of the study, why this particular person was selected, how his or her name was obtained, information about any remuneration, and when and how the potential participant will be contacted.

Participant remuneration. The topic of many studies may be vaguely interesting or beneficial to respondents, but often not to the extent that they feel gratified just to participate. Therefore, it is reasonable to compensate participants for their expert information and for the time required to do the interview.

Mailings. Frequent mailings can also help to build positive relationships with participants. Mailings can include letters announcing new assessment phases, cards confirming appointments, and thank-you letters accompanying payments, as well as birthday cards, season's greetings, letters of condolence, and newsletters about the study.

Ease of participation. Unless the use of complicated equipment is required or a standardized environment is necessary, interviewers should be flexible about times and locations of interviews; an interview should be done *when* and *where* it is most convenient for the participant, as long as the quality of the assessment and privacy can be assured.

Experience with previous interviewers. In the later assessment phases of an ongoing study, participants' willingness to continue depends to a large extent on their experiences with the previous interviewers. Therefore, interviewers should strive to make the interviews pleasant experiences for participants.

Locating participants. The task of locating individuals when they have moved from their original addresses is usually most difficult at the first assessment, when the information available may be limited to names and addresses of potential participants. If the researcher obtains a list of potential participants from an organization, it is helpful for that list to contain more than just names and addresses. The names of relatives, the individuals' professions, social security numbers, and other kinds of information can all be helpful for locating the people listed.

The groundwork for successful searching for follow-up assessments is established in the consent form, which asks permission from the participant to request new addresses from employers, schools, or institutions. This allows the researcher access to sources of information that would be unavailable without proof of permission from the participant.

At every assessment wave, the researcher should gather information about whether the participant plans to move and about names and addresses of friends and relatives who will always know the respondent's whereabouts. In addition, participants should be asked in each mailing to contact the project if they have moved, if their telephone numbers have changed, or if they are difficult to reach. All envelopes should request address correction from the postal service.

The final general principle is that the researcher should collect identifying information on participants as *much* and as *often* as possible. Seemingly factual information, such as names, birthdays, addresses, social security numbers, and family relationships, sometimes turns out to be surprisingly inaccurate or fleeting.

It is useful for researchers to develop systematic procedures for locating cases. In our studies, we find about 25% of the people who move simply by requesting address corrections when sending mail. If a piece of mail comes back without a new address, we require the interviewer to try to locate the participant, by consulting the telephone book and/or directory assistance or, if necessary, by visiting the site of the participant's last known residence. When an interviewer goes to an old—presumably incorrect—address, he or she sometimes finds the participant still there. If the person no longer lives at the address, the current resident, the building manager or owner, a local store clerk, or a neighbor may give helpful information. In our studies, interviewers solve about 25% of all search problems.

If the interviewer's search is unsuccessful, he or she turns the problem over to the office staff, who use information that is not accessible to interviewers because of its potential to influence the interviewer's view of the participant. Office staff members have access to the telephone numbers of friends and relatives provided by participants in previous interviews. Use of this information solves about 6% of the search cases. Contacting organizations and agencies for information about participants is also the task of the office staff. Previous interviews often give clues about the person's whereabouts. Professions, memberships in organizations, serious medical conditions, and unusual hobbies may form search starting points. For children, one of the best sources for a new address is their last known school. As a rule, schools are able to give the name and address of the school to which a student has moved. In our studies, about 22% of search cases are solved this way. The remainder of searches are solved with the help of employers, child protection agencies, welfare agencies, the military, the housing authority, the department of motor vehicles, and probation or social work departments. Social security numbers and, for adult populations, driver's licenses are also important tools for tracking. Furthermore, there are agencies that, for a fee, will track persons. These agencies use a large number of databases, and their services can be accessed by computer. Tracking agencies are particularly useful for finding people who are the easiest to find, such as people who obtain new driver's licenses when they move to another state, or who have bank accounts and telephones. Recently, CD-ROM telephone directories have become available that facilitate nationwide searching for telephone numbers. Current information on people with fewer ties to the middle class may not show up in electronic databases.

Because searching is time-consuming and most attempts are unsuccessful, it is important that the researcher try many avenues simultaneously, and not give up. When the researcher has tried every available method for finding a person, the only option is to *try everything again.*

Refusals and postponements. There are many reasons for refusals that interviewers can address to the satisfaction of potential participants. About half of the people who at one time say that they do not want to do an interview will later readily consent to be interviewed. It is therefore important that interviewers always leave the door open for future contacts. Once a person has decided not to participate, it is always necessary to *ask permission for further contacts.* Most of the time this permission is granted.

Another source of loss can be the end of an interview phase; it may not have been possible to schedule an interview in time, or the person may not have made up his or her mind to participate prior to the deadline. To achieve a high participation rate, the researcher should be prepared to spend a long time and considerable resources on the last 10% of the sample. If the researcher allows for sufficient time for the final stretch and can muster the necessary financial resources, creativity, persistence, and good humor, he or she can achieve high participation and retention rates.

■ Supervision of Interviewers

Continuous monitoring of the work of all members of the research staff is time-consuming but essential for the successful and timely completion of the

study and for obtaining high-quality data. Supervision of interviewers, however, requires particular attention, because in most situations they work away
from the office, which makes direct monitoring of their day-to-day efforts complicated.

Supervision of interviewers may be best described as providing solution-
oriented support while at the same time insisting on strict adherence to the
rules. Setting realistic standards for quantity and quality of the interviewers'
work is the key to successful supervision; interviewers will be productive and
are likely to try harder when they feel that they can meet the supervisor's
demands.

Supervision format. If a face-to-face supervision format is used, the interviewers should meet with their supervisors at set times, preferably once a week.
Frequent interaction between interviewer and supervisor prevents problems
from accumulating or from being deferred until they hamper the progress of the
study or until it becomes too late to take action. Even if interviewers have not
completed any cases in the previous week, they should be required to meet with
their supervisors and discuss the status of their work. Interviewers' missing or
trying to postpone weekly supervision is often an indication that they are not
following up on their cases and are having difficulty meeting standards.

There should also be a format in place for supervisors to communicate
regularly with interviewers when they are away from the office. Interviewers
are often hard to reach, and attempts to get in touch with them individually can
be time-consuming and frustrating. We require interviewers in our studies to
call the supervisor's answering machine *every day* to receive messages such as
address corrections or schedule changes called in by participants. Also, the
interviewers, without having to reach the supervisor, can leave messages on
the answering machine. For instance, they may need the assistance of the supervisor in obtaining clearance for an interview to be conducted in a prison, or
they may need some additional information on the whereabouts of a participant. They can also report, through answering machine messages, on scheduled
and completed cases, so that the office is provided with the most up-to-date
information on the field effort at all times. Interviewers should always leave
records of their calls on the answering machine so that supervisors can keep
track of who did and did not get the messages each day.

Monitoring interviewers' efforts. To monitor interviewer contacts with participants, the researcher should create a contact form on which will be recorded
basic information for contacting each participant as well as all field and office
efforts related to the case. For each contact, the interviewer then records the
date, the day of the week, and the time of day on this form. The interviewer also
records the method of contact (such as telephone, letter, or house contact), the
name of the individual with whom the interviewer talked, and what transpired
during the contact. Such documentation makes it easy for the supervisor to de-

tect an ineffective pattern of attempted contact, so that he or she can suggest a different plan of action, such as contacting the participant during the weekend or at a later time during the day. Recording search attempts should be a part of the contact form documentation. If an interviewer search proves to be unsuccessful and is taken over by a supervisor, the complete and detailed documentation on the contact form makes it possible for him or her to ascertain what was tried already, in which order, and at what time. If an interviewer is not able to convince a respondent to participate, the reason for the refusal should be recorded on the contact form as well.

Computerized tracking systems. In the supervision of a sizable number of interviewers, a computerized tracking system is useful for monitoring the field effort. Central to such a system is the continuous tracking of the most up-to-date status of each case, who has each case, when each case is issued, and when each case is targeted to be completed.

A computerized tracking system can generate an up-to-date performance report for each interviewer that highlights specific issues for the supervisor's attention. This report includes statistics on completed interviews and refusals as well as a list of outstanding cases. Interviews that require special attention, such as cases that have overdue target dates or have been in the interviewer's hands for too long, are flagged to alert the supervisor that the progress on these cases needs to be addressed.

Regular review of the overall progress of the study is also facilitated through the use of a computerized tracking system, which can produce a report with general statistics on the total number of completed interviews, refusals, searches, overdue cases, and cases that have been outstanding for longer than 4 weeks. Based on this information, the researcher can make decisions about whether staff need to be reallocated temporarily to catch up with the data collection effort. The report should also categorize the same information by individual interviewer. This enables the staff to recognize outstanding performance and also to make decisions about interviewers who are not completing enough cases or have incurred too many refusals. Finally, the report should identify problem cases by category. Outstanding searches are a particularly important category of problem cases, and a substantial part of the regular progress review should be devoted to brainstorming for new ways of finding lost participants.

Performance checks. The most immediate way to evaluate interviewers' performance is for supervisors to accompany them in the field. Observation interviews screen out those interviewers who have trouble with the administration of the interview or who need to improve their interactions with participants. Another way of monitoring interviewers' performance is to tape-record the interviews. If it is feasible, the investigator may decide to have every interview recorded, but then may select only certain interviews to be checked later. This strategy has the advantage of making interviewers feel that they always have to be on their best behavior because they never know which interviews will be evaluated. However, not all participants like the idea of being audio-taped. Another option is for the researcher to insert a "phantom" respondent into the participant pool. Interviewers will not know whether they are interviewing a "real" participant or the impostor, and the knowledge of the existence of a phantom participant may prevent them from deviating from the rules.

After the interviews are completed, the researcher should check on the interviewers' performance by having staff randomly call or visit about 10% of the participants. In this procedure, the participants should be asked again a few factual questions, to make sure that the interviews really took place, and should be asked to confirm whether the interviewers recontacted them when additional information needed to be obtained after their interviews were completed. When fraud is detected, the evidence should be so unequivocal and well documented that there can be no argument about the reason for the interviewer's dismissal.

During this verification process, some questions for the participants should address the interviewers' performance. This is particularly important when interviewers are paid per completed interview and supervisors want to make sure that interviewers have not rushed through interviews to make their employment as profitable as possible. Positive feedback from participants should be relayed to the interviewers as well. Hearing about enthusiastic reactions from satisfied participants can be a morale booster. In addition, it tells the interviewers that verification of their interviews is taking place.

End-of-phase strategies. To simplify the task of supervising the end of the data phase, it is a good strategy for the researcher to consolidate the final cases in the hands of just a few interviewers. For this task, supervisors should not only consider high producers but also interviewers who have low refusal rates, are tenacious, have excellent interpersonal and problem-solving skills, and have relatively few other commitments so that they have the flexibility to schedule interviews at any time. Also, interviewers who have a high success rate in turning around initially reluctant participants may be especially effective for the last part of the assessment phase. Because obtaining the final interviews is so important, and they usually require more time and energy to complete, the researcher may want to institute a bonus system that progressively adds more pay for each completed interview.

■ Data Management

The survival of a longitudinal study depends to a large extent on the researcher's ability to produce results in a timely fashion. Decisions concerning how the information resulting from the interviews will be processed, made available for data analysis, documented, and stored are central to data management and the final outcome of the project. The data must be handled with care, from the time of their arrival in the office to the final publications.

Identification of assessment materials. Assessment materials often consist of more than one interview booklet and may include loose sheets, such as consent forms and payment forms. Usually, not all materials will stay together; forms will be channeled to different people who take care of a variety of tasks. *All* pages of assessment materials should be uniformly marked with identification numbers, so that they can always be linked to particular participants when pages become detached. For studies with multiple assessment phases, all interview materials should also have some kind of assessment phase identifier. Materials may be color coded to distinguish assessment phases or samples, for example.

Tracking data processing. To make sure that all data processing steps—such as coding, data checking, and data entry—are completed, the researcher should document all steps, so that it is always possible to track which task was completed and who was responsible. One simple method of tracking is to require that the person who handles each data procedure date and initial the cover page of the interview booklet. It is even better to keep track of the different data steps in a computer file. This procedure has the advantage of allowing the researcher to trace the steps without having to look at the actual interview booklet.

Data checking. Even with the best training and the most user-friendly instruments, interviewers will make mistakes. Visual checking of interview materials can be cumbersome and prone to overlooking errors, especially when interview schedules contain complicated skip patterns. To circumvent such problems, the researcher can incorporate data checking into the data entry procedure. For this method of data checking to be effective, the computer program for data entry should be written in such a way that the visual display screens used for data entry closely resemble the pages in the interview schedule, so that missed questions can be detected easily. For instance, if an interviewer did not follow an instruction correctly and used the wrong skip pattern, the to-be-entered fields shown on the computer screen will be different from the questions filled out in the interview schedule. The data entry program should also check for out-of-range values and illogical answers. If data checking is incorporated into the first round of data entry, the second round of data entry can be used not only to verify the first entry but also to incorporate corrections made by interviewers to errors discovered during first entry.

Correcting errors. Correcting an error should be the responsibility of the interviewer. To distinguish information that was obtained during the interview from corrections and information obtained as a result of recontacting the participant, the interviewer should record all corrections and additional entries with a different color pen from that used to fill out the booklet initially. Supervisors should not assume that problems with the interview materials have been resolved correctly. They should always check corrections after an interviewer has dealt with them.

Dealing with missing data. An effective data management team quickly retrieves as much information as possible to complete missed questions and to clear up uncertainties in the participants' answers. Nonetheless, there are always errors that cannot be rectified, or there may be missing data because some participants did not know how to answer some questions or because particular questions did not apply to them. Missing data should be identified in such a way that the reason they are missing is clear from the coding scheme.

Handling identifiable information. Identifiable information, such as names and addresses, should be removed from interview schedules and stored in a locked place. In longitudinal studies, such information can be kept in participants' personal files together with contact and payment sheets and correspondence. Personal files that store information from different phases provide easy access to previous addresses, the names of former spouses, and telephone numbers of relatives, in case the researcher later has to search for the participants.

Data files. Each research project usually has to maintain a collection of data files that will be part of a *data bank* with a catalog that details the content of each file. In our projects, we distinguish among three sets of files. The first contains the assessment data in cleaned and coded format. The second set of files contains derived variables. In many instances, assessment data or raw variables are not used in analyses in their original format but are transformed or combined with other raw variables to create derived variables. For instance, responses to individual questions from a single measurement instrument may be added to form a summary score. A derived variable can also involve just a single raw variable that is recoded, as is the case when a continuous variable is dichotomized. Normalized variables or data where missing values have been imputed are also included in this category. The third set of files contains information related to the data collection effort, such as files that keep track of participants' addresses, payments, and consent status.

Keeping track of variables. Each researcher needs to develop a system for naming raw variables. We use a system that makes variable names unique and easy to trace within each data phase and across data phases. The name for each variable starts with the phase identifier, followed by the number for the instrument and the number of the question. The names of the files that store raw variables can be recognized by the phase identifier and the instrument number. The naming of derived variables should also be done systematically and may include the initial of the person who created the variable and an identifier for the phase(s) from which the raw data originated.

Many of the derived variables will simply be total scale scores for an assessment instrument. Computing these variables can take place at a set time—for instance, at the end of data cleaning. If the creation of these derived variables is integrated into data management as a routine procedure, it will be relatively easy to maintain a catalog of the variables with documentation that includes all arithmetic transformations, recoding procedures, value labeling statements, and routine procedures, such as internal reliability testing.

Derived variables that are constructed during the data analysis process are much harder to track. Documentation for these variables may be embedded in files with statistical analysis procedures or, worse, may not exist at all if they were created interactively without the existence of a log documenting the algorithms. The only way to keep track of derived variables constructed in the analysis process and to have the ability to reconstruct them is to request that, for each new derived variable, the analysis staff provide data management with procedural files that contain data transformation algorithms and the variables resulting from these transformations.

To keep track of derived variables, we have set up a data bank that is able to retrieve the following information about each variable: (a) description of the content, (b) the raw variables included in creating the derived variable, (c) the construction date, (d) the name of the procedural file that created the variable, (e) the person responsible for making the derived variable, and (f) the publication(s) in which the variable was used. This system facilitates the reconstruction of previously reported results. It enables any user of the data set to search for existing derived variables and avoids duplication of effort or the creation of slightly different variables intended to cover similar characteristics or behaviors.

When errors are discovered in raw variables, as inevitably will happen at times, the system permits the identification of all derived variables in which these flawed raw variables were included.

■ *Quality Control*

The quality of the data can be seen as the keystone of a project's success, and perfection should be the standard to strive for on all levels of the operation. Whenever there is a choice to be made between a strategy that would result in better, more complete data and one that is easier or less time-consuming, the researcher should automatically lean toward what will make the study more perfect. Inevitably, there will be circumstances that could not be foreseen that will make a study less than perfect; however, the researcher should not consciously add to these imperfections. In a large study, the researcher is tempted daily to make decisions that will slide the study a tiny notch away from the ideal. Each decision alone does not seem to be an important concession. Over time, however, many such unimportant decisions may compromise the study.

The attitude of striving for the best should be set from the top. Once the researcher sets such a climate, staff members know what is expected and may go to extraordinary lengths to do the best possible job. Concern for quality does not stop at the interviewers' level. Data cleaning, data analysis, and data documentation should be subject to the same scrutiny and the same standards. The goal is to ensure that the product of the study is not flawed because of sloppy decisions, carelessness, or errors that could have been prevented. A secondary goal is to be able to reconstruct what has happened to the data and to make it possible for others to use the data with the help of documentation. These are not trivial or easy-to-reach goals. Shapiro and Charrow (1989) have reported shortcomings in data management (quality control, documentation, and archiving) in more than 20% of routine data audits done on research conducted for the Food and Drug Administration in the United States. Other researchers have also noted an alarming number of instances of data mismanagement (see Stouthamer-Loeber & van Kammen, 1995). These lapses do not represent intentional deception or fraud in scientific research, but rather unintentional errors and carelessness in, or lack of the documentation of, data collection, data management, or analysis.

Freedland and Carney (1992) coined the expression "audit worthiness" to describe good housekeeping in data management and analysis. The larger the number of researchers working on a data set, the more difficult it is to impose accountability and to set uniform standards for data and analysis management, but the more necessary such standards become. Anyone who has ever indulged in a quick burst of data analysis and then after a month had difficulty reconstructing the analysis process knows how easy it is to just go ahead and not document and how difficult it is to make sense of one's work afterward.

Schwandt and Halpern (1988) have suggested that, even if the researcher does not expect a formal evaluation, he or she needs to form an audit trail that would allow an independent evaluator to assess procedures, decisions, and conclusions from the data.

We have written this chapter to guide the reader through some of the tasks involved in carrying out high-quality research and to convey the message that, with planning, the proper tools, a qualified, well-trained, and closely supervised research team, and continued care, even the most complex studies can be executed successfully.

■ *References*

Bailar, B. A. (1989). Issues in the design of panel surveys. In D. Kasprzyk, G. Duncan, G. Kalton, & M. P. Singh (Eds.), *Panel surveys.* New York; John Wiley.

Ball, J. C., & Brown, B. S. (1977). Institutional sources of data. In L. D. Johnston, D. N. Nurco, & L. N. Robins (Eds.), *Conducting follow-up research on drug treatment programs* (pp. 98-104). Washington, CD: Government Printing Office.

Capaldi, D., & Patterson, G.R. (1987). An approach to the problem of recruitment and retention rates for longitudinal research. *Behavioral Assessment, 9,* 169-177.

Cordray, S., & Polk, K. (1983). The implications of respondent loss in panel studies of deviant behavior. *Journal of Research in Crime and Delinquency, 20,* 214-242.

Davies, J. B., & Baker, R. (1987).The impact of self-presentation and interviewer bias effects on self-reported heroin use. *British Journal of Addiction, 82,* 907-912.

Davis, J. A., & Smith, T. W. (1992). *The NORC General Social Survey.* Newbury Park, CA: Sage.

Fowler, F. J., & Mangione, T. W. (1990). *Standardized survey interviewing: Minimizing interviewer-related error.* Newbury Park, CA: Sage.

Freedland, K. E., & Carney, R. M. (1992). Data management and accountability in behavioral and biomedical research. *American Psychologist, 47,* 640-645.

Groves, R. M. S. (1989). *Survey errors and survey costs.* New York: John Wiley.

Groves, R. M. S., Cialdini, R. B., & Couper, M. P. (1992). Understanding the decision to participate in a survey. *Public Opinion Quarterly, 56,* 475-495.

Hedrick, T. E., Bickman, L., & Rog, D. J. (1993). *Applied research design: A practical guide.* Newbury Park, CA: Sage.

Hornik, J. (1987). The effect of touch and gaze upon compliance and interest of interviewees. *Journal of Social Psychology, 127,* 681-683.

Jessor, R., & Jessor, S. L. (1977). *Problem behavior and psychosocial development: A longitudinal study of youth.* New York: Academic Press.

Kalton, G. (1983). *Introduction to survey sampling.* Beverly Hills, CA: Sage.

Menard, S. (1991). *Longitudinal research.* Newbury Park, CA: Sage.

Miller, D. C. (1991). *Handbook of research design and social measurement* (5th ed.). Newbury Park, CA: Sage.

Nurco, D. N., Robins, L. N., & O'Donnell, M. (1977). Locating respondents. In L. D. Johnston, D. N. Nurco, & L. N. Robins (Eds.), *Conducting follow-up research on drug treatment programs* (pp. 71-84). Washington, DC: Government Printing Office.

Schwandt, T. A., & Halpern, E. S. (1988). *Linking auditing and metaevaluation: Enhancing quality in applied research.* Newbury Park, CA: Sage.

Shapiro, M. F., & Charrow, R. P. (1989). The role of data audits in detecting scientific misconduct: Results of the FDA program. *Journal of the American Medical Association, 262,* 2505-2511.

Sieber, J. E. (Ed.). (1991). *Sharing social science data: Advantages and challenges.* Newbury Park, CA: Sage.

Sieber, J. E. (1992). *Planning ethically responsible research: A guide for students and internal review boards.* Newbury Park, CA: Sage.

Stouthamer-Loeber, M., & van Kammen, W. B. (1995). *Data collection and management: A practical guide.* Thousand Oaks, CA: Sage.

Swires-Hennessy, E., & Drake, M. (1992). The optimum time at which to conduct survey interviews. *Journal of the Market Research Society, 34,* 61-72.

Weinberg, E. (1983). Data collection: Planning and management. In P. H. Rossi, J. D. Wright, & A. B. Anderson (Eds.), *Handbook of survey research* (pp. 329-358). New York: Academic Press.

Weiss, C. H. (1968). Validity of welfare mothers' interview responses. *Public Opinion Quarterly, 32,* 622-633.

14

Mail Surveys

Thomas W. Mangione

■ *When Is a Mail Survey the Right Choice?*

This chapter is a short treatise on how to do mail surveys. The first step you must make is to decide whether a mailed survey is the appropriate data collection strategy for your research question. Although there are many problems to overcome, and many pitfalls lurking for the uneducated researcher, a mail survey is a very appropriate way of gathering data, and can produce high-quality information.

The advantages of mail surveys over other methods of data collection include the following:

- They are relatively inexpensive.
- They allow for large numbers of respondents to be surveyed in a relatively short period even if the respondents are widely distributed geographically.
- They allow respondents to take their time in answering and to look up information if they need to.
- They give privacy in responding.
- They allow for visual input rather than merely auditory input.
- They allow respondents to answer questions at times that are convenient.
- They allow respondents to see the context of a series of questions.
- They insulate respondents from the expectations of an interviewer.

In addition, mail surveys are a good choice when (a) you have limited human resources to help you conduct your study, (b) your questions are written in a closed-ended style, (c) your research sample has a moderate to high investment in the topic, and (d) your list of research objectives is modest in length.

■ *Reducing Error*

In this chapter, I will focus on methods and procedures for collecting data through mail surveys. In describing various strategies, my goal is to reduce the likelihood that errors will affect the quality of your data at any phase of the research project. There are four major types of errors that you want to guard against: sample selection bias, nonresponse error, item nonresponse error, and response error. By describing these four broad areas in which problems may arise, I am also introducing an important goal that you should keep in mind as you read this chapter: It is important that you design quality into all stages and parts of your mail survey project. If you cut corners in one area in order to do an excellent job in another, the final product may have significant quality problems. Quality is not an average of the efforts that you put in; rather, it is achieved only through concern for all phases of the project. This notion, of optimizing your efforts across all areas, has been referred to as "total survey design" (Biemer, Groves, Lyberg, Mathiowetz, & Sudman, 1991).

One area in which problems commonly arise is *sample selection bias.* A major fault can be introduced when you draw a sample from a list that is incomplete in a significant way. For example, a list may be out of date—people have left and new people have arrived, but the list does not represent these recent changes. Obviously, sampling from outdated lists will produce outdated samples.

Sometimes problems with lists are more subtle. You might use the wrong list. For instance, if you want to find out why people may or may not use a neighborhood health center, you might be tempted to draw a sample from patient files—some who have visited recently and some who have not. The real question being asked is, Why do people who live in the neighborhood either use the health center or not? Therefore, the sample that is most appropriate is a sample of neighborhood residents, not a sample of health center clients. Making sure that your list corresponds to the population you want to study is a critical point on the road to quality data.

Another important way to ensure that your sample is not biased is to use some method of random selection to draw a sample from the population in which you are interested. (Methods of selecting samples and a fuller discussion of the issues mentioned above are found in Henry, Chapter 4, this volume.)

A second problem area involves the *biased nature of the responding sample,* or *nonresponse error.* It does not matter how accurately and randomly you draw a sample if it turns out that returns come mainly from people biased in a particular way. Unfortunately, it is sometimes hard to know whether the responding sample is biased. The standard safeguard is to try to achieve a high response rate, somewhere near 75% or higher, if possible. With this type of response rate, the nonresponders would have to be very different from the responders to affect your overall estimates for the population. I will spend quite a bit of time later in this chapter describing how you can maximize your response rate.

Another general problem area is the *failure of respondents to answer individual questions,* or *item nonresponse error*—respondents leave questions blank, accidentally skip over items, do not follow instructions and so fill out answers incorrectly, or write marginal comments that cannot be equated with your printed answer categories. If this happens often enough, your remaining data may again be biased. I will discuss below some ways to ensure that respondents fill out your questionnaire properly.

The final broad area of problems comes from *respondents misunderstanding the wording of the questions as presented,* or *response error.* The central tenet of quantitative survey research is that all respondents should understand each question in the same way and can provide answers to each question. This is a simply stated goal, yet it is sometimes frustratingly difficult to achieve. Two general rules will help you to write good questions: (a) Make it clear, and (b) do not go beyond what is reasonable to expect people to remember. There are many new tools available to help you reach your goal of creating valid questions, but still it takes effort to get there. (For a good summary of the major issues you need to address, see Fowler, Chapter 12, this volume.)

■ Basic Mail Survey Procedures

There are a variety of basic elements and procedures that can ensure that a mail study is carried out well. These are described in turn below.

□ A Good Respondent Letter

Because most mail surveys arrive in the potential respondent's mail without any prior contact, the respondent letter has to do all the work of describing the study purposes, explaining the general procedures to be followed, and motivating the respondent to participate (Andreasen, 1970; Champion & Sear, 1969; Hornik, 1981; Houston & Nevin, 1977; Simon, 1967). It is critical that you produce a respondent letter that is "just right." Several characteristics and elements are important to a successful letter:

1. The letter should not be too long. Keep it to one page.

2. The letter should be printed on professionally produced letterhead; this makes it clear who is sending out the survey and what the supporting institution is. In the text, do not refer to the study name alone (e.g., the Healthy Family Study); instead, include the name of the university or research institution as well.

3. The letter should make it clear how the recipient can get in touch with you if he or she has questions. It should include the name of a contact person and a phone number, perhaps even a toll-free number or the instruction to "call collect."

4. The letter should have a "grabber" for a first sentence, something that encourages the recipient to read the rest of the letter. For example, in a study of police officers concerning gambling enforcement policies, we started our letter with: "We would like the benefit of your professional experience and ten minutes of your time!" For a corporate study of alcohol policies, we started with: "Many people are concerned about alcohol abuse in the workplace."

5. The letter should tell the respondent why this study is important and how the information may be used. Respondents want to participate only in things that they think are useful and that they feel relate to their lives in some specific way.

6. The letter should explain who is being asked to participate in the survey and how it was you got this person's name and address.

7. The letter should explain whether this is a confidential survey or an anonymous survey (they are not the same thing), and how that will be achieved.

8. The letter should mention that participation in the study is voluntary, but also should emphasize the importance of the recipient's participation.

9. The letter should make it clear how the respondent is to get the questionnaire back to you.

10. The letter should be easy to read, in terms of type size, layout, reproduction quality, and language level.

☐ *Return Postage*

It almost goes without saying that to get a good return rate you have to supply the respondent with a return envelope, already addressed to you, and return postage. Maybe because this is so obvious, few studies have explicitly tested this assertion. Those that have been done certainly confirm this point (Armstrong & Lusk, 1987; Blumberg, Fuller, & Hare, 1974; Ferris, 1951; Harris & Guffey, 1978; McCrohan & Lowe, 1981; Price, 1950; Yammarino, Skinner, & Childers, 1991).

There has been more research conducted on the types of postage put on the return envelope. The alternatives are to use some kind of business-reply franking or to put stamps on the return envelopes. The advantage of the business-reply method is that you get charged only for questionnaires that are actually returned. (By the way, the post office does charge a little extra for this service, something on the order of 7 cents per returned questionnaire, so you need to factor in this extra cost when comparing the costs of alternate postage mechanisms.) The disadvantage of this choice is that it appears more impersonal than the alternative.

Putting stamps on return envelopes seems to produce a small increase in return rates (Brook, 1978; Jones & Linda, 1978; Kimball, 1961; Watson, 1965). The reason for this is that respondents often do not want to "waste" stamps by not returning their questionnaires and yet are not crass enough to peel the stamps off and use them for their own purposes. Some studies have also shown that using pretty commemorative-type stamps has a slight advantage over the use of regular stamps (Henley, 1976; Jones & Linda, 1978; Martin & McConnell, 1970). The disadvantage of this approach is its cost. Not only do you pay for stamps that ultimately never get used, but it also costs time and money to obtain the stamps and affix them to all the envelopes.

☐ *Confidentiality/Anonymity*

Respondents are generally more likely to respond if they feel that their answers will be kept confidential instead of being attributed to them directly (Boek & Lade, 1963; Bradt, 1955; Childers & Skinner, 1985; Cox, Anderson, & Fulcher, 1974; Fuller, 1974; Futrell & Hise, 1982; Futrell & Swan, 1977; Kerin & Peterson, 1977; McDaniel & Jackson, 1981; Pearlin, 1961; Rosen, 1960; Wildman, 1977). There are some fairly direct methods for maintaining confidentiality. First, do not put any names or addresses directly on the questionnaires themselves. Instead, put code numbers on the surveys and keep a separate list of names and addresses with the corresponding code numbers; this list can be kept out of view of people who are not on the research team. Second, when the questionnaires come back, do not just leave them lying around for curious eyes to read. Keep them in file cabinets, preferably locked when you are not around, and lock your office when you are not there. Third, do not tell colleagues, friends, or family the answers you receive on individual questionnaires. Fourth, do not present the data, in reports or papers, in such a way that readers are able to figure out who individual respondents are. Sometimes this means describing individuals with characteristics somewhat different from those they really have, and sometimes it means not presenting information on very small groups of people. For example, in a company report you would not present data on a group of three vice presidents by saying, "Two-thirds of the senior management group reported thinking about changing jobs in the next year." Data for organizations such as companies, schools, and hospitals should be presented without the names of the organizations unless there has been a prior specific agreement that this would be done.

Maintaining anonymity is distinctly different from maintaining confidentiality. For confidentiality, you know who filled out which questionnaire, but you promise not to divulge that information to anyone outside the research team. For anonymity, even you do not know which questionnaire belongs to which person. You can achieve this by not putting code numbers on the questionnaires before they are sent out. This way there is no link between the questionnaires and any sample list you have.

It seems logical that studies offering true anonymity (no identification numbers on the questionnaires), compared with those offering only confidentiality (a promise of no disclosure), would produce better response rates, but studies have not clearly proved such an advantage (Andreasen, 1970; Boek & Lade, 1963; Bradt, 1955; Mason, Dressel, & Bain, 1961; Pearlin, 1961; Rosen, 1960; Scott, 1961). Perhaps this is too technical a distinction for respondents to understand. Perhaps they just assume that because you knew how to mail the questionnaire to them, you can somehow find them again if you want to. There is also the cynical interpretation: "They could figure out who I am by putting together several demographic characteristics, so their promise of anonymity is really not much more than a promise of confidentiality." Finally, many surveys are rather innocuous, and respondents do not care if people know what they think on these topics. It is probably best to provide anonymity if you can, as no one has shown that promising anonymity produces worse response rates. Even when the data are anonymous, you still must follow the other procedures described above to maintain confidentiality—that is, you should not leave questionnaires lying around for idle eyes to view and you cannot report data for small groups of respondents.

■ *Nonresponse Error*

The single biggest concern with mail surveys is nonresponse error, or the bias that comes about because you do not get returns from 100% of your sample. The size of this error is dependent, therefore, on how big the nonresponse is and how different the nonresponders are from the responders (Armstrong & Overton, 1977; Barnette, 1950; Baur, 1947; Blair, 1964; Blumberg et al., 1974; Brennan & Hoek, 1992; Campbell, 1949; Champion & Sear, 1969; Clausen & Ford, 1947; Cox et al., 1974; Daniel, 1975; Dillman, 1978; Donald, 1960; Eichner & Habermehl, 1981; Filion, 1975; Gannon, Northern, & Carroll, 1971; Gough & Hall, 1977; Jones & Lang, 1980; Larson & Catton, 1959; Newman, 1962; Ognibene, 1970; Reuss, 1943; Suchman & McCandless, 1940).

Nonresponse error is a particular risk for mail surveys. Unfortunately, in many studies very little is known about the nonresponders, and therefore we are left with uncertainty about the quality of the data. The solution to this concern is to do everything in your power to conduct a study that has a very high response rate. By obtaining a very high response rate, you reduce the likelihood that the nonresponders will have an impact on the validity of your population estimates, even if the nonresponders are different.

What is considered a high response rate? Certainly a rate of return in excess of 85% is viewed as excellent. With such a rate, it would take a peculiar set of circumstances to throw off your results by very much. Response rates in the 70% to 85% range are viewed as very good, and rates in the 60% to 70% range are considered acceptable, but at this level you should begin to be uneasy about the characteristics of nonresponders. Response rates between 50% and 60% are barely acceptable; at this level, you really need some additional information that can contribute to confidence about the quality of your data. Response rates below 50% are not scientifically acceptable—after all, at this level, the majority of the sample is not represented in the results.

Besides attempting to ensure high response rates, it is always useful to try to obtain information about the nonresponders, so that you can compare them with responders. Sometimes this information is available from the list that you originally sampled. For instance, city lists that are used to confirm eligibility for voter registration have each person's age, gender (not listed explicitly, but you can usually figure it out from the first name), occupation (in broad categories), precinct or voting district, whether the person is registered to vote or not, and, if registered, party affiliation. By keeping track of who has and has not responded from your original sample, you can compare the characteristics of those who have responded with those who have not.

Based on a number of studies (Baur, 1947; Campbell, 1949; Gannon et al., 1971; Gelb, 1975; Goodstadt, Chung, Kronitz, & Cook, 1977; Ognibene, 1970; Peterson, 1975; Robins, 1963; Suchman, 1962), we can get a picture of some common traits of nonresponders. Compared with responders, they tend to be less educated; they also tend to be elderly, unmarried, and male, or they have some characteristic that makes them seem less relevant to the study (e.g., abstainers for a drinking study, nondrivers for a traffic safety study, or lower-income people for a study about mortgages).

Nonresponse errors create problems for your study in two ways. First, if people who do not respond hold different views or behave differently from the majority of people, your study will incorrectly report the population average. It will also drastically underreport the number of people who feel as the nonresponders do. The basic problem is that nonresponders make your picture of the population wrong. How far off the mark you are depends on the pattern of nonresponse, but in any event your findings will not be accurate.

Second, even if nonresponders are not that different from responders, low response rates give the appearance of a poor-quality study and shake the consumer's confidence in the results of the study. The study becomes less useful or less influential just because it does not have the trappings of quality.

As I noted above, nonresponse error is a major problem with mail surveys. The primary reason mail surveys are vulnerable to nonresponse error is that it is *very* easy for recipients not to respond. It is not as if they have to close a door in someone's face, or even hang up the phone on a persistent interviewer; all they have to do is throw the survey in the wastebasket. In addition, some recipients of mail surveys become nonresponders simply because they never get around to filling out the questionnaire.

All levels of response rates are reported in the literature. It is safe to assume that some of the worst response rates never see the light of an academic journal. If the only thing you did was put questionnaires in envelopes and mail them to people with the request that they fill them out, it would be common to see response rates in the 20% range, and it would not be surprising to see them in the 5% range. This is a long way from the rate of 75% or so that can inspire confidence in the data. How do you get better response rates?

■ *Reminders*

Probably the single most important technique for producing high response rates is the use of reminders (Denton, Tsai, & Chevrette, 1988; Dillman, Carpenter, Christenson, & Brooks, 1974; Eckland, 1965; Etzel & Walker, 1974; Filion, 1976; Ford & Zeisel, 1949; Furse, Stewart, & Rados, 1981; House, Gerber, & McMichael, 1977; Jones & Lang, 1980; Kanuk & Berenson, 1975; Kephart & Bressler, 1958; Linsky, 1975; Yammarino et al., 1991). Even under the best of circumstances, you will not achieve acceptable levels of return if you do not send out any reminders. Actually, it is important to send out several reminders, and it is important to pay attention to their timing.

If you carefully keep track of your daily returns, you will see that an interesting pattern unfolds. For the first few days after you mail out the questionnaires, you get nothing back. This makes sense because it takes time for the surveys to be delivered, it takes a short period for respondents to fill them out, and then it takes a day or two to get them back to you in the mail (actually this can be a day or two longer if you use business-reply returns). About 5 to 7 days after you send out the initial mailing, you begin to get a few back; then in the next few days you get a lot more back, with more coming in each day than the day before. Around the 10th day after your mailing, the returns start to level off, and around the 14th day they start to drop off precipitously.

This drop-off in returns is a signal that whatever motivational influence your initial letter had is now fading. Respondents who have not returned the questionnaire by now are going to begin to forget about doing it, or they are going to misplace the survey under a pile of things on their desks. You want to plan your first reminder to arrive at the respondents' addresses just at this point in the return pattern, at about the 14th day.

After you send out the first reminder, you will see the same pattern repeats itself. A few days of no impact, then a burst of returns with more coming in each day, and then a precipitous decline at about 14 days after the second mailing (the first reminder).

The other interesting feature of this return pattern is that whatever return rate you got in the first wave (e.g., 40%), you will get about half that amount in the second wave (e.g., 20%), and so on for each succeeding wave. Therefore, because I recommend shooting for at least a 75% return rate, you should plan on at least four mailings—the initial mailing and three reminders. Each of these mailings should be spaced about 2 weeks apart. This gives you approximately the following pattern of returns:

$$40\% + 20\% + 10\% + 5\% = 75\%.$$

This means that your total mailing period will take about 8 to 9 weeks, because you have to leave time after your last reminder for the final returns to come in. Sending reminders out more frequently than every 2 weeks does not speed up the returns—all it does is waste time and money reminding people who were going to respond anyway.

Spreading two or three reminders out over a longer period than at 2-week intervals (to save money on postage) is not as effective in producing a good return rate. You do not keep building momentum among the nonresponders with your reminders because the gap in time is so long they have forgotten about the survey. Each reminder has to start all over again in getting people to decide to participate.

What is also interesting about this pattern is that the rate of returns and the number of reminders has nothing to do with the total size of your sample. You should follow the same procedures whether your sample size is 200 or 20,000. The only impact of size is that you have to have a bigger staff to help you get out the mailings in each round.

What should you put in each mailing? Is each reminder just a repeat of the first mailing? No. I recommend sending a complete package (respondent letter, questionnaire, return envelope) only in the first and third mailings. In the second and fourth mailings, you can limit yourself to a postcard or letter reminder.

In each of the four mailings, the letter addressed to the respondent should focus on slightly different issues. For the first mailing you want to be the most thorough, covering all the bases. In the second mailing you want to be gentle and friendly; for example, "Just a reminder in case you have not yet sent in your questionnaire. We would really like to hear from you." In the third mailing, you want to emphasize the confidentiality of responses and the importance of getting a good return so that all points of view are represented. You should also note that you are including another copy of the questionnaire in case the recipient misplaced the first one you sent. The fourth mailing should be a "last call." Set a specific deadline and encourage the recipient to send in the questionnaire so that his or her point of view can be represented.

□ *Who Should Receive Reminders?*

If you are using a procedure that promises confidentiality, you can keep track of the questionnaires being returned through their code numbers, and send reminders only to people who have not yet responded. This saves money on postage, printing, and supplies and keeps respondents from being annoyed (or confused) by reminders after they have already sent in their surveys.

If you want to use a procedure that gives respondents anonymity, then the steps to follow in sending reminders are a little more complicated. Because you do not know which of the people in your sample have sent back their questionnaires, you must use one of two alternate strategies for producing reminders. The first method is to send reminders to everyone, always including a line that says, "If you have already sent in your questionnaire, thank you very much."

You will probably also want to explain that, because the returns are anonymous, you do not know who has responded and who has not, and that is why you are sending reminders to everyone. I personally do not like to use this strategy because (a) it is wasteful of postage, supplies, and resources; (b) it irritates respondents to get reminders when they have returned their questionnaires; (c) it confuses some respondents and sometimes leads them to worry that their surveys got lost in the mail, so they fill out new ones (you do not want duplicate surveys, but you cannot remove them from your returns, because you have no way of knowing which might be someone's second questionnaire); and (d) it dilutes your reminder letter's message, because some of the verbiage is apologizing to people who have already returned their questionnaires and not just focusing on those who have yet to respond.

I prefer a method that I call the *reminder postcard strategy*. This method accomplishes two things at once: It maintains complete anonymity for the respondents' returned questionnaires while also letting you know who has and has not returned the questionnaire. This lets you send reminders only to those who have yet to respond. When using the reminder postcard strategy, you enclose with the questionnaire, in the original mailing, a postage-paid return postcard that has either an identification code or the recipient's name (or both) on it; the questionnaire itself has no identification on it. In the instructions, you tell the respondent explicitly that returning the postcard will tell you that he or she does not need any reminders. You also instruct the respondent to mail the postcard back *separately* from the questionnaire. By using this procedure, you know who has returned the questionnaire without having to put any identifying information on the questionnaire itself.

The first thing researchers worry about is, What if the respondent just sends back the postcard and not the questionnaire? That would be a problem, but in my experience that has never been the case. You usually get more questionnaires back than postcards. Some respondents forget to mail their postcards, some lose them, and some purposely do not send them back as a way of ensuring their anonymity. These last folks are willing to put up with getting reminders they do not need to guarantee their anonymity. Thankfully there are only a few who take this route (e.g., 5% or so), or else the method would not achieve its intended purpose of providing you information about who has responded while maintaining anonymity.

■ Incentives

Other than follow-up reminders, there is no technique more likely to improve your response rate than incentives. It turns out that the research findings hold some surprises concerning the various options available in providing incentives to respondents. The logic of offering an incentive is simple: Raise the stakes explicitly for the respondents by giving them something in return for filling out the questionnaire. The complications come in trying to figure out what to give respondents and when to give it to them.

Logically, one might assume that the respondents would receive their rewards after they return the questionnaires. They would be informed in the initial respondent letter that this is the deal, and more respondents would be motivated to participate because of the promise of this reward. Obviously, the respondent would have to value whatever is being offered, or it would have no motivational value. One disadvantage with this mechanism is that respondents receive delayed rewards; they get their rewards several weeks (probably) after their "good" behavior.

Another possibility is to offer the reward in advance, including it with the initial mailing in anticipation of the respondent's participation. The advantage here is that the impact is immediate; the respondent gets the benefit right away. We should not underestimate the motivational power of the implied contract: "They gave me this reward, so I had better do my part by filling out the questionnaire, or else I would not be living up to my end of the bargain." The disadvantage here (both financially and morally) is that some people get the reward but do not deserve it because they do not return the surveys anyway. Because of this problem, one goal in using this technique is to figure out the lowest value of the reward you need to give in order to achieve the effects that you want.

☐ *Monetary Rewards*

The simplest and most direct reward is money. A variety of studies and reviews of the literature have shown that the offering of monetary incentives tends to improve response rates (Duncan, 1979; Fox, Crask, & Kim, 1988; Heberlein & Baumgartner, 1978; Hopkins & Gullickson, 1992; Kanuk & Berenson, 1975; Linsky, 1975; Scott, 1961; Yammarino et al., 1991; Yu & Cooper, 1983). What is also clear from this research is that prepaid monetary incentives are more effective than promised monetary rewards (Blumberg et al., 1974; Hancock, 1940; Schewe & Cournoyer, 1976; Wotruba, 1966). There have been contradictory conclusions drawn about the impact of promised monetary rewards compared with no rewards, but there are examples of studies that have shown benefits for promised rewards although they are not as great as prepaid rewards (Yu & Cooper, 1983).

What is surprising about these research results is not that prepaid rewards have some impact, but that it does not seem to take a very big reward to stimulate an improved response rate. Many studies are reported in the literature that show the benefits of just 25 cents and 50 cents. However, many of these studies were done 15 to 20 years ago. It seems important to extrapolate the findings from these studies to the "current" value of the dollar. Hopkins and Gullickson (1992) conducted a review and equated these values to 1990 dollars, and still showed improvements for values less than 50 cents.

The question about whether there are increasing benefits for increasing dollar amounts is harder to answer definitively. It turns out that much of the experimentation that has been done to test alternate amounts have not tended to use monetary amounts more than $1.00, therefore the number of studies we have available to make generalizations about larger-sized incentives is relatively small. In their review, Hopkins and Gullickson (1992) did find an increasing percentage of improvement over "no incentive" control methods for greater incentive values, but their top group was designated as $2.00 or more and included only eight studies.

Another point that speaks to the issue of whether larger rewards (e.g., $5.00) or smaller rewards (e.g., $1.00) are better has to do with our understanding of the meaning of the reward to the respondent. With small amounts of money, people clearly do *not* interpret the reward as a fair market exchange for their time. Even a $1.00 reward for filling out a 20-minute questionnaire works out to only a $3.00 per hour rate of pay. Therefore, people must view the reward in another light; one idea is that it represents to the respondent a token of good faith or a "trust builder" (Dillman, 1978). The respondent feels that the research staff is nice to show their appreciation by giving the incentive and therefore feels motivated to reciprocate by filling out the questionnaire.

A few studies have reported on the provision of larger-sized rewards, and it looks as though response rates tend to be higher for these than for lesser amounts (Hopkins & Gullickson, 1992; Yu & Cooper, 1983). In particular, higher incentive amounts are reported in the literature for surveys conducted with persons in professional occupations, particularly doctors. Incentive amounts from $20.00 to $50.00 have been used (Godwin, 1979). In these circumstances, higher response rates are obtained with higher rewards (Berry & Kanouse, 1987). In addition, my own experience with a recent nonexperimental study dealing with alcohol use and work included one work site in which we used a $5.00 up-front incentive; the resulting response rate was 82%.

One final point about monetary incentives and their desired effects: The key to effectiveness seems to be to create a climate in which the prepaid incentive is seen as a feel-good thing rather than as a manipulative technique to coerce the respondent into participation.

Another variation on the idea of monetary rewards is the use of a "lottery" prize structure. This technique falls within the "promised reward" category, but with a twist. Respondents are offered a "chance" at a "big" prize, although they also have, of course, a chance of getting nothing. Again, research on this variation is limited, so definitive generalizations about its effectiveness are not possible (Hopkins & Gullickson, 1992; Gajraj, Faria, & Dickinson, 1990; Lorenzi, Friedmann, & Paolillo, 1988). The logic behind this idea is that the chance of hitting big will be such an inducement that respondents will fill out their surveys to qualify. This technique also works well if you are trying to encourage respondents to mail in their surveys by a particular deadline.

The other issue that must be dealt with if you want to use this technique is anonymity, or rather the lack of it. In order to have a drawing and give out prizes, you need to know the name and address associated with each returned survey. This lack of anonymity may be counterproductive in some circumstances. The postcard mechanism discussed above provides a solution to this dilemma. The surveys themselves are returned anonymously, but the postcards have the respondents' names and addresses on them. To be eligible for the lottery, the respondents would need to return their postcards. It seems like enterprising respondents would realize that all they really have to do to be eligible for the lottery is to turn in their postcards. You would not really be able to tell whether or not they had actually sent in their questionnaires. It seems that the more attractive the "prize," the more motivation there would be to cheat. However, respondents do not seem to do that. In my recent experience with this technique in 12 different work sites across the country, we never received more postcards back than we did questionnaires, even though we were offering three $250 lottery prizes at each work site.

☐   *Nonmonetary Rewards*

Of course, it is possible to reward respondents with things besides money (Brennan, 1958; Dommeyer, 1985; Furse & Stewart, 1982; Hansen, 1980; Hubbard & Little, 1988; Nederhof, 1983). All sorts of things have been, and can be, used, including ballpoint pens, cups, and movie tickets. The logic of giving a "gift" is similar to that for giving a token amount of money. The idea is to express to respondents that you are appreciative of their efforts and want to thank them for their participation. Again, as with money rewards, it is possible to think about the gift being given as a "prepaid" gift or as a "promised" gift that is sent after the survey is returned (Brennan, 1958; Pucel, Nelson, & Wheeler, 1971).

There has not been much research on the differences in response rates associated with prepaid and promised gifts, but one would assume that the effectiveness would follow the same pattern as with monetary rewards—prepaid gifts would probably have a better effect. Also, there has not been much research done on the "value" of gifts to see what the trends are with more valuable gifts. To some extent, the concept of value is less obvious with many types of gifts than it is with monetary rewards. Also, it is possible that a gift's perceived value may exceed the actual cost of the gift itself. This may arise because respondents may not have a good sense about how much particular gifts cost, or it may be because by buying in bulk you can get a discount. Movie passes are great in this regard, because they usually cost you about $4 although they are good at movies that cost $7 normally.

I recently had occasion to be part of a survey study in which respondents were asked to fill out a short questionnaire concerning their nutritional intake. The researchers also needed respondents to include clippings from their toenails. As an incentive, respondents were told that when they returned the survey they would receive detailed nutritional analyses of their own diets based on their reports and their toenail clippings. Returns were over 70% with only one reminder.

Another interesting incentive is to offer a contribution to charity in the respondents' names if surveys are returned (Robertson & Bellenger, 1978). Obviously, the perceived value of the charity might have some impact on the effectiveness of this incentive. This technique can be used on an individual or group basis. The individual strategy would be to contribute a certain amount (say $5.00) to a charity for each survey returned. Specific charities can be designated or you can allow respondents to check off among a few offerings, or you can ask them to write in their own suggestions. The group strategy would provide a significant payment to a charity if the sample as a whole provides a certain number or percentage of returns (e.g., a 70% return rate). My recent work site study included two sites in which we used the group strategy, a $750 contribution to charity, and wound up with response rates of 68% and 78%.

☐ *Incentives Versus Reminders*

Now that I have extolled the virtues of incentives as well as reminders, a legitimate question is whether incentives should be used instead of reminders. The question can be answered from the perspective of final response rates, cost-effectiveness, and quickness of returns. James and Bolstein (1990) conducted a study that offers some information on this issue. They ran an experiment using different amounts of incentives (none, 25 cents, 50 cents, $1.00, and $2.00) and kept track of the response rates at the end of each of their four mailings using a four-page questionnaire. The highest rates of returns resulted from the use of both methods in combination—four mailings and a $2.00 prepaid incentive. This strategy was also the most expensive. Good return rates (although a little lower than for the combination method) were also obtained through the use of two mailings and a $2.00 incentive, and from four mailings and no incentive. The no-incentive strategy was slightly less expensive than the incentive strategy, but of course it took more time for the additional waves of mailings to be administered. If time rather than money is the limiting factor, then using incentives may allow you to save some time; if money is the limiting factor, then planning for multiple mailings with no incentives may be the best. However, if a high response rate is your major goal, you should use multiple mailings and incentives together.

■ *Other Techniques*

There are other techniques beyond reminders and incentives that have been shown to improve response rates. Some have been associated with consistent improvements, whereas some have shown improvements only in some circumstances.

☐ *Length of the Questionnaire*

It almost goes without saying that you are likely to get a better response rate with a shorter questionnaire than with a longer one. Within this general recommendation, the real world is a little more complicated. It turns out that there are no clear demarcation points. It is not the case that a 12-page questionnaire will get a decent response rate but a 13-page questionnaire will not. There has been a fair amount of research on this issue, but the results are muddled because of several confounding factors (Berdie, 1973; Burchell & Marsh, 1992; Champion & Sear, 1969; Childers & Ferrell, 1979; Lockhart, 1991; Mason et al., 1961; Roscoe, Lang, & Sheth, 1975; Scott, 1961).

Part of the confusion has to do with how questionnaire length is measured. Is length determined by the number of questions, the number of pages, or some combination of the two? (For example, 30 questions on three pages may seem different from 30 questions on six pages.) Another confound is that different-length questionnaires may be perceived differently in terms of interest levels or in terms of importance. Longer questionnaires may actually be seen as more interesting or more important because they can get a fuller picture of a topic than a more cursory version. Even within one methodological study to test the effects of varying questionnaire length, it is hard to "hold constant" other factors that may play a role in response rates. Many studies that try hard to control these issues wind up comparing different-length questionnaires that are actually not that different. For example, Adams and Gale (1982) compared surveys with one page versus three pages versus five pages. They found no difference in response rates between one- and three-page surveys but did find a lower response rate for five-page surveys.

In addition, it is difficult to draw conclusions from findings on a series of studies because of the differences in topics covered, samples, reminder procedures, and so on. In an ambitious review covering 98 methodological studies, Heberlein and Baumgartner (1978) were unable to document any zero-order correlation between length measures and overall responses.

The message to take away from this is that length by itself is not the sole determining factor that decides response rates. No matter what the length of a questionnaire, other design factors can influence whether a good response rate is obtained or not. Within a specific design, however, I believe shorter questionnaires will on average do better than substantially longer versions. To put this statement in its proper context, however: My recent work site study, in which we used reminders and incentives, used a 24-page survey, and we wound up with an average response rate of 71% across all 16 work sites.

From my experience, I think the real issue for the researcher is to design a questionnaire that *efficiently* asks about all the elements that are important to the study. You want to avoid series of questions that seem off the topic; you want to avoid questions that are redundant; you want to avoid unnecessarily long sequences of questions that try to measure very minor differences in issues (e.g., asking about the actual length of time the respondent had to wait in a doctor's waiting room, plus how long he or she had to wait in the examining room before the doctor came in, plus asking how long the wait was overall, plus asking how satisfied the respondent was with the waiting time). There are also important issues of presentation and layout that can affect the perceived length of the questionnaire, which I will discuss below.

□ *Clarity of Instructions*

Practical Data
Collection
and Analysis
Methods

414

Another factor that contributes to perceived respondent burden and that in turn affects response rates is the clarity of the instructions that are part of the questionnaire. It is not surprising to find that forms with complicated or confusing or wrong instructions create frustration for respondents and that the result of this frustration is failure to return the questionnaire.

Instructions should be precise, short, and clearly visible. Various format aids—such as boldface type, boxes, and arrows—can supplement written directions and help the respondent to comply with instructions. In addition, it helps if you can have someone who has a graphic perspective review the layout of your questionnaire.

□ *Prenotification*

One interesting variation on the use of reminders is the prenotification of respondents—that is, contacting them before they receive the survey. In a sense, this is a reminder done ahead of time. Basically, prenotification consists of a contact by mail or phone that "warns" the respondent that he or she has been selected to be in a survey and to keep an eye open for its arrival in the mail a week or two in the future. The impact of prenotification has generally been found to be equivalent to one reminder (Allen, Schewe, & Wijk, 1980; Brunner & Carroll, 1969; Ford, 1967; Furse et al., 1981; Heaton, 1965; Jolson, 1977; Kerin & Peterson, 1977; Myers & Haug, 1969; Parsons & Medford, 1972; Schegelmilch & Diamantopoulos, 1991; Stafford, 1966; Walker & Burdick, 1977; Wynn & McDaniel, 1985; Yammarino et al., 1991).

This procedure provides one way to shorten the interval between the first mailing of the survey and the last reminder. You can "gain" 2 weeks on your return schedule by mailing out the prenotification letter a couple of weeks before you send out the questionnaire. You would send it out at about the same time the questionnaire goes off to the printer.

□ *Outgoing Postage*

The usual alternatives for types of outgoing postage are stamps or metered postage. A few studies have been done that show a slight advantage for stamps, particular commemorative stamps, on outgoing envelopes (Blumenfeld, 1973; Dillman, 1972; Hopkins & Podolak, 1983; Kernan, 1971; McCrohan & Lowe, 1981; Peterson, 1975; Vocino, 1977). The explanation for this difference is that respondents are less likely to assume a mailing is "junk mail" if there is a stamp on the envelope, and so are more likely actually to open the envelope. The only disadvantage of using stamps, again, is the extra cost of sticking them on the envelopes.

There is also a third option for outgoing postage, called a first-class indicia. It is like the business reply, except that it is used for outgoing first-class mail.

You set up a prepaid account with the postal service and print your account number and a first-class designation on your outgoing envelopes; the postal service keeps track of your mailings and deducts the postage amounts from your account. This is the least labor-intensive method of sending out your questionnaires, but it probably suffers somewhat from the same problem as metered mail in that it may be confused with junk mail.

There has also been some research on the value of using premium postage for mailings, such as special delivery or next-day delivery services. The research shows there to be some advantage to using this type of postage, but the costs are so substantial that many consider it prohibitive (Clausen & Ford, 1947; Kephart & Bressler, 1958). When special postage is used, it is most often used for final reminders. At least at this stage of the process you are mailing only to part of your sample.

□ *Study Sponsorship*

Respondents are more likely to respond to surveys that they consider important or prestigious (Doob, Freedman, & Carlsmith, 1973; Houston & Nevin, 1977; Jones & Lang, 1980; Jones & Linda, 1978; Peterson, 1975; Roeher, 1963; Watson, 1965), therefore they are more likely to respond to surveys that are sponsored by government agencies or well-known universities (Houston & Nevin, 1977; Jones & Lang, 1980; Jones & Linda, 1978; Peterson, 1975). Also, when the cover letter is on university or government agency letterhead, respondents may be less concerned that the survey is a ploy to sell them real estate or insurance.

□ *Personalization*

Another technique you might employ is personalization, either through the use of the respondent's name in the salutation (as opposed to a more anonymous greeting, such as "Dear Boston resident") or through the use of personally signed letters. Neither procedure has consistently shown benefits for response rates (Andreasen, 1970; Carpenter, 1975; Dillman & Frey, 1974; Frazier & Bird, 1958; Houston & Jefferson, 1975; Kawash & Aleamoni, 1971; Kerin & Peterson, 1977; Kimball, 1961; Rucker, Hughes, Thompson, Harrison, & Vanderlip, 1984; Simon, 1967; Weilbacher & Walsh, 1952). Indeed, some authors have commented that personalizing the letters may have just the opposite effect, because it calls attention to the fact that you know the respondent's name.

□ *Deadlines*

Providing the respondents with a deadline for responding has a nice appeal. The presumption is that respondents will try harder to return the questionnaire if there is a deadline, rather than putting it aside, meaning to get to it later, and then forgetting it. The use of a deadline gets a little complicated when you are also using reminders. You do not want to say that 2 weeks from now is the deadline for responding, and then send the respondent a reminder at that time saying, "Please respond—we are giving you 2 more weeks." On the other hand, you do not want to give a deadline of 8 weeks in the future, because that hardly serves any motivating purpose.

What research has been done on the use of deadlines does not show any particular advantage in final response rates. What it does show is that the returns come in a little faster (Futrell & Hise, 1982; Henley, 1976; Kanuk & Berenson, 1975; Linsky, 1975; Nevin & Ford, 1976; Roberts, McCrory, & Forthofer, 1978; Vocino, 1977). My suggestion is to use soft deadlines that also incorporate the information about subsequent reminders. For instance: "Please try to respond within the next week, so we will not have to send you any reminders."

■ Management

Because the mail survey process does not involve a staff of interviewers who need to be hired, trained, and supervised, researchers using mail surveys sometimes overlook the importance of managing the research process. There are two areas of management that need to be attended to: the design of a good schedule and the incorporation of a good quality control system.

□ The Schedule

Having a clear, precise, written schedule will aid you immeasurably in the management of the mail survey process. The schedule will enable you to appreciate how the various parts of the mail survey study have to fit together like a jigsaw puzzle for you to carry out the project in a timely fashion. By having a schedule you are also able to anticipate issues so that you are not overly rushed to get particular steps accomplished. A schedule can also serve as a checklist, to ensure that you do not forget anything.

In making up a schedule, you have to recognize that there are really several independent processes that come together to make a mail survey study. These include the sampling process, the development of the questionnaire, the development of other materials, the printing of the questionnaire (and other materials), the data collection period, and the coding and data entry process.

People have different preferences about how to construct a schedule. Some people like to start at the end—when the results are due—and work backward toward the start date. This assumes that the time window to conduct the study is fixed, and time is to be allocated among the various phases of the study within this fixed period. As components are allocated portions of time, those with fixed periods of time are entered into the schedule first. For example, we know that the data collection period is predetermined after you decide how many reminders you are going to send out and exactly how long you are going to wait between reminders. If you choose to do an original mailing and then three reminders with 2 weeks between mailings, then the data collection process will take 8 to 9 weeks.

Another common fixed period is how long it will take the printer to print the number of copies of the questionnaire you will need, encompassing the period from the day you give the pages to the printer until the day the surveys are delivered to you.

By using this mechanism to build your schedule, you can then allocate the remaining time to the other phases of the study. Inevitably, some phases begin to get scrunched for time. You may discover that you have only 2 weeks to develop your questionnaire, or you may find that you have only a 3-week period after the last questionnaire arrives to code, analyze, and write up your report. One way to deal with this scarcity of time is to overlap various functions in your schedule. For instance, you can be constructing your sample while you are developing your questionnaire. Also, you can begin the coding and data entry process even while questionnaires are still coming in.

An alternate way to construct a schedule is to start at the beginning of the project and allocate time to various phases based on your estimates of the time you will need. Again, for some phases you can be relatively certain about how much time will be required; for others you will need to make some educated guesses. As you get more experience, you will become better at estimating how long each phase may require.

As you put your schedule together, it is a very good policy to leave some time within it for unexpected issues or slippage, for when something does not go exactly as planned. Sometimes the printer does not come through with the questionnaires when promised, or sometimes you decide that you really want to pretest a particular section of troublesome questions one more time.

Often, researchers tend to consider their schedules to be "carved in stone," and it can be very anxiety provoking to see that one's project is getting off schedule. Instead, you should view the schedule as a dynamic list, such that when something changes, it may affect many subsequent dates that you have outlined. The important feature of the schedule is that it makes you aware of the implications of changes in the progress of your project and in the required adjustments in your activities.

☐ *Quality Controls*

Although you may have a clear schedule and much faith in those who are working for you, the creation of mechanisms to check the quality of the work being produced must be one of your primary concerns. There are many areas you need to consider. Everything that is word processed must be sent through a spell checker program. All materials must be carefully proofread before they are sent to the printer. Ideally, proofreading should be done by two individuals:

someone who is familiar with the project and someone who is not involved in the study on a day-to-day basis. Also, you need to be extremely careful about last-minute changes; sometimes in the rush to revise something, new errors are created.

Much of the mail survey process involves stuffing envelopes with various materials and putting mailing labels on the envelopes. Sometimes this phase involves relatively simple steps—insert a letter and a numbered questionnaire in an envelope, put a mailing label on the envelope, seal it, put postage on the envelope, and mail it. However, even in these simple processes, things can go wrong. Someone can forget to insert a letter; someone can misnumber or forget to number a questionnaire; someone can mix up the labels so that the wrong labels go with the wrong questionnaires; labels can be put on crooked; the postage can be wrong or not put on at all; the envelopes can be sent out without being sealed at all or with the seal not glued down well. You have to assume that if something can go wrong, it will go wrong sometimes. All of the above have happened at one point or another on the projects I have worked on, even though we were trying to be diligent.

The issues of potential mistakes can grow exponentially when the mailing process is more complicated or when the size of the study increases. As you get more steps to worry about and more people working on the mailing process, there are more opportunities for things to go wrong. One way you can help ensure the ultimate quality of your product is by analyzing the work flow of the questionnaire mailing assembly process. As you do so, think about the possible mistakes that could be made, then design the processes in a way that minimizes the potential for mistakes as well as maximizes your potential for checking the work of others.

■ Aesthetics

There are a variety of aesthetic issues that are important to attend to in the production of a mail survey (Blumenfeld, 1973; Ford, 1968). The reason you should be concerned with these issues, besides the inherent quest for beauty, is that attention to them can improve your response rates and the quality of your data. Your response rates will be better because an aesthetically pleasing questionnaire is more likely to be considered important and competently prepared. Neat and stylishly presented response alternatives and instructional messages make it easier for respondents to comply in a correct fashion.

□ Balance

The pages of your questionnaire should be balanced; that is, the margins at right and left and at top and bottom should be equal. Sometimes, the way the sequence of questions runs results in a page finished three-quarters of the way down, and the next question will not fit in the remaining space. It is important to make such a page look complete by increasing the space between items so that the page balances with the page it faces. The same principal applies to the use of pages with a two-column format. You want to make sure that both columns are equally "filled." In achieving balance, it is better to have more white space around questions than to produce an overly crammed or squeezed look.

□ *Type Style and Size*

You should choose a type style that is clean looking rather than overly fancy or scriptlike. The key issue, however, is type size. You should always use a type size that is large enough to be read easily. If your study focuses on elderly respondents, you may want to use a type size that is larger than normal. You should also make judicious use of such features as boldface type, underlining, and italicizing. For example, in a sequence of questions that are very similar except for one phrase, you may find it helpful to boldface the changing phrase. This will help the respondent to pick up the difference in the questions on the first reading. You should not go overboard with this mechanism, however. If you use it in every question, respondents will tend to become unresponsive to its message.

□ *Format of Questions*

Every question should have a question number, either applied sequentially throughout the whole questionnaire or numbered sequentially within sections (e.g., A1, A2 . . . B1, B2, and so on). By numbering each question, you provide a mechanism that helps the respondent move through the questionnaire efficiently. Sometimes researchers are tempted to leave follow-up, probing questions unnumbered, but I have found this to be a shortsighted strategy, because many respondents accidentally skip unnumbered questions.

You should also adopt a common style or format to be followed throughout the questionnaire. This style should encompass features such as the width of the margins, the number of spaces that you leave after question numbers, and the number of blank lines between response categories. One format I have used is to show all the questions completely in boldfaced type and the response categories in regular (medium) type. This style facilitates the respondent's eye scan from one question to another.

□ *Format of Response Categories*

Your response categories should have an established style. For example, you can display all the categories vertically in one column or horizontally in one row. If possible, you should avoid doubling up the categories into two columns or two rows, because this can create an ambiguous sequence for the reading of the categories. In addition, if you have a sequence of questions that all use the same response categories, these questions should all be lined up vertically on the page. Again, these seemingly small formatting issues can make or break the image of your questionnaire.

☐   *The Physical Dimensions of the Questionnaire*

Some have recommended that questionnaires be produced on sheets of paper that are smaller than $8\frac{1}{2}$ by 11 inches, to give the appearance of a "small" task. In general, I am supportive of that notion *if* it does not conflict with some of your other formatting goals. For instance, the type size should not be too small to compensate for the smaller page. Also, if the smaller pages result in significantly more pages, then it is not clear to me that there is a net benefit. Finally, smaller-sized questionnaires raise the issue of the size of the envelope. Standard-sized envelopes are made for dealing with $8\frac{1}{2}$-by-11-inch paper.

I definitely recommend printing on both sides of the pages, provided that the weight of the paper is sufficient to keep the print from bleeding through to the other side of the page. Printing pages back to back cuts the number of sheets needed in half, resulting in a questionnaire that looks "less weighty," which may help response rates. It also reduces postage costs.

You want your questionnaire to look like a booklet, so you should have the printer run the pages off on 17-by-11-inch paper (with the pages set up in the right order to run in sequence when the pages are folded) and then fold them in the middle. The staples go right in the fold (this is sometimes called saddle stitching).

Another style feature that will have a direct influence on the number of pages in your questionnaire is the use of a two-column, newspaper-type format. Many questions that have relatively short response categories (e.g., yes/no, agree/disagree) can easily be placed in a two-column format. The questions themselves may take up a few extra lines, but the response categories take up no more space. Using this technique can reduce the number of pages in your questionnaire by anywhere from 25% to 50%.

■ *Summary*

Now that you have reached the end of this chapter, it is important that you put all the facets together and make them work for you to produce a high-quality survey. I have focused here in turn on the various parts of the survey process and have tried to give you an in-depth understanding of the issues and procedures to follow. However, in the real world, one rarely gets the opportunity to conduct an "ideal" project—one where quality is maximized at each decision point. Instead, each project is a series of trade-offs and balancing efforts that tries to produce an optimum combination of decisions to produce the best total quality.

This process of trying to achieve an optimum balance is called a total survey design approach. An example of an inadequate attempt to apply the principles of total survey design would be a project in which a multistage, random sample of households is developed (very expensive but accurate) and used for a mail survey in which no follow-up reminders are sent (cheap but probably biased). What this example emphasizes is that you will do your project no good if you put all or most of your resources into one phase and, in so doing, leave yourself inadequate resources to undertake the other phases.

To review quickly, all mail surveys should include the following basic elements:

- A good respondent letter
- Return postage on a return envelope
- At least a guarantee of confidentiality (anonymity is even better)

To ensure good response rates, you should use one or both of the following:

- Reminders—up to three reminders spaced at 2-week intervals
- Prepaid incentives—usually a small amount of money ($1.00 to $5.00)

In addition, to maximize response rates, you should use as many of these procedures as possible:

- Keep your questionnaire modest in length.
- Work extra hard to make your instructions clear.
- Prenotify respondents of your survey.
- Use a pretty commemorative stamp on the *outgoing* envelope.
- Use a pretty commemorative stamp on the *return* envelope.
- Use letterhead that identifies your institutional sponsorship.
- Personalize the salutation or the signature.
- Mention a soft deadline in your respondent letter.

By following these procedures, you should be able to produce high-quality mail surveys.

■ References

Adams, L. L. M., & Gale, D. (1982). Solving the quandary between questionnaire length and response rate in educational research. *Research in Higher Education, 17,* 231-240.

Allen, C. T., Schewe, C. D., & Wijk, G. (1980). More on self-perception theory's foot technique in the pre-call/mail survey setting. *Journal of Marketing Research, 17,* 498-502.

Andreasen, A. R. (1970). Personalizing mail questionnaire correspondence. *Public Opinion Quarterly, 34*, 273-277.

Armstrong, J. S., & Lusk, E. J. (1987). Return postage in mail surveys. *Public Opinion Quarterly, 51*, 233-248.

Armstrong, J. S., & Overton, T. S. (1977). Estimating nonresponse bias in mail surveys. *Journal of Marketing Research, 14*, 396-402.

Barnette, W. L. (1950). Non-respondent problem in questionnaire research. *Journal of Applied Psychology, 34*, 397-398.

Baur, E. J. (1947). Response bias in a mail survey. *Public Opinion Quarterly, 11*, 594-600.

Berdie, D. R. (1973). Questionnaire length and response rate. *Journal of Applied Psychology, 58*, 278-280.

Berry, S., & Kanouse, D. (1987). Physicians' response to a mailed survey: An experiment in timing of payment. *Public Opinion Quarterly, 51*, 102-104.

Biemer, P. N., Groves, R. M., Lyberg, L. E., Mathiowetz, N. A., & Sudman, S. (Eds.). (1991). *Measurement errors in surveys*. New York: John Wiley.

Blair, W. S. (1964). How subject matter can bias a mail survey. *Mediascope, 8*(1), 70-72.

Blumberg, H. H., Fuller, C., & Hare, A. P. (1974). Response rates in postal surveys. *Public Opinion Quarterly, 38*, 113-123.

Blumenfeld, W. S. (1973). Effect of appearance of correspondence on response rate to a mail questionnaire survey. *Psychological Reports, 32*, 178.

Boek, W. E., & Lade, J. H. (1963). Test of the usefulness of the postcard technique in a mail questionnaire study. *Public Opinion Quarterly, 27*, 303-306.

Bradt, K. (1955). Usefulness of a postcard technique in a mail questionnaire study. *Public Opinion Quarterly, 19*, 218-222.

Brennan, M., & Hoek, J. (1992). Behavior of respondents, nonrespondents and refusers across mail surveys. *Public Opinion Survey, 56*, 530-535.

Brennan, R. (1958). Trading stamps as an incentive. *Journal of Marketing, 22*, 306-307.

Brook, L. L. (1978). Effect of different postage combinations on response levels and speed of reply. *Journal of the Market Research Society, 20*, 238-244.

Brunner, A. G., & Carroll, S. J., Jr. (1969). Effect of prior notification on the refusal rate in fixed address surveys. *Journal of Advertising Research, 9*, 42-44.

Burchell, B., & Marsh, C. (1992). Effect of questionnaire length on survey response. *Quality and Quantity, 26*, 233-244.

Campbell, D. T. (1949). Bias in mail surveys. *Public Opinion Quarterly, 13*, 562.

Carpenter, E. H. (1975). Personalizing mail surveys: A replication and reassessment. *Public Opinion Quarterly, 38*, 614-620.

Champion, D. J., & Sear, A. M. (1969). Questionnaire response rates: A methodological analysis. *Social Forces, 47*, 335-339.

Childers, T. L., & Ferrell, O. C. (1979). Response rates and perceived questionnaire length in mail surveys. *Journal of Marketing Research, 16*, 429-431.

Childers, T. L., & Skinner, S. J. (1985). Theoretical and empirical issues in the identification of survey respondents. *Journal of the Market Research Society, 27*, 39-53.

Clausen, J. A., & Ford, R. N. (1947). Controlling bias in mail questionnaires. *Journal of the American Statistical Association, 42*, 497-511.

Cox, E. P., III, Anderson, W. T., Jr., & Fulcher, D. G. (1974). Reappraising mail survey response rates. *Journal of Marketing Research, 11*, 413-417.

Daniel, W. W. (1975). Nonresponse in sociological surveys: A review of some methods for handling the problem. *Sociological Methods and Research, 3*, 291-307.

Denton, J., Tsai, C., & Chevrette, P. (1988). Effects on survey responses of subject, incentives, and multiple mailings. *Journal of Experimental Education, 56*, 77-82.

Dillman, D. A. (1972). Increasing mail questionnaire response in large samples of the general public. *Public Opinion Quarterly, 36,* 254-257.

Dillman, D. A. (1978). *Mail and telephone surveys: The total design method.* New York: John Wiley.

Dillman, D. A., Carpenter, E., Christenson, J., & Brooks, R. (1974). Increasing mail questionnaire response: A four state comparison. *American Sociological Review, 39,* 744-756.

Dillman, D. A., & Frey, J. H. (1974). Contribution of personalization to mail questionnaire response as an element of a previously tested method. *Journal of Applied Psychology, 59,* 297-301.

Dommeyer, C. J. (1985). Does response to an offer of mail survey results interact with questionnaire interest? *Journal of the Market Research Society, 27,* 27-38.

Donald, M. N. (1960). Implications of non-response for the interpretation of mail questionnaire data. *Public Opinion Quarterly, 24,* 99-114.

Doob, A. N., Freedman, J. L., & Carlsmith, J. M. (1973). Effects of sponsor and prepayment on compliance with a mailed request. *Journal of Applied Psychology, 57,* 346-347.

Duncan, W. J. (1979). Mail questionnaires in survey research: A review of response inducement techniques. *Journal of Management, 5,* 39-55.

Eckland, B. (1965). Effects of prodding to increase mail back returns. *Journal of Applied Psychology, 49,* 165-169.

Eichner, K., & Habermehl, W. (1981). Predicting response rates to mailed questionnaires. *American Sociological Review, 46,* 361-363.

Etzel, M. J., & Walker, B. J. (1974). Effects of alternative follow-up procedures on mail survey response rates. *Journal of Applied Psychology, 59,* 219-221.

Ferris, A. L. (1951). Note on stimulating response to questionnaires. *American Sociological Review, 16,* 247-249.

Filion, F. L. (1975). Estimating bias due to nonresponse in mail surveys. *Public Opinion Quarterly, 39,* 482-492.

Filion, F. L. (1976). Exploring and correcting for nonresponse bias using follow-ups on nonrespondents. *Pacific Sociological Review, 19,* 401-408.

Ford, N. M. (1967). The advance letter in mail surveys. *Journal of Marketing Research, 4,* 202-204.

Ford, N. M. (1968). Questionnaire appearance and response rates in mail surveys. *Journal of Advertising Research, 8,* 43-45.

Ford, R. N., & Zeisel, H. (1949). Bias in mail surveys cannot be controlled by one mailing. *Public Opinion Quarterly, 13,* 495-501.

Fox, R. J., Crask, M. R., & Kim, J. (1988). Mail survey response rate: A meta-analysis of selected techniques for inducing response. *Public Opinion Quarterly, 52,* 467-491.

Frazier, G., & Bird, K. (1958). Increasing the response of a mail questionnaire. *Journal of Marketing, 22,* 186-187.

Fuller, C. (1974). Effect of anonymity on return rate and response bias in a mail survey. *Journal of Applied Psychology, 59,* 292-296.

Furse, D. H., & Stewart, D. W. (1982). Monetary incentives versus promised contribution to charity: New evidence on mail survey response. *Journal of Marketing Research, 19,* 375-380.

Furse, D. H., Stewart, D. W., & Rados, D. L. (1981). Effects of foot-in-the-door, cash incentives, and followups on survey response. *Journal of Marketing Research, 18,* 473-478.

Futrell, C., & Hise, R. T. (1982). The effects on anonymity and a same-day deadline on the response rate to mail surveys. *European Research, 10,* 171-175.

Futrell, C., & Swan, J. E. (1977). Anonymity and response by salespeople to a mail questionnaire. *Journal of Marketing Research, 14,* 611-616.

Gajraj, A. M., Faria, A. J., & Dickinson, J. R. (1990). Comparison of the effect of promised and provided lotteries, monetary and gift incentives on mail survey response rate, speed and cost. *Journal of the Market Research Society, 32,* 141-162.

Gannon, M., Northern, J., & Carroll, S. J., Jr. (1971). Characteristics of non-respondents among workers. *Journal of Applied Psychology, 55,* 586-588.

Gelb, B. D. (1975). Incentives to increase survey returns: Social class considerations. *Journal of Marketing Research, 12,* 107-109.

Godwin, K. (1979). Consequences of large monetary incentives in mail surveys of elites. *Public Opinion Quarterly, 43,* 378-387.

Goodstadt, M. S., Chung, L., Kronitz, R., & Cook, G. (1977). Mail survey response rates: Their manipulation and impact. *Journal of Marketing Research, 14,* 391-395.

Gough, H. G., & Hall, W. B. (1977). Comparison of physicians who did and did not respond to a postal questionnaire. *Journal of Applied Psychology, 62,* 777-780.

Hancock, J. W. (1940). An experimental study of four methods of measuring unit costs of obtaining attitude toward the retail store. *Journal of Applied Psychology, 24,* 213-230.

Hansen, R. A. (1980). A self-perception interpretation of the effect of monetary and non-monetary incentives on mail survey respondent behavior. *Journal of Marketing Research, 17,* 77-83.

Harris, J. R., & Guffey, H. J., Jr. (1978). Questionnaire returns: Stamps versus business reply envelopes revisited. *Journal of Marketing Research, 15,* 290-293.

Heaton, E. E., Jr. (1965). Increasing mail questionnaire returns with a preliminary letter. *Journal of Advertising Research, 5,* 36-39.

Heberlein, T. A., & Baumgartner, R. (1978). Factors affecting response rates to mailed questionnaires: A quantitative analysis of the published literature. *American Sociological Review, 43,* 447-462.

Henley, J. R., Jr. (1976). Response rate to mail questionnaires with a return deadline. *Public Opinion Quarterly, 40,* 374-375.

Hopkins, K. D., & Podolak, J. (1983). Class-of-mail and the effects of monetary gratuity on the response rates of mailed questionnaires. *Journal of Experimental Education, 51,* 169-170.

Hopkins, K. D., & Gullickson, A. R. (1992). Response rates in survey research: A meta-analysis of the effects of monetary gratuities. *Journal of Experimental Education, 61,* 52-62.

Hornik, J. (1981). Time cue and time perception effect on response to mail surveys. *Journal of Marketing Research, 18,* 243-248.

House, J. S., Gerber, W., & McMichael, A. J. (1977). Increasing mail questionnaire response: A controlled replication and extension. *Public Opinion Quarterly, 41,* 95-99.

Houston, M. J., & Jefferson, R. W. (1975). The negative effects of personalization on response patterns in mail surveys. *Journal of Marketing Research, 12,* 114-117.

Houston, M. J., & Nevin, J. R. (1977). The effects of source and appeal on mail survey response patterns. *Journal of Marketing Research, 14,* 374-377.

Hubbard, R., & Little, E. (1988). Promised contributions to charity and mail survey responses replication with extension. *Public Opinion Quarterly, 52,* 223-230.

James, J. M., & Bolstein, R. (1990). Effect of monetary incentives and follow-up mailings on the response rate and response quality in mail surveys. *Public Opinion Quarterly, 54,* 346-361.

Jolson, M. A. (1977). How to double or triple mail response rates. *Journal of Marketing, 41,* 78-81.

Jones, W. H., & Lang, J. R. (1980). Sample composition bias and response bias in a mail survey: A comparison of inducement methods. *Journal of Marketing Research, 17,* 69-76.

Jones, W. H., & Linda, G. (1978). Multiple criteria effects in a mail survey experiment. *Journal of Marketing Research, 15,* 280-284.

Kanuk, L., & Berenson, C. (1975). Mail surveys and response rates: A literature review. *Journal of Marketing Research, 12,* 440-453.

Kawash, M. B., & Aleamoni, L. M. (1971). Effect of personal signature on the initial rate of return of a mailed questionnaire. *Journal of Applied Psychology, 55,* 589-592.

Kephart, W. M., & Bressler, M. (1958). Increasing the responses to mail questionnaires. *Public Opinion Quarterly, 22,* 123-132.

Kerin, R. A., & Peterson, R. A. (1977). Personalization, respondent anonymity, and response distortion in mail surveys. *Journal of Applied Psychology, 62,* 86-89.

Kernan, J. B. (1971). Are "bulk rate occupants" really unresponsive? *Public Opinion Quarterly, 35,* 420-424.

Kimball, A. E. (1961). Increasing the rate of return in mail surveys. *Journal of Marketing, 25,* 63-65.

Larson, R. F., & Catton, W. R., Jr. (1959). Can the mail-back bias contribute to a study's validity? *American Sociological Review, 24,* 243-245.

Linsky, A. S. (1975). Stimulating responses to mailed questionnaires: A review. *Public Opinion Quarterly, 39,* 82-101.

Lockhart, D. C. (1991). Mailed surveys to physicians: The effect of incentives and length on the return rate. *Journal of Pharmaceutical Marketing and Management, 6,* 107-121.

Lorenzi, P., Friedmann, R., & Paolillo, J. (1988). Consumer mail survey responses: More (unbiased) bang for the buck. *Journal of Consumer Marketing, 5,* 31-40.

Martin, J. D., & McConnell, J. P. (1970). Mail questionnaire response induction: The effect of four variables on the response of a random sample to a difficult questionnaire. *Social Science Quarterly, 51,* 409-414.

Mason, W. S., Dressel, R. J., & Bain, R. K. (1961). An experimental study of factors affecting response to a mail survey of beginning teachers. *Public Opinion Quarterly, 25,* 296-299.

McCrohan, K. F., & Lowe, L. S. (1981). A cost/benefit approach to postage used on mail questionnaires. *Journal of Marketing, 45,* 130-133.

McDaniel, S. W., & Jackson, R. W. (1981). An investigation of respondent anonymity's effect on mailed questionnaire response rate and quality. *Journal of the Market Research Society, 23,* 150-160.

Myers, J. H., & Haug, A. F. (1969). How a preliminary letter affects mail survey return and costs. *Journal of Advertising Research, 9,* 37-39.

Nederhof, A. J. (1983). The effects of material incentives in mail surveys: Two studies. *Public Opinion Quarterly, 47,* 103-111.

Nevin, J. R., & Ford, N. M. (1976). Effects of a deadline and a veiled threat on mail survey responses. *Journal of Applied Psychology, 61,* 116-118.

Newman, S. W. (1962). Differences between early and late respondents to a mailed survey. *Journal of Advertising Research, 2,* 37-39.

Ognibene, P. (1970). Traits affecting questionnaire response. *Journal of Advertising Research, 10,* 18-20.

Parsons, R. J., & Medford, T. S. (1972). The effect of advance notice in mail surveys of homogeneous groups. *Public Opinion Quarterly, 36,* 258-259.

Pearlin, L. I. (1961). The appeals of anonymity in questionnaire response. *Public Opinion Quarterly, 25,* 640-647.

Peterson, R. A. (1975). An experimental investigation of mail-survey responses. *Journal of Business Research, 3,* 199-209.

Price, D. O. (1950). On the use of stamped return envelopes with mail questionnaires. *American Sociological Review, 15,* 672-673.

Pucel, D. J., Nelson, H. F., & Wheeler, D. N. (1971). Questionnaire follow-up returns as a function of incentives and responder characteristics. *Vocational Guidance Quarterly, 19,* 188-193.

Reuss, C. F. (1943). Differences between persons responding and not responding to a mailed questionnaire. *American Sociological Review, 8,* 433-438.

Roberts, R. E., McCrory, O. F., & Forthofer, R. N. (1978). Further evidence on using a deadline to stimulate responses to a mail survey. *Public Opinion Quarterly, 42,* 407-410.

Robertson, D. H., & Bellenger, D. N. (1978). A new method of increasing mail survey responses: Contributions to charity. *Journal of Marketing Research, 15,* 632-633.

Robins, L. N. (1963). The reluctant respondent. *Public Opinion Quarterly, 27,* 276-286.

Roeher, G. A. (1963). Effective techniques in increasing response to mail questionnaires. *Public Opinion Quarterly, 27,* 299-302.

Roscoe, A. M., Lang, D., & Sheth, J. N. (1975). Follow-up methods, questionnaire length, and market differences in mail surveys. *Journal of Marketing, 39,* 20-27.

Rosen, N. (1960). Anonymity and attitude measurement. *Public Opinion Quarterly, 24,* 675-680.

Rucker, M., Hughes, R., Thompson, R., Harrison, A., & Vanderlip, N. (1984). Personalization of mail surveys: Too much of a good thing? *Educational and Psychological Measurement, 44,* 893-905.

Schegelmilch, B. B., & Diamantopoulos, S. (1991). Prenotification and mail survey response rates: A quantitative integration of the literature. *Journal of the Market Research Society, 33,* 243-255.

Schewe, C. D., & Cournoyer, N. D. (1976). Prepaid vs. promised incentives to questionnaire response: Further evidence. *Public Opinion Quarterly, 40,* 105-107.

Scott, C. (1961). Research on mail surveys. *Journal of the Royal Statistical Society, Series A, Part 2, 124,* 143-205.

Simon, R. (1967). Responses to personal and form letters in mail surveys. *Journal of Advertising Research, 7,* 28-30.

Stafford, J. E. (1966). Influence of preliminary contact on mail returns. *Journal of Marketing Research, 3,* 410-411.

Suchman, E. A. (1962). An analysis of "bias" in survey research. *Public Opinion Quarterly, 26,* 102-111.

Suchman, E. A., & McCandless, B. (1940). Who answers questionnaires? *Journal of Applied Psychology, 24,* 758-769.

Vocino, T. (1977). Three variables in stimulating responses to mailed questionnaires. *Journal of Marketing, 41,* 76-77.

Walker, B. J., & Burdick, R. K. (1977). Advance correspondence and error in mail surveys. *Journal of Marketing Research, 14,* 379-382.

Watson, J. (1965). Improving the response rate in mail research. *Journal of Advertising Research, 5,* 48-50.

Weilbacher, W., & Walsh, H. R. (1952). Mail questionnaires and the personalized letter of transmittal. *Journal of Marketing, 16,* 331-336.

Wildman, R. C. (1977). Effects of anonymity and social settings on survey responses. *Public Opinion Quarterly, 41,* 74-79.

Wotruba, T. R. (1966). Monetary inducements and mail questionnaire response. *Journal of Marketing Research, 3,* 398-400.

Wynn, G. W., & McDaniel, S. W. (1985). The effect of alternative foot-in-the-door manipulations on mailed questionnaire response rate and quality. *Journal of the Market Research Society, 27,* 15-26.

Yammarino, F. J., Skinner, S. J., & Childers, T. L. (1991). Understanding mail survey response behavior. *Public Opinion Quarterly, 55,* 613-639.

Yu, J., & Cooper, H. (1983). A quantitative review of research design effects on response rates to questionnaires. *Journal of Marketing Research, 20,* 36-44.

15

Methods for Sampling and Interviewing in Telephone Surveys

Paul J. Lavrakas

■ When and Why Use a Telephone Survey?

Surprising as it may seem, telephone survey methods have undergone serious development only in the past 25 years. Prior to that time, the proportion of households in the United States with telephones was too low to justify use of the telephone as a valid sampling medium. However, by the mid-1980s, telephone surveying had become commonplace, and in many instances it is the preferred approach to surveying. It is a methodology that has achieved respected status as a valid and reliable means of gathering information to aid research and effective decision making in both the public and private sectors (Lavrakas, 1993).

Why has telephone surveying gained prominence as a means of providing accurate measures on some topic of interest? Simply stated, in most cases its advantages far outweigh its disadvantages (see the delineation of the comparative strengths and weaknesses of different survey modes in Frey, 1989, p. 76). Although many fail to recognize or acknowledge it, by far the most important advantage of telephone surveying is the opportunity it provides for quality control over the entire data collection process. This includes sampling, respondent selection, the asking of questionnaire items, and, with computer-assisted telephone interviewing (CATI), data entry. It is this *quality control advantage* that recommends the telephone as the preferred mode for surveying, providing there are no overriding concerns that rule against its use. In particular, interviewing done by telephone can most closely approach the level of standardization that is the goal of all high-quality surveys (see de Leeuw & van der Zouwen, 1988; Fowler & Mangione, 1990).

In the early stages of the move away from personal interviewing to the telephone as the dominant mode for scientific surveying, there were concerns that data gathered by telephone would be of lower quality (more bias and/or variance) than data gathered in person. However, research in the past two decades has suggested that there are few consistent differences in data quality between the two modes, and whatever differences may have once existed appear to be getting smaller over time (de Leeuw & van der Zouwen, 1988; Groves, 1989).

A second major advantage to telephone surveying is its cost-efficiency. Telephone surveys can collect data far more efficiently than in-person interviewing. For example, in addition to the lack of travel expenses associated with telephone surveying, Groves (1989, p. 512) estimates that individual questionnaire items administered via telephone take 10-20% less time than the same items administered in person. Although telephone surveys are typically more expensive than mail surveys, their potential advantages for reducing total survey error (TSE) often outweigh this disadvantage.

The third major advantage of telephone surveying is the speed at which data can be gathered and processed. In a week or less, interviewers can gather data via telephone that might take a month or more using in-person interviews. An even longer period could be needed to conduct a mail survey, given the necessity of follow-up mailings to increase typically low response rates. For example, with as few as 10 experienced telephone interviewers, working 4-hour shifts, upward of 400-500 twenty-item questionnaires could be completed within 3 days (including allowance for at least some callbacks). If, for example, on Monday a mayor needed some information by the end of the week to aid her in making an important policy decision about citizen dissatisfaction with police services and whether she should fire the police chief, a good survey organization could complete a high-quality telephone survey of adult residents and provide results to the mayor by the deadline. High-quality data could not be gathered via mail or in-person surveys within this time frame for the same costs as the telephone survey.

A major disadvantage of telephone surveys, even when well executed, consists of the limitations they place on the complexity and length of the interview. Unlike in the dynamics of face-to-face interviewing, the average person (respondent) often finds it tiresome to be kept on the telephone for longer than 20-30 minutes. In contrast, personal interviewers do not seem to notice respondent fatigue, even with interviews that last 30-40 minutes or longer. Mail surveys also do not suffer from this disadvantage, as the questionnaires can be completed at the respondents' leisure over multiple sessions. Similarly, complicated questions, especially those that require the respondent to see or read something, have been impossible via the telephone (although with the advent of videophone technology this limitation may eventually start to diminish).

Other concerns about telephone surveys include potential coverage error, or the researcher's being unable to represent adequately the population of interest within the sampling frame used. Not everyone lives in a household with a telephone, and among those who do, not every demographic group is equally willing/able to be accounted for and/or interviewed via telephone. Thus telephone surveys are at a disadvantage in reaching certain segments of the general population. However, there are ways that information can be gathered via telephone about people who do not have telephones (see Frey, 1989, p. 46), making it possible to reach them in "mixed-mode" surveys. In contrast, regarding coverage error of persons within telephone households, Maklan and Waksberg (1988) report that well-conducted random-digit dialing telephone surveys do at least as well as the U.S. government's large in-person scale surveys in enumerating and interviewing all types of demographic groupings. (As described later in detail, random-digit dialing is a sampling technique for telephone surveys that allows any working telephone number to be reached within the geographic area in which a survey is being conducted. In the United States, this is accomplished through the use of a computer programmed with information about the three-digit telephone prefixes/exchanges that work in a given area and then programmed to add strings of random digits to complete the formation of seven-digit local numbers that might reach households. The cost trade-off is that the pool of numbers generated must be "cleaned" to eliminate those that are not in service or that reach nonresidences.)

Since the mid-1980s, there has been a significant increase in the use of, and thus knowledge about, multiple-frame or "mixed-mode" surveys (Dillman & Tarnai, 1988; Frey, 1989; Groves, 1989; Lavrakas, 1993). These are surveys that employ more than one mode to sample respondents and/or gather data. For example, in a school enrollment survey of more than 2,200 households conducted for a suburban Chicago school district, a 92% response rate was achieved by beginning with a mail survey, followed by telephone interviews and, when needed, in-person interviews of those who did not respond via the other modes (Lavrakas, 1990).

Telephone surveys and other survey modes should not be viewed as being in competition with each other. For example, telephoning can be used to encourage compliance with mail surveys or to screen for rare groups in the general population (e.g., blind adults) who are then interviewed in person. Thus, rather than viewing the choice of survey mode as an "either/or" decision, the modern survey researcher also should look for ways to combine modes creatively. As Dillman and Tarnai (1988) observe: "Each of the basic survey [modes] has certain limitations that defy solution. . . . The joint use of more than one [mode] offers promise for mitigating, if not overcoming, certain limitations of individual [modes]. Mixed mode survey designs offer the potential of using each [mode] to its greatest advantage while avoiding its onerous weaknesses" (pp. 509-510). Therefore, a challenge the researcher faces in planning a survey is to think how, if at all, he or she might best handle the various types of likely survey errors that can occur through the use of different modes of sampling and data collection, given the resources available.

As explained by other contributors to this volume, and as discussed in detail by Groves (1989), in addition to considerations of sampling error—the uncertainty (variance) that occurs in a survey merely because it is not a census—a careful survey researcher must attend to the potential effects of coverage error, nonresponse error, and measurement error. Together, all these potential sources of variance and bias constitute *total survey error* (see Fowler, 1993; Lavrakas, 1993, 1996). The researcher should consider each element of TSE separately when planning, implementing, and interpreting a survey.

Prudent concern about a survey's total error will lead the researcher to deploy methods that (a) are intended to reduce the likely sources of error and/or (b) will allow the measurement of the nature and size of potential errors. In the end, it remains the researcher's responsibility to allocate the resources available to conduct the survey so as to achieve the best-quality data possible within the finite budget. However, this often will require many difficult cost-benefit trade-offs, such as whether to use more resources to hire and train high-quality interviewers or, instead, to make additional callbacks to hard-to-reach respondents or to deploy a "refusal-conversion" process. A researcher will never have enough resources to attend fully to all potential sources of survey error, and so must make often difficult and onerous choices regarding what can be done and what simply cannot be done.

As it applies to telephone surveys, coverage error is the "gap" that often exists between the sampling frame (the list of telephone numbers from which a sampling pool is drawn) and the larger population the survey purports to represent. To the extent the group "covered" by the sampling frame differs from the group missed by the sampling frame, the survey will have coverage error in the form of bias. For example, all household telephone surveys use sampling frames that miss persons without telephones, and thus have the potential for coverage error if the researchers try to generalize findings to the general population.

Nonresponse error in a telephone survey results when those persons who are sampled, but not interviewed, differ as a group from those who are successfully interviewed. Nonresponse in telephone surveys is due to (a) failure to contact potential respondents, (b) contacts with potential respondents who refuse to participate, and (c) language and health problems. Despite what many appear to believe, if the nonresponders who are sampled, as a group, do not differ from the respondents from whom data are gathered, as a group, there is no nonresponse-associated error (bias), regardless of the actual response rate. However, researchers often are not able to estimate adequately the extent to which the responders and the nonresponders differ, and thus strive to achieve high response rates, hoping to minimize the chance/extent of nonresponse error.

Not all data that are recorded on a telephone survey questionnaire are accurate measures of the phenomenon of interest. These inaccuracies, in the forms of both bias and variance, may be due to errors associated with (a) the

questionnaire and/or (b) the interviewers and/or (c) the respondents (see Biemer, Groves, Lyberg, Mathiowetz, & Sudman, 1991). In thinking about these
potential sources of measurement error, the prudent telephone survey researcher will consider ways in which the nature and size of such errors might
be measured so that the researcher can consider post hoc adjustments to the
"raw data" gathered from respondents by interviewers.

Every telephone survey enterprise should be viewed as an endeavor with
a finite set of resources available. The challenge faced by the researchers is to
deploy these resources in the most cost-beneficial way possible, so as to maximize the quality of the data that are gathered. The TSE perspective can guide
the researchers through a series of choices (trade-offs) that often pit what they
know or assume about one source of potential error against what they know or
assume about another source of potential error. For novice researchers, these
considerations can seem forbidding or even overwhelming. When faced with
all the potential threats to a survey's validity, some may throw up their hands
and question the value of the entire survey enterprise. To do so, however, is to
fail to remember that highly accurate surveys are routinely conducted by surveyors who exercise the necessary care.

This chapter serves as an introduction to these considerations as they apply
to telephone surveys. This discussion of total survey error is meant to alert
researchers to the many challenges they face in conducting telephone surveys
that will be "accurate enough" for the purposes for which they are intended.
The message to the novice should be clear: Planning, implementing, and interpreting a survey that is likely to be accurate is a methodical and time-consuming process, but one well worth the effort.

■ Telephone Surveys and Telephone Usage in the United States

There are two sets of factors concerning the phenomenon of the telephone
that directly affect the success of telephone surveys: (a) technological factors
that physically determine the ability to reach respondents, and (b) social factors
related to the behavior of persons contacted via telephone. Furthermore, as
telecommunications technology rapidly changes, and as telemarketing and
telephone surveying continue to reach out to the public, we are experiencing
an evolution of the social norms of telephone-related behavior as these new
technologies interact with human dispositions and proclivities.

□ Physical Factors

By the mid-1940s, virtually all residential and business telephone lines in
the United States were interconnected across different telephone companies,
and it finally became possible for a telephone survey to reach any household
or business with a telephone regardless of the location of the survey organiza-

tion or the telephone being dialed. However, the prevalence of U.S. households with telephones as recently as the 1950s was too sparse to make possible the selection of a representative sample of Americans via telephone. (This "low" saturation level still precludes the valid use of telephone surveys in most of the countries of the world because of the coverage error that would result; see Trewin & Lee, 1988.)

Current estimates of the proportion of U.S. households with at least one telephone access line (i.e., a unique telephone number) suggest that the figure is about 95% (plus or minus 2%). Households without telephones do not mirror the demographic characteristics of the rest of the population: Not having a telephone is related to very low income, low education, rural residency, younger ages of household heads, and minority racial status. Therefore, anyone planning a telephone survey should make an explicit judgment about the potential error that noncoverage may introduce into the survey's findings. In particular, those conducting telephone surveys in local areas should be aware that the proportions of households with at least one telephone access line are not uniform throughout the United States. As of 1990, there were 10 states in which less than 90% of households had telephones: Alabama, Alaska, Arkansas, Kentucky, Louisiana, Mississippi, New Mexico, Oklahoma, Texas, and West Virginia (Congressional Information Service, 1990). Furthermore, lower-income inner-city neighborhoods typically have relatively low rates of telephone ownership (less than 90%).

Another physical factor that affects surveying the public via telephone is that of multiple-line households—about 15% of U.S. households as of 1996 (and growing). Whenever a random-digit dialing scheme is used for sampling, households with more than one telephone number have a greater probability of being sampled than do households with only one access line. (Note that whenever one is trying to measure the prevalence of some attribute in the population—such as the proportion of households that have home computers—one must measure the number of telephone lines per household in the interview and then take this into account when conducting post hoc statistical weighting adjustments.)

There remain other types of variations in telephone companies' services and policies throughout the nation that can affect the planning and conduct of telephone surveys. Thus a researcher's experience with a telephone survey in one geographic region may not necessarily apply when he or she samples another. As the telephone industry develops new hardware and software products and services (see Andrews, 1992), researchers must be alert to the need to adapt methods to these technological advances (e.g., caller ID, cellular phones, and pagers), in particular to assure high-quality sampling and interviewing. Currently, almost all high-quality telephone surveys of the general public sample respondents using their household telephone numbers. Thus, for example, telephone survey interviewers must be trained what to do when someone is "sampled" via a cellular phone number (in many surveys a cellular phone number constitutes an ineligible number—one at which an interview must not be conducted—

as interviewing persons reached at such numbers distorts the probabilities of respondent selection, which could violate sampling theory assumptions).

Possibly the biggest technological challenge to telephone surveyors in the next few decades will be the introduction of the videophone or some equivalent computer-based technology. Depending upon the extent to which this technology is embraced by the public and the business community, there likely will be a multiyear period during which some portion of respondents will have the technology and others will not, and telephone surveyors will need to devise procedures to accommodate this mixed-mode interviewing environment.

☐ *Social Factors*

As Frey (1989) notes, there are certain "behavioral norms" regarding the telephone that have traditionally worked to the advantage of telephone interviewers, although these appear to have started to break down in the past 10 years. The most important of these norms is that a ringing telephone will almost always be answered if someone is there. Granted, there is variation from household to household and from person to person in how quickly a telephone is answered. However, experience shows that if a telephone is answered, the median number of rings it takes is three or four, and more than 90% of the time it will be answered within seven to eight rings. Thus it has not been a problem in telephone surveys for potential respondents to allow ringing telephones to go unanswered. However, in a recent survey conducted for AT&T, approximately one in four residents in Illinois reported that at least once a week they let their home telephones ring without answering them or having them answered electronically (Lavrakas, Bauman, & Schejbal, 1994). With the advent of new technologies there is a small, but growing, proportion of the public using answering machines, voice mail, pagers, and/or caller ID systems to screen calls, thereby lowering response rates. We do not, however, have good estimates at present on the extent to which this happens. To the extent that any sizable proportion of the public comes to refuse to answer certain incoming calls routinely, nonresponse error in telephone surveys may become an increasingly serious concern.

Another norm has worked to the advantage of telephone surveying. Traditionally, it has been implicit in telephone conversations that it is the caller who determines the duration of the verbal interaction. That is, the caller has some purpose in placing the call, and courtesy dictates that the purpose should be fulfilled before the call is terminated. Obviously, not all persons practice this norm when answering their telephones, or telephone interviewers and telemarketers would not be refused as often as they are. However, this norm appears to be weakening, as suggested by the small but steady increase in telephone survey nonresponse due to refusals.

As demographic and behavioral changes continue to occur in society, they may have an impact on the practice of telephone surveying. For example, as a larger proportion of the U.S. population is made up of senior citizens, problems associated with aging (e.g., hearing loss and social disengagement) will increase for telephone surveys. If other social problems grow, such as those leading to fear of crime and concerns about the invasion of privacy, we can expect further trouble for telephone surveys, with increasing concern about potential coverage and nonresponse errors. These are trends that future telephone survey researchers must address; they must look for ways in which new telecommunications technologies might be used to reduce, rather than increase, total survey error.

■ *PAPI Versus CATI*

Traditionally, telephone surveys have been conducted by interviewers asking questions read from paper questionnaires and then recording the answers on the questionnaires with pencils. Despite what most appear to believe, there still are many telephone surveys in which paper-and-pencil interviewing (PAPI) remains the preferred mode because of time and/or cost considerations.

In computer-assisted telephone interviewing, human interviewers work at computer workstations that control the administration of the questionnaire and also may control the sampling process. CATI software can control the distribution of the sampling pool (the set of telephone numbers dialed by interviewers in a given survey), even to the point of dialing the appropriate telephone number for a "ready" interviewer. CATI has the potential to provide many types of statistics on interviewer productivity to aid supervisory staff. It can also be used only to administer the questionnaire, without also controlling the sampling pool. In presenting the questionnaire to the interviewer, CATI makes complicated skip patterns (question-sequence contingencies) very easy to use, compared with PAPI, and can randomly order sequences of items and incorporate previous answers into the wording of subsequent items. Of course, CATI also provides for simultaneous entry of the answers into a computer database.

However, despite what was expected of CATI in its early years, it has not been found generally to lower survey costs or to reduce the length of the field period (see Lavrakas, 1991, 1996). In fact, CATI often lengthens the average time an interview takes to complete, compared with PAPI, because with CATI the interviewer typically has less control over the speed at which the questionnaire is administered. Some surveyors, including many in marketing research, appear to have rushed to embrace CATI because of its "high-tech" image, without careful consideration of its cost-benefit mix (see Baker & Lefes, 1988; Catlin & Ingram, 1988; House & Nicholls, 1988; Nicholls, 1988; Weeks, 1988). CATI is not a panacea, but rather a tool that when properly implemented on appropriate studies has the potential to improve the quality of resulting data by reducing total survey error and/or more readily producing data that allow a researcher to conduct post hoc investigations of possible error sources.

Proper implementation of CATI calls for much more than merely purchasing computers, other hardware, and software. It also requires a substantial re-channeling of the physical and social environment within a survey facility. Ideally, the use of CATI should be based on a survey organization's desire to reduce total survey error (see Lavrakas, 1991, 1996). CATI offers great promise for those concerned with minimizing TSE, but it should never be viewed as a "technological fix" that replaces the need for intensive human quality control procedures. Just the opposite is true: When properly implemented, CATI allows for an increase in the quality control humans can impose on the telephone survey process.

■ *Steps in Conducting a Telephone Survey*

Anyone planning a telephone survey should develop a detailed administrative plan that lays out all the tasks that must be accomplished and identifies the personnel to be involved in each task (see Frey, 1989; Lyberg, 1988). These are the steps a researcher typically needs to perform in order to conduct high-quality telephone surveys:

1. Decide upon a sampling design, including identification of the sampling frame from which sampled units will be selected and the method of respondent selection within a sampling unit, if the sampling unit is not also the sampling element.

2. Choose a method to generate the set of telephone numbers that will be used in sampling (hereafter called the *sampling pool*) from the sampling frame.

3. Produce a call-sheet/record for each telephone number that will be used to track its call history during the field period.

4. Develop and format a draft questionnaire, typically on paper.

5. Develop a draft introduction/selection sequence and draft fallback statements for use by interviewers.

6. Pilot test and revise survey procedures and instruments.

7. Hire interviewers and supervisors, and schedule interviewer training and data collection sessions.

8. Print final questionnaires and other forms for PAPI or program them for CATI.

9. Train interviewers and supervisors.

10. Conduct fully supervised interviews.

11. Edit/code completed questionnaires and convert data into a computer-readable format if using PAPI.

12. Assign weights (if any) and perform data analysis, report preparation, and so on.

Once the topic and purpose of the survey are determined, and it is decided that a telephone survey affords the most cost-beneficial approach, the next step is to select a proper sampling design. This requires determining who will be sampled and how the sampling design will be implemented, including decisions about the population to which the survey will generalize, the sampling frame that will represent this population, and the specific method that will produce the sampling pool.

A draft questionnaire must be written and then formatted (laid out) in as user-friendly a manner as possible, so that interviewers' work will be facilitated, whether using PAPI or CATI. The sampling design will partly determine the nature and wording of questionnaire items. Along with a draft introductory "spiel" and any respondent selection sequence that must be used to select a respondent from within a sampling unit, the draft questionnaire should be pilot tested to identify potential problems and to estimate interviewer productivity (average number of completions per hour) and the average number of minutes per completion. Pilot testing of all materials and procedures is an extremely important part of any high-quality telephone survey; an adequate pilot test often can be accomplished with as few as 20-30 "practice" interviews. As part of the pilot stage, the researcher should hold a debriefing session with the interviewers who participated, the project management team, and (ideally) the survey sponsor, to identify any changes that are needed before the sampling scheme and the respondent selection procedures are finalized, and before final copies of the questionnaire and other survey forms are printed or programmed.

Before interviewing can begin, supervisory personnel and interviewers must be hired and decisions must be made about the scheduling of interviewing sessions. Training sessions must be held for supervisors and interviewers. Interviewing then begins under highly controlled conditions, as described later in this chapter. For example, supervisors listen to ongoing interviewing and constantly provide "on-the-job" training to interviewers as needed. Completed questionnaires later are coded (e.g., open-ended answers turned into quantitative categories), the data are entered into a computer-readable format if using PAPI, analyses are performed, and the findings are presented in whatever form may be required.

This entire process might need to be done in a few days or may play itself out over a year or longer.

■ *Sampling and Coverage Issues in Telephone Surveys*

As part of planning a telephone survey, the researcher must make a number of sampling design decisions. These include explicit identification of the following:

1. The population of inference (i.e., the group, setting, and time to which the findings must generalize)

2. The target population (i.e., the finite population that is supposedly surveyed)

3. The frame population or sampling frame (i.e., the operationalization, often in list form, of the target population)

4. The method by which a sampling pool (the actual set of telephone numbers dialed during the field period) will be created and deployed

5. The size of the final sample with whom interviews must be completed (see Groves, 1989, pp. 81-132; Henry, 1990; Kish, 1965; Lavrakas, 1993)

As part of this decision process, the researcher must choose between the use of a probability sample and the use of a nonprobability sample. As Henry (1990) notes, the great advantage of probability samples is that "the bias and likely error stemming from [their use] can be rigorously examined and estimated; [not so] for nonprobability samples" (p. 32; see also Chapter 4, this volume). As such, it is only with probability samples that the portion of total survey error that is due to sampling variance can be quantified. A probability sample provides every element in the sampling frame a known chance of selection (i.e., a known nonzero probability), whereas a nonprobability sample does not.

☐ *Sampling Frames and Generating Sampling Pools*

The sampling frame is the actual "list" that is used to represent the population being studied. If any part of the population is missing from the sampling frame, it is possible that the survey will have coverage error, as might result if a telephone directory is used as the sampling frame for a survey of the general public, because any directory will be missing unpublished/unlisted household numbers. Whether or not a person/household has a published number might be correlated with the variables being measured by the survey, and if it is, sampling from a directory will yield biased measures of the general public (e.g., in measuring political party affiliation and political attitudes, Democrats are underrepresented in a sampling frame of households with listed telephone numbers). It is from the sampling frame that the sampling pool is chosen.

The concept of a sampling pool is not often addressed explicitly in the survey methods literature. A naive observer might assume, for example, that a telephone survey in which 1,000 persons were interviewed actually sampled only those 1,000 persons and no others—but this is almost never the case, for many reasons, including the problem of nonresponse (as discussed later). Thus a surveyor is faced with the reality of often needing many more telephone numbers for interviewers to process than the total number of interviews the survey requires. What follows is a description of the major considerations and methods that are used to create telephone survey sampling pools. For more practical details about sampling in general, and about sampling for telephone surveys in particular, see Henry (1990; see also Chapter 4, this volume) and Lavrakas (1993, pp. 27-97).

Commercial List Vendors

Many organizations and persons who conduct telephone surveys nowadays purchase the telephone numbers (i.e., their sampling pools) from one of several companies that create lists (i.e., sampling frames) from which the sampling pools can be drawn. These lists include local telephone directories, master address lists, subscriber lists, customer lists, professional organization lists, and others. There are also companies that actually create a variety of telephone survey sampling pools, in addition to the sampling frames, for purchase, including numbers for random-digit dialing (RDD) surveying. (Many of these sampling pools can be generated so that they are stratified along some characteristic of interest to the surveyor, e.g., zip code.) However, as attractive as this may appear, a surveyor must be cautious in using telephone numbers assembled/created by outside parties, especially concerning possible coverage errors in the frames/lists. In particular, many sampling pools of the general public will contain mistakes in coverage—both errors of omission (households in the area but not sampled) and errors of commission (sampled households not in the area). This happens because telephone exchanges/prefixes do not always perfectly match geopolitical boundaries. Whereas the errors of commission can be handled through the addition of a geographic screening sequence to the survey's introduction, errors of omission by their very nature are hard to detect and correct.

If the surveyor chooses to purchase a sampling pool—or a sampling frame from which to generate his or her own sampling pool—the careful surveyor also must be a careful consumer. In particular, the surveyor should make certain that all questions are answered to his or her satisfaction regarding exactly how the master list (the sampling frame) and the purchased sampling pool were created. For example, Where does the firm get its original database information? How often is the information updated? What coverage problems does the firm acknowledge to exist in its own list? Remember that random sampling from a "master list" will not lead to a representative (valid) sample of the target population if coverage error is associated with the manner in which the master list was assembled. In sum, I heartily agree with Lepkowski's (1988) advice that "it is often unacceptable for this critical phase of survey operations [i.e., generating one's sampling pool] to be out of [the surveyor's] direct control" (p. 79).

Possible Coverage Error and the Prevalence of "Missing" Numbers

Assuming that telephone sampling will be done of the public at large, and that the purpose of the survey is to estimate population parameters within a given geographic area, two factors will often influence the researcher's decision of whether to use some form of RDD or to draw a probability sample from a directory or other listing. These factors are (a) the proportion of households with unlisted telephone numbers and (b) residential mobility within the area. Experience shows that surveys designed to gather valid estimates of population parameters in large cities will almost always require RDD, given that as many as half of all residential telephone numbers will not be published in the current directory; in many California municipalities, this figure often is closer to two-thirds of households with unlisted numbers (see Survey Sampling, 1992). In smaller cities and suburbs, the proportion of residential telephone numbers missing from the local directory is smaller, whereas in some rural areas it may be so small as to eliminate the need to employ RDD. But this varies a great deal across the United States.

To make an informed decision about directory sampling versus RDD, the researcher needs to know the approximate proportion of households whose numbers are not published. Sometimes local telephone companies will provide this information, but often they will not. In the latter instance, the surveyor needs to estimate this proportion. One approach to estimation is to determine the approximate number of residential telephone numbers in the local directory, adjust it for multiple household listings, and compare it to census statistics on the number of households in the sampling area. In general, if the proportion of unlisted numbers exceeds 20%, I would recommend the researcher use an RDD frame to be safe in sampling the general public.

If the surveyor decides to use a form of RDD, another important element he or she must consider in deciding what approach to use to generate the sampling pool is the amount of resources (including paid and unpaid person-time) available for generating sampling pools versus those available for interviewing. In some cases it may be cheaper to use a relatively inexpensive but inefficient RDD sampling pool—"inefficient" in that a relatively small proportion (less than 50%) of its numbers reach eligible households/persons—whereas in other cases it may be prudent to use a relatively expensive yet highly efficient sampling pool.

Random-Digit Dialing Sampling Pools

First proposed by Cooper (1964), random-digit dialing comprises a group of probability sampling techniques that provide a nonzero chance of reaching any household with a telephone access line in a sampling area (assuming all exchanges/prefixes in the area are represented in the frame), regardless of whether its telephone number is published or listed. RDD does not provide an equal probability of reaching every telephone household in a sampling area because some households have more than one telephone number. For households with two or more numbers, postsampling adjustments (weighting) typically need to be made before the data are analyzed to correct for this unequal probability of selection; thus data must be gathered via the questionnaire in RDD sampling about how many telephone numbers reach each household.

Recent estimates are that about one in three residential telephone numbers in the United States is unlisted (Survey Sampling, 1992). Despite what is often believed, it is lower-income, minority Americans, as a group, who are most likely to have unlisted telephone numbers. Thus income is generally inversely related to nonlisting. The unlisted problem is likely to increase total survey error in telephone surveys of the public if a directory is used because it does not represent a random subset of the citizenry that chooses not to list telephone numbers. In theory, using RDD eliminates the potential problem of coverage error that might result from missing households with unlisted telephone numbers.

Once the surveyor knows all telephone exchanges, or prefixes (i.e., the first three digits in a local telephone number), that ring within the sampling boundaries, he or she can use various techniques to add random suffixes (the last four digits of telephone numbers) to produce seven-digit local numbers. These RDD numbers may or may not be working and, if working, may or may not reach households. Thus the first step in generating a sampling pool for most RDD techniques is to assemble an exhaustive list of prefixes that ring within the geographic boundaries of the sampling area. This is often not a straightforward or easy task. Sometimes the boundaries of the sampling area and the boundaries of the prefixes that ring in the sampling area coincide exactly or at least closely; in other cases, the boundaries do not overlap closely. (In this instance, RDD sampling may have to be ruled out as too costly, because it may be impractical—too expensive and/or time-consuming—to screen accurately for geographically eligible households, which in turn may negate the value of conducting a telephone survey.)

Once a set of prefixes is assembled, the researcher can create an RDD sampling pool by having a computer randomly add four digits to each prefix, over and over again, until a large enough pool of numbers is created. The researcher should devise some way of eliminating duplicates, as occasionally they will be created by chance. If an RDD sampling pool is created by a surveyor who only knows/uses prefix information, only about one in four numbers will reach households. This leads to a lot of resources later being used to have interviewers dial nonworking and nonresidential numbers, and this is very inefficient, even though it does provide the "purest" RDD sampling possible. In order to create an efficient RDD sampling pool—one that reaches households with a majority of its numbers—the researcher must also know (a) the approximate number of residential telephone access lines in operation for each prefix in the sampling area and (b) the range of four-digit suffixes within which residential numbers have been assigned. Although there are many ways to use this information, the simplest is described below and is practical only to the extent that one or a few telephone directories cover the sampling area, as in the case of a citywide or metropolitan-area survey. For a statewide or national survey, this approach would be impractical, and readers are encouraged to seek other instruction, such as in Frey (1989) or Lavrakas (1993).

Using the most recent telephone directory in a local area, the surveyor systematically samples a "large number" of telephone numbers. For example, if the size of a sampling pool will need to be 3,000, then I would recommend sampling at least 500 or 600 numbers from the local directory. The surveyor enters these into a computer-readable file, which he or she can readily manipulate. (By *manipulate*, I mean the surveyor has some way of replacing the last two or three digits in the listed numbers with random digits, for example using the random-number functions in SPSSPC or some other software.) In this example, if the surveyor started with 500 listed "seed" numbers and wanted to end with 3,000 RDD numbers, he or she would need to create six "random replicates" with different final digits for each of the original seed numbers. This is by far the most efficient way to create an efficient RDD sampling pool, and basically this is what list vendors do when they create RDD sampling pools to sell.

However, before using this approach, the surveyor should decide whether or not there is likely to be coverage error resulting within a given sampling area. This could happen with this simple RDD technique if there are significantly differential proportions of numbers that are listed/unlisted on each prefix, and in many big cities, this will happen. If so, this approach to creating an RDD sampling pool will underrepresent those prefixes, and thus those people, that have the greatest proportions of unlisted numbers. For example, with Chicago's racially segregated neighborhoods, prefixes that disproportionately reach African Americans will be underrepresented in such a sampling pool, which in turn will lead to an undersampling of African Americans by the survey. (And this is exactly what happens in some purchased RDD sampling pools.)

If this is a serious concern, the researcher is urged to consider using a traditional multistage RDD sampling scheme, such as the Mitofsky-Waksberg RDD cluster sample (Mitofsky, 1970; Waksberg, 1978), which can be very complicated to implement. However, even this approach has its trade-off in somewhat increasing the survey's sampling error (see discussion of "design effects" in Groves, 1989; Henry, 1990; Kish, 1965; Lepkowski, 1988). However, in evaluating this trade-off, Groves (1989) observes that "despite the loss of precision for survey statistics from cluster samples, every major U.S. federal government household survey and almost all academic and commercial household surveys use cluster designs" (p. 260).

Sampling From a Directory or Other List

Depending on a survey's purpose, there are many instances in which RDD may be unnecessary and/or inappropriate to meet the surveyor's needs, such as in surveying rare population subsets in the public, customers or clients who have recently bought some product or used some service, or CEOs and other professionals at their places of work. Sampling in these instances will typically be more economical and feasible if done from a good list (the sampling frame). However, the main concern with this type of sampling is that accurate lists often are not available, and it may be very expensive for the surveyor to assemble a list that is without serious coverage problems. Therefore, it is best for the researcher in such a situation to proceed very carefully. In some instances the researcher may be forced to conclude that a valid telephone survey cannot be conducted with the resources that are available.

There are several problems associated with list sampling for telephone surveys, including restricted access, ineligible listings, duplicate listings, incorrect listings (errors of commission or "false positives"), and omitted listings (errors of omission or "false negatives"). The fact that approximately one in five Americans changes residence each year causes many lists to have outdated home telephone numbers. An example of creating a sampling pool from a list would be a telephone survey of members of a professional organization in which the organization has a complete enumeration of each member's home and/or business telephone number; this listing would serve as the sampling frame. Another example of list sampling would be a telephone survey of students currently enrolled at a university, in which a list from the registrar's office would be the sampling frame.

Forming a sampling pool through list sampling is uncomplicated and usually is done systematically—that is, using a "systematic simple random sample" or a "systematic stratified random sample" (each of these sampling strategies is described elsewhere in this book). This works as follows, using an example of a school district that wants to interview 200 teachers from a staff of 1,800, thus one-ninth of the staff should be sampled (assuming there would a 100% response rate). This fraction (1/9 or 1 in 9) is termed the *sampling interval.* After identifying the sampling interval, the researcher's next step is to select a random number from 1 through 9 and count that many names from the start of the alphabetical listing to sample the first teacher. After that, the researcher simply chooses every ninth name on the list. If the random start is the number 2, then the second teacher on the list would be the first name to enter the sampling pool. After that, the pool would include the 11th name, the 20th name, the 29th, the 38th, and so on. Nowadays, with many listings readily available in computer-readable form or easily put into such form, a researcher may use existing software (or write a simple program in BASIC) to avoid doing the sampling manually, especially if the list is a long one.

With list sampling, it is important that the researcher remember to employ a technique that chooses names throughout the entire listing, and that is exactly what systematic sampling accomplishes. Because lists are typically alphabetized, this results in a representative sampling pool chosen from throughout the alphabet. Similarly, if a list is ordered by seniority (or some other attribute), sampling across the entire listing will generate a stratified random sampling pool that is uncorrelated with length of membership and assures representation across the seniority variable (or whatever other attribute the list is ordered by). Furthermore, this stratification may lead to a reduction in sampling error (see Henry, 1990, p. 101).

For sampling households/persons within small geographic areas, such as neighborhoods, the researcher can use reverse directories—ones that have listings ordered by number and/or by address—in cases where RDD sampling would prove too costly, providing that coverage error (due to missing households with unlisted numbers) would not invalidate the survey's purpose. To determine the number of households to sample per block, it is best for the researcher to use a detailed street map. If the map shows actual housing units, then proportional sampling can be done to represent the approximate population per block in the final sample. If this level of information is not readily available, the surveyor may simply count the number of block faces in the geographic sampling area and divide the desired size of the sampling pool by this amount. The quotient would then be used as the number of telephone numbers to sample per block (although this approach does not take into account variable population density per block). The proper use of a reverse directory also requires that accurate information be available about the starting and ending address number on each block—thus the advantage provided by a detailed street-level map. (Such maps are often available from local government planning departments.)

In sum, the greatest concern that telephone surveyors face when using lists is the possibility of contributing coverage error to the survey because of what is missing from, or inaccuracies in, the lists. If the size of "noncoverage" is small and/or not likely to be correlated with whatever the survey is measuring, then list sampling is likely to be the most cost-beneficial approach to sampling. However, if the general public is being sampled, most telephone surveys will need to utilize RDD sampling pools.

☐   *Within-Unit Respondent Selection/Screening Techniques*

Some persons unfamiliar with valid telephone survey methods mistakenly assume that the person who initially answers the telephone is always the one who is interviewed. This is almost never the case with any survey designed to gather a representative "within-unit" sample of the general population. For example, although males and females are born at a near 50:50 rate, the adult population in most urban communities is closer to a 55:45 female/male split. A survey that strives to conduct interviews with a representative sample of an area's adult population must rely on a systematic respondent selection procedure to achieve a valid female/male balance, in part because, on average, a female is more likely than a male to answer the telephone when an interviewer calls. Thus always interviewing the first person who answers the telephone would lead to an oversampling of females.

Obviously, when sampling is done from a list and the respondent is known by name, "respondent selection" requires merely that the interviewer ask to speak with that person. But in many instances with list sampling, and with all RDD sampling, the interviewer will not know the name of the person within the household who should be interviewed, unless this has been learned in a previous contact with the household. Therefore, a survey designed to gather estimates of person-level population parameters (as opposed to household-level measures) must employ a systematic selection technique to maximize external validity by lessening the chance of within-unit noncoverage error.

As a rule, interviewers should neither be allowed to interview the first person who answers the telephone nor be allowed to interview anyone who is merely "willing" to be surveyed. Instead, the interviewer should select one designated respondent in a systematic and unbiased fashion from among all possible "eligible respondents" within the unit; generally, "possibly eligibles" are all persons within the unit who meet the survey's demographic/experiential definition of a respondent.

Respondents can be selected within a sampling unit using a true probability sampling scheme—one that gives every possibly eligible respondent a known and nonzero chance of selection—although surveyors will not always need nor necessarily want to employ such an approach. For the purposes of most surveys, it is acceptable to use a procedure that systematically balances selection along the lines of both gender and age. Because most sampling units (e.g., households) are quite homogeneous on many other demographic characteristics (e.g., race, education, religion), random sampling of units should provide adequate coverage of the population on these other demographic factors.

During the past 30 years, most of the techniques that commonly have been employed for respondent selection were devised to be minimally intrusive about gathering personal information at the start of the interviewer's contact with the household, while attempting to provide a demographically balanced sample of respondents across an entire survey. Because asking for "sensitive" information before adequate trust has been developed by the interviewer can seriously increase refusals, and thus nonresponse, surveyors have tried to strike a somewhat difficult balance in their respondent selection techniques, between avoiding coverage error and avoiding nonresponse error.

The Kish Method of Random Selection

The most rigorous respondent selection method that has been used in many sample surveys, and the accepted standard for in-person interviews, was developed by Kish (1949, 1965). This method can also be used in telephone surveys that require as complete a representation as possible of all eligibles from within sampling units. The Kish method minimizes noncoverage within sampling units compared with other less rigorous selection methods, although, due to its intrusive nature, it may increase refusal/nonresponse rates, especially when used by relatively unskilled interviewers.

In the Kish selection method, immediately after reading the introductory spiel, the interviewer identifies all eligibles within the sampling unit. In most cases this means determining all persons living in the household who meet the survey's age criterion. Some surveyors prefer to have interviewers identify eligibles in terms of the familial relationships within the household, whereas others have interviewers ask for eligibles' first names. Either way, it is typical for the interviewer to begin by identifying the household head(s) and then follow by listing other eligibles. For example, assuming the survey is sampling adults, an interviewer will most commonly begin by recording the "husband" and the "wife," because this is the most frequent adult composition in U.S. households. After the interviewer has made certain that all eligibles are accounted for, he or she asks for and records the age of each person listed. The interviewer then pauses, briefly, to check that the age of each person listed meets the age requirements of the survey, eliminating any who do not meet the requirements from further consideration. Then the interviewer rank orders all eligibles according to the following traditional rule: oldest male numbered 1, next-oldest male (if there is one) numbered 2, and so on through all males listed, then followed by oldest female, next-oldest female, and so forth. The interviewer next consults one of several versions of a "selection table" to determine which one person should be interviewed for that household. Of course, with Kish, as with any selection method, if there is only one eligible person in the household, then that person automatically becomes the selected respondent. Used across an entire survey, Kish comes very close to providing a truly random within-unit selection of all possible eligible respondents in the units that are sampled. (More details about using the Kish method in telephone surveys are explained in Lavrakas, 1993, pp. 108-111.)

Birthday Methods for Respondent Selection

In the past two decades, a different and much more streamlined approach for yielding, in theory, a probability selection of respondents within sampling units has been explored (see Lavrakas, Merkle, & Bauman, 1993; Oldendick, Sorenson, Tuchfarber, & Bishop, 1985; O'Rourke & Blair, 1983; Salmon & Nichols, 1983). In using these "birthday" methods, the interviewer asks either for the eligible person within the sampling unit whose birthday was "most recent" or for the eligible who will have the "next birthday." Due to their nonintrusive nature and the heterogeneous within-unit sample they produce, birthday selection methods have been widely embraced in telephone surveys by academic, public sector, and private sector surveyors. Because birthday selection methods are neither intrusive nor time-consuming and are easy for interviewers to administer, their appeal is great. In particular, it is thought that nonresponse is lessened by such an easy, nonintrusive approach to respondent selection.

After reading the introductory spiel, the interviewer using a birthday selection method asks for a respondent with wording such as the following: "For this survey, I'd like to speak with the person in your household, 18 years of age or older, who had the last birthday." (Note that interviewers should be trained to explain, if necessary, that *last* means most recent.) There is evidence suggesting that the birthday methods lead to the correct eligible being interviewed in most, but not all, cases (Lavrakas et al., 1993); however, these errors appear to be random across a sample. More research is needed before we can be certain of the validity of these techniques, but in the meantime researchers should continue to consider the use of this widely popular respondent selection method.

Systematic Quota Selection Methods

Troldahl and Carter (1964) have proposed a method that is less intrusive than the Kish approach for systematically (not randomly) selecting respondents (however, compared with the birthday methods, it too is quite intrusive). Bryant (1975) has suggested a modification of the Troldahl-Carter method to try to compensate for the undersampling of males that seems to result with the original approach.

As described here, the Troldahl-Carter-Bryant (T-C-B) selection method reflects a further refinement based on the findings of Czaja, Blair, and Sebestik (1982). The T-C-B method requires the interviewer to ask two questions as part of the introduction/selection sequence: (a) How many persons _____ years or older live in your household, including yourself? (b) How many of these are women? The age delimiter used in the first question is determined by the needs of each particular survey, but in most cases it is 18 (i.e., adults are selected). Somewhat as in the Kish approach, the interviewer then uses one of several versions of a "selection table" to select objectively one respondent in each sampled unit. In theory, by mixing the versions of the selection matrices a survey will end with a proper balance (quota) of females and males and of younger and older adults compared with the target population. However, in practice even the prescribed combination of versions typically results in a slight undersampling of males, unless adjustments are made throughout the survey period.

(Other within-unit respondent quota sampling techniques are described in Lavrakas, 1993, pp. 113-116, but their use is not generally recommended, as none of them appear superior to the birthday methods.)

Other Criteria for Respondent Selection

Whenever a telephone survey requires only a certain type of respondent (e.g., women between the ages of 30 and 49 who are college graduates), the researcher will need to employ other respondent selection (or screening) methods. Some surveys require interviews only with heads of households, or taxpayers, or registered voters, for example. For other surveys, researchers may need to select people who live within a relatively small geographic boundary, or some unique subsample of the general population. For more information about how to sample within households for "head of household," "likely voters," and other subsets of the adult population, including those who live within certain small area boundaries, see Lavrakas (1993, pp. 116-120).

Regardless of the respondent selection method the researcher chooses, the method should be tested along with the questionnaire in any pilot study that is implemented. This will provide the researcher with a chance to look for evidence that the method and its interaction with the group of interviewers being used and respondents being sampled may be contributing errors of omission or commission.

In sum, respondent selection is a nonissue for any telephone survey in which respondents are sampled by name. However, in a survey that does not sample people by name, the researcher's purpose in using a systematic within-unit respondent selection procedure is to choose one and only one person from within each sampling unit in an unbiased fashion—one that will not contribute to possible coverage error.

□ *How CATI Can Help with Potential Coverage Error*

There is little computer-assisted telephone interviewing can do to affect the potential for unit coverage error in a telephone survey (i.e., potential error that may result from the use of a sampling frame that does not fully cover the target population). However, CATI can be deployed so as to lessen the chance of within-unit coverage error through the control it can afford over the respondent selection process (Lavrakas, 1996). Depending upon the complexity of the respondent selection sequence used to choose one respondent to interview per sampled unit, and/or the complexity of any screening sequence used to qualify a unit, use of CATI for these tasks should reduce the potential for within-unit coverage-related errors. For example, a survey of the public that uses RDD with geographic screening to reach households within a relatively small area of a city will require interviewers to take each household informant through a series of questions to determine whether or not the household is located within the survey's target boundaries. The more complicated the sequence, the greater the advantage that CATI (versus PAPI) can have in leading interviewers and respondents to complete it properly, thus avoiding errors of omission and commission. Selection of respondents from within the sampling unit among all eligible unit members should also be accomplished more accurately with CATI. For example, use of a Kish randomized selection procedure with CATI should not only be easy for interviewers to implement to select correct respondents, but random assignment of the eight versions of the Kish selection tables can more be readily achieved in their prescribed proportions with CATI than with PAPI.

□ *Sampling and Coverage in Mixed-Mode Surveys*

The past decade has seen a growing interest in surveys that combine two or more modes of sampling and data collection. The appeal of combining different survey modes—personal, telephone, and/or mail—follows the reasoning that total survey error may be reduced if the limitations of one mode are offset by the strengths of another (see Dillman & Tarnai, 1988).

For the surveyor who is planning how a sampling pool will be generated, use of a mixed-mode approach may require additional time and resources to assemble the sampling frame(s) but in the end may bring the payoff of better coverage of the population. For example, a survey of a specific community that does not conform well with the geographic boundaries of the telephone prefixes that reach the area might employ a "dual-frame" approach by combining the mail and telephone modes. The sampling pool for the part to be done by telephone could be selected systematically from a reverse directory; this would cover only households with listed telephone numbers at the time the directory was printed. The sampling pool for the part to be done via mail could be generated from block/address maps obtained from the city's housing department, also with systematic random sampling. (Note that it would be necessary to eliminate possible duplicate households sampled via both methods.) Because each of the households in the telephone sampling pool has a listed address, advance letters could be mailed to inform residents they have been selected for the telephone survey, to reduce nonresponse (as explained in the next section). The mail portion would require several follow-up mailings to reduce nonresponse and should include an item asking whether or not the household has a telephone and, if so, if the number is listed or unlisted. This information would allow the surveyor to investigate any differences that may exist in the data associated with each mode.

All in all, it remains the responsibility of the researcher to determine how best to use the survey's fixed budget so as to balance the possibility of reducing coverage error by using a mixed-mode approach versus the cost of doing so— that is, whether the potential for gains is "justified when costs and other error considerations are taken into account" (Lepkowski, 1988, p. 98).

■ *Nonresponse Issues in Telephone Surveys*

A high-quality telephone survey must have a formal system in place to control the use of numbers released from the sampling pool in order to avoid the considerable nonresponse that would likely result if interviewers were allowed simply to choose telephone numbers from the sampling pool at will. For example, only through use of a highly routinized callback system will hard-to-reach respondents be recontacted a requisite number of times. If this is not done, the final interviewed sample will include a disproportionate number of easier-to-contact respondents. Because harder-to-contact respondents in a survey of the general population are more likely to be younger and male, and easier-to-contact respondents are more likely to be older and female, the potential threat of nonresponse error attributable to noncontacts would be increased and the external validity of the final sample may be compromised. This may happen because demographic factors typically associated with noncontacts (e.g., age and gender) are often correlated with the topical focus of a survey.

A similar concern exists for potential nonresponse error associated with refusals, unless a formal system is in place to control the processing of the sampling pool. A formal system also improves interviewer efficiency by removing the burden of scheduling callbacks from interviewers, regardless of whether the survey involves CATI or PAPI. Furthermore, if efforts are made to "convert" initial refusals (i.e., calling back those who initially refused to complete the interview in order to try to convince them to do so), these refusal-conversion callbacks can be individually rescheduled at times deemed best by the supervisory personnel controlling the sampling pool.

□ *Controlling Sampling Pools*

In a PAPI telephone survey, the control and sorting of processed telephone numbers from the sampling pool is done manually. Even in CATI environments, there are many firms that control their sampling pools by hand, rather than by computer, using the computer only to control the administration of the questionnaire and data entry. Thus the approach discussed here is instructive regardless of whether PAPI or CATI will be used, including a full-CATI system that also controls the sampling pool.

There are three basic steps to controlling a sampling pool manually: (a) Each interviewer is given a relatively small group of telephone numbers with which to start each interviewing session; (b) a supervisor provides additional numbers, as needed, to interviewers during the interviewing session; and (c) before the next session begins, someone must "sort" the group of numbers processed during the previous session. Experience strongly recommends that one person should be given responsibility for this final step, assuming the size of the surveying effort makes this feasible. (For example, if 100 interviews are completed per day, the size of the sampling pool that is being processed each day can easily be managed by one person. However, if several hundred interviews are being completed each day, one person cannot manage this alone.) The preferred way for the researcher to institute this level of control over the sampling pool is through the use of a separate call-sheet (as shown in Figure 15.1), sometimes called a call record or interviewer report form, for each telephone number released from the sampling pool. If there is a unique call-sheet for each number dialed by interviewers, a dialing history can be constructed that explains what happened each time a particular number was tried.

Even with full-CATI systems, there is an on-screen equivalent of the call-sheet that controls and facilitates interviewers' processing of the numbers in the sampling pool. Where full-CATI differs from PAPI in how a sampling pool is controlled is the automatic scheduling rules that can be programmed into the system, which replace some of the human decision making needed with PAPI.

Every telephone number released from the sampling pool in a PAPI survey should be printed on a separate call-sheet on which interviewers record information that allows supervisory personnel to decide what to do with each number that has been processed. To clarify the meaning of the phrase *released from*

User Supplied Title

Telephone Number ###-#### Questionnaire #: __ __ __ __

Contact attempts	Date	Time	Disposition code	Interviewer ID
1	__/__	__:__	__ __	__ __
2	__/__	__:__	__ __	__ __
3	__/__	__:__	__ __	__ __
4	__/__	__:__	__ __	__ __
5	__/__	__:__	__ __	__ __
6	__/__	__:__	__ __	__ __
7	__/__	__:__	__ __	__ __
8	__/__	__:__	__ __	__ __
9	__/__	__:__	__ __	__ __
10	__/__	__:__	__ __	__ __

NOTES

1. ______________________________
2. ______________________________
3. ______________________________
4. ______________________________
5. ______________________________
6. ______________________________
7. ______________________________
8. ______________________________
9. ______________________________
10. ______________________________

Figure 15.1. Example of a Call-Sheet

the sampling pool, I should remind readers that it is not necessary to process all numbers in the sampling pool. Whereas it is highly recommended that the entire sampling pool be generated in advance of the start of interviewing (as discussed in Lavrakas, 1993, pp. 55-58), telephone numbers from the sampling pool are released to interviewers only as needed.

To reduce the size of the survey's nonresponse and the possibility of nonresponse error, supervisors should see to it that all numbers released from the sampling pool are fully processed (i.e., called back an adequate number of times). Neither nonresponse error nor total survey error is inflated when all the numbers originally generated to reach the desired number of completions are not released, assuming the numbers that were released are a random subset of all those generated.

Figure 15.1 is an example of a basic call-sheet. The purpose of the call-sheet is to provide interviewers with a formalized structure for recording important information about every dialing of each telephone number that is released from the sampling pool. The information to be written on the call-sheet includes the date, time, and disposition of each dialing. Information on the disposition takes the form of a code (e.g., for ring-no answer, busy, out of order, refusal, completed, or callback). The interviewer also should record her or his ID number with each dialing. Finally, the form provides space for annotations, which can be extremely helpful to both the person who sorts the call-sheets and any interviewer who may subsequently redial the telephone number.

A call-sheet is attached to a questionnaire only after an interview has been completed. As shown in Figure 15.1, the telephone number can be printed in the upper-left corner and space is provided toward the upper right so that a unique questionnaire identification number (or case number) can be assigned. Call-sheets for different surveys should be printed with different titles and on different colored paper when a group of interviewers is conducting two or more surveys simultaneously. It is important that interviewers record the date and time of each call, because this information can aid in subsequent decisions that are made about the call-sheet. For example, because call attempts are spaced throughout the period the survey is being fielded, having the date and time recorded allows supervisory personnel to determine best when to reprocess a number. In some cases, especially with numbers that consistently ring without answer, the person controlling the sampling pool must hold aside call-sheets for particular days and times. Accountability is the primary reason for having interviewers record their ID numbers.

The most important information that is recorded on the call-sheet is found in the disposition codes that indicate the outcomes of every dialing. The disposition codes allow supervisors to sort the call-sheets quickly and efficiently after each interviewing session. The set of disposition categories and their associated numerical codes may be fairly exhaustive for most telephone surveys; these can be easily collapsed into broader categories or expanded into more discrete categories (see Table 15.1 for an example of some disposition codes). The critical point for most telephone surveys is that a numerical coding scheme should be used by interviewers in order to enhance the ability of supervisory personnel to control the sampling pool. (For more detailed information about the different dispositions that can be expected in telephone survey dialing and how they can affect the size of the nonresponse that remains at the end of the field period, see Lavrakas, 1993, pp. 61-78.)

A goal of every high-quality telephone survey should be to achieve as high a response rate as resources allow, while balancing this against other survey error considerations. And it is only through a well-planned and well-implemented scheme to control the sampling pool that high response rates will result.

☐ *Introductory Spiels*

The introduction that the interviewer reads upon first making contact with a potential respondent is critical for the success of the survey. A poorly worded introductory spiel will lead to many refusals and can increase nonresponse error to a point that entirely invalidates the survey. There are differing opinions among survey professionals regarding how much information should be given in the introductory spiel, and the research literature does not provide a definitive answer (see Groves & Lyberg, 1988, pp. 202-210). I side with those who

Table 15.1 Example of Disposition Codes for Controlling a Sampling Pool

Disposition Code	Explanation
10	No answer after seven rings
11	Busy, after one immediate redial
12	Answering machine (residence)
13	Household language barrier
14	Answered by nonresident
15	Household refusal: Use 15H for immediate hang-up without comment
20	Disconnected or other nonworking
21	Temporarily disconnected
22	Business, other nonresidence
23	No one meets eligibility criteria
30	Contact only: Use 30A for appointment
31	Selected respondent temporarily unavailable
32	Selected respondent unavailable during field period
33	Selected respondent unavailable due to physical/mental disability
34	Language barrier with selected respondent
35	Refusal by selected respondent
36	Partial interview: Use 36R for refusal
37	Completed interview

believe the introduction should be reasonably brief, so that the respondent can be actively engaged via the start of the questionnaire. Exceptions to this rule exist, as in cases where introductions must contain instructions regarding how the questionnaire is organized or about unusual types of questions. Furthermore, although the content of the spiel is important, how well interviewers deploy it is probably even more important.

I recommend that an introductory spiel contain enough information to reduce as much as possible any apprehension and uncertainty on the part of the person answering the telephone who hears that a stranger is calling to conduct a survey interview (see Frey, 1989, pp. 125-137). In other words, the credibility of the interviewer (and thus the survey effort) must be established as soon as possible, and it is the task of the introduction to do this. At the same time, experience demonstrates that it is easier to get someone's full cooperation once he or she begins the questionnaire—somewhat like the "foot-in-the-door" technique. Thus logic suggests that the longer the introduction and the more a potential respondent must listen without active involvement, the greater the

---

INTRODUCTION/SELECTION SHEET: EVANSTON ANTICRIME SURVEY

Hello, my name is _____, and I'm calling from the Northwestern University Survey Laboratory. We are conducting a short random survey of Evanston residents in cooperation with the Evanston Police Department. The purpose of the survey is to determine how people feel about the safety and security of their neighborhoods, so that the city can plan better anticrime programs. (Your cooperation is voluntary, but we'd greatly appreciate your help.)

Before I continue, may I please verify that this is _____? **[VERIFY TELE-PHONE NUMBER]**

User Supplied Selection Procedure

Figure 15.2. Example of an Introductory Spiel

chance he or she will lose interest before questioning even begins (Dillman, Gallegos, & Frey, 1976).

Although survey researchers may differ in the exact ways they prefer to word introductions, I strongly recommend the inclusion in every telephone survey introduction of the following information, consistent with the disclosure guidelines of the American Association for Public Opinion Research (1991) and the National Council on Public Polls (Gawiser & Witt, 1992): (a) identification of the interviewer, the interviewer's affiliation, and the survey's sponsor; (b) a brief explanation of the purpose of the survey and its sampling area (or target population); (c) some "positively" worded phrase to encourage cooperation; and (d) verification of the telephone number dialed by the interviewer.

Figure 15.2 provides an example of an introduction/selection sequence with a typical introductory spiel. This spiel begins with the interviewer's introducing her- or himself by name, identifying where the call is originating, and why the call is being made. Included in the wording about the purpose of the call is a reference to the sampling area and the survey sponsor. Whenever possible, some implicit or explicit statement should be made in the introduction about the use of the findings, unless that might confound the answers given by respondents. If the questionnaire is a short one (say under 10 minutes), I recommend mentioning its brevity in the introduction; otherwise it is best for the interviewer not to say anything about length unless asked by the respondent. Finally, the introduction must explicitly or implicitly inform the respondent that participation is voluntary and that no harm will come to him or her regardless of whether the respondent chooses to participate or not.

The introductory spiel should also include a verification of the telephone number the interviewer dialed to further professionalize the contact and to assist quality control of the processing of the sampling pool. By positioning the number verification "low" in the introductory spiel, the opportunity is created for the interviewer to develop some rapport with the respondent before this question is asked. It is especially important that the number dialed is verified in RDD surveys, both for sample control purposes and to avoid the problems that call forwarding can create (e.g., call forwarding alters the probability of selection in unknown ways).

In most surveys it is unnecessary, and thus highly inadvisable, to devise an introductory spiel that contains a detailed explanation of what the survey is about, as this is likely to increase nonresponse. For those respondents who want to know more about the survey before making a decision to participate, interviewers should be given an honest, standardized explanation to read or paraphrase. For those respondents who seem reluctant to participate, interviewers should be trained to exercise discretion and possibly to convey an even more detailed explanation of the survey's purpose.

There are some basic types of information-seeking exchanges that are occasionally initiated with interviewers by prospective respondents (see Lavrakas & Merkle, 1991). The word *occasionally* is important to keep in mind: If interviewers were asked these questions often, it would be wise to incorporate the information conveyed in the answers into the introductory spiel read to everyone. The types of information respondents sometimes ask for include (a) the purpose of the survey and how the findings will be used; (b) how the respondent's number was selected; (c) more about the survey firm and/or sponsor than simply a name; and (d) why the particular respondent selection method is being used. For each of these questions, written "fallback statements" should be provided to interviewers to enable them to give honest, standardized answers to respondents who ask them. The goal of fallback statements is to help interviewers convince potential respondents that the survey is a worthwhile (and harmless) endeavor; this should be kept in mind by the person who composes the statements. (For more details on telephone survey introductions and fallback statements, see Frey, 1989, pp. 125-137; Lavrakas, 1993, pp. 100-105.)

☐   *Callbacks*

The majority of times that interviewers dial telephone numbers, especially with RDD sampling, they will not complete interviews. In fact, on many of the dialings in sampling the general public, interviewers will not reach anyone at all—the telephone will ring without being answered. For example, most RDD surveys with which I have had experience in the past 15 years have shown that between one-third and one-half of all dialings result in the number ringing but not being answered. The number of rings interviewers should allow before hanging up depends partly on the surveyor's preference. On the low side, four or five rings should occur before an interviewer hangs up (see Frey, 1989, p. 228; Smead & Wilcox, 1980); it is not cost-effective for interviewers to allow numbers to ring many more times. An exception would be telephone numbers that have been dialed on several previous occasions without ever being answered.

Ring-no answers and other dispositions that do not end up reaching the designated respondent should be reprocessed, interviewing session after session, until a predetermined number of callbacks have been made. How many callbacks should be made is based in part on the resources available to support the survey and on the length of the field period (i.e., the number of days from start to finish for the survey). In general, the fewer callbacks that are budgeted, the greater the proportion of numbers that will never be answered by a human (as opposed to an answering machine). The difficult trade-off a surveyor faces is to spend relatively more resources on additional callbacks, which typically yield diminishing returns the more callbacks that are made (i.e., proportionately fewer households will be reached on the 10th call attempt than on the 5th, for example).

In their seminal test of RDD sampling, Groves and Kahn (1979) estimate that only 5% of the numbers dialed more than 12 times were households. This low hit rate of households among numbers unanswered after many dialings is routinely encountered in many large-scale government-sponsored RDD studies (Maklan & Waksberg, 1988). Yet potential nonresponse error associated with these hardest-to-contact households could contribute substantially to total survey error if they are not interviewed. Interested readers are referred to Sebold's (1988) more detailed discussion of the perplexing issue of how to handle unanswered numbers in telephone surveys.

Telephone surveys of the public and of special populations will experience differing patterns of final dispositions, depending on the number of callbacks that are planned/budgeted. In market research, three callback attempts appear to be considered more than adequate by many surveyors. In contrast, many academic-based and federal government-sponsored telephone surveys typically allow for 10 or 20 or even more callbacks (see Traugott, 1987). It should be obvious that the distribution of final dispositions will differ markedly between the former case (few callbacks) and the latter.

Multivariate analyses on the number of callbacks in RDD surveys show that those persons who are reached with only a few call attempts (e.g., three or fewer) are significantly more likely to be female, less educated, unemployed, married, and older, and to report being in relatively poorer health (Merkle, Bauman, & Lavrakas, 1991). To the extent that such factors are correlated with the substantive focus of a survey, there will almost certainly be nonresponse error (bias) in the findings of any survey that conducts relatively few callbacks. Whether this bias will be large or small often is not obvious, and it remains the responsibility of the surveyor to make an a priori decision about the relative importance of the allocation of resources for more or fewer callbacks.

□   *Refusals and Refusal Conversions*

Even a telephone survey that makes numerous callbacks to minimize that number of noncontacts at the end of the field period will have a sizable minority of sampled persons/households refuse to participate. In the 1990s, in good RDD surveys of the public, refusals typically make up two-thirds or more of a survey's nonresponse and typically occur in least 20% of the households contacted. For telephone surveys that use poorly skilled and/or poorly trained interviewers and/or that have poorly crafted introductory spiels, refusals can occur at the majority of the households reached.

It is noteworthy that the vast majority of telephone survey refusals occur within the first 20-30 seconds of contact with a respondent—that is, during the introduction, before the questionnaire has begun to be administered. Traditionally, good telephone surveys have invested many resources to reduce the number of refusals, in hopes that nonresponse error that might otherwise be associated with refusals will be markedly reduced. The most important of these are the resources spent on (a) developing an effective introductory spiel and (b) employing a skilled and well-trained group of interviewers.

Refusal Avoidance Training

The single factor that seems to differentiate the best of interviewers from those who are not so good is the ability to handle difficult respondents and outright refusals. This is one of the reasons I believe that, in most cases, interviewers should not be required to read an introductory spiel exactly as it is written, but should be allowed to convey the information accurately to the respondent in some of their own words (of course, this freedom in wording accorded an interviewer is unacceptable when it comes to the reading of the actual survey items). The part of the interviewer's training that covers general expectations therefore should include a detailed discussion of the nature of refusals and explicit advice on how to be "politely persuasive" without being overly aggressive. Interested readers are encouraged to study Groves's (1989, pp. 215-236) review of the social science literature on persuasion and compliance as it relates to respondents' willingness to participate in surveys and interviewing strategies to reduce nonresponse.

Based upon two decades of experience with telephone interviewing, I believe that it is best to assume that all potential respondents need to be provided incentives for participating. Fortunately, with many respondents it seems to be enough incentive if they are told they are being helpful by providing answers. For others, it appears to make them feel important to know that it is *their* opinions that are being sought. However, for approximately one-third of all potential respondents in surveys of both the general public and special populations, interviewers will have to work harder at "selling" the interview.

In these challenging cases, one option is to assume that the timing of the contact is wrong and to suggest calling back on another occasion. Interviewers might be trained to make a statement such as, "I'm sorry we've bothered you at what is apparently a bad time." Interviewers then must exercise discretion on a case-by-case basis concerning asking if there is a better time to call back, simply stating that a callback will be made, or not saying anything else. Another option is for the interviewer to "plead" with the potential respondent. When a telephone questionnaire is a relatively short one (i.e., can be administered in 10 minutes or less), an interviewer can try to convince a reluctant respondent that it will not take very long. Another tactic for countering reluctance is to state that any question the respondent is uncomfortable answering may be left unanswered. Or interviewers can be trained to give several levels of assurance of both the legitimacy and importance of the survey through use of the survey's fallback statements. However, the simple provision of assurances, such as offering the respondent the name and phone number of the project director, often goes a long way toward alleviating the concerns of a reluctant respondent. As a last resort, the interviewer might consider reminding the respondent that by cooperating, the respondent is helping the interviewer earn a living (or, for the unpaid interviewer, the respondent is helping the interviewer fulfill her or his obligation). By personalizing the issue of cooperation, the interviewer is neither referring to an abstract incentive, such as "to help plan better social programs," nor appealing in the name of another party (the survey organization or sponsor).

In addition to training interviewers about *what* to say to minimize the refusals they experience, researchers should train them in *how* to say it—in terms of both attitude and voice. Collins, Sykes, Wilson, and Blackshaw (1988) found that less successful interviewers, when confronted with problems such as reluctant respondents, "showed a lack of confidence and a tendency to panic; they seemed unprepared for problems, gave in too easily, and failed to avoid 'deadends' " (p. 229). The confidence that successful interviewers feel is conveyed in the way they speak. Oksenberg and Cannell (1988) have reported that "dominance" appears to win out, with interviewers with low refusal rates being "generally more potent" (p. 268), rather than trying to be overly friendly, ingratiating, and/or nonthreatening. In terms of interviewers' voices, Oksenberg and Cannell found that those who spoke somewhat faster, louder, with greater confidence, and in a "falling" tone (declarative versus interrogative) had the lowest refusal rates.

Refusal Conversions

Due in part to small but continuing difficulties in eliciting respondent cooperation over the past two decades, procedures have been developed and tested that are designed to lessen the potential problems refusals may cause (see Lyberg & Dean, 1992). One approach involves the use of a structured refusal report form (RRF) that the interviewer completes after encountering a refusal. This form can provide information that may help the sampling pool controller and interviewers in subsequent efforts to convert refusals—calling back at another time to try to convince a respondent to complete the interview after a refusal was previously encountered—and may help the surveyor learn more about the size and nature of potential nonresponse error. If a surveyor chooses to incorporate an RRF into the sampling process, it is not entirely

---

User Supplied Title

Interviewer #: _____

1. Did the person who refused have the last (most recent) birthday?
   Yes 35
   No/Uncertain 15

2. Demographics of the person refusing:

GENDER	*AGE*	*RACE*
Female 1	Child 0	Asian 1
Male 2	Adult < 30 1	Black 2
Uncertain 9	30-59 Yrs 2	Hispanic 3
	60 or Older 3	White 4
	Uncertain 9	Uncertain 9

3. Reason for refusal: _____
   _____

4. Strength of refusal: VERY WEAK 1 2 3 4 5 6 7 VERY STRONG
   Respondent attitude: VERY POLITE 1 2 3 4 5 6 7 VERY RUDE
                    NOT AT ALL ANGRY 1 2 3 4 5 6 7 VERY ANGRY

5. Did you tell the person:

		YES	*NO*
A.	How he or she was sampled?	1	 2
B.	The nature/purpose of survey beyond the *standard* intro?	1	 2
C.	Confidentiality?	1	 2
D.	How the data would be used?	1	 2
E.	Verification with supervisor/sponsor? . .	1	 2

6. What can you recommend, if anything, for gaining respondent/household cooperation if a conversion attempt were made?
   _____
   _____
   _____

[PLEASE STAPLE TO CALL-SHEET AND RETURN TO SUPERVISOR]

Figure 15.3. Example of a Refusal Report Form

obvious what information should be recorded. That is, as of the mid-1990s, use of these forms has not received much attention in the survey methods literature. With this in mind, I urge interested readers to consider the following discussion of RRFs as suggestive, and to follow the future literature on this topic.

Figure 15.3 is an example of an RRF that my organization typically uses (a form such as this could be deployed in either PAPI or CATI surveys). The interviewer completes the RRF immediately after encountering a refusal. Using the RRF shown in Figure 15.3, the interviewer would begin by recording who it was within the household who refused, although this is not always obvious and depends upon information the interviewer is able to glean prior to the termination of the call. The interviewer might also code some basic demographics about the person refusing, but only if the interviewer has some degree of certainty in doing so. Research suggests that interviewers can do this accurately in a majority of cases for gender, age, and race (Bauman, Merkle, & Lavrakas, 1992; Lavrakas, Merkle, & Bauman, 1992). To the extent that this demographic information is accurate, the supervisor can use it to make decisions about which interviewers should attempt which subsequent refusal conversions. For example, my own experience and research suggests that an interviewer of the same race as the person who initially refused will have better success in converting a refusal. Furthermore, to the extent that respondent demographic characteristics correlate with survey measures, the surveyor could investigate the effects of nonresponse by considering the demographic characteristics of the unconverted refusals; however, much more needs to be learned before the validity of this strategy is known. The interviewer can also rate the "severity" of the refusal, as shown in Figure 15.3, as well as add comments and answer other questions that may help to explain the exact nature of the verbal exchange (if any) that transpired prior to the termination of the call.

In my own organization, we do not recontact households in which someone has told the interviewer at the initial refusal, "Don't call back!" or some such explicit comment. Short of that, however, we will attempt conversions with other initial refusals, with the exception of those that are so hostile that prudence suggests not doing so; these very strong refusals appear to represent approximately 10-15% of initial refusals in RDD surveys.

No definitive evidence exists about the success rate of refusal-conversion attempts, although Groves and Lyberg (1988) place it in the 25-40% range; my own experience leads me to put it in the 25-30% range. In making decisions about whether or not to attempt to convert refusals, the surveyor is faced with this trade-off: the investment of resources to convert refusals, so as to possibly decrease potential nonresponse error, versus the possible increase in other potential sources of survey error that otherwise might be reduced if those same resources were invested differently (e.g., paying more to have better-quality interviewers or refining the questionnaire more with additional pilot testing).

□ *How CATI Can Help With Potential Nonresponse Error*

CATI offers considerably greater potential than PAPI telephone surveys to reduce nonresponse and thereby lessen the potential of nonresponse error, but these benefits will not accrue unless the researcher makes explicit plans to achieve them.

Noncontacts

The great advantage that a full-CATI system—one that includes automatic distribution and control of the sampling pool—offers in reducing the number of sampled units that are not contacted is its facility to reschedule callbacks at optimal days/times, taking into account a telephone number's previous call-attempt history. In telephone interviews of elites, specific appointments are typically required to fit the executives' busy schedules. CATI can accurately schedule callbacks at the proper times, thereby increasing the chances that sampled respondents will be available to be interviewed. The most sophisticated

CATI software uses statistical algorithms to calculate probabilities that prioritize which telephone number is "served up" to an available interviewer on a given day and time. Not only can the computer implement this with greater accuracy than can be done manually, but the added advantage is that this frees up valuable administrative staff time (and cost) to be used on tasks that can be done best (or only) by humans, such as monitoring ongoing interviews and providing corrective/instructive feedback to interviewers.

Refusals

CATI also has the potential to provide interviewers, in real time, with unit/respondent-specific information and unit/respondent-specific persuasive spiels to decrease the chances that refusals will occur. Or if a refusal has occurred and a refusal conversion is attempted, CATI can increase the chances that the conversion attempt will succeed if its potential to provide the interviewer with more respondent/household-specific cues is actualized. A CATI system that controls the introductory sequence affords the researcher the opportunity to tailor the suggested wording of the spiel read to the individual respondent. For example, in a panel survey in which information is known about respondents from their previous interviews, the researcher can compose targeted respondent-specific introductions that incorporate, and thereby personalize, data about respondents that were obtained in an earlier wave.

☐ Response Rates

An important indicator of a survey's likely quality is its response rate(s); that is, of all the telephone numbers dialed and households/persons sampled, how many were actually interviewed? Currently, most survey professionals agree that response rates are best considered as a range rather than a single value. In general, response rates are affected by the survey topic, the length of the questionnaire, the caliber of the organization and interviewing staff conducting the survey, the length of the field period, rules for callbacks and refusal conversions, and other factors. Furthermore, Groves (1989, p. 133) correctly warns that these rates, in themselves, are *not* a direct measure of nonresponse error, the latter being a function of (a) the response/nonresponse rate and (b) whatever differences may exist on the survey variables between those who responded and those who did not. (For additional discussion of these issues, see Fowler, 1993; Frey, 1989; Groves & Lyberg, 1988; Lavrakas, 1993.)

One type of quality-of-response indicator is the sampling pool's efficiency in reaching eligible persons. Another is the proportion of "possibly eligible" persons/households sampled that were interviewed. Here it is important to recognize that almost all telephone surveys will process numbers from the sampling pool about which nothing will have been learned by the end of the field period, including whether or not particular numbers reached eligible respondents (i.e., the numbers will simply ring without answer). Due to this uncertainty, another useful rate to calculate is the proportion of "known eligibles" interviewed. Finally, it is informative to calculate the ratio of refusals to completions, sometimes called the *cooperation rate*. With the RDD surveys my colleagues and I have been conducting in the 1990s, our rates for these four indicators typically are about 55% (efficiency), 60% (all possible eligibles), 65-70% (all known eligibles), and 1:3 (refusals to completions).

■ *Measurement Issues in Telephone Surveys*

Measurement issues in surveying include the effects of the questionnaire, the interviewers, the respondents, and the survey mode. However, this section on measurement issues in telephone surveys focuses almost entirely on the interviewer and on how a surveyor can plan to minimize the potential error (bias and variance) that interviewers can contribute in telephone surveys.

As Groves (1989) notes, "Interviewers are the medium through which measurements are taken in [personal and telephone] surveys" (p. 404). This includes not only asking questions and recording responses, but also processing the sample and securing respondent cooperation. Given the central role of interviewers, it is not surprising that they can add significant bias and variance to survey measures. However, there are many strategies for reducing interviewer-related error (see Fowler & Mangione, 1990, p. 9) that too often go unused.

Interviewing is a part of the telephone survey process that, to date, has been much more a craft than a science. The quality of interviewing starts with the caliber of the persons recruited/hired to serve as interviewers, includes pre-interviewing training, and continues through supervisor monitoring and constant on-the-job training. I have long held the view that the great strength of the telephone survey method is its *potentially* large advantage over other modes of gathering survey data to reduce measurement error through centralized data collection (Lavrakas, 1987, 1993). Surprisingly, although many surveyors appear to recognize the importance of a representative sampling pool, a low rate of nonresponse, and a well-constructed questionnaire, they often are lax in the control they institute over the telephone interviewing process. Cost appears to be the primary reason for the lack of adequate attention given to rigorous control of interviewing in telephone surveys. Although it is expensive to institute strict and constant controls over telephone interviewers, in the absence of such a system, the researcher should be concerned that money spent on other parts of the survey enterprise (e.g., sampling) may be money wasted.

☐ *Interviewer Recruitment, Training, and Monitoring*

Recruitment

A basic consideration regarding interviewers is whether they are paid for their work or unpaid, such as volunteers or students who do interviewing as part of their course work. When a telephone survey employs paid interviewers, there should be a greater likelihood of higher-quality interviewing, due to several factors. In situations in which interviewers are paid, the surveyors can select carefully from among the most skilled individuals. With unpaid interviewers, surveyors have much less control over who will not be allowed to interview. Paid interviewers are more likely to have an objective detachment from the survey's purpose. In contrast, unpaid interviewers often have expectancies of the data; that is, volunteers by nature are often committed to an organization's purpose in conducting a survey and may hold preconceived notions of results, which can alter their behavior as interviewers and contribute bias to the data they gather. Similarly, students who interview for academic credit often have an interest in the survey outcomes, especially if the survey is their class's own project.

Regardless of whether interviewers are paid or unpaid, I recommend that each interviewer be asked to enter into a written agreement with the surveyor. This agreement should include a clause about not violating respondents' confidentiality. Also, the surveyor must make it very clear to all prospective interviewers that telephone surveys normally require "standardized survey interviewing" (see Fowler & Mangione, 1990)—a highly structured and rather sterile style of interviewing. Standardized survey interviewing does not allow for creativity on the part of interviewers in the ordering or wording of particular questionnaire items or in deciding who can be interviewed. Furthermore, the surveyor should inform all prospective telephone interviewers that constant monitoring will be conducted by supervisors, including listening to ongoing interviews. The surveyor's informing prospective interviewers of features such as these in advance of making a final decision about their beginning to work will create realistic expectations. In the case of paid interviewers, it may discourage those who are not likely to conform to highly structured situations from applying. Good-quality telephone interviewers are best recruited through the use of a careful personnel screening procedure and the offer of a good wage to attract persons with ability and experience who might otherwise not be interested in telephone interviewing. Simply stated, the more the surveyor pays interviewers, the more he or she can (and should) expect from them, in terms of both quality and quantity. (For more details about these matters, see Lavrakas, 1993, pp. 126-129.)

Survey administrators may be concerned with whether there are any demographic characteristics that are associated with high-quality interviewing—such as gender, age, or education—and whether they should take these characteristics into account in making hiring decisions. Within the perspective of wanting to avoid hiring practices that might be discriminatory, it should be noted that, "other than good reading and writing skills and a reasonably pleasant personality, [there appear to be] no other credible selection criteria for distinguishing among potential interviewers" (Fowler & Mangione, 1990, p. 140). Even in the case of strong regional accents, Bass and Totora (1988) report no interviewer-related effects. On the other hand, if the survey topic is related to interviewer demographics, there is consistent evidence that interviewer-respondent effects can and do occur that can increase total survey error (see Fowler & Mangione, 1990, pp. 98-105). For example, a telephone survey about sexual harassment found that male respondents were twice as likely to report having sexually harassed someone at work if they were interviewed by a male versus a female (Lavrakas, 1992). In such cases, hiring criteria certainly should take into account the needs of the survey and should consider interviewer demographics in a nondiscriminatory manner.

Training

The training of telephone survey interviewers, prior to the on-the-job training they should constantly receive by working with their supervisors, has two distinct components: general training and project-specific training. New interviewers should receive general training to start their learning process. General training also should be repeated, or at least "refreshed," for experienced interviewers. Project-specific training is given to everyone, no matter what seniority or ability they have as interviewers.

The following issues should be addressed in the part of training that covers general practices and expectancies:

1. What makes a good telephone interviewer, including behaviors related to processing the sampling pool, introducing the survey, selecting and securing the cooperation of the correct respondent, avoiding refusals, and administering the questionnaire in a standardized fashion

2. How the survey group's CATI system hardware and software works, if one is being used

3. How interviewing is monitored, including an explication of standards for quality and quantity

4. Ethical considerations in survey research

5. The particulars of employment with the organization or person conducting the survey

If CATI is used, interviewers should be trained so as to understand that their "primary job is interviewing, not operating a CATI system" (House & Nicholls, 1988, p. 427). In training interviewers on CATI, it also is beneficial to explain how CATI is expected to improve interviewing and thereby lower interviewer-related error (see Groves, 1989, pp. 377-378; Lavrakas, 1991).

All interviewers must be trained in the particulars of each new survey. Generally, this second, project-specific, part of training should be structured as follows:

1. An explanation of the purpose of the survey

2. A review of how the sampling pool was generated and how telephone numbers will be processed

3. An explanation of the use of the introduction/selection sequence

4. A review of fallback statements

5. An explanation of the refusal report form, if one is used

6. A detailed explanation of the questionnaire, including role-playing practice in its use

With CATI, any atypical software sequences should be clearly explained and ample time allotted for on-line practice. (For more details of the substance of each of these training areas, see Lavrakas, 1993, pp. 140-144.)

Fowler and Mangione (1990) suggest that prospective interviewers cannot be expected to behave acceptably as standardized survey interviewers with fewer than 20-30 hours of training. Researchers planning for interviewer training and the costs associated with it should take this into consideration. (For more suggestions on the general training telephone survey interviewers might receive, see Lavrakas, 1993, pp. 130-140.)

Monitoring

The demands on supervisors in high-quality telephone survey operations are great. It is the responsibility of supervisors to ensure the integrity of sampling and the quality of the data that are gathered. For these reasons, researchers should employ energetic and skilled persons in supervisory positions, and should pay them accordingly. In general, considering both costs and data quality, an optimal ratio should be one supervisor for every 8 to 10 experienced interviewers (see Groves, 1989, pp. 61-62). Supervisors are responsible for maintaining the quality of the interviewing that occurs during their sessions, and interviewers should clearly perceive that their supervisors feel and display this responsibility.

Supervisors should themselves be trained to determine the levels at which interviewing-related problems occur (Cannell & Oksenberg, 1988). It may be that an interviewer has yet to receive adequate training, and therefore is unfamiliar with proper techniques. Or it may be that the interviewer knows what to do, but not exactly how to operationalize it. Or the interviewer may know how something is supposed to be done, but lacks the skill/ability to do it properly. Unless the supervisor can judge accurately the level of the problem, she or he is not likely to be able to propose an effective solution to the interviewer. The rapport that supervisors develop with interviewers will affect the quality of data produced. To achieve a high level of quality, there must be constant verbal and/or written feedback from supervisors to interviewers, especially during the early part of a field period, when on-the-job training is critical.

Whenever possible, a telephone survey should use a centralized bank of telephones with equipment that allows the supervisor's telephone to monitor all interviewers' lines. There are special telephones that can be used to monitor an ongoing interview without the interviewer or respondent being aware of it. With CATI surveys, monitoring ongoing interviews often is a supervisor's primary responsibility. With PAPI, monitoring ongoing interviews should be a secondary, but nevertheless high-priority, supervisory responsibility. Regardless of the use of CATI or PAPI, monitoring can be done formally, with the use of a structured interviewer monitoring form (IMF), or informally, without a structured procedure. Supervisors need not listen to complete interviews, but rather should systematically apportion their listening, a few minutes at a time, across all interviewers, concentrating more frequently and at longer intervals on less-experienced ones. All aspects of interviewer-respondent contact should be monitored, including the interviewer's use of the introduction, the respondent selection sequence, fallback statements, and administration of the questionnaire itself. An IMF can (a) aid the supervisor by providing documented on-the-job feedback to interviewers, (b) generate interviewer performance data for the field director, and (c) provide the surveyor with a valuable type of data for investigating item-specific interviewer-related measurement error (see Cannell & Oksenberg, 1988; Groves, 1989, pp. 381-389).

In addition to noting whether or not interviewers are reading the items exactly as they are written, supervisors should pay special attention to the ways in which interviewers probe incomplete, ambiguous, or irrelevant responses, and to whether or not interviewers adequately repeat questions and define/clarify terms respondents may not understand in an unbiased fashion, if the latter is appropriate for the survey. Supervisors also need to pay close attention to anything interviewers may be saying or doing (verbally) that might reinforce certain response patterns that may bias answers. With some CATI systems, monitoring an ongoing interview includes being able to view the interviewer's use of the keyboard as it happens. Listening to ongoing interviewing and providing frequent feedback is especially important in the early stages of the field period and with new interviewers, and at these times extra supervisors may be needed. (For more detail about monitoring telephone survey interviewers, see Lavrakas, 1996.)

☐ *How CATI Can Help With Potential Measurement Error*

CATI offers considerable potential for reducing the extent that the questionnaire, interviewers, and/or respondents will contribute measurement error, thereby lowering, and possibly entirely undermining, survey validity. Just as important, CATI facilitates the incorporation of methodological measurements into the data collection process to estimate the effects of potential sources of measurement error. However, this does not happen by itself just because a survey group has a CATI system. The researcher must actively exploit and intelligently implement the CATI system in order to reap these potential benefits (see Lavrakas, 1996).

The Questionnaire

CATI's obvious early attraction was the control it affords over the administration of the questionnaire. CATI offers broad flexibility concerning the order in which survey items can be presented. This provides for the possibility that any order effects might cancel each other out. CATI also makes it easier for a surveyor to estimate later the magnitude of possible order effects. However, a questionnaire has to be devised and deployed in a way that generates the type of data that make these analyses possible, and too often this potential is not exploited by survey researchers.

Interviewers and Supervisors

There are myriad ways in which CATI offers the potential to reduce and/or to measure interviewer-related error in telephone surveys. In training interviewers on CATI, researchers should emphasize explicitly that CATI is expected to improve interviewing, thereby lowering interviewer-related error. CATI also provides considerable potential for producing statistics on interviewer productivity. Linked to this, supervisory personnel can have a greater quantity of timely information with which to make informed decisions about what types of additional attention given interviewers may require.

Respondents

To the extent that CATI enhances the ability of interviewers to concentrate on their interaction with the respondent, interviewers should be trained to detect more accurately those instances in which (a) an item should be reread, (b) a respondent is really a "don't know," and/or (c) a respondent does not appear to be answering in a reliable fashion.

In sum, it is the researcher's responsibility to see that CATI is used in ways that exploit its potential to increase survey accuracy. Because this often can be done at no added cost, the use of CATI can only produce benefits within a total survey error perspective.

■ Conclusion

☐ Survey Quality and Basic Cost Considerations

Every telephone survey has a finite budget, and the key challenge the surveyor faces is to get the most accurate data from these finite resources. As suggested earlier, I believe that the surveyor can do this best by explicitly considering all sources of survey error and making careful a priori trade-off decisions about how best to allocate fixed resources. As Groves (1989) explains, efforts to reduce and/or measure the potential effects of the various types of survey error have real cost implications. In closing, I want to remind readers of the basic distinction between approaches intended to reduce potential errors and approaches intended to measure their potential effects. That is, whereas it may be too expensive for the researcher to implement procedures that may eliminate (or substantially reduce) a potential source of error, he or she might be able to implement procedures to measure its approximate size, and thus take it into account when interpreting the survey's findings. (I encourage more advanced readers and practitioners to study and restudy Groves's challenging but nonetheless excellent 1989 volume, *Survey Errors and Survey Costs.*)

For novice survey researchers, these considerations can seem forbidding or even overwhelming. When faced with all the potential threats to a survey's validity, some may question the value of the entire survey enterprise. However, to do so is to fail to remember the fact that highly accurate surveys are routinely conducted by experienced surveyors who exercise the necessary care. This chapter is meant to serve as an introduction to many of these considerations as they apply to telephone surveys. This discussion is not meant to lower the esteem that good telephone surveys merit or to dissuade anyone from conducting a good survey. Rather, it is meant to alert readers to the many challenges a researcher faces in conducting a telephone survey that will be "accurate enough" for the purposes for which it is meant. My message should be clear: Planning, implementing, and interpreting a telephone survey that is likely to be accurate is a methodical, time-consuming process, but one well worth the effort.

□ *Ethical Considerations and Pseudopolls*

High-quality telephone surveys practice the principal of "informed consent." Respondents are informed, either explicitly or implicitly, that their participation is voluntary and that no harm will come to them regardless of whether they choose to participate or not. In addition to practicing these ethical standards, legitimate telephone surveys assure respondents that the answers they provide will be confidential; that is, no one other than the survey organization will know "who said what," unless respondents explicitly provide permission for their answers to be linked with their names.

In the mid-1990s, unfortunately, many unethical survey practices are masquerading as legitimate surveys (see Traugott & Lavrakas, 1996). For example, there are so-called push-polls (political propagandizing disguised as legitimate polling, but using biased question wording solely to expose "respondents" to a highly partisan viewpoint), "FRUGing" (fund-raising under the guise of surveying), and "SUGing" (selling under the guise of surveying). With these telemarketing scams occurring, it is no wonder that many citizens hold negative (albeit uninformed) views of telephone surveying. Thus all legitimate telephone surveyors face the dual challenge of having to work to counter the negative effects of these pseudopolls and having to make certain they do nothing inadvertent to compromise the integrity of ethical surveying.

■ References

*Practical Data
Collection
and Analysis
Methods*

470

American Association for Public Opinion Research. (1991). *Code of professional ethics and practices.* Ann Arbor, MI: Author.

Andrews, E. L. (1992, March 15). Emboldened phone companies are pushing the frills. *New York Times,* p. F8.

Baker, R. P., & Lefes, W. L. (1988). The design of CATI systems: A review of current practice. In R. M. Groves, P. N. Biemer, L. E. Lyberg, J. T. Massey, W. L. Nicholls, & J. Waksberg (Eds.), *Telephone survey methodology* (pp. 387-402). New York: John Wiley.

Bass, R. T., & Totora, R. D. (1988). A comparison of centralized CATI facilities for an agricultural labor survey. In R. M. Groves, P. N. Biemer, L. E. Lyberg, J. T. Massey, W. L. Nicholls, & J. Waksberg (Eds.), *Telephone survey methodology* (pp. 497-508). New York: John Wiley.

Bauman, S. L., Merkle, D. M., & Lavrakas, P. J. (1992). *Interviewer estimates of refusers' gender, age, and race in telephone surveys.* Paper presented at the annual meeting of the Midwest Association for Public Opinion Research, Chicago.

Biemer, P. N., Groves, R. M., Lyberg, L. E., Mathiowetz, N. A., & Sudman, S. (Eds.). (1991). *Measurement errors in surveys.* New York: John Wiley.

Bryant, B. E. (1975). Respondent selection in a time of changing household composition. *Journal of Marketing Research, 12,* 129-135.

Cannell, C. F., & Oksenberg, L. (1988). Observation of behavior in telephone interviews. In R. M. Groves, P. N. Biemer, L. E. Lyberg, J. T. Massey, W. L. Nicholls, & J. Waksberg (Eds.), *Telephone survey methodology* (pp. 475-496). New York: John Wiley.

Catlin, G., & Ingram, S. (1988). The effects of CATI on costs and data quality: A comparison of CATI and paper methods in centralized interviewing. In R. M. Groves, P. N. Biemer, L. E. Lyberg, J. T. Massey, W. L. Nicholls, & J. Waksberg (Eds.), *Telephone survey methodology* (pp. 437-452). New York: John Wiley.

Collins, M., Sykes, W., Wilson, P., & Blackshaw, N. (1988). Nonresponse: The UK experience. In R. M. Groves, P. N. Biemer, L. E. Lyberg, J. T. Massey, W. L. Nicholls, & J. Waksberg (Eds.), *Telephone survey methodology* (pp. 213-232). New York: John Wiley.

Congressional Information Service. (1990). *American statistical index.* Bethesda, MD: Author.

Cooper, S. L. (1964). Random sampling by telephone: An improved method. *Journal of Marketing Research, 1*(4), 45-48.

Czaja, R., Blair, J., & Sebestik, J. (1982). Respondent selection in a telephone survey. *Journal of Marketing Research, 19,* 381-385.

de Leeuw, E. D., & van der Zouwen, J. (1988). Data quality in telephone and face to face surveys: A comparative meta-analysis. In R. M. Groves, P. N. Biemer, L. E. Lyberg, J. T. Massey, W. L. Nicholls, & J. Waksberg (Eds.), *Telephone survey methodology* (pp. 283-300). New York: John Wiley.

Dillman, D. A., Gallegos, J., & Frey, J. H. (1976). Reducing refusals for telephone interviews. *Public Opinion Quarterly, 40,* 99-114.

Dillman, D. A., & Tarnai, J. (1988). Administrative issues in mixed mode surveys. In R. M. Groves, P. N. Biemer, L. E. Lyberg, J. T. Massey, W. L. Nicholls, & J. Waksberg (Eds.), *Telephone survey methodology* (pp. 509-528). New York: John Wiley.

Fowler, F. J., Jr. (1993). *Survey research methods* (2nd ed.). Newbury Park, CA: Sage.

Fowler, F. J., Jr., & Mangione, T. W. (1990). *Standardized survey interviewing: Minimizing interviewer-related error.* Newbury Park, CA: Sage.

Frey, J. H. (1989). *Survey research by telephone* (2nd ed.). Newbury Park, CA: Sage.

Gawiser, S. R., & Witt, G. E. (1992). *Twenty questions a journalist should ask about poll results.* New York: National Council on Public Polls.

Groves, R. M. (1989). *Survey errors and survey costs.* New York: John Wiley.

Groves, R. M., & Kahn, R. L. (1979). *Surveys by telephone: A national comparison with personal interviews.* New York: Academic Press.

Groves, R. M., & Lyberg, L. E. (1988). An overview of nonresponse issues in telephone surveys. In R. M. Groves, P. N. Biemer, L. E. Lyberg, J. T. Massey, W. L. Nicholls, & J. Waksberg (Eds.), *Telephone survey methodology* (pp. 191-212). New York: John Wiley.

Henry, G. T. (1990). *Practical sampling.* Newbury Park, CA: Sage.

House, C. C., & Nicholls, W. L. (1988). Questionnaire design for CATI: Design objectives and methods. In R. M. Groves, P. N. Biemer, L. E. Lyberg, J. T. Massey, W. L. Nicholls, & J. Waksberg (Eds.), *Telephone survey methodology* (pp. 421-426). New York: John Wiley.

Kish, L. (1949). A procedure for objective respondent selection within the household. *Journal of the American Statistical Association, 44,* 380-387.

Kish, L. (1965). *Survey sampling.* New York: John Wiley.

Lavrakas, P. J. (1987). *Telephone survey methods: Sampling, selection, and supervision.* Newbury Park, CA: Sage.

Lavrakas, P. J. (1990). *Morton Grove District 70 enrollment study.* Unpublished manuscript, Northwestern University Survey Lab, Evanston, IL.

Lavrakas, P. J. (1991). Implementing CATI at the Northwestern survey lab: Part I. *CATI News, 4*(1), 2-3ff.

Lavrakas, P. J. (1992). *Attitudes towards and experiences with sexual harassment in the workplace.* Paper presented at the annual meeting of the Midwest Association for Public Opinion Research, Chicago.

Lavrakas, P. J. (1993). *Telephone survey methods: Sampling, selection, and supervision* (2nd ed.). Newbury Park, CA: Sage.

Lavrakas, P. J. (1996). To err is human. *Marketing Research, 8*(1), 30-36.

Lavrakas, P. J., Bauman, S. L., & Schejbal, J. A. (1994). *The costs and benefits of refusal-conversions in telephone surveys.* Paper presented at the annual meeting of the Midwest Association for Public Opinion Research, Chicago.

Lavrakas, P. J., & Merkle, D. A. (1991). *A reversal of roles: When respondents question interviewers.* Paper presented at the annual meeting of the Midwest Association for Public Opinion Research, Chicago.

Lavrakas, P. J., Merkle, D. A., & Bauman, S. L. (1992). *Refusal report forms, refusal conversions, and nonresponse bias.* Paper presented at the annual meeting of the American Association for Public Opinion Research, St. Petersburg, FL.

Lavrakas, P. J., Merkle, D. A., & Bauman, S. L. (1993). *The last birthday selection method and within-unit coverage problems.* Paper presented at the annual meeting of the American Association for Public Opinion Research, St. Charles, IL.

Lepkowski, J. M. (1988). Telephone sampling methods in the United States. In R. M. Groves, P. N. Biemer, L. E. Lyberg, J. T. Massey, W. L. Nicholls, & J. Waksberg (Eds.), *Telephone survey methodology* (pp. 73-98). New York: John Wiley.

Lyberg, L. E. (1988). The administration of telephone surveys. In R. M. Groves, P. N. Biemer, L. E. Lyberg, J. T. Massey, W. L. Nicholls, & J. Waksberg (Eds.), *Telephone survey methodology* (pp. 453-456). New York: John Wiley.

Lyberg, L. E., & Dean, P. (1992). *Methods for reducing nonresponse rates: A review.* Paper presented at the annual meeting of the American Association for Public Opinion Research, St. Petersburg, FL.

Maklan, D., & Waksberg, J. (1988). Within-household coverage in RDD surveys. In R. M. Groves, P. N. Biemer, L. E. Lyberg, J. T. Massey, W. L. Nicholls, & J. Waksberg (Eds.), *Telephone survey methodology* (pp. 51-72). New York: John Wiley.

Merkle, D. M., Bauman, S. L., & Lavrakas, P. J. (1991). *Nonresponse bias: Refusal conversions and call-backs in RDD telephone surveys.* Paper presented at the annual meeting of the Midwest Association for Public Opinion Research, Chicago.

Mitofsky, W. J. (1970). *Sampling of telephone households.* Unpublished manuscript, CBS News, New York.

Nicholls, W. L. (1988). Computer-assisted telephone interviewing: A general introduction. In R. M. Groves, P. N. Biemer, L. E. Lyberg, J. T. Massey, W. L. Nicholls, & J. Waksberg (Eds.), *Telephone survey methodology* (pp. 377-386). New York: John Wiley.

Oksenberg, L., & Cannell, C. F. (1988). Effects of interviewer vocal characteristics on nonresponse. In R. M. Groves, P. N. Biemer, L. E. Lyberg, J. T. Massey, W. L. Nicholls, & J. Waksberg (Eds.), *Telephone survey methodology* (pp. 257-272). New York: John Wiley.

Oldendick, R. W., Sorenson, S. B., Tuchfarber, A. J., & Bishop, G. F. (1985). *Last birthday respondent selection in telephone surveys: A further test.* Paper presented at the annual meeting of the Midwest Association for Public Opinion Research, Chicago.

O'Rourke, D., & Blair, J. (1983). Improving random respondent selection in telephone surveys. *Journal of Marketing Research, 20,* 428-432.

Salmon, C. T., & Nichols, J. S. (1983). The next-birthday method for respondent selection. *Public Opinion Quarterly, 47,* 270-276.

Sebold, J. (1988). Survey period length, unanswered numbers, and nonresponse in telephone surveys. In R. M. Groves, P. N. Biemer, L. E. Lyberg, J. T. Massey, W. L. Nicholls, & J. Waksberg (Eds.), *Telephone survey methodology* (pp. 247-256). New York: John Wiley.

Smead, R. J., & Wilcox, J. (1980). Ring policy in telephone surveys. *Public Opinion Quarterly, 44,* 115-116.

Survey Sampling, Inc. (1992). *A survey researcher's view of the U.S.* Fairfield, CT: Author.

Traugott, M. W. (1987). The importance of persistence in respondent selection for preelection surveys. *Public Opinion Quarterly, 51,* 48-57.

Traugott, M. W., & Lavrakas, P. J. (1996). *The voter's guide to election polls.* Chatham, NJ: Chatham House.

Trewin, D., & Lee, G. (1988). International comparisons of telephone coverage. In R. M. Groves, P. N. Biemer, L. E. Lyberg, J. T. Massey, W. L. Nicholls, & J. Waksberg (Eds.), *Telephone survey methodology* (pp. 9-24). New York: John Wiley.

Troldahl, V. C., & Carter, R. E., Jr. (1964). Random selection of respondents within households in phone surveys. *Journal of Marketing Research, 1*(4), 71-76.

Waksberg, J. (1978). Sampling methods for random digit dialing. *Journal of the American Statistical Association, 73,* 40-46.

Weeks, M. F. (1988). Call scheduling with CATI. In R. M. Groves, P. N. Biemer, L. E. Lyberg, J. T. Massey, W. L. Nicholls, & J. Waksberg (Eds.), *Telephone survey methodology* (pp. 403-420). New York: John Wiley.

16

Ethnography

David M. Fetterman

Ethnography is the art and science of describing a group or culture. The description may be of a small tribal group in some exotic land or of a classroom in middle-class suburbia. The task is much like the one taken on by an investigative reporter, who interviews relevant people, reviews records, weighs the credibility of one person's opinions against another's, looks for ties to special interests and organizations, and writes the story for a concerned public as well as for professional colleagues. A key difference between the investigative reporter and the ethnographer, however, is that where the journalist seeks out the unusual—the murder, the plane crash, the bank robbery—the ethnographer writes about the routine, daily lives of people. The more predictable patterns of human thought and behavior are the focus of inquiry.

Ethnographers are noted for their ability to keep an open mind about the groups or cultures they are studying. However, this quality does not imply any lack of rigor. The ethnographer enters the field with an open mind, not an empty head. Before asking the first question in the field, the ethnographer begins with a problem, a theory or model, a research design, specific data collection techniques, tools for analysis, and a specific writing style. The ethnographer also begins with biases and preconceived notions about how people behave and what they think—as do researchers in every field. Indeed, the choice of what problem, geographic area, or people to study is in itself biased. Biases serve both positive and negative functions. Controlled, biases can focus and limit the research effort. Uncontrolled, they can undermine the quality of ethnographic research. To mitigate the negative effects of bias, the ethnographer must first make specific biases explicit. A series of additional quality controls, such as triangulation, contextualization, and a nonjudgmental orientation, place a check on the negative influence of bias.

An open mind also allows the ethnographer to explore rich, untapped sources of data not mapped out in the research design. The ethnographic study allows multiple interpretations of reality and alternative interpretations of data throughout the study. The ethnographer is interested in understanding and describing a social and cultural scene from the emic, or insider's, perspective. The ethnographer is both storyteller and scientist; the closer the reader of an ethnography comes to understanding the native's point of view, the better the story and the better the science.

■ *Overview*

This chapter presents an overview of the steps involved in ethnographic work (see Fetterman, 1989, for additional detail). The process begins when the ethnographer selects a problem or topic and a theory or model to guide the study. The ethnographer simultaneously chooses whether to follow a basic or applied research approach to delineate and shape the effort. The research design then provides a basic set of instructions about what to do and where to go during the study. Fieldwork is the heart of the ethnographic research design. In the field, basic anthropological concepts, data collection methods and techniques, and analysis are the fundamental elements of "doing ethnography." Selection and use of various pieces of equipment—including the human instrument—facilitate the work. This process becomes product through analysis at various stages in ethnographic work—in field notes, memoranda, and interim reports, but most dramatically in the published report, article, or book.

This chapter presents the concepts, methods and techniques, equipment, analysis, writing, and ethics involved in ethnographic research. This approach highlights the utility of planning and organization in ethnographic work. The more organized the ethnographer, the easier his or her task of making sense of the mountains of data collected in the field. Sifting through notepads filled with illegible scrawl, listening to hours of tape recordings, labeling and organizing piles of pictures and slides, and cross-referencing disks of data are much less daunting to the ethnographer who has taken an organized, carefully planned approach.

The reality, however, is that ethnographic work is not always orderly. It involves serendipity, creativity, being in the right place at the right or wrong time, a lot of hard work, and old-fashioned luck. Thus, although this discussion proceeds within the confines of an orderly structure, I have made a concerted effort to ensure that it conveys as well the unplanned, sometimes chaotic, and always intriguing character of ethnographic research.

Whereas in most research analysis follows data collection, in ethnographic research analysis and data collection begin simultaneously. An ethnographer is a human instrument and must discriminate among different types of data and analyze the relative worth of one path over another at every turn in fieldwork, well before any formalized analysis takes place. Clearly, ethnographic research involves all different levels of analysis. Analysis is an ongoing responsibility and joy from the first moment an ethnographer envisions a new project to the final stages of writing and reporting the findings.

■ *Concepts*

The most important concepts that guide ethnographers in their fieldwork include culture, a holistic perspective, contextualization, emic perspective and multiple realities, etic perspective, nonjudgmental orientation, inter- and intra-cultural diversity, structure and function, symbol and ritual, micro and macro, and operationalism.

□ *Culture*

Culture is the broadest ethnographic concept. Definitions of culture typically espouse either a materialist or an ideational perspective. The classic materialist interpretation of culture focuses on behavior. In this view, culture is the sum of a social group's observable patterns of behavior, customs, and way of life (see Harris, 1968, p. 16). The most popular ideational definition of culture is the cognitive definition. According to the cognitive approach, culture comprises the ideas, beliefs, and knowledge that characterize a particular group of people. This second—and currently most popular—definition specifically excludes behavior. Obviously, ethnographers need to know about both cultural behavior and cultural knowledge to describe a culture or subculture adequately. Although neither definition is sufficient, each offers the ethnographer a starting point and a perspective from which to approach the group under study.

Both material and ideational definitions are useful at different times in exploring fully how groups of people think and behave in their natural environments. However defined, the concept of culture helps the ethnographer search for a logical, cohesive pattern in the myriad, often ritualistic behaviors and ideas that characterize a group.

Anthropologists learn about the intricacies of a subgroup or community in order to describe it in all its richness and complexity. In the process of studying these details, they typically discover underlying forces that make the system tick. These cultural elements are values or beliefs that can unite or divide a group, but that are commonly shared focal points. An awareness of what role these abstract elements play in a given culture can give the researcher a clearer picture of how the culture works.

Many anthropologists consider cultural interpretation ethnography's primary contribution. Cultural interpretation involves the researcher's ability to describe what he or she has heard and seen within the framework of the social group's view of reality. A classic example of the interpretive contribution involves the wink and the blink. A mechanical difference between the two may not be evident. However, the cultural context of each movement, the relationship between individuals that each act suggests, and the contexts surrounding the two help define and differentiate these two significantly different behaviors. Anyone who has ever mistaken a blink for a wink is fully aware of the significance of cultural interpretation (see Fetterman, 1982, p. 24; Geertz, 1973, p. 6; Wolcott, 1980, pp. 57, 59).

☐ *Holistic Perspective and Contextualization*

Ethnographers assume a holistic outlook in research to gain a comprehensive and complete picture of a social group. Ethnographers attempt to describe as much as possible about a culture or a social group. This description might include the group's history, religion, politics, economy, and environment. No study can capture an entire culture or group. The holistic orientation forces the fieldworker to see beyond an immediate cultural scene or event in a classroom, hospital room, city street, or plush offices in Washington, D.C., New York, or Chicago. Each scene exists within a multilayered and interrelated context.

Contextualizing data involves placing observations into a larger perspective. For example, in one of my studies of an alternative high school for dropouts, policy makers were contemplating terminating one dropout program because of its low attendance—approximately 60-70%. My reminder that the baseline with which to compare 60-70% attendance was zero attendance—these were students who systematically skipped school—helped the policy makers make a more informed decision about the program. In this case, contextualization ensured that the program would continue serving former dropouts (see Fetterman, 1987a).

☐ *Emic and Etic Perspectives*

The emic perspective—the insider's or native's perspective of reality—is at the heart of most ethnographic research. The insider's perception of reality is instrumental to understanding and accurately describing situations and behaviors. Native perceptions may not conform to an "objective" reality, but they help the fieldworker understand why members of the social group do what they do. In contrast to a priori assumptions about how systems work from a simple, linear, logical perspective—which might be completely off target—ethnography typically takes a phenomenologically oriented research approach.

An emic perspective compels the recognition and acceptance of multiple realities. Documenting multiple perspectives of reality in a given study is crucial to an understanding of why people think and act in the different ways they do. Differing perceptions of reality can be useful clues to individuals' religious, economic, or political status and can help a researcher understand maladaptive behavior patterns.

An etic perspective is an external, social scientific perspective on reality. Some ethnographers are interested only in describing the emic view, without placing their data in an etic or scientific perspective. They stand at the ideational and phenomenological end of the ethnographic spectrum. Other ethnographers prefer to rely on etically derived data first, and consider emically derived data secondary in their analysis. They stand at the materialist and positivist philosophical end of the ethnographic spectrum. At one time, a conflict about whether the causes of human actions are motivated primarily by ideas (ideational, typically emically oriented perspective) or by the environment (materialist, often etically based perspective) consumed the field. Today, most ethnographers simply see emic and etic orientations as markers along a continuum of styles or different levels of analysis. Most ethnographers start collecting data from the emic perspective, then try to make sense of what they have collected in terms of both the native's view and their own scientific analysis. Just as thorough fieldwork requires an insightful and sensitive cultural interpretation combined with rigorous data collection techniques, so good ethnography requires both emic and etic perspectives.

☐ *Nonjudgmental Orientation and Inter- and Intracultural Diversity*

A nonjudgmental orientation requires the ethnographer to suspend personal valuation of any given cultural practice. Maintaining a nonjudgmental orientation is similar to suspending disbelief while watching a movie or play, or reading a book—one accepts what may be an obviously illogical or unbelievable set of circumstances in order to allow the author to unravel a riveting story.

Intercultural diversity refers to the differences between two cultures, *intracultural diversity* to the differences between subcultures within a culture. Intercultural differences are reasonably easy to see. Compare the descriptions of two different cultures on a point-by-point basis—their political, religious, economic, kinship, and ecological systems and other pertinent dimensions. Intracultural differences, however, are more likely to go unnoticed.

These concepts place a check on our observations. They help the fieldworker see differences that may invalidate pat theories or hypotheses about observed events in the field. In some cases, these differences are systematic patterned activities for a broad spectrum of the community, compelling the fieldworker to readjust the research focus; to throw away dated and inappropriate theories, models, hypotheses, and assumptions; and to modify the vision of the finished puzzle. In other cases, the differences are idiosyncratic but useful in underscoring another, dominant pattern—the exception that proves the rule. In most cases, however, such differences are instructive about a level or dimension of the community that had not received sufficient consideration. (For an illustration of intracultural diversity in qualitative research, see Fetterman, 1988.)

☐ *Structure and Function and Symbol and Ritual*

Structure and function are traditional concepts that guide research in social organization. *Structure* here refers to the social structure or configuration of the group, such as the kinship or political structure. *Function* refers to the social relations among members of the group. Most groups have identifiable internal structures and established sets of social relationships that help regulate behavior.

Ethnographers use the concepts of structure and function to guide their inquiry. They extract information from the group under study to construct a skeletal structure and then thread in the social functions—the muscle, flesh, and nerves that fill out the skeleton. A detailed understanding of the underlying structure of a system provides the ethnographer with a foundation on and frame within which to construct an ethnographic description.

In addition, ethnographers look for symbols that help them understand and describe a culture. Symbols are condensed expressions of meaning that evoke powerful feelings and thoughts. A cross or a menorah represents an entire religion, a swastika represents a movement, whether the original Nazi movement or one of the many neo-Nazi movements. A flag represents an entire country, evoking both patriotic fervor and epithets.

Rituals are repeated patterns of symbolic behavior that play a part in both religious and secular life. Ethnographers see symbols and rituals as a form of cultural shorthand. Symbols open doors to initial understanding and crystallize critical cultural knowledge. Together, symbols and rituals help ethnographers make sense of observations by providing a framework in which to classify and categorize behavior (see Dolgin, Kemnitzer, & Schneider, 1977).

☐ *Micro or Macro and Operationalism*

A micro study is a close-up view, as if under a microscope, of a small social unit or an identifiable activity within the social unit. Typically, an ethnomethodologist or symbolic interactionist will conduct a microanalysis (see Denzin, 1989). The areas of proxemics and kinesics in anthropology involve micro studies. Proxemics is the study of how the socially defined physical distance between people varies under differing social circumstances. Kinesics is the study of body language. A macro study focuses on the large picture. In anthropology, the large picture can range from a single school to worldwide systems. The typical ethnography focuses on a community or specific sociocultural system. The selection of a micro or macro level of study depends on what the researcher wants to know, and thus what theory the study involves and how the researcher has defined the problem under study.

Operationalism, simply, means defining one's terms and methods of measurement. In simple descriptive accounts, saying that "a few people said this and a few others said that" may not be problematic. However, establishing a significant relationship between facts and theory, or interpreting "the facts," requires greater specificity. Operationalism tests ethnographers and forces them to be honest with themselves. Instead of leaving conclusions to strong impressions, the fieldworker should quantify or identify the source of ethnographic insights whenever possible. Specifying how one arrives at one's conclusions gives other researchers something concrete to go on, something to prove or disprove.

In this section of the chapter I have provided a discussion of some of the most important concepts in the profession, beginning with such global concepts as culture, a holistic orientation, and contextualization and gradually shifting to more narrow concepts—inter- and intracultural diversity, structure and function, symbol and ritual, and operationalism. In the next section, I detail the ethnographic methods and techniques that grow out of these concepts and allow the researcher to carry out the work of ethnography.

■ *Methods and Techniques*

The ethnographer is a human instrument. Ethnographic methods and techniques help to guide the ethnographer through the wilderness of personal observation and to identify and classify accurately the bewildering variety of events and actions that form a social situation.

□ *Fieldwork*

Fieldwork is the hallmark of research for both sociologists and anthropologists. The method is essentially the same for both types of researchers—working with people for long periods of time in their natural setting. The ethnographer conducts research in the native environment to see people and their behavior given all the real-world incentives and constraints. This naturalist approach avoids the artificial response typical of controlled or laboratory conditions. Understanding the world—or some small fragment of it—requires studying it in all its wonder and complexity. The task is in many ways more difficult than laboratory study, but it can also be more rewarding.

The fieldworker uses a variety of methods and techniques to ensure the integrity of the data. These methods and techniques objectify and standardize the researcher's perceptions. Of course, the ethnographer must adapt each one of the methods and techniques discussed below to the local environment. Resource constraints and deadlines may also limit the length of time for data gathering in the field—exploring, cross-checking, and recording information.

□ *Selection, Sampling, and Entry*

The research questions shape the selection of a place and a people or program to study. The ideal site for investigation of the research problem is not always accessible. In that event, the researcher accepts and notes the limitations of the study from the onset. Ideally, the focus of the investigation shifts to match the site under study.

The next step is to decide how to sample members of the target population. Most ethnographers use the big-net approach conducive to participant observation—mixing and mingling with everyone they can at first. As the study progresses, the focus narrows to specific portions of the population under study. The big-net approach ensures a wide-angle view of events before the microscopic study of specific interactions begins.

Ethnographers typically use informal strategies to begin fieldwork, such as starting wherever they can slip a foot in the door. (An introduction by a member is the ethnographer's best ticket into the community.) The most common technique is judgmental sampling; that is, ethnographers rely on their judgment to select the most appropriate members of the subculture or unit, based on the research question. Some experienced ethnographers use a rigorous randomized strategy to begin work—particularly when they already know a great deal about the culture or unit they are studying. However, using a highly structured randomized design without a basic understanding of the people under study may cause the researcher to narrow the focus prematurely, thus eliminating perhaps the very people or subjects relevant to the study.

□ *Participant Observation*

Participant observation characterizes most ethnographic research and is crucial to effective fieldwork. Participant observation combines participation in the lives of the people under study with maintenance of a professional distance that allows adequate observation and recording of data.

Participant observation is immersion in a culture. Ideally, the ethnographer lives and works in the community for 6 months to a year or more, learning the language and seeing patterns of behavior over time. Long-term residence helps the researcher internalize the basic beliefs, fears, hopes, and expectations of the people under study. The simple, ritualistic behaviors of going to the market or to the well for water teach how people use their time and space, how they determine what is precious, sacred, and profane. The process may seem unsystematic; in the beginning, it is somewhat uncontrolled and haphazard. However, even in the early stages of fieldwork the ethnographer searches out experiences and events as they come to his or her attention. Participant observation sets the stage for more refined techniques—including projective techniques and questionnaires—and becomes more refined itself as the fieldworker understands more and more about the culture. Ideas and behaviors that were only a blur to the ethnographer on entering the community take on a sharper focus. Participant observation can also help clarify the results of more refined instruments by providing a baseline of meaning and a way to reenter the field to explore the context for those (often unexpected) results.

In applied settings, participant observation is often noncontinuous, spread out over an extended time. Often contract research budgets or time schedules do not allow long periods of study—continuous or noncontinuous. In these situations, the researcher can apply ethnographic techniques to the study, but cannot conduct an ethnography.

□ *Interviewing*

The interview is the ethnographer's most important data-gathering technique. Interviews explain and put into a larger context what the ethnographer sees and experiences. General interview types include structured, semistructured, informal, and retrospective interviews.

Formally structured and semistructured interviews are verbal approximations of a questionnaire with explicit research goals. These interviews generally serve comparative and representative purposes—comparing responses and putting them in the context of common group beliefs and themes. A structured or semistructured interview is most valuable when the fieldworker comprehends the fundamentals of a community from the "insider's" perspective. At this point, questions are more likely to conform to the native's perception of reality than to the researcher's.

Informal interviews are the most common in ethnographic work. They seem to be casual conversations, but where structured interviews have an explicit agenda, informal interviews have a specific but implicit research agenda. The researcher uses informal approaches to discover the categories of meaning in a culture. Informal interviews are useful throughout an ethnographic study for discovering what people think and how one person's perceptions compare with another's. Such comparisons help the fieldworker to identify shared values in the community—values that inform behavior. Informal interviews are also useful for establishing and maintaining healthy rapport.

Retrospective interviews can be structured, semistructured, or informal. The ethnographer uses retrospective interviews to reconstruct the past, asking informants to recall personal historical information. This type of interview does not elicit the most accurate data. People forget or filter past events. In some cases, retrospective interviews are the only way to gather information about the past. In situations where the ethnographer already has an accurate understanding of the historical facts, retrospective interviews provide useful information about individuals.

All interviews share some generic kinds of questions. The most common types are survey or grand tour, detail or specific, and open-ended or closed-ended questions. Survey questions help identify significant topics to explore. Specific questions explore these topics in more detail. They determine similarities and differences in the ways people see the world. Open- and closed-ended questions help the ethnographer discover and confirm the participant's experiences and perceptions.

□ *Survey Questions*

A survey question—or what Spradley and McCurdy (1972) call a grand tour question—is designed to elicit a broad picture of the participant or native's world, to map the cultural terrain. Survey questions help the ethnographer to define the boundaries of a study and plan wise use of resources. The participant's overview of the physical setting, universe of activities, and thoughts helps to focus and direct the investigation.

Once survey questions reveal a category of some significance to both fieldworker and native, specific questions about that category become most useful. The difference between a survey question and a specific or detailed question depends largely on context.

Specific questions probe further into established categories of meaning or activity. Whereas survey questions shape and inform a global understanding, specific questions refine and expand that understanding. Structural and attribute questions—subcategories of specific questions—are often the most appropriate approach to this level of inquiry. Structural and attribute questions are useful to the ethnographer in organizing an understanding of the native's view. Structural questions reveal the similarities that exist across the conceptual spectrum—in the native's head. (See Spradley & McCurdy, 1972, for additional information about the construction of taxonomic definitions.) Attribute questions—questions about the characteristics of a role or a structural element—ferret out the differences between conceptual categories. Typically, the interview will juxtapose structural with attribute questions. Information from a structural question might suggest a question about the differences among various newly identified categories.

Ethnographic research requires the fieldworker to move back and forth between survey and specific questions. Focusing in on one segment of a person's activities or worldview prematurely may drain all the ethnographer's resources before the investigation is half done. The fieldworker must maintain a delicate balance of questions throughout the study; in general, however, survey questions should predominate in the early stages of fieldwork, and more specific questions in the middle and final stages.

☐ *Open-Ended or Closed-Ended Questions*

Ethnographers use both open-ended and closed-ended questions to pursue fieldwork. An open-ended question allows participants to interpret it. Closed-ended questions are useful in trying to quantify behavior patterns. Ethnographers typically ask more open-ended questions during discovery phases of their research and more closed-ended questions during confirmational periods. The most important type of question to avoid is the stand-alone vague question.

☐ *Interviewing Protocols and Strategies*

A protocol exists for all interviews—the product of the interviewer's and the participant's personalities and moods, the formality or informality of the setting, the stage of research, and an assortment of other conditions. The first element common to every protocol is the ethnographer's respect for the culture of the group under study. In an interview or any other interaction, ethnographers try to be sensitive to the group's cultural norms. This sensitivity manifests itself in apparel, language, and behavior. Second, an overarching guide in all interviews is respect for the person. An individual does the fieldworker a favor by giving up time to answer questions. Thus the interview is not an excuse to interrogate an individual or criticize cultural practices. It is an opportunity to learn from the interviewee. Further, the individual's time is precious: Both the industrial executive and the school janitor have work to do, and the ethnographer should plan initial interviews, whether formal or informal, around their work obligations and schedules. Later, the fieldworker becomes an integral part of the work.

In formal settings—such as a school district—a highly formalized, ritualistic protocol is necessary to gain access to and to interview students and teachers. Structured interviews require a more structured protocol of introductions, permission, instructions, formal cues to mark major changes in the interview, closure, and possible follow-up communications.

Informal interviews require the same initial protocol. However, the researcher casually and implicitly communicates permission, instructions, cues, closure, and follow-up signals. Pleasantries and icebreakers are important in both informal interviews and formally structured interviews, but they differ in the degree of subtlety each interview type requires. Sensitivity to the appropriate protocol can enhance the interviewer's effectiveness.

Particular strategies or techniques can also enhance the quality of an interview. The most effective strategy is, paradoxically, no strategy. Being natural is much more convincing than any performance (see Fetterman, 1989, for detail in this area).

☐ *Key Actor or Informant Interviewing*

Some people are more articulate and culturally sensitive than others. These individuals make excellent key actors or informants. *Informant* is the traditional anthropological term; however, I use the term *key actor* to describe this individual, to avoid both the stigma of the term *informant* and its historical roots. In the social group under study, this individual is one of many actors, and may not be a central or even an indispensable community member. Yet this individual becomes a key actor in the theater of ethnographic research and plays a pivotal role, linking the fieldworker and the community.

Key actors can provide detailed historical data, knowledge about contemporary interpersonal relationships (including conflicts), and a wealth of information about the nuances of everyday life. Although the ethnographer tries to speak with as many people as possible, time is always a factor. Therefore, anthropologists have traditionally relied most heavily on one or two individuals in a given group.

Typically, the key actor will find many of the ethnographer's questions obvious or stupid. The fieldworker is asking about basic features of the culture—elementary knowledge to the key actor. However, such naive questions often lead to global explanations of how a culture works. Such responses point out the difference between the key actor and a respondent. The key actor generally answers questions in a comprehensive, albeit meandering, fashion. A respondent answers a question specifically, without explanations about the larger picture and conversational tangents, with all their richness and texture. Interviewing a respondent is usually a more efficient data collection strategy, but it is also less revealing and potentially less valid than discussions with a key actor.

Key actors require careful selection. They are rarely perfect representatives of the group. However, they are usually members of the mainstream—otherwise, they would not have access to up-to-date cultural information. Key actors may be cultural brokers, straddling two cultures. This position may give them a special vantage point and objectivity about their culture. They may also be informal or formal leaders in the community. Key actors come from all walks of life and all socioeconomic and age groups.

Key actor and ethnographer must share a bond of trust. Respect on both sides is earned slowly. The ethnographer must take the time to search out and spend time with these articulate individuals. The fieldworker learns to depend on the key actor's information—particularly as cross-checks with other sources prove it to be accurate and revealing. Sometimes key actors are initially selected simply because they and the ethnographer have personality similarities or mutual interests. Ethnographers establish long-term relationships with key actors who continually provide reliable and insightful information. Key actors can be extremely effective and efficient sources of data and analysis.

At the same time, the ethnographer must judge the key actor's information cautiously. Overreliance on a key actor can be dangerous. Every study requires multiple sources. In addition, the fieldworker must take care to ensure that key actors do not simply provide answers they think the fieldworker wants to hear. The ethnographer can check answers rather easily, but must stay on guard against such distortion and contamination. Another, subtler problem occurs when a key actor begins to adopt the ethnographer's theoretical and conceptual framework. The key actor may inadvertently begin to describe the culture in terms of this a priori construct, undermining the fieldwork and distorting the emic or insider's perspective. (For further discussion of the role of key informants, see Dobbert, 1982; Ellen, 1984; Freilick, 1970; Goetz & LeCompte, 1984; Pelto, 1970; Spradley, 1979; Taylor & Bogdan, 1984.)

☐ *Life Histories and Expressive-Autobiographical Interviews*

Key actors often provide ethnographers with rich, detailed autobiographical descriptions. These life histories are usually quite personal; the individual is usually not completely representative of the group. However, how a key actor weaves a personal story tells much about the fabric of the social group. Personal description provides an integrated picture of the target culture.

Many of these oral histories are verifiable with additional work. However, in some instances the life history may not be verifiable or even factually accurate. In these cases, the life history is still invaluable because the record captures an individual's perception of the past, providing a unique look at how the key actor thinks and how personal and cultural values shape his or her perception of the past. Together with observation and interviewing, taking life histories allows the ethnographer to assemble a massive amount of perceptual data with which to generate and answer basic cultural questions about the social group.

The life history approach is usually rewarding for both key actor and ethnographer. However, it is exceedingly time-consuming. Approximations of this approach, including expressive-autobiographical interviewing, are particularly valuable contributions to a study with resource limitations and time constraints (see Spindler & Spindler, 1970, p. 293).

☐ *Lists and Forms*

A number of techniques can stimulate the interviewer's recall and help to organize the data. During a semistructured interview, the ethnographer may find a protocol or topical checklist useful. Printed or unobtrusively displayed on a portable computer screen, such a list usually contains the major topics and questions the ethnographer plans to cover during the interview. A checklist can be both a reminder and a mechanism to guide the interview when a more efficient approach is desirable. Similarly, after some experience in the field, the fieldworker can develop forms that facilitate data capture.

Checklists and forms help to organize and discipline data collection and analysis. Their construction should rely on some knowledge from the field to ensure their appropriateness and usefulness. Checklists and forms also require consistent use. However, such lists and forms are not cast in stone; new topics emerge that merit exploration. New conceptualizations arise, and different forms are necessary for collection and analysis of the relevant data.

☐ *Questionnaires*

Structured interviews are close approximations of questionnaires. Questionnaires represent perhaps the most formal and rigid form of exchange in the interviewing spectrum—the logical extension of an increasingly structured interview. However, questionnaires are qualitatively different from interviews because of the distance between the researcher and the respondent. Interviews have an interactive nature that questionnaires lack. In filling out a questionnaire, the respondent completes the researcher's form without any verbal exchange or clarification. Knowing whether the researcher and the respondent are on the same wavelength, sharing common assumptions and understandings about the questions, is difficult—perhaps impossible.

Misinterpretations and misrepresentations are common with questionnaires. Many people present idealized images of themselves on questionnaires, answering as they think they should to conform to a certain image. The researcher has no control over this type of response and no interpersonal cues to guide the interpretation of responses. Other problems include bias in the questions and poor return rates.

Despite these caveats, questionnaires are an excellent way for fieldworkers to tackle questions dealing with representativeness. They are the only realistic way of taking the pulses of hundreds or thousands of people. Anthropologists usually develop questionnaires to explore specific concerns after they have a good grasp of how the larger pieces of the puzzle fit together. The questionnaire is a product of the ethnographer's knowledge about the system, and the researcher can adapt it to a specific topic or set of concerns. Ethnographers also use existing questionnaires to test hypotheses about specific conceptions and behaviors. However, the ethnographer must establish the relevance of a particular questionnaire to the target culture or subculture before administering it.

☐ *Projective Techniques*

Projective techniques supplement and enhance fieldwork, they do not replace it. These techniques are employed by the ethnographer to elicit cultural and often psychological information from group members. Typically, the ethnographer holds an item up and asks the participant what it is. The researcher may have an idea about what the item represents, but that idea is less important than the participant's perception. The participant's responses usually reveal individual needs, fears, inclinations, and general worldview.

Projective techniques, however revealing, rarely stand alone. The researcher needs to set these techniques in a larger research context to understand the elicited responses completely. Projective techniques can elicit cues that can lead to further inquiry or can be one of several sources of information to support an ongoing hypothesis. Only the ethnographer's imagination limits the number of possible projective techniques. However, the fieldworker should use only those tests that can be relevant to the local group and the study.

☐ *Additional Eliciting Devices*

A variety of other tools are available with which the fieldworker can elicit the insider's classification and categorization of a target culture. Ethnographers ask participants to rank order people in their communities to understand the various social hierarchies. The semantic differential technique (Osgood, 1964) elicits an insider's rating of certain concepts. Cognitive mapping is also useful in eliciting the insider's perspective. Asking a student to map out his or her walk to school with various landmarks—for example, a route that identifies gang territories by block—provides insight into how that individual sees the world. As with projective techniques, the ethnographer requires some baseline knowledge of the community before he or she can design and use such techniques.

☐ *Unobtrusive Measures*

I began this section on methods and techniques by stating that ethnographers are human instruments, dependent on all their senses for data collection and analysis. Most ethnographic methods are interactive: They involve dealing with people. The ethnographer attempts to be as unobtrusive as possible to minimize effects on the participant's behavior. However, data collection techniques—except for questionnaires—fundamentally depend on that human interaction.

A variety of other measures, however, do not require human interaction and can supplement interactive methods of data collection and analysis. These methods require only that the ethnographer keep eyes and ears open. Ranging from outcroppings to folktales, these unobtrusive measures allow the ethnographer to draw social and cultural inferences from physical evidence (see Webb, Campbell, Schwartz, & Sechrest, 1966).

Outcroppings

Outcropping is a geological term referring to a portion of the bedrock that is visible on the surface—in other words, something that sticks out. Outcroppings in inner-city ethnographic research include skyscrapers, burned-out buildings, graffiti, the smell of urine on city streets, yards littered with garbage, a Rolls-Royce, and a syringe in the schoolyard. The researcher can quickly estimate the relative wealth or poverty of an area from these outcroppings. Initial inferences are possible without any human interaction. However, such cues by themselves can be misleading. A house with all the modern conveniences and luxuries imaginable can signal wealth or financial overextension verging on bankruptcy. The researcher must place each outcropping in a larger context. A broken syringe can have several meanings, depending on whether it lies on the floor of a doctor's office or in an elementary schoolyard late at night. On the walls of an inner-city school, the absence of graffiti is as important as its presence.

Changes in a physical setting over time can also be revealing. For example, an increase in the number of burned-out and empty buildings on a block indicates a decaying neighborhood. Conversely, an increase in the number of remodeled and revitalized houses may be indicative of gentrification, in which wealthy investors take over the neighborhood. The fieldworker must assess this abundant information with care, but should not ignore it or take it for granted.

Written and Electronic Information

In literate societies, written documents provide one of the most valuable and timesaving forms of data collection. In studies of office life, I have found past reports, memoranda, and personnel and payroll records invaluable. Mission statements and annual reports provide the organization's purpose or stated purpose and indicate the image the organization wishes to present to the outside world. Internal evaluation reports indicate areas of concern. Budgets tell a great deal about organizational values. Electronic mail is often less inhibited than general correspondence and thus quite revealing about office interrelationships, turf, and various power struggles. Proper use of this type of information can save the ethnographer years of work.

Proxemics and Kinesics

Proxemics is the analysis of socially defined distance between people, and kinesics focuses on body language (see Birdwhistell, 1970; Hall, 1974). In American culture, a salesperson speaking about a product while standing 2 inches away from a prospective buyer's face has probably intruded on the buyer's sense of private space. A skillful use of such intrusion may overwhelm the customer and make the sale, but it is more likely to turn the customer off.

Sensitivity to body language can also be instrumental in ethnographic research. A clenched fist, a student's head on a desk, a condescending superior's facial expression, a scowl, a blush, a student sitting at the edge of a chair with eyes fixed on the lecturer, and many other physical statements provide useful information to the observant fieldworker. In context, this information can generate hypotheses, partially confirm suspicions, and add another layer of understanding to fieldwork.

Folktales

Folktales are important to both literate and nonliterate societies. They crystallize an ethos or a way of being. Cultures often use folktales to transmit critical cultural values and lessons from one generation to the next. Folktales usually draw on familiar surroundings and on figures relevant to the local setting, but the stories themselves are facades. Beneath the thin veneer is another layer of meaning. This inner layer reveals the stories' underlying values. Stories provide ethnographers with insight into the secular and the sacred, the intellectual and the emotional life of a people.

All the methods and techniques discussed above are used together in ethnographic research. They reinforce one another. Like concepts, methods and techniques guide the ethnographer through the maze of human existence. Discovery and understanding are at the heart of this endeavor. The next section explores a wide range of useful devices that make the ethnographer's expedition through time and space more productive and pleasant.

■ *Equipment*

Notepads, computers, tape recorders, cameras—all the tools of ethnography are merely extensions of the human instrument, aids to memory and vision. Yet these useful devices can facilitate the ethnographic mission by capturing the rich detail and flavor of the ethnographic experience and then helping to organize and analyze these data. Ethnographic equipment ranges from simple

paper and pen to high-tech laptop and mainframe computers, from tape recorders and cameras to videocassette recorders. The proper equipment can
make the ethnographer's sojourn in an alien culture more pleasant, safe, productive, and rewarding.

☐ *Pen and Paper*

The most common tools ethnographers use are pen and paper. With these
tools, the fieldworker records notes from interviews during or after each session, sketches an area's physical layout, traces an organizational chart, and
outlines informal social networks. Notepads can hold initial impressions, detailed conversations, and preliminary analyses. Most academics have had a
great deal of experience with these simple tools, having taken extensive notes
in classes. Note-taking skill is easily transferable to the field. Pen and paper
have several advantages: ease of use, minimal expense, and unobtrusiveness.
The drawbacks are obvious: The note-taking fieldworker cannot record every
word and nuance in a social situation, has difficulty maintaining eye contact
with other participants, and must expend a great deal of effort to record data
legibly and in an organized manner.

☐ *Laptop Computers*

The laptop computer is a significant improvement over pen and notepad.
Laptop computers are truly portable computers for use in the office, on a plane,
or in the field. I often use one in lieu of pen and paper during interviews. In a
technologically sophisticated setting, a laptop is rarely obtrusive or distracting
if the fieldworker introduces the device casually and with consideration for the
person and the situation. Laptop computers can save ethnographers time they
can better spend thinking and analyzing. They greatly reduce the fieldworker's
need to type up raw data interview notes every day, because the fieldworker
enters these data into the computer only once, during or immediately after an
interview. These notes can then be expanded and revised with ease. The files
can be transferred from the laptop to a personal computer or mainframe with
an external disk drive, appropriate software, and/or a high-speed modem. These
files can then be merged with other field data, forming a highly organized
(dated and cross-referenced), cumulative record of the fieldwork.

Laptops also provide the ethnographer with an opportunity to interact with
participants at critical analytic moments. Ethnographers can share and revise
notes, spreadsheets, and graphs with participants on the spot. I routinely ask
participants to review my notes and memoranda as a way to improve the accuracy of my observations and to sensitize me to their concerns.

The laptop computer is not a panacea, but it is a real time-saver and is
particularly useful in contract research. An ethnographer who conducts multi-
site research can carry a laptop to the sites and send files home via modem

linkup with a home computer. Laptops also greatly facilitate communication from the field to the research center through interactive electronic mail systems. Laptops have drawbacks, of course, as any equipment does. The fieldworker must learn the operating system, word processing, and so on. Using a laptop is not as easy as using a pen and paper. In addition, the fieldworker needs to take time to acquaint people with the device before thrusting it before them. Certain people will explicitly or implicitly prohibit the use of even a pen and notepad, never mind a laptop or other device. Also, the clatter of the keyboard can be distracting and obtrusive in certain situations. In most cases, however, a brief desensitization period will make people feel comfortable with the equipment. In fact, the laptop can be an icebreaker, helping the fieldworker to develop a strong rapport with people and at the same time inuring them to its presence. Given a careful introduction, laptops or any other useful pieces of equipment can greatly facilitate ethnographic work.

☐ *Desktop Computers*

Many researchers use laptops to compose memos, reports, and articles, to conduct interviews, and for general data collection, and then upload or send their files to a desktop computer with more storage capacity for extensive manipulation. However, an increasing number of researchers are using their laptop or notebook-type computers as their primary computers, because they are as powerful as the larger systems but more convenient.

☐ *Database Software*

Database programs enable the ethnographer to play a multitude of what-if games, to test a variety of hypotheses with the push of a button (and a few macros—strings of commands—assigned to that button). I have used a variety of database programs to test my perceptions of the frequency of certain behaviors, to test specific hypotheses, and to provide new insights into the data. NUDIST, Ethnograph, HyperQual, HyperResearch, AskSam, Qualpro, and Atlas/ti are some programs that are well suited to ethnographic research. Dataease and Lotus are less suitable for field notes, but are useful for more limited data sets and manipulation. (See Weitzman & Miles, 1995, for a detailed review of qualitative data analysis software.)

☐ *Videoconferencing Technology*

Videoconferencing technology allows geographically disparate parties to see and hear each other—around the globe. Free or inexpensive software programs, including CU-SeeMe, are available that allow videoconferencing online over the Internet, with no satellite or long-distance charges. With only this software and a small, relatively inexpensive digital camera plugged directly into a personal computer, individuals can videoconference through their computer screens with any other similarly equipped users worldwide. I use videoconferencing to conduct follow-up interviews and observations at remote sites, after initially interviewing on-site and establishing rapport in person (see Fetterman, 1996, for additional details).

Ethnographers have conducted fieldwork for generations without the benefit of laptop and desktop computers, printers, database software, and videoconferencing, and continue to conduct it without them. However, these tools are becoming indispensable in many disciplines, and few anthropologists conduct research without the use of some type of computer. Yet computers have limitations: They are only as good as the data the user enters. They still require the eyes and ears of the ethnographer to determine what to collect and how to record it, as well as how to interpret the data from a cultural perspective. (For further information about computing in ethnographic and qualitative research, see Brent, 1984; Conrad & Reinharz, 1984; Fischer, 1994; Podolefsky & McCarthy, 1983; Sproull & Sproull, 1982; Weitzman & Miles, 1995; also see "Computer-Assisted Anthropology," 1984. My web page provides a list of ethnographic resources on the Internet at http://www.stanford.edu/~davidf/ethnography.html.)

☐ *Tape Recorders*

Ethnographers attempt to immerse themselves in the field, working with people rather than devices. Tools that free the ethnographer from recording devices, whether pen and paper or laptop computers, are welcome. Tape recorders allow the ethnographer to engage in lengthy informal and semistructured interviews without the distraction of manual recording devices. Tape recorders effectively capture long verbatim quotations, essential to good fieldwork, while the ethnographer maintains a natural conversational flow. Audiotapes can be analyzed over and over again. In all cases, however, the fieldworker should use the tape recorder judiciously and only with consent.

Tape recorders can inhibit some individuals from speaking freely during interviews. Some individuals may fear reprisals because their voices are identifiable on tape. The ethnographer must assure these people of the confidentiality of the data. Sometimes, easing into the use of tape recorders slowly can avoid unnecessary tension. I usually begin with pen and pad, and then ask if I can switch to the tape recorder simply because I cannot write fast enough to catch every word. I also stop the tape recorder whenever I touch on a topic that the interviewee thinks is too sensitive. A quick response to such requests highlights the ethnographer's sensitivity and integrity, and strengthens the bond between ethnographer and participant.

Tape recorders are useful icebreakers. On several occasions, I have recorded students' songs on the tape recorder and played the music back for them before asking them about the school under study. During group interviews, I typically ask students to pass the tape recorder around and introduce themselves on it as though they were celebrities. This approach often makes them eager to participate in the discussion and usually makes them comfortable with the machine. It also enables me to identify accurately each participant's words long after I have left the field.

Tape recorders do, however, have some hidden costs. Transcribing tapes is an extremely time-consuming and tedious task. Listening to a tape takes as much time as making the original recording—hours of interview data require hours of listening. Transcribing tapes adds another dimension to the concept of time-consumption. Typically, the fieldworker edits the tapes, transcribing only the most important sections. A carefully selected professional transcriber can remove this burden if funds are available.

☐ *Cameras*

Cameras have a special role in ethnographic research. They can function as a can opener, providing rapid entry into a community or classroom (see Collier, 1967; Fetterman, 1980). They are a known commodity to most industrialized and many nonindustrialized groups. I use cameras to help establish an immediate familiarity with people. Cameras can create pictures useful in projective techniques or can be projective tools themselves. They are most useful, however, for documenting field observations.

Cameras document people, places, events, and settings over time. They enable the ethnographer to create a photographic record of specific behaviors. As Collier (1967) explains:

> Photography is a legitimate abstracting process in observation. It is one of the first steps in evidence refinement that turns raw circumstances into data that are manageable in research analysis. Photographs are precise records of material reality. They are also documents that can be filed and cross-filed as can verbal statements. Photographic evidence can be endlessly duplicated, enlarged or reduced in visual dimension, and fitted into many schemes or diagrams, and by scientific reading, into many statistical designs. (p. 5)

Photographs are mnemonic devices. During analysis and writing periods, photographs and slides can bring a rush of detail that the fieldworker might not remember otherwise. By capturing cultural scenes and episodes on film at the beginning of a study—before he or she has a grasp of the situation—the ethnographer can use the pictures to interpret events retroactively, producing a rare second chance. Also, the camera often captures details on film that the human eye has missed. Although the camera is an extension of the subjective eye, it can be a more objective observer, less dependent on the fieldworker's biases and expectations. A photographic record provides information that the fieldworker may not have noticed at the time. Photographs and slides are also excellent educational tools, both in the classroom and in a sponsor's conference room.

The use of the camera or any photographic or audio recording mechanisms in fieldwork requires the subjects' permission. Some people are uncomfortable having their pictures taken; others cannot afford exposure. The ethnographer may enter the lives of people on their terms, but may not invade individual privacy. Photography is often perceived to be an intrusion. People are usually self-conscious about their self-presentation and concerned about how and where their pictures will be seen. An individual's verbal permission is usually sufficient to take a picture. However, written permission is necessary to publish or to display that picture in a public forum. Even with verbal and written permission in hand, the ethnographer must exercise judgment in choosing an appropriate display and suitable forum. Cameras, too, can be problematic. Inappropriate use of cameras can annoy and irritate people, undermining rapport and degrading the quality of the data. Cameras can also distort reality. A skillful photographer uses angles and shadows to exaggerate the size of a building or to shape the expression on a person's face. The same techniques can present a distorted picture of an individual's behavior. (See Becker, 1979, for an excellent discussion of photography and threats to validity. See also the visual anthropology journal *Studies in Visual Communication.*)

□ *Videotape Recorders*

Videotape recordings are extremely useful in micro ethnographic studies. Ethnographers usually have a fraction of a second to reflect on a gesture or a person's posture or gait. Videotape provides the observer with the ability to stop time. The ethnographer can tape a class and watch it over and over again, each time finding new layers of meaning or nonverbal signals from teacher to student, from student to teacher, and from student to student. Over time, visual and verbal patterns of communication become clear.

Videotape equipment is essential to any micro ethnographic research effort. Gatekeeping procedures (Erickson, 1976) and the politics of the classroom (McDermott, 1974) are some elements of complex social situations that the fieldworker can capture on tape. However, the fieldworker must weigh the expense of the equipment and the time required to use it against the value of the information it will capture. Many ethnographic studies simply do not need fine-grained pictures of social reality. In addition, the expense of using videotape equipment—including camera, videotapes, and videotape recorder/player—is not a trivial consideration. This equipment is also notably obtrusive. Even after participants have spent time with the ethnographer with and without the equipment, mugging and posing for the camera are not uncommon. The most significant hazard in using videotape equipment is the risk of tunnel vision. Ideally, the ethnographer has studied the social group long enough to know what to focus on. The ethnographer may need months to develop a reasonably clear conception of specific behaviors before deciding to focus on them for a time. The videotape can focus in on a certain type of behavior to the exclusion of almost everything else. Thus the ethnographer may arrive at a very good understanding of a specific cultural mechanism but achieve little understanding of its real role in a particular environment.

☐ *Cinema*

The use of cinema or movies in ethnographic research remains rare. In ethnography, movies primarily present finished pictures of cultural groups; they are not tools that researchers use to compose these pictures. Cost and the expertise needed to function as a filmmaker and editor are probably the primary reasons underlying this emphasis. Ethnographic films have rigorous requirements, ranging from actual time sequencing to authenticity of the events recorded. Heider (1976, pp. 46-117) has produced a scale of "ethnographicness" with which to judge ethnographic films.

The brief review of ethnographic equipment offered in this section is certainly not exhaustive. For example, many novel computer-aided design tools provide three-dimensional pictures of objects—an extremely useful tool for anthropologists working in space exploration. However, the tools discussed here are the ones that an ethnographer will most often use in the field. As aids to the ethnographer's own senses and abilities, they ease the difficult task of analysis, which is the subject of the next section of this chapter.

■ *Analysis*

Analysis is one of the most engaging features of ethnography. It begins at the moment a fieldworker selects a problem to study and ends with the last word in the report or ethnography. Ethnography involves many levels of analysis. Some are simple and informal; others require some statistical sophistication. Ethnographic analysis is iterative, building on ideas throughout the study. Analyzing data in the field enables the ethnographer to know precisely which methods to use next, as well as when and how to use them. Through analysis, the ethnographer tests hypotheses and perceptions to construct an accurate conceptual framework about what is happening in the social group under study. Analysis in ethnography is as much a test of the ethnographer as it is a test of the data.

☐ *Thinking*

First and foremost, analysis is a test of the ethnographer's ability to think—to process information in a meaningful and useful manner. The ethnographer confronts a vast array of complex information and needs to make some sense of it all—piece by piece. The initial stage in analysis involves simple perception. However, even perception is selective. The ethnographer selects and isolates pieces of information from all the data in the field. The ethnographer's personal or idiosyncratic approach, together with an assortment of academic theories and models, focuses and limits the scope of inquiry. However, the field presents a vast amount of material, and in understanding day-to-day human interaction, elementary thinking skills are as important as ethnographic concepts and methods.

A focus on relevant, manageable topics is essential and is possible through the refinement of the unit of analysis. But then the fieldworker must probe those topics by comparing and contrasting data, trying to fit pieces of data into the bigger puzzle—all the while hypothesizing about the best fit and the best picture.

The ethnographer employs many useful techniques to make sense of the forests of data, from triangulation to the use of statistical software packages. All these techniques, however, require critical thinking skills—notably, the ability to synthesize and evaluate information—and a large dose of common sense.

☐ *Triangulation*

Triangulation is basic in ethnographic research. It is at the heart of ethnographic validity, testing one source of information against another to strip away alternative explanations and prove a hypothesis. Typically, the ethnographer compares information sources to test the quality of the information (and the person sharing it), to understand more completely the part an actor plays in the social drama, and ultimately to put the whole situation into perspective. (See Webb et al., 1966, for a detailed discussion of triangulation.)

☐ *Patterns*

Ethnographers look for patterns of thought and behavior. Patterns are a form of ethnographic reliability. Ethnographers see patterns of thought and action repeat in various situations and among various players. Looking for patterns is a form of analysis. The ethnographer begins with a mass of undifferentiated ideas and behavior, and then collects pieces of information, comparing, contrasting, and sorting gross categories and minutiae until a discernible thought or behavior becomes identifiable. Next the ethnographer must listen and observe, and then compare his or her observations with this poorly defined model. Exceptions to the rule emerge, variations on a theme are detectable. These variants help to circumscribe the activity and clarify its meaning. The process requires further sifting and sorting to make a match between categories. The theme or ritualistic activity finally emerges, consisting of a collection of such matches between the model (abstracted from reality) and the ongoing observed reality.

Any cultural group's patterns of thought and behavior are interwoven strands. As soon as the ethnographer finishes analyzing and identifying one pattern, another pattern emerges for analysis and identification. The fieldworker can then compare the two patterns. In practice, the ethnographer works simultaneously on many patterns. The level of understanding increases geometrically as the ethnographer moves up the conceptual ladder—mixing and matching patterns and building theory from the ground up. (See Glaser & Strauss, 1967, for a discussion of grounded theory.)

The observer can make preliminary inferences about the entire economic system by analyzing the behavior that is subsumed within the pattern, as well as the patterns themselves. Ethnographers acquire a deeper understanding of and appreciation for a culture as they weave each part of the ornate human tapestry together, by observing and analyzing the patterns of everyday life.

☐ *Key Events*

Key or focal events that the fieldworker can use to analyze an entire culture occur in every social group. Geertz (1973) eloquently used the cockfight to understand and portray Balinese life. Key events come in all shapes and sizes. Some tell more about a culture than others, but all provide a focus for analysis (see also Geertz, 1957).

Key events, like snapshots or videotapes, concretely convey a wealth of information. Some images are clear representations of social activity; others provide a tremendous amount of embedded meaning. Once the event is recorded, the ethnographer can enlarge or reduce any portion of the picture. A rudimentary knowledge of the social situation will enable the ethnographer to infer a great deal from key events. In many cases, the event is a metaphor for a way of life or a specific social value. Key events provide lenses through which to view a culture.

Key events are extraordinarily useful for analysis. Not only do they help the fieldworker understand a social group, but the fieldworker in turn can use them to explain the culture to others. The key event thus becomes a metaphor for the culture. Key events also illustrate how participation, observation, and analysis are inextricably bound together during fieldwork.

☐ *Maps, Flowcharts, Organizational Charts, and Matrices*

Visual representations are useful tools in ethnographic research. Having to draw a map of the community tests an ethnographer's understanding of the area's physical layout. It can also help the ethnographer chart a course through the community. Flowcharts are useful in studies of production line operations. Flowcharting a social welfare program is also common in evaluation. The analytic process of mapping the flow of activity and information can also serve as a vehicle to initiate additional discussions. Drawing organizational charts is a useful analytic tool. It tests the ethnographer's knowledge of the system, much as drawing a map or a flowchart does. Both formal and informal organizational hierarchies can be charted for comparison. In addition, organizational charts can measure changes over time, as people move in and out or up and down the hierarchy. Organizational charts clarify the structure and function of any institutional form of human organization.

Matrices provide a simple, systematic, graphic way to compare and contrast data. The researcher can compare and cross-reference categories of information to establish a picture of a range of behaviors or thought categories. Matrices also help the researcher to identify emerging patterns in the data. (See Miles & Huberman, 1994, for detailed presentation of the use of matrices in qualitative research.) Maps, flowcharts, organizational charts, and matrices all help to crystallize and display consolidated information.

□ *Content Analysis*

Ethnographers analyze written and electronic data in much the same way they analyze observed behavior. They triangulate information within documents to test for internal consistency. They attempt to discover patterns within the text and seek key events recorded and memorialized in print.

Ethnographers may subject internal documents to special scrutiny to determine whether they are internally consistent with program philosophy. Reviews may also reveal significant patterns. It is often possible for the ethnographer to infer the significance of a concept from its frequency and context in the text.

□ *Statistics*

Ethnographers use nonparametric statistics more often than parametric statistics because they typically work with small samples. Parametric statistics require large samples for statistical significance. The use of nonparametric statistics is also more consistent with the needs and concerns of most anthropologists. Anthropologists typically work with nominal and ordinal scales. Nominal scales consist of discrete categories, such as sex and religion. Ordinal scales also provide discrete categories as well as a range of variation within each category—for example, reform, conservative, and orthodox variants within the category of Judaism. Ordinal scales do not determine the degree of difference between subcategories. The Guttman (1944) scale is one example of an ordinal scale that is useful in ethnographic research.

The chi-square test and the Fisher exact probability test are popular nonparametric statistical tools in anthropology. However, all statistical formulas require that certain assumptions be met before the formulas may be applied to any situation. A disregard for these variables in the statistical equation is as dangerous as neglect of comparable assumptions in the human equation in conducting ethnographic fieldwork. Both errors result in distorted and misleading efforts at worst, and waste valuable time at best.

Ethnographers use parametric statistics when they have large samples and limited time and resources to conduct all the interviews. Survey and questionnaire work often requires sophisticated statistical tests of significance. Ethnographers also use the results of parametric statistics to test certain hypotheses, cross-check their own observations, and generally provide additional insight. (See Fetterman, 1989, for discussion of problems with statistics.)

☐ *Crystallization*

Ethnographers crystallize their thoughts at various stages throughout an ethnographic endeavor. The crystallization may bring a mundane conclusion, a novel insight, or an earth-shattering epiphany. The crystallization is typically the result of a convergence of similarities that spontaneously strike the ethnographer as relevant or important to the study. Crystallization may be an exciting process or the result of painstaking, boring, methodical work. This research gestalt requires attention to all pertinent variables in an equation.

Every study has classic moments when everything falls into place. After months of thought and immersion in the culture, the ethnographer discovers that a special configuration gels. All the subtopics, miniexperiments, layers of triangulated effort, key events, and patterns of behavior form a coherent and often cogent picture of what is happening. One of the most exciting moments in ethnographic research is when an ethnographer discovers a counterintuitive conception of reality—a conception that defies common sense. Such moments make the long days and nights worthwhile.

Analysis has no single form or stage in ethnography. Multiple analyses and forms of analyses are essential. Analysis takes place throughout any ethnographic endeavor, from the selection of the problem to the final stages of writing. Analysis is iterative and often cyclical in ethnography (see Goetz & LeCompte, 1984; Hammersley & Atkinson, 1983; Taylor & Bogdan, 1984). The researcher builds a firm knowledge base in bits and pieces, asking questions, listening, probing, comparing and contrasting, synthesizing, and evaluating information. The ethnographer must run sophisticated tests on data long before leaving the field. However, a formal, identifiable stage of analysis does take place when the ethnographer physically leaves the field. Half the analysis at this stage involves additional triangulation, sifting for patterns, developing new matrices, and applying statistical tests to the data. The other half takes place during the final stage of writing an ethnography or an ethnographically informed report.

■ *Writing*

Ethnography requires good writing skills at every stage of the enterprise. Research proposals, field notes, memoranda, interim reports, final reports, articles, and books are the tangible products of ethnographic work. The ethnographer can share these written works with participants to verify their accuracy and with colleagues for review and consideration. Ethnography offers many intangibles, through the media of participation and verbal communication. However, written products, unlike transitory conversations and interactions, withstand the test of time.

Writing good field notes is very different from writing a solid and illuminating ethnography or ethnographically informed report. Note taking is the rawest kind of writing. The note taker typically has an audience of one. Thus, although clarity, concision, and completeness are vital in note taking, style is not a primary consideration.

Writing for an audience, however, means writing to that audience. Reports for academics, government bureaucrats, private and public industry officials, medical professionals, and various educational program sponsors require different formats, languages, and levels of abstraction. The brevity and emphasis on findings in a report written for a program-level audience might raise some academics' eyebrows and cause them to question the project's intellectual effort. Similarly, a refereed scholarly publication would frustrate program personnel, who would likely feel that the researcher is wasting their time with irrelevant concerns, time that they need to take care of business. In essence, both parties feel that the researcher is simply not in touch with their reality. These two audiences are both interested in the fieldwork and the researcher's conclusions, but have different needs and concerns. Good ethnographic work can usually produce information that is relevant to both parties. The skillful ethnographer will communicate effectively with all audiences—using the right smoke signals for the right tribe. (See Fetterman, 1987b, for discussion of the ethnographer as rhetorician. See also Yin, 1994, for discussion of differing audiences in the presentation of a case study.)

Writing is part of the analysis process as well as a means of communication (see also Hammersley & Atkinson, 1983). Writing clarifies thinking. In sitting down to put thoughts on paper, an individual must organize those thoughts and sort out specific ideas and relationships. Writing often reveals gaps in knowledge. If the researcher is still in the field when he or she discovers those gaps, the researcher needs to conduct additional interviews and observations of specific settings. If the researcher has left the field, field notes and telephone calls must suffice. Embryonic ideas often come to maturity during writing, as the ethnographer crystallizes months of thought on a particular topic. From conception—as a twinkle in the ethnographer's eye—to delivery in the final report, an ethnographic study progresses through written stages. (For additional discussions of ethnographic writing, see Fetterman, 1989; Wolcott, 1990.)

■ *Ethics*

Ethnographers do not work in a vacuum, they work with people. They often pry into people's innermost secrets, sacred rites, achievements, and failures. In pursuing this personal science, ethnographers subscribe to a code of ethics that preserves the participants' rights, facilitates communication in the field, and leaves the door open for further research.

This code specifies first and foremost that the ethnographer do no harm to the people or the community under study. In seeking a logical path through the cultural wilds, the ethnographer is careful not to trample the feelings of natives or desecrate what the culture calls sacred. This respect for social environment ensures not only the rights of the people, but also the integrity of the data and a productive, enduring relationship between the people and the researcher. Professionalism and a delicate step demonstrate the ethnographer's deep respect, admiration, and appreciation for the people's way of life. Noninvasive ethnography is not only good ethics, it is also good science (see American Anthropological Association, 1990; Rynkiewich & Spradley, 1976; Weaver, 1973). Basic underlying ethical standards include the securing of permission (to protect individual privacy), honesty, trust (both implicit and explicit), and reciprocity (see Sieber, Chapter 5, this volume).

☐ *Permission*

Ethnographers must formally or informally seek informed consent to conduct their work. In a school district, formal written requests are requisite. Often the ethnographer's request is accompanied by a detailed account of the purpose and design of the study. Similarly, in most government agencies and private industry, the researcher must submit a formal request and receive written permission. The nature of the request and the consent changes according to the context of the study. For example, no formal structure exists for the researcher to communicate within a study of tramps. However, permission is still necessary to conduct a study. In this situation, the request may be as simple as the following embedded question to a tramp: "I am interested in learning about your life, and I would like to ask you a few questions, if that's all right with you." In this context, a detailed explanation of purpose and method might be counterproductive unless the individual asks for additional detail.

☐ *Honesty*

Ethnographers must be candid about their task, explaining what they plan to study and how they plan to study it. In some cases detailed description is appropriate, and in others extremely general statements are best, according to the type of audience and the interest in the topic. Few individuals want to hear a detailed discussion of the theoretical and methodological bases of an ethnographer's work. However, the ethnographer should be ready throughout the study to present this information to any participant who requests it. Deceptive techniques are unnecessary and inappropriate in ethnographic research. Ethnographers need not disguise their efforts or use elaborate ploys to trick people into responding to specific stimuli.

☐ *Trust*

Ethnographers need the trust of the people they work with to complete their task. An ethnographer who establishes a bond of trust will learn about the many layers of meaning in any community or program under study. The ethnographer builds this bond on a foundation of honesty, and communicates this trust verbally and nonverbally. He or she may speak simply and promise confidentiality as the need arises. Nonverbally, the ethnographer communicates this trust through self-presentation and general demeanor. Appropriate apparel, an open physical posture, handshakes, and other nonverbal cues can establish and maintain trust between an ethnographer and a participant.

Actions speak louder than words. An ethnographer's behavior in the field is usually his or her most effective means of cementing relationships and building trust. People like to talk, and ethnographers love to listen. As people learn that the ethnographer will respect and protect their conversations, they open up a little more each day in the belief that the researcher will not betray their trust. Trust can be an instant and spontaneous chemical reaction, but more often it is a long, steady process, like building a friendship.

☐ *Pseudonyms*

Ethnographic descriptions are usually detailed and revealing. They probe beyond the facade of normal human interaction. Such descriptions can jeopardize individuals. One person may speak candidly about a neighbor's wild parties and mention calling the police to complain about them. Another individual may reveal the arbitrary and punitive behavior of a program director or principal. Each individual has provided invaluable information about how the system really works. However, the delicate web of interrelationships in a neighborhood, a school, or an office might be destroyed if the researcher reveals the source of this information. Similarly, individuals involved in illegal activity—ranging from handling venomous rattlesnakes in a religious ceremony to selling heroin in East Detroit in order to build a gang empire—have a legitimate concern about the repercussions of the researcher's disclosing their identities.

The use of pseudonyms is a simple way to disguise the identities of individuals and protect them from potential harm. Disguising the name of the village or program can also prevent the curious from descending on the community and disrupting the social fabric of its members' lives. Similarly, coding confidential data helps to prevent them from falling into the wrong hands. However, there are limits to confidentiality in litigation.

☐ *Reciprocity*

Ethnographers use a great deal of people's time, and they owe something in return. In some cases, ethnographers provide a service simply by lending a sympathetic ear to troubled individuals. In other situations, the ethnographer may offer time and expertise as barter—for example, teaching a participant English or math, milking cows and cleaning chicken coops, or helping a key actor set up a new computer and learn to use the software. Ethnographers also offer the results of their research in its final form as a type of reciprocity.

Some circumstances legitimate direct payment for services rendered, such as having participants help distribute questionnaires, hiring them as guides on expeditions, and soliciting various kinds of technical assistance. However, direct payment is not a highly recommended form of reciprocity. This approach often reinforces patterns of artificial dependence and fosters inappropriate expectations. Direct payment may also shape a person's responses or recommendations throughout a study. Reciprocity in some form is essential during fieldwork (and, in some cases, after the study is complete), but it should not become an obtrusive, contaminating, or unethical activity.

□   *Guilty Knowledge and Dirty Hands*

During the more advanced stages of fieldwork, the ethnographer is likely to encounter the problems of guilty knowledge and dirty hands. *Guilty knowledge* refers to confidential knowledge of illegal or illicit activities. *Dirty hands* refers to situations in which the ethnographer cannot emerge innocent of wrongdoing (see Fetterman, 1983, 1989; Klockars, 1977, 1979; Polsky, 1967). Ethics guide the first and last steps of an ethnography. Ethnographers stand at ethical crossroads throughout their research. This fact of ethnographic life sharpens the senses and ultimately refines and enhances the quality of the endeavor. (See Fetterman, 1989, for detailed discussion of the complexity of ethical decision making in ethnography.)

■ *Conclusion*

This chapter has provided a brisk walk through the intellectual landscape of ethnography, leading the reader step by step through the ethnographic terrain, periodically stopping to smell the roses and contemplate the value of one concept or technique over another.

Each section of the chapter has built on the one before—as each step on a path follows the step before. Discussion about the selection of a problem or issue has been followed by a detailed discussion of guiding concepts. The ethnographer's next logical step is to become acquainted with the tools of the trade—the methods and techniques required to conduct ethnographic research and the equipment used to chisel out this scientific art form. A discussion of analysis in ethnographic research becomes more meaningful at this stage, once the preceding facets of ethnography have laid the foundation. Similarly, I have discussed the role of writing in the second-to-last section of this chapter because writing is one of the final stages in the process and because the meaning of writing in ethnography is amplified and made more illuminating by a series of discussions about what "doing ethnography" entails. Finally, ethics comes last because the complete ethnographic context is necessary to a meaningful discussion of this topic. Step by step, this chapter provides a path through the complex terrain of ethnographic work.

■ References

American Anthropological Association. (1990). *Principles of professional responsibility.* Arlington, VA: Author.

Becker, H. S. (1979). Do photographs tell the truth? In T. D. Cook & C. S. Reichardt (Eds.), *Qualitative and quantitative methods in evaluation research.* Beverly Hills, CA: Sage.

Birdwhistell, R. L. (1970). *Kinesics and context: Essays on body motion communication.* Philadelphia: University of Pennsylvania Press.

Brent, E. (1984). Qualitative computing approaches and issues. *Qualitative Sociology, 7,* 61-74.

Collier, J. (1967). *Visual anthropology: Photography as a research method.* New York: Holt, Rinehart & Winston.

Computer-assisted anthropology [Special section]. (1984). *Practicing Anthropology, 6*(2), 1-17.

Conrad, P., & Reinharz, S. (1984). Computers and qualitative data. *Qualitative Sociology, 7, 1-2.*

Denzin, N. K. (1989). *Interpretive interactionism.* Newbury Park, CA: Sage.

Dobbert, M. L. (1982). *Ethnographic research: Theory and application for modern schools and societies.* New York: Praeger.

Dolgin, J. L., Kemnitzer, D. S., & Schneider, D. M. (1977). *Symbolic anthropology: A reader in the study of symbols and meanings.* New York: Columbia University Press.

Ellen, R. F. (1984). *Ethnographic research: A guide to general conduct.* New York: Academic Press.

Erickson, F. (1976). Gatekeeping encounters: A social selection process. In P. R. Sanday (Ed.), *Anthropology and the public interest: Fieldwork and theory.* New York: Academic Press.

Fetterman, D. M. (1980). Ethnographic techniques in educational evaluation: An illustration. In A. Van Fleet (Ed.), Anthropology of education: Methods and applications [Special issue]. *Journal of Thought, 15*(3), 31-48.

Fetterman, D. M. (1982). Ethnography in educational research: The dynamics of diffusion. *Educational Researcher, 11*(3), 17-29.

Fetterman, D. M. (1983). Guilty knowledge, dirty hands, and other ethical dilemmas: The hazards of contract research. *Human Organization, 42,* 214-224.

Fetterman, D. M. (1987a). Ethnographic educational evaluation. In G. D. Spindler (Ed.), *Interpretive ethnography of education: At home and abroad.* Hillsdale, NJ: Lawrence Erlbaum.

Fetterman, D. M. (1987b, November 18-22). *Multiple audiences reflect multiple realities.* Invited presentation at the 86th Annual Meeting of the American Anthropological Association, Chicago.

Fetterman, D. M. (1988). *Qualitative approaches to evaluation in education: The silent scientific revolution.* New York: Praeger.

Fetterman, D. M. (1989). *Ethnography: Step by step.* Newbury Park, CA: Sage.

Fetterman, D. M. (1996). Videoconferencing on-line: Enhancing communication over the Internet. *Educational Researcher, 25*(4), 23-26.

Fischer, M. D. (1994). *Applications in computing for social anthropologists.* New York: Routledge.

Freilick, M. (Ed.). (1970). *Marginal natives: Anthropologists at work.* New York: Harper & Row.

Geertz, C. (1957). Ritual and social change: A Javanese example. *American Anthropologist, 59,* 32-54.

Geertz, C. (1973). *The interpretation of cultures: Selected essays.* New York: Basic Books.

Glaser, B. G., & Strauss, A. L. (1967). *The discovery of grounded theory: Strategies for qualitative research.* Chicago: Aldine.

Goetz, J. P., & LeCompte, M. D. (1984). *Ethnography and qualitative design in educational research.* New York: Academic Press.

Guttman, L. (1944). A basis for scaling qualitative data. *American Sociological Review, 9,* 139-150.

Hall, E. T. (1974). *Handbook for proxemic research.* Washington, DC: Society for the Anthropology of Visual Communication.

Hammersley, M., & Atkinson, P. (1983). *Ethnography: Principles in practice.* London: Tavistock.

Harris, M. (1968). *The rise of anthropological theory.* New York: Thomas Y. Crowell.

Heider, K. G. (1976). *Ethnographic film.* Austin: University of Texas Press.

Klockars, C. B. (1977). Field ethics for the life history. In R. S. Weppner (Ed.), *Street ethnography: Selected studies of crime and drug use in natural settings.* Beverly Hills, CA: Sage.

Klockars, C. B. (1979). Dirty hands and deviant subjects. In C. B. Klockars & F. W. O'Connor (Eds.), *Deviance and decency: The ethics of research with human subjects.* Beverly Hills, CA: Sage.

McDermott, R. P. (1974). Achieving school failure: An anthropological approach to illiteracy and social stratification. In G. D. Spindler (Ed.), *Education and cultural process: Toward an anthropology of education.* New York: Holt, Rinehart & Winston.

Miles, M. B., & Huberman, A. M. (1994). *Qualitative data analysis: An expanded sourcebook* (2nd ed.). Thousand Oaks, CA: Sage.

Osgood, C. (1964). Semantic differential technique in the comparative study of cultures. In A. K. Romney & R. G. D'Andrade (Eds.), Transcultural studies in cognition [Special issue]. *American Anthropologist, 66.*

Pelto, P. J. (1970). *Anthropological research: The structure of inquiry.* New York: Harper & Row.

Podolefsky, A., & McCarthy, C. (1983). Topical sorting: A technique for computer assisted qualitative data analysis. *American Anthropologist, 85,* 886-890.

Polsky, N. (1967). *Hustlers, beats, and others.* Chicago: Aldine.

Rynkiewich, M. A., & Spradley, J. P. (1976). *Ethics and anthropology: Dilemmas in fieldwork.* New York: John Wiley.

Spindler, G. D., & Spindler, L. (1970). *Being an anthropologist: Fieldwork in eleven cultures.* New York: Holt, Rinehart & Winston.

Spradley, J. P. (1979). *The ethnographic interview.* New York: Holt, Rinehart & Winston.

Spradley, J. P., & McCurdy, D. W. (1972). *The cultural experience: Ethnography in complex society.* Palo Alto, CA: Science Research Associates.

Sproull, L. S., & Sproull, R. F. (1982). Managing and analyzing behavior records: Explorations in nonnumeric data analysis. *Human Organization, 41,* 283-290.

Taylor, S. J., & Bogdan, R. C. (1984). *Introduction to qualitative research methods: The search for meanings.* New York: John Wiley.

Weaver, T. (1973). *To see ourselves: Anthropology and modern social issues.* Glenview, IL: Scott, Foresman.

Webb, E. J., Campbell, D. T., Schwartz, R. D., & Sechrest, L. (1966). *Unobtrusive measures: Nonreactive research in the social sciences.* Chicago: Rand McNally.

Weitzman, E. A., & Miles, M. B. (1995). *A software sourcebook: Computer programs for qualitative data analysis.* Thousand Oaks, CA: Sage.

Wolcott, H. F. (1980). How to look like an anthropologist without really being one. *Practicing Anthropology, 3*(2), 56-59.

Wolcott, H. F. (1990). *Writing up qualitative research.* Newbury Park, CA: Sage.

Yin, R. K. (1994). *Case study research: Design and methods* (2nd ed.). Thousand Oaks, CA: Sage.

17

Focus Group Research

Exploration and Discovery

David W. Stewart
Prem N. Shamdasani

Focus group research is among the most common research methods used by marketers, policy analysts, political consultants, and other social scientists to gather information. A focus group involves a group discussion of a topic that is the "focus" of the conversation. The contemporary focus group interview generally involves 8 to 12 individuals who discuss a particular topic under the direction of a professional moderator, who promotes interaction and assures that the discussion remains on the topic of interest. A typical focus group session will last from $1\frac{1}{2}$ to $2\frac{1}{2}$ hours.

The most common purpose of a focus group interview is to stimulate an in-depth exploration of a topic about which little is known. Focus group research is uniquely suited for quickly identifying qualitative similarities and differences among customers, for determining the language customers use when thinking and talking about products and services, and for suggesting a range of hypotheses about the topic of interest. Focus groups may be useful at virtually any point in a research program, but they are particularly useful for exploratory research when rather little is known about the phenomenon of interest. As a result, focus groups tend to be used very early in research projects,

AUTHORS' NOTE: This chapter is an updated adaptation of Stewart and Shamdasani (1990) and Shamdasani and Stewart (1992). Comments and correspondence regarding this chapter should be directed to David W. Stewart, University of Southern California, Department of Marketing, Los Angeles, CA 90089-1421. Telephone (213) 740-5037; fax (213) 740-7828; e-mail DSTEWART@SBA.USC.EDU.

505

and are often followed by other types of research that provide more quantifiable data from larger groups of respondents.

Focus groups have also been proven useful following the analysis of a large-scale, quantitative survey. In this use, the focus group facilitates interpretation of quantitative results and adds depth to the responses obtained in the more structured survey. Focus groups also have a place as a confirmatory method that may be used for testing hypotheses. This application may arise when the researcher has strong reasons to believe a hypothesis is correct, and where disconfirmation by even a small group would tend to result in rejection of the hypothesis.

Although focus group research can produce quantitative data, focus groups are almost always carried out with the collection of qualitative data as their primary purpose. This is their advantage, because focus groups produce a very rich body of data expressed in the respondents' own words and context. There is a minimum of artificiality of response, unlike in survey questionnaires that ask for responses expressed on 5-point rating scales or other constrained response categories. Participants can qualify their responses or identity important contingencies associated with their answers. Thus responses have a certain ecological validity not found in traditional survey research. This makes the data provided by focus groups idiosyncratic, however.

Although focus groups can be conducted in a variety of sites, ranging from homes to offices, it is most common for focus groups to be held in facilities designed especially for focus group interviewing. Such facilities provide one-way mirrors and viewing rooms where observers may unobtrusively observe an interview in progress. Focus group facilities may also include equipment for audio- or videotaping interviews and perhaps even small receivers for moderators to wear in their ears, so that observers may speak to them and thus have input into interviews. Such facilities tend to be situated either in locations that are easy to get to, such as just off a major commuter traffic artery, or in places like shopping malls, where people tend naturally to gather.

Focus groups are in use almost everywhere around the globe, but they are particularly important research tools in nations where survey research is difficult to conduct due to the unavailability of lists of representative customers, norms governing contact via telephone or mail, unreliable mail or telephone service, or language and literacy problems. In such settings, focus groups often become the only practical vehicle for collecting information, even when other methods might be more appropriate.

A variety of research needs lend themselves to the use of focus group interviews. Among the more common uses of focus groups are the following:

1. Obtaining general background information about a topic of interest

2. Generating research hypotheses that can be submitted to further research and testing using more quantitative approaches

3. Stimulating new ideas and creative concepts

4. Diagnosing the potential for problems with a new program, service, or product

5. Generating impressions of products, programs, services, institutions, or other objects of interest

6. Learning how respondents talk about the phenomenon of interest (which may, in turn, facilitate the design of questionnaires, survey instruments, or other research tools that might be employed in more quantitative research)

7. Interpreting previously obtained quantitative results

■ *Philosophical Perspectives on Focus Group Research*

Focus groups are particularly well suited for answering questions about "what kind." This is their advantage, because it is impossible to answer quantitative questions efficiently—such as "how many," "how much," and "how often"—without first knowing "what kinds" to quantify. In this regard, qualitative and quantitative research complement one another, because the former helps identify important types of phenomena and the latter provides a means of assessing the frequency and/or magnitude of the types of phenomena. Individual depth interviews also help answer "what kind" questions. However, focus groups are more efficient, in terms of time and budgetary considerations, for providing a quick overview of differences, range of ideas, and so on. Further, as with individual interviews, focus groups produce a rich body of data expressed in the respondents' own words and context.

If focus groups can be used for both exploration and confirmation, the question arises of how focus groups differ from other tools of science—What purposes do they serve that are not served by other methods? The answer lies in the nature or character of the data generated by focus group interviews. Krippendorf (1980) distinguishes between two types of data: emic and etic. Emic data are data that arise in a natural or indigenous form. They are only minimally imposed by the researcher or the research setting. Etic data, on the other hand, represent the researcher's imposed view of the situation. Little of the research that is actually carried out can be described as completely etic or completely emic. Even the most structured type of research will be influenced to some extent by the idiosyncratic nature of the respondent and his or her environment. On the other hand, even the most natural of situations may not yield data that are completely emic, because the researcher must make decisions about what to attend to and what to ignore. Thus it is perhaps more useful to think of a continuum of research, with some methods lying closer to the emic side of the continuum and some techniques lying closer to the etic side.

Focus groups, along with a few other techniques such as unstructured individual depth interviews, provide data that are closer to the emic side of the continuum, because they allow individuals to respond in their own words using their own categorizations and perceived associations. They are not completely void of structure, however, because the researcher does raise questions of one type or another. Survey research and experimentation tend to produce data that are closer to the etic side of the continuum, because the response categories used by the respondent are generally prescribed by the researcher. These responses categories may or may not be those with which the respondent is comfortable, though the respondent may still select an answer. And even when closed-ended survey questions are the only options available, some respondents elect to give answers in their own words, as most experienced survey researchers have discovered.

Neither emic nor etic data are better or worse than the other; they simply differ. Both kinds of data have their place in social science research; they complement each other, each compensating for the limitations of the other. Indeed, one way to view social science research is as a process that moves from the emic to the etic and back, in a cycle. Phenomena that are not well understood are often first studied with tools that yield more emic data. As a particular phenomenon is better understood and greater theoretical and empirical structure is built around it, tools that yield more etic types of data tend to predominate. As knowledge accumulates, it often becomes apparent that the exploratory structure surrounding a given phenomenon is incomplete. This frequently leads to the need for data that are more emic, and the process continues. (Further discussion of the philosophical issues associated with the use of focus group research and the complementarity of structured and unstructured approaches to social science research can be found in Bliss, Monk, & Ogborn, 1983; Bogdan & Biklen, 1982; Maxwell, Chapter 3, this volume.)

Focus groups are widely used because they provide useful information and offer researchers a number of advantages. This information and the advantages of the technique come at a price, however. We review the relative advantages and limitations of focus group research below. We then present a discussion of the steps involved in the use and design of focus groups.

■ *Advantages and Limitations of Focus Group Research*

☐ *Advantages*

The use of focus groups provides a number of advantages relative to other types of research:

1. Focus groups can collect data from a group of people much more quickly and at less cost than would be the case if each individual were interviewed separately. They can also be assembled on much shorter notice than would be required for a more systematic, larger survey.

2. Focus groups allow researchers to interact directly with respondents. This provides opportunities for clarification and probing of responses as well as follow-up questions. Respondents can qualify responses or give contingent answers to questions. In addition, researchers can observe nonverbal responses,

such as gestures, smiles, and frowns, that may carry information that supplements and, on occasion, even contradicts, verbal responses.

3. The open response format of focus groups provides researchers the opportunity to obtain large and rich amounts of data in the respondents' own words. Researchers can determine deeper levels of meaning, make important connections, and identify subtle nuances in expression and meaning.

4. Focus groups allow respondents to react to and build upon the responses of other group members. This synergistic effect of the group setting may result in the production of data or ideas that might not have been uncovered in individual interviews.

5. Focus groups are very flexible. They can be used to examine a wide range of topics with a variety of individuals and in a variety of settings.

6. Focus groups may be one of the few research tools available for obtaining data from children or from individuals who are not particularly literate.

7. The results of focus group research are usually easy to understand. Researchers and decision makers can readily understand the verbal responses of most respondents. This is not always the case with more sophisticated survey research that employs complex statistical analyses.

8. Multiple individuals can view a focus group as it is conducted, or review video- or audiotape of the group session. This provides a useful vehicle for creating a common understanding of an issue or problem. Such an understanding can be especially helpful for team building and for reducing conflict among decision makers.

☐ *Limitations*

Although the focus group technique is a valuable research tool and offers a number of advantages, it is not a panacea for all research needs. It does have significant limitations, many of which are simply the negative sides of the advantages listed above:

1. The small numbers of respondents that participate in even several different focus groups and the convenience nature of most focus group recruiting practices significantly limit generalization to larger populations. Indeed, persons who are willing to travel to a locale to participate in a 1- to 2-hour group discussion may be quite different from the population of interest.

2. The interaction of respondents with one another and with the moderator has two potentially undesirable effects. First, the responses from members of the group are not independent of one another, which restricts the generalizability of results. Second, the results obtained in a focus group may be biased by a very dominant or opinionated member. More reserved group members may be hesitant to talk.

3. The "live" and immediate nature of the interaction may lead a researcher or decision maker to place greater faith in the findings than is actually warranted.

There is a certain credibility attached to the opinion of a live respondent that is often not present in statistical summaries.

4. The open-ended nature of responses obtained in focus groups often makes summarization and interpretation of results difficult. Statements by respondents are frequently characterized by qualifications and contingencies that make direct comparison of respondents' opinions difficult.

5. A moderator, especially one who is unskilled or inexperienced, may bias results by knowingly or unknowingly providing cues about what types of responses and answers are desirable.

Focus group research has been the subject of much controversy and criticism. Such criticism is generally associated with the view that focus group interviews do not yield "hard" data and the concern that group members may not be representative of a larger population, because of both the small numbers and the idiosyncratic nature of the group discussion. Such criticisms are unfair, however. Although focus groups do have important limitations of which researchers should be aware, limitations are not unique to focus group research; all research tools in the social sciences have significant limitations. The key to using focus groups successfully in social science research is assuring that their use is consistent with the objectives and purpose of the research. It is also important to recognize and appreciate the philosophical underpinnings of focus group research.

■ *Designing, Conducting, and Analyzing Focus Group Research*

☐ *Predesign Considerations*

An important decision faced by all researchers concerns the amount and type of data and analysis required to address the research question at hand. The amount and type of data and analysis will vary with the purpose of the research, the complexity of the research design, and the extent to which conclusions can be reached easily based on simple analyses. Nevertheless, it is especially important that a researcher have a well-framed research question prior to initiating focus group research. This research question will guide the type of selection of respondents, the types of questions posed during the group session, and the types of analyses conducted following the group session. The exploratory nature of focus group research makes it tempting for researchers to use it as a substitute for constructing clear research questions. Such use of focus group research is likely to produce highly unsatisfactory results, however. Unfocused questions addressed to an inappropriate set of respondents by an ill-prepared moderator may not only fail to produce useful information, but actually mislead the researcher. Focus groups are designed to do exactly what the name implies—focus.

A focus group is not a freewheeling conversation among group members; it has focus and a clearly identifiable agenda. Problem definition requires a clear statement of what kinds of information are desirable and from whom this information should be obtained. A clear understanding of the problem, or general research question, is critical because it gives rise to the specific questions that should be raised by the moderator and identifies the population of interest. Thus the first step in the design of focus group research, as it should be for any other type of research, is specification of the research question.

☐ *Group Composition*

Once the researcher has generated a clear statement of the research question, he or she can move to the second stage of focus group research. As for a survey, it is important for the researcher to identify a sampling frame—that is, a list of people (households, organizations) the researcher has reason to believe is representative of the larger population of interest. The sampling frame is the operational definition of the population. The identification of a sound sampling frame is far more critical in large-scale survey research than it is for focus group research, however. Because it is generally inappropriate to generalize far beyond the members of focus groups, the sampling frame need only be a good approximation of the population of interest. Thus if the research is concerned with middle-class parents of schoolchildren, a membership list for the local PTA might be an appropriate sampling frame.

Indeed, random samples, which are the rule in much survey research, are less frequently employed in focus group research. The reason for this is that the topics of some focus group discussions are topics that require special expertise, experience, or unique knowledge. For example, a random sample of the population of any given country would be unlikely to produce individuals who could talk knowledgeably about the direction of information technology over the next 50 years or persons who could discuss their feelings about having contracted AIDS. Thus purposive sampling, in which respondents are purposely selected because they have certain characteristics, is often used in focus group research. Random sampling is also common in recruiting focus group participants, but it is important to recognize that the representativeness of any set of focus group participants is diminished by their participation in the group experience.

Unlike survey research, where data are obtained from respondents who are independent of one another, the design of focus group research must also include consideration of the likely dynamics that will be produced by any particular combination of individuals (Carey & Smith, 1994). For example, the interaction among a group of 15-year-olds will be very different when their parents are a part of the group versus when they are alone. Similarly, men may respond differently in groups composed only of other men from the way they would in groups made up of a mixture of men and women. Care also needs to be exercised in mixing groups across cultures. For example, in a 90-minute focus group session involving strangers, participants from more aggressive cultures are likely to dominate. Therefore, where possible, the best strategy would be to avoid such mixing of participants from diverse cultures. Additionally, some topics and issues (e.g., sexual habits and contraception use) are perceived to be more personal and sensitive by members of some cultural groups than by others (Asians compared with Westerners, for instance). Thus the moderators of focus groups investigating such sensitive topics need to exercise a great deal of tact and diplomacy, because members of some cultures are quite reserved and reluctant to discuss openly behaviors and issues that may lead to embarrassment or "loss of face."

A recent trend in research on focus groups has been the examination of their use with various special populations. Such research has examined the unique issues that arise in the use of focus groups in various developing nations (Folch-Lyon, de la Macorra, & Schearer, 1981; Fuller, Edwards, Vorakitphokatorn, & Sermsri, 1993; Knodel, 1995), with children (Hoppe, Wells, Morrison, Gillmore, & Wilsdon, 1995), and among low-income and minority populations (Jarrett, 1993; Magill, 1993). Although such populations do require some adaptation of technique, they have all been included successfully in focus group research.

There is no "best" mix of individuals in a focus group. Rather, the researcher needs to consider what group dynamic is most consistent with the research objectives. If the interaction of children and their parents is important for purposes of the research, then groups should be composed of parents and their children. On the other hand, if the focus of the research is on adolescents' perspectives on a topic, the presence of parents in the group may reduce the willingness of the adolescents to speak out and express their feelings. In the latter case, it would be more consistent with research objectives for the researcher to design groups that include only adolescents.

The interaction among members of a focus group adds a dimension to data collection that is not common in other forms of social science research. Because the results obtained from a group are the outcome of both the individuals in the group and the dynamics of the group interaction, it is common for focus group researchers to use several groups that differ with respect to composition. Indeed, it is uncommon for focus group research to use only a single group. More often, the research includes multiple groups composed of different types of individuals and different mixes of individuals. The specific number of groups that may be included in any research project is a function of the number of distinct *types of individuals* from which the researcher wishes to obtain data and the number of *mixtures of individuals* of interest to the researcher.

☐ *The Interview Guide*

Although focus groups are relatively unstructured compared with the typical survey or other types of quantitative research, they are not completely without structure. The group's discussion needs to be guided and directed so that it remains focused on the topic of interest. The moderator plays an important role in maintaining this focus, but an especially important tool for creating the agenda for a focus group discussion is the interview guide. The interview guide for a focus group discussion generally consists of a set of very general open-ended questions about the topic or issue of interest. It does not include all of the questions that may be asked during the group discussion; rather, it serves to introduce broad areas for discussion and to assure that all of the topics relevant to the research are included in the research. The interview guide is not a script for the discussion, nor should it be regarded as an immutable agenda. Rather, it is simply a guide, and it may be modified in response to the discussion and interaction among the respondents.

A typical interview guide for a 90-minute discussion seldom includes more than 12 to 15 questions. Generally, questions of a more general nature are raised first, and more specific issues are raised later in the guide. This assures that background information, context, and broader issues are discussed before the group focuses on very specific issues. The use of very specific questions early in a discussion often results in a premature narrowing of the focus of the group and reduces the richness of the information that is obtained.

☐ *The Role of the Focus Group Moderator*

The moderator is the key to assuring that the group discussion goes smoothly. The focus group moderator is generally a specialist who is well trained in group dynamics and interview skills. Depending on the intent of the research, the moderator may be more or less directive with respect to the discussion, and often is quite nondirective, letting the discussion flow naturally as long as it remains on the topic of interest. Indeed, one of the strengths of focus group research is that it may be adapted to provide the most desirable level of focus and structure. If the researcher is interested in how parents have adapted to the child-care requirements created by dual careers, the moderator can ask very general and nonspecific questions about the topic in order to determine the most salient issues on the minds of the participants. On the other hand, if the researcher is interested in parents' reactions to a very specific concept for child care, the moderator can provide specific information about the concept and ask very specific questions.

The amount of direction provided by the moderator influences the types and quality of the data obtained from the group. The moderator provides the agenda or structure for the discussion by virtue of his or her role in the group. When a moderator suggests a new topic for discussion by asking a new question, the group has a tendency to comply. This is important for assuring that all of the topics of interest are covered in the time available. A group discussion might never cover particular topics or issues unless the moderator intervenes. On the other hand, the frequency and type of intervention by the moderator clearly affects the nature of the discussion. This raises the question of the most appropriate amount of structure for a given group. There is, of course, no best answer to this question, because the amount of structure and the directiveness of the moderator must be determined by the broader research agenda that gave rise to the focus group: the types of information sought, the specificity of the information required, and the way the information will be used.

There is also a balance that must be struck between what is important to members of the group and what is important to the researcher. Less structured groups will tend to pursue those issues and topics of greater importance, relevance, and interest to the group. This is perfectly appropriate if the objective of the researcher is to learn about the things that are most important to the group. Often, however, the researcher has rather specific information needs. Discussion of issues relevant to these needs may occur only when the moderator takes a more directive and structured approach. It is important for the researcher to remember that when this occurs, participants are discussing what is important to the researcher, not necessarily what they consider significant.

□ *Analysis and Interpretation of Focus Group Research*

The most common analyses of focus group results involve transcripts of the group interviews and discussions of the conclusions that can be drawn. There are occasions, however, when transcripts are unnecessary. When decisions must be made quickly and the conclusions of the research are rather straightforward, a brief summary may be all that is necessary and justifiable. In some cases there may be time or budget constraints that prevent detailed analysis. In other cases, all interested parties and decision makers may be able to observe or participate in the groups, so there may be little need for detailed analyses or reports.

Aside from the few occasions when only short summaries of the focus group discussions are required, all analytic techniques for focus group data require transcription of the interviews as a first step. Transcription not only facilitates further analysis, it establishes a permanent written record of the interviews that can be shared with other interested parties. The amount of editing an analyst does on a transcribed interview is a matter of preference. Transcriptions are not always complete, and the moderator may want to fill in gaps and missing words, as well as correct spelling and typographical errors. There is a danger in this, of course, because the moderator's memory may be fallible or knowledge of what was said later in the course of the interview may color his or her memory of what happened earlier. Although editing may increase readability, it is important that the character of the respondents' comments be maintained, even if at times they use poor grammar or appear to be confused. Because one use of focus group interviewing is to learn how respondents think and talk about a particular issue, too much editing and cleaning of the transcript is undesirable. Too much editing and cleaning tends to censor ideas and information, often based on the analyst's preconceived ideas.

It should be noted, however, that the transcript does not reflect the entire character of the discussion. Nonverbal communication, gestures, and behavioral responses are not reflected in a transcript. Thus the interviewer or observer may wish to supplement the transcript with some additional observational data that were obtained during the interview, such as a videotape or notes by an observer. Such observational data may be quite useful, but they will be available only if their collection is planned in advance. Preplanning of the analyses of the data to be obtained from focus groups is as important as it is for any other type of research.

As with other types of research, the analysis and interpretation of focus group data require a great deal of judgment and care. Unfortunately, focus group research is easily abused and often inappropriately applied. A great deal of the skepticism about the value of focus groups probably arises from (a) the perception that focus group data are subjective and difficult to interpret and (b) the concern that focus group participants may not be representative of a larger population because of both the small numbers and the idiosyncratic nature of the group discussion.

The analysis and interpretation of focus group data can be as rigorous as the analysis and interpretation generated by any other method. Focus group data can even be quantified and submitted to sophisticated mathematical analyses, though the purpose of focus group interviews seldom requires this type of analysis. Indeed, there is no one best or correct approach to the analysis of focus group data. The nature of the analysis of focus group interview data should be determined by the research question and the purpose for which the data are collected. This in turn, has implications for the validity of the findings generated from focus groups. Researchers should constantly be aware of the possible sources of bias at various stages of the focus group research process and take appropriate steps to deal with threats to the validity of the results.

A number of books and papers on focus group research have appeared in recent years (e.g., Agar & MacDonald, 1995; Carey, 1995; Flores & Alonso, 1995; Goldman & McDonald, 1987; Greenbaum, 1993; Krueger, 1988; Morgan, 1993, 1996; Templeton, 1987). Although these publications are useful, their focus has tended to be more on the mechanics of the interviews themselves rather than on the analysis of the data generated in focus group sessions (see Stewart & Shamdasani, 1990, for an exception). Where analysis is treated, the discussion is often limited to efforts to identify key themes in focus group sessions. Researchers interested in more sophisticated approaches have limited options. They can consult the rather voluminous literature on content analysis that exists outside the marketing domain, but this literature is not always readily accessible to researchers, particularly those outside of academic settings. The more common approaches to content analysis are described below.

The Cut-and-Sort Technique

The cut-and-sort technique is a quick and cost-effective method for analyzing a transcript from a focus group discussion. This process may also be readily carried out on any computer with a word processing program. Regardless of whether scissors or a personal computer is employed, this method yields a set of sorted materials that provides the basis for the development of a summary report. Each topic is treated in turn, with a brief introduction. The various pieces of interview transcription are used as supporting materials and incorporated within an interpretative analysis.

Although the cut-and-sort technique is useful, it tends to rely very heavily on the judgment of a single analyst. This analyst determines which segments of the transcript are important, develops a categorization system for the topics discussed by the group, selects representative statements regarding these topics from the transcript, and develops an interpretation of what it all means. There is obviously much opportunity for subjectivity and potential bias in this approach. Yet it shares many of the characteristics of more sophisticated and time-consuming approaches. It may be desirable to have two or more analysts independently code the focus group transcript. The use of multiple analysts provides an opportunity to assess the reliability of coding, at least with respect to major themes and issues. When determination of the reliability of more detailed types of codes is needed, more sophisticated content-analytic coding procedures are required.

Formal Content Analysis

Every effort to interpret a focus group represents analysis of content. Some efforts are more formal than others, however. There are rigorous approaches to the analysis of content, approaches that emphasize the reliability and replicability of observations and subsequent interpretation (Bertrand, Brown, & Ward, 1992). These approaches include a variety of specific methods and techniques that are collectively known as content analysis (Krippendorf, 1980). There are frequent occasions when the use of this more rigorous approach is appropriate for the analysis of data generated by focus groups. In addition, the literature on content analysis provides the foundation for computer-assisted approaches to the analysis of focus group data. Computer-assisted approaches to content analysis are increasingly being applied to focus group data because they maintain much of the rigor of traditional content analysis while greatly reducing the time and cost required to complete such analysis. It is important to note that in addition to verbal communication, there is a great deal of communication that takes place in a focus group discussion that is nonverbal and that is not captured in the written transcript. It is therefore desirable to videotape focus group sessions, so that the nonverbal behavior of participants can be recorded and coded. If videotaping is not possible, an observer may be used to record nonverbal behavior. By subjecting nonverbal communication to content analysis, the researcher can enhance the overall information content of the focus group research.

Janis (1965) defines content analysis as "any technique (a) for the classification of the sign-vehicles (b) which relies solely upon the judgments (which theoretically may range from perceptual discrimination to sheer guesses) of an analyst or group of analysts as to which sign-vehicles fall into which categories, (c) provided that the analyst's judgments are regarded as the report of a scientific observer" (p. 55). A sign-vehicle is anything that may carry meaning, though most often it is likely to be a word or set of words in the context of a focus group interview. Sign-vehicles may also include gestures, facial expressions, or any of a variety of other means of communication, however. Indeed, such nonverbal signs may carry a great deal of information and should not be overlooked as sources of information.

A substantial body of literature now exists on content analysis, including books by Krippendorf (1980), Gottschalk (1979), and Ericsson and Simon (1984). A number of specific instruments have been developed to facilitate content analysis, including the Message Measurement Inventory (Smith 1978) and the Gottschalk-Gleser Content Analysis Scale (Gottschalk, Winget, & Gleser, 1969). The Message Measurement Inventory was originally designed for the analysis of communications in the mass media, such as television programming and newsmagazines. The Gottschalk-Gleser Content Analysis Scale, on the other hand, was designed for the analysis of interpersonal communication. Both scales have been adapted for other purposes, but they are generally representative of the types of formal content analysis scales that are in use.

Although content analysis is a specific type of research tool, it shares many features in common with certain types of research. The same stages of the research process are found in content analysis as are present in any research project (Krippendorf, 1980): data making, data reduction, inference, analysis, validation, testing for correspondence with other methods, and testing hypotheses regarding other data.

Data making. Data used in content analysis include human speech, observations of behavior, and various forms of nonverbal communication. The speech itself may be recorded, and, if video cameras are available, at least some of the behavior and nonverbal communication may be permanently archived. Such data are highly unstructured, however, at least for the purposes of the researcher. Before the researcher can analyze the content of a focus group session, he or she must convert it into specific units of information. The particular organizing structure a researcher chooses will depend on the particular purpose of the research, but there are specific steps in the structuring process that are common to all applications. These steps are unitizing, sampling, and recording.

Unitizing involves defining the appropriate unit or level of analysis. It would be possible to consider each word spoken in a focus group session as a unit of analysis. Alternatively, the unit of analysis could be a sentence, a sequence of sentences, or a complete dialogue about a particular topic. Krippendorf (1980) suggests that in content analysis there are three kinds of units that must be considered: sampling units, recording units, and context units. Sampling units are those parts of the larger whole that can be regarded as independent of each other. Sampling units tend to have physically identified boundaries. For example, sampling units may be defined as individual words, complete statements of an individual, or the totality of an exchange between two or more individuals.

Recording units tend to grow out of the descriptive system that is being employed. Generally, recording units are subsets of sampling units. For example, the set of words with emotional connotations would describe certain types of words and would be a subset of the total words used. Alternatively, individual statements of several group members may be recording units that make up a sampling unit that consists of all of the interaction concerned with a particular topic or issue. In this latter case, the recording units might provide a means for describing those exchanges that are hostile, supportive, friendly, and so forth.

Context units provide a basis for interpreting a recording unit. They may be identical to recording units in some cases, whereas in other cases they may be quite independent. Context units are often defined in terms of the syntax or structure in which a recording unit occurs. For example, in marketing research it is often useful to learn how frequently evaluative words are used in the context of describing particular products or services. Thus context units provide a reference for the content of the recording units.

Sampling units, then, represent the way in which the broad structure of the information within the discussion is divided. Sampling units provide a way of organizing information that is related. Within these broader sampling units, the recording units represent specific statements and the context units represent the environment or context in which the statement occurs. The way in which these units are defined can have a significant influence on the interpretation of the content of a particular focus group discussion. These units can be defined in a number of different ways. The definition of the appropriate unit of analysis must be driven by both the purpose of the research and the ability of the researcher to achieve reliability in the coding system. The reliability of such coding systems must be determined empirically, and in many cases involves the use of measures of interrater agreement.

It is seldom practical to try to unitize all of the discussion that arises in a focus group. When multiple focus groups are carried out on the same general topic, complete unitization becomes even more difficult. For this reason, most content analyses of focus groups involve some sampling of the total group discussion for purposes of analysis. The analyst may seek to identify important themes and sample statements within themes, or use some other approach, such as examining statements made in response to particular types of questions, or at particular points in the conversation. Like other types of sampling, the intent of sampling in content analysis is to provide a representative subset of the larger population. It is relatively easy for a researcher to draw incorrect conclusions from a focus group if he or she does not take care to ensure representative sampling of the content of the group discussion. One can support almost any contention by taking a set of unrepresentative statements out of the context in which they were spoken. Thus it is important for the analyst to devise a plan for sampling the total content of group discussions.

The final stage of data making is the recording of the data in such a way as to ensure their reliability and meaningfulness. The recording phase of content analysis is not simply the rewriting of a statement of one or more respondents. Rather, it is the use of the defined units of analysis to classify the content of the discussion into categories such that the meaning of the discussions is maintained and explicated. It is only after the researcher has accomplished this latter stage that he or she can claim actually to have data for purposes of analysis and interpretation.

The recording phase of content analysis requires the execution of an explicit set of recording instructions. These instructions represent the rules for assigning units (words, phrases, sentences, gestures, and so on) to categories. These instructions must address at least four different aspects of the recording process (Krippendorf, 1980):

1. The nature of the raw data from which the recording is to be done (transcript tape recording, film, and so on)
2. The characteristics of coders (recorders), including any special skills such as familiarity with the subject matter and scientific research
3. The training that coders will need in order to do the recording
4. The specific rules for placing units into categories

The specific rules referred to above are critical to the establishment of the reliability of the recording exercise and the entire data-making process. Further, it is necessary that the researcher make these rules explicit and demonstrate that the rules produce reliable results when used by individuals other than those who developed them in the first place. Lorr and McNair (1966) question the practice of reporting high interrater reliability coefficients when they are based solely on the agreement of individuals who have worked closely together to develop a coding system. Rather, these researchers suggest that the minimum requirement for establishing the reliability of a coding system is a demonstration that judges using only the coding rules exhibit agreement.

Once a set of recording rules has been defined and demonstrated to produce reliable results, the researcher can complete the data-making process by applying the recording rules to the full content of the material of interest. Under ideal circumstances, recording will involve more than one judge, so that the coding of each specific unit can be examined for reliability and sources of disagreement can be identified and corrected. There is a difference between developing a generally reliable set of recording rules and assuring that an individual element in a transcript is reliably coded.

The assessment of the reliability of a coding system may be carried out in a variety of ways. As noted above, there is a difference between establishing that multiple recorders are in general agreement (manifest a high degree of interrater reliability) and establishing that a particular unit is reliably coded. The researcher must decide which approach is more useful for the given research question. It is safe to conclude that in most focus group projects, general rater reliability will be more important, because the emphasis is on general themes in the group discussion rather than specific units.

Computation of a coefficient of agreement provides a quantitative index of the reliability of the recording system. There exists a substantial literature on coefficients of agreement. Treatment of this literature and issues related to the selection of a specific coefficient of agreement are beyond the scope of this chapter. Among the more common coefficients in use are kappa (Cohen, 1960) and pi (Scott, 1955). Both of these coefficients correct the observed level of agreement (or disagreement) for the level that would be expected by chance alone. Krippendorf (1980) offers a useful discussion of reliability coefficients in content analysis, including procedures for use with more than two judges (see also Spiegelman, Terwilliger, & Fearing, 1953).

Data making tends to be the most time-consuming of all the stages in content analysis. It is also the stage that has received the greatest attention in the content analysis literature. The reason for this is that content analysis involves data making after observations have been obtained, rather than before. Content analysis uses the observations themselves to suggest what should be examined and submitted to further analysis, whereas many other types of research establish the specific domain of interest prior to observation. In survey research, much of the data making occurs prior to administration of the survey. Such data making involves identification of reasonable alternatives from which a respondent selects an answer. Thus data making is a step in survey research, and all types of research, but it occurs prior to observation. In content analysis, data making occurs after observation.

Data analysis. The recording or coding of individual units is not content analysis. It is merely a first stage in preparation for analysis. The specific types of analyses that might be used in a given application will depend on the purpose of the research. Virtually any analytic tool may be employed, ranging from simple descriptive analysis to more elaborate data reduction and multivariate associative techniques. Much of the content analysis work that occurs in the context of focus group data tends to be descriptive, but this need not be the case. Indeed, although focus group data tend to be regarded as qualitative, proper content analysis of the data can make them amenable to the most sophisticated quantitative analysis. This is well illustrated by development of computer-assisted methods for content analysis.

Computer-assisted content analysis. Content analysts were quick to recognize the value of the computer as an analytic tool. The time-consuming and tedious task of data making can be greatly facilitated through use of the computer. Computers can be programmed to follow the data-making rules described earlier. The importance of assuring that these rules are well designed is made even clearer in the context of their use by a computer. In recent years, computer-assisted interpretation of focus group interviews has received attention and has built upon the earlier foundations of research on content analysis.

The computer is capable of a great deal more than automation of search, find, and cut-and-paste activities. One problem with simple counting and sorting of words is that these procedures lose the contexts in which the words occur. For example, a simple count of the frequency with which emotionally charged words are used loses information about the objects of those emotional words. Because the meanings of words are frequently context dependent, it is useful to try to capture context. This is one reason content analysts recommend the identification and coding of context units as a routine part of content analysis.

One computer-assisted approach to capturing the context as well as content of a passage of text is the key-word-in-context (KWIC) technique. In the KWIC approach, the computer is used to search for key words, which are then shown along with the text that surrounds them. The amount of text obtained on either side of the key word can be controlled by specification of the number of words or letters to be printed. One of the earliest computer programs for KWIC analyses was the General Inquirer (Stone, Dunphy, Smith, & Ogilvie, 1966), which is still in use today. The General Inquirer uses a theoretically derived dictionary for classifying words. A variety of similar systems have since been developed, and many use specially designed dictionaries for particular applications. Some of these programs are simply designated as KWIC, whereas others are named for particular applications for which KWIC may be used. Among the more frequently cited software programs for content analysis are TEXTPACK V, the Oxford Concordance Program (Hockey & Marriott, 1982), and the Key-Word-in-Context Bibliographic Indexing Program (Popko, 1980). Software for text analysis is frequently reviewed in the journal *Computers and the Humanities*. Specialized dictionaries for use in conjunction with text analysis programs like the General Inquirer and TEXTPACK V are also available. Weber (1985) provides a brief introduction to several of these specialized dictionaries, including successful applications of content analysis.

More recent work on content analysis has built on the research on artificial intelligence and in cognitive science. This more recent work recognizes that associations among words are often important determinants of meaning. Further, meaning may be related to the frequency of association of certain words, the distance between associated words or concepts (often measured by the number of intervening words), and the number of different associations. The basic idea in this work is that the way people use language provides insights into the way people organize information, impressions, and feelings in memory, and thus how they tend to think. The view that language provides insight into the way individuals think about the world has existed for many years. The anthropologist Edward Sapir (1929) has noted that language plays a critical role in how people experience the world. Social psychologists have also long had an interest in the role language plays in the assignment of meaning and in adjustment to the environment (see, e.g., Bruner, Goodnow, & Austin, 1956; Chomsky, 1965; Sherif & Sherif, 1969). In more recent years, the study of categorization has become a discipline in its own right and has benefited from research on naturalistic categories in anthropology, philosophy, and developmental psychology, and the work on modeling natural concepts that has occurred in the areas of semantic memory and artificial intelligence (see Mervis & Rosch, 1981, for a review of this literature).

This research has recently been extended to the examination of focus groups. Building on theoretical work in the cognitive sciences (Anderson, 1983; Grunert, 1982), Grunert and Bader (1986) developed a computer-assisted procedure for analyzing the proximities of word associations. Their approach builds on prior work on content analysis as well. Indeed, the data-making phase of the approach uses the KWIC approach as an interactive tool for designing a customized dictionary of categories. The particular computer program they use for this purpose is TEXTPACK V (Mohler & Zull, 1984), but other computer packages are also available for this purpose.

The construction of a customized dictionary of categories is particularly important for the content analysis of focus groups because the range and specificity of topics that may be dealt with by focus group interviews is very broad, and no general-purpose dictionary or set of codes and categories is likely to suit the needs of a researcher with a specific research application. For example, to analyze focus group sessions designed to examine the way groups of respondents think and talk about computer workstations, the researcher will need to develop a dictionary of categories that refer specifically to the features of workstations, particular applications, and specific work environments. To analyze focus groups designed to examine the use of condoms among inner-city adolescents, it is likely that a dictionary of categories that includes the slang vernacular of the respondents will be required to capture the content of the discussion. Although the dictionaries developed for other applications may provide some helpful suggestions, the specificity of the language used by particular groups of respondents to discuss specific objects within given contexts almost always means that the focus group analyst will have to develop a customized categorization system.

Once the data-making phase is complete, the researcher can analyze the associative structure of the discussion content. He or she accomplishes this by counting the distances between various cognitive categories. Distance, or the proximity of two categories of content, is defined as the number of intervening constructs. Thus two constructs that appear next to one another would have a distance of 1. To simplify computations, Grunert and Bader (1986) recommend examining categories that are at a maximum value of 10. This maximum value is then used as a reference point and distances are subtracted from it in order to obtain a numeric value that varies directly (rather than inversely) with intensity of association. This procedure yields a proximity value rather than a distance measure; that is, the higher scores represent closer associations among categories. Because most categories appear more than once, the measures of association are summed over all occurrences to obtain a total proximity score for each pair of constructs. These proximity data may then be used for further analysis.

Whether the amount of effort needed for further analysis is justified in focus group applications depends on a variety of factors—time and budget constraints, the nature of the research question, and the availability of a computer and the necessary software. The important point is that the level and detail of analysis of focus group data can be increased considerably through the use of the computer. At the same time, the computer can be an extremely useful tool for data reduction. It can also be used to uncover relationships that might otherwise go unnoticed. Thus, like most of the research tools in the social sciences, the focus group interview has benefited from the advent of the computer. Users of focus group interviews have also become increasingly facile in the use of the computer as an aid to the analysis, summarization, and interpretation of focus group data.

Electronic Focus Groups

A recent development involving the use of computer technology in focus group research is the electronic focus group. In contrast to a traditional focus group, an electronic focus group utilizes a real-time, interactive computer system to enhance group discussion (Gormley, 1989). One such group decision support system is the OptionFinder (from Option Technologies, Inc., 1988). A group decision support system (GDSS) can be defined as "a set of interactive, computerized tools designed to support semi- and unstructured decisions made by groups as well as group work in general" (Beauclair, 1990, p. 153).

By using GDSS tools, electronic focus groups are able to facilitate face-to-face group discussions and problem solving by incorporating a variety of discussion-focusing features, such as large video displays and information storage and retrieval software and hardware that help overcome communication barriers (DeSanctis & Gallupe, 1987; Gormley, 1989). During the course of an electronic focus group session, a moderator has several opportunities to ask participants to vote anonymously on relevant stimulus items that have been either preprogrammed or generated during the session. Results can be immediately displayed in charts or graphs that provide the moderator with additional stimulus for discussion and interpretation of perceptual similarities and differences. This advantage of electronic focus groups enables researchers to include demographically diverse respondents in the same focus groups as well as to initiate discussion of controversial topics, as participants are not "forced" to defend or explain their personal observations or opinions (Williams, Toy, & Gormley, 1990).

By ensuring respondent anonymity and the availability of instantaneous records of individual and group responses (qualitative and quantitative), electronic focus groups help enhance the validity of group findings. Validity is enhanced through the reduction of the effects of two sources of bias: moderator bias and respondent bias due to group reaction. In the final analysis, however, the advantages of electronic focus groups for enhancing the validity of results will depend ultimately on the researcher's skill and judgment and his or her ability to accomplish the purpose of the research objectively.

■ *Conclusion*

With the advent of computer-assisted analysis and real-time, interactive electronic focus groups, the issue of validity in focus group research may on the surface seem to occupy a higher plane of importance and sophistication now that it is "technologically" more accessible. However, the use of computers alone does not ensure validity. Like other quantitative techniques, computer analysis of focus group results also suffers from the GIGO (garbage in, garbage out) problem. Therefore, it is worthwhile for social science researchers to take note of Brinberg and McGrath's (1985) succinct reminder that validity "is not a commodity that can be purchased with techniques. . . . Rather validity is like integrity, character, or quality, to be assessed relative to purposes and circumstances" (p. 13).

In this regard, the validity of focus group findings should be assessed relative to the research objectives and circumstances that gave rise to the research. Further, the issue of validity needs to be addressed throughout the focus group research process—from planning and data collection to data making, analysis, and interpretation. The execution of each step of this research process has the potential to influence the validity of focus group findings, either positively or negatively. Understanding the limitations and possible sources of bias at each stage of the focus group process will enable the researcher to take appropriate measures to deal objectively with threats to the integrity of the research results.

■ *References*

Agar, M., & MacDonald, J. (1995). Focus groups and ethnography. *Human Organization, 54,* 78-86.

Anderson, J. R. (1983). *The architecture of cognition.* Cambridge, MA: Harvard University Press.

Beauclair R. (1990). Group decision support systems and their effect on small group work. In G. Phillips (Ed.), *Teaching how to work in groups* (pp. 151-172). Norwood, NJ: Ablex.

Bertrand, J. E., Brown, J. E., & Ward, V. M. (1992). Techniques for analyzing focus group data. *Evaluation Review, 16,* 198-209.

Bliss, J., Monk, M., & Ogborn, J. (1983). *Qualitative data analysis for educational research.* London: Croom Helm.

Bogdan, R. C., & Biklen, S. K. (1982). *Qualitative research for education: An introduction to theory and methods.* Boston: Allyn & Bacon.

Brinberg, D., & McGrath, J. E. (1985). *Validity and the research process.* Beverly Hills, CA: Sage.

Bruner, J. S., Goodnow, J. J., & Austin, J. G. (1956). *A study of thinking.* New York: John Wiley.

Carey, M. A. (Ed.). (1995). Issues and applications of focus groups [Special issue]. *Qualitative Health Research, 5,* 413-530.

Carey, M. A., & Smith, M. (1994). Capturing the group effect in focus groups: A special concern in analysis. *Qualitative Health Research, 4,* 123-127.

Chomsky, N. (1965). *Aspects of the theory of syntax.* Cambridge: MIT Press.

Cohen, J. (1960). A coefficient of agreement for nominal scales. *Educational and Psychological Measurement, 20,* 37-46.

DeSanctis, G., & Gallupe, B. (1987). A foundation for the study of group decision support systems. *Management Science, 33,* 589-609.

Ericsson, K., & Simon, H. A. (1984). *Protocol analysis: Verbal reports as data.* Cambridge: MIT Press.

Flores, J. G., & Alonso, C. G. (1995). Using focus groups in educational research. *Evaluation Research, 18,* 84-101.

Folch-Lyon, E., de la Macorra, L., & Schearer, S. B. (1981). Focus group and survey research on family planning in Mexico. *Studies in Family Planning, 12,* 409-432.

Fuller, T. D., Edwards, J. N., Vorakitphokatorn, S., & Sermsri, S. (1993). Using focus groups to adapt survey instruments to new populations: Experience in a developing country. In D. L. Morgan (Ed.), *Successful focus groups: Advancing the state of the art* (pp. 89-104). Newbury Park, CA: Sage.

Goldman, A. E., & McDonald, S. S. (1987). *The group depth interview: Principles and practice.* Englewood Cliffs, NJ: Prentice Hall.

Gormley, R. R. (1989). *An exploratory study of electronic focus group processes as represented and implemented using OptionFinder, an electronic, decision-assist tool.* Unpublished master's thesis.

Gottschalk, L. A. (1979). *The content analysis of verbal behavior.* Jamaica, NY: Spectrum.

Gottschalk, L. A., Winget, C. N., & Gleser, G. C. (1969). *Manual of instructions for using the Gottschalk-Gleser Content Analysis Scales.* Berkeley: University of California Press.

Greenbaum, T. L. (1993). *The practical handbook and guide to focus group research.* Lexington, MA: Lexington.

Grunert, K. G. (1982). Linear processing in a semantic network: An alternative view of consumer product evaluation. *Journal of Business Research, 10,* 31-42.

Grunert, K. G., & Bader, M. (1986). *A systematic way to analyze focus group data.* Paper presented at the summer Marketing Educator's Conference of the American Marketing Association, Chicago.

Hockey, S., & Marriott, I. (1982). *Oxford Concordance Program Version 1.0 users' manual.* Oxford: Oxford University Computing Service.

Hoppe, M. J., Wells, E. A., Morrison, D. M., Gillmore, M. R., & Wilsdon, A. (1995). Using focus groups to discuss sensitive topics with children. *Evaluation Review, 19,* 102-114.

Janis, I. L. (1965). The problem of validating content analysis. In H. D. Lasswell, N. Leites, & Associates (Eds.), *Language of politics* (pp. 42-67). Cambridge: MIT Press.

Jarrett, R. L. (1993). Focus group interviewing with low-income, minority populations: A research experience. In D. L. Morgan (Ed.), *Successful focus groups: Advancing the state of the art* (pp. 184-201). Newbury Park, CA: Sage.

Knodel, J. (1995). Focus groups as a qualitative method for cross-cultural research in social gerontology. *Journal of Cross-Cultural Gerontology, 10*(1-2), 7-20.

Krippendorf, K. (1980). *Content analysis: An introduction to its methodology.* Beverly Hills, CA: Sage.

Krueger, R. A. (1988). *Focus groups: A practical guide for applied research.* Newbury Park, CA: Sage.

Lorr, M., & McNair, D. M. (1966). Methods relating to evaluation of therapeutic outcome. In L. A. Gottschalk & A. H. Auerbach (Eds.), *Methods of research in psychotherapy.* Englewood Cliffs, NJ: Prentice Hall.

Magill, R. S. (1993). Focus groups, program evaluation, and the poor. *Journal of the Sociology of Social Welfare, 20,* 103-114.

Mervis, B., & Rosch, E. (1981). Categorization of natural objects. *Annual Review of Psychology, 32,* 89-115.

Mohler, P. P., & Zull, C. (1984). *TEXTPACK, Version V, release 2.* Mannheim: ZUMA.

Morgan, D. L. (Ed.). (1993). *Successful focus groups: Advancing the state of the art.* Newbury Park, CA: Sage.

Morgan, D. L. (1996). Focus groups. *Annual Review of Sociology, 22,* 129-152.

Popko, E. S. (1980). *Key-Word-in-Context Bibliographic Indexing: Release 4.0 users manual.* Cambridge, MA: Harvard University, Laboratory for Computer Graphics and Spatial Analysis.

Sapir, E. (1929). The status of linguistics as a science. *Language, 5,* 207-214.

Scott, W. A. (1955). Reliability of content analysis: The case of nominal coding. *Public Opinion Quarterly, 19,* 321-325.

Shamdasani, P., & Stewart, D. W. (1992). Analytical issues in focus group research. *Asian Journal of Marketing, 1*(1), 27-42.

Sherif, M., & Sherif, C. W. (1969). *Social psychology.* New York: Harper & Row.

Smith, R. G. (1978). *The Message Measurement Inventory: A profile for communication analysis.* Bloomington: Indiana University Press.

Spiegelman, M. C., Terwilliger, C., & Fearing, F. (1953). The reliability of agreement in content analysis. *Journal of Social Psychology, 37,* 175-187.

Stewart, D. W., & Shamdasani, P. N. (1990). *Focus groups: Theory and practice.* Newbury Park, CA: Sage.

Stone, P. J., Dunphy, D. C., Smith, M. S., & Ogilvie, D. M. (1966). *The General Inquirer: A computer approach to content analysis.* Cambridge: MIT Press.

Templeton, J. F. (1987). *Focus groups: A guide for marketing and advertising professionals.* Chicago: Probus.

Weber, R. P. (1985). *Basic content analysis.* Beverly Hills, CA: Sage.

Williams, J. D., Toy, D. R., & Gormley, J. (1990). *Using electronic focus groups to evaluate cultural diversity advertising in higher education.* Greenwich, CT: JAI.

18

Graphing Data

Gary T. Henry

Audiences for research findings expect to find graphs when they read about a study. From newspapers and magazines to technical journals, authors infuse their writing with graphs and charts. Graphs such as trend lines and bar charts can set the stage for a discussion, convey a message, or reinforce a central point. Data-based, analytic graphs are essential tools of the sciences, and they often convey data in a concise and readily digestible format. Now, software programs for producing graphs are available for most personal computers. These programs allow researchers to generate graphical displays, sometimes good ones, sometimes bad, with little time or effort.

It is fortunate that the means for producing graphical displays has come at a time when researchers are coming to appreciate the power and utility of such displays. The focus of this chapter is the communication of quantitative data through graphical displays. I will use the terms *graph, graphical display, chart,* and *graphic* more or less interchangeably. All these terms refer to graphs that are based on quantitative data and have the purpose of visually displaying data. The power of graphs comes from their ability to convey data directly to the viewer. In this sense, graphs reveal data to viewers. Viewers use their spatial intelligence to retrieve the data from graphs, a different source of intelligence from the language-based intelligence of prose and verbal presentations. The data become more credible and more convincing when the audience can see them and have a direct interaction with them. The communication process becomes more direct and immediate through graphical displays.

The power that stems from using graphs to communicate data directly with an audience can be thwarted, however. Badly designed or poorly executed graphs can obscure the data and try the patience of even a motivated audience. Most people have the ability to retrieve data from a well-composed graph: One

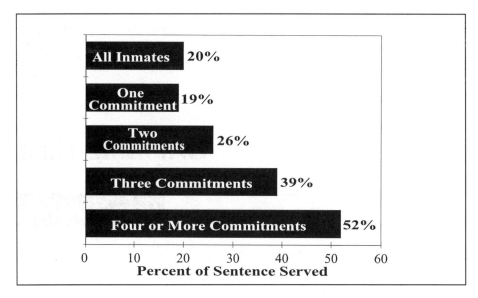

Figure 18.1. Sentences Served at Parole Eligibility
SOURCE: Joint Legislative Audit and Review Commission (1991, p. 3).

education theorist goes so far as to state that this ability is "hardwired" into the brain (Wainer, 1992). Unfortunately, producing a good graph is not as easy as retrieving information from it, and, in many cases, reliance on the default graphics of some software programs will not produce readily usable graphs. In this chapter, I will address the production of graphics that fulfill their communication purpose.

■ Using Graphs: From Description to Analysis

Graphical displays function as descriptive information sources as well as analytic tools. Presentation graphics are most often employed to describe major study findings. These graphs are frequently used in briefings and allow the audience to access descriptive data visually while a speaker communicates verbally. Usually presentation graphs contain a limited amount of data, which allows the audience to retrieve the message in a quick scan. Figure 18.1 presents a good example of a simple, descriptive display.

The graphic in Figure 18.1 was used by the staff of a legislative oversight commission to convey data on parole eligibility efficiently to legislators and the public. The graphic shows that inmates are serving a small fraction of their actual sentences, on average 20%, before being considered eligible for parole. For first-time offenders, this amounts to 19% of their sentences; those who have been to prison four or more times become eligible for parole after serving 52% of their sentences. A quick scan of the graph, independent of the text, communicates this basic information. The graph allows those in the audience

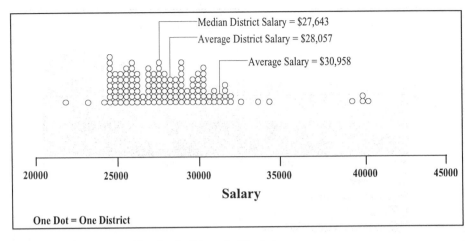

Median District Salary = $27,643

Average District Salary = $28,057

Average Salary = $30,958

20000   25000   30000   35000   40000   45000

Salary

One Dot = One District

Figure 18.2. Average Teacher's Salary in Virginia

SOURCE: Data from the Virginia Department of Education (1988).

to form their own conclusions about parole policies that lead to these results, and, just as important, it invites other questions: What is the percentage of the *sentence* actually served? Is the number of commitments the only cause of the variation in the percentage of sentence served before the inmate is eligible for parole? A quick scan communicates the basic point, but the graph also shows some additional information. For example, most of the inmates must be serving their first commitments, as the average for all inmates is only slightly higher than that for those serving their first commitments.

Data graphics should communicate information by facilitating the transfer of information from the researcher to the audience. In turn, graphs should stimulate interest and enhance the understanding of the audience. Graphs such as the one in Figure 18.1 present a limited amount of data using a common type of display, the bar chart. But as Figure 18.2 shows, more can be done with graphics; they can be used for more detailed description as well as for analytic purposes.

Figure 18.2 invites the audience to analyze the salaries of teachers in Virginia. The graphic depicts the average salary in each of the state's 133 school districts. Each dot represents the salary in one school district. The reader can quickly grasp the level and the variation of average salaries among the districts. Several norms or averages are shown: the median of the 133 district averages, the average salary of the district averages, and the average salary in the state. The form of the graphic and the amount of data presented allow the audience to go beyond the information available from a scan and to break down the salary variation further. The audience can examine the relationships among the norms and between the norm and the extremes. Only 13 districts pay more than the average salary. The average district salary is significantly higher because of these districts, indicating that they must be very large and employ many teachers. Twelve districts pay less than $25,000 on average. After a close examination of the graph, some may ponder why teachers' salaries vary so much across the state.

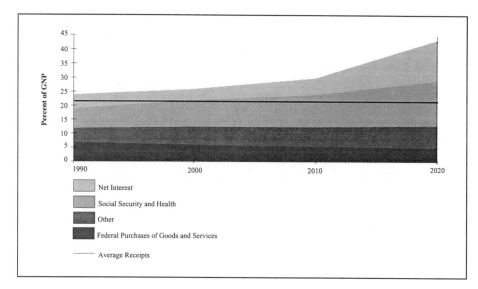

Figure 18.3. Federal Expenditures in the No-Action Scenario
SOURCE: U.S. General Accounting Office (1992, p. 60).

Good graphs answer some questions and encourage other questions. However, some graphs hide more than they show. Sometimes the ability to communicate graphically is inhibited by the graphical designer's trying to do too
much in a single graph. In other instances, communication fails because the
designer is unsure of the purpose of the graph. One principal reason for the
failure of a graph to communicate is improper execution of the basics of graphical design. Figure 18.3 is a reproduction of an original graph that obscures the
data and inhibits more detailed probing.

The purpose of the graph shown in Figure 18.3 was to raise concerns about
the rapidly increasing federal deficit and to motivate Congress to take action
to reduce it. In the publication in which this graph originally appeared, the text
referring to the graph states, "The deficit explodes to 20.6 percent of GNP by
2020, due in part to the projected dramatic rise in spending" (U.S. General
Accounting Office, 1992, p. 60). Yet the graph appears anything but explosive
and dramatic. Subtle differences in shading make the four trend lines, arranged
in a cumulative fashion, difficult to distinguish. The scale of the graph—too
wide for its height—stretches the display across the page and reduces the visual
impact of the increase, thus contradicting the written message.

The effect of this graph is reduced further in the original by the fact that
the 20.6% figure does not appear directly on the graph, although with some
effort the viewer can obtain it from the graph, by subtracting the line that represents average receipts from the top of the cumulative line for the year 2020.
The authors missed the potential to tie the graph to the text. A further problem
arises from failure to consider how the graph was to be incorporated into the
report. The report, which was published in a bound, 8½-by-11-inch format,
obscured the right side of the graph (the "explosion"), because that portion of

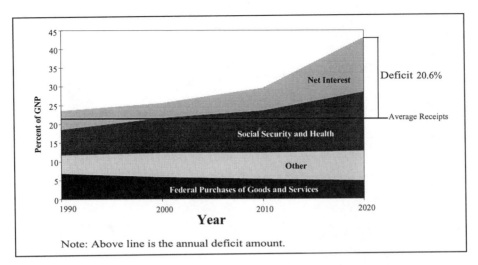

Figure 18.4. Federal Expenditures in the No-Action Scenario (Revised
Presentation)
SOURCE: Data from the U.S. General Accounting Office (1992, p. 60).

the graph fell behind the curve created by the report's binding. Figure 18.4
represents an attempt to marry the graph with the text. The viewer now gets
the impression that the growth in net interest payments produces most of the
increase, which now appears more dramatic.

These figures presented thus far, although they have progressively added
more information, principally summarize the data. On the continuum of purposes for graphics (Fienberg, 1979), these graphs are aligned progressively
from the point anchored at one end by descriptive displays toward the other
end, anchored by those that lend themselves to analysis of data. Tukey (1988)
points to two types of graphs with descriptive purposes: graphs that substitute
for tables and graphs that show the result of some other technique. The trend
line, which Tufte (1983) has found to be the most popular kind of graph, and
the bar chart are two examples of graphs generally used for descriptive purposes.

The multivariate trend lines presented in Figure 18.4 assist in breaking the
cumulative deficit increase into its component parts, which allows the viewer
to begin to analyze the sources for the increasing deficit. This graph goes beyond description to encourage the reader to analyze the data contained in it.
Tukey (1988) describes the graphs further toward this end of the continuum as
"graphs to let us see what may be happening over and above what has already
been described (analytical graphs)" (p. 38). The two-variable plot in Figure
18.4 moves further into the analytic realm.

Plotted in Figure 18.5a are the percentages of students eligible for free or
reduced-price lunches and students failing first-grade readiness tests, by school
districts. This figure shows the relationship between free lunch eligibility,
which is a measure of poverty, and first-grade readiness at the school district
level. Clearly, there is a relationship between the percentage of children who

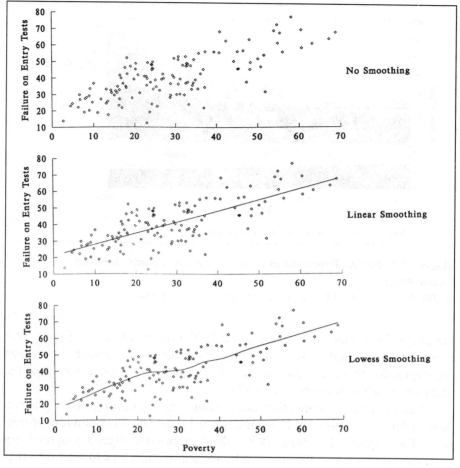

Figure 18.5. School District Percentage of Students Eligible for Free Lunch and
Entry Test Failures

are living in poverty in a school district and the percentage that fail at least one
school readiness exam. The relationship appears to be strong, positive, and
linear. Although we can quibble about the measures, it seems clear that school
districts with high proportions of disadvantaged students have significant challenges compared with other districts. One could reasonably conclude that the
difficulty of educating students increases in proportion to the amount of poverty in a school district.

In Figure 18.5b, a line has been added using standard linear (least squares)
regression and summarizing the relationship between the level of poverty and
the percentage of entry test failures. This line adds the "norm," or the predicted
percentage of entry test failures, for each level of students living in poverty.
An author could communicate information about this line by listing the coefficient estimates from the regression output, but the graph with the line is much
more compelling and quickly assimilated by viewers, especially by a lay audience. The graph also retains the visual sense of variation in the level of poverty

and failure of test scores in the districts and variation from the "norm." In addition, the graph draws viewers' attention to the three cases that appear to have very low entry test failures for the level of poverty among students' families. These three districts, with levels of poverty at about 23%, 38%, and 51%, and percentages of failures well below the line, appear to be unusual, or outliers. Outlier analysis, or the identification of unusual or anomalous cases, is readily done with graphs such as these.

Figure 18.5c introduces an analytic procedure that is uniquely graphical. The line drawn through this graph is computed by a smoothing technique called LOWESS smoothing, developed by Cleveland (1979). The LOWESS line is straight when the relationship is linear, and thus allows the researcher to assess whether the relationship between two variables is linear. In this case, the assumption of linearity required for ordinary least squares regression is supported. This type of diagnostic analysis is most readily performed by graphical means.

The graphs presented in Figure 18.5 are located more toward the analytic end of the continuum. However, it is not only the form of the graph that determines its place on the continuum. The choice of form can limit the sophistication of the graphical information displayed; for example, pie charts are capable only of breaking a whole into its component parts, whereas bivariate plots, such as those in Figure 18.5, can show relationships between two variables, the "norm" for the relationship, and outliers. Together with the graphical form, the amount and type of information displayed affect the viewer's ability to penetrate the data further.

In addition to purpose, graphs can be categorized by function (Henry, 1995): displays of parts of a whole (e.g., Figure 18.1), displays of multiple units (e.g., Figure 18.2), trends or time series (e.g., Figures 18.3 and 18.4), and relational graphs (e.g., Figure 18.5). Although there is much more to understand about the way in which we perform the tasks of retrieving information from graphs (see, e.g., Bertin, 1967/1983; Henry, 1995; Simkin & Hastie, 1987; Wainer, 1992), the focus of this chapter is on the preparation of better graphs. In the following sections, I offer examples and practical guidance on the construction of graphs for the three most common graphical functions: parts of a whole, displays of multiple units, and trends. Relational graphs have the greatest potential for analytic purposes, but exploration of these graphical forms is better left to a forum where more in-depth discussion can be provided (see Chambers, Cleveland, Kleiner, & Tukey, 1983; Henry, 1995; Tufte, 1983, 1990). I close the chapter with a brief discussion of the elements researchers must consider as they polish graphs into final form.

■ *Parts of a Whole*

Applied social researchers often use graphs to provide summaries or overviews of data that represent parts of the whole. The primary purpose of these displays is descriptive. Bar charts and pie charts are the most frequently used formats for displaying parts of a whole. Such displays can serve several purposes for the audience:

1. They orient viewers to the subject or topic.

2. They point out a problem or issue central to the study.

3. They provide an overview of the group being studied.

4. They justify the study's concentration on a part of the topic or a subgroup of the population.

5. They allow viewers to generate questions and issues for themselves that the researcher will address in the study.

6. They expose a commonly held myth or misconception about the population or topic.

Too often, rather than offering a stimulating lead-in to draw the audience into the study, a pie chart is used to present the first categorical breakdown of data that comes to the researcher's mind—or, worse yet, is simply an interesting design that the publications staff comes up with. In these cases, graphics serve a purpose other than those mentioned above—rote decoration.

Pie graphs are limited to showing percentage or proportional distributions of categorical data. Bar graphs can display the same data, but they can also be used to convey more complex data, such as responses to a series of items that use a common scale, the values of a single variable over multiple units, or distributional characteristics of a continuous variable (sometimes called histograms) for a batch of data. Obviously, these basic formats are limited in the types of data they can present, especially pie graphs. Bar graphs, however, have a considerable range of uses, and researchers should consider the significant variations in bar graph design in the development of summaries. Bar graphs have an advantage over some other more complex graphical formats, because they are used so commonly—the bar format is likely to be stored in long-term memory for many members of the audience. Thus the information processing to be done by the audience can be more readily accomplished.

Since at least the time of Eells's (1926) article in the *Journal of the American Statistical Association,* statistical graphers have pondered the relative merits of bar and pie graphs. For at least one task—the breakdown of a variable into distributions by category, such as government expenditures by categories (defense, social security, debt maintenance, and so on)—either seems adequate. In cases where either is usable, is there evidence to suggest that one is better than the other?

Two recent empirical studies have found that bars are indeed better than pies. Cleveland and McGill (1984) and Simkin and Hastie (1987) found a preference for bar charts based on accuracy and processing time, respectively. But test the differences for yourself. In Figure 18.6, which is adapted from Cleveland and McGill (1984), cover all but Figure 18.6a and try to pick the largest slice of the pie. Then make the same comparison using the horizontal bar chart

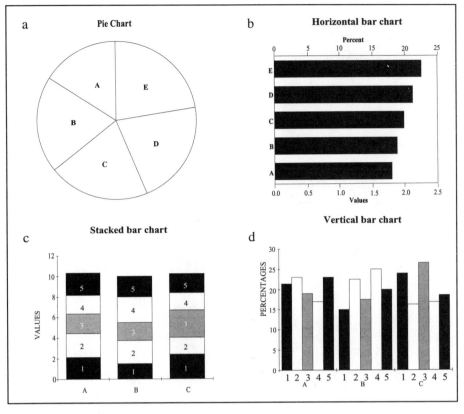

Figure 18.6. Displays of Parts of the Whole
SOURCE: Cleveland and McGill (1984).

(Figure 18.6b). Both the graphs display the same data, but clearly the differences are more quickly discernible in the bar graph. Thus, for questions that fall into the first level of graphicacy—questions of level, count, or amount—bars are preferable. It is simply quicker and more accurate for the viewer to read the values from a bar than from slices of a pie.

Both Cleveland and McGill (1984) and Simkin and Hastie (1987) went further in their studies and considered stacked bar charts. It is more difficult to make accurate judgments about stacked bar charts than about either of the other forms. In Figures 18.6c and 18.6d, the divided bar chart is compared to a grouped bar chart for ease and accuracy of determining the order of the proportions. Once again, the same data are plotted. Clearly, it is easier to retrieve data from the horizontal bar (18.6b) and the vertical grouped bars (18.6d) than from their respective counterparts, the pie and the stacked bar.

Simple, unadorned pie charts, such as the one shown at the top of Figure 18.7, have been shown to present more perceptual difficulties than alternative graphical formats. For this reason they are shunned by many graphics experts. Pie charts do what they were designed to do; as Bertin (1967/1983) notes, "The essential point of the information—the relationship to the whole—is depicted,"

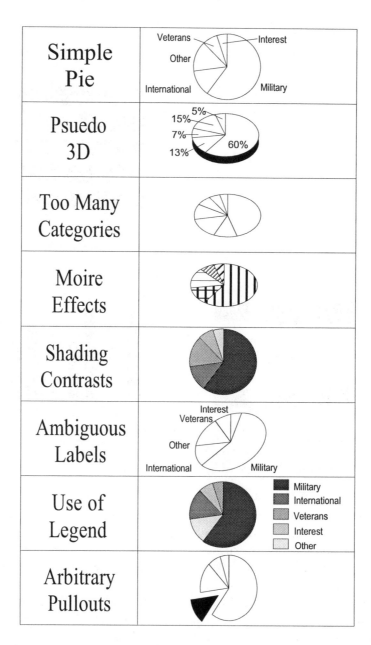

Figure 18.7. Common Problems With Pie Charts

as long as no external comparisons are needed and the categories are few in number (p. 200). But as used in practice, pies often present design features that further impede audience comprehension. Figure 18.7 illustrates seven common problems with pie charts that cause data to be distorted: fake 3D perspective, too many categories, moire effects, imperceptible shading contrasts, ambiguous labels, legends, and arbitrary pullouts. Rather than enabling a graphic to reveal data, these elements can distort comprehension.

Bar graphs are the most highly recommended format for presenting parts of the whole. There are a number of design variations that may be used in bar graphs, including orientation, grid lines, axes, tick marks on the axes, fill, and order of the bars. These are considerations that should not be left to software default settings.

- *Orientation:* In a bar chart, *orientation* refers to whether the bars run vertically or horizontally. Figure 18.8 shows the same data presented as a vertical bar chart and then repeated as a horizontal chart with some additional refinements. One major advantage of horizontal bar charts is the ease of reading labels set on the left side of the bars, rather than labels below, which are often abbreviated or set at an acute angle.

- *Grid lines:* Figure 18.8b shows the same data as Figure 18.8a, but with grid lines. Most standards call for grid patterns, but offer little guidance about their number or spacing. Tufte (1983) strongly suggests the minimalist approach. With a few bars, many software packages allow the user to show percentages within the bars or just beyond them. If the percentages are written on the graph, grid lines are redundant and therefore unnecessary. Research has shown that with numbers provided on graphs, readers use graphs as accurately as tables, but readers can use tables more accurately than they can graphs without the numbers (Jarvenpaa & Dickson, 1988).

- *Axes and tick marks:* Axes such as those that appear in Figure 18.8a provide a frame for the bars; to some eyes, this gives the appearance of "completeness." To my eye, they act as arbitrary caps on the percentages (or values of the variables in other graphs) and so should not be used. Adding box around the entire graph presents a finished look without interfering with the data.

- *Fill:* Another option for simple bar charts is fill. Without filling in the bars, as shown in Figure 18.8a, the graph appears anemic, less dramatic. To gain the advantage of fill without encouraging misleading comparisons, it is best to use thin bars.

- *Order:* Figure 18.8 also illustrates one other design variation, the changing of the order of the bars. In Figure 18.8b, the expenditure categories are presented in ascending order, from smallest to largest. Bertin (1967/1983) suggests ordering to imprint a pattern in the mind of the viewer. By reading the categories from top to bottom, the viewer obtains ordinal data about the categories. In this case, ascending order provides the largest expenditure category as a base for judging the relative size of the other categories. For data displaying multiple units, descending order has the virtue of putting the largest unit on top and emphasizing the large units, as we tend to read from top to bottom. Alternatively, some data such as Figure 18.1 have a natural order.

■ *Displaying Multiple Units*

Applied social researchers often have data on cases that they wish to be able to compare case by case. For example, educational researchers now collect

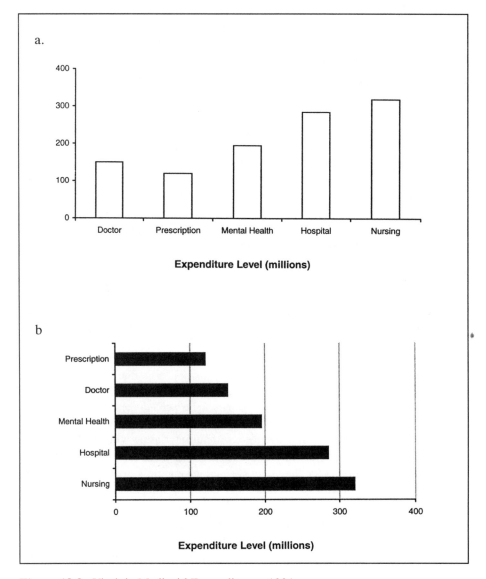

Figure 18.8. Virginia Medicaid Expenditures, 1991

data on student achievement and attainment at the school and school district levels. To understand how patterns of outcome variables differ from one school to the next, it is important to compare them. Graphical displays of these data, such as that shown in Figure 18.9, could reveal patterns in the data as well as communicate performance levels to a wide variety of people interested in schools and education. The literature is replete with other examples.

Graphical comparisons can express patterns and substantive differences in ways that complement and enhance traditional statistical analyses. Applied researchers generally analyze the data and report the results of the statistical analyses as estimates, sometimes with confidence intervals and statistical tests

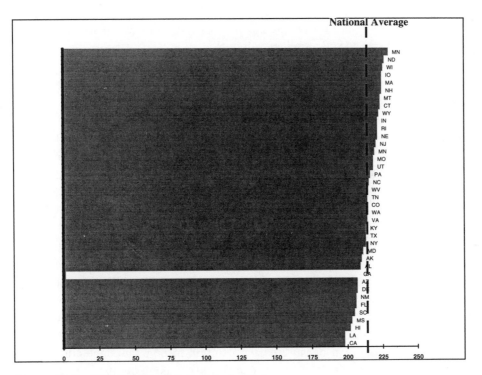

Figure 18.9. 1992 NAEP Math Results by State

of significance. These analyses are summaries, and, as such, they provide very few data about specific cases. We may know the average of all cases or the percentage of variance explained by an independent variable, but we do not find out anything about a particular case, whether it fits the pattern or if it is a relative outlier. Usually, when researchers deem it important to provide the results for individual cases, they do so by recording them in tables. Before we turn to graphical approaches, let us consider this approach.

☐ *Data Tables*

Often, applied research and evaluation reports (and reports of social statistics) are filled with pages of tables. Although the intention of providing consumers with the "actual data" is admirable, their access to the information is limited by the format. It is difficult, even for motivated consumers of information, to go beyond reading values for particular cases from the table without exhausting their time and energy and coming to unwarranted or inaccurate conclusions. Data tables are excellent methods for storing data, but difficult media for communicating and analyzing data. Wainer (1992, p. 21) provides useful suggestions for improving tables:

1. Order the columns and rows in a way that makes sense, such as by placing cases and variables likely to be of most interest first or in natural sequence.

2. Round the data as much as possible, as two digits are about all humans comprehend and all most data will justify.

3. Include summaries and averages as a means for making comparisons.

Table 18.1 illustrates these suggestions using some school district performance data from 14 school districts in Virginia. The group was selected by a benchmark selection technique that uses five variables to select the districts that are most similar to a "seed" district, in this case Fairfax County, the district highlighted (Henry, McTaggart, & McMillan, 1992). In Table 18.1, the 14 districts are ordered based on their poverty level, as measured by the percentages of students eligible for free lunches. Fairfax County is sixth in poverty, slightly lower than the median, with 13%. Poverty being related to school performance sets up a rough indicator of expectations for judging the performance of these districts, which have already been determined to be similar. Looking at the median for each variable that appears at the bottom of the table, we can quickly see that Fairfax County schools are above the median for all five performance indicators, and in fact are in the top four on every indicator as shown by the rankings in parentheses.

The indicators that measure participation in foreign language courses are grouped together so that the reader can quickly make a comparison between overall participation and participation of minority students. Although Fairfax County ranks well on both indicators, the proximity allows the reader to note that Fairfax County has the lowest difference in the two percentages, indicating a substantial degree of "equity." Such features can improve the audience's ability to access information contained in a table, but they do not make it easy to perform analysis with tables, especially if there are more cases than in this example.

Many applied research projects have a need to report data on multiple cases, such as the data in Figures 18.2 and 18.9. In the latter case, it was important to identify each of the cases; in the former, it was more important to grasp the overall shape of the distribution of the values, that is, the relative frequency with which certain salaries occur. Other formats for obtaining a picture of the data, as well as some statistical information on the spread of the data, are the box and whisker plot (Benjamini, 1988; Tukey, 1977) and the stem and leaf plot Tukey (1977; Tufte, 1983). Although packed with information, these formats are difficult for nontechnical audiences to grasp, and so they are limited to use mainly by researchers themselves.

In Figure 18.9, data on the National Assessment of Education Progress (NAEP) are presented, with the states sorted in descending order from top to bottom. Bertin (1967/1983) recommends this sorting or "repartitioning" to simplify the image in a way that results in "a quantitative series which tends toward a straight line" (p. 104). The graphic is oriented horizontally to facilitate reading of the labels. The viewer's ability to read the labels also depends on the number of units in the display, the size of the display, and the type font

Table 18.1   Student Performance Data for Fairfax County School District and Its Benchmark Districts

	Students Eligible for Free Lunch	Absent Fewer Than 10 Days (6th-8th Grade) Attendance	Literacy Passport 6th-Grade Pass Rate	Taking Foreign Language by 8th Grade	Minority Students Taking Foreign Language by 8th Grade	8th-Grade Standardized Test Scores Above the 75th Percentile
1. Poquoson	4	79 (5)	68 (12)	21 (13)	—[a] —[a]	53 (1)
2. Chesterfield	10	75 (7)	76 (5)	36 (11)	24 (9)	38 (10)
3. Roanoke Co.	10	89 (1)	70 (8)	44 (6)	23 (10)	40 (8)
4. Falls Church	11	79 (5)	80 (2)	58 (1)	35 (6)	53 (1)
5. Stafford	11	66 (13)	72 (7)	30 (12)	16 (12)	38 (10)
6. Fairfax Co.	12	81 (2)	79 (3)	46 (4)	42 (2)	53 (1)
7. Prince William	12	67 (11)	69 (10)	40 (9)	29 (7)	40 (8)
8. Manassas	14	53 (14)	83 (1)	20 (14)	9 (13)	44 (5)
9. York	17	81 (2)	73 (6)	43 (7)	37 (5)	43 (7)
10. Henrico	18	73 (8)	63 (14)	46 (4)	38 (4)	38 (10)
11. Virginia Beach	20	81 (2)	70 (8)	48 (3)	40 (3)	33 (14)
12. Williamsburg	24	71 (9)	69 (10)	42 (8)	21 (11)	37 (13)
13. Harrisonburg	30	67 (11)	79 (3)	40 (9)	27 (8)	44 (5)
14. Arlington	33	68 (10)	67 (13)	58 (1)	44 (1)	45 (4)
Median	13	74	71	42.5	29	41.5

SOURCE: Virginia Department of Education (1993).

NOTE: All variables in the table are percentages. The rank for each variable is in parentheses.

a. Too few cases in denominator to be reliable.

541

used. For the display area on an 8½-by-11-inch page, about 40 units can be displayed. Type size that is adequate when printed on a high-quality laser printer will wash out with copying or if transferred to a transparency for an overhead. A larger typeface is required for such uses, and fewer units can be displayed. Also, remember that legibility on the computer monitor does not imply legibility on the printed page. When individual units are important, the graphic designer should examine the printed graph, checking for legibility, and make a copy of a copy before finalizing it.

Cleveland (1984) has made an interesting point concerning bar charts such as that shown in Figure 18.9. The length of the bar conveys the score for each state; therefore, the scale of the x axis must be set to make the minimum point 0. This eliminates the confusion between length and position of the end of the bar in making comparisons. Without doing this or using another format, such as Cleveland's (1984) dot chart, differences in the scores can be exaggerated and some bars can appear to be twice as long as others (Henry, 1995).

In some cases, researchers wish to compare two groups. An experiment with one treatment group and a control group is a common example. Another example is the comparison of a single case or site to a norm or typical case. Comparing two demographic groups, such as males and females, as in Figure 18.10, is yet another example. Figure 18.10 shows responses to a student survey concerning potential issues involved in the relocation of university classrooms and faculty offices. Clearly, the women students had greater concerns about security than did the men. This indicated the need to pay special attention to women's concerns during security planning. The graph also shows that parking and building security were major concerns and that students were less concerned about getting to faculty offices than to other campus locations—unsurprising results for an urban, commuter campus, but useful for security planning.

The graphical technique used in Figure 18.10, aligning the responses of two groups along a common vertical spine, is extremely useful for promoting comparisons both across items for a group and between groups on an item. The technique is limited to comparisons of two groups and items that are measures on the same scale. Often, however, more than two groups or cases are involved in a given study. In addition, variables of interest to the analyst and the audience are not necessarily measured on a common scale. For example, an audience interested in public school performance indicators may wish to see test scores, dropout rates, and attendance rates and to compare them graphically. In this case, multivariate, multiple-case graphics are needed. Multivariate graphs, which I have discussed in detail elsewhere (Henry, 1993; Henry et al., 1992), are relatively easy for nontechnical audiences to decode, as has been shown for four-variable plots, and a powerful tool for empowering lay audiences to do their own analyses.

When considering the use of a graph to display multiple units and multiple variables, the designer must work through a number of steps. First, the number of cases or units is important. For two units or groups, there are more graphical options. With more than two cases, the next issue is the importance of identi-

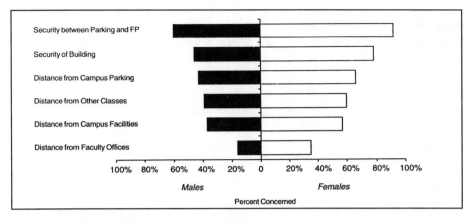

Figure 18.10. Security Concerns in Fairlie-Poplar (Male Versus Female)

fying individual cases. Histograms, box plots, stem and leaf plots, and histograms with dots are useful univariate summaries for multiple cases. When multiple cases must be displayed with individual cases identified, bar charts with a zero base are useful, but they are limited to one variable. Moving to multivariate displays in which individual cases can be identified is possible, but it increases the complexity of the display. Clearly, the graphic designer must carefully consider the type and amount of data, the level at which the audience is expected to "read" the graph, the type of display, and the audience.

■ Trends

The most common type of graphical display is the trend line or time series graph (Tufte, 1983). Trend graphs usually have a measure of time (years, months, weeks, days) on the horizontal or x axis and one or more dependent variables on the vertical or y axis.

Trend graphs were the first to use the x-y plane to represent data that do not have complete and direct physical analogies. Earlier graphical depictions were maps and charts in which the plane of the paper itself is intended as an accurate physical representation of spatial relationships. Trend lines change the x-y plane from the two-dimensional representation of space to a more abstract, symbolic representation of the level of a variable at set intervals of time. Time is charted across the horizontal axis, moving from left to right.

Time series graphs began to be popularized in the late 1700s, according to Beniger and Robyn (1978). Most graphical historians attribute the popularization of the innovation of time series with economic and social data to William Playfair in his *Commercial and Political Atlas* (1786), where the first bar chart was also presented.

Perhaps the basic simplicity of the trend graph is what has led it to be so abused in the hands of graphic designers over the years. With important data, some elementary mathematics, and graph paper, almost anyone can construct a time series graph. However, an overemphasis on entertainment and an underemphasis on displaying data to facilitate the exchange of information seems to have spawned numerous faulty designs. After slogging through numerous examples of time series charts trying to retrieve the data and trends supposedly presented in them, I believe the straightforward advice of Edward Tufte (1983) regarding the presentation of good graphics is important: "Above all else show the data" (p. 92).

☐ *Displaying Trend Data*

Often, a designer will construct a times series graph by using all of the available data and a default plot. A plot of this type depicting a jail population series is shown in Figure 18.11a. These data seem to have too much fluctuation to imprint an image in short-term memory that goes beyond an overall upward trend. This graph does not allow the viewer to ascertain the differences in the rates of increases from one group of months to another. The designer can reinforce the trend and make analysis of specific time periods possible by drawing a linear smoothing line, as shown in Figure 18.11b. For this plot the line is restricted to the range of the data to avoid the appearance of forecasting or backcasting the data using this simplistic method. In general, it is good practice for researchers to avoid extrapolating beyond the range of the data with a simple linear smoothing unless they have good reason for doing so.

From Figure 18.11 we can see that the jails across the state have had to accommodate about 690 additional inmates each year during this time period. In the early 1980s, the growth appears insignificant; in the middle of the series, a drop in jail populations is evident; and in the most recent months, the increase seems greater than the linear trend for the entire series. However, we are not sure that the trend is linear. Cleveland has developed another type of smoothing using locally weighted sum of squares (LOWESS) (see Chambers et al., 1983). LOWESS computes a curve that is dependent on the predicted values from a weighted average of the y values that lie near each x value. A LOWESS curve follows the trend in data from one period to the next and gives the graph viewer a good idea if the data are linear. The LOWESS curve for this series is shown in Figure 18.11c. The curve appears to be close to linear, but the slope is increasing somewhat over time, given the slightly convex appearance. This curve fits both ends of the series better than the straight line regression.

In addition to drawing lines to orient the viewer to the overall trend, the graphic designer can smooth the data themselves. In Figure 18.12, the same series is displayed three ways. The original data appear in Figure 18.12a. Then the data have been converted to a four-period moving average. One calculates the moving average by taking the average of the first four observations in the time series for the first value, then removing the first observation and adding the fifth in the ordered series and recomputing the average. One continues this

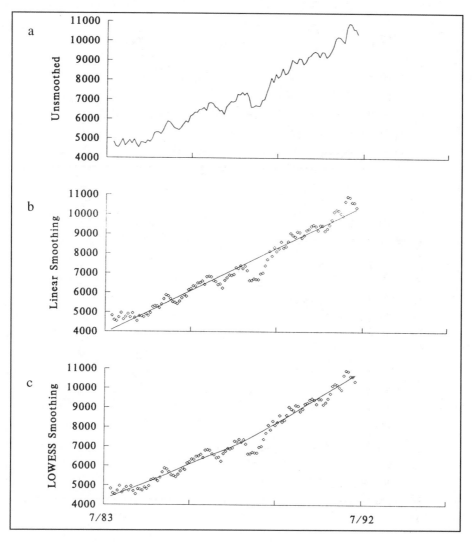

Figure 18.11. Inmate Population in Local Jails: Smoothing

process, deleting the earliest observation and adding the next data point throughout the entire series. The moving average plot focuses attention on the two distinct series: the ripples in the first 60 to 70 observations and the increased slope of the trend thereafter (see Figure 18.12b).

The moving average assists in removing some of the random fluctuation of the data, which enables the viewer's eyes to follow the overall trend. For data with more fluctuations, a more robust method of taking moving averages can be done by using running medians. The original data are smoothed by a four-period running median in Figure 18.12c. The process is similar to moving averages except that medians are computed rather than means. The curves are

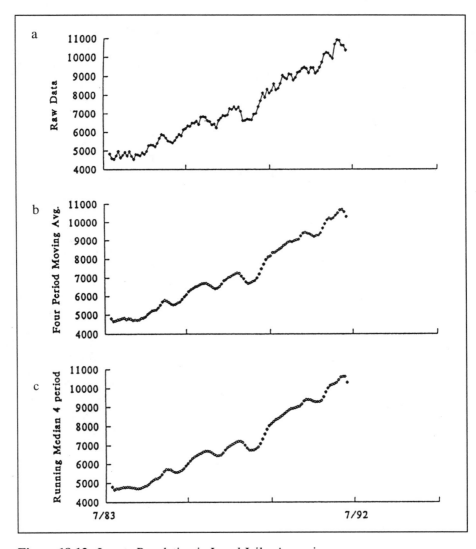

Figure 18.12. Inmate Population in Local Jails: Averaging

smoother than before. This method works especially well with series that have
occasional outliers, which tend to distract attention from the images in the data.

■ *Sizing the Graph*

Two graphing principles concern the size of a graphic: data density and
distortion of effect size. Data density should be maximized (Tufte, 1983). In
other words, data should be packed into as small a display space as possible.
Of course, human perception places real limits on the size of the marks used
to plot the data and how close they can be and still be distinguished. Along with

the limitations on legibility come other limitations, such as the quality of common photocopier reproductions and the aesthetic appeal of the graph in a publication. Dense graphs are preferred, but the degree to which they can be condensed depends on legibility, method of reproduction, and the aesthetic appeal of the graph.

In addition to the overall size of the graph, the relationship between the length and width of the graph, or the scale, also has implications for its size. Tufte and Cleveland have different ways of approaching the relationship between the length and width of the graph. For Tufte (1983), it is a matter of proportion. He refers to the "golden rectangle" from ancient philosophy, Playfair's work, and some very practical issues about labeling to come to the conclusion that graphs should be wider than tall: "Graphs should tend toward the horizontal" (p. 186). The golden rectangle would have us draw graphs approximately 1.618 times longer than tall. Tufte seems to set his limits for a ratio firmly between 1.2 times and 2.2 times wider than tall. Figures 18.13a and 18.13b show these two ratios for the crime rate data in a minimum overall size. Obviously, the choice of scale will affect the viewer's perception of the trend in the data: Figure 18.13b makes the crime rate appear to be gradually increasing, whereas Figure 18.13a visually depicts a steep increase. Most graphics software allows the analyst to manipulate length and width, enabling sizing of graphs for particular publication spaces and for appropriateness of the message that is intended to be conveyed.

Cleveland (1984) takes another approach to the size issue based upon the slope of the data. He has developed a method for computing the dimensions of the graph to achieve an absolute median slope of 1. The graph plotted in Figure 18.13c uses his method and has a ratio of 2.32. Having used this method on several time series graphs, I find it yields a graph at the upper end of Tufte's (1983) recommended ratio, above the golden rectangle. As a general rule, for a 5-inch-wide graph, which is commonly used in a report on $8\frac{1}{2}$-by-11-inch paper, the graph should be about $2\frac{1}{4}$ to $2\frac{1}{2}$ inches tall. Many software programs seem to default to the square, which gives an impression of urgency.

■ *Minding the Details*

Ambiguity is the greatest enemy of useful graphics. Attention to the details of graphics thwarts ambiguity. However, details are those time-consuming nuisances the minding of which comes after the creative work is done. "I know what it says and they'll figure it out when I explain it," reflects an attitude that may cause a researcher to miss out on an opportunity to communicate data to an important audience. It also misses the fundamental point that Bertin (1967/1983) makes about the power of graphical displays. They are atemporal. They can be viewed and reviewed as the interests and curiosity of audience members are piqued. To possess atemporality, a graph must stand on its own, as a complete entity.

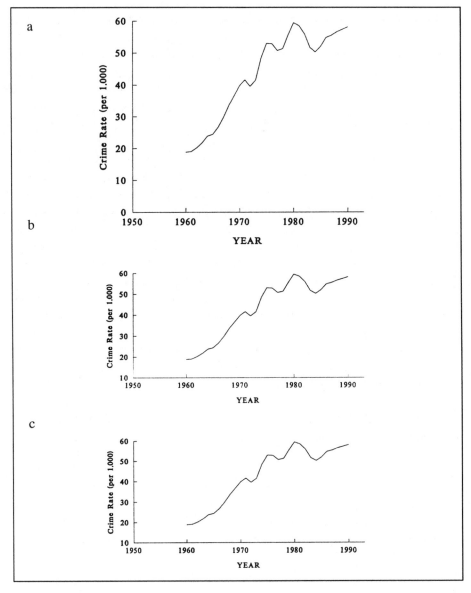

Figure 18.13. Reported Crime Rate in the United States (Three Scales)
SOURCE: Federal Bureau of Investigation (1991).

Completeness in a graphic involves a number of essential items:

■ *Title:* The title should describe the variable(s) and the population being plotted.
■ *Axes:* Both axes for the graph should be clearly labeled with the variable name or measure.
■ *Axis lines:* The minimum number of axis lines should be used. Usually two will suffice, if any are needed at all.

- *Scale:* Scales should be marked and labeled at intervals on both axes that permit interpolation of points from the graph for the viewer to retrieve specific data points.
- *Line labels:* Lines should be labeled at the end when the series is multivariate, using the gestalt principle of continuity; the use of line symbols, such as dashed or dotted lines with a legend, makes reading the graph more difficult.
- *Source:* The source of the data should be noted at the bottom of the graphic for the viewer's convenience.
- *Grid lines:* Grid lines distract the eye from the data and, when placed at arbitrary intervals on a time series, do little to aid the retrieval of data; they should be minimized or taken out entirely.

■ *Multivariate Time Series*

Multivariate time series can take three forms: cumulative time series, difference time series, and multiple series time series. The Medicaid expenditures depicted in Figure 18.14 are one example of a cumulative time series, although they are plotted as individual series with the total also on the graph in this example. This example shows that it is often difficult to read the data from a three-dimensional design such as this. Difference time series are two time series whose difference is meaningful for analysis. Import-export, balance-of-trade graphics (Henry, 1995; Playfair, 1786; Tufte, 1983) are examples of this type of time series. Multiple series time series are usually two trends between which the researcher posits a cause-effect relationship. This type of graph usually involves plotting two different metrics on the vertical scale, which makes graphing very tricky. In this section, I will address only the cumulative time series, which is a set of related time series that are actually parts of a whole.

The cumulative time series is a data series of the components of the whole over time. Although this type of multivariate time series seems easily graphed because the series are in the same metric, it can be quite challenging. The Medicaid data presented in Figure 18.15 provide an opportunity to review the design choices for cumulative multivariate graphs. First, we must decide if the total is needed. Figure 18.15a shows the five categories of Medicaid expenditures for 1983-1991 graphed as multiple time series without the total included. This graph allows the viewer to follow the individual categories, noting the dramatic rise in inpatient expenditure and the similar pattern in physician and drug expenditures until 1990. In Figure 18.15b, the total is added. The increases in the individual components over time produce a dramatic rise in the total that was not apparent without adding in the total. However, some of the detail for individual categories is lost.

Because of the scale differences between the components and the total, the ability to track individual categories over time is diminished in Figure 18.15b. One solution is to use a log scale to graph the six series, including the total, as depicted in Figure 18.15c. In this graph the log scale values are replaced by the

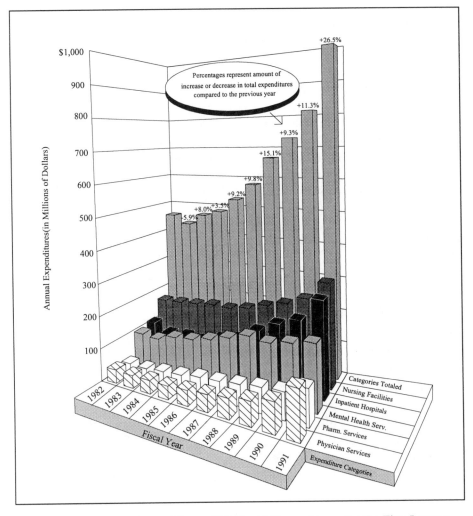

Figure 18.14. Comparison of Annual Medicaid Expenditures for the Five Largest
Medical Care Categories, FY 1982-FY 1991

SOURCE: Joint Legislative Audit and Review Commission (1992, p. 36); JLARC staff depiction of
Department of Medical Assistance Services medical care expenditure worksheet, derived from un-
audited financial statements.

original metric, but the vertical axis is clearly identified as a log scale. The log
scale is useful to those familiar with its properties, but it reduces the slopes
significantly, as we can see by comparing the total series in Figures 18.15b and
18.15c. Figure 18.15d shows a cumulative graph. This graph appears to be the
most pleasing, but it too has its drawbacks. To look at a category of expenditures other than the nursing expenditures at the bottom of the graph, the eye
must judge the differences between two curves, a notoriously difficult task
(Cleveland & McGill, 1984, p. 549). For this type of graph, it is important to
put the category that is the primary focus of attention at the bottom. However,
if this category has considerable fluctuation over the time period, it will make
the other categories too difficult to retrieve. In this case, the most stable cate-

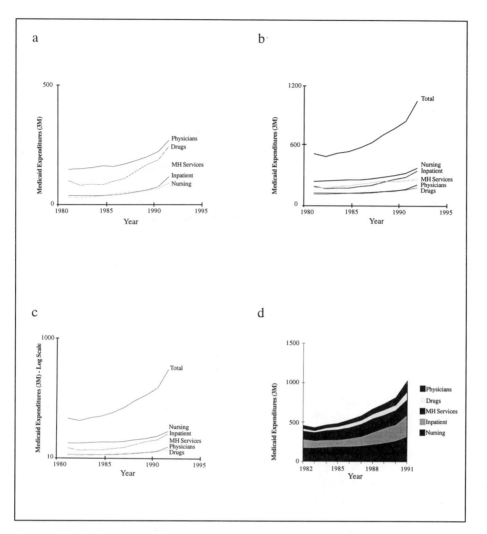

Figure 18.15. Annual Medicaid Expenditures in Virginia

gories should be placed at the bottom, and the category of interest at the top, where the fluctuations can be observed without the perception of the other data being affected.

Time series graphs represent a significant step in the evolution of graphical displays. They were the first graphs that did not rely on spatial analogies as had their predecessors—maps and diagrams. They set the stage for two-variable, or Cartesian, plots, which are the most abstract and first truly relational graphs. The two types of displays share many similar properties, as the time can be regarded as a particular variable graphed on the horizontal axis. Relational graphs have great potential for analytic work, including allowing audiences for the research to analyze the data for themselves; interested readers are referred to other sources for further discussion of this topic (Chambers et al., 1983; Henry, 1995; Tufte, 1983, 1990; Tukey, 1977).

■ Principles for Preparing Useful Graphics

□ Give Primacy to the Data

Show the data. The purpose of graphical data displays is to inform viewers. To inform, the displays must contain meaningful data and the display format must provide access to the data. The data that applied researchers collect have been acquired at a cost of time and human effort. If they are worthy of collection, they are worthy of being displayed and analyzed properly. In presenting meaningful data, the graphical designer should keep one central idea in mind: Comparisons are the means by which graphical information is digested. Graphicacy, or the ability of the viewer to retrieve data from a display, can be summed up in terms of the following comparisons:

- *Level 1 graphicacy* is the ability to make a comparison between the position of the graphical symbol used to represent the data and the position or other graphical device that encodes the value of the data. An accurate description of the observation, developed through the comparison, is the objective of Level 1 graphicacy.

- *Level 2 graphicacy* is the ability to compare the position of multiple graphical symbols and discern a norm. The norm may be an average, a trend, or a slope. For a time series graph, the norm is the overall trend; for a bar chart, it is the average or point estimate. Level 2 graphicacy assumes Level 1 skills. The viewer must compare all the elements to formulate the norm.

- *Level 3 graphicacy* is the ability to make comparisons between trends or between patterns and specific cases. In carrying out Level 3 graphicacy, the viewer goes from describing the subject to analyzing the data. The pattern of data in the 10 most recent time periods might be compared with the earlier trends using a time series graph. The comparison forces the question, Why?

Showing the data amounts to facilitating comparisons. Viewers should be able to retrieve specific data from the graph; they should be able to construct a norm; they should be able to analyze the data from the graph by comparing trends, patterns, and observations. Of course, not all graphs will place equal emphasis on each of the three types of exercises. The researcher must ask, What is the most meaningful, most important exercise for the audience to carry out with these data? It may not be possible for one graph to facilitate all the meaningful comparisons. Attempting to do too much with a single graph may hide the data.

□ Design Information-Rich Graphics

Applied researchers should strive to produce graphics that reveal the underlying complexity of the subjects with which they deal. Graphs can show relationships that exist and dispel myths about relationships that do not. Graphical displays show patterns and exceptions to those patterns. Graphs give meaning to statistical summaries. They enhance the credibility of findings: Seeing is believing, after all. But graphs can perform these functions only when they contain the data necessary to carry them out.

In practice, carrying out these functions will require abstract graphical forms and high data densities. Relational graphics are needed to show the relationship between two variables. Both variables can be individually described with simpler graphical forms, such as bar charts, but their covariance is most directly presented through the use of the two-variable plot. Graphs will often display large, multivariate batches of data. All other things being equal, greater data densities are preferred. But as we learn from economics, all things are never equal. Audiences less familiar with decoding graphical data may find the cost of retrieving information from data-dense graphical displays too dear. A novel or unusual graphical display will also limit the optimal data densities. These conditions should not deter the researcher from using data-dense graphs. Rather, the researcher should use them to assess what he or she is attempting to convey and to tailor designs to the data *and* the audience. As audience members become more adroit at reading graphical displays—that is, as their graphicacy skills increase—the researcher can increase the data density.

☐ *Tailor Designs to Reveal Data*

Taking the primary purpose of graphs as informing their audience, applied researchers should tailor designs to the data and the audience. Often this will involve many iterations of the display, with the researcher testing one improvement after another. And just as often, improvements do not work out. Fortunately, researchers can use three criteria in the iterative process of graphical production to judge the success of a new graphical idea: Does it avoid distortion? Does it enhance clarity? Does it encourage important comparisons? Each of these criteria should be applied as successive versions of the graph are produced.

Avoid Distortion

The size of the effect, be it indicated by a difference or a slope, should be equivalent to the size displayed in the graph. This phenomenon is measured by the "lie factor," or the amount of distortion in the display of the effect (Tufte, 1983). Distortion can occur as the result of a willful, malicious act; through the actions of a graphical designer who values the medium more than the message; or—and I suspect most commonly—through unintentional actions.

Using size or color saturation to convey quantitative information can also cause distortion. Perception of the differences in size is a function of the actual difference in size. Unfortunately, the relationship is not one to one. Differences in size are perceived as less than the actual differences recorded in the graph. Therefore, even if the graph accurately conveys differences, it is likely to be misperceived. Using lengths such as bars and the distances from the axes in two-variable plots to convey most information seems to be safe.

One additional comment is in order. Sometimes it is not clear what the information-carrying symbol is. For example, in a pictogram, a graphical device that uses a picture of an object to convey information, it can be unclear whether the height of the picture, the size (area) of the picture, or the volume of the picture provides the visual cue. Researchers can avoid some such confusion by avoiding pictograms entirely. But confusion also can arise when three-dimensional or even two-dimensional bars are used to convey information. Are the data represented by the height of the bar or its area? By convention, we expect it to be height, and it generally is. But bars should be thin to avoid this confusion.

Enhance Clarity

In tailoring designs, the importance of clarity cannot be overstated. The designer must continually ask: What is the purpose of this graph? In the iterative process of tailoring a display, it is easy to lose sight of the original purpose and whether the graph is achieving that purpose. Clarity in graphical displays requires the avoidance of ambiguity. Some potential sources of ambiguity have been discussed above, such as ambiguity about which physical aspects of the display convey the information—length, size, or volume? Also important are variations in labels, titles, and legends.

A graphical display should be able to stand on its own. In addition to the data represented symbolically, there should be enough information for the audience to construct meaning from the display. Not enough technical information about the measures and the data collected can be provided to answer all questions, but it should be sufficient for viewers to decode the graph.

Legends are generally difficult for viewers to use. Legends needed to identify graphical symbols require viewers to shift their eyes back and forth as if they were watching a Ping-Pong match. The constant effort of using a legend can be a distraction, an inconvenience, and a source of error in retrieving the data. The use of a legend for two or three symbols is tolerable, but any more can cause a processing overload. Many graphics packages allow the labeling of symbols within the display space, as in the bar graph in Figure 18.1, or extended directly from the line. When proximate labels are not possible, the designer should take care to make the symbols as distinct as possible. Bertin (1967/1983) provides some advice on this, such as the use of the dot (·), dash (−), and plus (+) as the most easily distinguished point symbols. Lines are more difficult to make distinct, and areas may produce moire effects when hatching or cross-hatching is used. Figure 18.4 presents a desirable alternative for a cumulative time series graph. In any case, legends for graphical symbols require memorization, allow ambiguity to creep in, and slow down the decoding of information.

Encourage Important Comparisons

Important comparisons are encouraged when the items to be compared are placed in close proximity. This is the concept behind grouping multiple bar charts. If the bars are grouped, the viewer compares the responses within the groups most easily. If the bars are arranged by response categories, between-group comparisons are made most readily. Proximity is one key to encouraging comparisons, but other considerations enter into the process.

It is essential that data be displayed on identical scales if comparisons are to be made accurately. The scaling question enters in several ways. For time series data, the intervals in the display must be equivalent. Equally important is the use of identical scales on every graph that is to be compared. This some-times causes less-than-optimal scaling on individual graphs, but the data are directly comparable.

☐ *Remember the Audience*

Achieving competent graphical displays is an interactive process. Viewers are active participants in the retrieval of information, and it is the unique char-acteristic of graphical data displays—that is, atemporality—that provides viewers access to the information on their own terms. Graphical data cannot be force-fed. Graphs are a medium of a free exchange of information. Data graphers are seeking to stimulate the demand for their product among audience members. This must be done carefully.

The graphic designer must take care to respect the current level of graphi-cacy of the audience and must constantly seek to foster greater levels of graphi-cacy and greater comfort with the data. Respect for the audience is paramount in graphical display. As Tufte (1983, pp. 80-81) has noted, researchers must consider the viewers of their graphs to be as intelligent as themselves. A cynical or condescending view of the audience taints the graphical design process and leads to failed graphs. Graphs developed under these circumstances are weight-less, without heft or substance. They display facts, but just facts. It is not nec-essary for the designer to present graphical iterations to the audience, but it may be useful to begin with a familiar format and then move to a more chal-lenging one to develop graphicacy with increasingly sophisticated formats. When the format for a graphic is unique and different, it requires some expla-nation.

■ *References*

Benjamini, Y. (1988). Opening the box of a boxplot. *American Statistician, 42,* 257-262.

Beniger, J. R., & Robyn, D. L. (1978). Quantitative graphics in statistics: A brief history. *American Statistician, 32,* 1-11.

Bertin, J. (1983). *Semiology of graphics: Diagrams networks maps* (W. J. Berg, Trans.). Madison: University of Wisconsin Press. (Original work published 1967)

Chambers, J. M., Cleveland, W. S., Kleiner, B., & Tukey, P. A. (1983). *Graphical methods for data analysis.* Boston: Duxbury.

Cleveland, W. S. (1979). Robust locally weight regression and smoothing scatterplots. *Journal of the American Statistical Association, 74,* 829-836.

Cleveland, W. S. (1984). Graphical methods for data presentation: Full scale breaks, dot charts, and multibased logging. *American Statistician, 38,* 270-280.

Cleveland, W. S., & McGill, R. (1984). Graphical perception: Theory, experimentation, and application to the development of graphical methods. *Journal of the American Statistical Association, 79,* 531-554.

Eells, W. C. (1926). The relative merits of circles and bars for representing component parts. *Journal of the American Statistical Association, 21,* 119-132.

Federal Bureau of Investigation. (1991). *Uniform crime reports for the United States.* Washington, DC: Government Printing Office.

Fienberg, S. E. (1979). Graphical methods in statistics. *American Statistician, 33,* 165-178.

Henry, G. T. (1993). Using graphical displays for evaluation data. *Evaluation Review, 17,* 60-78.

Henry, G. T. (1995). *Graphing data: Techniques for display and analysis.* Thousand Oaks, CA: Sage.

Henry, G. T., McTaggart, M. J., & McMillan, J. H. (1992). Establishing benchmarks for outcome indicators: A statistical approach to developing performance standards, *Evaluation Review, 16,* 131-150.

Jarvenpaa, S. L., & Dickson, G. W. (1988). Graphics and managerial decision making: Research based guidelines. *Communications of the ACM, 31,* 764-774.

Joint Legislative Audit and Review Commission. (1991). *Review of Virginia's parole process* (Senate Document No. 4). Richmond: Virginia General Assembly Bill Room.

Joint Legislative Audit and Review Commission. (1992). *Review of Virginia Medicaid program* (Senate Document No. 27). Richmond: Virginia General Assembly Bill Room.

Playfair, W. (1786). *Commercial and political atlas.* London.

Simkin, D., & Hastie, R. (1987). An information-processing analysis of graph perception. *Journal of the American Statistical Association, 82,* 454-465.

Tufte, E. R. (1983). *The visual display of quantitative information.* Cheshire, CT: Graphics.

Tufte, E. R. (1990). *Envisioning information.* Cheshire, CT: Graphics.

Tukey, J. W. (1977). *Exploratory data analysis.* Reading, MA: Addison-Wesley.

Tukey, J. W. (1988). Some graphic and semigraphic displays. In W. S. Cleveland (Ed.), *The collected works of John W. Tukey* (pp. 37-62). Pacific Grove, CA: Wadsworth & Brooks.

U.S. General Accounting Office. (1992). *Budget policy: Prompt action necessary to avert long-term damage to the economy* (Publication No. GAO/OCG 92-2). Washington, DC: Government Printing Office.

Virginia Department of Education. (1988). *Teacher salary survey.* Richmond: Author.

Virginia Department of Education. (1993). *Outcome accountability project: 1993 Virginia summary report.* Richmond: Author.

Wainer, H. (1992). Understanding graphs and tables. *Educational Researcher, 21*(1), 14-23.

Index

EDITOR'S NOTE: Page references followed by *t* or *f* indicate tables or figures, respectively. Page numbers followed by "n" indicated endnotes.

*Handbook
of Applied
Social
Research
Methods*

560

Handbook
of Applied
Social
Research
Methods

562

Publication, 329
Public Health Service Act, 145
Public hearings, 275, 276, 278
Public presentation, 323
Purposes, 73-76
Push-polls, 469

QAV. *See* Quantitative assignment variable
Qualitative integration rules, 278-279
Qualitative methods, xvii, 86
Qualitative research, 69-73
   advantages of, 76
   conceptual context, 71
   designing, 69-100
   generalization in, 95-96
   methods, 71
   prestructuring, 85-86
   proposal model for, 72
   purposes, 71, 75
   questions, 71
   validity, 71
Quality control, 329-330, 333-334
   case study design, 242
   interview, 395-396
   mail survey, 417-418
   telephone survey, 429, 468-469
Quantitative assignment variable, 212-213,
   214-215
Quantitative integration rules, 279-281
Quantitative methods, xvii
Quasi-experimentation, 193-228
   description and purpose, 16
   designs, 16-17
   key features, 16
   limitations, 17
   practical considerations, 220-221
   strengths, 17
   variations, 16-17
   when to use, 17
Quasi-statistics, 94-95
Questionnaires, 485-486
   length of, 412-413
   physical dimensions of, 420
   telephone survey, 467-468
Questions, 71, 80-85, 170-172
   articulation of, 233-234
   asking, 244
   broad *vs* narrow, xi
   case study research, 233-236
   clarifying, 8-9
   closed-ended, 482
   examples, 233
   format, 419
   functions of, 81-85
   grand tour, 481
   identifying, 8
   open-ended, 482

secondary, 171
sensitive, 354
survey, 343-374, 481-482
time and, 28
Quota selection methods, 448

Random assignment, 105, 177-179
Random-digit dialing, 440, 441-443
Randomized clinical trials, 164
Randomized experiments, 162-163, 164
   between-group design, 211-212
   design, 173-187
   design elements, 173-174
   elements of, 170-187
   for evaluation and planning, 161-191
   illustrative, 164-170
   two-group, 211
Randomized social experiments, 164
Randomized tests, 164
Random selection, 446-447
Rank orders, 279-280, 282n10, 361-362
Rapport, 132-133
Ratings, 355f, 357-360
RDD. *See* Random-digit dialing
Reactivity, 92
Recall, 351-352
Recipients:
   differential effects across, 222
   See also Participants; Respondents
Reciprocity, 501-502
Recording process, 519
Recruitment, interviewer, 463-465
Reflexivity, 86
Refusals, 389, 457-461, 462
   avoidance training, 458-459
   conversions, 432, 459-461
   handling, 384
   report form, 459-461, 460f
Regression-discontinuity design, 212f, 212-215,
   213f, 214f
Regression toward mean, 202
Regulations, 383-384
Relevance ratings, 274, 274f
Reliability, 20-21, 54-55, 344
   case study tactic for, 242, 243t
Remembering, 350-353
Reminders, 406-408, 412
Remission, spontaneous, 202
Remuneration, participant, 387, 409-411
   reciprocity, 501-502
Repeated measures, 51-52
Replication logic, 240
Reports and reporting, 185-187
   case study, 255-258
   composing, 257-258
   fundamental issues in, 185
   illustrative structures for, 257-258

*Handbook
of Applied
Social
Research
Methods*

572

About the Editors

Leonard Bickman is Professor of Psychology, Psychiatry, and Public Policy at Vanderbilt University, where he directs The Center for Mental Health Policy. He is the coeditor of the **Applied Social Research Methods Series** and is the editor of a new journal, *Mental Health Services Research*. He has published over 15 books and monographs and more than 120 articles and chapters. Dr. Bickman's research has been supported by several federal and state agencies as well as foundations over the past 25 years and he has received several awards recognizing the contributions of his research. He is the immediate past president of the American Evaluation Association and was president of the Society for the Psychological Study of Social Issues. He was a Senior Policy Advisor at the U.S. Substance Abuse and Mental Health Services Administration where his contribution was recognized with the 1997 Secretary's Award for Distinguished Service.

Debra J. Rog, Ph.D., directs the Washington, D.C. office of Vanderbilt University's Institute for Public Policy Studies, Center for Mental Health Policy. She has nearly 20 years of experience in program evaluation and applied research. As a Research Fellow and Director of VIPPS-DC since 1990, Dr. Rog has directed numerous multisite evaluations and research projects. Her areas of research include homelessness and supportive housing, collaboration and systems change, mental health, and the development of applied research methodology. Dr. Rog also consults with several Federal agencies and foundations on various evaluation studies and provides evaluation TA to local housing and service providers. Prior to joining VIPPS, she served as the Associate Director in the National Institute of Mental Health Office of Programs for the Homeless Mentally Ill, where she developed the first research and evaluation programs in this area. Dr. Rog has to her credit numerous publications on evaluation methodology, homelessness, poverty, mental health, and program and policy development and is

Handbook
of Applied
Social
Research
Methods

574

coeditor of the **Applied Social Research Methods Series**. Currently, Dr. Rog is on the Board of Directors of the American Evaluation Association, and a member of the American Psychological Association and the American Public Health Association. She recently completed an appointment on the Advisory Committee of Women's Services for the U.S. Substance Abuse and Mental Health Services Administration, and has been recognized for her evaluation work by the National Institute of Mental Health, the American Evaluation Association, and the Knowledge Utilization Society.

About the Contributors

Robert F. Boruch is University Trustee Chair Professor of the Graduate School of Education and the Statistics Department at the Wharton School at the University of Pennsylvania. He is an expert on research methods for evaluating programs and projects. In his international work, he chaired the National Academy of Sciences Education Statistics delegation to China and has contributed to seminars on program evaluation in Sweden, Israel, Colombia, India, Côte D'Ivoire, and Kenya. He has been a consultant to the World Health Organization on AIDS research, and to UNESCO and USAID on project evaluation. His work on evaluating social and educational programs has received recognition from the American Educational Research Association (Research Review Award) and the American Evaluation Association (Gunnar and Alva Myrdal Award). For his work on survey research methods, he was elected a Fellow of the American Statistical Association. He has been a Fellow at the Center for Advanced Study in the Behavioral Sciences and a Rockefeller Foundation Bellagio Fellow. He is the author of over 130 articles in research journals and author or editor of more than 10 books. His most recent volume is *Randomized Experiments for Planning & Evaluation.* He serves on advisory groups to the National Center for Education Statistics, the Office of Planning and Evaluation for the U.S. Department of Education, the William T. Grant Foundation, and the U.S. General Accounting Office.

Harris M. Cooper is Professor of Psychology at the University of Missouri-Columbia. He received his Ph.D. in social psychology from the University of Connecticut and has been a visiting scholar at Harvard University, Stanford University, the University of Oregon, and the Russell Sage Foundation. He is the author of *Integrating Research: A Guide for Literature Reviews,* a book on procedures for conducting scientific reviews of research literature, and is coeditor of *The Handbook of Research Synthesis* (with

*Handbook
of Applied
Social
Research
Methods*
576

Larry Hedges). He is a Fellow of the American Psychological Association and the American Psychological Society. He was the first recipient of the American Educational Research Association's Early Career Award for Programmatic Research and has also received AERA's Interpretive Scholarship Award. He is or has been an advising editor for *Psychological Bulletin, Journal of Educational Psychology, Elementary School Journal, Journal of Experimental Education,* and *Personality and Social Psychology Bulletin.*

David M. Fetterman is Professor, Director of Research at the California Institute of Integral Studies, Director of the M.A. Policy Analysis and Evaluation Program at Stanford University, and a member of the faculty at Sierra Nevada College. He was formerly a Principal Research Scientist at the American Institutes for Research and a Senior Associate and Project Director at RMC Research Corporation. He received his Ph.D. from Stanford University in educational and medical anthropology. He works in the fields of educational evaluation, ethnography, and policy analysis, studying programs for dropouts and gifted and talented education. His most recent research efforts have focused on developing empowerment evaluation—to help people help themselves. He is a past president and former program chair of both the American Evaluation Association and the American Anthropological Association's Council on Anthropology and Education. He has been elected a Fellow of the American Anthropological Association and the Society for Applied Anthropology, and has received the Myrdal Award for Evaluation Practice. He has also received the George and Louise Spindler Award for outstanding contributions to educational anthropology as a scholar and practitioner, the Ethnographic Evaluation Award from the Council on Anthropology and Education, and the President's Award from the Evaluation Research Society for contributions to ethnographic education evaluation. He is the author of *Excellence and Equality: A Qualitatively Different Perspective on Gifted and Talented Education*; *Educational Evaluation: Ethnography in Theory, Practice, and Politics*; *Ethnography in Educational Evaluation*; and *Ethnography: Step by Step.* He has also contributed to a variety of encyclopedias, including the *International Encyclopedia of Education* and *The Encyclopedia of Human Intelligence.*

Floyd J. Fowler, Jr., received a Ph.D. in social psychology from the University of Michigan in 1966. He has led survey studies related to religion, crime, housing, urban problems, and numerous other topics. His recent work has focused particularly on measuring how medical treatments affect quality of life. He also has been engaged in primary methodological studies of how to reduce interviewer-related error and how to evaluate survey questions. He has taught survey research methods at the Harvard School of Public Health and elsewhere. He is the author of *Survey Research Methods, Standardized Survey Interviewing: Minimizing Interviewer-Related Error* (with Thomas W. Mangione), and *Improving Survey Questions: Design and Evaluation,* three widely used books on survey methods. For 14 years he was Director of the Center for Survey Research at the University of Massachusetts-Boston, where he currently serves as a Senior Research Fellow.

Terry E. Hedrick is a former Assistant Comptroller General for Program Evaluation of the U.S. General Accounting Office (GAO). Prior to this position she served as Director of GAO's Training Institute, managing the agency's education efforts in support of evaluation, audit, information management, and financial accounting work for Congress. During a 17-year career, she conducted and managed program evaluation work for state and county government, the federal government, and the private sector. After receiving her doctorate in social psychology from the University of Missouri and completing a postdoctoral appointment in program evaluation methods at Northwestern University, she spent two years as Assistant Professor in Psychology at Kent State University, served as a Staff Associate in Employment Policy at The Brookings Institution, and held appointments in the evaluation offices in the Employment and Training Administration, Department of Labor, and the Food and Nutrition Service, Department of Agriculture. Throughout her career, she has been especially interested in the problems associated with bringing rigorous and unbiased applied research approaches to complex social issues.

Gary T. Henry, Ph.D., is Director of the Applied Research Center and Professor in the Departments of Public Administration and the Department of Political Science at Georgia State University. The Applied Research Center, part of the newly formed School of Policy Studies at Georgia State, is one of the largest academic survey research facilities in the southeastern United States. He is the author of *Practical Sampling* and *Graphing Data: Techniques for Display and Analysis,* and has published multiple articles in *Evaluation Review, Public Administration Review,* and education journals such as *Educational Measurement: Issues and Practice, Educational Evaluation and Policy Analysis* and *Phi Delta Kappan.*

Paul J. Lavrakas is Professor of Communication and Journalism in the College of Social and Behavioral Sciences at the Ohio State University. He is also Director of the OSU's new survey research center. Prior to the 1996-1997 academic year, he was Professor of Communications Studies, Journalism, Statistics, and Urban Affairs at Northwestern University, where he was employed starting in 1978. In 1982, he founded the Northwestern University Survey Laboratory and served as its director through the summer of 1996. He received his B.A. in social science from Michigan State University, and his M.A. and Ph.D. in research psychology from Loyola University of Chicago. Since the early 1980s, a main focus of his scholarship and teaching has been survey research methods, in particular those used in telephone surveys. His book *Telephone Survey Methods: Sampling, Selection, and Supervision* has been used extensively by telephone survey researchers for the past decade. In addition, he is coeditor of two book on election polls and the news media: *Polling and Presidential Election Coverage* (1991) and *Presidential Polls and the News Media* (1995). He is also coauthor, with M. W. Traugott, of *The Voter's Guide to Election Polls* (1996).

James J. Lindsay is a Ph.D. candidate studying social psychology at the University of Missouri. His interests include aggression, responsible environmental behavior, and meta-analysis.

Mark W. Lipsey is Professor of Public Policy at Vanderbilt University's Peabody College where he serves as Co-Director of the Center for Evaluation Research and Methodology at the Vanderbilt Institute for Public Policy Studies. He was chairman of the Public Affairs Psychology Program at Claremont Graduate School from 1984-1989 and a Fullbright Lecturer at the University of Delhi in 1985-1986. His research and teaching interests are in the areas of public policy, program evaluation research, social intervention, field research methodology, and research synthesis. The foci of his recent research have been the efficacy of juvenile delinquency intervention and issues of methodological quality in program evaluation research. He has published three books and more than 50 articles and technical reports in these areas and has consulted with numerous organizations and projects. He is a former editor-in-chief of *New Directions for Program Evaluation*, a journal of the American Evaluation Association, and has served on the editorial boards of *Evaluation Review, Evaluation Studies Review Annual,* and *Evaluation and Program Planning.* He is a member of the American Evaluation Association and was its Paul Lazarsfeld Award Recipient in 1996.

*Handbook
of Applied
Social
Research
Methods*
578

Thomas W. Mangione is Senior Research Scientist at JSI Research and Training Institute in Boston. He obtained his Ph.D. in organizational psychology from the University of Michigan in 1973. He has had more than 25 years of survey research experience using in-person, telephone, and self-administered data collection modes. At JSI his own work has focused on two areas: substance abuse and needs assessments of HIV-positive populations. He has also served as a consultant on questionnaire design for a wide range of studies. Before coming to JSI, he worked as a Senior Research Fellow at the University of Massachusetts's Center for Survey Research. There he worked on more than 100 different survey projects spanning a wide range of topics, including environmental health risks, alcohol use, AIDS knowledge and risk behaviors, crime and fear, and mental health. As a graduate student, he worked on several national surveys of employment at Michigan's Survey Research Center. He has two books on survey research methodology: *Mail Surveys* (1996) and, with Floyd J. Fowler, Jr., *Standardized Survey Interviewing* (1990). He also teaches classes in survey research methodology at both the Boston University and Harvard University Schools of Public Health.

Melvin M. Mark is Professor of Psychology at the Pennsylvania State University. He serves or has served on the editorial boards of several evaluation journals and on the board of directors of the American Evaluation Association. He has published numerous papers and chapters on the design of evaluations. His publications include the coedited books *Social Science and Social Policy* and *Multiple Methods in Program Evaluation*. He and Charles Reichardt are coauthors of a forthcoming book on quasi-experimentation, and, with Gary Henry and George Julnes, he also has a volume forthcoming on emergent realist theory of evaluation.

Joseph A. Maxwell is Associate Professor in the Graduate School of Education at George Mason University, where he teaches courses on research and evaluation methods. He has been employed in both academic and applied settings; his applied work includes research and evaluation in medical education, the evaluation of gender equity programs, and consulting work for schools and a range of educational projects. He has a Ph.D. in anthropology from the University of Chicago, and continues to see himself as an anthropologist and social theorist, as well as a research methodologist. His publications include *Qualitative Research Design: An Interactive Approach* (1996) and numerous papers on research and evaluation methods, medical education, Native American social organization, and diversity.

Jack McKillip is Professor of Applied Experimental Psychology and Associate Dean of the Graduate School at Southern Illinois University at Carbondale. His research interests include certification evaluation, environmental determinants of college student alcohol use, and methodological aspects of program evaluation and need assessment. He has published more than 40 journal articles and book chapters on these topics. He is also the author of *Need Assessment: Tools for the Human Services and Education* (1987) and coauthor, with G. F. Pitz, of *Decision Analysis for Program Evaluators* (1984).

Charles S. Reichardt is Professor of Psychology at the University of Denver. His research concerns research methodology and statistics in general, and the logic and practice of causal inference in particular. He is coeditor of *Qualitative and Quantitative Methods in Evaluation Research* (with Tom Cook), *Evaluation Studies Review Annual* (Volume 12) (with Will Shadish), and *The Qualitative-Quantitative Debate: New Perspectives* (with Sharon Rallis).

Prem N. Shamdasani is Senior Lecturer at the School of Management, National University of Singapore. He received his Ph.D. in marketing from the University of Southern California. His publications have appeared in the *Journal of Marketing, Singapore Marketing Review, Journal of Consumer Satisfaction, Asian Journal of Marketing, Dissatisfaction and Complaining Behavior,* and other international journals and published proceedings. His teaching interests include international marketing, consumer behavior, marketing strategy, and advertising.

Joan E. Sieber is Professor of Psychology at California State University, Hayward, and the recipient of that University's Outstanding Professor Award for 1991. A social psychologist by training, her area of specialization is the study of emerging ethical and value problems in social research and intervention. She has also researched related areas such as data sharing and whistle blowing. Her main interest is in the development of procedural and methodological solutions to ethical problems in human research that otherwise would limit the value of social science. In addition to her work on ethical issues in human research, she currently researches the relationship of the elderly with the business and professional community that ostensibly serves them. She is a fellow of the American Psychological Association/American Psychological Society Joint Task Force to Revise Ethical Principles in the Conduct of Research with Human Participants. She has chaired human subjects ethics committees for both academic and private corporate organizations. She is the author of the Sage volumes *Sharing Social Science Data: Advantages and Challenges, Planning Ethically Responsible Research: A Guide for Students and Internal Review Boards,* and coeditor with Barbara Stanley of the Sage volume *Social Research on Children and Adolescents,* as well as author of numerous other books, chapters, and articles.

David W. Stewart, Ph.D., is Robert E. Brooker Professor of Marketing and Chairperson of the Department of Marketing in the Gordon Marshall School of Business at the University of Southern California. Prior to moving to Southern California in 1986, he was Senior Associate Dean and Associate Professor of Marketing at the Owen Graduate School of Management, Vanderbilt University. He is a past president of the Society for Consumer Psychology and a Fellow of both the American Psychological Association and the American Psychological Society. He is Chairman of the Section on Statistics in Marketing of the American Statistical Association and President-Elect of the Academic Council and a member of the board of directors of the American Marketing Association. He has authored or coauthored more than 150 publications and six books, including *Secondary Research: Sources and Methods* (second edition, 1993), *Effective Television Advertising: A Study of 1000 Commercials* (1986), and *Focus Groups: Theory and Practice* (1990). He serves or has served on the editorial boards of many professional journals, including the *Journal of Marketing Research, Journal of Advertising, Journal of Marketing,* and *Journal of Public Policy and Marketing.* His research has examined a wide range of issues, including marketing strategy, the analysis of markets, consumer information search and decision making, effectiveness of marketing communications, and methodological approaches to the analysis of marketing data. His research and commentary are frequently featured in the business and popular press.

Magda Stouthamer-Loeber is Co-Director of the Life History Studies Group at Western Psychiatric Institute and Clinic of the University of Pittsburgh Medical Center. An Associate Professor of Psychiatry and Psychology at the University of Pittsburgh, she has conducted several studies requiring data collection by interviewers in the field. She completed her M.A. degree in psychology in the Netherlands and received her doctorate in clinical psychology from Queen's University, Kingston, Ontario, Canada, in 1979. She spent 5 years as a Research Associate at the Oregon Learning Center in Eugene, Oregon, where she helped conduct a pilot study for a longitudinal study. From Oregon, she moved to her current position in Pittsburgh. She is currently codirecting the Pittsburgh Youth Study, a longitudinal study of inner-city boys. Throughout her career, she has been interested in the nuts and bolts of conducting high-quality research in the area of the development of antisocial behavior.

Welmoet Bok van Kammen received her B.A. in the Netherlands and her Ph.D. from Johns Hopkins University in 1977. Her first job related to longitudinal research was as a Research Coordinator of the Schizophrenia Research Unit at the Highland Drive Veterans Administration Medical Center in Pittsburgh, Pennsylvania. From 1987 until 1997, she worked for the Pittsburgh Youth Study, University of Pittsburgh Medical Center, as Program Director. With Magda Stouthamer-Loeber, she was responsible for the day-to-day management of the project. She has been involved in a variety of studies dealing with relapse prediction in schizophrenia, psychological sequelae of war-related stress, and substance use in children and adolescents. At present, she is working as a research scientist for Macro International in Atlanta.

Brian T. Yates received his Ph.D. in psychology from Stanford University in 1976. He is a tenured Associate Professor in the Department of Psychology of the College of Arts and Sciences at American University in Washington, D.C., where he has worked since 1976. He has published more than 50 articles and book chapters; most apply cost-effectiveness or cost-benefit analysis to the systematic evaluation and improvement of human services. His book *Improving Effectiveness and Reducing Costs in Mental Health,* published in 1980, laid the groundwork for his present integration of program evaluation with economics and operations research in *Analyzing Costs, Procedures, Processes, and Outcomes in Human Services,* his fifth book. He has conducted cost-procedure-process-outcome-analysis for service enterprises and research initiatives in treatment of heroin and cocaine addiction, residential programs for urban youth, intermediate care facilities for mentally retarded adults, suicide prevention, psychiatric inpatient treatment of schizophrenic adolescents, and prevention of alcohol, tobacco, and other substance abuse. Currently he is publishing his research on the cost and cost-effectiveness of two substance abuse treatment programs in the District of Columbia.

Robert K. Yin has contributed frequently on the topic of the case study method and its use in evaluation. Currently, he is directing several major evaluations, mainly focusing on community or university partnerships and collaboratives of one sort or another, using both case studies and quantitative analyses involving nested data. Previously, he served as a Visiting Scholar to the U.S. General Accounting Office (Program Evaluation and Methodology Division). He has been the President of COSMOS Corporation for more than 16 years; previously he worked at the RAND Corporation for nearly 8 years. He has a Ph.D. from the Massachusetts Institute of Technology in brain and cognitive sciences and a B.A. (magna cum laude) from Harvard College.